# THE
# GUIDE TO
# CLASSIC
# RECORDED
# JAZZ

# THE GUIDE TO CLASSIC RECORDED JAZZ

# TOM PIAZZA

University of Iowa Press Ψ Iowa City

University of Iowa Press,

Iowa City 52242

Copyright © 1995 by Tom Piazza

All rights reserved

Printed in the United States of America

Design by Richard Hendel

Printed on acid-free paper

Library of Congress Cataloging-in-Publication Data

Piazza, Tom, 1955–

The guide to classic recorded jazz / by Tom Piazza.

p.    cm.

Includes index.

ISBN 0-87745-489-2 (acid-free paper)

1. Jazz – Discography.    2. Sound recordings – Reviews.    I. Title.

ML156.4.J3P53    1995

016.78165′0266 – dc20                          94-36373

CIP

MN

01   00   99   98   97   96   95   P   5   4   3   2   1

FOR MY MOTHER AND FATHER

*and for everybody in the woodshed*

# CONTENTS

## The Reed Section

## The Piano

# INTRODUCTION

**JAZZ MUSIC** is more popular now than it has been in many years. New York's Lincoln Center has made it a permanent part of its agenda along with the New York Philharmonic and the Metropolitan Opera, big-budget movies have been made about it, talented young musicians seem to arrive in New York City weekly, and record companies have been issuing classic as well as newly recorded material at an astonishing rate. Everybody seems to be curious about jazz, but it can be a little hard to know where to begin.

The book you are holding is designed to serve as a guide to the territory, to give you a sense of how jazz developed, who has played it, what they think about when they play it, and what their best recordings are. It concentrates on artists and recordings from the period in which the idiom's greatest and most definitive statements were made – the period roughly between 1920 and 1970. With the boom in jazz reissues that has coincided with the introduction of the compact disc, a staggering number of classic jazz recordings are once again available, often with greatly improved sound. *The Guide* is intended to be a companion to that great body of work. In writing it, I have concentrated on the recordings that have endured, that are as vital today as they were when they were first recorded.

*The Guide* is different in conception from other books on the subject. It is the only book of its scope and purpose to have been written entirely by one author. Most books on recorded jazz have consisted of encyclopedia-style entries written by a number of different writers. It can be tricky in such books to know who's talking when and what their assumptions are. The artists are discussed briefly and their recordings are rated, but the larger picture is often lacking. *The Guide*, on the other hand, discusses more than eight hundred recordings in stylistic and chronological context rather than merely offering capsule evaluations in a vacuum. The judgments and evaluations here are all, for better or worse, those of the author.

*The Guide* is organized into two main sections, the first called Ensembles and the second called Soloists. Each section takes a complete pass through the period covered, but from a different vantage point. Some musicians – such as bandleaders Fletcher Henderson and Jelly Roll Morton – have been more important as leaders of ensembles than as instrumentalists, and some – trumpeter Roy Eldridge or saxophonist Charlie Parker, for instance – have been more important as soloists. Some have been significant both as solo voices and as ensemble thinkers, Miles Davis being probably the best example.

*The Guide*'s Ensembles section begins by looking at the New Orleans ensemble tradition exemplified by King Oliver's Creole Jazz Band, then investigates the adaptation of that style for the larger ensembles of the 1920s and 1930s, such as those of Fletcher Henderson, Duke Ellington, Benny Goodman, and Count Basie, traces the stripping-down process that went along with what was called bebop in the recordings of Dizzy Gillespie, Charlie Parker, Tadd Dameron, and others, and explores the ensemble styles that developed out of bebop in the 1950s, especially in the work of Art Blakey, Thelonious Monk, Charles Mingus, and Miles Davis. Finally, it looks at the major groups of the 1960s, like those of Davis, John Coltrane, and Ornette Coleman, which, while using the stripped-down instrumentation of the bebop ensemble, returned to something very much like New Orleans group improvisation.

*The Guide*'s Soloists section discusses the major soloists on the main solo instruments – trumpet, saxophone, and piano – in chronological order. The discussion of trumpeters, for example, begins with Louis Armstrong and his contemporaries of the 1920s, proceeds through the flowering of great trumpeters of the 1930s whom he inspired, looks at Roy Eldridge's innovations, then the work of Dizzy Gillespie, Fats Navarro, Clifford Brown, and so on. Most guides discuss only a musician's recordings as leader, but much of almost any great soloist's best work is done as a sideman on other musicians' recordings. In *The Guide*, each musician's important recordings as both leader and sideman are discussed together.

Above all, *The Guide* is meant to be both useful and enjoyable. It can be read as a narrative history of the music's development or used as a buyer's guide to available jazz recordings. All of the book's musical examples are tied to specific available recordings, including label and catalog numbers for easy reference.

You can find the recordings of any artist by looking in the Table of Contents. If, for example, you want to know what recordings by Roy Eldridge are discussed, look up his name in the Trumpets section under Soloists and turn to the appropriate pages in *The Guide*; there you will find a discussion of his style as well as an in-depth look at important recordings he made both as leader and as sideman. You will also be steered to especially characteristic or exciting solos on specific discs. If you want to know what recordings to seek out by Art

Blakey's Jazz Messengers, with that band's procession of major sidemen and classic albums, look up Blakey in the Ensembles section of the Table of Contents, then turn to the pages listed there, where you will find a discussion of the development of the style he represented, as well as evaluations of his most important albums.

In trying to write a book that could fit between two covers, I have concentrated on what I considered to be classic recordings from the 1920s through about 1970. By classic, I mean recordings that have formed or that exemplify the definitive elements of the jazz style, in as undiluted a form as possible. In the past twenty-five years or so, many hybrid forms of jazz have been popularized, most notably what has been called jazz fusion, a form which incorporates heavy electronics and rock elements into a context of instrumental improvisation. In recent years, forms of indigenous music from around the world have offered techniques and approaches which some jazz musicians have used.

All of this is healthy and inevitable, but it is telling that the use of the word "jazz" persists throughout all of this hybridization. Even the term "jazz fusion" implies that there is something called jazz, which has been fused with something else. My concern here has been to discuss recordings that, taken together, might say something essential about what is meant by the word "jazz."

That has become a thorny issue lately. Surprisingly loud arguments have been conducted in print over the meaning of the word and even over whether it has a meaning. Many of the people who use the word most vociferously insist on a usage for it that is so broad as to be, in my mind, meaningless. I think it is true to say that, no matter what "style" of jazz one is playing or listening to, certain specific musical techniques and structures tend to be present consistently. The writer Stanley Crouch has made a short but useful list of the essential musical elements that jazz musicians deal with: the blues, the romantic ballad, Afro-Hispanic rhythms, and the attitude toward the passage of time (at slow, medium, and fast tempos) that is called swing. To these I would add that jazz always demonstrates a call-and-response sensibility derived originally from the African American church and which is present in the music's most basic structures. These elements are discussed in this book; at times they are used as a kind of acid test to decide whether certain recordings or the work of certain musicians is or isn't jazz.

For the sake of The Guide's length, I have made the decision not to include a separate section devoted to singers. Singers form a special case within the music; often, the work of even the most jazz-steeped of singers ranges from heavily jazz influenced to essentially pop work, and the difference is usually dictated by the musicians around them. So Billie Holiday, Dinah Washington, Sarah Vaughan, and many other singers are touched on here, but only in the context of discussions of the major instrumentalists or bands with whom they recorded.

In order to make *The Guide* most useful, I have based my discussion on easily available recordings, for most of which you should have to look no farther than a good record store in a medium-sized or even small city. The catalog numbers given for the recordings are always those of the compact disc issue. The cassette catalog numbers of these sets are usually identical to the compact disc number, except for a different numerical suffix indicating the different format. In a very few cases, where important material is still available only on LP, I have noted it as such.

In the past few years, since the development of the compact disc, there has been an explosion in the amount of classic material available; for a time, many new titles seemed to arrive in stores every week. Since I began *The Guide*, that flow has slowed somewhat, with certain companies even beginning to trim some titles from their lists. I have kept adding material to *The Guide* until as close to publication as possible, but new titles will inevitably be available by the time it is published. Likewise, some of what I've listed will almost certainly go out of print. But most of this material will remain in print, in one form or another, for as long as people listen to sound recordings. *The Guide* will prove useful, I hope, as a comprehensive overview of the music's classic recordings for years to come.

# ACKNOWLEDGMENTS

**NO PROJECT** like this could get off the ground without the cooperation of record companies large and small. I am indebted to all the following, who were very understanding and more than generous in making available the recordings I needed: Terri Hinte of Fantasy; Kevin Gore, Monica Shovlin, and Arthur Levy of CBS/Sony Music; Marilyn Laverty of Shore Fire Media; Steve Backer, Marilyn Lipsius, and David Goldfarb of RCA/BMG; Michael Cuscuna of Blue Note; Michael Bloom of GRP; Don Lucoff of DL Media; Richard Seidel and Mary Stone of Polygram; Joe Fields of Muse; Didier Deutsch of Atlantic; Don Schlitten of Xanadu; James Austin of Rhino; the late Martin Williams and Tom Dube of Smithsonian; Andy McKaie and Don Thomas of MCA; P. J. Littleton of Bainbridge Records; Carrie Svingen of Rykodisc; Jerry Valburn of Merrit Record Society; Will Friedwald of Stash; Hugh Fordin of DRG; Steve Wagner of Delmark; Glenn Dicker of Rounder; and a special thanks to Michael Cuscuna (again) and Charlie Lourie of Mosaic Records, who have brought a new level of sophistication and commitment to jazz reissues.

Many people helped in different ways, knowingly and unknowingly, to make this book, but none helped more than my mother and father, who supported and encouraged an interest they must have had trouble understanding. I got interested in jazz when I was about eleven years old, and they always managed, somehow, to find the records I wanted for Christmas and my birthday. And a special thanks to my mother for spending those long Saturday afternoons ferrying me to antique stores on Long Island looking for old 78s. Thanks, Mom; thanks, Dad.

My editor, Paul Zimmer, and everyone at the University of Iowa Press have shown an inspiring understanding of what I tried to do here, and I want to thank them for the energy and faith they showed in bringing this project to fruition. John Hasse, of the Smithsonian Institution, made very valuable comments on the manuscript, for which I am grateful. Erroll McDonald of Pantheon Books was a supporter of this project in its earliest stages and made it possible for me to develop the initial outline.

Several other people played special parts in the evolution of this book. I'd like to thank Stanley Crouch for fifteen years of great conversation and enduring friendship. Peter Keepnews provided me with invaluable leads at record companies, as well as much moral support. Dan Morgenstern, now the director of the Institute of Jazz Studies at Rutgers University, was kind enough to publish my juvenilia in *Down Beat* while I was still in high school, encouraging me to think I might have something to say about this music.

I'd also like to thank Albert Murray for all his reading lists and for the insights contained in what is still the best book about jazz music, *Stomping the Blues* (Da Capo Press). Thanks, too, to the writers and commentators on the music, whose work I've admired and learned from through the years: Stanley Dance, Leonard Feather, Dan Morgenstern, Ira Gitler, Ed Beach, Whitney Balliett, Ralph Ellison, Martin Williams, David Himmelstein, and Hsio Wen Shih (wherever he may be). And, for various kindnesses, thanks to Lorraine Gordon, Norman Mailer, George Wein, Jeff Rosen, Stew Bernstein, Ross and Sally Keegan, Hank O'Neal, Jack Meltzer, Leonard Kunstadt, Red Metzger, Carl Kendziora, Bob Altschuler, and Wendy Cunningham.

Lastly, I would like to thank the many musicians, alive and deceased, who have spent time talking, hanging out, and sometimes playing music with me; I could never list them all, but I could never leave out Milt Hinton, Buddy Tate, Dicky Wells, Rudy Powell, Mary Lou Williams, Tommy Flanagan, Hank Jones, Jo Jones, Budd Johnson, Barry Harris, Wynton Marsalis, Jimmy Owens, Chris White, Warren Smith, Ernie Wilkins, Jaki Byard, Bennie Morton, Roy Eldridge, Lonnie Hillyer, Jay McShann, Al Hibbler, Bernard Addison, Ruby Braff, Jerry Dodgion, Eddie Jefferson, Billy Mitchell, Clifford Jordan, Walter Davis, Jr., Marcus Roberts, Walter Booker, Thad Jones, Mel Lewis, Jimmy Rowles, and especially my piano teacher, the late Sanford Gold. To them I owe more than I could put into words.

# MANY VOICES

**IN A JAZZ GROUP**, as in any community, certain roles need to be filled. Someone has to play the melody (if there's a melody), someone has to keep time, someone has to suggest the harmonic context. Often these jobs overlap. In jazz, each instrumentalist has to understand his or her role in the group well enough so that he or she can improvise on it and not just follow directions. Playing in a jazz group involves both responsibility and freedom; freedom consists of understanding your responsibility well enough to act independently and still make the needed contribution to the group. As such, a jazz performance is a working model of a democracy.

Of course, the notion of who fills what role in the ensemble changes with time, as it does in any community. And the way the community supports individual voices, accompanies, so to speak, a soloist, also changes. This section looks at the changes in these attitudes.

In the earliest jazz bands on record, the approach to the ensemble was polyphonic, or many-voiced. Each melody instrument – typically one or two trumpets, a trombone, and a clarinet – played its own melody, or line, in an ongoing counterpoint, sometimes worked out, often improvised. Sometimes the instruments all played different lines; sometimes they doubled up together for a while.

The so-called rhythm instruments – usually a piano, banjo or guitar, drums, and a string bass or tuba – hammered out the underlying rhythm. At the same time, they spelled out the harmonic underpinning – the piano and guitar playing chords, the bass or tuba hitting the appropriate low notes.

This instrumentation, except for the piano, was derived from that of the typical New Orleans marching band. These bands played most often for parades and were an integral part of the life of the community; their music was indispensable for weddings, funerals, and holiday festivities. Their repertoire consisted of spirituals, marching tunes, ragtime tunes, light opera, blues, French and Spanish songs, and just about everything else.

These bands evolved a way of playing that delegated the melody to the trumpet, the instrument that was simultaneously most powerful and most flexible, the one that could be heard above the others at a fairground or in a noisy street parade. The trombone, lower-pitched and less agile, played long, held harmony notes and simple answering phrases. The clarinet and saxophone, considered more fluid but possessed of less volume, played more notes, embroidering around the melody work of the trumpets. In the course of playing this way, depending on the occasion, the musicians would make variations in their parts. But New Orleans trumpeters learned to play a melody straight, or they didn't eat regularly.

This same instrumentation, more or less, was employed in dance halls and other good-time places, and there the fare was raunchier and designed specifically for dancing. It's hard today to know what this music actually sounded like; by the time most of the earliest musicians got a chance to record they had already heard and been influenced by performers in later styles, by bands such as those led by King Oliver, Jelly Roll Morton, and, later, Charlie Parker, Duke Ellington, and Miles Davis.

Out of the rhythmic and melodic gumbo created from the marching and honky-tonk bands, a first era of classic jazz materialized. It didn't emphasize solos, as we think of them; the emphasis was on group interplay and rhythmic coherence. The first jazz records were, in fact, made in 1917 by a white band from New Orleans, the Original Dixieland Jazz Band. Their early records, available as *Original Dixieland Jazz Band: The 75th Anniversary* (RCA/Bluebird 61098-2-RB), are full of energy and fun, if a little thin musically. They were, however, a commercial sensation, and for several years record companies recorded all kinds of nonjazz syncopated dance music under the name of jazz. It wasn't until the early 1920s that bands that could deliver the genuine article began recording.

You can find and enjoy the whole range of approaches to small-band polyphony in the recordings of King Oliver's Creole Jazz Band and Jelly Roll Morton's Red Hot Peppers; both bands were led by men from New Orleans. The Creole Jazz Band records are, by and large, primitively recorded, but they contain fantastic music once you get used to the sound. It takes some concentrating at first to hear what's going on, but the fire, the assurance, and the excitement of the band belong to a style that is at its peak.

The Morton records are a little less wild sounding at first, a little more orchestrated in a more refined manner, but they are as exciting in their own way, and they are easier to listen to. They also feature the piano of the leader, who was, in many respects, one of the most interesting figures in the history of jazz.

## KING OLIVER

Joe "King" Oliver was one of the most famous cornet (a smaller version of the trumpet in common use in the early days of jazz) players in New Orleans, where the title "King" is not bestowed lightly. He was a strong leader, and some of New Orleans's best musicians played under him – clarinetist Johnny Dodds and his brother, drummer Baby Dodds, clarinetist Jimmie Noone, and others. Oliver left New Orleans for Chicago in 1918 to play as a sideman for a couple of years before organizing what would be called the Creole Jazz Band. The first incarnation of the Creole Jazz Band spent a year in California before returning to Chicago in 1922, where they were joined by Oliver's protégé from New Orleans, Louis Armstrong.

Armstrong joined them in July 1922, but the band didn't record until April 1923. So the band that finally recorded the first truly classic jazz records had time to get its signals straight. The band's very first recordings, made for a small company called Gennett, showed the power and inventiveness of the band, as well as its flexibility. They are available on *Louis Armstrong and King Oliver* (Milestone MCD-47017-2). Gennett, by the way, was responsible for many of the most important early jazz records. Its primitive recording studio was located next to the railroad tracks in Richmond, Indiana, and whenever a train was scheduled to go by, the musicians had to stop recording. Although the sound on the Gennetts is extremely low fidelity, the music is worth any effort.

The first tune, "Just Gone," is New Orleans polyphony all the way, with the two cornets playing the lead, or melody, the clarinet playing embroidery around this line, and the trombone playing held harmony notes and sometimes simple countermelodies. The piano and banjo players and drummer Baby Dodds, who plays woodblocks throughout the Gennetts, hammer out the tempo and the chords. As the performance goes on, the cornets begin making variations on the melody; the performance is a two-and-a-half-minute jam. The drive that Oliver and Armstrong generated together, the bite of the two cornets, which you can hear as they come in after Johnny Dodds's clarinet solo on "Canal Street Blues," gave a lesson to everyone who listened and formed the basis for the distribution of roles in the early swing big bands, in which most often the trumpet section carried the lead, the reeds played a countermelody, or embroidery, and the trombones played harmony and simple counterrhythms.

Listen to Oliver's solos and breaks on "Mandy Lee Blues" and "Dippermouth Blues." This onomatopoeically named wa-wa style, achieved by manipulating the rubber part of a standard bathroom plunger over the opening in the bell of the horn, was a way of imitating vocal tone and increasing the horn's expressiveness. It influenced Armstrong heavily, especially in his accompaniments to blues singers (listen to Armstrong answering and commenting on Bessie Smith's singing on "Reckless Blues" and "You've Been a Good Old Wagon" on *Bessie Smith/The Collection* [Columbia CK 44441]). This style was refined and extended by the brass section of Duke Ellington's orchestra; today, Wynton Marsalis continues this tradition. An example of his plunger playing can be heard on the title track of his album *The Majesty of the Blues* (Columbia CK 45091,) which also includes a stylized re-creation of a New Orleans funeral.

Oliver's solo on "Dippermouth Blues" (Dippermouth, or Dipper, was one of Armstrong's early nicknames, before the famous Satchmo) became the standard solo to play on the tune, which was transposed for big band by Don Redman and renamed "Sugar Foot Stomp." But in these recordings, generally, the concern with solos is subordinated to the ensemble. And the sheer flat-out drive that the group as a whole could generate, especially on a tune like "Snake Rag," was hard to believe and even today does not sound dated.

### BREAKS

"Snake Rag" incorporates another basic compositional technique of jazz: the break, a moment in which the rhythm section stops playing and an instrument or, in this case, instruments (Oliver's and Armstrong's cornets) play alone but in tempo. It is a test of skill, equilibrium, and presence of mind; think of it as the moment when a ski jumper takes off from the end of the ramp or an Olympic diver leaves the diving board for an intricately executed series of moves. Except in a jazz break, more often than not, the moves are improvised rather than carefully worked out in advance.

Most of the giants of jazz have been masters of the break. Louis Armstrong certainly was; his Hot Five and Hot Seven recordings are full of stunning breaks, especially "Wild Man Blues," a slow, minor-key number recorded four years after the Oliver records, in which Armstrong takes break after break of phenomenal intensity (available on *The Hot Fives and Hot Sevens, Volume 2* [Columbia CK 44253]).

Lester Young, the tenor saxophonist whose graceful, inventive solos with the Count Basie band changed musicians' conception of melody, was also a master of this device; his 1939 solo on "Clap Hands, Here Comes Charlie" (on *The Essential Count Basie, Volume 2* [Columbia CK 40835]) begins with a break using only one note, repeated and accented, like a bull stamping the ground before charging, and his solo on his own composition "Tickle Toe," on the same set, also begins with a startling break. His masterpiece "Lester Leaps In" (also on *The Essential Count Basie, Volume 2*) contains a chorus consisting of one break after another in which the rhythm section is silent except for a chord on the first beat of every other measure; this kind of series of breaks, where the soloist plays basically over suspended time, is called stop-time. Armstrong does it, too, on his "Potato Head Blues" solo (on *The Hot Fives and Hot Sevens, Volume 2*). For a more recent example of stop-time, listen to Sonny Rollins's tenor solo on "I Know That You Know" on Dizzy Gillespie's *Sonny Side Up* (Verve 825 674-2).

Charlie Parker, the alto saxophone genius who revolutionized the music yet again and was originally a disciple of Lester Young's, also recorded some classic breaks, the most famous of which was on his 1946 "A Night in Tunisia." The originally issued version (on *The Legendary Dial Masters, Volume 1* [Stash ST-CD-23]) is fantastic, but on a previous take he took a break that was so great it quickly became a legend among musicians and fans alike; it was issued by itself, fading up just before the break and fading out just afterward, and is included on *The Legendary Dial Masters, Volume 2* (Stash ST-CD-25). He also plays perfect breaks on both takes of "Victory Ball," recorded in 1949 with an all-star band including trumpeters Dizzy Gillespie and Miles Davis and available on *The Metronome All-Star Bands* (RCA/Bluebird 7636-2-RB). And for just one example of John Coltrane's aptitude for breaks, listen to "Liberia" on *Coltrane's Sound* (Atlantic 1419-2). The point is that the break is a basic compositional element of jazz music, and it can be found in the work of musicians of every period of jazz. In any case, the Creole Jazz Band's version of "Snake Rag" is studded with two-cornet breaks by Oliver and Armstrong, which caused a sensation in Chicago and are still sly, fresh, and exhilarating.

## MORE OLIVER

"Froggie Moore" is a fine band reading of a piano rag composed by Jelly Roll Morton. You can hear the composer's solo version of the same tune, recorded eight months later (also for Gennett), on *Jelly Roll Morton 1923/24* (Milestone MCD-47018-2).

Another of the Gennetts, "Weather Bird," is an Armstrong composition, which he recorded five years later as a duet with pianist Earl Hines (available on *Louis Armstrong, Volume 4: Louis Armstrong and Earl Hines* [Columbia CK 45142]). Listening to the Creole Jazz Band version and the Armstrong/Hines duet back to back, there is much to learn about ensemble playing.

As great as the drive is in the band version, that of the duet is probably greater, with Armstrong abstracting the cornet parts of the original and Hines gamboling percussively and fluently around Armstrong's lead, sometimes like the clarinet, sometimes like the trombone, sometimes head-to-head like another trumpet (his style used to be called trumpet-style piano). At the end they trade a series of breaks. The duet makes an interesting contrast with a duet between Oliver and Jelly Roll Morton on Morton's "King Porter Stomp" (like so many New Orleans/Chicago standards, this later became a staple for many swing big bands, as arranged by Fletcher Henderson), also included on the Armstrong/Oliver Milestone set.

Both duets show that an irresistible pulse can be generated without drums and even without a rhythm section. On the Creole Jazz Band Gennetts, the rhythm is spelled out more by Lil Armstrong's piano and Bill Johnson's banjo than by drummer Baby Dodds, who plays woodblocks, instead of a regular trap drum set, in such a manner as to make them almost a part of the frontline counterpoint. Later musicians such as Charles Mingus and Ornette Coleman would explore this approach, in which the so-called rhythm instruments would play an almost melodic role in the music as opposed to a strictly timekeeping one (see, for example, "Folk Forms No. 1" on *Mingus Presents Mingus* [Candid CD 9005]).

The recordings the Oliver band made for Columbia and OKeh are currently very hard to find; many of the same qualities present in the Gennetts are to be found here, too, usually with marginally better sound. Baby Dodds plays the snare drum on the OKehs, rather than woodblocks. The prize OKehs include "Buddy's Habit," which resembles pianist James P. Johnson's "Carolina Shout," and "Tears," which has some startling Armstrong breaks, one of which he later used on his recording of "Potato Head Blues." "High Society Rag," with its echoes of New Orleans street parades, employed a clarinet solo (devised by New Orleans clarinet master Alphonse Picou) that has been used in every performance of the tune to this day. Charlie Parker liked to quote it and did so, in fact, in his epochal "Ko Ko" (available on *Original Bird – The Best of Bird on Savoy* [Savoy ZDS 1208]). And then there is "I Ain't Gonna Tell Nobody," maybe the most exciting Creole Jazz Band performance, where the two cornets leap and dance around each other, a real time in the sun, a moment of glory.

Oliver never again made recordings as important or influential as the Creole Jazz Band sides; in fact, by a year or two after their release, the style they represented was already considered old-fashioned by most younger musicians. He did, however, make an excellent series of recordings beginning in 1926, some of the best of which are available as *King Oliver and His Dixie Syncopators: Sugar Foot Stomp* (Decca/GRPGRD-616). The band has the Creole Jazz Band's instrumentation but with three saxophone players (who doubled on clarinet) in most cases, rather than a lone clarinetist; the music still sounds like New Orleans music in some ways, but it reflects the larger-band sound that was then becoming the cutting edge of the music, as orchestrated by Fletcher Henderson and his ace arranger, Don Redman (often using tunes borrowed from the repertoire of Oliver himself). The recordings are very successful, musically, from the eerie moods on "Snag It," "Jackass Blues" (two more that were adapted by Henderson), and "Showboat Shuffle," to the great drive of "Deep Henderson" (no relation to Fletcher) and "Wa-Wa-Wa."

A handsome-looking reissue entitled *King Oliver: The New York Sessions 1929–1930* (RCA/Bluebird 9903-2-RB) is nonetheless disappointing musically, presenting Oliver in a steep technical decline in musical settings that lack the sting of the Dixie Syncopators sides. This set is mainly worth having for historical interest and for a few solos by New Orleans trumpeter Henry "Red" Allen. An RCA/Bluebird compilation called *Great Trumpets: Classic Jazz to Swing* (6753-2-RB) supposedly presents Oliver trying to re-create Louis Armstrong's opening cadenza to "West End Blues," an Oliver composition that Armstrong made his own the previous year. The trumpeter on this track, however, is not Oliver but Louis Metcalf, a very active New York trumpeter of the time. The misattribution is yet another irony in the career of a true giant of the music whose fate it was not to profit from the advances made by others on foundations he had laid down. Oliver died in poverty in 1938.

## JELLY ROLL MORTON

The recordings of Jelly Roll Morton's Red Hot Peppers occupy as important a place in the history of jazz as Oliver's. The Peppers were not a working band, as Oliver's band was, but rather a group with shifting personnel and instrumentation, brought together beginning in 1926 only for recording purposes. Morton was the first real jazz composer. Oliver wrote many tunes – "Someday Sweetheart," "West End Blues," and plenty of others – but Morton was a composer: he clearly heard the shape of an entire, varied performance in his mind, and the Peppers recordings are all full aesthetic statements made within the three-minute limit of the standard 10-inch 78-rpm records of the time.

Partly this may have been because of Morton's training as a pianist. Trained pianists learn to carry rhythm, melody, and accompaniment all at the same time; in a sense they are taught to function as an entire orchestra. And any pianist who is trained learns how to approach the treatment of entire compositions. It's no coincidence that most of jazz's preeminent composer-arrangers have been pianists. One exception to this "rule" is Charles Mingus, a bass player (although, in fact, he made several recordings playing piano), who, for all his worship of Duke Ellington, in many ways more closely resembled Morton, personally as well as musically. Mingus recorded tributes to Morton on his albums *Mingus Ah Um* (Columbia CK 40648) and *Blues and Roots* (Atlantic 1305-2), the latter one of the best jazz albums ever made.

There is a greater range of mood available in these Morton performances than in Oliver's. There is also a greater variety of instrumental approach. Instead of giving every instrument a different line, there is a more intricate, premeditated attempt to vary the group sound; the performances are more carefully shaped and paced. This is not to say that there is anything haphazard about Oliver's, only that there is more of a single organizing consciousness behind Morton's.

But along with that, perhaps paradoxically, perhaps not, comes more space for solo statements, albeit solos often composed in advance. In the version of musical democracy that Morton was working out, there was more space for flamboyant individuals (of which Morton was one of the prime examples in the history of a music full of individualists). Morton was working toward a place where the individual's voice would become part of a carefully orchestrated whole; the tension between the soloist's statement, the ensemble's commentary, and the composer's direction was part of the sound. This attitude was the basis of early big-band jazz and found its best expression in the work of jazz's greatest composer, Duke Ellington, who even at the time of these recordings was starting to work out his own grand notion of the balance between individual liberty and group meaning.

You can hear Morton's best early recordings on *The Pearls* (RCA/Bluebird 6588-2-RB). Most of these performances begin with New Orleans–style ensembles, with the trumpet or cornet playing the lead, the clarinet playing a fluid embroidery around that, and the trombone playing harmony notes. Because the recording quality is much better than that of the Oliver records, you can sort out the various instruments more easily. Morton uses the full panoply of devices that Oliver used, including breaks, stop-time choruses, and group polyphony, but there is more variety in the routining, more ingenuity in combining instruments, as in the haunting clarinet harmony with wailing trombone at the end of "Dead Man Blues." There is also more dramatic contrast between sections of the pieces.

Another crucial difference is that, on many of these tracks, Morton uses a string, or upright, bass – rather than a tuba – to fill in the harmonic underpinnings of the music and also to make the rhythm more flexible. On "Black Bottom Stomp," for example, the bass plays the customary New Orleans street-parade two beats per measure, on the first and third beats of each measure, as a tuba might have. But at certain points, the bass begins playing on all four beats of each measure, imparting a different, more runaway kind of rhythmic drive, more like the forward movement of a train or a car on a highway than the stop-and-go strut of paraders making their way down a street on a hot day. (On Mingus's "My Jelly Roll Soul" on *Blues and Roots* [Atlantic 1305-2], Mingus alternates between a two-four and a four-four feeling in his own bass playing; it's worth comparing it to "Black Bottom Stomp" for a lesson in the nature of swing.)

But on most of the tunes, Morton uses the more typical two-beat approach. You can learn something about the way his piano style relates to his arranging style by comparing the 1928 band version of "Kansas City Stomps" with his solo version, recorded for Gennett in 1923 (available on *Jelly Roll Morton 1923/24* [Milestone MCD-47018-2]). If you listen closely to the solo version (and you have to listen closely, because the sound is primitive), you can hear that Morton's left hand is playing a bass/chord, bass/chord pattern most of the time, which was characteristic of most ragtime pieces and of stride piano (to hear the stride style clearly, listen to the piano solos "Handful of Keys" and "Carolina Shout" as played by Fats Waller on the album *The Joint Is Jumpin'* [RCA/Bluebird 6288-2-RB]).

On the band version of "Kansas City Stomps," the left-hand way of keeping the beat is delegated to the tuba and drums: the tuba plays the bass note, and drummer Tommy Benford hits his snare drum with brushes on what would be the chord beat. On "Georgia Swing," the banjo takes over the part played by the snare drum. On "Kansas City Stomps," which has a beautiful, dancing, swinging feeling, you can hear both the tuba and the trombone play the occasional melodic punctuations that Morton's left hand interjects on his solo version. "The Pearls," "Grandpa's Spells," "Wolverine Blues," and "Mr. Jelly Lord" also make instructive comparisons to the piano solo versions.

Morton's piano is a constant presence on these recordings, commenting, underlining, embroidering, and propelling the ensemble, not to mention taking some fine solos. On "Sidewalk Blues," listen to the way Morton improvises gorgeous filigrees underneath the closely harmonized trio section for trumpet, clarinet, and trombone. The first time through this section, by the way, a break is actually taken by an automobile horn – a real novelty in 1926. Morton often used humorous effects like the car horn and comic dialogues; it was part of Morton's understanding of himself as an entertainer, not just as an artist.

Jelly Roll Morton had no trouble swinging from low comedy to high art. You can see this, too, on "Dead Man Blues," which begins with a parody of a New Orleans funeral march, probably the first on record, and then opens, like a flower, into a lilting, swinging blues with a melancholy overtone.

### RIFFS

Morton also used riffs imaginatively, an essential ingredient in jazz. A riff is a repeated phrase usually used to give momentum, encourage forward movement, or set a groove. At the end of "Georgia Swing," for example, the little figure the trumpet and clarinet play is a riff. Riffs often focus the rhythmic feeling of a particular number. The riff is derived from the repeated patterns of call-and-response that developed in the African-American church, not only in the singing but in the way a preacher uses repeated phrasings, varied slightly, for emphasis. Louis Armstrong organizes his famous solo on "S.O.L. Blues" (available on *The Hot Fives and Hot Sevens, Volume 3* [Columbia CK 44422]) around a riff pattern that could have been translated directly from the rhythms of a sanctified preacher.

Riffs are an integral part of the three versions of Morton's own "King Porter Stomp," recorded by Fletcher Henderson and available together on *A Study in Frustration: The Fletcher Henderson Story* (Columbia/Legacy C3K 57596). The tune became a standard of the swing-era dance band. In fact, the entire third disc of this three-disc set is a kind of graduate seminar in riffs, especially the apocalyptic "Yeah Man!," in which the brass and reed sections engage in thrilling call-and-response. Perhaps even more exciting is "Toby" by Bennie Moten's Kansas City Orchestra (featuring some wild stride piano by a young Count Basie), available on *Bennie Moten's Kansas City Orchestra (1929–1932): Basie Beginnings* (RCA/Bluebird 9768-2-RB).

Riffs were the meat and potatoes of the big swing dance bands of the 1930s, but small groups used them to their own advantage as well; listen, for just one example, to "Swing Is Here" by Gene Krupa's Swing Band, recorded in 1936 by a small group including trumpeter Roy Eldridge, tenor saxophonist Chu Berry, and Benny Goodman on clarinet (available on the collection *Swing Is Here: Small Band Swing 1935–1939* [RCA/Bluebird 2180-2-RB]). At the end, they use a series of rapid-fire riffs to create tension and ease it at the same time. Soloists, too, could use riffs to generate propulsion; as tenor saxophonist Coleman Hawkins enters his solo on "Crazy Rhythm" (available on *Coleman Hawkins and Benny Carter in Paris* [DRG/Swing CDSW 8403]), he sets up a repeated phrase that provides an exciting momentum.

The so-called bebop players of the 1940s were less interested in riffs than they were in long, intricate melodic lines that didn't repeat, but they used riffs in their own way. One example is Dizzy Gillespie's famous "Salt Peanuts," built on a swing-era riff, and his tune "Dizzy Atmosphere," available on *Bebop's Heartbeat* (Savoy ZDS 1177). Bebop tunes such as "A Night in Tunisia" and Thelonious Monk's "Epistrophy," "52nd Street Theme," "Straight, No Chaser," and "Thelonious" are all built on riffs. Gillespie's big band of the late 1940s also used riffs to great effect on tunes such as "Ow!" and "Jumpin' with Symphony Sid," available on *The Bebop Revolution* (RCA/Bluebird 2177-2-RB).

Certain players of the 1950s brought riffs back as an integral part of their performances. Miles Davis's famous recording of "Blue 'N' Boogie" (available on *Walkin'* [Prestige/OJC-213]), as well as having a repeated riff for a melody (originally recorded by Dizzy Gillespie), has a number of exciting riffs set behind Lucky Thompson's tenor saxophone solo. These riffs were originally used in Coleman Hawkins's 1944 recording of "Disorder at the Border," behind Hawkins's tenor solo (available on *Dizzy Gillespie: The Development of an American Artist* [Smithsonian Collection R004]).

Horace Silver, the pianist on the *Walkin'* session, was a bandleader and composer in his own right, and he practically built his whole style on riffs, producing such tunes as "Sister Sadie" and "Filthy McNasty." His piano accompaniments to solos often consisted of little more than a series of riffs, as you can hear on "Filthy McNasty" from *Doin' the Thing: The Horace Silver Quintet at the Village Gate* (Blue Note 84076). Charles Mingus, too, frequently used riffs to create a turbulent and compelling swing in his compositions. Maybe the best example is "E's Flat, Ah's Flat, Too" on *Blues and Roots* (Atlantic 1305-2), in which each instrument enters separately playing a different riff, overlaying them until a dense, exciting pattern is set up. "Folk Forms No. 1" (available on *Mingus Presents Mingus* [Candid CD 9005] as well as on *The Complete Candid Recordings of Charles Mingus* [Mosaic MD3-111]) is an improvised performance built entirely off of one repeated rhythmic figure; "MDM," in the Mosaic set, is an extended study in riffs as well.

### MORE MORTON

On "The Chant," Morton gives the performance unity by having the ensemble play the same riff at the end of each chorus (the "Hold That Tiger" phrase they play is one of Morton's favorite devices; he uses it in many different arrangements as a way of gearing up for a new solo or chorus) and by having the banjo and the trombone play much the same solo. But there is so much to listen for on these sides: the booting clarinet-piano-drum trio version of "Shreveport Stomp," the modern-sounding piano solo "Freakish," the exuberant "Tank Town Bump," and two good band sides from 1939, close to the end of Morton's career and life, on which he sings evocative, swaggering vocals on "Winin' Boy Blues" and "I Thought I Heard Buddy Bolden Say" (also known as "Buddy Bolden's Blues"). *The Pearls* (RCA/Bluebird 6588-2-RB) is truly one of the essential jazz albums.

All of the recordings on *The Pearls* are also included on a five-disc set released by RCA in the fall of 1990 for the hundredth anniversary of Morton's birth. *The Jelly Roll Morton Centennial* (RCA/Bluebird 2361-2-RB) contains all the recordings, along with all known alternate takes, made under Morton's leadership for Victor. The alternate takes follow the originally released takes, so listening to the set straight through involves hearing each tune twice in a row; *The Pearls* is much easier to listen to for pleasure. But *The Jelly Roll Morton Centennial* is an important set for serious students of the music.

Morton continued to record through the early 1930s, but his style, like Oliver's, had been shouldered out of the commercial picture by a big-band style that was refining and expanding concepts that he had delivered into the jazz language. Unable to really adapt himself to these extensions, he became an anachronism. He was also an egotistical man, hard to get along with by all reports, with no tendency to undervalue his own contributions. Many people just didn't like him. He was rediscovered briefly in the late 1930s, but it didn't pan out into anything resembling a new lease on life.

Despite all his hard times, Morton had a last laugh of sorts. In the summer of 1938 he was interviewed by folklorist Alan Lomax for the Library of Congress. During the five weeks over which the interviews were conducted, Morton reminisced about growing up in New Orleans, told stories about the colorful characters he knew there, illustrated with his own piano playing and singing how jazz developed from early marching band music, blues, quadrilles, and Spanish music, underscored his own role in that process, and played his compositions at length.

Rounder Records has issued every bit of music from these sessions on four CDs – *The Library of Congress Recordings, Volume 1 (Kansas City Stomp)* (CD 1091), *Volume 2 (Anamule Dance)* (CD 1092), *Volume 3 (The Pearls)* (CD 1093), and *Volume 4 (Winin' Boy Blues)* (CD 1094). The discs are all worth having, especially *Volume 1,* which includes Morton's demonstration of the way in which "Tiger Rag" developed from a French quadrille, and *Volume 4,* which has extended demonstrations of what Morton called the "Spanish tinge," a Latin rhythmic inflection used as accenting throughout jazz. Unfortunately, since Rounder chose to issue only the musical selections, Morton's fascinating autobiographical and musicological monologues are missing, and they are in some ways the most valuable part of the Library of Congress material, especially the half-hour-long "Discourse on Jazz." The small New Orleans label Solo Art has issued at least one volume of integrated talking and playing, but they seem to have given up issuing the rest of it in the face of Rounder's set. If you are really interested, the Library of Congress material is available on LP from both Swaggie (Australian) and Classic Jazz Masters (Swedish), labels available only through specialty shops. They are worth tracking down; as musicology, as history, and as storytelling at its best, they are one of the glories of American cultural history.

Not long after the sessions at the Library of Congress, Morton made a series of commercial recordings for the small label General, which were later released as *New Orleans Memories* (available under that title, but hard to find, on Commodore [6.24062 AG]). Morton talks a little, sings beautiful songs like "Don't You Leave Me Here" and "2:19 Blues," and plays some infectious piano solos. This is a thoroughly enjoyable set, a haunting coda to one of the most important and fascinating careers in jazz.

Depending on how much you like this style, you might want to check out the recordings of the New Orleans Rhythm Kings, a white band from New Orleans that included clarinetist Leon Rappolo. Their style is a little more staid than Oliver's but is basically in the same vein; their recordings are available, in ultra-low fidelity, on *New Orleans Rhythm Kings* (Milestone MCD-47020-2). *The Sound of New Orleans,* a three-record boxed set (Columbia Special Products JC3L 30), may be hard to track down but has a lot of unusual material by important early bands such as Sam Morgan's, Oscar "Papa" Celestin's, and A. J. Piron's, along with music from the likes of King Oliver, Louis Armstrong, Wingy Manone, and others less celebrated.

## BREAKING OUT

Several important things happened as the New Orleans style started to get disseminated, both in Chicago and in New York. For one, small recording combinations began making records that had a New Orleans ensemble sound, but these groups placed more emphasis on solos than the New Orleans ensembles did. For another, big dance bands of nine to twelve pieces began to adapt the New Orleans ensemble approach to the larger, more urbane framework of the dance orchestra. The pivotal figure in both trends was Louis Armstrong.

In June 1924 Armstrong had left King Oliver to become a featured soloist with the preeminent black dance band of the day, Fletcher Henderson's. In the band at the time Armstrong joined was Coleman Hawkins, who would become the first important soloist on the tenor saxophone. Both as an incubator of solo talent and as a lab for the development of a big-band style, Henderson's was by far the most important band of the 1920s. His innovations, and those of his principal arrangers (Don Redman, Horace Henderson, and Benny Carter), became the blueprint for the swing era. Fletcher Henderson arrangements formed the foundation of the band books for both the Benny Goodman and Count Basie orchestras at their inceptions. But in the early 1920s Henderson was still finding his direction as a bandleader.

In the band's early days, there weren't many musicians who could sustain a solo over eight bars, much less a full chorus of a popular tune. So the arranger bore most of the brunt of the work, as you can hear in pre–Louis Armstrong Henderson recordings. If you can stand it, listen to cuts like "Charleston Crazy" and "War Horse Mama" (compare the stiff trumpet solo with Armstrong's work from just seven months later) on *Rarest Fletcher* (MCA-1346). An interesting performance from this era is "Dicty Blues" (available on both the MCA release and on the best Henderson compilation, *A Study in Frustration: The Fletcher Henderson Story* [Columbia/Legacy C3K 57596]), in which the Henderson band has the sound and even the instrumentation (substantially) of the Oliver band.

But after Armstrong arrived, there was a quantum leap in the amount of information potential soloists had to work with, and the art of soloing advanced very quickly. Compare solos by the pre-Armstrong trumpeters with any of Armstrong's and it's very clear what he brought to the activity. He wasn't the first to try and make things up as he went along, but he had such a sure sense of how to aim for the next phrase. Each of his phrases followed naturally and logically from the previous one, as sentences flow from a great conversationalist. That sureness of phrasing also influenced the arrangers, and the sections soon had a bite and crispness they had lacked until then. Armstrong, for all he was featured when he was with Henderson, still had limited solo space. But you can hear the authority in his solos on otherwise forgettable records like "Copenhagen" and "Shanghai Shuffle" (both available on the Columbia/Legacy Henderson set).

Armstrong rubbed off on his bandmates, especially Coleman Hawkins. On recordings from 1923 and 1924, like "Dicty Blues," Hawkins sounds stiff and unswinging, but by 1926 he was playing mature solos. The fullest, most impressive statement he made that year was on "The Stampede" (available on the Columbia/Legacy set). This Don Redman arrangement employed all sections of the orchestra in unison as well as in polyphonic ways. Hawkins and trumpeters Rex Stewart and Joe Smith take wonderful solos, and the ending is jammed in truly polyphonic New Orleans style.

Armstrong, emerging star that he was as well as genius virtuoso, needed more room to stretch out than just the occasional eight- or sixteen-bar solo. He left Henderson in November 1925 and got work with the big bands of Erskine Tate and Carroll Dickerson in Chicago, which featured him as a star but still didn't let him stretch out in a flat-out jazz context. So he started making some small-group jazz records that mixed the New Orleans polyphonic group sound with a more stripped-down instrumentation, as well as more solo space. The records he made with this group, which was called the Hot Five, shook up the world.

The recordings of the Hot Five and the slightly later Hot Seven are available in four volumes on Columbia: *The Hot Fives, Volume 1* (CK 44049), *The Hot Fives and Hot Sevens, Volume 2 and Volume 3* (CK 44253 and CK 44422), and *Louis Armstrong, Volume 4: Louis Armstrong and Earl Hines* (CK 45142). They are all essential; their vitality and genius make them just as enjoyable today as they must have been then. The recordings are discussed in detail with the rest of Armstrong's records in the Soloists section, but they were also important in the development of ensemble styles.

In the first recordings the group made (on *Volume 1*), Armstrong's cornet is an equal member of the front line, along with Johnny Dodds's clarinet and Kid Ory's trombone; in fact, the overall group approach is similar to Oliver's Creole Jazz Band recordings except that there is only one cornet. Solo space for Armstrong is at a minimum, but his presence is the animating factor in the front line. He plays the melody as the clarinet and trombone do their traditional jobs from the New Orleans ensemble. In the later choruses of tunes like "My Heart" and "Yes, I'm in the Barrel," Armstrong varies his lead so much that it could stand on its own as a solo, and he takes several concise breaks in which there isn't a tentative note.

But beginning with the session of February 26, 1926, things are a little different. Armstrong is more out front in the recording mix, louder than the trombone and clarinet, and he is featured more. He takes his famous scat singing chorus on "Heebie Jeebies," and on "Oriental Strut" and, especially, "Cornet Chop Suey" takes stop-time solos that were far beyond what any other trumpeter of the time could have conceived. Musicians all over the country studied these records; Armstrong was serving notice that soloists didn't exist just as a spice in a big-band arrangement but could create new, original melodies of their own. He extended this idea as the Hot Five and Hot Seven series went along. By May 1927, when the Hot Seven recorded "Wild Man Blues" and "Potato Head Blues," Armstrong was the idol of musicians everywhere, and jazz soloists had truly come into their own.

It should be noted that the New Orleans–born clarinetist and soprano saxophonist Sidney Bechet was, if anything, ahead of Armstrong as a soloist in the early 1920s. On the recordings he made with Clarence Williams's Blue Five in July 1923 (currently very difficult to find), only three months after the Oliver band's first records (and two and a half years before the first Hot Fives), Bechet's soprano is as strong and brilliant a part of the front line as Armstrong's cornet was later to be. He also takes several breaks, especially on "Wild Cat Blues," that are every bit as assured and imaginative as Armstrong's were with Henderson. Bechet, however, spent lots of time in Europe throughout the 1920s, so his influence wasn't felt to anything like the extent that Armstrong's was. Also, he lacked the extraordinary kind of personal projection Armstrong had.

The two met, however, at a session arranged by pianist and composer Clarence Williams, in a telling match of wits and imagination. "Cake Walkin' Babies," a head-to-head New Orleans front-line jam, with high-wire breaks, stop-time passages, and thrilling trading back and forth of the lead, was recorded twice, first in December 1924 and again in January 1925. Both sessions are available on *The Essential Sidney Bechet, Volume 1* (Musicmemoria CD 30229). The second version is one of the great examples of competition raising two voices up above their own heads, really one of the most thrilling moments in jazz. This shows as well as anything could what the tension between an ego straining at the leash and the commitment to overall musical sound can produce when the tension is perfect.

For more excellent New Orleans-by-way-of-Chicago small-group playing, try *Johnny Dodds – South Side Chicago Jazz* (Decca/MCA MCAD-42326), which features Dodds's totally individual clarinet playing in trio settings, in a quartet with Armstrong, pianist Jimmy Blythe, and washboard player Jimmy Bertrand, and in other fascinating settings that give a good sense of the various shapes the style could take. *Great Trumpets: Classic Jazz to Swing* (RCA/Bluebird 6753-2-RB) has some examples of this style under the nominal leadership, variously, of trumpeters Tommy Ladnier, Lee Collins, and Sidney De Paris.

New Orleans clarinetist Jimmie Noone was one of the most influential players on that instrument in the late 1920s. His band, which for a time featured piano innovator Earl Hines, played an extended engagement at Chicago's Apex Club and made a series of recordings in 1928 and 1929 using arranging devices à la Morton, along with more flat-out group improvisation à la the Hot Five. They are available on *Jimmie Noone: Apex Blues* (Decca/GRP GRD-633), a set that is well worth owning. Chicago trumpeter Jabbo Smith, a fiery player who set himself up as competition for Armstrong, led an exciting small band on a series of recordings available on the possibly hard-to-find *The Ace of Rhythm* (MCA-1347, cassette only).

## SETTLING DOWN

Like trains on parallel tracks, the understanding of how to orchestrate jazz and the increased understanding of solo possibilities picked up momentum simultaneously. The big dance bands learned more and more how to integrate the new hot sounds into their repertoire by featuring both solos and arrangements that made use of the accenting and instrumental-distribution strategies learned from New Orleans jazz (and then expanded upon in ways more appropriate for the larger ensembles).

As the dance-oriented big-band sound increasingly became the apparent wave, it gathered more of the financial resources. Everybody wanted to hire the larger ensembles; there was a lot of money around, people wanted to go out dancing, and most emerging (and established) musicians of the day found work with the large dance bands. Some of the bands were closer to the spirit of jazz than others, and the sometimes very thin line between so-called hot bands and so-called sweet bands continued to be drawn throughout the swing era.

Fletcher Henderson's band was the best of the late 1920s. He insisted on top-flight musicianship; the sections were crisp and defined. The trumpets most often played a melody, which would be set against a countermelody in the saxophones, with harmony parts and accents provided by the trombones. Henderson's band could combine the abandon of a New Orleans street-parade band with the precision of an Air Force drill team. The band's always impressive roster of soloists by this time included Coleman Hawkins, Rex Stewart, Jimmy Harrison, Bobby Stark, and others. The combination of crack ensemble work with strong solo statements was irresistible.

Henderson's repertoire, at least on records, consisted of popular tunes of the day, blues, specially composed rhythm numbers often concocted of riffs, and New Orleans standards like "Sugar Foot Stomp," "Milenburg Joys," and "King Porter Stomp" updated for the new big-band style. By far the best all-around collection is *A Study in Frustration: The Fletcher Henderson Story* (Columbia/Legacy C3K 57596). The collection spans Henderson's career from the period before Armstrong's arrival to the end of the 1930s, when his band included such greats as Roy Eldridge, Chu Berry, and Ben Webster. The examples of the band's work range from highly arranged pieces like "The Henderson Stomp" (featuring Fats Waller as guest star on piano) and "Rocky Mountain Blues" to loosely worked-up masterpieces like "New King Porter Stomp." There is plenty of solo work by Hawkins and Louis Armstrong, as well as by important players like trumpeters Red Allen, Tommy Ladnier, and Joe Smith, trombonists Jimmy Harrison and J. C. Higginbotham, and many others, and plenty of opportunities to study the kinds of backgrounds Henderson and his arrangers could write to encourage and set off the soloists.

At a time when the Henderson band was developing and refining its notion of what a large ensemble could do, it also did a series of recordings emphasizing its roots in flat-out jazz. *Fletcher Henderson and the Dixie Stompers 1925–1928* (DRG/Swing SW8445/6) has some outstanding and uninhibited jazz (some of the most uninhibited jazz of the 1920s) featuring Coleman Hawkins, Rex Stewart, the little-heard trumpeter Bobby Stark, Joe Smith, and all of Henderson's other stars. While not exactly a small group (it was the full Henderson band), it gave much more free rein to the soloists. Unfortunately, the album notes list the wrong personnel.

A valuable set, especially for its generous sampling of the 1936 band with Roy Eldridge and Chu Berry, is *Hocus Pocus: Fletcher Henderson and His Orchestra 1927–1936* (RCA/Bluebird 9904-2-RB). Some of the material here sounds very dated, like "Roll On, Mississippi, Roll On" and "Strangers" (which, nevertheless, has an excellent Coleman Hawkins solo). But the set includes a strong version of "Sugar Foot Stomp" by the 1931 band, as well as some fine swing arrangements by the 1936 band, including the infectious "Knock, Knock, Who's There?" and the blistering "Jangled Nerves."

An interesting set of sides recorded by Henderson's band in 1931 for the small Crown label is *Fletcher Henderson: The Crown King of Swing* (Savoy SJL 1152), on which the repertoire includes such popular songs as "Stardust" and "After You've Gone" and older jazz items such as "Tiger Rag" and "Milenburg Joys." Four first-rate 1933 Henderson titles are available on *Ridin' in Rhythm* (DRG/Swing CDSW 8453/4). Coleman Hawkins's exercise in the whole-tone scale, "Queer Notions," is here, as is his outstanding solo on "It's the Talk of the Town." "Nagasaki" has a great vocal by Red Allen; he plays the trumpet solo as well, not Bobby Stark as the album credits claim.

Throughout these sides, Hawkins's tenor gives the entire saxophone section its character. But by that time he was already a star and would soon be leaving for Europe, where he would be hailed internationally. The same orchestra under the direction of Horace Henderson has six sides in the *Ridin' in Rhythm* set, containing fine solos by Hawkins, Red Allen, and trombone virtuoso Dicky Wells, as well as good riff-based writing for all the sections.

Henderson arranger Don Redman later led a very influential band with the period name McKinney's Cotton Pickers, which had tremendous ensemble finesse and interesting arrangements. *McKinney's Cotton Pickers (1928–1930): The Band Don Redman Built* (RCA/Bluebird 2275-2-RB) shows the band at its best, with guest stars like Coleman Hawkins and Fats Waller; this is an invaluable document of the late-1920s New York big-band scene.

A collection that shows the influence, and the wide range of interpretation possible, of the Henderson/Redman style is *Early Black Swing – The Birth of Big Band Jazz: 1927–1934* (RCA/Bluebird 9583-2-RB). It includes fascinating glimpses of such luminaries as Earl Hines, Jimmie Lunceford, and Duke Ellington in relatively obscure early performances and less well known bands such as The Missourians (which became the Cab Calloway orchestra) and Charlie Johnson's Paradise Ten. The arrangements are as formal as Will Hudson's "White Heat," performed by Jimmie Lunceford's orchestra, and as informal as Charlie Johnson's "Hot Tempered Blues," which, informal though it is, features all kinds of combinations: notated duets for trumpets and clarinets, a violin solo with a clarinet background, and a jammed last chorus.

A perfectly encapsulated summation of what happened in the music in the time period covered by the set can be found by comparing the set's two performances by Bennie Moten's Kansas City Orchestra, "South" and "Moten Swing." "South," recorded in 1928, is a performance steeped in the New Orleans rhythmic feeling, with its characteristic sense of hesitation followed by a burst of movement ahead, like a parade beat. For "Moten Swing," however, recorded four years later, the tuba of the earlier session has been replaced by the string bass of Walter Page, playing four even beats per measure instead of the tuba's two, and the banjo has been replaced by a guitar, all of which make the beats more subtle, lighter, and forward-moving.

The Moten band, in fact, was seminal in the transition from the heavy, sometimes jerky rhythmic efforts of the first jazz big bands to the streamlined, forward-moving rhythmic feel of the best of the late swing bands and, through them, to the bebop of Charlie Parker. The band's work after Count Basie joined as its pianist is documented on *Bennie Moten's Kansas City Orchestra (1929–1932): Basie Beginnings* (RCA/Bluebird 9768-2-RB). The most enjoyable tracks, and the most modern sounding, are the ones recorded at the same 1932 session that produced "Moten Swing." One thing to listen for is the lightness of the beats in the rhythm section. Most big bands at the time sounded like a runner landing hard on every footfall; Moten's sounded like a runner landing only hard enough to propel him or her into the next stride. An interesting tune here is Moten's treatment of the New Orleans standard "Milenburg Joys," which begins with Walter Page's bass hitting on one and three, like a street-parade tuba, and then shifting into the sleekest of straight four-four.

A listen to the band's phrasing on their treatment of Rodgers and Hart's "The Blue Room" provides an insight into the nature of swing. It will be helpful for readers without a musical background to know that each of the four beats per bar can be divided in half; you can count the rhythm one *and* two *and* three *and* four (*and* one . . .). The one, two, three, and four beats, which the rhythm section, particularly the bass, usually articulates, are called the down beats. The *and* half of the beat is called the up beat. The arrangement of "The Blue Room" here tends to accent the up beats rather than the down beats; this also gives the performance a forward-moving rather than a heavy-footed feeling.

But of all the big bands at the time and of all the arrangers, the one who was destined to make the greatest contribution by far was Duke Ellington.

## DUKE ELLINGTON, PART I

There is no way to do justice to the work of Duke Ellington in a book this size, even if the whole book were to concern itself solely with his music. Ellington's achievement was quintessentially American and was accomplished under the conditions of life of the American itinerant bandleader – constant movement, constant management problems, and, be it said, constant inspiration from both the panorama of American life, high and low, to which he was exposed and the experience of having his music played back to him almost instantaneously by a group of some of the most talented and individualistic instrumentalists in history.

Ellington created at the highest levels throughout the whole span of a recording career that ran from 1924 to 1974. At every stage he busied himself with synthesizing what had been done and what was being done by the musicians who preceded and surrounded him, and his music, of every period, stands apart from, and above, that of his contemporaries.

From the beginning, Ellington's music dealt with formal, compositional aspects that were beyond even the very best of the day's arrangers; his choices of instrumentation, of dynamics, and of contrast between sections of a piece showed that he was thinking, from the beginning, as a composer, not just as an arranger of dance hall pieces, although almost all of what he did functioned as the highest-level kind of dance hall music as well as repaying serious formal study. Like Shakespeare, whom he resembled above all, Ellington worked on several levels at once, filling the needs of storytelling, entertainment, instruction, beautification of his chosen language, intellectual stimulation, and the presentation of emotional truth.

In the late 1920s and very early 1930s Ellington investigated all the basics of the large-band format he was working in – the sounds of sections, the role of a soloist, instrumental sonorities, dance rhythms, the New Orleans tradition, the blues, two-four versus four-four, swing – and from 1926 on produced music unlike anyone else's. A shock may be had by turning from the Fletcher Henderson arrangements, great as they are, to *Duke Ellington and His Orchestra – The Brunswick Era, Volume 1 (1926–1929)* (Decca/MCA MCAD-42325). From the brooding opening strains of his theme song of the time, "East St. Louis Toodle-Oo," through a wild and, at times, hilarious two-part deconstruction of the New Orleans standard "Tiger Rag," Ellington has his way with the conventions of the day and invents more than one or two of his own.

Each of these pieces is more than just a showpiece for a band; each has a specific mood – often more than one – that it conveys. "East St. Louis Toodle-Oo," for example, begins with a somber minor-key figure played by tuba and saxophone in a very low register. Over this swelling minor-key theme, Bubber Miley's plunger-muted growl trumpet comes in with the first theme. When the piece goes into major for the bridge, it is as if the sun has come out. When it goes back into minor for the last eight bars, it does so with all the drama of bad luck coming back to stay. Then the key shifts to major again for a second theme, played by Tricky Sam Nanton on trombone; there are solos from clarinet, a trumpet duet, a clarinet trio, and then a final, dramatic repetition of the first melody. The piece, in other words, goes in and out of two contrasting moods, uses a startling range of instrumental timbre and coloration, tells a complete story by developing two separate themes, and does it all in under three minutes.

The same kind of range of contrasting colors can be found in other early classics, such as "Black and Tan Fantasy" and "The Mooche," both of which Ellington returned to throughout his career. There are more conventional stomp pieces, such as "Birmingham Breakdown," "Jubilee Stomp," and "Doin' the Frog," included here, but also a little remarked upon masterpiece called "Immigration Blues" (only on the CD issue of the set), which begins with a fanfare from the trumpets, answered by the reeds, goes into a short three-note blues phrase, answered by the tuba and the piano's left hand, goes into a trumpet solo, then an alto solo over a Spanish beat, then another trumpet solo over a background in which the time is turned around (the tuba and other rhythm instruments accent two and four, when they had been accenting one and three). Underneath a trombone solo later, Ellington has arranged the reeds playing at the bottom of their ranges for an unusual sonority, like the low horn of an ocean liner. The last chorus is a sort of jam, with reprises of the original tuba theme as well as a brief taste of the time turnaround and a coda from the growl trumpet. Not to be overlooked are several early lyrical themes stated by muted trumpet over a hushed reed background – "Take It Easy," the beautiful and durable "Black Beauty," and "Awful Sad" – which show his melodic and lyric genius, his sensitivity, and also his awareness of dynamics;

rare was the band of that day that could approach lyricism this delicate without falling off into sentimentality.

*Early Ellington 1927–1934* (RCA/Bluebird 6852-2-RB) has alternate versions of "East St. Louis Toodle-Oo," "Black and Tan Fantasy," "The Mooche," and "Black Beauty," as well as early incarnations of such Ellington classics as "Mood Indigo," "Rockin' in Rhythm," "Ring Dem Bells," "Solitude," and "Creole Love Call." We hear the band's major voices as they join: baritone saxophonist Harry Carney, trumpeter Cootie Williams, alto saxophonist Johnny Hodges; we also hear how the solo statements are made a part of the ensemble sound. The individual is always allowed to make a contribution in a context that helps him make sense, and to which he has to relate in turn, or risk making no sense at all. In this way, too, Ellington's music is democratic in its essence; the individual has a responsibility for making the whole group make sense, and the group has a responsibility for giving meaning to its individual members.

The extraordinary moments in this set are too many to mention, but listen to "Saturday Night Function," with its pedal-point, or drone, effect from Wellman Braud's extremely well recorded bass. Even on a number like this, which is essentially a string of solos, the background makes a pointed statement. "Shout 'Em Aunt Tillie," with its AAB minor theme stated by both brass and reeds, the ingenious routining of "Old Man Blues" (based, as Dan Morgenstern points out in his liner notes, on "Old Man River"), especially the way the bridge is treated, the unique instrumental voicings of "Mood Indigo" and "Solitude," the shockingly apt railroad onomatopoeia (writer Albert Murray's phrase) of "Daybreak Express," the infectious jump tunes "Stompy Jones" and "Cotton Club Stomp," and the eight-and-a-half-minute "Creole Rhapsody" (two sides of a 12-inch 78-rpm record), one of Ellington's earliest extended works, in which multiple tempos, varied orchestrations of the same melodic material, and dynamic contrast contribute to a fully realized extended work, demonstrate the genius of Ellington in its early flowering. An essential set.

The most comprehensive collection of early Ellington is certainly *The OKeh Ellington* (Columbia C2K 46177), a two-disc set of material recorded between 1927 and 1930, not all of which was issued on the Columbia-affiliated OKeh label. This set includes pieces like "Hop Head," "Stack O'Lee Blues," and "Bugle Call Rag," a couple of versions apiece of classics like "East St. Louis Toodle-Oo," "Black and Tan Fantasy," and the thrilling "Hot and Bothered," and a number of rare collector's items. The set is especially valuable for showing the widely varying approaches Ellington would use in revisiting the same tunes and for showing the band's development over a three-and-a-half-year period. The album notes, by Ellington expert Stanley Dance, are very informative as well.

Both RCA and MCA have issued second volumes of Ellington material, neither of which is as valuable as either *Early Ellington* or *The Brunswick Era, Volume 1*. But *Jungle Nights in Harlem 1927–1932* (RCA/Bluebird 2499-2-RB) and *The Jungle Band: The Brunswick Era, Volume 2 1929–1931* (Decca/MCA MCAD-42348) document an Ellington band that had been honed by an extended engagement at Harlem's Cotton Club, where they played a trademark "jungle music" for white patrons who came to see all-black floor shows. There is much excellent music on both sets, but any of the three previously mentioned collections would be a better place to start listening to the early band.

Ellington's Columbia material from the early and mid-1930s is somewhat hard to find, although much of it has been issued on the European Classics label. But make sure you listen to the 1932 "Lazy Rhapsody" on *The 1930s: Big Bands* (Columbia CK 40651), a unique essay in instrumental sonority in which the solo voices of clarinet, alto, baritone sax, piano, and even Cootie Williams's wordless vocal come out of a background that they fade back into. Also of interest, and a must for the Ellington fan, is *Reflections in Ellington* (Natasha Imports NI 4016), which contains two medleys recorded by the 1932 band in stereo – not reprocessed stereo but the real thing, recorded on two machines and then synchronized. The fascinating story of the discovery of this material is told in the liner notes.

Ellington occupied the same position in every era of jazz that he did in the late 1920s and very early 1930s. We'll revisit him periodically.

## LONELY MELODY

Jazz-oriented bands weren't the only ones to hire what were called hot soloists in those days. Every band needed one or two musicians who could provide at least a semblance of a jazz solo. As a gross generalization, the black big bands tended to have a higher jazz quotient than the white bands, but even the sweetest of the sweet (with the possible exception of Guy Lombardo) usually had at least one hot soloist. Probably the most famous example was the orchestra of Paul Whiteman.

Whiteman was called the King of Jazz by a public and press that equated the word with the uninhibited excess and license of the 1920s life-style. Whiteman's was basically a dance band with pretensions, and little of its enormous output would be recognizable as jazz today. But throughout the late

1920s and 1930s, he hired some very good musicians indeed, including violinist Joe Venuti, the Dorsey brothers, saxophonist Frank Trumbauer, trombonist Jack Teagarden, and, perhaps the best known, cornetist Bix Beiderbecke.

Most of the best of Whiteman's records were orchestrated by the great arranger Bill Challis. Records like "Changes," "Lonely Melody," and "From Monday On" have beautiful, complete statements by the short-lived Beiderbecke; they are collected on *Bix Lives!* (RCA/Bluebird 6845-2-RB). In listening to the cuts collected here, note how the jazz aspect of the performances fades in and out, like a radio station just on the edge of its range. At times, as in "San," the jazz wing of the band is given full freedom. At other times, Beiderbecke takes his solo over crooning voices, or his solo stands out in the middle of lush string arrangements like the Statue of Liberty in a cornfield. One of the most interesting cuts is "You Took Advantage of Me," which has a full chase chorus of two-bar exchanges between Bix and his soulmate Frank Trumbauer on C-melody saxophone. But the jazz element is rarely integrated fully into the performance; the violins and other sweet elements provide a sentimental spin that was temperamentally foreign to what bands like Henderson's were trying to bring off.

Other orchestras, such as those of Roger Wolfe Kahn and, especially, Ben Pollack, could generate considerable jazz feeling when they wanted to. Pollack's most serious jazz soloists were trombonist Jack Teagarden and a young clarinetist from Chicago named Benny Goodman, who joined the Pollack orchestra when he was only seventeen. You can hear Teagarden with the Pollack and Kahn bands, as well as on several sides recorded during his mid-1930s tenure with Whiteman, on *Jack Teagarden/That's a Serious Thing* (RCA/Bluebird 9986-2-RB), which also includes some flat-out small-group jazz with the trombonist.

Good as those sides are, Teagarden gets even more of a chance to shine – alongside Goodman himself – on *Benny Goodman and Jack Teagarden: B.G. and Big Tea in NYC* (Decca/GRP GRD-609). This collection of tracks recorded between 1929 and 1934 shows what happened when the best hot soloists from the white dance orchestras of the time were turned loose to play more or less as they wished. Most of the bands on this collection were recording-studio-only affairs made up of the likes of Goodman, Teagarden, violin master Joe Venuti, the brilliant guitarist Eddie Lang, and the much-recorded trumpeter Red Nichols. Probably the best tracks here are the four 1931 sides – "Beale Street Blues," "After You've Gone," "Farewell Blues," and "Someday Sweetheart" – by Venuti and Lang and their All-Star Orchestra. Teagarden takes wonderful, characteristic vocals on the first two, and both he and Goodman shine throughout one of the best small-group jazz dates of the early 1930s.

Also included on the collection are four tracks by Irving Mills's Hotsy-Totsy Gang, which featured Bix Beiderbecke in his second-to-last recording session. A highly recommended set.

One surprising figure who made records spotlighting jazz musicians such as Benny Goodman, Muggsy Spanier, Fats Waller, and clarinetist Frank Teschemacher was the entertainer Ted Lewis, who usually sang sentimental songs. "I'm Crazy 'Bout My Baby" (available on *The 1930s: The Singers* [Columbia CK 40847]) is performed by Lewis's band with Fats Waller on piano and vocal; the arrangement is a little stiff, but Waller has fun, and there's a glimpse of young Benny Goodman, too.

Some elegant and durable jazz was recorded by small groups drawn from the ranks of large dance bands such as Whiteman's. Some of the best of these were made under the leadership of Frank Trumbauer and featured Bix Beiderbecke. Probably the most famous single side they cut was the 1927 "Singin' the Blues," a beautiful song with a graceful harmonic structure that was made for storytelling. Taken at a very relaxed, underplayed medium tempo, it is an early example of a cool approach to hot jazz. (Whiteman arranger Bill Challis transcribed the entire performance and orchestrated it for the Fletcher Henderson orchestra in 1931; you can hear it on the Henderson album *Hocus Pocus: Fletcher Henderson and His Orchestra 1927–1936* [RCA/Bluebird 9904-2-RB].)

The Beiderbecke original is available on *Bix Beiderbecke, Volume 1: Singin' the Blues* (Columbia CK 45450), along with a number of other excellent items and some not so excellent. A notable factor here is the careful routing and arranging effects on even the most jazz-intensive sides, such as "Clarinet Marmalade." The soloists on most of these performances are accorded little more freedom, in fact, than they had in the big bands with which they usually worked. On some of the more ambitious ones, such as "Krazy Kat" and "Humpty Dumpty," attempts are made at futuristic effects that haven't aged well. But the most relaxed tunes, such as "Riverboat Shuffle," with its carefully arranged New Orleans–style touches, "Ostrich Walk," with its fine saxophone writing and haunting Beiderbecke solo, and "Way Down Yonder in New Orleans," swing along very nicely and have extremely beautiful statements from Beiderbecke.

## SWINGING OUT

**IF "STOMP" WAS** the most common word for the characteristic rhythm of celebration of the late 1920s and early 1930s (as in "Black Bottom Stomp," "Sugar Foot Stomp," "King Porter Stomp," "Cotton Club Stomp," etc.), then the 1930s saw it change to "jump," and, especially, in the word that gave the era its name, "swing." The names weren't arbitrary; they betrayed a bias in rhythmic feeling: just as a stomp might suggest a heavy emphasis on a down beat, a jump might suggest an impulse in the up direction. And swing suggests that what is being planned is a movement forward, not just up and down.

And that is what the mid-1930s was about – finding a way to step lightly on the beat and to keep moving forward. This had a lot to do with the introduction of electric microphones, which encouraged the use of the upright bass in place of the tuba (the string bass could continue to play a legato four beats per bar long after a tuba player would have run out of breath) and the replacement of the banjo with the springier-sounding guitar. These two changes alone insured that the rhythmic difference in the music would be every bit as marked as the difference between Bennie Moten's 1930 "New Moten Stomp" and his 1932 "Moten Swing" (both available on *Bennie Moten's Kansas City Orchestra (1929–1932): Basie Beginnings* [RCA/Bluebird 9768-2-RB]).

It is perhaps no accident that this new rhythmic sense in the music was being introduced – pioneered, you might say – by musicians from the Midwest and Southwest. The New Orleans beat was designed to echo the stop-and-go strut of paraders making their way down a street on a hot day; parades were occasioned by holidays, funerals, celebrations – the milestones of life in a circumscribed community with an established and full sense of the cyclical rhythms of life and death.

But the pure four-four that came to identify the best of the so-called swing bands, above all Count Basie's, which grew out of Bennie Moten's, was music of the road and the train. The Midwest – Kansas, Missouri, Oklahoma – still partook of a frontier mythology of possibility, mobility, and independence. The music the midwesterners brought with them was redolent of optimism, possibility, a better life just down the road – a message that was sure to be popular during the Great Depression.

## RIFFING

Not all of the swing big bands played in straight four-four all the time, and few held the beat as lightly as the Count Basie orchestra, but the era was defined by a quick sense of how to impel forward movement. The use of riffs became a kind of science; the best arrangers could use them to create an irresistible momentum of swing. *The 1930s: Big Bands* (Columbia CK 40651) is a perfect introductory sampler to the syles of most of the important jazz-oriented big bands of the time. The majority of the performances in the collection, from Claude Hopkins's 1932 "Mush Mouth" to Benny Goodman's 1939 Fletcher Henderson–arranged "Stealin' Apples," rely on the accretion of riffs for their character and effect. Musicians were learning how to use the expectations set up by the even four beats per bar to create a new kind of tension, surprise, and satisfaction, as in the wild Cab Calloway performance of "The Man from Harlem," when the trumpets alter the accents of Chopin's *Funeral March* to increase the effect of forward momentum. (Calloway exhorts the band through a series of exciting riff choruses, too.) Louis Armstrong had known this secret at least since his first recordings with Fletcher Henderson, but his knowledge was being integrated into every musician's vocabulary.

One of the ways of creating tension and release was to alternate long, held notes with phrases consisting of short, punchy notes; Fletcher Henderson's "Can You Take It?" uses this strategy. The tune "Let's Get Together," by drummer Chick Webb's band, uses a similar technique – the alternation of a simple two-note motif with an answering phrase of more complexity. These techniques derive from the incantatory call-and-response patterns of the African-American church and create the same climate of involvement and community that call-and-response and percussive incantation always point toward. They also reflect the instrumental strategy of the New Orleans ensembles, with the trumpets playing simpler lines which are answered by the reeds.

"Passionette," by the important but little-known band of Teddy Hill (which included such greats as trombonist Dicky Wells and trumpeter Frankie Newton), is built entirely on riffs and, in its main theme, shows another way of creating suspense: the countering of a series of up-beat accents with an answering phrase beginning on the down beat, which creates a feeling of tumbling forward. In the late choruses of "St. Louis Wiggle Rhythm," by the Blue Rhythm Band, call-and-response technique has been telescoped into simultaneous riffs dovetailed over one another; this became standard operating procedure, a kind of counterpoint of riffs. (Charles Mingus took this principle to its logical extreme in his recording of "E's Flat, Ah's Flat, Too," available on *Blues and Roots* [Atlantic 1305-2], in which every horn in the ensemble plays a different riff simultaneously.) This set is an essential one-volume survey of the genre.

Another excellent overview of big-band styles is the two-disc set *An Anthology of Big Band Swing 1930–1955* (Decca/GRP GRD-2-629). It includes representative tracks by seminal jazz big bands such as those of Fletcher Henderson, Luis Russell, Count Basie, Duke Ellington, Earl Hines, and Jimmie Lunceford, strongly jazz-inflected performances by Jan Savitt, Artie Shaw, the Dorsey brothers, and others, and echoes of New Orleans and Chicago in performances by the orchestras of Bob Crosby, Muggsy Spanier, and Noble Sissle (whose "Polka Dot Rag" features a raging solo by Sidney Bechet). Because the set ranges so far and wide, it affords a broad view of the way in which jazz techniques were used, alluded to, and transmuted by the big dance bands. A bonus in this set is a booklet full of very intelligent commentary by saxophonist and musicologist Loren Schoenberg.

## THE COUNT

Possibly no band ever swung more than Count Basie's, which grew out of the Kansas City bands of Bennie Moten and Walter Page. The recordings they made between 1937 and 1940 demonstrate that Basie's was one of the greatest ensembles in jazz history. It contained some of the most individual voices in jazz, yet together they contributed to one of the most relaxed, roomy, exhilarating group sounds ever heard. An excellent introduction to the basic Basie sound is *One O'Clock Jump* (Decca/MCA MCAD-42324), which contains the big band's first studio recordings. The band's strategy in its ensemble playing was the archetypal one of the swing era; the trumpet, saxophone, and trombone sections were set against each other, playing riffs that interlocked to create an exquisite and exciting rhythmic tension and balance, as on the final choruses of "Honeysuckle Rose," in which the trumpets play a simple repeated riff against a repeated saxophone melody.

Many of these tunes are what used to be called head – i.e., unwritten – arrangements, in which members of the different sections would set up riffs for their respective sections. But even the early Basie band's written arrangements had the loose, stripped-down quality of head arrangements. This set is full of such gems, especially the title track, which is a perfect capsule version of the approach. The brass soloists are backed by subdued riffs from the saxes, and the saxophone soloists are backed by subdued brass riffs. After the soloists there is a chorus of pure "walking," or four-beats-to-the-bar timekeeping, from the bass player, Walter Page, while guitarist Freddie Green strums four to the bar as well, drummer Jo Jones keeps time on the high-hat, or "sock," cymbal, and Basie plays short, stabbing treble piano accents which sound very much like short trumpet riffs. Basie and the others sound absolutely cool and unruffled as they delineate the outlines of one of the greatest mysteries in life – time itself. Then the band rides out with the trumpets, trombones, and saxophones all playing their own riffs in one of the most famous passages in jazz. The combination of relaxation and excitement is characteristic of the Basie approach to swing.

Basie's piano is a constant presence here, commenting on the solos, playing riffs against the ensemble passages, and taking an active solo role as well, in an instantly identifiable manner built on riffs and the right-hand style of Fats Waller. Green, Page, and Jones were such an absolutely authoritative unit that Basie didn't need to worry about hammering out time; he could pick his spots, comment on the action, feed a soloist things to think about. A good tune on which to study his approach at length is "Roseland Shuffle," in which Basie and tenor saxophonist Lester Young go head-to-head, exchanging ideas in a fascinating dialogue for three exhilarating choruses. After they finish, listen to Basie's right hand answering the ensemble riffs at the end. Jimmy Rushing's vocals, both on blues material like "Good Morning Blues" and "Boogie-Woogie" as well as on pop songs like "Pennies from Heaven" and "Boo-Hoo," are a gas, and the seldom-heard baritone saxophone pioneer Jack Washington has some fine solos, as does Lester Young. But the stars of this collection are Basie's piano and the band itself, combining a new rhythmic propulsion with a new degree of relaxation.

Good as *One O'Clock Jump* is, all jazz fans owe it to themselves to acquire *Count Basie: The Complete Decca Recordings* (Decca/GRP GRD-3-611), a three-CD set that includes everything on *One O'Clock Jump* as well as forty-six more tracks, many of them the original recordings of eternal Basie classics such as "Jumpin' at the Woodside," "Shorty George," "Doggin' Around," and "Jive at Five." Tenor saxophonist Lester Young really comes into his own here, soloing on these tunes and many others, including "Texas Shuffle," on which he plays clarinet, and "You Can Depend on Me," on which his exchanges with Basie and trumpeter Shad Collins are a thing of priceless beauty. Young's solos on these early Deccas would be quoted in other jazz musicians' solos for decades to come. Young's sectionmate Herschel Evans is heard in his classic tenor solo on "Blue and Sentimental," and Jimmy Rushing sings classic blues in "Blues in the Dark" and "Sent for You Yesterday." In addition, this set includes a series of blues recorded by only Basie and the rhythm section; these exemplary recordings, like "How Long Blues" and "The Fives," reach way back into jazz's deep blues background. Fantastic stuff, all of it; I would urge anyone with even a moderate taste for the swing style to spend the extra money and get *The Complete Decca Recordings.*

The band's further adventures are documented on Columbia's *The Essential Count Basie, Volume 1* (CK 40608), *Volume 2* (CK 40835), and *Volume 3* (CK 44150). By the time of the first big-band recordings on this set (March 1939), the band steps even more lightly on the beat, Basie has become even more elliptical, and arrangements such as "Rock-A-Bye Basie" and "Easy Does It" are miracles of relaxation. The band's full complement of soloists is in place (with the fine Buddy Tate replacing tenor saxophonist Herschel Evans, who died in February 1939), and much of the time they are accompanied by a rhythm that is implied as much as stated.

"Miss Thing (Parts 1 & 2)" on *Volume 1* is one of the band's greatest performances, beginning with one of Lester Young's best solos. But the band's playing of riffs is what makes this a masterpiece of light-stepping propulsion, especially at the end of part one (this was issued on two sides of a 78-rpm record). In part two, the band shows a phenomenal mastery of dynamics, moving from a roaring, shouting riff chorus down to a whisper, down to an even lower whisper, until just Harry Edison and the rhythm section are playing, finally leaving Jo Jones playing his high-hat cymbal with the band woofing at him. A real moment of glory.

"Taxi War Dance," also on *Volume 1*, is just as good, with full-chorus statements from Young and trombonist Dicky Wells and effortless riffing from the full band. *Volume 2* finds the band continuing its winning streak into 1940, with classics like Lester Young's "Tickle Toe" and the powerhouse "Blow Top." By this time, the band's ensemble playing had become tighter, more "professional," even glossy, and some performances, such as "Louisiana," are a little dated-sounding, almost as if the band were copying itself. But then Lester Young comes in and everything is right with the world again. He leaves the band midway through *Volume 3*, but not before making some great noises on "The World Is Mad" and "Broadway." His place is taken by the fine stylist Don Byas. There is a version of "Moten Swing" that makes an interesting comparison to the Moten version from 1932. And on two tracks, "9:20 Special" and "Feedin' the Bean," the band is joined by special guest Coleman Hawkins.

Two other Kansas City bands that were widely admired for the high quality of their musicianship, arrangements, ensemble feel, and soloists were Andy Kirk's and Jay McShann's. If you like Basie's characteristic blues-based, riff-oriented approach, you might want to check out *Jay McShann Orchestra: Blues from Kansas City* (Decca/GRP GRD-614). The McShann band is best remembered as the first to feature Charlie Parker on recordings; on this set, "Swingmatism," "Hootie Blues," "The Jumpin' Blues," and "Sepian Bounce" feature Parker playing short but classic solos that brought him to the attention of all who had ears to hear. But this set's 1941–1943 recordings are also worthwhile for their irresistible ensemble swing, the leader's excellent blues piano, and the sly blues vocals of Walter Brown.

Andy Kirk's Clouds of Joy was distinguished above all by the piano playing and arranging of one of jazz's giants, Mary Lou Williams. The set *Andy Kirk and Mary Lou Williams: Mary's Idea* (Decca/GRP GRD-622) gives a full and convincing sense of the band's range, with good tenor solos on many tracks from the little-known Dick Wilson, as well as large helpings of Williams's piano. Not to be missed on this set is "Walkin' and Swingin'," a 1936 Williams masterpiece of adventuresome ensemble writing and harmonic insight.

## BENNY GOODMAN

Benny Goodman made a huge contribution to the music, both as a nonpareil clarinetist (since his first recordings with Ben Pollack's orchestra in 1926) and as the longtime leader of a swinging band with extremely high musical standards. Along with much good jazz, he recorded a lot of popular ephemera – forgettable songs that he was unwilling to grant a higher life to, as artists such as Fats Waller and Billie Holiday routinely did with substandard material.

Still, his bands, when they were at their best, could hold their own with almost any band of the time, especially when playing arrangements by Fletcher Henderson, who laid the foundation for the band's repertoire, as well as arrangements by aces such as Jimmy Mundy and Edgar Sampson. Much of the Goodman available today, and there is a lot, mixes the gold with the schmaltz in a way that will be satisfying only to true Goodman freaks. So what follows is a highly selective introduction to Goodman's jazz side, after which you're on your own.

The best single document of the Goodman big band at work in the recording studio is undoubtedly *Benny Goodman and His Orchestra: Sing, Sing, Sing*

(RCA/Bluebird 5630-2-RB). This is the 1936–1938 Goodman band in all its glory, performing big-band arrangements by Fletcher Henderson, Mary Lou Williams, Jimmy Mundy, and others with a precision and verve that were rarely equaled, featuring soloists like trumpeters Bunny Berigan and Harry James, saxophonist Vido Musso, and pianist Jess Stacy. Most of Goodman's best-known recordings of the time are included – "King Porter Stomp," "Sometimes I'm Happy," "Don't Be That Way," "Down South Camp Meeting," "Bugle Call Rag," his theme song "Goodbye," and the title track, with its throbbing tom-tom work by drummer Gene Krupa, an eight-minute-plus performance originally issued on both sides of a 12-inch 78. A cornerstone set.

*Roll 'Em, Volume 1* (Columbia CK 40588) is valuable for six broadcast performances by the 1937–1938 band, five of which are top-level big-band jazz featuring the likes of trumpeters Harry James and Ziggy Elman, drummer Krupa, and Goodman himself turning in fiery solos and ensemble work in arrangements by Henderson, Mundy, and, on the title cut, Williams. "Down South Camp Meeting," a riff-based Henderson arrangement, shows the crispness and bite of the band's section work, as well as its great buoyancy and drive, heavier than Basie's largely because of Krupa's drumming. "Ridin' High" is one of the Goodman band's great recorded performances, with take-no-prisoners execution by the band and electrifying exchanges between Goodman and Harry James. Notice how much more keyed-up the band sounds than Basie's, which played at tempos like these with insouciant cool. "St. Louis Blues" features some shout-chorus riffing by the band and a dramatic, swaggering solo by James. Finally, "Roll 'Em," a sort of translation of piano boogie-woogie for big band, builds up a tremendous head of steam.

Performances like these show why people couldn't help dancing in the aisles at concerts and why they clustered around the bandstand to listen at dances. The rest of the album consists of comparatively tepid studio recordings of popular tunes, with the exception of an important version of "Honeysuckle Rose" featuring the electric guitar genius Charlie Christian. The album notes mistakenly attribute the solo to the band's section guitarist, Arnold Covey, who is inexplicably called "the father of modern jazz guitar playing." This is one case where we know the father for sure, and it was Christian.

One of Goodman's most famous recordings, and still one of the best for its moments of spontaneity and high drama, is *Benny Goodman Live at Carnegie Hall* (Columbia G2K 40244), a two-CD set. One of the first concerts to feature jazz music in Carnegie Hall, the 1938 evening presented Goodman's full band and his trio and quartet with Teddy Wilson, Lionel Hampton, and Gene Krupa, as well as guest stars from the Basie and Ellington bands. There are a number of high points, including a long jam session on "Honeysuckle Rose" featuring Lester Young, Ellington altoist Johnny Hodges, and Count Basie himself at the keyboard, but none more storied than the long patrol on "Sing, Sing, Sing," during the twelve minutes of which the band finds its way into various grooves both high-voltage and mysterioso, propelled by Krupa's famous tom-tom work. Pianist Jess Stacy's wholly impromptu solo on this is one of the magic moments in the history of jazz.

*Benny Goodman and Sid Catlett "Roll 'Em!"* (Vintage Jazz Classics VJC 1032-2) contains 1941 broadcast performances by the full Goodman band featuring Big Sid Catlett, one of the greatest drummers in the history of the music. The album contains no fewer than three versions of the title track, the first of which is the version to end all versions. Catlett's swing and way of driving a band were unmatched by almost anyone, and the band had a different kind of lift for the few months when he was with it. Very revealing is the version of "Sing, Sing, Sing," which makes an interesting contrast with Krupa's approach, Catlett playing a Spanish-flavored beat on the tom-toms (check out his duet with Goodman).

Some good studio performances from roughly the same period are contained in *Benny Goodman, Volume 2: Clarinet à la King* (Columbia CK 40834), with readings of solid jazz themes such as "The Earl," "Pound Ridge," and "Superman," on which ex-Ellington trumpeter Cootie Williams steps into the spotlight. Also important here is an alternate take of "Solo Flight," a full-band feature for Charlie Christian. (The originally issued take is on *Charlie Christian: The Genius of the Electric Guitar* [Columbia CK 40846].)

*Air Play* (Signature AGK 40350) contains high-quality broadcast performances from 1937 and 1938, with the band in the prime of life, kicking out on Fletcher Henderson arrangements of "Japanese Sandman" and "I Want To Be Happy." The 1938 sides feature the wonderful Dave Tough, a graceful and distinctive big-band drummer. This is a recommended set.

## FLETCHER, EARL, CHICK, AND CAB

Fletcher Henderson had been forced to disband his orchestra briefly late in 1934. To pay the bills, he had found a ready customer for arrangements in Benny Goodman. But Henderson wanted his own orchestra, and he assembled one in 1935; this band's recordings, through 1936 and 1937, are classic swing, and in trumpeter Roy Eldridge and tenor saxophonists Chu Berry and, later, Ben Webster, he had soloists equal to any he had ever had, with the exception of Armstrong and Hawkins.

Ten tunes by this band show up on *Hocus Pocus: Fletcher Henderson and His Orchestra 1927–1936* (RCA/Bluebird 9904-2-RB), ranging from crisply arranged pop tunes like "Moonrise on the Lowlands" and "I'll Always Be in Love with You," both of which are lessons in how to make conventional melodies swing, to white-knuckle flag-wavers like "Jangled Nerves" and "Riffin'." Not to be overlooked is the novelty tune "Knock, Knock, Who's There?," with a fantastic solo by Chu Berry on baritone sax instead of his customary tenor. Most of the arrangements here were done by Fletcher Henderson's brother, Horace.

An example of how ten years can change a band's approach to the same material is Fletcher Henderson's 1937 arrangement of "The Stampede," which his orchestra had originally recorded in 1926 in a Don Redman arrangement. Available in a collection called *The Jazz Arranger, Volume 1* (Columbia CK 45143), a fine overview of various big-band styles, it provides a neat summary of some of the rhythmic changes in the music when played back-to-back with the earlier version.

Four excellent cuts by the 1936 band, "Christopher Columbus," "Blue Lou," "Stealin' Apples," and "Big Chief De Sota," are available on the highly recommended *Roy Eldridge – Little Jazz* (Columbia CK 45275). This is classic big-band swing, with searing solos by one of the most influential musicians in jazz. The first three of these tunes are also available on the Columbia/Legacy Henderson set (discussed earlier). After 1937, for the rest of his life Henderson would have difficulty keeping a band together; for a while he even joined Goodman's band as pianist and arranger. Yet few make as large a contribution to any art as Henderson did to jazz.

Pianist Earl Hines also fronted an important big band throughout the 1930s and early 1940s. It combined crack section work with the forward-thinking, brilliant arranging talents of saxophonist Budd Johnson, one of jazz's unsung heroes. A good cross section of the band's work from 1939 to 1942 is *Piano Man: Earl Hines, His Piano and His Orchestra* (RCA/Bluebird 6750-2-RB). The leader's piano is a thrilling force throughout, especially on "G. T. Stomp," which also features some nice trumpet playing from Walter Fuller, "Piano Man," from which the band's opening fanfare and the first few notes of Hines's opening piano statement have been inexplicably shaved off, and "Boogie Woogie on 'St. Louis Blues,'" on which trumpeter George Dixon exhorts the leader to "play it 'til 1951."

This was a band in which the soloists truly existed as part of the ensemble; listen to the give-and-take between John Ewing on trombone and Budd Johnson on tenor and the exciting and ingenious ensemble writing (by Johnson) on "Grand Terrace Shuffle," to name just one example. And no one should go through life without hearing Billy Eckstine's unbelievably suave blues vocal on "Jelly, Jelly." For all-around enjoyment, assuming you like big-band jazz at all, this collection is tops. (It also includes five solo performances by Hines and a trio performance with clarinet master Sidney Bechet.) Excellent single performances by Hines's 1934 and 1937 bands may be found on Columbia's *The Jazz Arranger, Volume 1* (CK 45143) and *The 1930s: Big Bands* (CK 40651), respectively.

Entertainer and singer Cab Calloway led one of the best bands of the 1930s, which featured his wild vocals set off by hot arrangements and solos by the likes of Chu Berry, Jonah Jones, Dizzy Gillespie, and others. A decent introduction to his brand of jive is *Cab Calloway – Best of the Big Bands* (Columbia CK 45336), a mix of early-1930s sides and later things, none of which are identified beyond their titles. (Would it have been that much extra work to provide dates and personnel for the performances?) You'll hear good solos from Chu Berry on "Bye Bye Blues" and young Dizzy Gillespie on "Pickin' the Cabbage" (mistitled on the disc), and two Calloway vocal classics in "Reefer Man" and "The Jumpin' Jive," although the 1942 version presented here of his biggest hit, "Minnie the Moocher," is inferior to his 1931 original, despite what the notes say. A shoddy production but probably the easiest Calloway set to find.

Much better, although in an earlier stylistic vein, is *Cab Calloway – Mr. Hi De Ho 1930–1931* (MCA 1344, cassette only). Calloway really lets it hang out on such masterpieces of jazz surrealism as "Trickeration," "Doin' the Rhumba," "St. Louis Blues," and the original version of "Minnie the Moocher." Don't miss this if you can find it. Many of the same tracks can be found on *Kicking the Gong Around* (Living Era AJA 5013). A really wild Calloway cut is "The Man from Harlem," from 1932, on *The 1930s: Big Bands* (Columbia CK 40651); despite the bizarre period-lyrics, Calloway and the band generate a phenomenal swing. In a different vein is the haunting nonvocal "Ebony Silhouette," very unusual for the time (1941) in being a full-band showcase for a bassist – one of the masters of the instrument, Milt Hinton. Available on *The Jazz Arranger, Volume 1* (Columbia CK 45143), the performance, in which Hinton switches back and forth between plucking the bass and bowing it, had bassists shaking their heads in awe for years; it stands as a landmark of the jazz bass and also of the big-band concerto form, in which an entire arrangement would be built around one soloist.

Chick Webb and Jimmie Lunceford led two of the most popular jazz-based big bands of the late 1930s; Webb's has a special place in jazz history because it introduced singer Ella Fitzgerald to the public. Lunceford's band is still spoken of with wonder by those who saw it. The primary function of both bands was to get people to dance, and both were at the very top of that game. My feeling is that they are not quite as interesting to sit and listen to today as the bands I've been discussing. This is to take nothing away from the extremely high level of musicianship in both bands. And certainly anyone who has a special affinity for big-band music will want to check out their recordings.

The best single Chick Webb collection is *Spinnin' the Webb* (Decca/GRP GRD-635), a mixed bag of instrumentals recorded between 1929 and 1939, featuring trumpeters Bobby Stark and Taft Jordan. Included is Webb's famous feature on Benny Carter's arrangement of "Liza." Edgar Sampson's big-band arranging talents are also well displayed here. Two discs' worth of early Ella Fitzgerald with the Webb band, vintage 1935–1938, may be found on *Ella Fitzgerald: The Early Years – Part One* (Decca/GRP GRD-2-618). Jimmie Lunceford's fine band is heard to good advantage on *Stomp It Off* (Decca/GRP GRD-609), a collection of solid jazz tracks from the mid-1930s. Lunceford's exquisite "Uptown Blues," with a timeless solo by altoist Willie Smith, is included on Columbia's *The 1930s: Big Bands* (CK 40651). Maybe someday Columbia will reissue the great collection *The Lunceford Special*, with classics like "Cheatin' on Me" and "Tain't Whatcha Do."

Lunceford's arranger Sy Oliver was one of the finest all-around musicians of the time, and his services were in demand by more orchestras than just Lunceford's, among them the very popular Tommy Dorsey orchestra; a number of Dorsey performances of Oliver arrangements are collected on *Tommy Dorsey/Yes, Indeed!* (RCA/Bluebird 9987-2-RB). Tunes such as "Swanee River" and "Deep River" are valuable for their perfect ensemble phrasing. The busy version of "Easy Does It" here makes an interesting comparison with Basie's minimalist take on the same tune (on *The Essential Count Basie, Volume 2* [Columbia CK 40835]), but the most valuable cut in the set is "The Minor Goes Muggin'," on which Duke Ellington sits in on piano with the band. Loren Schoenberg's notes to this set are a bonus, an example of what liner notes should be.

Drummer Gene Krupa achieved such stardom with Benny Goodman's band that he left in 1938 to form his own big band, a pattern followed by many prominent sidemen – with varied results, both artistically and commercially. Krupa's was one of the success stories; he led an excellent band which, for a while, boasted the services of Roy Eldridge as both singer and trumpet player, in the days when it was still rare to have racially mixed groups performing in public. The records Eldridge made with Krupa and singer Anita O'Day hold up very well and have been collected in *Roy Eldridge with the Gene Krupa Orchestra – Uptown* (Columbia CK 45448). Along with hits like "Let Me Off Uptown," with its playful vocal banter between O'Day and Eldridge and the trumpeter's thrilling climactic solo (worth the price of the set by itself), "Rockin' Chair," and "After You've Gone," both of which have solos by Eldridge, there is the little-known 1949 gem "Swiss Lullaby," on which

Eldridge is cast as an irate neighbor awakened by the saccharine vocal. He finally decides that it's no use trying to get any sleep and that he "might as well get my horn out and practice a little"; the tempo doubles, and Eldridge tears the roof off the chalet.

Lionel Hampton, too, used his success with Goodman as a springboard from which to launch his own big band, which had even more artistic (and perhaps commercial) success than Krupa's – it was certainly longer-lived. Two good collections are *Lionel Hampton: Flying Home* (Decca/MCA MCAD-42349) and *Midnight Sun* (Decca/GRP GRD-625), the former covering the years 1942–1945 and the latter covering 1946–1947. *Lionel Hampton: Flying Home* includes two versions of Hampton's signature tune, "Flying Home," with tenor solos by, respectively, Illinois Jacquet and Arnett Cobb, along with Hampton standbys like the nascent-bop-flavored "The Lamplighter" and "Blow Top Blues," with a vocal by Dinah Washington. *Midnight Sun* includes the legendary "Mingus Fingers," a 1947 showcase for the bass of Charles Mingus, one of the greatest figures in postwar music.

## COUNTLESS BLUES

Krupa and Hampton were hardly the only big-band sidemen to make a name for themselves in the swing era. A soloist who was able to play something rhythmic or acrobatic or moving inspired awe in people; there was something magical about the ability to stand up and extemporize in that way, and for the first time members of the general population were being exposed to the phenomenon on a mass scale. People developed a taste for those individual voices, and that created a demand for them as musical personalities in their own right.

The late 1930s saw the rise of what would prove to be an enduring phenomenon – the all-star band, chosen by magazine polls and assembled for recording purposes. Musical fan magazines, of which *Down Beat* and *Metronome* were the best known (*Down Beat* is still going), started popping up in the mid-1930s to service a public for whom musicians were a kind of movie star. *Metronome* began conducting polls to find out its readers' favorite players and then putting together recording dates to feature them – as magazines such as *Esquire* and *Playboy* would do later. A document of this phenomenon is *The Metronome All-Star Bands* (RCA/Bluebird 7636-2-RB), a collection of sessions recorded between 1937 and 1949 and featuring musicians such as Benny Goodman, Coleman Hawkins, Benny Carter, Johnny Hodges, Dizzy Gillespie, and Charlie Parker, often playing in unusual juxtaposition to one another.

The musicians' stardom also created an audience for performances in which they could stretch out a little more than they could with the big bands and be heard at greater length. I'll discuss a number of these recordings here as a phenomenon of group play, but the best of them will be discussed at greater length under the appropriate soloist sections.

Musicians from the Basie and Goodman bands made some of the most famous of these recordings. In fact, tenor saxophonist Lester Young first recorded, in 1936, with a small group including Basie himself on piano. Young's first recordings are available only in scatter-shot form; the two most important are "Shoe Shine Swing" on *The 1930s: Small Combos* (Columbia CK 40833) and "Oh, Lady Be Good" on *The Essential Count Basie, Volume 1* (Columbia CK 40608). Musicians on all instruments studied these recordings carefully because Young was doing something very different in his accenting and tone (see the discussion of Young in the Soloists section); they would study his later solos with the full Basie band the same way.

Several tunes by a small group made up of members of the 1939 Basie band are on *The Essential Count Basie, Volume 1*, but more famous by far are two sides included on *The Essential Count Basie, Volume 2* (Columbia CK 40835): "Lester Leaps In" and "Dickie's Dream," which spotlighted, as the titles indicate, two of the band's star soloists (the other was trombonist Dicky Wells). Not quite as famous, but perhaps even better musically, are the recordings of the Kansas City Six, a small group from the Basie band with Eddie Durham's guitar replacing Basie's piano. Available on *Lester "Prez" Young and Friends – Giants of the Tenor Sax* (Commodore CCD 7002), the tunes they recorded – "Countless Blues," "Them There Eyes," "Pagin' the Devil," "Way Down Yonder in New Orleans," and "I Want a Little Girl" – are models of relaxed group interplay, with Young's matchless inventive abilities at a peak. Young, on clarinet, engages Buck Clayton's muted trumpet in an exquisite, improvised dialogue at the end of "Way Down Yonder in New Orleans." "Countless Blues" is a riff piece with more fantastic clarinet from Young, and "Pagin' the Devil," named for bassist Walter Page, is a slow, muted blues at a walking tempo that sets a very mysterioso groove; both, by the way, have perfect blues solos by Buck Clayton. "Them There Eyes" contains great solos by Young on both tenor and clarinet. These sides are hard evidence that riffs can be used to set a quiet groove and not just to build to a climax.

For a change of pace, Goodman featured his own small groups as part of his regular big-band performances. The Benny Goodman Trio, with regular band drummer Gene Krupa and pianist Teddy Wilson, who toured only as a member of the trio, was a popular element of Goodman's presentations, and the group became even more popular when vibraphonist Lionel Hampton joined to make it a quartet. Even with no bass, the two small groups could generate a great bounce and drive on rhythm numbers, as well as a sustained mood on ballads like "Body and Soul" and "More Than You Know," a tribute to the musicianship of all involved. Some of their early studio recordings are collected on *The Original Benny Goodman Trio and Quartet Sessions, Volume 1: After You've Gone* (RCA/Bluebird 5631-2-RB).

Good as these are, the trio and quartet are a lot more exciting and unfettered by time constraints on *Benny Goodman Live at Carnegie Hall* (Columbia G2K 40244), where the versions of "China Boy," "Avalon," and several other tunes create a wild head of steam. The trio and quartet were reunited regularly through the years, almost always with special results; one of these occasions was *The Benny Goodman Quartet Together Again* (RCA/Bluebird 6283-2-RB), recorded in 1963 in stereo. The recordings in this set are generally a little less successful than the earlier ones, largely because Krupa keeps time on the ride cymbal rather than on the snare drum, as he did twenty-five years earlier. Still, it is a good set, and the version of "Runnin' Wild" (on which Krupa switches to brushes) is worth the price of admission.

Both Teddy Wilson and Lionel Hampton led a series of extremely important and enjoyable all-star recording sessions in the mid- to late 1930s, Wilson for Brunswick and Hampton for Victor. Some of these symposia are collected under Hampton's name on *Hot Mallets, Volume 1* (RCA/Bluebird 6458-2-RB) and *Jumpin' Jive, Volume 2* (RCA/Bluebird 2433-2-RB). Musicians from the Basie, Ellington, Hines, Henderson, Calloway, and Goodman bands contribute a mixture of solos and arrangements, all to the end of swinging – first hard, then harder, which is the only way it ever is when Hampton is around.

These are essential collections; no one should miss the fantastic drive generated by Cootie Williams, Lawrence Brown, and Johnny Hodges on "Buzzin' Around with the Bee" and "Stompology," or Chu Berry's tenor solo on "Shufflin' at the Hollywood," or the four tunes included from a 1939 session with a sax section consisting of Benny Carter, Coleman Hawkins, Chu Berry, and Ben Webster, with young Dizzy Gillespie on trumpet and Charlie Christian on guitar. The swing on almost all these sides is definitive, as Hampton used the best rhythm players, often Cozy Cole on drums and either John Kirby, who would soon be leading an important band of his own, or Cab Calloway's Milt Hinton on bass.

Unfortunately, there is at present no collection from Columbia (who owns the Brunswick material of that time) devoted to Wilson's small-band work, which included musicians from all the major bands in extremely satisfying small-group situations. Much of it is available, however, as part of the series of recordings on which Wilson led groups accompanying singer Billie Holiday; these have been collected as *The Quintessential Billie Holiday, Volume 1*

(Columbia CK 40646), *Volume 2* (Columbia CK 40790), *Volume 3* (Columbia CK 44048), *Volume 4* (Columbia CK 44252), *Volume 5* (Columbia CK 44423), and *Volume 6* (Columbia CK 45449) and constitute some of the most sublime jazz ever recorded.

*Volume 1* is notable especially for the way Roy Eldridge and either Ben Webster or Chu Berry barbecue silly 1935 songs like "Yankee Doodle Never Went to Town" and "Eeny Meeny Miney Mo" – a good, if extreme, example of the way jazz musicians can transform almost any material into gold. *Volume 4* contains the masterpieces "Easy Living," "Foolin' Myself," "Me, Myself, and I," and others on which Holiday and Lester Young achieve a level of musical togetherness that has never been surpassed. The only less-than-perfect thing about these sets is the fussy and self-indulgent annotation. Beginning with *Volume 6*, Holiday is less a part of a total group effect and more the main attraction – still great, but turning more into a torch singer.

Four super Wilson-led sides from 1936 are included on *Roy Eldridge – Little Jazz* (Columbia CK 45275), featuring Eldridge and some bandmates from the Fletcher Henderson organization, including Chu Berry and drummer Sid Catlett. Especially good are "Blues in C Sharp Minor," with its brooding and insistent ostinato bass figure from Israel Crosby and intense, beautiful solo work from everyone, and "Warmin' Up," an extremely exciting, up-tempo series of solos in which we can hear the musicians, some of the best of their time, exulting in what they've learned about the expectations set up by the four-four beat – how they can hammer on the beat to create emphasis and excitement, then play off the beat for surprise and implied cross-rhythms. Listen, in the last eight bars of Eldridge's fiery solo, how Catlett cranks up the emphasis on the two and four beats of each measure, to telling effect. This was a time when the style had found an equilibrium and was at its peak; the grammar and syntax had been established, and musicians were concerned with refining their abilities to make coherent statements within the common language.

Much the same can be said for at least two of four sides recorded under the leadership of drummer Gene Krupa in 1936, with several of the same principals. Available on a collection entitled *Swing Is Here: Small Band Swing 1935–1939* (RCA/Bluebird 2180-2-RB), "Swing Is Here" and "I Hope Gabriel Likes My Music" were recorded three months before the Wilson session just discussed. They lack the Olympian grandeur of "Blues in C Sharp Minor," but in its place there is a go-for-broke energy that was matched by few if any similar recording combinations. Roy Eldridge, Chu Berry, and Benny Goodman show how the big-band riff style could be adapted for small groups as intelligently as the New Orleans style had been translated for big bands in the previous decade. When each instrument is playing a different riff, the style turns into a new version of the old New Orleans polyphonic approach to ensembles.

The collection is useful, also, for showing the broad range of small group approaches that were open at the time, when the language of Louis Armstrong had become a universal medium of exchange. In fact, several of the sessions from which the album draws mate New Orleans–style players like Wingy Manone and Mezz Mezzrow with big-band stalwarts like Chu Berry and Sy Oliver. Especially good are two dates pairing trumpeter Frankie Newton with two of the greatest Harlem stride pianists, Willie "The Lion" Smith and James P. Johnson, respectively, in settings that combine a characteristic swing rhythm section feeling with a loose, jammed, New Orleans polyphonic ensemble style. A highly recommended set.

Somewhat less focused but still excellent is *The 1930s: Small Combos* (Columbia CK 40833), a collection that spans the entire decade, with glances at early 1930s all-star groups like Benny Carter's Chocolate Dandies with Coleman Hawkins, the Rhythmakers with trumpeter Red Allen and the unique clarinetist Pee Wee Russell, and working bands such as those of violinist Stuff Smith, Roy Eldridge, and bassist John Kirby. The collection also includes the great "Shoe Shine Swing" from Lester Young's first recording session and "Blues in E Flat" by a studio-only group led by xylophonist Red Norvo and including Bunny Berigan, Chu Berry, and Teddy Wilson.

Some of the most pleasing small-group jazz of the time was made by a loosely knit group of musicians, most of whom made their living playing in big bands but whose stylistic roots lay in the late-1920s Chicago dialect of New Orleans–style ensemble playing. Often brought together for recordings and concerts by guitarist and impresario Eddie Condon, musicians like trumpeters Bobby Hackett, Wild Bill Davison, and Max Kaminsky, trombonist Lou McGarity, clarinetists Pee Wee Russell and Edmond Hall, and saxophonist Bud Freeman, among others, made beautiful music together by applying the jammed ensemble feel of the Chicago style to high-quality popular tunes by Gershwin and others, as well as to older jazz tunes of the 1920s. A nice set containing twenty representative 1939–1946 tracks by this gang is *Eddie Condon: Dixieland All-Stars* (Decca/GRP GRD-637).

## FATS WALLER

Not all the small-group recording activity of the time was by these specially assembled studio bands; some of the best swing was recorded by regularly working small bands that had worked out their own balances between ensemble philosophy and solos. Of all these, the swingingest was led by one of the greatest pianists (and singers) in jazz history, Thomas "Fats" Waller.

The name his bands usually recorded under, Fats Waller and His Rhythm, is revealing and apt; Waller was one of the preeminent stride piano players, a school that dictated that a pianist should be able to create a driving, riff-based performance with no accompaniment at all. Anchoring his band around his own piano playing, along with rhythm guitar, bass, and drums, Waller added saxophone, trumpet, and often clarinet to make a flexible yet full-sounding setting that could swing out as a band and provide accompaniment for his vocals.

One of the most common observations made about Waller is that he was given the worst pop songs of Tin Pan Alley to sing because he was the only one who could do anything with them. He took inane lyrics and stretched them like Silly Putty, singing them in a mock-operatic voice, singing them in mock-falsetto, inserting one-liners and commentary, becoming inappropriately belligerent in the middle of a love song, or treating a novelty tune with a bizarre gravity. Yet it is very clearly a mask of ridicule he is wearing; we know it's a mask because Waller never loses his equilibrium, the audience is always let in on the joke, and everything, even the most bizarre interjections, swings like a through freight train.

A perfect introduction to Waller is *The Joint Is Jumpin'* (RCA/Bluebird 6288-2-RB). The album contains a number of piano solos in which Waller establishes his credentials as an unalloyed jazz pianist and shows why he was the idol of Count Basie and Art Tatum (his piano style is discussed at greater length in the Soloists section). Especially formidable are the stride pieces "Handful of Keys" and James P. Johnson's "Carolina Shout." The collection also reminds us that Waller was one of jazz's best composers; the piano solos "Alligator Crawl" and "Viper's Drag" show this, as do the versions of Waller compositions, such as "Honeysuckle Rose" and "Ain't Misbehavin'."

But it is on the classic band sides with vocals, like "The Joint Is Jumpin'," "Your Feets Too Big," "I'm Crazy 'Bout My Baby," and "Lulu's Back in Town," that we get a sense of his infectious way of driving a band with his piano, his gusto for life, and his wild humor. Listen to his accompaniment to the solos on "Lulu" – simple, like muted brass riffs, behind the clarinet, switching to a tremelo to build suspense behind the first part of the trumpet solo, and finally more complex riffs as the trumpet moves into its final eight bars. When the clarinet and trumpet join, after the trumpet solo, to jam sixteen bars before Waller comes back in with his vocal, the pianist stays out of the way with his right hand, knowing that the melodic counterpoint is already dense enough. This kind of understanding is what made him a great band pianist. Listen also to how, toward the end of "I'm Crazy 'Bout My Baby," when the horns come in again after his second piano solo, he plays a repeated bass figure that the drummer picks up on, sort of a riff behind the horns. This version, by the way, is really taken from a 1939 radio transcription, not the 1936 performance listed on the disc.

You can hear him doing the same thing on all the band numbers, including the riotous title cut, which is a stylized simulation of a wild Harlem party of the time (1937), with Waller ruling over everything like the master of the revels, exhorting the band members, talking to the women, commenting on the action for our benefit, telling one of the partiers to "get rid of that pistol – get rid of that pistol!" while people scream in the background and the band works up a hot jam session. At the end he says, "I got bail if we go to jail; I said this joint is jumpin'!" If this sounds as if it might be corny or dated, it's not. Waller always seemed to be laughing at himself laughing at everything; his temper is modern in that sense. He was hip to the highest degree, and his best recordings are a full-strength antidote to the blues.

If you like Waller at all, a necessary investment is *Fats Waller and His Rhythm/The Middle Years, Part 1 (1936–38)* (RCA/Bluebird 66083-2). This three-disc set shows the Waller group at the height of its popularity, turning an endless procession of chintzy pop tunes (and some very good ones as well) into pure gold. It includes some things that will be familiar to confirmed Waller fans, like "Havin' a Ball," "Nero," his surprisingly straight vocal on "Our Love Was Meant To Be," and his wild "She's Tall, She's Tan, She's Terrific." But the set also includes many items that have lain out of print for years and which only the most fanatical Waller collector will already own. Good as the material here is, one can hardly wait for further volumes in the series; Waller's mid-1930s recordings are the heart of his legacy, even more than these somewhat later gems. Keep your eyes peeled for the 1934–1937 material.

Waller recorded very little worthless music; almost all of it is collected on *Fats Waller and His Rhythm/The Last Years (1940–1943)* (RCA/Bluebird 9883-2-RB), another three-CD set. Great as his talent for burlesque was, even he could do nothing with junk like "Abercrombie Had a Zombie," "The Bells of San Raquel," "Liver Lip Jones," and "Your Socks Don't Match," songs so bad that they were already burlesques of themselves. Or maybe he was just getting tired after years of turning garbage into treasure. Still, there's good stuff here, including extremely wacked-out performances of "You Run Your Mouth, I'll Run My Business" and "Eep, Ipe, Wanna Piece of Pie" and real gems like "Winter Weather," "Cash for Your Trash," "Up Jumped You with Love," and "Fats Waller's Original E Flat Blues."

A good single-disc collection is *The Definitive Fats Waller, Volume 1 – His Rhythm, His Piano* (Stash ST-CD-528). A mix of solo piano, duets with clarinetist Rudy Powell, and band tracks, this set presents Waller at his most re-laxed and includes several partial takes and false starts. *Fats Waller in London* (DRG/Swing CDXP 8442) is interesting for a look at Waller playing organ on a series of spirituals, as well as for some funny sides with a group of English musicians who try valiantly to generate the feeling of Waller's own band, mostly unsuccessfully. As if in compensation, Waller turns in some truly baroque vocals, especially on "A Tisket, a Tasket."

## OTHER IDEAS

Three other small bands, which took different tacks, have to be mentioned: John Kirby and His Orchestra, Muggsy Spanier and His Ragtime Band, and the Quintet of the Hot Club of France, featuring the great gypsy guitarist Django Reinhardt. Kirby's small band, with its tight arrangements, its occasional references to the classics, its limited solo work, and its conscious use of the form suggested by the three-minute 78-rpm record of the time, was a real attempt to integrate the soloist and the ensemble more fully; this places it in the tradition of the Beiderbecke/Trumbauer recordings of the late 1920s, Miles Davis's *Birth of the Cool* sessions, and the Modern Jazz Quartet. Kirby was one of the best bassists of the time and a veteran of the Fletcher Henderson orchestra; his band was advanced harmonically and extremely sophisticated in its use of arrangements that were as involved and carefully routined as those of any big band of the time. *John Kirby: The Biggest Little Band 1937–1941* (Smithsonian Collection R013) is a scholarly, thorough, and very enjoyable survey of the band's development.

Muggsy Spanier was a great cornetist who came up in the 1920s and played in many big bands but whose heart was in New Orleans music of the type played by King Oliver. In 1939 he made a series of recordings that blended the Oliver ensemble style with a swing rhythm section feeling and greater space for soloists, including saxophones. The combination of styles comes off extremely well in Spanier's hands, and the results are on *At the Jazz Band Ball – Chicago/New York Dixieland* (RCA/Bluebird 6752-2-RB). Don't let the word "Dixieland" scare you; there is nothing corny about these recordings. They burst with energy and underline the flexibility of the jazz tradition. The leader, on cornet, plays solo after beautiful solo in the classic manner, and the ensembles are a joy. Highly recommended.

Just as appealing is the work of the Quintet of the Hot Club of France, which featured the guitar work of Django Reinhardt. The quintet consisted of Reinhardt and one of jazz's greatest violinists, Stephane Grappelli, as the lead voices, along with two rhythm guitars and a bass – no piano and no drums.

The swing they could generate was compelling, their own version of mid-1930s straight four-four, and their group sound was unique. Django's was a plaintive, extremely expressive sound that swung very hard in a way that was all his own – staccato, heavily accented, yet light-footed.

The band had several incarnations, but its greatest, as well as the greatest work of Django, was that of the years from 1936 through 1940, the years covered by the essential *Djangologie/USA, Volume 1* (DRG/Swing CDSW 8421/3 [blue cover]) and *Volume 2* (DRG/Swing CDSW 8424/6 [yellow cover]), each volume consisting of two CDs. Of the two, *Volume 1* is better overall, containing one full disc of quintet sides like "Swing Guitars," "You're Driving Me Crazy," and "Chicago," and a second disc containing two stunning solo tracks by Django ("Parfum" and "Improvisation"), along with some duets with the American violinist Eddie South, more quintet sides including "Mystery Pacific," a classic if somewhat melodramatic evocation of the railroad, and four timeless sides by an all-star band led by Coleman Hawkins, with arrangements by Benny Carter, recorded in Paris (see the discussion of Coleman Hawkins in the Soloists section). *Volume 2* is more of a mixed bag, with more South material, later quintet stuff, including the beautiful "Nuages," and some small-group sides with visiting Americans Benny Carter and Ellington trumpeter Rex Stewart.

These two sets are not to be confused with *Djangology 49* (RCA/Bluebird 9988-2-RB), a collection of material from a decade later, in which Reinhardt is reunited with violinist Grappelli, along with a conventional piano-bass-drums rhythm section. The performances here lack the charm and grace of the earlier ones; there isn't the same group unity, although Django can still be devilishly inventive. Something just doesn't gel, but there are good moments, especially on the ballads "I'll Never Be the Same" and "I Surrender, Dear."

### SOLO FLIGHT

Reinhardt was the only jazz guitarist to record a large body of single-string melodic solo work until a young man from Oklahoma named Charlie Christian joined Benny Goodman's band at the behest of impresario and fan John Hammond. Great as Reinhardt was, Christian was the real founder of modern guitar playing; his playing was much more steeped in the blues than Reinhardt's, and it swung harder, in a hornlike, behind-the-beat way that made it more a part of the jazz mainstream, a contribution that affected all instrumentalists, not just guitarists.

Beginning in 1939, Goodman led a sextet (in addition to his full band) which featured Christian. The sextet had a shifting personnel; the earliest group featured Fletcher Henderson at the piano and Lionel Hampton on vibes. Later, the vibes were supplanted by Cootie Williams's trumpet and Georgie Auld's tenor sax, making it a septet rather than a sextet, although it continued to be called by the original name. But the group's main attraction is unquestionably Christian's work, set in a relaxed, riff-based format reminiscent of the Count-less Kansas City Six recordings of 1938, discussed earlier. In fact, many of the sextet's best sides feature Basie himself guesting at the piano.

Two Columbia collections document the sextet's studio work: *The Benny Goodman Sextet Featuring Charlie Christian – 1939–1941* (CK 45144) and *Charlie Christian: The Genius of the Electric Guitar* (CK 40846). Both contain a good cross section of the group's work; the former centers more on standards, ballads, and the vibes configuration, and the latter contains more of the rhythm numbers, especially those with Basie, and the trumpet/tenor configuration. The second volume has a bit of an edge over the first; the trumpet/tenor version of the group had more drive and a more varied sound. The second set also has the original version of the big-band "Solo Flight," as well as two warm-up tunes from a sextet session, recorded while the men were waiting for their leader (hence the title "Waiting for Benny").

But both volumes are worthwhile and point to some of the changes that were going on in group playing at the time. For one thing, in jazz, whenever a period of major change has taken place, instruments from the rhythm section have come to prominence as solo instruments, as if to signal that the group democracy was being reevaluated. Christian was an important figure from this standpoint, as his work signaled a new relation between melodic playing and rhythm (since the guitar, once thought of primarily as a rhythm instrument, was now playing melodies, and melodies unlike almost anything in common currency at the time). It is no coincidence, seen in this light, that bassist Jimmy Blanton, who joined the Ellington band at almost the same time Christian joined Goodman, made the same kinds of revolutionary strides on his hitherto mainly rhythm instrument as Christian was making on his. (Sadly, both men died only a couple of years later, both at tragically young ages.)

For a fascinating and immediate glimpse of the kind of effect Christian was having on other instrumentalists, listen to pianist Kenny Kersey's solo on "Breakfast Feud" (on *The Benny Goodman Sextet Featuring Charlie Christian – 1939–1941* [Columbia CK 45144]), recorded in December 1940 after Christian had been with the band for over a year. Kersey, a highly regarded pianist, plays a solo in which his attack, phrasing, rhythmic feel, harmonic sense, and even note choice are all Christian's; in fact, his piano solo amounts to a translation of Christian for the piano's right hand.

Christian can also be heard, playing acoustic guitar, on one of the most interesting small-group jazz dates of the time (1941); available on *The Complete Edmond Hall/James P. Johnson/Sidney De Paris/Vic Dickenson Blue Note Sessions* (Mosaic MR6-109), the session teams Christian with Edmond Hall, one of jazz's finest clarinetists, bassist Israel Crosby (who set the groove on Teddy Wilson's "Blues in C Sharp Minor"), and boogie-woogie piano player Meade Lux Lewis playing not piano but the delicate-toned celeste. The unorthodox instrumentation and lack of drums made this a unique date; "Edmond Hall Blues" and "Profoundly Blue" have a mellow mood unlike almost anything else in jazz (the closest thing might be "Pagin' the Devil" by the Kansas City Six), but "Jammin' in Four" and "Celestial Express" swing as hard as anything you've ever heard. The rest of this six-record set is also excellent, by the way.

Clarinetist Artie Shaw was Goodman's biggest direct competition as a bandleader; a brilliant instrumentalist and a maverick type of personality, he was willing to try anything he thought would sound good. In 1940 he formed a jazz small group to supplement his sometimes very commercial big-band performances; it was his answer, in effect, to the Goodman sextet, and he called it the Gramercy Five (named for a New York City telephone exchange). The group's total output is available on *The Complete Gramercy Five Sessions* (RCA/Bluebird 7637-2-RB). Actually, it was two groups; the eight sides recorded in 1940 feature Billy Butterfield on trumpet and Johnny Guarnieri (who was a member, intermittently, of Goodman's sextet as well) on, believe it or not, harpsichord. The 1945 sides feature Roy Eldridge on trumpet and modernist Dodo Marmarosa on piano. Some of this music is, as you might guess, very unusual sounding.

All of these recordings reflect the growing understanding of, and fascination with, the soloist. As four-four time got evened out, soloists were able to be ever more subtle in their approach to phrasing, and players like Christian, Lester Young, and Roy Eldridge began to construct longer phrases in which the notes of the solo of an earlier style would show up as the accented notes in a long melodic line. The most forward-looking leaders were trying to strike a balance between the demands of the soloist and the need to have an ensemble cohesion, as well as a formal aspect to the music, based on more than just solos. The public and musicians alike were more and more interested in what soloists were saying, but one genius had worked out a way to incorporate that interest into an ensemble fabric and formal design that would constitute perhaps the greatest achievement in jazz for the next thirty years. His name, of course, was Duke Ellington.

# DUKE ELLINGTON, PART 2

Just as he had with the New Orleans and early big-band traditions a decade earlier, in the mid-1930s and 1940s Duke Ellington used all the conventions of the swing big band to create a music that was steeped in the idiom, functioned the same way as swing music was supposed to function (i.e., as dance music), yet also stood apart from and above all other contemporary work, both in formal interest and in mastery of the tone colors and rhythmic flexibility available to an orchestrator for typical big-band instrumentation. Ellington recorded so much great music during this period, with so much variety, that it is hard to believe. Sadly, at present there is no collection from Columbia of Ellington's work of the mid-1930s (for an example of the kind of thing that is presently languishing in the vaults, listen to "Lazy Rhapsody" on *The 1930s: Big Bands* [Columbia CK 40651]). The end of the decade, however, has been well documented by a couple of collections.

The most readily available one is *Duke Ellington: Braggin' in Brass – The Immortal 1938 Year* (Portrait R2K 44395), a two-CD compendium of items that shows Ellington's range at the time, extending his understanding of riff pieces, mood pieces, song form, and instrumental sonority. We also watch Ellington's band members evolving into a repertory company of instantly identifiable voices, and we get a number of pieces designed to feature one or another of them, such as "Slap Happy," for baritonist Harry Carney, "Boy Meets Horn," a famous feature for cornetist Rex Stewart, and "Blue Light," presented in two takes, a showcase for Barney Bigard's clarinet.

Tunes like "Steppin' into Swing Society," "Hip Chic," and "Buffet Flat" seem initially to be conventional swing-era pieces, designed for dancing, but even these have unusual orchestrations and formal devices that create a unity that was not found in the conventional dance-band orchestrations of the time. "Steppin'," for example, sounds at first as if it is going to be a typical swing-era performance based on simple riffs. It begins with an ordinary-enough riff from the saxophones, which lasts eight bars. The saxophones are then accompanied by muted trumpets for another eight bars. Then the saxophones drop out, and the muted trumpets take over with their own mysterious riff for eight bars, after which the trombones surreptitiously creep in behind them for another eight bars, before taking over on the next eight bars, and so on. In other words, one section after another "steps in" to the picture, easing out the previous section; Ellington pulls all this together at the end by an ingenious dovetailing of the sections, culminating in a simple statement of the first theme. This kind of witty and brilliant formal play is found throughout the 1938 sides.

Also not to be missed here are stunning displays of ensemble virtuosity, like the title cut, and fine readings of Ellington popular tunes, like "I Let a Song Go Out of My Heart" and "Prelude to a Kiss." Unfortunately, the set is a fairly careless production, lacking a personnel listing for the band, although soloists are listed, and Nat Hentoff's liner notes aren't much help in understanding the music. The same exact program can be found on the first of four two-LP sets still available from the Smithsonian – *Duke Ellington 1938* (Smithsonian Collection R003), with very good liner notes by composer and conductor Gunther Schuller, author of two recommended studies of jazz, *Early Jazz* and *The Swing Era*; the other Smithsonian sets, *Duke Ellington 1939* (R010), *1940* (R013), and *1941* (R027), are impossible to recommend highly enough. All have liner notes that help you hear more in the music, adding the all-important aspect of the intellect (which was ever present in Ellington's work) to the easily available emotional component of the music, which requires no explication.

The Smithsonian's *1939* set contains material that supports the same kinds of remarks I've made about the 1938 sides; Ellington continues to extend and refine the essential aspects of the swing big-band style in tunes like "Old King Dooji" and "Solid Old Man"; but listen to the way in which, in "Dooji," the initial two-note phrase the saxophones play is echoed, twisted, and reharmonized throughout the piece. Ellington would use this kind of motivic development throughout his career, one of the most notable examples being his extended piece "A Tone Parallel to Harlem" (available on both *Ellington Uptown* [Columbia CK 40836] and *The Great Paris Concert* [Atlantic 304-2]), in which the initial two-note trumpet pronunciation of the word "Harlem" is the figure in the carpet for the entire composition, showing up in numberless guises.

But something new was also beginning to happen in 1939; listen to the ensemble blend on "Way Low," for example. Ellington's grasp of how to combine instruments from different sections of the band to create unique sonorities (which he had explored to startling effect on "Mood Indigo") was getting more and more sophisticated. By this time, Billy Strayhorn, a classically trained pianist, orchestrator, and lyricist who was to be Ellington's musical alter ego for the rest of Strayhorn's life (he died in 1967), had joined the band, and it is possible that Ellington was stretching out even farther because he had someone new, and of a higher level than ever, to strut his stuff for. Listen, too, to the wild chords on "Bouncing Buoyancy," Ellington's satire on the boogie-woogie craze that was sweeping the country.

Late in the year, another important element of the band fell into place with the arrival of bassist Jimmy Blanton. Blanton's sound and technique, the clarity of his sound, and the logic of his note choices gave the band a new kind of rhythmic life. But even more than that, he was able to play solos that were as fleet and coherent as horn solos, radically expanding the potential role for the bass in any jazz ensemble. In "Tootin' through the Roof," Blanton's sound swells behind the band, heating things up, and in two duets between Ellington and Blanton, "Blues" and "Plucked Again," you can hear Blanton's technique, taste, swing, and ideas in sharp relief. He was to be featured extensively with the full band very soon thereafter.

### SEPIA PANORAMA

As good as the 1939 sides are, they are only a warm-up for the stunning series of recordings Ellington made for Victor beginning the next year. The presence of Strayhorn, the advent of Blanton, and the arrival of a new member of the saxophone section, tenorist Ben Webster, created a critical mass of new possibilities that pushed Ellington into an even higher creative orbit. *Duke Ellington: The Blanton-Webster Band* (RCA/Bluebird 5659-2-RB) presents all of Ellington's big-band commercial recordings for Victor made from 1940 until 1942 and is certainly one of the essential sets of jazz music. There is far too much on this three-CD set to go into here; an entire book could be written on these recordings alone. But a number of remarks are in order.

For one, Ellington seemed to be able to do anything he wanted at this point with the sound of his orchestra. Partly this had to do with the addition of Webster to the saxophone section. A group of five rather than four reeds gave more possibility for body, especially at the bottom end of the reeds' range, and a wider range of harmonic extension. The kinds of textural richness that Ellington was getting on pieces like "Jack the Bear" (a Blanton feature as well) and, especially, "Ko-Ko," in which the brass and reed voices mix, at the end, like layers of paint applied with a palette knife, were, and are, the kind of thing that inspires awe in other arrangers and orchestrators.

Along with the increased command of instrumental sonority comes a greater range, depth, and precision of emotional rendering. Ellington, as has been observed numerous times, always had something in mind that he wanted to convey – a mood, a picture, a moment – and this is what makes his work more than a collection of brilliant technical devices. Here, in 1940, we find the greatest resources ever arrayed in jazz at the service of a breathtaking human grandeur and sensitivity. "Dusk," for example, is shot through with unusual and exquisite writing for all the sections (such as the organlike reed chords behind Rex Stewart's cornet solo, which hark back to the foghorn chords on "Immigration Blues" on *Duke Ellington and His Orchestra – The Brunswick Era, Volume 1 (1926–1929)* [Decca/MCA MCAD-42325]), which creates a mood that is indescribable. Another performance of this stripe is Ellington's classic of erotic geography, "Warm Valley."

Ellington's piano is right up front as a part of the ensemble, commenting, shaping, paraphrasing, and echoing the band's parts and providing its own motivic thread through the pieces, as it does on both "Dusk" and "All Too Soon," on which material from his piano introduction is echoed periodically throughout the piece, usually functioning as a reminder of some earlier mood. Ellington truly thought as an orchestrator when he was playing piano, as did Count Basie.

Ellington continued to use one section to comment on what another section was saying, not just in typical swing-era riff-counterpoint fashion but as competing personalities that undercut, egg on, or italicize what another section or soloist is saying. He had done this for a long time, but he was raising the technique to new heights, as on "Conga Brava," in which muted trumpets seem to mock Juan Tizol's decorous opening melody statement. Another factor in the ascendant as the year went on was the writing of Billy Strayhorn, who produced mood pieces like the beautiful "Chelsea Bridge" as well as more up-tempo compositions with characteristic Ellingtonian richness of form, such as "Raincheck" and "Johnny Come Lately," which uses some of the same kinds of unusual intervals as earlier Ellington items like "Old King Dooji."

The number of compositions here that came to be regarded as Ellington classics is staggering. Others that can't go unmentioned include the up-tempo Ben Webster feature on "Cottontail," in which Webster gallops through the "I Got Rhythm" changes, giving way to some fantastic shout choruses from reeds and brass at the end. "Across the Track Blues," at first glance a string of solos on a relaxed, medium-tempo blues, becomes something more in the perfect, tasteful subtlety of the background and the sheer simplicity of the routine. "Across the Track Blues" seems to refer back, musically, to the 1929 "Saturday Night Function," available on *Early Ellington 1927–1934* (RCA/ Bluebird 6852-2-RB), which, with its brooding mood and serial solos from clarinet, cornet, and trombone over simple backgrounds, transcended the form in much the same way.

"Harlem Airshaft" is another masterwork, a swinging dance tune with fantastic reed writing and a use of riffs and breaks that seems to telescope the entire jazz tradition. Ellington continues a series of portraits of black show business figures, which already included tributes to dancer Florence Mills ("Black Beauty") and stride pianist Willie "The Lion" Smith ("Portrait of The Lion"), with "A Portrait of Bert Williams" and "Bojangles (A Portrait of Bill Robinson)." "Main Stem" is an apocalyptic riff-based tune that builds up a momentum that must have occasioned many a heroic moment on the dance floors of the time. And there is also the original recording of the band's theme, "Take the 'A' Train," by Billy Strayhorn, with its solo by trumpeter Ray Nance, the replacement for Cootie Williams, who had just left to join Benny Goodman's orchestra. This became the classic solo, played note for note even by Cootie Williams after Cootie rejoined the band in 1962.

The Smithsonian's *1941* set also includes a select number of alternate versions of classics such as "Take the 'A' Train," "Chelsea Bridge," Ray Nance's violin feature "Bakiff," and Mercer Ellington's fine tunes "Jumpin' Punkins" and "Blue Serge" recorded for Standard Transcriptions, which are very worth owning. The entire series of 1941 Standard Transcriptions recordings, including a number that were left off the Smithsonian set, are available on CD as *Take the 'A' Train – The Legendary Blanton-Webster Transcriptions* (Vintage Jazz Classics VJC-1003-2).

## SMALL GROUPS

A number of small-group performances from the era I've been discussing are available, some classic and some forgettable. Absolutely necessary is *The Great Ellington Units* (RCA/Bluebird 6751-2-RB), a collection of sides made in 1940 and 1941 under the nominal leadership of Johnny Hodges, Rex Stewart, and Barney Bigard, yet all bearing the unmistakable Ellington stamp.

These are much more "shaped" performances than the average small-group jazz date of the same period; compare them, as a group, with the material on the Lionel Hampton *Hot Mallets, Volume 1* (RCA/Bluebird 6458-2-RB) collection, for example. Whereas the Hampton-led performances – including the ones using Ellington band members – are, with some exceptions, light frameworks for blowing, these tend to be complete performances, with careful backgrounds, variation in mood, and unusually structured material, yet with a greater emphasis on the solo voice than in most of the Ellington big-band arrangements of the time. In that sense, these may be seen as an extension of the big-band concerto performances, such as "Concerto for Cootie," in which a full-dress context is designed to set off one or another of the band's major voices. The twenty-two performances on this CD are some of the most satisfying small-group jazz ever recorded.

One of the constants in the set is the bass of Jimmy Blanton, heard to especially good advantage in this more stripped-down setting. On Hodges's up-tempo "Squatty Roo," Blanton nearly jumps out of the speakers at you from behind Hodges's swaggering alto solo. On a piece like "Passion Flower," a Strayhorn effort, his bass is used to add another harmonic and even contrapuntal element to the ensemble.

There are great solo moments by Ray Nance, Lawrence Brown, and Ben Webster (lots of good Webster here), as well as some fine Ellington piano. My favorites, this year, are the Rex Stewart sides, especially the blues-drenched

"Mobile Bay" and the lyrical and poignant "Some Saturday," not to mention "Poor Bubber," a tribute to early Ellington trumpeter Bubber Miley, with its chanting saxophone background, and Webster's solo on "Linger Awhile." But then, there are also Bigard's "Charlie the Chulo," in which the leader's clarinet engages Ellington's piano in a riveting dialogue, the mysterious Ellington composition "Lament for Javanette," Hodges's exquisite playing on "Day Dream," and the first recording of Mercer Ellington's "Things Ain't What They Used To Be."

*The Duke's Men – Duke Ellington Small Groups, Volume 1* (Columbia C2K 46995) is a two-CD mixed bag of recordings from 1934 through 1938, led by Rex Stewart, Cootie Williams, Barney Bigard, Johnny Hodges, and Ellington himself. Much of it can stand comparison with the material on *The Great Ellington Units,* especially some Ellington mood pieces such as "Indigo Echoes," the haunting "Blue Reverie," with its chromatic introduction and soprano saxophone filigrees by Johnny Hodges (another version of this tune may be found on *Benny Goodman Live at Carnegie Hall* [Columbia G2K 40244] – as played by the members of the Ellington orchestra guesting that night, including this session's Hodges, Harry Carney, and Cootie Williams), and Williams's growl specialty "Echoes of Harlem." The set also boasts quite a few swingers in which the small-group horns are arranged imaginatively around the soloists. There's some less interesting material here, too, but the set is well worth having. The liner notes by Helen Oakley Dance, who produced many of the sessions represented in the set, are a bonus, with valuable and engaging insights into the band and the mechanics of the recording process.

A much less satisfactory set is *The Duke Ellington Small Bands – Back Room Romp* (Portrait RK 44094), which duplicates a number of items from *The Duke's Men.* Although the set contains some good music, it is hard to recommend since the sound is atrocious and the producer didn't even bother to include personnel listings.

One of the most original of all the Ellington small groups had only two members: Ellington and Jimmy Blanton. They recorded two duets for Columbia, mentioned earlier, and included in the Smithsonian's *1939* set, but a feast of their duet work is available on *Duke Ellington: Solos, Duets, and Trios* (RCA/Bluebird 2178-2-RB). They recorded four sides in October 1940, when Blanton was just shy of his twenty-second birthday; all are included here in at least two takes, for a total of nine performances, and the alternate versions make for fascinating comparison with the master takes.

The first of the duets is "Pitter Panther Patter." Other bassists before Blanton, especially Wellman Braud, Walter Page, John Kirby, and Milt Hinton, had played the instrument with great drive and definition, but none had mastered the possibilities in melodic lines to the extent that Blanton had; his arrival had the same effect on bassists that Charlie Christian had on guitarists. "Pitter" is taken at a medium bounce tempo, and the two voices trade back and forth like a practiced tap-dance duet, Ellington's stride playing and augmented chords suspending the time for Blanton to make incredible double-time runs and blues phrases that reach way down into the gutbucket. You have to go back to the Armstrong/Hines "Weather Bird" to hear anything comparable.

The other tunes from the session are no less astonishing. "Body and Soul" and "Sophisticated Lady" are ballad tours de force in which Blanton shows his ability both arco and pizzicato ("Pitter" is all plucked). "Mr. J. B. Blues" is a medium walking blues with a rock-steady tempo which seems as natural as can be until you realize that Blanton only actually walks (plays four-to-a-bar) for a total of about four bars in the first take and not at all in the brighter-tempo second. It is a tribute to the absolute rhythmic sense of orientation of both men that the tempo is never in doubt although it is almost never overtly articulated. An amusing moment in take two is when Blanton quotes Buck Clayton's trumpet solo from Count Basie's recording of "One O'Clock Jump." Blanton plays two bowed choruses on the blues, too. These duets sum up a moment in the music when the range of options available to every player was being radically expanded.

### BLACK, BROWN, AND BEIGE

After the last of the recordings in *Duke Ellington: The Blanton-Webster Band* (RCA/Bluebird 5659-2-RB) were made, there was a hiatus of about two years in Ellington's studio activity due to a strike called by the musicians' union against recording companies. By the time Ellington got back into the studio, certain key members of the band had departed – notably Ben Webster and Barney Bigard – and there had been something of a falling-off in the level of sustained brilliance and originality in the three-minute form that marked *The Blanton-Webster Band* recordings.

Partly this must have been because nobody could have kept going at that pace without a rest, partly because of the personnel changes. Although this period of the mid- to late 1940s has usually been deprecated by critics, what Ellington was doing was still in a class of its own, and many of these recordings are extraordinary in their own right. Another reason, though, why the level of originality and sustained invention in the short form had leveled off at this time may have been that Ellington was beginning to investigate long forms in earnest. The first result of this aspect of his career was the monumental "Black, Brown, and Beige," a nearly fifty-minute-long work premiered at Ellington's first Carnegie Hall concert in January 1943.

Ellington had, almost from the beginning of his career, been intrigued with longer forms and had recorded a number of pieces that were issued on two or more sides of 10- or 12-inch 78-rpm recordings. Among these were "Creole Rhapsody" on *Early Ellington 1927–1934* (RCA/Bluebird 6852-2-RB), the less formal two-part "Tiger Rag" on *Duke Ellington and His Orchestra – The Brunswick Era, Volume 1 (1926–1929)* (Decca/MCA MCAD 42325), and "Reminiscing in Tempo," currently unavailable, which took up four record sides. But these longer forms were an outgrowth of the formal concern that Ellington had shown in his earliest masterpieces, such as "Black and Tan Fantasy" and "East St. Louis Toodle-Oo."

Still, nothing Ellington had written or recorded to that point matched "Black, Brown, and Beige" in scope. You can hear the piece in its entirety, as it was performed at Carnegie Hall, on *The Duke Ellington Carnegie Hall Concerts – January 1943* (Prestige P-34004), which includes many other excellent items from a period when Ellington's band wasn't in the recording studio. Leonard Feather's liner notes discuss the piece and the significance of the concert. The sound, however, leaves something to be desired.

"Black, Brown, and Beige" was not, as some have mistakenly claimed, an attempt by Ellington to use European structures in his writing but was rather a highly successful use of American forms such as the blues, popular song forms, riffs, and other vernacular elements in assembling a longer form. Ellington's longer works will be discussed in the next Ellington section, but for now understand that Ellington was, and had been, engaged in taking what he needed from the European conceptual bag (the concerto and concerto grosso pieces, for example, as well as rondo forms and miniaturized sonata-like contrasting-form pieces such as "Black and Tan Fantasy") and asking himself what an American version would sound like.

When Ellington finally did get back into the studio in December 1944, almost the first thing he did was to record some sections from his large work. These four long sections, collected on the three-CD *Black, Brown and Beige* (RCA/Bluebird 6641-2-RB), present a good look at some of the thematic material Ellington offered in the piece, particularly the famous "Come Sunday," but leave out the sense of the composition's whole structure. Still, the sound is excellent, much better than the Carnegie Hall material, and the set is very worthwhile. Most of the Bluebird set is devoted to shorter-form material from the 1944–1946 band. As mentioned, much of this material can't match the 1940–1941 sides for sheer breathtaking timelessness, but there is still so much material to listen to here of such high quality. Included are the new Ellington compositions "Blue Cellophane," "Transblucency," and "Rockabye River," along with another long-form piece, "The Perfume Suite."

The set also includes revisitations of Ellington standards like "Mood Indigo," "Black and Tan Fantasy," and "It Don't Mean a Thing (If It Ain't Got That Swing)," which show that Ellington was engaged in an ongoing dialogue with the implications of his own past work and was never satisfied with anything in its final shape. One fine 1946 track should be mentioned, although it is not an Ellington composition: Hal Mooney's "Swamp Fire," with its fabulous and well-recorded bass playing by Oscar Pettiford, probably the greatest bassist in jazz after Blanton and an off-and-on member of the Ellington constellation. Another good reason to pick up this set is the accompanying booklet, with outstanding notes by Ellington expert Andrew Homzy.

Ellington's Carnegie Hall concerts were regular events, and Prestige has issued three sets in addition to the *January 1943* collection. Collectively titled *The Duke Ellington Carnegie Hall Concerts*, each one presents a mixture of Ellington standards, new pieces, and, usually, an extended work composed for the occasion. *December 1944* (Prestige P-24073), *January 1946* (Prestige P-24074), and *December 1947* (Prestige P-24075) are all stunning examples of the composer's range, and that of his band, and include many of Ellington's spoken introductions as well as pieces unavailable in other incarnations.

# CHASIN' THE BIRD

**THE YEARS OF WORLD WAR II** brought a new approach to group playing, one that had been brewing for several years and was implicit in the sound of the Count Basie rhythm section as well as in the playing of tenorist Lester Young, guitarist Charlie Christian, bassist Jimmy Blanton, and several others. It had been hammered out, rhythmically and harmonically, in jam sessions in Harlem by a group of younger musicians including Christian, Thelonious Monk, Dizzy Gillespie, and Charlie Parker. The first recordings of the kind of music they worked out, called bebop, or just bop, show what they were aiming toward – precision of execution at high speeds, harmonic sophistication, a closer wedding of the accents a musician played to the harmony, and a more contrapuntal, front-line role for the rhythm section instruments, especially the piano and drums.

Although a number of big bands played music that made use of the harmonic and rhythmic devices (and, often, the clichés) favored by the modernists, bebop was, finally, music of the small group. Jazz had always placed a premium on inventiveness and presence of mind, but Parker, Gillespie, Fats Navarro, Bud Powell, and a handful of others upped the ante considerably. Their music demanded virtuosity, and, like a self-fulfilling prophecy, virtuosity, brilliance, ideas – the ability to think quickly on one's feet and exhibit grace and wit under great pressure – became part of the aesthetic.

To play the new music correctly, musicians had to be able not only to swing but to articulate complicated melodic material that fit all the extra harmonic nooks and crannies that were being discovered and explored, sometimes at speeds that placed unbelievable demands on their coordination and presence of mind. The essential grammar of the style was made up of the lines of legato eighth notes perfected by Lester Young and Charlie Christian, but with an important difference.

An improvising musician works with a sort of harmonic map of a certain song in his or her head. The map is usually referred to as the song's "changes," short for chord changes; the song is a progression through changing harmonic territory, the nature of which is designated in a harmonic shorthand of chords. Chords are groupings of three or four (or more) notes that outline a certain harmonic gravity or tension and sometimes indicate a new harmonic direction. If I give you directions to get somewhere, I may give you a succession of route numbers, with some indication of how long to stay on each road – "Get on I-95 until you see the sign for Route 3, get off and make a right and go two miles until you hit the overpass for County Highway 103 . . ." In jazz, certainly in bebop, musicians usually indicate these routes by a series of chord names. Some chords, to follow the metaphor, stand for roads, some stand for the signs or landmarks that you have to look for, some are destinations, some are turning points.

But these chords are only a shorthand, just as saying "Route 3" gives no sense of the ups and downs of the road, its character, the sights you see, or whether it's a main road or a tributary. To each chord are attached scales, which give a more fleshed-out sense of the harmonic terrain, and musicians really think of these scales when they address the harmonic map of a tune. To make things more complex, often several scales are appropriate to any given chord, and a large number of chords can fit on the same scale. This may sound confusing, but it gives some sense of the kinds of knowledge a musician has to have metabolized beyond any conscious level in order to play coherently.

In the scales, certain notes and note groupings are like landmarks that let you know what road you're on. In a jazz solo, a musician tends to accent these characteristic notes, even though he or she plays many other notes of the scales. In the swing players' grammar, the accents and the characteristic notes tended to fall on the down beat. One thing that distinguished the true bebop players of the mid-1940s from even the most forward-looking of the swing players was that their accented notes as often as not fell on the up, or "and," beat. This more flexible system of accenting, combined with a tendency to play many more notes, gave a more detailed picture of the harmonic landscape's contours, just as a topographical map will be more detailed the more rings per inch there are or a newspaper photo will have more definition the more dots there are per square inch.

Just as the swing players learned to use the expectations set up by the relentless four beats per measure, the boppers learned how to set up rhythmic expectations by accenting certain places in each measure during a solo passage, which would become a sort of code for the accompanying musicians, who would use it to shape the choices they made. In Charlie Parker's "Ko Ko" (available on *Bird: The Savoy Original Master Takes* [Savoy ZDS 8801]), Parker plays a series of figures that resemble the melody of "Tea for Two," leading the ear to expect the same rhythmic pattern to be repeated. Then he staggers it, doubles up on it, just as a boxer will set up a pattern of expectations with a certain kind of punch or combination, then surprise his opponent by breaking the pattern unexpectedly.

The new style required the technical ability to accent certain notes within very long melodic lines; this meant great control over fingerings, for pianists, and great breath control for players of wind instruments. Bird played long melodic lines over a complicated harmonic background the way a skier traces a particularly daring but logical path over difficult terrain at high speeds. You could think of the accents as the places where one cuts one's legs left or right. Listen, for example, to his Savoy recording of "Warming Up a Riff" on *Bird: The Savoy Original Master Takes*, recorded as a rehearsal on the chord changes of Ray Noble's popular song "Cherokee." You can hear how Parker accents certain notes in his extraordinarily long lines and how the accented notes act as pivot points for the tonal direction the music takes.

But bop wasn't the total revolution many made it out to be. At first, at least, it used all the compositional devices jazz had always used – riffs, breaks, polyphony, blues, and chord changes of popular tunes – but it infused them with a somewhat different sensibility and emphasis. The earliest bebop records, like "Woody'n You" and "Disorder at the Border," by Coleman Hawkins with Dizzy Gillespie and Max Roach (available on *Dizzy Gillespie: The Development of an American Artist* [Smithsonian Collection R004]) still used conventions from big bands – riffs, large ensembles, arranged interludes. And the first recordings by Dizzy Gillespie's small groups, like "Groovin' High," "Salt Peanuts," "Dizzy Atmosphere," and "Blue and Boogie" (available on *Dizzy Gillespie and His Sextets and Orchestra: "Shaw 'Nuff"* [Musicraft MVSCD-53]), carry on this technique. Throughout the late 1940s, Gillespie led a big band of the standard instrumentation which played an exciting, highly arranged version of the new music; some excellent examples of the band's work can be found on both the Musicraft set and *The Bebop Revolution* (RCA/Bluebird 2177-2-RB). But the typical bop ensembles left maximum space for improvisation and eventually stripped away even the interludes and arranged parts that had been there in the early Gillespie records, leaving nothing but the classic bebop format: head (or melody), solos, head.

A perfect session in which to hear the classic bebop small-group approach was recorded under Charlie Parker's leadership in May 1947, with young Miles Davis on trumpet, Bud Powell, the most influential pianist of the time, Tommy Potter on bass, and Max Roach, the genius of modern drumming. The four tunes they recorded – "Donna Lee," "Chasin' the Bird," "Cheryl," and "Buzzy" – give a good sampling of the approach. Several takes of each may be heard on the three-CD set *The Complete Charlie Parker Savoy Studio Sessions* (Savoy ZDS 5500).

The repertoire is revealing in itself. "Donna Lee" is a quintessential bebop melody: a test of dexterity (in fact, a famous Charlie Parker head was entitled "Dexterity") full of long lines of trickily accented eighth notes interspersed with triplets, a mixture of scales, and arpeggios, based on chord changes borrowed from a popular song, in this case "Indiana." "Chasin' the Bird" is one of two contrapuntal lines Parker wrote, the other being "Ah-Leu-Cha" (in both, Parker plays one melody on alto and Miles Davis plays another on trumpet). "Cheryl" is a bouncing, medium-tempo blues with a heavily accented melody, and "Buzzy," another blues, is a riff tune.

We can notice two things right off the bat about these recordings. One is that the focus is, superficially at least, very much on the soloists. There is, in each case, a statement of the head in unison (except on "Chasin' the Bird," where the head is in counterpoint), and then there are solos all the way until it's time for the head again. There are no arranged backgrounds, no tempo changes or changes in dynamics – only the soloists showing their prowess and powers of inventiveness over the harmonic map.

The other thing to notice, after an initial fascination with the soloists' brilliance, is that the pianist and drummer are much more actively involved with what the soloists are playing than they tended to be in earlier forms of jazz. Max Roach puts in accents on his bass and snare drums, anticipating and echoing the accents in Parker's melodic lines. Bud Powell does the same at the piano, answering and commenting on the soloists' lines, sometimes jabbing, à la Basie, like trumpet accents in a big-band arrangement, sometimes like a saxophone section background, always responding, both harmonically and rhythmically, to what the soloists are playing (and, when his solo comes, his right-hand lines are a translation, for piano, of the horn players' styles, but with a more percussive element).

The implication of this kind of group interplay was, to those who were equipped to think in these terms, a new gloss on New Orleans polyphony, a kind of collective group counterpoint based on an agreed-upon harmonic map, modified by collectively evolved choices in how to negotiate that map. This approach, at its best, makes for tremendously exciting music because one hears a number of musicians thinking at full creative tilt at once, reacting to each other's ideas and shaping a coherent group sound as they go.

This approach, and the possibilities it opened, formed the basis of jazz group playing, except for those who chose to play in earlier styles, through the 1950s and into the 1960s. You can hear examples of it, in its early incarnations, in the following albums, all of which are recommended: *Sonny Stitt/Bud Powell/J. J. Johnson* (Prestige/OJC-009), *Fats Navarro: Fat Girl* (Savoy SJL 2216), *Dexter Gordon: Long Tall Dexter* (Savoy SJL 2211), *J. J. Johnson: Mad Bebop* (Savoy SJL 2232), and *The Bebop Boys* (Savoy SJL 2225). The music on the albums is discussed in somewhat greater detail under the appropriate instrumentalists' names in the Soloists section.

## NO ROOM FOR SQUARES

Bebop created a lot of confusion – and hostility – at first, and for quite a while thereafter, among people who had grown up on earlier forms of the music. Bop sounded jarring to many of them; the new harmonic landscape produced what sounded to them like wrong notes, and the up-front role of what had been considered supporting instruments produced what they thought was a cacophony. But there was something else underneath these elements that increased the hostility.

Most of the music of the swing era, no matter how sophisticated, was inclusive music, music for communal experience. Primarily, it was music for dancing, music that was finally functional in that it got people together in a social context and provided the lubrication on the gears of romance and good times. People danced and celebrated to it, and its repertoire depended heavily on the current romantic songs, often complete with lyrics sung by the band's singer.

Bebop, on the other hand, was harder to penetrate. Its tempos were often too fast to dance to, and its melodies were often difficult for the uninitiated even to hear as melodies. Even when they were based on the harmonies of popular tunes, the new melodies the boppers made were extended out of recognition. Sometimes, as in Charlie Parker's recordings of "Klaunstance," "Bird Gets the Worm," and "Merry-Go-Round" (all on *The Complete Charlie Parker Savoy Studio Sessions* [Savoy ZDS 5500]), there was no melody played at all; the performance would start right in on a white-hot, up-tempo improvisation. Some true bop bands, among them those led by Gillespie and by composer-arranger Tadd Dameron, had singers, and Parker and his contemporaries occasionally played for dances. But bop was primarily a musicians' music. You had to know all kinds of harmonic and rhythmic passwords to be "in"; the very aesthetic of the music was based on difficulty – dexterity, technique, harmonic sophistication, and an understanding of a new and complex system of accenting. To those who didn't understand, the surface of the music could be as opaque as the trademark sunglasses that many bop musicians wore night and day.

If the 1930s in jazz were about finding a way to step lightly on the beat and keep moving forward – music of the road, with all the social mobility and possibility of the frontier and the Midwest and Southwest of the time – then the music of Kansas City's own Charlie Parker was an unprecedented extension of that mobility. If the background tempo and harmonic structure in a jazz performance are the axis of the community assumptions of the jazz ensemble, then the melodic inventiveness and resourcefulness of the soloist are the axis of the individual's ability to function against the background of a given social organization at a given time. The tempos that Bird was able to play at – liked to play, practically defined a style by playing (listen to the 1947 "Dizzy Atmosphere" on *Bebop's Heartbeat* [Savoy ZDS 1177] or "Lester Leaps In" on *Live at the Rockland Palace* [Charlie Parker Records CP(2)502]) – were sometimes so fast as to be nearly meaningless. This post–World War II, post-atom-bomb four-four was no longer really about the elegant, triumphant possibilities of mobility but about mobility being taken to its limit, apocalyptic mobility, mobility exhausted by its own logic. Bebop at its most characteristic struck a chord of peculiarly American tragic lyricism – a sense of the exhaustion waiting at the end of all that optimistic mobility – that had found expression in earlier years in the Melville of *Moby Dick*, in the Fitzgerald of *The Great Gatsby*, and in Hemingway. It would remain for John Coltrane to come along and play Ahab in the obsessive chase to boat the harmonic white whale, but that is a story for later.

If the incredibly fast bebop tempos (and accompanying harmonic complexity) were, in effect, an echo of a society that was changing too quickly for anyone but a true adept to keep up with, then the soloist, the individual who had prepared himself or herself to be part of an elite that could deal with that complexity, was the real cultural hero of that movement, and that fact was to lend a certain character to jazz until the late 1950s, when there was another swing of the pendulum.

## RHYTHM IN A RIFF

Big bands didn't just dry up and blow away with the coming of the new style; many of the established ones incorporated bop elements into their arrangements, and others were part of the new music from the beginning. One in the latter category was the justly famous big band of singer Billy Eckstine.

Eckstine, whose early hits "Jelly, Jelly" and "Stormy Monday Blues," recorded with the Earl Hines orchestra, can be heard on *Piano Man: Earl Hines, His Piano and His Orchestra* (RCA/Bluebird 6750-2-RB), was popular enough soon thereafter to form his own short-lived band, which was a haven for the younger players, among them Dizzy Gillespie, Charlie Parker, Fats Navarro, Sonny Stitt, Dexter Gordon, and Gene Ammons, to name just a few. *Mr. B. and the Band* (Savoy ZDS 4401) shows Eckstine's powerhouse band of 1945–1946 wailing on tunes like "Lonesome Lover Blues," "I Love the Rhythm in a Riff," and "The Jitney Man," all of which feature exuberant vocals by Eckstine along with exciting solos by Gordon, Ammons, and Navarro. At a party in the late 1980s, I heard drummer Roy Haynes sing Dexter Gordon the entire arrangement of "Rhythm in a Riff," including Gordon's solo, from memory, while Gordon sat on a kitchen chair grinning and keeping time by snapping his fingers; the band had a special meaning for the musicians who were around at the time. An equally good reason to buy *Mr. B. and the Band* is the presence of such ultra-romantic Eckstine ballads as "A Cottage for Sale," "Last Night," and "Prisoner of Love."

A truly great big band, with a style that took up where the Eckstine band's left off, was trumpeter Dizzy Gillespie's band of the late 1940s. Some good tunes by the big band are included on *Dizzy Gillespie and His Sextets and Orchestra: "Shaw 'Nuff"* (Musicraft MVSCD-53), especially bassist Ray Brown's Blantonesque feature on "One Bass Hit" and the wild "Things to Come." But a better bet for the real excitement of the band are the sides they recorded for RCA a bit later. Some of the best are available on *The Bebop Revolution* (RCA/Bluebird 2177-2-RB), including Ray Brown's second at-bat, entitled "Two Bass Hit," the riffy "Ow!," and the Afro-Cuban specialties "Woody'n You," "Cubana Be," and "Manteca," which utilize the explosive talents of the Cuban conga drummer Chano Pozo.

Pozo's conga accents underlined the characteristic accents of the bebop rhythmic pattern and also gave a special seasoning to the forefront of the music that had been there since the early New Orleans days, as Jelly Roll Morton says in the Library of Congress recordings. Jazz and Afro-Spanish rhythms had always fed each other, but the relationship hadn't been stressed as much during the 1930s, when musicians were trying primarily to refine straight-ahead four-four swing. With that having been brought to a full boil, the Afro-Cuban element reintroduced an important rhythmic component into jazz. By the way, the tune titled "Cubano Be" on *The Bebop Revolution* is really another tune entirely, the excellent "Cool Breeze." The tune labeled "Cubano Bop" on the collection is really "Cubana Be."

Despite this mixup, the music is great. "Manteca" is the Latin equivalent of a riff tune, but Gillespie's good humor and spirit infuse the band, particularly the brass section, which will lift the top of your head off. The straight-ahead swinging tunes, especially "Cool Breeze" (titled "Cubano Be" on the set, don't forget) and "Jumpin' with Symphony Sid" (another riff tune), all contain stop-on-a-dime section work from the band and virtuoso trumpeting from Gillespie. An essential set.

A band that had been around for a while but which incorporated many of the devices of the new style was Woody Herman's. A good sampling of his band's mid-1940s work can be found on *Woody Herman – The Thundering Herds, 1945–1947* (Columbia CK 44108). The 1945 band, which takes up most of the set, was basically a swing band for whom the arrangers threw in a few bop clichés, mostly high-note work for the trumpets and a couple of characteristic rhythmic devices. The band's weakness was a penchant for corniness, but tunes like "Apple Honey" and "Your Father's Moustache" really surge along, powered by Chubby Jackson's bass. The lovely "Bijou," written by Ralph Burns, is a unique Latin-flavored mood piece. "The Goof and I" and "Four Brothers," both by the thoroughly bop-oriented 1947 band, are still fresh-sounding and have fine solos by baritone saxophonist Serge Chaloff and the young tenorists Zoot Sims and Stan Getz. The 1949 Herman band, with its Four Brothers saxophone section of Al Cohn, Zoot Sims, Stan Getz, and baritonist Serge Chaloff, is heard on *Woody Herman – Keeper of the Flame: The Complete Capitol Recordings of the Four Brothers Band* (Capitol CDP 7 98453 2). This nice set includes the boppish "That's Right" and "Lemon Drop," Ralph Burns's beautiful "Early Autumn" (featuring Stan Getz), and "More Moon" (based on "How High the Moon"), on which tenorist Gene Ammons is featured.

Stan Kenton's band also came up around this time. Kenton was much beloved by his sidemen and had a solid, even fanatical following among a segment of jazz fans. Extremely serious and dedicated to the art form of jazz, he attracted many highly skilled musicians to his band. Sometimes – much of the time – he was solemn or ponderous instead of just serious, and his music could reflect that. His band, despite what some say, was able to swing sometimes, but swing wasn't uppermost in his or his arrangers' minds. *New Concepts of Artistry in Rhythm* (Capitol CDP 7 92865 2) is a sampler of his band in 1952, with arrangements by stalwarts like Gerry Mulligan, Bill Holman, and Bill Russo.

A collection entitled *The Bebop Era* (Columbia CK 40972) contains bop-flavored big-band efforts by Herman, Gene Krupa, Claude Thornhill, Elliot Lawrence, and, in one of the first recorded performances of a composition by Thelonious Monk ("Epistrophy," from 1942), ex-Ellington trumpeter Cootie

Williams. There are also fine small-group performances here involving Dizzy Gillespie, Miles Davis, Charlie Parker, Bud Powell, and Fats Navarro, including a stunning "Ornithology," recorded live at Birdland in 1950 and featuring Parker, Powell, and Navarro in a real summit meeting.

### DAMERONIA

A big-band arranger who became one of the greatest composers in jazz and whose small groups had an immediately distinguishable sound because of his arranging was Tadd Dameron. His mastery of harmony was absolute, and some of his melodies are among the most durable of the late 1940s. *The Fabulous Fats Navarro, Volume 1* (Blue Note 81531) and *Volume 2* (Blue Note 81532) contain material from several Dameron-led sessions featuring trumpeter Navarro, which show instantly what set Dameron's work apart. Among bebop dates, these were really something special, full of carefully worked-out ensembles, introductions, and codas, yet still with plenty of stretching room for the soloists.

Dameron's writing gives a strong framework to all the players, including not only Navarro but, variously, altoist Ernie Henry and tenorists Charlie Rouse, Dexter Gordon, Allen Eager, and Wardell Gray. Listen to how large an ensemble sound he gets on "Our Delight" (Gillespie's big band recorded this as well; it's on the Musicraft set listed earlier) and "Dameronia" (both on *Volume 1*), even though the ensemble includes only one more voice (the tenor sax) than Charlie Parker's Savoy quintet recordings. Drummer Shadow Wilson's work on these sides is not to be overlooked, either.

The same remarks apply to "Sid's Delight" and the gorgeous "Casbah," on both of which Dameron has a slightly larger ensemble to work with. He takes advantage of it, layering on a sound with a rich bottom to it due to the presence of a trombone and baritone saxophone. Both tunes have a Latin influence enhanced by the presence of bongo and conga drums; "Casbah" has a wordless vocal by singer Rae Pearl for an additional tone color. "Jahbero," on *Volume 2*, also features the Spanish tinge via the conga drums of Chano Pozo; its sessionmate, "Lady Bird," is another richly voiced Dameron standard, with a beautiful introduction and an excellent arranged interlude preceding Dameron's piano solo. Such touches only add to the brilliant solo work by Navarro and the others and put these recordings in a class of their own for the period.

Dameron should have had a much higher profile in jazz than he did as time went on; he was plagued by drug problems and was never as widely known by the jazz public, let alone the general public, as he should have been. Two later albums show his arranging and composing talents to good advantage. *Fontainebleau* (Prestige/OJC 055) is well worth owning; recorded in 1956 with a band including trumpeter Kenny Dorham, three saxophones, and trombone, the album gives Dameron a chance to work out at greater length than he could on the previous decade's three-minute 78-rpm records. The title cut is a miniature suite, a through-composed mood piece with shifting textures and themes. "Delirium" is an up-tempo cooker, with plenty of solo space for Dorham and tenorist Joe Alexander; "The Scene Is Clean" is a walking-tempo thing with typically rich Dameron ensemble voicings.

Even better is *The Magic Touch* (Riverside/OJC-143), a 1962 set on which Dameron gets a chance to score for a full big band including trumpeter Clark Terry, tenor saxophonist Johnny Griffin, and pianist Bill Evans. The program consists of Dameron favorites like "On a Misty Night," "Our Delight," and his great ballad "If You Could See Me Now," along with a good amount of new material and a reorchestrated version of "Fontainebleau." The writing here is as rich as fine cognac; the solos are set off by imaginative backgrounds and interludes. Dameron put his own stamp on everything he touched, and whatever he touched was made beautiful.

## BOPLICITY

Bebop as such – the stripped-down small-group performances consisting of a unison head and a series of solo choruses – held the floor for a relatively short time before musicians began to look for ways to use bop's rhythmic and harmonic discoveries in the service of more supple, expressive, and complete aesthetic statements. Not long after the music arrived, the LP form came into being (up until then, performances had been limited by the time constraints of the 78-rpm record), and musicians began to use the longer forms that became available with increased recording time as part of the aesthetic.

To be sure, the harmonic and rhythmic vocabulary developed by the boppers dominated the 1950s, but the form began to mutate almost as soon as it started. The elements of Parker's work, like Armstrong's in the 1920s, spread like a dandelion's seeds; both men's discoveries were so fundamental that players of many different personalities could express themselves in the language they developed. Of all the musicians who grew up around Bird, the ones who did the most to expand the possibilities of the bop based ensemble were trumpeter Miles Davis and bassist-composer Charles Mingus.

Davis's career is treated in detail in the Soloists section, but certain ensemble projects he was involved in should be discussed here. The 1949–1950 recordings known collectively as the *Birth of the Cool* (Capitol CDP 7 92862 2) rank as some of the most interesting in jazz. Involved were such luminaries, or luminaries-to-be, as Gerry Mulligan, Gil Evans, Lee Konitz, Max Roach, and John Lewis; the instrumentation included baritone saxophone, French horn, and tuba, making for fascinating instrumental possibilities that were explored imaginatively, to say the least.

In many ways, the *Birth of the Cool* sides were to the rest of the modern movement what the 1927 Bix Beiderbecke/Frank Trumbauer sides were to the small-group jazz of their day: underplayed, lyrical, legato, and with worked-out ensemble sections existing in an ongoing give-and-take with the solo sections. All of the tunes, even the most bebop oriented, like "Move" and "Budo," are richly orchestrated and give a kind of air-cushioned effect, often achieved by doubling a melody line as played by trumpet or alto saxophone with a unison line played one or two octaves lower by tuba, baritone sax, or French horn, for the same kind of tonal effect Davis and Parker (in a rare appearance on tenor saxophone) achieved on the 1947 "Milestones" session (available on *First Miles* [Savoy ZDS 1196]).

On "Boplicity," arranged by Gil Evans, with whom Davis would collaborate again later in the 1950s, the melody is orchestrated so that all the instruments play different notes but in rhythmic unison; the effect is contrapuntal, even though the various instruments' lines match each other rhythmically. John Carisi's "Israel" makes intriguing use of counterpoint as well, in a different way. "Moon Dreams," arranged by Evans, underscores by contrast the fact that much bebop had a frantic quality about it; this music peeled off the more apocalyptic aspects of the modernist temper. At a time when bop's emphasis on solo dexterity had led a lot of players into minimalist ensemble settings, this band, like Dameron's, came along and showed that a whole range of textures and emotions could be achieved within a small-band format.

Throughout the 1950s Davis also brought an important lyrical element to his small-band performances. He always had an ear for pretty and neglected popular tunes; he played the melodies of medium-tempo standards and slow ballads with an assured personal phrasing that, at its best, was the equal of Louis Armstrong's and Billie Holiday's rephrasing of popular material. He took this approach especially with his great quintet of the late 1950s, with John Coltrane, in which he would often use the Harmon mute to devastating emotional effect. An album he made just before forming the quintet, *The Musings of Miles* (Prestige/OJC-004), shows this approach on "I See Your Face Before Me" and "A Gal in Calico." This approach also pointed away from the strict bop approach and toward a more lyrical, accessible group sound.

Davis was one of the first jazz musicians to begin using the longer performance time available on LPs to offer extended solos from all the band members, as well as in the service of mood pieces. (Later, Davis would be one of the first to use the whole LP as a form in itself.) And, although Davis was saddled in the popular imagination with the "cool" label, he led many recording dates in which the music snapped, crackled, and popped. The 1951 sides with Sonny Rollins and young Jackie McLean, available as *Miles Davis Featuring Sonny Rollins: Dig* (Prestige/OJC-005), are an early and very satisfying example of this, as are the 1953 sides on *Collectors' Items* (Prestige/OJC-071), teaming Davis with both Parker (again on tenor) and the up-and-coming tenor player Sonny Rollins.

The 1953 session is worth looking at in some detail as a typical example of 1950s group playing. Perhaps the biggest reason for this is the rhythm section. Pianist Walter Bishop, Jr., was one of the great bop accompanists; he understood how to feed accents at just the right places. (You might think of a pianist as playing chords the same way you'd nudge a basketball that you are spinning on your finger. A nervous accompanist spins it too much and wastes energy. An incompetent one hits it at the wrong time or place and knocks it off. A great accompanist knows how to feed chords to a soloist at just the right moments to keep the rhythmic and harmonic momentum going.) Percy Heath was, and is, one of the greatest bassists in jazz because of his big tone, his swing, and the variety of his lines; Heath's presence on a 1950s recording date practically guarantees excellent music from all concerned.

But perhaps the one to watch closest here is drummer Philly Joe Jones, who would later join Davis's late-1950s quintet. Like Art Blakey, one of the most swinging drummers of the time, Jones tended to accent on the second and fourth beats of each measure with his high-hat cymbal, as well as maintaining a crackling pace on the ride cymbal. Jones also was developing a constantly ready repertoire of snare drum accents with which to answer, goad, underline, and comment upon the soloists' statements. This brought up the temperature of any session he was involved in, because the soloist could have an ongoing rhythmic dialogue with the drums.

The most exciting track of the session is probably the first one they recorded, Davis's up-tempo cooker "Compulsion." From the opening ensemble, Jones adds little fills and accents on the snare. The riffs behind each soloist help generate momentum, too. Bird plays a deep-toned pair of choruses, with Heath providing giant rubber tires for him to drive on, then Rollins comes in like the cavalry coming over the ridge in a western. Listen to the way in which, after Rollins's long opening phrase, which covers almost his full first eight bars, Jones answers with a "bump-de-bump" figure on the bass drum and Bishop answers Jones with an "uh-huh" on the piano. Also, under that first long opening phrase, listen to how Percy Heath plays an ascending line, going higher on the bass in order to build up excitement. (Generally, ascending lines build up tension, and descending lines discharge it.)

Rollins really plays to Jones on this track, as he does throughout, and Jones plays back, answering many of Rollins's phrases with little snare drum figures, as if to say "uh-huh," or "yeah," or "say it again." Listen for these figures throughout the date; they are a perfect example of how a mature bop-oriented rhythm section plays together. The ideas go back and forth, too, as in Rollins's solo on the second take of "The Serpent's Tooth," where Jones plays a rhythmic figure before Rollins's first bridge, and Rollins immediately follows with a melodic figure based on exactly the same rhythm.

This was the archetypal 1950s way of playing in, and with, a rhythm section. Davis's late-1950s quintet, with John Coltrane, pianist Red Garland, bassist Paul Chambers, and Philly Joe Jones, would refine the approach and stylize it perhaps to the point where nothing much further could be done with it, at least until some more discoveries were brought into the picture. They made a number of albums for Prestige, all of which are excellent, and they were comfortable with high-voltage cookers as well as romantic ballads. *Cookin'* (Prestige/OJC-128), *Workin'* (Prestige/OJC-296), and *Steamin'* (Prestige/OJC-391) are classic statements. The Columbia quintet material is at least as good. *'Round about Midnight* (Columbia CK 40610) contains Parker's contrapuntal line "Ah-Leu-Cha," Tadd Dameron's "Sid's Delight" (renamed "Tadd's Delight"), Monk's "'Round Midnight," and several standards; *Milestones* (Columbia CK 40837), which adds altoist Cannonball Adderley, is even better – a last look at the bebop group concept before Davis began to lead his group in another direction. (See the discussion of Davis in the Soloists section.)

## EAST COAST, WEST COAST; HOT AND COOL

The "cool" that the *Birth of the Cool* gave birth to was never a particularly well defined school; it was more a temperamental tendency. Perhaps the quintessential cool recordings were those made in California in 1952 and 1953 by baritone saxophonist Gerry Mulligan (who was in on the *Birth of the Cool*) and trumpeter Chet Baker. Some feature them with only bass and drum accompaniment; some involve a band that harks back directly to the Davis sides. Available on *The Complete Pacific Jazz and Capitol Recordings of the Original Gerry Mulligan Quartet and Tentette with Chet Baker* (Mosaic MR5-102), these recordings use many of the same stylistic elements that the Davis recordings used – unison lines with a high voice and a low voice, counterpoint (both written and improvised), written backgrounds for solos (especially on the Tentette recordings), and a legato, very lightly accented rhythmic orientation.

To the extent that these recordings are to be compared with the Davis recordings (the Tentette instrumentation, which includes French horn and tuba but no piano, is very similar), they are less interesting. The rationale for leaving the piano out was that its absence would afford greater harmonic and rhythmic freedom to the soloist (a dubious notion in itself), but these recordings are not notable for their great harmonic or rhythmic adventurousness. The absence of a piano, widely hailed at the time because it was so unusual, makes for a certain sameness of sound, which Mulligan tried to balance with various ensemble devices – switches between unison, harmony, and counterpoint and occasional tempo variation (as on the quartet's "Lullaby of the Leaves"). The problem was that the piano is not just a harmonic factor but a rhythmic factor.

In order to maintain interest in a pianoless context, the drummer must be very inventive, and the drummer here (either Chico Hamilton or Larry Bunker) does little more than keep subdued time. Without the piano to provide accenting, the ensemble texture becomes very monotonous. This holds true even for soloists who are much more interesting than either Mulligan or Baker were then. On a number of the tracks here, the Mulligan/Baker quartet is joined by altoist Lee Konitz, who was, and is, a truly inventive improviser; these sides are somewhat more interesting because of his presence. (For a couple of examples of pianoless groups that really work, check out Sonny Rollins's 1957 *A Night at the Village Vanguard, Volume 1* [Blue Note 46517] and *Volume 2* [Blue Note 46518], which feature the great drummer Elvin Jones, as well as Jones's own 1968 *Puttin' It Together* [Blue Note 84282].)

The Mulligan records, and much of the so-called West Coast music that took its inspiration from them as well as from the *Birth of the Cool* recordings, are admirable for their attempt to keep the ensemble in the forefront of things and for their high standards of musicianship. But finally, they are weak, as jazz, for the simple reason that there is very little blues feeling in them, which is to say very little blues-idiom, dance-oriented accenting. Without that, a music's roots in jazz will be very shallow.

Some music was about to be recorded on the East Coast that seemed designed to underline this last observation. Actually, such music had never stopped being recorded; the previously mentioned Davis sides with Parker, Rollins, and Jackie McLean are obvious examples, as are all of Charlie Parker's recordings of the time and more others than I could possibly mention here (although I have to mention the sextet sides by trombonist J. J. Johnson, with trumpeter Clifford Brown, on *The Eminent Jay Jay Johnson, Volume 1* [Blue Note 81505] and an explosive Miles Davis session with Johnson, saxophonist Jimmy Heath, and Art Blakey on drums on *Miles Davis, Volume 2* [Blue Note 81502]). But beginning in 1954, Art Blakey, who had powered the Eckstine band and had been a drummer of choice for many of the best of the modernists, would be at the helm of a series of groups that constantly reaffirmed jazz's roots in the blues and even gospel music and that swung as if their collective lives depended on it.

## JAZZ MESSENGERS

The idea behind the Jazz Messengers seemed from the beginning to be implied in the group's name: there was more to jazz than just a set of musical conventions; something further, spiritual, was embodied in the music and constituted a "message" that jazz alone could deliver. That "message" was one that went back to the roots of jazz, to blues and gospel music, and was in danger of getting lost when the music got too far from those roots. Art Blakey and pianist Horace Silver, who were the core of the original Jazz Messengers, both made careers out of keeping those roots watered and vital.

You can hear the two of them together in early 1954, in a group under Blakey's leadership, on *A Night at Birdland, Volume 1* (Blue Note 46519) and *Volume 2* (Blue Note 46520). One of the earliest live recordings in jazz and still one of the best, the album is a sort of apotheosis of the early-1950s approach. It features perhaps the greatest trumpeter of the decade, Clifford Brown, the soulful Parker disciple Lou Donaldson on alto, and a rhythm section that includes ex-Parker bassist Curly Russell in addition to Blakey and Silver.

For the most part, the group takes the familiar head-solos-head approach – but what solos and what group interplay! The horn players' work is discussed in the appropriate Soloists sections, but there is something to notice in the rhythm section. Whereas bop pianists like Bud Powell or Al Haig might surgically insert chords here and there as an answer to a particular line or like crisp trumpet-section accents, Silver tended to accompany a soloist like a big band riffing away in the out chorus of a flag-waver or like a gospel pianist playing behind a choir. His voicings tended to be elemental and his rhythm very churchy. He was the perfect foil for Blakey, whose high-hat cymbal accented on two and four and who liked to use the tom-toms for African-sounding, riff-style accents behind a soloist. These were the seeds of what later came to be called hard bop, which was basically a bebop group conception laced heavily with blues tonality and an accent on the second and fourth beat of the bar, an intensely rhythmic orientation.

The heat this group generates on "Split Kick," the fast blues "Wee Dot," and almost everything else is hard to believe; Blakey and Silver spur Donaldson and, especially, Brown to inspired heights of cogency and momentum. Blakey always had very strong trumpet players, and he liked to play off trumpeters' phrases when they played percussive ideas; Brown played peppery, flowing lines that were lyrical and percussive at the same time. The music on this set can't be recommended highly enough. This same rhythm section, by the way, can be heard to very interesting effect accompanying two of the giants of the swing era, Coleman Hawkins and Roy Eldridge, on the probably hard-to-find *Coleman Hawkins – Disorder at the Border* (Spotlite 121, LP only).

Later that year, the Jazz Messengers proper recorded their first album for Blue Note, under the leadership of Horace Silver. Blakey played drums, and the front line consisted of the ex-Parker trumpeter Kenny Dorham and a young tenor player named Hank Mobley, from whom much more would be heard. Doug Watkins, one of the 1950s finest bassists, rounded out the group. The album, *Horace Silver and the Jazz Messengers* (Blue Note 46140), lays out almost all the directions that both Silver and Blakey would go on to explore in more depth. Silver wrote all but one of the eight tunes.

The first tune, "Room 608," has two themes; the first, stated at the beginning, is a fairly typical bebop line, but the second, which separates Silver's piano solo and Mobley's tenor solo, is something different – a gospel-influenced call-and-response between the horns and the rhythm section. Listen, too, to the change in Silver's accompanying style behind Mobley; both his rhythms and his harmonies suggest a gospel pianist. "Creepin' In" is an archetypal walking-tempo minor-key blues-based tune on which Silver's piano answers the short phrases of the horns. "To Whom It May Concern" contrasts a typical bluesy repeated figure with a Latin interlude; "Stop Time," "Hippy," and "Hankerin'" are all cookers. "The Preacher," probably the most famous item from the session, is a simple theme over very simple gospel-type chords, on top of a New Orleans–inflected two-beat rhythmic background that shifts into straight-ahead four-four during the solos. All of this – the shifting rhythms, the interest in Latin rhythms and gospel-flavored tunes and harmonies, the simple, short-lined blues themes, and the sheer joy in swinging – would go on to mark the work of both Blakey's and Silver's groups.

Late in 1955 the same band recorded a live performance that was released as *The Jazz Messengers at the Cafe Bohemia, Volume 1* (Blue Note 46521) and *Volume 2* (Blue Note 46522). Neither volume has the quality of a complete statement that *Horace Silver and the Jazz Messengers* has; what we get instead is a chance to look at this group philosophy as it plays itself out over a typical evening in a club. The program is a mix of standards ("Like Someone in Love," "Yesterdays," "Just One of Those Things") and originals by Dorham and Mobley.

One departure that this style made from classic bebop was that it tended to employ shorter phrases in the melodies, which were used for their rhythmic, or percussive, effect (see Mobley's "Decifering the Message" or "Hank's Symphony" here, or "Stop Time," "Hippy," or, especially, "The Preacher" on the Silver album). Compare these to such classic Parker lines as "Donna Lee" (on *The Complete Charlie Parker Savoy Studio Recordings* [Savoy ZDS 5500]) or "Quasimodo" (on *The Legendary Dial Masters, Volume 2* [Stash ST-CD-25]), which wind and twist, making an aesthetic point by their complexity. Silver's piano style, too, echoes this approach by relying mainly on arpeggios and melodic fragments used rhythmically.

This idea of setting up percussive melodic patterns becomes a principle of group interplay as well; Blakey or Silver would set up what was essentially a riff pattern in the background, and the soloist would incorporate the pattern into the solo, and vice versa, with the piano and drums sometimes answering a rhythmic pattern the soloist set up. This gave a motivic continuity and interest to performances which were essentially strings of solos and which could have become boring, since most of the time the solos didn't relate to the melody or to each other. For just one example of the technique, listen to Blakey and Mobley on "Sportin' Crowd," a blues riff once known as "Royal Roost" and later to become more famous as "Tenor Madness," as recorded by Sonny Rollins and John Coltrane (*Tenor Madness* [Prestige/OJC-124]). Behind Dorham, on this same cut, the dialogue is primarily between Blakey and Silver. Drum fans will want to check out "Hank's Symphony," a virtual anthology of patented Blakey devices.

Blakey and Silver parted company after this session; Silver formed his own band, and Blakey went on to lead many different incarnations of the Jazz Messengers. It would be impossible to look in detail here at the complete work of both men, but we can trace the concerns that were laid out in these early records through the high points of their careers as their concepts developed. Blakey, in particular, made countless albums.

One Blakey album that is worth listening to even though it is hardly characteristic is *Art Blakey's Jazz Messengers with Thelonious Monk* (Atlantic 1278-2). Monk sits in with the 1957 Messengers in a program made up almost entirely of Monk compositions. Blakey was always one of the best accompanists to the unconventional pianist-composer; listening to this record after any of the records with Silver underscores the point that Monk, for all his supposed difficulty, was as much of a back-to-basics thinker as Blakey and Silver were.

In fact, Monk uses the piano in much the same way as Silver does, although the sound is different. Whereas Silver tended to play a lot behind a soloist, Monk would sometimes drop out altogether or just play his version of Basie/

Powell surgical-strike trumpet-section punctuations. But, given that difference, both liked to use voicings with only two or three notes, both used repeated melodic fragments percussively, both were essentially riff-based players, and both liked to set up rhythmic patterns for the soloist to work off of; listen to Monk and Blakey behind trumpeter Bill Hardman on Monk's "I Mean You." But the album was recorded before the Messengers had really jelled into what Blakey was looking for. *Theory of Art* (RCA/Bluebird 6286-2-RB) also features this 1957 band, plus alto saxophonist Jackie McLean. Good as all the musicians involved are, this set never really lifts off.

*Moanin'* (Blue Note 46516), recorded in October 1958, is a whole other story; Blakey had found the sound here and came up with one of the classic albums in jazz. The title tune, composed by the group's pianist, Bobby Timmons, is a call-and-response gospel number which switches into a heavily two-and-four accented, straight-ahead rhythm for the solos. Bassist Jymie Merritt goes back and forth between playing only on one and three and walking all four beats. Trumpeter Lee Morgan and tenor saxophonist Benny Golson both take impassioned, preaching solos.

The rest of the album is hardly a letdown; Benny Golson contributes four originals, including the almost cool-sounding "Along Came Betty" and the famous "Blues March," a full-dress blues performance over Blakey's relentlessly martial drums. There are also a ballad, "Come Rain or Come Shine," recast as a medium-tempo blowing vehicle, "Are You Real," a bright-tempo Golson original with a beautiful harmonic progression and nice contrasts in dynamics, and Golson's "Drum Thunder Suite," a showcase for Blakey. Throughout, Golson, Morgan, and Timmons burst with ideas and energy, and the group approach has really jelled; this is an essential album.

Blakey recorded a number of other excellent albums for Blue Note. *The Big Beat* (Blue Note 46400) has tenor saxophonist and composer Wayne Shorter, who would be one of the preeminent figures of the 1960s and 1970s, in place of Golson. The album is a collection mining the same veins as *Moanin'*: a gospel number (Bobby Timmons's "Dat Dere"), a back-beat, or shuffle rhythm, tune ("The Chess Players"), a standard recast as a blowing number ("It's Only a Paper Moon"), and two bright-tempo originals, both by Shorter. "Lester Left Town," especially, is a beautiful composition.

*Indestructible* (Blue Note 46429) expands the Messengers' front line to include trombonist Curtis Fuller, and Cedar Walton replaces Bobby Timmons on piano. This album is mostly based on vamps, which are essentially riffs played by the bass. On "The Egyptian," a representative example, the horn melodies create a kind of counterpoint with the rhythm section's vamp. Vamps tend to undercut the forward-moving tendency of the music and point toward a more static time feel; the exploration of this technique would be one of the main events of the 1960s. Much New Orleans music was based on vamps.

Often such a rhythmic feel is accompanied by a harmonic vocabulary, based on suspended chords, that makes the harmonic destination ambiguous. The suspended chords can be centered in a number of tonalities, or modes, which are essentially single scales that musicians play in for a while until a new scale is designated. This is different from the chord-changes approach because that approach used transitional chords and scales to draw you into the next harmonic gravity, implying cause and effect. The new harmonic/rhythmic technique downplayed the role of cause and effect over time. "Calling Miss Khadija" is probably the most exciting track on the album. Another vamp tune, a blues in structure, it is cast in six-four time rather than the customary four-four, for a very refreshing, unexpected rhythmic vitality.

*Mosaic* (Blue Note 46523) extends some of the same techniques of *Indestructible* but is perhaps an even more interesting album overall. It is essentially the same edition of the Messengers but with the significant replacement of Lee Morgan by the equally fiery Freddie Hubbard. Almost all the tunes here use vamps as a basis, but the variety and interest are deep. The title track is a fast swinger that goes through shifting rhythmic terrain – a fast Latin vamp, straight-ahead swing, and a repeated technique of playing a half-note triplet rhythmic figure against the four-four time for a feeling of superimposed meters. Freddie Hubbard's own composition "Crisis" is also first-rate, making use of a bass vamp that undergoes a number of mutations, along with a very effective use of dynamics. There is, of course, strong soloing from everyone concerned; all in all, this is one of the best Blakey albums.

This same group, with Reggie Workman on bass in place of Jymie Merritt, recorded several albums for Riverside, the best of which is probably *Caravan* (Riverside/OJC-038), with nice ballad features for Hubbard ("Skylark") and Fuller ("In the Wee Small Hours of the Morning") and two excellent Shorter originals, "Sweet 'n' Sour," a waltz full of interesting arranged touches for the rhythm section, and "This Is for Albert," a personal favorite of mine, with its poignant theme, ingenious voicings, and fine use of dynamics. *Ugetsu* (Riverside/OJC-090), recorded live at Birdland, is very much Shorter's album; he contributes four originals and has a ballad feature to himself on "I Didn't Know What Time It Was." A fine set but not quite as focused as some of the studio efforts and not quite as fiery as some of the other live stuff.

Blakey went on to record countless albums and to introduce many important young players. In the 1980s Blakey gave early public exposure to Wynton and Branford Marsalis, altoist Bobby Watson, trumpeter Terence Blanchard, altoist Donald Harrison, pianist Geoff Keezer, and many others. His career ended only with his death in 1990, but his influence and spirit will be felt for many years to come.

## MORE MESSAGES

Art Blakey was hardly the only one affirming the values of blues tonality and cohesive group sound at the time. Blakey alumnus Benny Golson, the tenor saxophonist and composer who did so much to make *Moanin'* (Blue Note 46516) a classic album, formed a band with Art Farmer, one of the most talented and lyrical trumpeters of the 1950s, called the Jazztet, which paid close attention to routining, ensemble backgrounds to solos, original compositions, and mood pieces. Their album *Meet the Jazztet* (MCA/Chess-91550) is a perfect summation of their style. A mix of Golson originals ("Blues March," originally recorded on *Moanin'*, "I Remember Clifford," the beautiful ballad tribute to trumpeter Clifford Brown, the neglected but exquisite ballad "Park Avenue Petite," and a classic portrait of a hustler, "Killer Joe," with its unique shifting mood) and standards ("Avalon," "Easy Living," "It Ain't Necessarily So," and "It's All Right with Me"), with a Farmer original and an adaptation of Leroy Anderson's "Serenata" thrown in for good measure, it is a thoroughly satisfying set, with excellent solo work from both leaders as well as trombonist Curtis Fuller and the young McCoy Tyner on piano.

Blakey's cofounder of the Jazz Messengers, Horace Silver, would go on to establish his own quintet as an even longer-lasting ensemble. Silver's groups always emphasized the same rhythmic and harmonic virtues that Blakey's did, in an even more elemental form, if that's possible. At his best, Silver could generate an absolutely irresistible rhythmic drive, and his were among the most popular jazz recordings of the late 1950s and early 1960s.

Probably the two best and most characteristic are *Doin' the Thing: The Horace Silver Quintet at the Village Gate* (Blue Note 84076) and *Song for My Father* (Blue Note 84185). The former is a flat-out, take-no-prisoners cooker of an album, the latter a more varied program from several years later, with a more reflective cast to much of it. Together, they show the range of unique flavorings that Silver could cook up with his riff-based style.

*Doin' the Thing* is comprised of two wild up-tempo pieces and two in a rocking medium tempo. Probably the most famous of these is the set's opener, "Filthy McNasty," on which the group (made up of Blue Mitchell on trumpet, Junior Cook on tenor, Silver at the piano, Gene Taylor on bass, and the underappreciated Roy Brooks on drums) hits a groove, a rhythmic pocket, and doesn't let up for a moment. The track is a good place to notice the effect of this heavily accented rhythmic approach when used by skilled musicians.

Just as Roy Eldridge and Chu Berry used the heavy four-to-the-bar beat of "Swing Is Here" (on *Swing Is Here: Small Band Swing 1935–1939* [RCA/Bluebird 2180-2-RB]) to set up expectations that they would then alternately fulfill and subvert, Mitchell and especially Cook constantly set up rhythmic patterns that lead you to expect them to play an accented note in a certain place but leave your ear to hear only the rhythm section at that point, giving an experience of surprise, much the same as a juggler will set up patterns that lead your eye to expect to see something in a certain place at a certain time, then vary the pattern, causing interest and excitement to build up.

*Song for My Father* has some tracks by this same group and some by a later one, which included trumpeter Carmell Jones and the hugely talented tenor saxophonist Joe Henderson. The title tune, with its undulating rhythm and Latin-flavored theme voiced simply in thirds, sets a languorous, tropical mood that heats up as it goes through a succession of solos. "The Natives Are Restless Tonight" is an up-tempo romp through a minor-key blues, with Silver and drummer Roger Humphries setting exciting rhythmic patterns behind the horn soloists. Henderson, in particular, is interested in using the building blocks of his phrases as rhythmic elements. The balance of the album consists mainly of tunes based, like "Calcutta Cutie" and "Que Pasa," on simple melodies over rhythm section vamps; Henderson's up-tempo "The Kicker" and Silver's beautiful trio performance of his original ballad "Lonely Woman" (not to be confused with the Ornette Coleman tune of the same title) round out a great set.

Also excellent if not quite on the same level is *Blowin' the Blues Away* (Blue Note 46526), by the same group that recorded *Doin' the Thing* but with Louis Hayes replacing Roy Brooks at the drums – a mix of hot up-tempo things like the title track, "Break City," and "Baghdad Blues," the gospel-flavored "Sister Sadie" (a Silver classic), and the Silver ballad "Peace." Silver, it should be noted, was a composer of great ballads, which he would play in chords and which would all be good vehicles for lyrics; this side of his musical personality is often overlooked because of his ability at generating heat.

*Six Pieces of Silver* (Blue Note 81539) is also a recommended set, recorded mostly in 1956 by the original Silver quintet, including tenorist Hank Mobley and bassist Doug Watkins from the Silver/Blakey Jazz Messengers, along with trumpeter Donald Byrd and drummer Louis Hayes. It contains the usual mix of cookers (including "Camouflage," which is especially tasty for its passages of stop-time playing, and the well-known "Senor Blues") and ballads, including "Shirl," a trio track, like "Peace," played by Silver mostly in chords, faintly reminiscent of Duke Ellington's unique "Melancholia" (available on *Duke Ellington: Piano Reflections* [Capitol Jazz CDP 7 92863 2]).

*Finger Poppin'* (Blue Note 84008) is a very good set, a true cooker, especially on the exciting "Cookin' at the Continental," featuring the same band that recorded *Blowin' the Blues Away. Horace-Scope* (Blue Note 84042), with the *Doin' the Thing* band, is likewise excellent and includes the fine Latin-flavored Silver standard "Nica's Dream." *The Cape Verdean Blues* (Blue Note 84220) features the 1965 band, with Woody Shaw on trumpet and Joe Henderson on tenor and with trombonist J. J. Johnson as guest artist on three tracks. Like *Song for My Father*, much of the album's material is written in simple phrases over vamps.

## MJQ

Obviously, the mid-1950s was a kind of golden age for small-group jazz, but we haven't even looked at some of the most important of these ensembles yet. The Miles Davis quintet and sextet of the late 1950s and 1960s is discussed under the trumpeter's name in the Soloists section. The great quintets that percussionist Max Roach led in the late 1950s, first with trumpeter Clifford Brown, then, after Brown's untimely death in 1956, with Kenny Dorham and Booker Little, are discussed in the sections on trumpet players.

One group that formed in the mid-1950s and that enjoyed great longevity and popularity was the Modern Jazz Quartet, commonly known as the MJQ. Led by pianist-composer John Lewis and including vibraharp master Milt Jackson, bassist Percy Heath, and drummer Connie Kay, the MJQ stood above all for an attention to order, organized group interplay, and control.

Partly this had to do with the lack of horns in the instrumentation, in which the vibes and the sober right hand of leader Lewis often engaged in Bach-like counterpoint over the rolling bass of Heath and the nonexplosive drums of Kay. Partly this had to do with a compositional conception that didn't place the highest premium on swinging; everything is very careful in their records, Lewis is in total control of the conception. But, to me, the music is just not very compelling.

Still, the group features Percy Heath's buoyant bass and the blues-drenched playing of Milt Jackson who, if he ever played an unswinging phrase, did it in private. When they wanted to, the MJQ could generate considerable momentum. One recording on which they consistently do just that is *The Complete Last Concert* (Atlantic 7 81976-2), a two-disc set recorded at their farewell concert in 1974, which marked the end of nineteen years playing together as a unit (they subsequently joined forces again in 1981). This set contains some of their hardest swinging and most lyrical playing on a program of popular and jazz standards, including "Summertime," "What's New," "A Night in Tunisia," and " 'Round Midnight," as well as well-known John Lewis compositions such as "Django," "Skating in Central Park," and "The Golden Striker."

One of their very best and most varied studio efforts is *Lonely Woman* (Atlantic 7 90665-2). This set shows the group at their peak in 1962; they had been playing together for seven years and knew each other very well musically. There is a lot to listen for here: the shifting tempos on "New York 19," the flat-out drive of Milt Jackson on "Belkis," Lewis's and Jackson's fine blues playing on "Why Are You Blue?" (Lewis is usually at his best on slow tempos, particularly on the blues; listen to his solo on Charlie Parker's "Parker's Mood" on *Bird: The Savoy Original Master Takes* [Savoy ZDS 8801]), and the deliciously relaxed mood of "Lamb, Leopard (If I Were Eve)." The title tune is one of the best-known compositions of Ornette Coleman, the alto saxophonist who was making a very large stir in the jazz world at the time this record was made; the MJQ's version of it shows, paradoxically, by taking a very different tack, the tonal implications of Coleman's "free" approach. I recommend this set very highly. Also excellent is *Pyramid* (Atlantic 1325-2), with its characteristic Bachian counterpoint on "Vendome," a fine reading of Lewis's "Django," and a unique, nearly eleven-minute performance of the title tune, a slow, gospel/blues-flavored piece by bassist Ray Brown.

## THELONIOUS MONK

One of the greatest presences of the 1950s and 1960s was pianist and composer Thelonious Monk. Monk participated in the legendary jam sessions at Minton's Playhouse in Harlem in the very early 1940s, along with Charlie Christian and Dizzy Gillespie, at which some of the ideas of Christian, Lester Young, and Roy Eldridge – the longer melodic lines, the substitute harmonies, the off-the-beat accenting – were being refined and extended into what would eventually be called bebop.

Monk was already composing back then, and several of his tunes were recorded by other musicians. (Cootie Williams, the great Ellington trumpeter, recorded two of Monk's tunes when he led his own band, " 'Round Midnight" and "Epistrophy." The latter, recorded in 1942, is available on *The Bebop Era* [Columbia CK 40972], which also includes a Charlie Parker reading of " 'Round Midnight.") " 'Round Midnight" was the most popular, followed closely by "52nd Street Theme," recorded by Bud Powell and many others. But most of his tunes, as everyone was to find later, demanded more of the musicians who played them than the standard bebop line demanded; Monk's compositions had characteristic harmonies and rhythmic devices that needed to be incorporated, or at least taken into account, when a player was soloing.

And the ensemble, as well, had to pay attention to a number of fine points. Almost everything Monk recorded is worth owning.

Monk's first sessions as a leader, recorded in 1947, are available as *Thelonious Monk – Genius of Modern Music, Volume 1* (Blue Note 81510) and show his unique ensemble and compositional conception at work from the beginning. Very few others, at a time when Bird was recording "Donna Lee" and other complex lines, would have recorded a song – "Thelonious" – the main theme of which consisted essentially of only two notes. And no other pianist would have recorded the introduction Monk put on his "In Walked Bud" – a skittering, descending run that sounds at first just like a rapidly played scale but which actually functions to set the tempo for the band (listen closely to the way he accents certain notes as he descends).

Monk always did the unexpected and usually tried to figure out a way to use material that had been taken for granted in some way to a different effect. His harmonic individuality and rhythmic devices marked him as a modernist of the time, but he was a member of no school; he was himself, and he took the entire history of jazz as his province. His solo on "Thelonious," for example, sounds a lot like Count Basie in the way it uses space, in its percussive, trumpet-riff right-hand accents, in its economy, even in the way he plays a brief stride passage. The collection has a number of other tunes that Monk would return to throughout his career as well: "Well You Needn't," "Off Minor," and the beautiful "Ruby, My Dear" were all Monk standards. The performances of two haunting slow pieces, "Monk's Mood" and the perennial " 'Round Midnight," are especially interesting. "Monk's Mood" is a whole composition, not just a melody over some chord changes, with short counter-melodies and characteristic harmony notes from the piano in between the horn players' reading of the melody. " 'Round Midnight" is one of the greatest mood pieces in the history of jazz, beginning with the piano answering the horns' melancholy calls in the introduction and the piano stating the unforgettable melody over the horns' held notes.

*Milt Jackson* (Blue Note 81509) contains eight tracks from a 1948 session pairing Monk with the great vibraharp master, including two takes of Monk's blues "Misterioso." Listen to how, on both takes, Monk uses the same accompaniment strategy, based on a flatted seventh interval, to Jackson's solo. Also interesting here is Monk's version of "Epistrophy," in which the piano, vibes, and drums give the feeling of playing in three different meters. Some of the best of the Blue Note Monk material is to be found on *Thelonious Monk – Genius of Modern Music, Volume 2* (Blue Note 81511), recorded in 1951 and 1952. Monk is joined, again, by Jackson for half the album and by an all-star group including trumpeter Kenny Dorham, the underappreciated tenor saxophonist Lucky Thompson, and Max Roach on drums for the other half. The set points up how funny Monk could be in his writing, as in the devilishly intricate "Four in One" and the well-known "Straight, No Chaser." Both use unexpected, unorthodox linear strategies that nobody else would have thought of. They are surprising but logical, which is a good way of characterizing everything Monk did.

For another surprise, check out "Skippy" here; the performance starts with what seems to be an improvised Monk solo, playing another funny line that twists back on itself and uses all kinds of odd intervals. At the end of the piece, the horns come in playing the same line. The ensembles throughout this set are expertly played, and there is fine solo work from Dorham and Thompson.

Over the next couple of years Monk made a number of records for Prestige, one of the most important independent jazz record companies of the 1950s. *Thelonious Monk* (Prestige/OJC-010), *Monk* (Prestige/OJC-016), and *Thelonious Monk and Sonny Rollins* (Prestige/OJC-059) all showcase Monk's hardest swinging side, generally in relatively informal settings. *Thelonious Monk* is a set of trio performances with either Art Blakey or Max Roach on drums, which highlight Monk's percussive approach to the piano. Included here is the original version of "Little Rootie Tootie"; Monk's solo on this was transcribed by Hall Overton and performed by a large ensemble at a 1959 Town Hall concert (available on *The Thelonious Monk Orchestra at Town Hall* [Riverside/OJC-135]). *Monk* has four tracks recorded by a quintet including Basie tenorist Frank Foster and trumpeter Ray Copeland, along with Blakey (he was one of Monk's most compatible drummers) and bassist Curly Russell. This is Monk at his most swinging, especially on "Hackensack," his reworking of "Lady, Be Good." Foster really rolls here, Monk urging him on with strong, pushing chords. Notice how, when the higher-pitched trumpet comes in, Monk moves up the keyboard, playing high, bell-like sounds in the upper register. Also in this set are three tracks by a quintet including tenorist Sonny Rollins and French horn player Julius Watkins which have a loose, relaxed feeling about them. Watkins was an excellent player; the unusual sonority of the French horn makes these sides especially interesting. *Thelonious Monk and Sonny Rollins* includes two fantastic extended 1954 tracks ("The Way You Look Tonight" and "I Want To Be Happy") on which Rollins plays and plays and plays, a fountain of fresh ideas and rhythmic assurance. Monk is in a supporting role here, but he fills it extremely well. The set also includes two trio tracks ("Nutty" and the very unusual "Work"), along with another one of Monk's pieces that use repitition to humorous effect ("Friday the Thirteenth").

Monk's best material, it is generally agreed, was recorded for Riverside

Records beginning in 1955. Producer Orrin Keepnews gave Monk the opportunity to play in many different kinds of settings; he recorded him live, solo, in several trio sessions, as well in ambitious projects with larger ensembles. Because there is so much, I will concentrate on the highlights and only sketch in the minor efforts. If you'd like to eliminate the suspense of buying the discs one at a time, pick up the Grammy-winning *Thelonious Monk: The Complete Riverside Recordings* (Riverside RCD-022-2), a twelve-disc set containing every bit of music that Monk laid down for that label. Otherwise, check out the following discs.

Probably the all-around best record Monk ever made was *Brilliant Corners* (Riverside/OJC-026). It contains some extremely challenging writing for the five-piece band on the title track, a mysterious theme that includes several tempo changes and is a killer to play at the faster speed. Monk gets a huge sound out of the front line of alto and tenor sax. A long blues, entitled "Ba-Lue Bolivar Ba-Lues-Are," contains great solos from Sonny Rollins, who spins his solo out of a motif Monk plays in his solo, altoist Ernie Henry (a dedicated Parker disciple), and bassist Oscar Pettiford. Max Roach is the drummer on the session. On "Pannonica," a languorous, sophisticated ballad named for the Baroness Pannonica de Koenigswarter, otherwise known as Nica, who was a special friend to many jazz musicians, Monk plays celeste as well as piano. Rollins takes a phenomenal solo here, too. In addition, Monk plays a fine solo version of the standard "I Surrender Dear," and trumpeter Clark Terry signs on for a version of "Bemsha Swing," on which Max Roach plays timpani. For the breadth of its sounds and the depth of the music, this is really one of the essential albums.

*Monk's Music* (Riverside/OJC-084) is another ambitious outing, perhaps most notable for the presence of tenor patriarch Coleman Hawkins, one of three saxophonists at the date (the other two were tenor giant-to-be John Coltrane and altoist Gigi Gryce). The program includes readings by the full band (which also included trumpeter Ray Copeland) of "Off Minor," "Crepuscule with Nellie," "Epistrophy," and a famous version of "Well You Needn't," on which Monk calls out "Coltrane, Coltrane" to cue the tenorist for his solo. (On the twelve-disc Riverside set, there is a fascinating short breakdown take of "Well You Needn't," on which you can see how difficult Monk's music could be; his piano introduction, which sounds as if it's in a different tempo from the rest of the song is, in fact, in tempo, only accented so that it sounds as if it's in a different tempo. At one point Monk says to someone in the band, "You can't hear that, man? Or do you just want to be obstinate?" The second time through, Art Blakey plays the basic tempo underneath the intro, so the others can hear how it works.) There is also a priceless version of "Ruby, My Dear" on which Hawkins plays only with the trio.

*Thelonious Monk with John Coltrane* (Jazzland/OJC-039) contains alternate takes of "Off Minor" and "Epistrophy" from the *Monk's Music* session, but the real prizes here are three tracks by the quartet Monk led at the New York club the Five Spot in the summer of 1957, with Coltrane, bassist Wilbur Ware, and drummer Shadow Wilson. The version of "Ruby, My Dear" makes a fascinating comparison with the one Hawkins recorded a month earlier; both are beautiful, in completely different ways. The tune certainly draws out Coltrane's lyrical side. His more searching side comes out on the intricate "Trinkle, Tinkle," where Coltrane explores every corner of the harmonies and rhythms; at one point Monk drops out, leaving Coltrane to play with just bass and drum accompaniment. The set also includes one of Monk's best solo piano performances, the long blues titled "Functional."

In 1993 Blue Note released a CD containing recently unearthed live performances recorded by the Monk-Coltrane quartet at the Five Spot in the summer of 1957, with Ahmed-Abdul Malik and Roy Haynes taking the places of Ware and Wilson. *The Thelonious Monk Quartet Featuring John Coltrane – Live at the Five Spot: Discovery!* (Blue Note CDP 0777 7 99786 2 5) is made up of performances of "Trinkle, Tinkle," "In Walked Bud," "I Mean You," "Epistrophy," and "Crepuscule with Nellie," recorded in ultra-low fidelity. You can, however, hear what is going on well enough; Monk was in a swinging, extroverted mood that night, and Coltrane was breathing fire. The historical significance of these recordings perhaps exceeds the listening pleasure afforded by them, but if you are a Monk or Trane fan, they provide all the pleasure you need.

One of the most enjoyable Monk albums is *The Thelonious Monk Orchestra at Town Hall* (Riverside/OJC-135), which features Monk in front of a large ensemble playing expanded versions of some of his best tunes, including "Monk's Mood" and a version of "Little Rootie Tootie" transcribed from his trio recording of the tune. The ensemble includes trumpet, trombone, French horn, tuba, and alto, tenor, and baritone saxes. There are fine solos by trumpeter Donald Byrd, altoist Phil Woods, and baritonist Pepper Adams on "Little Rootie Tootie," which is one of the most infectious jazz performances ever recorded. This is also the first meeting on record of Monk and tenor saxophonist Charlie Rouse, who would work with Monk throughout the 1960s.

Two albums recorded live at the Five Spot in 1958, *Thelonious in Action* (Riverside/OJC-103) and *Misterioso* (Riverside/OJC-206), feature the Monk quartet with tenorist Johnny Griffin, an energetic, multinote player, as well as drummer Roy Haynes. Both sets are worth having but are not among the very best of Monk; Griffin was, and is, a sort of "show me the changes and let me blow" player, and Monk's music needed players who were more oriented toward melodic invention based either on motivic development or some other way of extending melodic ideas – a theme-and-variations approach. Griffin, an excellent musician, is from a different school. But there is some fine music here anyway, especially on *Thelonious in Action,* which includes the lovely and rarely played "Light Blue" and good versions of the Monk standards "Rhythm-A-Ning" and "Blue Monk."

One pairing that worked out surprisingly well was the meeting of Monk and baritone saxophonist Gerry Mulligan. I say "surprisingly" because Mulligan was, at the time, associated in most people's minds with cool or West Coast jazz, temperamentally quite different from Monk's roots-oriented music. Released as *Mulligan Meets Monk* (Riverside/OJC-301), the session has a relaxed, conversational feel about it and is enjoyable to listen to, although Mulligan's ideas are sometimes a little corny – they wrap up too neatly and obviously. But he swings, aided not a little by Monk's bassist and drummer from the Five Spot, Wilbur Ware and Shadow Wilson, respectively.

Another unusual pairing is that of Monk and Ellington trumpeter Clark Terry, who made a guest appearance on "Bemsha Swing" on *Brilliant Corners* (Riverside/OJC-026). Monk appears as a sideman on Terry's album *In Orbit* (Riverside/OJC-302), and it is an opportunity to hear him addressing someone else's originals (there's only one Monk tune on the album). He sounds enthusiastic; Sam Jones plays bass, and Philly Joe Jones plays drums, so things swing real well. Monk also plays some gospel-flavored piano on "One Foot in the Gutter." The same words – relaxed and conversational – that apply to the Mulligan album apply to this one. It has been relatively overlooked in discussions of Monk's work, probably because it has only one of his compositions on it, but it is excellent.

*5 by Monk by 5* (Riverside/OJC-362) would be worth picking up if only for the beautiful reading of Monk's ballad "Ask Me Now," which should be played for anyone who needs proof that Charlie Rouse was a great tenor player. Trumpeter Thad Jones, from the Count Basie orchestra and an excellent composer in his own right, is also present here and delivers a very hip solo on the roiling version of Monk's highly unusual piece "Jackie-ing," on which Sam Jones and Art Taylor strike a hot groove. *Thelonious Monk Quartet Plus Two: At the Blackhawk* (Riverside/OJC-305) adds trumpeter Joe Gordon and tenorist Harold Land to Monk's Rouse–John Ore–Billy Higgins quartet for nice but hardly earthshaking results. It's worth having, but there's a lot of Monk to get to before you pick this up.

The group that Monk kept together the longest – for nearly a decade – was his quartet, with Charlie Rouse on tenor saxophone, either Larry Gales or John Ore on bass, and either Ben Riley or Frankie Dunlop on drums. Rouse had a smoky tone and a taste for certain intervals in his playing that seemed to lay well with Monk's harmonies. The quartet recorded mostly for Columbia, although a good amount of material recorded on a 1961 European tour is available on the Riverside box. Their first Columbia album, recorded in 1962 and one of their best, is *Monk's Dream* (CK 40786). The quartet from the beginning was an extremely graceful group; although critics have eternally reached into the same tiny bag of adjectives to describe Monk – angular, jagged, weird – Monk's music was as natural as breathing. I once heard bassist Larry Ridley, who played with Monk in the 1970s, illustrate the rhythmic feel of Monk's music with the image of two bicycle pedals going up and down, easily and regularly. Monk, Rouse, and Frankie Dunlop engage in an ongoing, three-way call-and-response conversation, a lesson in integrated rhythm section playing. On the title track, as well as on "Bright Mississippi" (based on "Sweet Georgia Brown"), "Bolivar Blues" (a remake of "Ba-Lue Bolivar Ba-Lues-Are," from *Brilliant Corners* [Riverside/OJC-026]), "Bye-Ya," and the others, Monk's music stands as just what it is – music. The set also includes two excellent piano solos on "Body and Soul" and "Just a Gigolo."

Almost as good is *Criss-Cross* (Columbia CK 48823), Monk's second Columbia album, with Rouse, Ore, and Dunlop. Much of the music in this set – Monk standards like "Hackensack," "Eronel," and "Rhythm-A-Ning" – has a very hard-charging feel about it. All but two of the tracks are well under five minutes long, though, and sometimes I wish the group had more of a chance to build up some steam. One of the highlights here is Monk's solo version of "Don't Blame Me."

*Underground* (Columbia CK 40785), recorded five years after *Monk's Dream*, is also excellent, although Rouse plays on only three of the tunes (his replacement on "In Walked Bud" is Jon Hendricks, who sings his original lyrics to the tune and then engages in some strong scat singing). The album was notable at the time because it contained four new Monk compositions, an unusual event, since Monk tended to play the same tunes over and over. One of the originals is a waltz called "Ugly Beauty." Monk's music is so honest; there is never anything faked or thrown in just for effect. "Easy Street" is a fine trio performance of a lesser-known popular tune. All in all, an excellent set.

At present, such fine Columbia quartet albums as *Straight, No Chaser* and

*It's Monk's Time* are available only in European issues. Two good compilations that include material from several of the 1960s albums have been released, one titled *Standards* (Columbia CK 45148), the other *The Composer* (Columbia CK 44297). *Standards* is mostly solo piano and is highly recommended for Monk's thoroughly individualistic readings of "I Hadn't Anyone Till You," "Between the Devil and the Deep Blue Sea," and "Memories of You." *The Composer* has blazing versions of "Bemsha Swing" and "Straight, No Chaser" from a Japanese concert. The two discs together make an excellent introduction to Monk. Also worthwhile is *Music from the Motion Picture "Straight, No Chaser"* (Columbia SC 45358), a collection of interesting odds and ends, mostly live performances taken from the soundtrack to a documentary about Monk's life and work.

One other item that must be mentioned is a set called *Thelonious Monk and Herbie Nichols* (Savoy ZDS 1166), which contains four tunes recorded by a quartet led by the fine alto-playing Bird disciple Gigi Gryce, with Monk on piano, Percy Heath on bass, and Art Blakey on drums. Three of the four tunes – "Brake's Sake," "Gallop's Gallop," and "Shuffle Boil" – are Monk originals rarely heard elsewhere; the fourth, "Nica's Tempo" (another tribute to the Baroness de Koenigswarter), is a very good Gryce original. Predictably, given the personnel, the session is a smoker.

As should be obvious, I can't recommend Monk's music highly enough. Several of his solo and trio records are discussed in the Soloists section.

## CHARLES MINGUS

Bassist Charles Mingus was certainly one of the most important composers and bandleaders to appear in the wake of Charlie Parker. Like Monk, he was active in the 1940s (Lionel Hampton recorded his big-band arrangement of "Mingus Fingers" in 1947), but his real impact wasn't felt until well into the 1950s.

Mingus understood perhaps better than anyone that the real implication of Charlie Parker's style was a constantly evolving group counterpoint ideal rather than the soloist-with-rhythm approach taken by so many. Mingus's idol was Duke Ellington, and he was steeped in jazz history, recording tributes to Ellington, Jelly Roll Morton, Lester Young, Charlie Parker, Dizzy Gillespie, and others. At a time when many were obsessed with the latest sound, Mingus made his horn players use plunger mutes and other devices associated with a so-called older form of jazz, as if to remind everyone that the music was a continuum – or, as pianist Mary Lou Williams liked to say, that "all eras in the history of jazz were modern."

As a bandleader, Mingus always urged his band members to find something of their own to say. Many musicians have stressed how important their tenure with Mingus was in helping them grow and find their own voices. His compositions and performances were marked by a turbulence that all who knew him say echoed the turbulence inside him. He was a volatile person, known on more than one occasion to physically strike a band member who wasn't pulling his weight, and yet he could be gentle, charming, and very funny as well. Mingus above all didn't like to let assumptions rest unchallenged, whether they were other people's assumptions about who they were or assumptions about the role an instrument was to play. His recordings vary in quality, too; some are very tight and well planned, and some are positively raggedy sounding. Some of the loosest-seeming are, in actuality, some of the tightest. But that was Mingus in a nutshell – a bunch of heroic contradictions.

One of the very best Mingus albums is *Blues and Roots* (Atlantic 1305-2), a collection of six Mingus originals that address the fundamentals of jazz: its roots in gospel and blues, group counterpoint, and swing in both four-four and two-four. Mingus said that, instead of writing out the music for the nine-piece ensemble, he played each musician's part on the piano and had him commit it to memory, so that the ensembles would have a looser, more spontaneous feeling than they would have if he had written the parts out. Certainly the record is remarkable for its combination of fire and urgency with a very focused group conception.

"Wednesday Night Prayer Meeting" is Mingus's six-eight impression of sanctified church music, a rolling, boiling performance in which the instrumental voices come out of the ensemble like voices in a church congregation. During Booker Ervin's tenor solo the background rhythm stops, and he is accompanied only by hand clapping; throughout, you can hear Mingus hollering like someone catching the spirit in church. "Moanin'," not to be confused with the Bobby Timmons composition of the same name recorded by Art Blakey, is a surging, medium-tempo composition on which all the horn players play different melodic lines, in a sort of reaching back to New Orleans polyphony. At times Mingus's bass comes up into the higher register behind one of the horn solos or plays a counterrhythm, like a whale coming up from the depths for some air; the vitality of the music and Mingus's involvement in it are tremendous. "Tensions" is another performance at the same surging medium tempo, with exceptional solos from Mingus on bass, altoist Jackie McLean, Booker Ervin, and baritone saxophonist Pepper Adams.

"E's Flat, Ah's Flat, Too" uses the same device as "Moanin'," that of having each instrument play a separate line; here they do it at a ferocious up-tempo. The piece starts off with the baritone playing its line for one fast blues chorus, then each succeeding chorus adds one instrument with a new line – tenor, trombone, another trombone, then the altos – until six horns are playing different lines in counterpoint over a savagely swinging rhythm section background. The lines the horns play, by the way, are riffs, not long, nonrepeating lines; in this way, it is Mingus's extension of the swing players' extension of New Orleans polyphony. "My Jelly Roll Soul" is Mingus's tribute to Jelly Roll Morton, a two-melody contrapuntal theme played by the saxophones versus the trombones. The main theme is played once over a parade-ground two-beat feeling, then over a straight-ahead four-four feeling, and is a perfect example of the difference that accenting makes in a performance. During the solos, too, the metric feel shifts, from two to four, at one point into a march as well. All in all, *Blues and Roots* is a grand statement, one of the most enjoyable jazz records ever made – not background music, not hors d'oeuvres, but a full plate of meat and potatoes. Mingus's music was so strong because he understood all the fundamentals of the jazz idiom, as he demonstrates here. Don't miss this album.

Another essential Mingus set is *The Complete Candid Recordings of Charles Mingus* (Mosaic MD3-111), a three-CD set containing everything Mingus recorded for the independent label Candid under the supervision of writer Nat Hentoff. The set shows Mingus simultaneously at his most emotionally raw and his most focused. The best-known tracks in the collection – also available as a separate CD called *Mingus Presents Mingus* (Candid CD 9005) – are four by the quartet he led in 1960 at a Greenwich Village club called the Showplace, which included Eric Dolphy on alto saxophone, flute, and bass clarinet, Ted Curson on trumpet, and Dannie Richmond on drums; they are some of the most extraordinary jazz performances ever recorded.

"Folk Forms No. 1" is a themeless blues based on one short rhythmic motif, which all the instruments play with, extend, modify, twist, and shout throughout a thirteen-minute performance. The motif is basically a gospel figure, but the form of the piece is a blues; over the course of it, all the instruments contribute as if they are part of the front line. Sometimes Mingus walks on the bass and Richmond plays tempo, but much of the rest of the time the instruments are engaged in dialogues with each other – in groups of two, three, and four, sometimes all of them improvising at once. Since they all know the basic accenting structure of the piece, based on the motif, they can play things with each other that make sense and have a truly improvised counterpoint. To hear Dolphy and Curson blowing their heads off over Mingus's and Richmond's stormy swing is a jazz experience you'll never forget.

"Fables of Faubus" is an eerie theme dedicated to the governor of Arkansas at that time, a notorious racist. Mingus and Richmond sing some mocking lyrics, and the tune is full of tempo shifts and changes in dynamics. Also notice that here, as throughout these four sides, the instruments aren't locked into their customary roles; Mingus and Richmond are not merely backing up the soloists but are constantly at work behind them, playing little arranged sections and other kinds of commentary, as well as playing solos themselves. They do the same thing on "What Love," a long, languorous theme, seemingly out of tempo. Under the main theme, listen closely for Mingus's bass countermelody, which gets repeated and transmuted over the course of the piece behind the various solos. This track is also famous for a startling duet between Mingus's bass and Dolphy's bass clarinet; the two instruments so closely approximate two human voices having an argument that you can practically tell what they are saying. The last tune, "All the Things You Could Be by Now If Sigmund Freud's Wife Was Your Mother," is a wild ride through tempo changes, Charleston vamps, stop-time sections, and more, distinguished above all by the nearly telepathic interplay between Mingus and Richmond.

It would be worth having the Mosaic set for these four tracks alone, but there is so much more here. The quartet is augmented by various horns for a number of other excellent performances, including two takes of Mingus's ode to Charlie Parker, entitled "Reincarnation of a Lovebird," featuring altoist Charles McPherson, a straight-ahead bop line called "Bugs," on which the bass and drums play contrapuntal figures under the horns' reading of the head, and "Vassarlean," also recorded as "Weird Nightmare" and, in a fantastic version by Miles Davis with Mingus on piano, as "Smooch" (available on Davis's *Blue Haze* [Prestige/OJC-093]). But the most exciting of these is probably "MDM," subtitled "Monk, Duke, and Mingus," which features the full band (Ted Curson and Lonnie Hillyer, trumpets; Eric Dolphy on both alto sax and bass clarinet; Charles McPherson, alto; Booker Ervin, tenor; Jimmy Knepper and Britt Woodman, trombones; Nico Bunick, piano; and Mingus and Dannie Richmond) on a cooking, up-tempo blues. The soloists are paired off – the two trombones follow each other, then the altos, etc. They play just with rhythm, then they are accompanied by different riffs. After all the soloists have played, they are brought around again for a round of four-bar exchanges in which inspiration runs high. This is real jazz improvising at the highest pitch on the most basic of materials, one of the most swinging recordings ever made. Notice also that the trombones use the plunger mute in their solos to give the New Orleans–based vocalized quality that Ellington used to such advantage in his bands and which Mingus loved so much.

The balance of the set contains material recorded by an improbable ensemble including Mingus, Dolphy, and Knepper, along with trumpeter Roy Eldridge, pianist Tommy Flanagan, and Jo Jones, the drummer of the Count

Basie orchestra. The results are very harmonious and once again underscore the uselessness of rigid stylistic categories when talking about great musicians. All concerned here understood the fundamentals of jazz and had even defined one or two, and the program, made up of blues and a couple of standards, including two fine Eldridge features on "Body and Soul," is in the timeless arena that is the property of all true jazz musicians. *The Complete Candid Recordings of Charles Mingus* is an essential set.

Some of the same material is dealt with on *Mingus at Antibes* (Atlantic 90532-2), which features the Mingus-Curson-Dolphy-Richmond band with Booker Ervin added on a highly charged program including both "What Love" and "Folk Forms No. 1," as well as "Wednesday Night Prayer Meeting." The performances aren't quite up to the level of the Candid sides, but then very little is. The set is especially enjoyable for the presence of Bud Powell, in very good shape, sitting in on a long version of "I'll Remember April," on which he emits chorus after chorus of characteristic Powell melody; it is also a treat to hear him accompanying the other horn players. At the end, Dolphy and Ervin engage in some four-bar exchanges, then two-bar exchanges; you can hear, at one point, Mingus yell out "ones," and the two go into a section of one-bar exchanges. As they do, Mingus signals to Richmond, and they break up the background tempo. The tune ends with the three horns blowing simultaneously, giving a good example of the kind of spontaneity that was part of a Mingus performance.

If you're not quite ready to set off for such deep waters, a good place to start might be *Mingus Ah Um* (Columbia CK 40648). This set contains nine tunes, most of which last under five minutes and which show the most organized side of Mingus; it is one of his least wild sets, no shouting and wailing, and most of the loose ends have been tucked neatly back into place. That's not to say that it's a subpar album; it stands as one of Mingus's classics. Several tunes here are available in other versions that are perhaps more interesting (the version of "Fables of Faubus" on *The Complete Candid Recordings of Charles Mingus* [Mosaic MD3-111], for example, blows this one out of the water, at least for intensity), but this set does contain the achingly beautiful slow theme dedicated to Lester Young, called "Goodbye Pork Pie Hat," definitely one of the most haunting things Mingus ever recorded, and "Self-Portrait in Three Colors," another singing, slow melody of the type Mingus was so good at spinning. "Open Letter to Duke" goes through several moods and tempos in under five minutes – an up-tempo solo section for Booker Ervin, a ballad section with the alto in the lead à la Johnny Hodges, backed with shifting chromatic harmony and tone clusters, and finally a Latin section. My favorite on the set is "Pussy Cat Dues," a slow, sly, good-humored blues that evokes a late night in a club; the ensemble is lightly contrapuntal, clarinet and trombone both playing countermelodies to an effect that sounds loose and jammed but is carefully planned. "Jelly Roll" is a recasting of "My Jelly Roll Soul" from *Blues and Roots* (Atlantic 1305-2). A companion set, entitled *Mingus Dynasty* (Columbia CK 52922), is in the same vein and just as good.

One of the best things Mingus ever did is *New Tijuana Moods* (RCA/Bluebird 5644-2-RB). An impression of a trip to Tijuana, Mexico, the music is full of shifting rhythms, abrupt changes in dynamics and tempo, and wild contrasts in mood. Nothing in the best of Mingus's music stays the same for long; his music is always changing, arguing with itself, posing alternatives and questions. On "Ysabel's Table Dance," for instance, a piano and bass vamp based on a fast flamenco rhythm underlies a series of tumultuous ensemble passages in which castanets twitch and all the instruments blow at once, then slowly die out; solo instrumental interludes come along, only to give way again to the crashing, whirling ensemble. Yet toward the end a lyrical, melancholy theme for trumpet floats over all the tumult. It is unique music.

"Los Mariachis (The Street Musicians)" likewise goes through a series of contrasting themes and sections, yet always returns to the same theme. As Martin Williams says in his section of the liner notes, observing how full-sounding Mingus makes the relatively small (six pieces, plus percussion) ensemble, "There has been nothing like this, I think, since the golden days of the New Orleans style. Even with one horn in solo, there is a denseness to the performance, a feeling of total movement that is never distracting, always integrated." The same goes for the slowest of slow tunes, as here, on a poignantly bittersweet version of the ballad "Flamingo," with Clarence Shaw's muted trumpet evoking all the melancholy of the end of a trip, the view of a place through the eyes of someone who is about to leave it with a mixture of good memories and disappointments. For anyone who really wants to sit and listen, this is an extremely rewarding set. (Note: the set is called *New Tijuana Moods* because alternate takes of four of the five tracks are included.)

*Pithecanthropus Erectus* (Atlantic 8809-2) contains some of the first examples of a technique that would become very common in jazz, a replacement of the chord-changes approach with one in which players play only off of one scale, instead of a series of them, for as long as they like, at which point they cue the other members to switch to another scale. "Love Chant" here alternates between this approach and the earlier chord-oriented approach and produces some interesting sounds from altoist Jackie McLean and the rarely heard J. R. Monterose on tenor. The title piece also uses the new idea, usually called the modal approach, in a long piece in progressive sections. "A Foggy Day" is described by Mingus as a walk through San Francisco with all the noises of the city – car horns, police whistles, fog horns – behind the soloists as they make their way through the streets; it's a charming performance. "Profile of Jackie" is a nice, short ballad feature for the altoist. Miles Davis's 1959 album *Kind of Blue* (Columbia CK 40579) was the record that really prompted widespread investigation of the modal approach.

Two other Atlantic Mingus sets, *The Clown* (7 90142-2) and *Oh Yeah* (7 90667-2), are somewhat less interesting, although *The Clown* has the great "Haitian Fight Song" on it, which opens with a huge-toned, extremely strong bass solo from the composer before the musicians come on playing the menacing, fanfarelike theme. Notice the marchlike stop-time section under the soloists, a direct echo of the introduction to "(Yes!) I'm in the Barrel" on *The Hot Fives, Volume 1* (Columbia CK 44049). The title cut is a long piece with narration by radio personality Jean Shepard. *Oh Yeah* is a big favorite with some for its loose, spirited ensemble, which produces a sound something like that of Bob Dylan's "Rainy Day Women #12 and #35" (and just about as together, musically), Mingus's Ray Charles–inflected piano playing, and Mingus vocals(!) on "Eat That Chicken" and "Oh Lord Don't Let Them Drop That Atomic Bomb on Me." To me, Mingus's singing sounds like he had just spent a long, rough night in a club with a leaky roof. The idea seems to have been to have a really loose, fun session, but the ensemble seems to be looking for direction from Mingus that isn't forthcoming. The album might have been fun if they had thought a little more about it beforehand.

*Changes One* (Rhino/Atlantic R2 71403) and *Changes Two* (Rhino/Atlantic R2 71404) are two of Mingus's best and most listenable small-group sets, simultaneously very pulled-together and very relaxed, recorded with a quintet including trumpeter Jack Walrath, tenorist George Adams, pianist Don Pullen, and Mingus's favorite drummer, Dannie Richmond. *Changes One* may have a slight edge, with a varied program consisting of four new Mingus compositions – the bright, bittersweet "Remember Rockefeller at Attica," "Sue's Changes," a mood piece that shifts between languid ballad sections, medium-tempo swing, shuffle rhythms, and turbulent group improvisation, "Devil Blues," a shuffle blues with a humorous vocal from tenorist George Adams, and the gorgeous ballad "Duke Ellington's Sound of Love." *Changes Two* has a short version of this last tune with a vocal by Jackie Paris and two non-Mingus tunes that are performed well. But this disc is essential Mingus for the seventeen-and-a-half-minute version of one of his best compositions, "Orange Was the Color of Her Dress, Then Silk Blue," which appears in another incarnation on *Mingus at Monterey* (Prestige P-34001). This tune is one of the greatest mood pieces in the literature of jazz, and here it gets a classic reading, the small ensemble negotiating the changing tempos as if they were thinking with one mind. Don't miss this. *Mingus Moves* (Rhino/Atlantic R2 71454), a quintet set from 1973, is considerably less interesting than either of the *Changes* albums, with only three Mingus compositions out of the nine tracks. The two most spirited tracks here didn't appear on the original LP: "Big Alice," a Don Pullen tune that sounds like a meeting of Horace Silver and some New Orleans Mardi Gras Indians, and a swinger called "The Call."

*Let My Children Hear Music* (Columbia CK 48910) is another of Mingus's best recordings, a brilliant 1971 presentation of Mingus compositions with large-orchestra arrangements by Sy Johnson. Highlights include the stately, mournful theme of "The Shoes of the Fisherman's Wife Are Some Jive Ass Slippers," a reworking of a Mingus composition originally called "Once Upon a Time There Was a Holding Corporation Called Old America," as well as the surging, insistent "Hobo Ho" and the lyrical "Adagio Ma Non Troppo." A certain aspect of Mingus – the side of him that composed "Reincarnation of a Lovebird" and "Peggy's Blue Skylight" – is more fully represented in this album than it is anywhere else – a romantic, lyrical sound full of both optimism and melancholy that is completely Mingus's own. My personal favorite track here is "The I of Hurricane Sue," with its extended solos by alto saxophonist Charles McPherson and tenorist Bobby Jones.

*Mingus Revisited* (EmArcy 826 496-2) is a collection I keep wishing were better than it is; Mingus has a big band with the cream of New York's musicians (Clark Terry, Eric Dolphy, Roland Hanna, Booker Ervin, et al.) at his disposal. But six of the eight tracks are under four minutes, and things always seem to stop just as they get going. There are a couple of showbizzy vocals that don't add much and two tracks on which tunes are set against each other in counterpoint; the first combines "Take the 'A' Train" and "Exactly Like You," and the second is an Ellington medley of an unusually up-tempo "Do Nothing Till You Hear from Me" overlaid with "I Let a Song Go Out of My Heart." It's fun but a bit of a parlor trick. The most substantial tracks are the Ellington-influenced "Bemoanable Lady," which features Eric Dolphy on alto sounding like Johnny Hodges on laughing gas, and an eight-minute-long contemporary classical piece by Mingus called "Half-Mast Inhibition," which is very ambitious and successful on its own terms but isn't primarily jazz influenced. Not to be overlooked here is "Mingus Fingus No. 2," first recorded as "Mingus Fingers" in 1947 with Lionel Hampton's big band (available on *Midnight Sun* [Decca/GRP GRD-625]), a choppy but interesting big-band chart.

A favorite album of many Mingus fans is *The Black Saint and the Sinner Lady* (MCAD-5649 JVC-462), an extended work in six parts that seems to have been written to accompany dancers. This is very romantic music, lushly scored for ensemble, with Charlie Mariano's florid alto handling most of the lead. Much of the work is based on vamps, churning riffs stated by the horns as well as the rhythm section, and is based harmonically on a pedal tone, or a bass note that forms the root of a number of different harmonic directions the group might take; the approach is very close in effect to the modal approach. As a result, perhaps, I find the music a little hard to listen to; it feels monotonous to me, and the melodic element seems weak. Generally, if the harmonic and rhythmic bases of the music are going to be relatively static, there should be a lot of melodic inventiveness to provide interest. Mingus seems here to be working mainly with incantatory patterns based on vamps, and I don't think it really comes off. Lots of people do, though.

A more successful large-ensemble performance is *Mingus at Monterey* (Prestige P-34001), recorded at the 1964 Monterey Jazz Festival. The focus of interest here is on two long pieces, "Meditations on Integration" and "Orange Was the Color of Her Dress, Then Blue Silk." "Meditations" is an intricate, emotional work lasting more than twenty-eight minutes, with a beautiful, brooding main theme, including variations full of tumult and shouting, solos overlapping with backgrounds, and Mingus's customary tempo shifts and dynamic turns. The recording quality is less than satisfactory, though, and in many places it is hard to really hear what's happening. "Orange," on the other hand, is a lyric masterpiece, a blues-tinged theme with delicious harmonies, which the ensemble plays, bending and stretching the notes. The centerpiece of this performance is a long alto solo by Charles McPherson that sets and sustains a fantastic mood, balanced perfectly between languor and tension. It is worth owning the set just for this track. The album also includes a twenty-four-minute medley of Duke Ellington material, including a long version of "Take the 'A' Train."

A different approach to "Meditations" can be heard on *Town Hall Concert* (Jazz Workshop/OJC-042), retitled "Praying with Eric (Meditations for a Pair of Wire Cutters)." This isn't the large ensemble bombardment that the Monterey version is but rather a long patrol by a small band, including Johnny Coles on trumpet, Eric Dolphy on flute and bass clarinet, Clifford Jordan on tenor, and Jaki Byard on piano, along with Mingus and Dannie Richmond, into the heart of an ever-shifting composition, ballad sections of great gentleness giving way to surging, cooking sections. It is a really extraordinary example of extended-form improvisation.

A very good album is *Mingus, Mingus, Mingus, Mingus, Mingus* (MCAD-39119), which is often overlooked because there isn't a lot of new material on it. "Hora Decubitus" is "E's Flat, Ah's Flat, Too" by another name; "Theme for Lester Young" is a reworking of "Goodbye Pork Pie Hat." But there is some great playing here by two large ensembles containing two trumpets, trombone, tuba, three or four saxophones, and rhythm, and they give a strong reading to even the familiar themes. A highlight of the record is a shockingly beautiful ballad called "I X Love," in which Mingus wrote some exquisite Ellingtonian voicings behind Charlie Mariano's alto lead; check out, too, the trombone's countermelody to the muted trumpet solo. A strong album, if not a groundbreaking one.

The most ambitious Mingus record ever made was recorded ten years after his death. *Epitaph* (Columbia C2K 45428) is a two-hour performance by a thirty-piece ensemble of some of the best musicians in New York, recorded live in a 1989 concert conducted by composer-musician-writer Gunther Schuller. The recording represents a phenomenal amount of detective work, since much of the piece was unfinished at the time of Mingus's death, having been merely sketched out by him. The booklet that comes with the set is full of information and wonderful photographs of Mingus.

## EZZ-THETIC

Several other composer-arrangers must be mentioned here, each of whom used a large talent for orchestration to create unorthodox and stimulating situations for other instrumentalists to play in. One of the most highly regarded is George Russell, whose "Cubana Be" and "Cubana Bop" were recorded by Dizzy Gillespie's big band in 1947. Russell, who was only a limited instrumentalist himself (he played what is sometimes called arranger's piano), evolved a complex theory of harmony that involved modes rather than chords and which gave much less of a sense of rootedness in a tonal center than traditional harmony did. Beginning in the mid-1950s, Russell led a number of recording ensembles in performances of his original material.

*The George Russell Smalltet – Jazz Workshop* (RCA/Bluebird 6467-2-RB) is certainly one of the best of these. Recorded with a small group including trumpeter Art Farmer and pianist Bill Evans, the extremely varied program is a refreshing change of pace from just about everything else being recorded at the time. Russell uses vamps, swing tempo, arranged backgrounds, and all the materials in the arranger's palette to set off the excellent solo work of all concerned. The set includes the famous "Ezz-thetic," dedicated to boxer Ezzard Charles, and a startling feature for Evans, "Concerto for Billy the Kid." All of the Russell albums reissued by Riverside/OJC are interesting; 1961's *Ezz-thetics* (Riverside/OJC-070) is especially noteworthy for the presence of alto saxophonist Eric Dolphy, who plays beautifully on Russell's arrangement of Thelonious Monk's ballad " 'Round Midnight."

Russell's *New York, N.Y.* (Decca/MCA MCAD-31371) is fun, a sort of postbop *Manhattan Tower*, a stylized late-1950s sound portrait of New York's jazz world, with a spoken narration by singer Jon Hendricks. Here and there the proceedings are spiced with appearances by soloists such as John Coltrane, Benny Golson, Art Farmer, Bill Evans, amd Max Roach. Despite the stellar cast, this is probably more worth having as a period curio with some high points than as something to provide sustained listening pleasure.

Russell's writing can also be heard on two compilations, *The Jazz Arranger, Volume 2* (Columbia CK 45445) and *The RCA Victor Jazz Workshop – The Arrangers* (RCA/Bluebird 6471-2-RB). His offering on the Columbia set is the multilayered and multisectioned "All About Rosie," which, again, features an extended solo from pianist Bill Evans. The Russell material on the RCA set, recorded under the leadership of altoist Hal McKusick, involves a group similar to that on the other Russell RCA set, augmented by several more horns. The Russell tracks here share the spotlight with the McKusick group's treatment of two originals by another great orchestrator of the day, Gil Evans.

Evans had made a name for himself by orchestrating several of Charlie Parker's tunes for Claude Thornhill's big band in the late 1940s and had later turned in some very impressive work for the Miles Davis *Birth of the Cool* sessions (available on Capitol CDP 7 92862 2). He is still probably most famous for his late-1950s collaborations with Davis, *Miles Ahead* (Columbia CK 40784), *Porgy and Bess* (Columbia CK 40647), and *Sketches of Spain* (Columbia CK 40578), for which he produced beautiful large-orchestra frameworks for Davis's trumpet.

But Evans made a number of recordings under his own name that are worth hearing in their own right. His grasp of orchestration was masterful, and he always surrounded himself with the best musicians. *Gil Evans and Ten* (Prestige/OJC-346) has Evans at the piano directing a fine ensemble, including soprano saxophonist Steve Lacy, altoist Lee Konitz, and bassist Paul Chambers, in a mixed program of ballads and cookers, with a gorgeous feature for trombonist Jimmy Cleveland on Tadd Dameron's "If You Could See Me Now" and a fascinating translation of the folk ballad "Ella Speed" into a rolling, medium-tempo performance with excellent work from Lacy.

*New Bottle Old Wine* (Pacific Jazz/EMI-Manhattan CDP 7 46855 2) is a sort of extended concerto for alto virtuoso Cannonball Adderley in a program consisting of material by "the great jazz composers," including Jelly Roll Morton's "King Porter Stomp," Monk's " 'Round Midnight," and Lester Young's "Lester Leaps In." Some of the writing here, like the fey scoring of parts of "King Porter Stomp," sounds a little corny or contrived; the opening of Dizzy Gillespie's Afro-Cuban cooker "Manteca," which is done practically sotto voce with mysterious flutes and guitar played mandolin-style, seems to be straining for an effect that isn't natural to the material. But there is some excellent stuff here; I especially like the writing on Charlie Parker's "Bird Feathers," which makes wholesale use of improvised Parker lines very deftly scored for the ensemble. Adderley and trombonist Frank Rehak play fine solos.

*Great Jazz Standards* (Pacific Jazz CDP 7 46856 2), recorded the next year (1959), is better, more relaxed and naturally conceived. The recording balance is better, too. The album is organized along the same lines as *New Bottle Old Wine*: new treatments of tunes by Bix Beiderbecke ("Davenport Blues"), Clifford Brown ("Joy Spring"), Don Redman ("Chant of the Weed"), and others. Trumpeter Johnny Coles is the primary soloist here, although Budd Johnson just about steals the show, both on clarinet ("Chant of the Weed") and on tenor sax ("La Nevada" – a solo not to be missed). Coming at a transitional time in the music, this album and its predecessor were significant, reaffirming the continuum of the work of the jazz masters from the earliest times until then. Also good is *Out of the Cool* (MCA/Impulse MCAD-5653), which contains another version of "La Nevada," this one much longer than that on *Great Jazz Standards*, including some very Miles Davisian trumpet from Johnny Coles and another wailing Budd Johnson tenor solo.

In 1961 Oliver Nelson, a talented alto saxophonist, composer, and arranger, went into the studio with a seven-piece band – made up of himself on alto and tenor saxophones, Freddie Hubbard on trumpet, Eric Dolphy on alto and flute, George Barrow on baritone, Bill Evans on piano, Paul Chambers on bass, and Roy Haynes on drums – and recorded one of the strongest albums of the early 1960s, *Blues and the Abstract Truth* (MCA/Impulse MCAD-5659). The set consists entirely of Nelson originals, including the lovely medium-tempo "Stolen Moments," which went on to become something of a standard, all orchestrated imaginatively, economically, and tastefully by Nelson. The music swings hard and is steeped in the blues, and the solo work from all concerned cuts right to the heart of the matter. "Cascades" is an up-tempo scalar piece based, according to Nelson, on a saxophone exercise, and "Hoe-Down," despite the title, is a gospel-based piece that shifts into a fast swing tempo for the solos. The other four tunes, including "Stolen Moments," are either blues or are derived from the blues, in different tempos, and there is never any question of monotony. Throughout, the drumming of Roy Haynes is exciting, sensitive, and appropriate to the material; he is, to this day, one of the best and most underappreciated drummers in jazz.

Almost as good – maybe better, in some respects – is *More Blues and the Abstract Truth* (MCA/Impulse MCAD-5888), recorded in 1964 with all-star personnel including Thad Jones on trumpet, Phil Woods on alto, Pepper Adams on baritone, and Richard Davis on bass. The session doesn't have as unified a feeling as the earlier date – several of the tunes aren't by Nelson at all, including two less-than-thrilling pieces by Dave Brubeck – and there is a very humdrum blues line by Ellington altoist Johnny Hodges. But there is a relaxed, at-home feeling about the solo work, fine accompaniment by the rhythm section, which includes the seldom-heard Roger Kellaway on piano, and guest appearances on two tracks by Ben Webster which are worth the price of admission by themselves. Phil Woods, Pepper Adams, and the ever-unusual-sounding Thad Jones are all in great shape, too.

## DUKE ELLINGTON, PART 3

Although there are different schools of thought on the relative merits of the various periods of Ellington's creative life, it is my opinion that the period beginning with the 1951 "A Tone Parallel to Harlem" and ending with Ellington's death in 1974 was by far the richest artistic time of his career. There is no denying the genius of the 1940–1941 recordings or the heights reached by the mid-1930s band. But by the 1950s Ellington had developed farther, and he was still in possession of seemingly limitless energy. The extended works he had begun producing, mostly suites of interrelated short pieces, contained some of the most brilliant music ever written in America, and the band, after Johnny Hodges rejoined in 1955 (he had departed for several years in 1951), was arguably the greatest Ellington ever had.

The sheer amount of material recorded by Ellington and his band in the last twenty-five years of his life makes a full survey here impossible. I'll confine myself to some of the highlights and then point you in the direction of the rest. Many of his late-1950s albums for Columbia are available only on hard-to-find imports; I will briefly discuss some of the best of these as well.

### UPTOWN AND AROUND

*Ellington Uptown* (Columbia CK 40836), recorded in 1951 and 1952, is notable mainly for its definitive version of Ellington's "A Tone Parallel to Harlem," which had been originally commissioned by Arturo Toscanini for the NBC Symphony. This performance, nearly fourteen minutes long, shows how formidable Ellington's compositional abilities had become by this time. The word "Harlem," intoned initially by plunger-muted trumpet, reappears as a compositional motif as the suite winds its way through a kaleidoscopic terrain representing the boulevards, back alleys, and even the churches of New York City's famous black neighborhood. The piece, also known as the "Harlem Suite," remains one of Ellington's greatest compositions.

*Uptown* also includes the two-part "The Controversial Suite," an occasionally satiric tour through jazz history, and a feature for Louis Bellson's drums, "Skin Deep." The set, like another early-1950s Ellington set entitled *Ellington Masterpieces* (not available in a domestic version), also includes extended versions of several Ellington standards. The most famous of those on *Uptown* is undoubtedly "Take the 'A' Train," with Betty Roche's buoyant vocal. *Masterpieces* is worth hunting up, especially for "The Tattooed Bride," an extended work that rivals "Harlem" for imagination and coherence.

A further investigation of Ellington's extended-form works might begin with *Three Suites* (Columbia CK 46825), a set composed of three 1960 collaborative efforts by Ellington and Billy Strayhorn: the brilliant and underrated "Suite Thursday," based on characters and themes from the work of author John Steinbeck, and their ingenious reworkings of *The Nutcracker* and the *Peer Gynt* suites. This entire disc could be used as an orchestration text; throughout it, Ellington and Strayhorn manage to elicit an amazing variety of sonorities from the band, all of which make musical sense. Those familiar with *The Nutcracker* will be especially pleased by the ingenuity and wit shown in this reworking. The *Peer Gynt* selections are less well known, somewhat less playful, but also great music. "Suite Thursday" turns up in an even more exciting performance on *The Great Paris Concert* (Atlantic 304-2), as does "A Tone Parallel to Harlem."

*The Ellington Suites* (Pablo/OJC-446) is most notable for "The Queen's Suite," which Ellington composed after a 1958 meeting with Queen Elizabeth. The version on this disc is the same one that he recorded in 1959 at his own expense, pressed in a single copy as a gift for the Queen, and refused to issue in his lifetime. It is certainly one of the best things he ever composed, containing within it a dazzling variety of moods and textures, from the lyricism of "Sunset and the Mocking Bird" to the percussive "Apes and Peacocks," by way of the lusciously scored reed-section showpiece "Le Sucrier Velours." Also part of the suite is Ellington's beautiful and unique piano solo (with bowed bass accompaniment), "The Single Petal of a Rose." "The Uwis Suite" (composed in honor of a 1972 residency at the University of Wisconsin) is probably best known for the train movement called "Loco Madi," although there is an interesting polka movement here, too.

At present, the stunning 1957 Shakespearean suite *Such Sweet Thunder* is not easily available, but it is worth paying for an imported issue if you can find one. It is to be hoped that Columbia will decide to issue *Such Sweet Thunder* domestically, along with such other late-1950s extended-form masterpieces as *A Drum Is a Woman* and *Black, Brown and Beige* with Mahalia Jackson.

Possibly the greatest of Ellington's late-1950s Columbias was his score for an otherwise forgettable 1959 Otto Preminger movie starring Jimmy Stewart and Lee Remick. In a 1988 article for the *New Republic*, I called *Anatomy of a Murder* (Rykodisc RCD 10039) "the closest thing we have to a vernacular American symphony," and I think that still holds true. This disc will repay as much close listening as you care to give it. Ellington integrates, with consummate skill and profundity, the two main themes (the first theme being the bluesy melody found in "Flirtibird," "Way Early Subtone," and "Almost Cried," the second theme being the ballad melody found in "Low Key Lightly," "Midnight Indigo," "Grace Valse," and "Haupe"), which are in fact mirror images of one another. Each time they appear they are reorchestrated for very different effects. In addition, he uses a wealth of other melodic and motivic material to maximum effect. Ellington wastes nothing here; even a brief bass ostinato figure in "Midnight Indigo" shows up later, transposed and played by baritone saxophonist Harry Carney, in "Sunswept Sunday." Rykodisc, which licensed the material from Columbia, did a brilliant remastering job, and you need this disc.

Ellington continued working in extended forms up until his death. *The Far East Suite* (RCA/Bluebird 7640-2-RB), a collaboration with Strayhorn from 1966, cannot be recommended highly enough. Anchored around three long pieces – "Tourist Point of View," the beautiful "Mount Harissa," and the epic "Ad Lib on Nippon" – the suite presents a fantastic mix of rhythms and moods, using all the resources of that great orchestra. "Isfahan" and "Agra," features for Johnny Hodges's alto saxophone and Harry Carney's baritone, respectively, are two of Ellington's ballad masterpieces. Ellington's piano is featured heavily on "Mount Harissa" and, especially, "Ad Lib on Nippon." This set is a cornerstone of any jazz library.

*New Orleans Suite* (Atlantic 1580-2), from 1970, is one of Ellington's lesser works. This is only to say that it doesn't have the staggering variety of timbral approaches and melodic invention that his greatest works do. There's some very good stuff here, though, including the surging "Second Line" and "Blues for New Orleans," which was Johnny Hodges's last recorded performance.

*Latin American Suite* (Fantasy/OJC-469), from 1968, is one of the lesser-known Ellington suites, but it is one of the best, almost as good as *The Far East Suite*. It lacks a single track as grand in conception as "Mount Harissa" or "Ad Lib on Nippon," but it is swimming in fresh and striking melodic ideas, brilliant orchestration, and rhythmic intrigue. The leader's piano is at center stage to an even greater extent than in *The Far East Suite*, especially on the gorgeous, tango-laced "Tina," a musical impression of Argentina recorded in 1970. This set is a neglected gem.

Even better, perhaps, is the music on *Duke Ellington – The Private Collection,*

*Volume 5: The Suites, New York 1968 and 1970* (SAJA 7 91045). "The Degas Suite," written as a soundtrack for a 1968 film, and "The River," composed in 1970 for choreographer Alvin Ailey, both contain music as good as anything Ellington wrote. In both suites, his lyrical, meditative side gets the strongest workout; "Race" and "Daily Double" from "The Degas Suite" contain beautiful ballad melodies played by Johnny Hodges and tenorist Harold Ashby, and the opening section of "The River" is a piano solo organized around one tone, in which the tonality constantly shifts, like a jewel showing its facets. This set is a must for any serious Ellington fan.

*Afro-Bossa* (Discovery 71002), although not billed as a suite, might be viewed as one, as it is an extended study in different rhythmic grooves and orchestral techniques. This is a real musicians' album, full of fascinating sounds, deployed brilliantly. Many different percussion instruments are used here to set up the various rhythmic patterns, and, purely as a matter of taste, I get a little burnt out on the percussion by about the third track. It's as if too much of some spice had been added to a great stew. Still, it is a unique and valuable set.

### BLUES IN ORBIT

Not all of Ellington's extended works cover an entire album; a number of Ellington's albums of the 1950s and 1960s contain minisuites along with other material. *Ellington at Newport* (Columbia CK 40587), recorded live at the 1956 Newport Jazz Festival, is one of Ellington's most famous recordings, mainly because of the extended version of his 1937 "Diminuendo and Crescendo in Blue," featuring Paul Gonsalves's legendary twenty-seven chorus tenor saxophone solo. This rocking blues is one of the greatest jazz performances ever recorded. The set includes the neglected but excellent "Newport Jazz Festival Suite," a three-part piece. It also includes a feature for altoist Johnny Hodges on his old hit "Jeep's Blues." Taken as a whole, this disc is certainly one of the essential recordings.

*Ella Fitzgerald Sings the Duke Ellington Song Book* (Verve 837 035-2) is just what it sounds like; for about half the disc, the great singer is accompanied by the Ellington band, singing mostly the better-known items from the Ellington-Strayhorn oeuvre but throwing in a few neglected beauties as well, like "Clementine" and "Lost in Meditation." For the other half, Fitzgerald is backed by a fine non-Ellington small band including violinist Stuff Smith and tenorist Ben Webster. "Portrait of Ella Fitzgerald," a suite in four parts on which Fitzgerald doesn't perform, is also included and is another of the least recognized Ellington-Strayhorn masterpieces. Sit down with "Portrait" and follow the motifs through the four movements and have a musical ball.

*Jazz Party* (Columbia CK 40712) is a bit of a grab bag, containing, among other things, one suite ("Toot Suite," which climaxes with a fire-breathing Paul Gonsalves solo), two interesting compositions featuring a nine-member percussion section in addition to regular drummer Sam Woodyard, a blues featuring singer Jimmy Rushing, and the definitive version of Billy Strayhorn's masterpiece "U.M.M.G.," which features Dizzy Gillespie sitting in on trumpet and which builds to a tremendous climax. This set would be worth having for "U.M.M.G." if for nothing else.

Another grab bag is *Blues in Orbit* (Columbia CK 44051), a collection of items from 1958 and 1959, which makes up in memorable individual performances what it lacks in overall coherence. Special highlights are the great and unique train piece "Track 360," the minor-key swinger "Villes Ville Is the Place, Man," Johnny Hodges's ballad feature on "Sentimental Lady" (also known as "I Didn't Know about You"), and the unusual and ingenious "Blues in Blueprint." There is other Ellington to pick up before this one, but it is a very satisfying set nonetheless.

*The Great Paris Concert* (Atlantic 304-2), a two-disc set from 1963, is an extremely strong picture of the band in action, live. As mentioned, it contains very good versions of both "A Tone Parallel to Harlem" and "Suite Thursday," but it also has a roaring, apocalyptic rendition of "Rockin' in Rhythm," as well as several excellent Hodges features, very well recorded. Ellington specialists will dig the versions of "Rose of the Rio Grande," "Echoes of Harlem," and a great "Tutti for Cootie," featuring Cootie Williams in a graduate seminar on the plunger mute. Very highly recommended.

Ellington and his band spent much, or most, of their time playing for audiences who wanted most to hear the great standards Ellington had composed and to dance to them, as well as to other popular music arranged by Ellington. *Ellington Indigos* (Columbia CK 44444), by the 1957 band, contains stunningly beautiful versions of Ellington's "Solitude," "Mood Indigo," and "Prelude to a Kiss" (one of Johnny Hodges's best performances), as well as suave and deep versions of pop tunes like "Where or When" (featuring Paul Gonsalves's tenor), "Dancing in the Dark," and "Tenderly." This set is one of the cornerstones of late-1950s Ellington and might get overlooked in the wave of very welcome interest in Ellington's extended works. Don't overlook it. (For more in this vein, Ellington's currently hard-to-find late-1950s set *At the Bal Masque* presents ingenious arrangements of fine standards like "Alice Blue Gown," "Poor Butterfly," and "Indian Love Call.")

Another one that absolutely must not be overlooked is . . . *And His Mother Called Him Bill* (RCA/Bluebird 6287-2-RB), a 1967 recording consisting entirely of compositions by Billy Strayhorn, who had died earlier in the year. It shows the band at its very best, playing incomparable material composed by Ellington's alter ego. Trumpeter Clark Terry joins the band on fluegelhorn for this set, to good effect. The emotional high point here is "Blood Count," Strayhorn's last composition; Johnny Hodges and the entire band combine to make a thing of supernatural beauty. Ellington's solo piano version of "Lotus Blossom" is also enormously moving, but if I were to start singling out tracks, I'd have to continue through the whole disc. Please don't miss this.

For some unique small-band performances from 1957 and 1958, check out *Happy Reunion* (Signature/Sony Music AK 40030). The 1957 tracks here are by a septet including Johnny Hodges on alto and Clark Terry on trumpet and include the swinger "Rubber Bottom" and the haunting "Where's the Music?" The 1958 titles feature tenorist Paul Gonsalves alone with the Ellington–Jimmy Woode–Sam Woodyard rhythm section, playing two takes apiece of "In a Mellotone" and the fine ballad "Happy Reunion," as well as thirty-one hot choruses of blues billed as a version of the "wailing interval" from "Diminuendo and Crescendo in Blue."

But the ultimate treasure trove of unusual late Ellington is certainly the ten-volume series called *Duke Ellington – The Private Collection* (SAJA 7 91041–91045 and 91230–91234). It would be impossible here to detail everything in this amazing mix of live and studio recordings from the 1950s and 1960s, most of which was recorded by Ellington himself, at his own expense. Almost every volume contains tunes unheard elsewhere or familiar material in radically altered arrangements. Stanley Dance's liner notes provide fascinating glimpses into the actual circumstances of the recordings.

Some highlights, briefly noted: *Volume 1* contains studio material recorded in 1956, with Johnny Hodges and Paul Gonsalves heavily featured. Notable here are the furiously swinging "Feet Bone" and the bop-flavored "Short Sheet Cluster," on which Clark Terry plays brilliantly. *Volume 2* features a very loose 1958 band playing for a dance at a California Air Force base. The sound here isn't that great, and Ellington doesn't get to the piano until the fifth track. Johnny Hodges and trumpeter Cat Anderson were both missing, and this gets my vote for least interesting set of the series. *Volume 3* is one of the best and most interesting of the series, with a number of previously unreleased tunes, including Billy Strayhorn's arrangement of Thelonious Monk's "Monk's Dream" and Ellington's Monk tribute called "Frere Monk." Gonsalves is featured heavily in these 1962 tracks, to especially good effect on the very fast "ESP" that opens the set.

*Volume 4* is another excellent set, consisting of studio tracks from 1963 on which cornetist Ray Nance is the most prominent voice; on most, he is the only brass voice, along with the reeds and the rhythm section. He even is allowed to take over the Hodges feature "Jeep's Blues." Also check out the jumping version of "Harmony in Harlem," with the bass of the undersung Ernie Shepard. *Volume 5* consists of the two suites discussed earlier. *Volume 6* consists of live tracks from yet another California dance gig for the Air Force, on the night after the one featured on *Volume 2*. This set is somewhat more pulled together, although Hodges's presence is still missed. The band does some interesting things, like "Such Sweet Thunder" and "Blues To Be There," which is from the "Newport Jazz Festival Suite." *Volume 7* is something of a grab bag, full of tracks from several 1957 and 1962 studio sessions, with Gonsalves again prominent. His chase choruses with Clark Terry on "Circle of Fourths" are very exciting.

*Volume 8* contains some very unusual studio things, all but one of which date from the mid-1960s, including three tunes with the drums playing heavy-handed rock/funk rhythms, which make the tracks sound dated. The good news on this one is all the Johnny Hodges there is to hear, especially "Banquet Scene" from "Timon of Athens" and the oddly titled "Rod La Rocque." *Volume 9* would be worth having if only for the informal "Sophisticated Lady" by Hodges and the rhythm section. These 1968 studio tracks also include a fine "I Can't Get Started" by tenorist Harold Ashby and an Ellington piano solo on his "Meditation." Finally, *Volume 10* contains almost a full reading of "Black, Brown, and Beige," recorded mostly in 1965, and extremely important for an understanding of Ellington's work. It also contains a reading of "Harlem" that is not quite up to the versions on either *Ellington Uptown* (Columbia CK 40836) or *The Great Paris Concert* (Atlantic 304-2) and an alternate version of "Ad Lib on Nippon," the definitive version of which is to be found on *The Far East Suite* (RCA/Bluebird 7640-2-RB).

# TRANSITION

**IN THE LATE 1950S** many musicians' ideas about the passage of time and about the roles instruments should fill in the jazz group began to change. The music they had been playing up to that point was basically a metaphor for the cycle of voyage and return. Its essential harmonic devices were linked to the idea of finding home; a tension was set up by a chord or chords, then finally resolved, if only momentarily.

That metaphor for voyage and return was also built into the music's structure – the organization into choruses, whether the twelve-measure chorus of the blues or the usual thirty-two-measure chorus of the standard popular song. Choruses were little stories, the plots of which consisted of the way-onto-way of the harmonic pulls and rests; they ended in resolution, then began again. It was music of cause-and-effect over time; the sense of mastery of time was a big part of the satisfaction the music delivered. But in the late 1950s a number of elements of the music began to undercut the sense of movement through time.

One of those elements was the use of gospel harmonies and vamps in the work of Art Blakey and Horace Silver. In gospel-based tunes such as "Moanin'" and "The Preacher," the harmonic background was simpler than in much bebop, with fewer turns in the map. Part of the notion underneath this was to ground the music again in the community it had come from, in the bedrock sounds of African-American life – the church and the blues. It was less about venturing out, as the midwestern swing of the 1930s and Charlie

Parker's music were, and more about reaffirming something. And it was supposed to be more accessible to people, more popular, more involved in the community at large in that sense, too, instead of a being a hermetic music that only in-group members could properly play or understand.

If, as I said earlier, the background tempo and harmonic structure in a jazz performance are the axis of the community, then the melodic inventiveness and resourcefulness of the soloist are the axis of the individual's ability to function against the background of a given social organization at a given time. The complex bop harmonies and fast tempos inevitably reflected the kinds of social and even class contrasts that were becoming more commonplace in the wake of World War II, and they also reflected a faith in the individual's ability to master the rules of that increasingly complex social (harmonic, rhythmic) system. For whatever mix of reasons, the music that Blakey and Silver were making was pointing less toward social (harmonic, rhythmic) contrast and more toward simplicity and stasis.

As their music developed, it went farther in this direction. They began using vamps, the repeated phrases in the rhythm section that make for an incantatory quality, which comes from religious music. Vamps usually imply little or no harmonic movement. They don't move you through time; they immerse you in the present. Vamps are associated with ritual and myth, and ritual and mythic time is eternal, as opposed to historical time, which is contingent.

Another element that began to undercut the sense of movement through time was the modal approach used by Charles Mingus on *Pithecanthropus Erectus* (Atlantic 8809-2) and, most famously, by Miles Davis on *Kind of Blue* (Columbia CK 40579). Instead of an intricate harmonic map, musicians played off of one scale, or mode, either for a preordained number of measures or until someone signaled to change to another scale. But staying in one scale kept the harmony static and weakened the sense of time passing.

At the same time, what were once accompaniment or rhythm instruments were being integrated into the total group sound. At its most extreme, the tendency was to eliminate the distinction between lead and accompaniment altogether. The Mingus quartet with Eric Dolphy, Ted Curson, and Dannie Richmond, as heard in *Mingus Presents Mingus* (Candid CD 9005), was a very well realized example. This approach made the group fully polyphonic again, like the New Orleans bands, where the various voices contributed to a group counterpoint. Only now the drums and bass, along with the so-called melody instruments, were front-line instruments.

This amounted to a full-scale overhaul of the group democracy. Whereas once, by mutual agreement, certain instruments took the lead and certain instruments filled a formalized accompanying role, now all instruments were in the foreground. Also, since the rhythm instruments weren't necessarily keeping time, the lead instruments had to assume responsibility for thinking about that as well.

Along with this came a tendency in many jazz groups to eliminate the piano. The piano implicitly gives at least a harmonic context for what everyone else does. A horn player's single-note melodic lines can often be in several keys at once. Or if there is a pedal tone from the bass, the horns can play in several keys off of that, switching at will. The piano puts the notes that the other instruments are playing into the context of a chord. It sets boundaries and arranges everything into a vertical hierarchy, and to many players at the time it felt like a straitjacket. Without the piano, they felt, each instrument had maximum flexibility in harmonic direction; you could play in a number of harmonic valences at once, like 3-D tic-tac-toe.

Such seminal recordings as the Mingus Candid quartet records, Sonny Rollins's *A Night at the Village Vanguard, Volume 1* (Blue Note 46517) and *Volume 2* (Blue Note 46518), *Freedom Suite* (Riverside/OJC-067), and *Way Out West* (Contemporary/OJC-337), and Ornette Coleman's *The Shape of Jazz to Come* (Atlantic 1317-2) and *Free Jazz* (Atlantic 1364-2) had no piano. The groups that did have pianists often began using them in different ways. The important pianists of the time were players like McCoy Tyner, Andrew Hill, Herbie Hancock, and Bill Evans, who used lots of tone clusters and suspensions that made the harmonic destination ambiguous.

The effect of this, too, was to lessen the emphasis on movement through time. If three people are developing their own lines, without someone to tell them where they are going, there will be a shift from a focus on forward movement to a focus on the nature of group dynamics. The group began, figuratively, to stay in one place and examine itself.

With these developments, we are a long way from the regal smile on Count Basie's drummer Jo Jones's face, which said that time had been tamed, which assured us that time went forward and that conquering it was something worth doing, that there was order and hierarchy, a happy and willing acquiescence to the directives of the Count (or the Duke or Mr. Jelly Lord). As America's faith in its own manifest destiny began to break down, the relationship between the individual and the group, as well as between the spontaneous and the planned, inevitably began to tilt.

## CHASIN' THE TRANE

The career of John Coltrane illustrates several of the questions, frustrations, and aspirations many musicians had in the late 1950s. In a sense, Coltrane was an extreme embodiment of some of the bebop principles; perhaps as a result, he became an extreme embodiment of some of the reactions to those principles. But at each phase of his development, at least up until the final one, he was able to play exquisitely beautiful and lyrical things on ballads, for example, and he never failed to address the blues and four-four swing. His career is studied in more detail in the Soloists section; this is a study of one aspect of it.

Trane was extremely preoccupied with the nature of the harmonic maps, the chord changes, of the music. He was obsessed with scales, and he liked to play lots of notes, as if he was trying to play as many permutations of the scales in as short a space as possible. On his album *Blue Train* (Blue Note 46095), you can hear him attacking the chord changes of the title tune, a blues, as if he is trying to scour every corner of the harmonic pot. It seemed, too, as if the standard rate of chord progressions wasn't dense enough for him; on that same album, his tune "Moment's Notice" has a harmonic map on which the routes change more quickly than in almost any tune written up until that time, sometimes twice in a measure for several bars at a stretch. It was as if, with his great mastery of scales, he needed a more complex obstacle course thrown at him in order to maintain interest. Musicians puzzled over "Moment's Notice" for quite a while. That was in 1957.

By the next spring Coltrane was playing with a technique that critic Ira Gitler dubbed "sheets of sound," in which he played so fast over a medium-tempo background that he sounded almost out of tempo. "Sweet Sapphire Blues" on the album *Black Pearls* (Prestige/OJC-352) is only one example, but a startling one. Red Garland and the trio play chorus after chorus of a medium-tempo, swinging blues, a finger-popping groove designed for maximum swing. When Coltrane finally enters, he plays one or two choruses that actually address the tempo, then he goes off into a cascading, tumbling reading of what seems every possible chord change, inversion, and permutation, as if trying to quench something that couldn't be quenched. Listening to it is an odd experience; Coltrane seems to be banging his head against a wall. He had learned all the changes, mastered them better than anyone, and still there was this huge, even unmanageable hunger expressed in his playing. The bebop group organization, he seemed to be saying, couldn't provide him with a satisfactory framework of meaning; what the rhythm section is doing on "Sweet Sapphire" is designed for something very different from what he is doing. What he had spent his career trying to do was turning into a dead end for him.

The next year he recorded *Giant Steps* (Atlantic 1311-2), which took the "Moment's Notice" idea to its logical extreme; the title tune rolled chord changes at the soloist at an unprecedented rate, two per measure at a furious up-tempo, and with a set of interchordal relationships that was uncommon, to boot. Coltrane eats the changes up on the record; the power and fire with which he tears through them shock listeners even to this day. A measure of the tune's difficulty is that Tommy Flanagan, the session's pianist and one of the best in jazz, seems dumbfounded in his solo, struggling to keep up.

At the same time that Coltrane made *Giant Steps* he was participating, as a member of Miles Davis's group, in the sessions for the album *Kind of Blue* (Columbia CK 40579), which would make a clear and totally successful use of modal improvisation. On tunes like "So What" and "Flamenco Sketches," the group improvised over only one scale instead of over a series of changes; instead of being challenged to run the changes, one was challenged to make a coherent melody over a static harmonic backdrop. This provided a way out for Coltrane, at least temporarily. "Giant Steps" represented the farthest he could go in the domination of time; harmonic time, in terms of the changing of chords, was passing as fast as time could pass under him, and he still dominated it, and there was still that hunger. After *Kind of Blue*, the mainstream of his playing would be in the direction of one chord or no chord, a burning present, an eternal moment.

That change seemed to stand for the frustration many were having with the assumptions that had been in force for a decade or more. If forward movement is a manifestation of faith in the visible, knowable world, Coltrane had worked his way to the logical conclusion of bop's technological aspect. His was the musical equivalent of a real spiritual crisis, which seems to have had its parallel in Coltrane's extramusical life. After he left Miles Davis, his music would become increasingly spiritual and less and less based on an illusion of forward movement. In Coltrane's classic quartet of the early and mid-1960s, with McCoy Tyner, Jimmy Garrison, and Elvin Jones, all the instruments, as often as not, participated in an incantatory and pointedly spiritual approach, often grounded in vamps, as on his famous *A Love Supreme* (MCA/Impulse MCAD-5660 JVC-467). Solos stopped being lines that led from one place to another and began to seem more like chants, the object of which was a meditation upon higher things, an escape from the world of contingency.

While few of the New Thing, or avant-garde, players of the 1960s could approach the profundity of Coltrane's spiritual dimension, most of them had also begun questioning the point of movement through time, echoing or anticipating in that questioning the period of self-examination that was in store for a nation that was about to be severely shown its limits for the first time in over thirty years.

## TOMORROW IS THE QUESTION

What was happening in jazz, belatedly, was what had been happening in painting since the turn of the century. The hierarchical convention of background and foreground broke down at the same time as the convention of representation. In jazz, the equivalent of the illusion of representation was, and is, the illusion of the passage of time, a sort of hyper-real time that is measured not by the clock but by the implicit rate of beats passing within the bar line. The illusion of the passage of time began to feel like a prison to many of the younger musicians.

Part of that breaking down of illusion in painting was the breaking down of distinctions between foreground and background. Elements that were background were made an equal part of the design elements of the picture with the foreground objects. In jazz, too, as the illusion of the passage of time broke down, the rhythm instruments were brought up to become an integral part of the composition and not just as background for soloists.

When Ornette Coleman made his first records with his pianoless quartet, which included trumpeter Don Cherry, bassist Charlie Haden, and either Billy Higgins or Ed Blackwell on drums, many people had trouble believing that he was serious. His melodies often seemed at first to have nothing to do with the background that the bass and drums were playing. Sometimes the bass and drums seemed to be playing the melody along with the horns. Sometimes they played in a conventional group structure, but nobody could tell where in the form the soloist was.

There was nothing contrived about Coleman's music, however; it was extremely natural, and it addressed the fundamentals of the jazz tradition: it swung in slow, medium, and fast tempos, it was steeped in the blues, and it used Afro-Hispanic rhythms. And there was nothing vague or experimental about it. Everything that Coleman played was very definite. Today the music still sounds fresh and invigorating, unlike much music that is consciously designed to be new.

Although a closer look at Coleman's work will be found in the Soloists section, two of his records bear looking at here strictly for their ensemble work. *The Shape of Jazz to Come* (Atlantic 1317-2) is probably the best single album by the quartet, and you can hear most of the elements that seemed so odd when compared to the bop-oriented playing everyone was used to. The first track, "Lonely Woman," begins with Higgins playing a very fast tempo on the ride cymbal and Charlie Haden strumming an almost flamenco-sounding, insistent, droning bass figure in what sounds like a much slower tempo. When Coleman and Cherry come in to state the theme, it seems to float way above either tempo, almost as Louis Armstrong does at the end of "I Gotta Right to Sing the Blues" on *Laughin' Louie* (RCA/Bluebird 9759-2-RB). So even though the drums are articulating what would usually be taken to be a very fast, forward-moving up-tempo on the ride cymbal, it is undercut by the theme itself, as well as by the different tempo superimposed by the bass. This in itself was a fascinating discovery – that you could neutralize the conventions of the passage of time by superimposing two different time schemes. Coleman would use this to supreme effect on *Free Jazz* (Atlantic 1364-2). (When the Modern Jazz Quartet performed "Lonely Woman," they underlined the melody not with simultaneous tempos but with ominous chords out of tempo, to much the same effect.)

Almost all the other tunes on *The Shape of Jazz to Come* undercut the sense of the passage of time in a variety of ways. "Peace," for example, seems tempoless at first; the bass and drums come in and out, sometimes playing the actual theme with the horns, sometimes playing straight time, sometimes being silent. The first solo is Charlie Haden bowing very soft whole notes at the bottom of his range, then the horns restate the theme. Notice that Coleman's solo is very melodic, but it would be very difficult to put chord changes behind it. When Sonny Rollins plays with only bass and drums on *A Night at the Village Vanguard, Volume 1* (Blue Note 46517) and *Volume 2* (Blue Note 46518), you can almost always hear the tune and its harmonic progression implied in what he plays. Coleman here doesn't outline a set of chord changes; he lets his melodic imagination lead wherever it wants to go.

Despite the newness of much of *The Shape of Jazz to Come*, it sounds fairly conventional next to *Free Jazz* (Atlantic 1364-2), recorded in December 1960 and subtitled *A Collective Improvisation by the Ornette Coleman Double Quartet*. A first listening to this album may seem to reveal total chaos, but a closer listening shows an ingenious scheme. The first copy I owned of this record, when I was something like fourteen years old, was in mono, and I had no idea what was going on. In stereo, however, it is easier to see what the "double quartet" amounts to. On the left channel, Coleman, Cherry, bassist Scott La Faro, and drummer Billy Higgins are grouped; on the right, Eric Dolphy on bass clarinet, Freddie Hubbard on trumpet, Charlie Haden on bass, and Ed Blackwell on drums. What seems like a chaos of tempos on first listening is, in fact, two very regular tempos being played simultaneously: Charlie Haden's medium-tempo walking bass (in a low register), with Blackwell keeping time in that tempo, versus Scott La Faro's bass walking twice as fast as Haden's, mostly in the bass's upper register, with Higgins keeping time in La Faro's tempo. Both drummers add fills, accents, and all the other devices of the bop and postbop bag. But, as on "Lonely Woman," the superimposition of times gives an effect of stasis. Each musician gets a solo section in which he plays essentially in the time frame of the bass and drums from his own quartet, with the drummer and sometimes the horn players from the other quartet offering commentary as they see fit.

*Free Jazz*, once you really hear what's going on, addresses all the fundamentals of the music; you listen for the same things in it that you listen for in earlier jazz – you just have to listen a little harder because there's more stuff overlaid on it. There are riffs, polyphony, swing, melody, blues tonality. In fact, it helps to have listened to a good amount of jazz from all styles before you try it, or it won't make sense easily. But if you've listened to King Oliver, Lester Young, Charlie Parker, and the Miles Davis quintet of the late 1950s, you're ready for it.

A highly regarded (by many) pianist and composer associated with jazz is Cecil Taylor. Much of his music has always sounded like contemporary European classical music with drums added, and I have reservations about associating it with the jazz tradition because I think that once Taylor began producing his most characteristic work, he stopped addressing the fundamentals of African-American musical expression. Many people disagree with this notion, though quite a few agree with it; you can make up your own mind by listening. His 1966 *Unit Structures* (Blue Note 84237) shows some approaches he took in his composing and performing. "Steps," the first piece, demonstrates clearly why this music was of the avant-garde – all the instruments are in the foreground, and the lines don't move forward through time. The horns have lines written out for them, and Taylor's playing is all over the place, splashing, skittering, and commenting on what the horns are playing. There is a pulse running through it, but no tempo.

"Enter Evening" has an entirely different mood; it's softer and much less dense. Muted trumpet, oboe, alto, and arco bass all play discrete lines, seemingly out of tempo, although, again, there is a discernible pulse. Taylor pays much attention to density, instrumental timbre, and dynamics in his music. In some respects it seems to have less in common with jazz than with the modern dance of someone like Merce Cunningham, a situation in which everyone seems to be doing something different over a static temporal background but with echoes, rhythmic and motivic, that serve as organizing figures. Still, this music is not primarily grounded in jazz, by my criteria, as Coleman's indisputably is. But it is careful music, worked out music, and worth hearing. If you like *Unit Structures*, you might want to try his subsequent *Conquistador* (Blue Note 84260), which many Taylor fans hold in high regard.

Both *Free Jazz* and *Unit Structures*, although they cut the cord on the standard four-four passage-of-time format, have a pulse running through the performances; the listener is in another time zone, not the zone of the clock but of musical time. But Chicago saxophonist Roscoe Mitchell's 1966 *Sound* (Delmark DS-408) rips the innards out of any clock you care to use. There is no illusion whatsoever of time passing in any other way than it ordinarily passes. There is no rhythmic momentum, no groove or anything to orient you. Suddenly you're in a room full of strangers who are all doing their own thing, and you have to deal with it.

Or you can take the record off. But if you listen to it for what it is, it has its virtues; at its best, its virtue is a sense of humor. "The Little Suite" is an example of this. It appears to be random sounds at first; there's a harmonica, a saxophone, bass sounds, drum rattle. The sounds get denser, then sparser. You hear police whistles, shouts. After a while, it feels like you're sitting on a porch in a strange neighborhood – you hear people fighting, a truck going by, a siren in the distance, a chicken being strangled, a five-car pileup, a drunken barbershop quartet, and then that guy walking by with the harmonica again . . . It's funny, I think. But it sounds, finally, as if it was more fun to make than it is to listen to.

One leader whose unorthodox approach is championed by some and derided by others is the pianist Sun Ra, who, with his Arkestra, made extraordinary music for well over thirty years. His music has much in common with the avant-garde but also much in common with rhythm and blues, big-band swing, bebop, African music, and anything else he chose to use. Probably the best all-around introduction to Sun Ra is one of his first albums, *Sound of Joy* (Delmark DS-414). The program includes tunes laden with percussion instruments and cross-rhythms, as well as a baritone saxophone bebop battle ("Two Tones"). "El Is a Sound of Joy" has characteristically ethereal harmonies in the first theme, then shifts into a swinging, rhythm-and-blues-flavored riff for baritone, accompanied by hand clapping. "Saturn" is an up-tempo big-band chart with interesting backgrounds to a series of good solos. Maybe the most interesting tune on the record is "Planet Earth." It begins with a slow, lyrical melody over a slow tempo, which continues to be played at the original tempo as the rhythm section shifts into a much faster tempo. Recorded in 1957, it anticipates Ornette Coleman's subversion of the time scheme by a couple of years. Sun Ra and his Arkestra were very active up until his death in 1993. His shows often included dancers, stilt walkers, acrobats, singers, costumes, and group singing, as well as band work that ran the gamut, literally, from Fletcher Henderson to planet Neptune.

*Albert Ayler in Greenwich Village* (Impulse MCAD-39123) is a document of one of the best-known New Thing saxophonists in two different playing situations in 1966 and 1967. The first two tracks feature Ayler on alto saxophone with a group consisting of two basses, a cello, and, on one track, drummer Beaver Harris. The tunes "For John Coltrane" and "Change Has Come" do not use jazz-based rhythm at all; the overall effect, as with Cecil Taylor's music, is more or less that of contemporary European chamber music. The tunes are completely out of tempo, and all instruments improvise at once.

The other two tracks feature Ayler on tenor, with his brother Donald on trumpet and a violinist, two bassists, and a drummer. Here, partly because of the presence of the trumpet and drums, the music sounds less like European chamber music and more like a Salvation Army band. "Truth Is Marching In" and "Our Prayer" are arranged around one tonal center, and the horns play held notes in simple major-scale relation to the tonal center. There is no tempo, and the other instruments contribute as they please. After a beginning in which the horns play meditative held notes, they move into an extended section of playing that is outside the conception of notes altogether, in which Ayler plays with all the other sounds – squawks, screeches, double tones, overtones, etc. – that his horn can produce. With the drone effect, the music has an incantatory aspect, as one might expect from the spiritual orientation of the titles. Ayler had a very piercing and unique sound on the saxophone, which can be very affecting, but the group concept goes nowhere, which was probably the point.

Archie Shepp's 1965 *Fire Music* (Impulse MCAD-39121) is a different story. One of the New Thing's most outspoken musicians, Shepp was closely associated with John Coltrane and many of the other New York avant-gardists of the 1960s. *Fire Music* is much more worked-out than the Ayler or Roscoe Mitchell sets and much more rooted in the jazz tradition than either their work or that of Cecil Taylor. Much of it sounds, in fact, like a combination of the formal concern and surging rhythms of Charles Mingus and the melodic freedom of Ornette Coleman.

"Hambone," for example, begins with a bass vamp over a little repeated cymbal figure, over which the trumpet and trombone play a very free, mournful melody; this segues almost immediately into a countertheme, a heavily rhythmic riff played by the ensemble (which consists of trumpet, trombone, and alto sax) and answered by Shepp's tenor. The drums play a critical role here in setting the groove; it is blues-based music, and it swings hard. After repeats of the slow theme and the riff, there is a trumpet solo over a chanted ensemble riff played on top of a trickily accented six-eight rhythm. It has some of the same effect of a Mingus piece like "Wednesday Night Prayer Meeting." The trumpet soloist, by the way, is Ted Curson, who contributed so much to the quartet sides on Mingus's Candid recordings. Then comes a shuffle-rhythm section for Shepp's tenor, which is steeped in the blues tradition. The track shows a willingness and ability to address the whole spectrum of approaches to jazz and bring something fresh to it.

"Los Olvidados," a more lyrical piece, likewise has a number of sections which go in and out of a swing feeling, including a fast waltz. There are also versions of Ellington's "Prelude to a Kiss," the popular Brazilian song "The Girl from Ipanema," and a tenor, bass, and drums performance of a Shepp composition dedicated to Malcolm X. All in all, this is a satisfying set, a good example of the avant-garde using its head as well as its emotions and keeping its mind on its roots.

## WHAT'S NEW?

The approaches we've just glanced at, as taken by Cecil Taylor, Roscoe Mitchell, the Ayler brothers, and others, were by no means the work of more than a small minority of the people playing jazz, even at the height of the New Thing. The mid-1960s work of John Coltrane (see the Soloists section) had a broader impact, as did Ornette Coleman's work, but most musicians continued to play with the basic vocabulary of bebop, with some harmonic alterations stemming from the modal approach taken by Miles Davis and Charles Mingus.

Still, some of jazz's most basic assumptions had been challenged, and the music that was seen as being on the cutting edge had, in fact, brought jazz to the end of a long first cycle that had begun in New Orleans. For the most part, the New Thing signaled a retreat from the notion of time as something that moves forward, as well as from a cosmopolitan vision of the music as a symbol of literal social mobility.

Yet the avant-garde of the 1960s, with a few exceptions, for all its tribal overtones and egalitarian conception of group organization, did not succeed in putting together a new aesthetic that worked in terms of the challenges already laid down by the music. The community music of New Orleans was spiritual music that was involved with the rituals of people's day-to-day lives, the weddings, parades, and funerals that marked their progress through the world. The music of the 1960s avant-garde lacked the ritual basis of the spiritual authority it seemed to want to claim. It was a nonhierarchical group music, the justification of which was an increased freedom to pursue individual revelation, and it never managed to resolve that paradox successfully *in musical terms*. The logical extreme of the most extreme edge of the music, as heard in Coltrane's *Meditations* (MCA/Impulse MCAD-39139) and Ayler's work, never really caught on with the black community in the way the musicians wanted it to, and musically it produced a very passionate chaos. It offered a group meaning based exclusively on individual freedom, and that paradox leads to meaninglessness if there isn't also a clear vision of the needs of the ensemble.

Throughout the 1970s people continued to make music that sounded like all the various styles of jazz, but we have had to wait until fairly recently to hear musicians who would again begin addressing a group concept that could reflect the complexities of a democracy in the terms that the landmarks of the music outlined. Those terms involve the maintenance of a constant and delicate tension between the freedom of the individual and the coherence of the group.

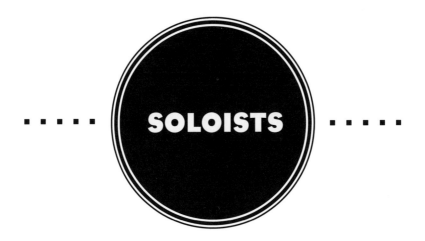

SOLOISTS

## THE TRUMPET SECTION

### LOUIS ARMSTRONG

Louis Armstrong – also known as Pops, Satchelmouth, Satchmo, and Dippermouth – was the most important jazz instrumentalist who ever lived. He more than anyone else developed the idea of the jazz solo and brought to it a shape and grandeur of conception that all who followed have had to take into account. The details of Armstrong's life, from his birth at the turn of the century in poverty in New Orleans to his death as an international celebrity in 1971, are well known. Countless people have heard his music, but relatively few, still, know just how deep, broad, and significant Armstrong's work was – not just in the 1920s, when he was defining the agenda for every jazz instrumentalist, but throughout his life.

Armstrong's recording career had several stages. The first consists of the years in the early and mid-1920s when he recorded as a sideman with the bands of King Oliver and Fletcher Henderson and as an accompanist to numerous blues singers, including the immortal Bessie Smith. After that came the Hot Five and Hot Seven recordings of the late 1920s, a time of virtuoso soloing. From the very late 1920s through the years of World War II, Armstrong played almost exclusively in front of big bands and became a world famous singer, musician, and personality. The years after World War II saw him break up his big band in favor of a small group, called the All Stars, which he would lead, with shifting personnel, for the rest of his life. During this latter period, which lasted some twenty-five years, he recorded in many different kinds of settings in addition to his work with the All Stars.

### DIPPERMOUTH BLUES

The 1923 recordings of Armstrong with King Oliver's Creole Jazz Band are discussed in detail in the Ensembles section. Of all of them, only two contain Armstrong solos; one – "Chimes Blues" – is available on *Louis Armstrong and King Oliver* (Milestone MCD-47017-2). But a close listen to the band's ensemble approach, as well as to the cornet playing of his mentor, King Oliver, will help you understand where Armstrong was coming from. The New Orleans emphasis on playing a clear lead, a defined melody with a strong rhythmic basis – and on having a strong, singing tone – set Armstrong's course for life and, with it, the traditional role of the trumpet in the jazz group, small and large.

The Milestone set also includes several blues performances on which Armstrong accompanies singer Alberta Hunter. On three tracks, this ensemble (called the Red Onion Jazz Babies) is joined by the New Orleans clarinetist and soprano saxophonist Sidney Bechet, who was the only musician at the time who could give Armstrong some competition as a soloist; the most exciting performance is "Cake Walking Babies from Home," on which Armstrong and Bechet engage in a famous battle of wits.

For the finest examples of Armstrong's way with blues accompaniments, proceed directly to *Bessie Smith/The Collection* (Columbia CK 44441). Four 1925 titles – "St. Louis Blues," "Reckless Blues," "You've Been a Good Old Wagon," and "I Ain't Gonna Play No Second Fiddle" – feature Armstrong accompanying the greatest blues singer of the time. Armstrong's cornet dances around Smith's strong vocal lines, echoing them and sometimes puckishly mocking them; the coupling of these two artists was one of the high points in American music. Also in this set, don't miss the work of trumpeter Joe Smith, especially on "Young Woman's Blues." A tragically short-lived contemporary of Armstrong, Joe Smith was one of the stars of the Fletcher Henderson band.

When Armstrong joined the Fletcher Henderson orchestra, the premier black dance band of its day, in September 1924, his career, as well as his influence on the course of the music, began to skyrocket. On *A Study in Frustration: The Fletcher Henderson Story* (Columbia/Legacy C3K 57596), you can hear examples of the band's work both before Armstrong arrived and afterward. In early solos with the band, such as those on "Copenhagen" and "Shanghai Shuffle," Armstrong provides electrifying, swinging moments in the midst of otherwise dated or pedestrian performances. The somewhat later "T.N.T." is a more integrated performance, with Armstrong and the band played off against each other. (Joe Smith has some good moments here, too, as he does on the set's version of "The Stampede.")

But in the Henderson band, Armstrong was still one soloist among many, and in November 1925 he left to be featured as a star with the large orchestras of Erskine Tate and, later, Carroll Dickerson in Chicago. He can be heard raising the roof with the Tate band in May 1926 on "Stomp Off, Let's Go" and the thrilling "Static Strut" on the possibly hard-to-find *Young Louis, the Side Man* (MCA-1301, cassette only) and with the Carroll Dickerson band, playing "Symphonic Raps" and "Savoyagers' Stomp" on *Louis Armstrong, Volume 4: Louis Armstrong and Earl Hines* (Columbia CK 45142). But by far the most important activity he engaged in immediately after leaving Henderson was a series of recording sessions with the small groups he called the Hot Five and the Hot Seven.

### HOTTER THAN THAT

Possibly the most influential series of recordings in the history of jazz, certainly one of the very greatest and definitely one of the most enduringly enjoyable, the Hot Fives and Hot Sevens are available from Columbia in four volumes: *The Hot Fives, Volume 1* (CK 44049), *The Hot Fives and Hot Sevens, Volume 2* (CK 44253) and *Volume 3* (CK 44422), and *Louis Armstrong, Volume 4: Louis Armstrong and Earl Hines* (CK 45142). Every side that Armstrong made with these bands has moments worth singling out, but there is space here only to point to the most important highlights. *Volume 1* begins with a masterpiece of group playing, "My Heart," on which Armstrong's cornet leads the band with a buoyancy that is as fresh today as when it was recorded. Notice that he doesn't solo here, although he takes some ingenious breaks. A couple of months later, however, they recorded "Cornet Chop Suey," on which he takes a solo of fantastic power and definition. On the same day, he recorded "Heebie Jeebies," the first example of scat, or wordless, singing on record. Also worth pointing out are Armstrong's minor-key blowing on "King of the Zulus," a piece of period New Orleans jive, and the original version of the New Orleans standard "Muskrat Ramble."

*Volume 2* finds Armstrong switching to the brighter-toned trumpet for some performances that to this day have the power to thrill and surprise, foremost among them "Potato Head Blues," on which Armstrong takes what may be his most famous solo over a full chorus of stop-time rhythm, a marvel of controlled tension and structure. "Potato Head Blues" is something you live with as a jazz fan; you listen to it periodically, and it grows in meaning over the years.

But one could say that about many of the sides contained in *Volume 2*: "Big Butter and Egg Man," with its ecstatic lead playing, certainly "Wild Man Blues," on which Armstrong takes break after break of amazing invention and daring in a slow tempo, and "Weary Blues," with the most misleading title in jazz history, on which the excitement of a style at its peak jumps out of the speakers at you. "Potato Head Blues," "Wild Man Blues," and "Weary Blues" are by the Hot Seven, which was the Hot Five augmented by tuba and drums (and recorded in the new electric process, which gave the music more presence). And don't miss Armstrong's startling deconstruction of the hackneyed Tin Pan Alley melody "Twelfth Street Rag."

*Volume 3* contains "S.O.L. Blues," on which he constructs a burning blues solo from a series of phrases all beginning with the same high note. This set contains the first and best recording of the Armstrong standard "Struttin' with Some Barbecue" (with another stunning stop-time solo), the exuberant "Hotter than That," on which Armstrong scats a chorus in duet with Lonnie Johnson's guitar, and "Savoy Blues," a slower blues with a meditative trumpet solo. In addition, *Volume 3* has the first four sides Armstrong recorded with pianist Earl Hines, a pairing that would provide some of the most exciting moments in jazz. "Skip the Gutter" is especially good, featuring a series of breaks traded back and forth between Armstrong and Hines in an escalating test of rhythmic and harmonic wits.

*Volume 4* is devoted entirely to that partnership. In Hines, Armstrong had found an instrumentalist who was a worthy match for him as an innovator and improviser. Hines played what was called trumpet-style piano, his right hand punching out adventuresome original melodies as opposed to the riffs that most pianists used. Hines's harmonic sense was very sophisticated, and he stimulated Armstrong to some truly inspired work. Probably the greatest side on this set is "West End Blues." Armstrong's opening cadenza, played solo and out of tempo, is a miracle of balance and invention.

Three other high points in a set full of high points are "Beau Koo Jack," an arrangement by Alex Hill full of tricky ensemble passages featuring a high-wire Armstrong solo studded with fantastic breaks, "Muggles" (a slang term for marijuana), on which Pops plays two choruses of smoldering blues under which he turns up the heat gradually and relentlessly, egged on by Hines's barrelhouse licks, and "Weather Bird Rag," a duet between Armstrong and Hines in which they hand the lead back and forth in a miniature symphony of breaks and improvised counterpoint.

The Hot Fives and Hot Sevens are matchless, but if you want more Armstrong from that period, he makes some guest appearances on *Johnny Dodds – South Side Chicago Jazz* (Decca/MCA MCAD-42326). Dodds was the clarinetist in the Hot Five (as well as in King Oliver's Creole Jazz Band) and a great blues player; he and Armstrong complemented each other well, Dodds providing a classic New Orleans clarinet embroidery around Armstrong's lead. On this set, Armstrong is subdued on "Easy Come, Easy Go Blues" and "The Blues Stampede," but he can be heard at length on the four sides by Johnny Dodds's Black Bottom Stompers, which include three tunes also recorded by the Hot Seven – "Weary Blues," "Wild Man Blues," and "Melancholy" – along with "New Orleans Stomp," which seems the best of the lot, perhaps because it doesn't suffer by comparison to a Hot Seven performance. This version of "Wild Man Blues" is quiet and almost conversational compared to the brooding Hot Seven version. An alternate take of it may be heard on *Louis Armstrong of New Orleans* (Decca/MCA MCAD-42328).

### LAUGHIN' LOUIE

The Armstrong-Hines sides were all recorded in 1928, and they marked a spectacular farewell, for Armstrong, to the small-group style of which they were a high water mark. Beginning in 1929, Armstrong would spend most of his time fronting one or another big band, playing arrangements designed to spotlight both his trumpet playing and his singing, which by now had grown to almost equal importance, and his repertoire would shift from jazz specialties and New Orleans tunes to the popular songs of the time. Some critics have suggested that the most important part of Armstrong's career came to an end when this shift occurred, but I strongly disagree. Armstrong's conception continued to grow in magnitude throughout his life; he seemed the kind of person who was made deeper and wiser, humanly and artistically, by his experience, and it came out in his music from all periods.

The series of big-band sides that he recorded for OKeh records from 1929 through 1932, which include some of his best recordings in this genre, are available in three volumes from Columbia in a continuation of the series begun with the Hot Fives. *Volume 5: Louis in New York* (Columbia CK 46148), *Volume 6: St. Louis Blues* (Columbia CK 46996), and *Volume 7: You're Drivin' Me Crazy* (Columbia CK 48828) are all worth having, to say the least.

*Volume 5* contains classic versions of pop tunes like "Ain't Misbehavin'," "When You're Smiling," and two takes of a blazing "Some of These Days." The version with the vocal climaxes with a two-chorus Armstrong solo that starts in the lower register and climbs higher, building in intensity all the while. The solo is remarkable from a structural as well as an emotional standpoint; usually the progress of a solo that builds the way this one does, in this style, is to move from a close paraphrase of the melody to more and more extended variations that move farther from the melody. Here Armstrong's first chorus is a pensive, completely original chorus in the lower and middle registers; the second is more or less an upper-register reading of the melody, yet Armstrong invests it with so much drama and tension purely by his phrasing that it has more excitement than the first.

*Volume 6* includes "Dallas Blues," "Blue, Turning Grey over You," "Tiger Rag," and a gorgeous "Body and Soul." "Dear Old Southland" is a haunting duet with pianist Buck Washington. "I'm in the Market for You" is a neglected but excellent pop tune which Armstrong does wonderfully by, but the standout on this set is "I'm a Ding Dong Daddy from Dumas," a jive song that Pops grills to a crisp at the end with four choruses of electrifying trumpet playing, each chorus building on the previous one and including an incredible break. No collection is complete without a copy, somewhere, of "Ding Dong Daddy."

The greatest of the three volumes, however, is probably *Volume 7*, which consists of some of the best of Armstrong's 1930–1932 masterpieces. None of these stands higher than the versions of "Stardust," on which Armstrong makes completely different variations on the melody in his spectacular vocal and trumpet solos. "Sweethearts on Parade," too, contains one of Armstrong's towering statements, the closing trumpet solo a lesson in the management of aesthetic tension and its release. The set also boasts gems like "The Lonesome Road," in which he becomes "Reverend Satchelmouth" and conducts a small church service, complete with testimonials from his band members, all over a mellow, walking tempo with throbbing saxophone harmony in the background, "I Got Rhythm," on which he introduces the band members one by one for short solos and then bats cleanup, and a spectacular up-tempo version of "Chinatown, My Chinatown," on which he leads into his trumpet solo by saying, "Well I'm ready, I'm ready, so help me, I'm ready . . ." He wasn't lying, either.

You can really hear, in this set, how at-home Armstrong was with an audience, even if it was just the hypothetical audience sitting in front of their Victrolas in their living rooms. He addresses the listener in terms that exude well-being and controlled excitement and a sense of life's humor and mystery. He's also very funny.

The set also includes a number of ballad performances on good popular tunes such as "All of Me," "Home," and "Between the Devil and the Deep Blue Sea," and another Armstrong masterpiece in "Blue Again," a rarely done but fine pop tune; Armstrong takes a cadenza at the beginning of this tune that is almost as rhythmically daring as his opening cadenza on "West End Blues."

Two other sets – *Stardust* (Portrait RK 44093) and *Louis and the Big Bands* (Swing/DRG CDXP 8450) – consist of tracks included on the three Columbia sets and are worth picking up if you can't find the Columbias.

Later in 1932, Armstrong began a series of large-band recordings for the Victor company which haven't received the same kind of critical attention as the OKeh sides. They deserve it, even though some of the material is inferior to the fine pop tunes he did for OKeh. *Laughin' Louie* (RCA/Bluebird 9759-2-RB) is a document of this Victor period and an indispensable Armstrong item. A couple of the best things, however – "Hobo, You Can't Ride This Train" and "Laughin' Louie" – are presented in alternate takes that are somewhat inferior to the classics that had been available for years. It is wonderful to have new versions of these tunes but not at the expense of the old ones; the effect is like going to the Louvre and seeing a preliminary study for the *Mona Lisa* hanging in place of the original.

That being said, the music here is fantastic and is presented in great sound quality as well. The trumpet solo at the end of "I've Got a Right to Sing the Blues" is still one of Armstrong's grandest statements; he floats above the tempo, singing on his horn with a relaxation and absolute control that have never had any peer. His theme statement on "Hustlin' and Bustlin' for Baby" is a sharp paraphrase of the tune, and "Some Sweet Day" contains one of his most exuberant vocals, a swinging and exquisitely phrased set of variations on the melody.

Also remarkable is Armstrong's wordless vocal on "Basin Street Blues," as well as his thrilling trumpet solo on the same tune, but every track has moments that make you shake your head in wonder. Two more that have to be mentioned are the alternate takes of "Hobo, You Can't Ride This Train" and "Laughin' Louie." "Hobo" is a minor pop tune that Armstrong brings alive with his spoken introduction, exhortations to the band, and fabulous trumpet solo. "Laughin' Louie" is a unique performance in which the guys in the band heckle Pops good-naturedly, and there's a lot of laughter and high spirits – as well as two haunting unaccompanied solos by Armstrong. For good measure, make sure you check out "Sweet Sue," with its chorus of "viper's language" sung by tenor saxophonist Budd Johnson. A viper in the slang of the day was a marijuana smoker; the viper's language is a tricky kind of pig Latin that Johnson executes with great aplomb, after which the tempo goes way up and Pops deep-fries a chorus.

### SWING THAT MUSIC

After the Victor sides were made, Armstrong stayed out of the recording studio for a while, except for a handful of sides in Europe, including the unearthly "Song of the Vipers," unavailable at present. When he started recording again, it was for Decca. His Decca years found him in almost every playing situation imaginable, from straight-ahead big-band concertos for trumpet and voice, to guest appearances with the Mills Brothers vocal group, to records with Hawaiian bands.

The best single collection of Decca material is probably *Heart Full of Rhythm* (GRP/Decca GRD-620), which includes one fabulous Armstrong performance after another on tunes like "Lyin' to Myself," "Ev'ntide," "Jubilee," and "The Skeleton in the Closet." The set contains two versions of his signature tune, "Swing That Music," a virtuoso performance featuring Armstrong almost all the way, singing and playing and ending with a series of high notes calculated to bring an audience to its feet. The set also includes "I've Got a Heart Full of Rhythm," on which Armstrong's solo consists only of a subtle rephrasing of the melody so that it carries the same kind of power as his out chorus on the OKeh "Some of These Days."

An excellent set is *Louis Armstrong of New Orleans* (Decca/MCA MCAD-42328), which contains a wide spectrum of material recorded between 1926 and 1950, focusing on Armstrong's continuing treatment of songs associated with the New Orleans repertoire. It includes two Hot Five performances from 1926 under the group name Lil's Hot Shots (Armstrong's wife at the time, the former Lillian Hardin, had been the pianist with King Oliver's band and subsequently with the Hot Five) and a 1940 small-band session on which Armstrong was once again matched with New Orleans clarinetist and soprano saxophonist Sidney Bechet, which produced some fine music but not the epochal results one might expect.

Some of the best music in the set comes on the six big-band versions of such Armstrong classics as "Mahogany Hall Stomp" (on which New Orleans bassist Pops Foster does some slap-bass playing behind the ensemble), "Struttin' with Some Barbecue" (with another daring opening cadenza by Pops, as well as a glorious pair of out-chorus variations), and "West End Blues." A standout is the 1940 "Wolverine Blues," on which drummer Big Sid Catlett really boots the big band of Luis Russell. An especially interesting performance for those who have listened to the King Oliver Creole Jazz Band sides is "Dippermouth Blues," where Armstrong is backed by the Jimmy Dorsey orchestra on a medium-tempo re-creation of the Oliver version that really captures the feel of the original – no small achievement with a big band. (Drummer Ray McKinley even plays woodblocks à la Baby Dodds on the opening choruses.)

### ALL STARS

*Louis Armstrong of New Orleans* (Decca/MCA MCAD-42328) also contains three 1950 tunes by the group that, with a number of personnel changes, Armstrong would perform and travel with for the rest of his life. The three tunes, "My

Bucket's Got a Hole in It," "Panama," and "New Orleans Function" (not really a tune but a miniature suite re-creating a New Orleans funeral, narrated by Armstrong himself), are by the most "all-star" edition of Armstrong's All Stars, with trombonist Jack Teagarden (who takes a typically sly vocal and masterful blues-inflected solo on "Bucket"), ex-Ellington New Orleans clarinetist Barney Bigard, pianist Earl Hines, bassist Arvell Shaw, and drummer Cozy Cole. After World War II, when times got hard for big bands, Armstrong formed the All Stars as a more economically viable touring group.

A very good set documenting this transitional period in Armstrong's career is *Pops: The 1940s' Small-Band Sides* (RCA/Bluebird 6378-2-RB), featuring Armstrong in a variety of situations in 1946 and 1947, most of which find him paired with Teagarden for some real vocal and instrumental high points. Five tunes recorded at Armstrong's famous May 1947 Town Hall concert are standouts, especially "Back O' Town Blues" and Pops and Tea's duet on "Rockin' Chair." Other highlights are the small-band versions of "I Want a Little Girl" and "Sugar," recorded with trombonist Vic Dickenson, and two performances of tunes written for the movie *New Orleans* (which starred Billie Holiday in addition to Armstrong): "Where the Blues Were Born in New Orleans" and the well-known "Do You Know What It Means to Miss New Orleans?" The former, a fairly corny tune, contains three thrilling out choruses with Pops reaching simultaneously for the stars and into the gutbucket. The album notes, by Dan Morgenstern, are another good reason to pick this one up.

The All Stars can be heard at the top of their game in two albums recorded for Columbia in 1954 and 1955: *Louis Armstrong Plays W. C. Handy* (CK 40242) and *Satch Plays Fats* (CK 40378). Both feature Armstrong at his best, playing compositions by the legendary "Father of the Blues," Handy, and by stride pianist, singer, and entertainer Fats Waller. The Handy set is remarkable for the utter relaxation of Armstrong's vocals and horn playing on "Aunt Hagar's Blues," "Beale Street Blues," "Memphis Blues," "Hesitating Blues," and the others, and for the range of moods available in this kind of treatment of the blues form. A few changes have been made for this new issue of the material, with several previously unissued takes replacing the ones that had been there; one unfortunate choice is the elimination of a great moment when, through tape overdubbing, Armstrong sang a duet with himself on the bouncing "Atlanta Blues." But the mood throughout this set, of elegant barrelhouse sophistication and relaxed concentration, is still unmatched.

*Satch Plays Fats* is as good, although the mood is a hair less deep than on the Handy set; Armstrong gives the royal treatment to the cream of Waller, including "Honeysuckle Rose," "Ain't Misbehavin'," and "Black and Blue," as well as perhaps less known gems such as "Blue Turning Grey Over You" and

"I'm Crazy 'Bout My Baby." The buoyancy Armstrong achieves in his phrasing, both on horn and in his vocals, is a marvel and is a perfect answer to anybody who still thinks that Armstrong's later work somehow represents a decline.

A true feast for fans of the All Stars is Decca's four-CD set *Louis Armstrong: The California Concerts* (Decca/GRP GRD-4-613), which shows the performing side of the band. The first disc and a half contain the results of an evening with the Teagarden-Bigard-Hines All Stars at the Pasadena Civic Auditorium in 1951 doing a mix of pop tunes ("Honeysuckle Rose," "Just You, Just Me") and Armstrong standards ("Some Day," "Back O' Town Blues"). The rest of the set is taken up with a mighty demonstration of the 1955 band, with Trummy Young in place of Teagarden and Billy Kyle in place of Hines, in action over the course of one evening at Hollywood's Crescendo Club, performing their standard program of New Orleans tunes, pop tunes, and Armstrong favorites. Armstrong's energy and presence are phenomenal throughout.

### OTHER SETTINGS

Although the All Stars were Armstrong's touring and performance band for most of the last twenty-five years of his life, he recorded in many other settings, including with big bands, string orchestras, and choirs and in encounters with such eminences as Ella Fitzgerald and Duke Ellington.

An excellent collection drawing mainly from the 1950s and focusing on Armstrong's singing is *Louis Armstrong/The Best of the Decca Years, Volume 1: The Singer* (MCA MCAD-31346). It contains such hits as "A Kiss to Build a Dream On," "Blueberry Hill," and "La Vie en Rose," as well as "That Lucky Old Sun," recorded with a large choir in 1949, "Gone Fishin'," a duet between Pops and Bing Crosby, "You Rascal You," a running dialogue with singer and alto saxophonist Louis Jordan, and "The Gypsy," a pop tune that Pops raises to the heights. These sides present Armstrong as the perfect fusion of entertainer and jazz master.

Even better is the material collected on *Louis Armstrong: The Silver Collection* (Verve 823 446-2). Culled from two albums recorded in 1957 with a large orchestra conducted by Russ Garcia, it presents the trumpeter and singer as an interpreter of the best kind of popular standards, both well known and lesser known. Armstrong weaves pure magic on "Body and Soul," "Have You Met Miss Jones," "East of the Sun," "You're Blasé," "I've Got the World on a String," and ten others from the likes of Irving Berlin, Harold Arlen, Cole Porter, and Duke Ellington. His singing was never richer, and his trumpet playing hits the bull's-eye every time. His phrasing invariably illuminates sides of the melodies that one wouldn't hear with other singers. This is one of the very best Armstrong items available.

Three late-1950s sets that match Armstrong with one of the few singers who could give him a run for his money are *Ella Fitzgerald and Louis Armstrong: Ella and Louis* (Verve 825 373-2), *Ella and Louis Again* (Verve 825 374-2), and *Porgy and Bess* (Verve 827 475-2). The repertoire on the first two again consists of excellent popular standards. The combination of their two contrasting vocal timbres makes for a perfect ying and yang balance, and they are heard in a small-group setting that affords them maximum elbow room. *Ella and Louis* has gems like "Can't We Be Friends," "Moonlight in Vermont," and "Cheek to Cheek," but *Ella and Louis Again* may have a slight edge, if only for the riotous version of "Stompin' at the Savoy." The subtle one-upsmanship on "A Fine Romance" and the perfect groove on "I'm Putting All My Eggs in One Basket" aren't bad either. The *Porgy and Bess* set has orchestrations by Russ Garcia that nicely show off the lyrical qualities of Gershwin's music. Armstrong's high spots include "Summertime," on which he accompanies Fitzgerald's closing chorus with a sublime wordless vocal, "Bess, You Is My Woman Now," and "It Ain't Necessarily So," which he invests with a brooding grandeur in his trumpet solo.

One cake that didn't rise as well as some of the others is *Louis Armstrong Meets Oscar Peterson* (Verve 825 713-2), a collection of fine standards in a promising small-group setting of pianist Peterson, guitarist Herb Ellis, bassist Ray Brown, and drummer Louis Bellson. But to my ears it never reaches the level one might expect, except on an impromptu duet between Armstrong and Ellis on "There's No You."

I would almost say the same thing about another summit meeting from which one might have expected apocalyptic results. *Louis Armstrong and Duke Ellington: The Complete Sessions* (Roulette CDP 7938442) is the document of two 1961 sessions on which Ellington sat in on piano with the Armstrong All Stars in a program consisting entirely of Ellington compositions. The results are a little disappointing, as if very little thought went into the proceedings beforehand. The session's producers could have at least tuned the piano. Still, there are some amazing moments here – Armstrong's vocals on "I'm Just a Lucky So and So" and the rarely heard "Azalea" are fantastic, as is his trumpet lead on "Drop Me Off in Harlem." The standout of the entire set is a version of "I Got It Bad (And That Ain't Good)," on which Armstrong plays a full trumpet chorus accompanied only by Ellington's piano, then sings a definitive vocal. The set is more than worth having, but if only they had been able to record Armstrong with the full Ellington band . . .

Armstrong's universality and durability have never been so startlingly shown as when his recording of the pop ditty "Hello, Dolly" reached the top of the popular music charts in 1964, beating out the most popular group in the world, the Beatles. The album *Louis Armstrong's Hello, Dolly!* (MCA MCAD-538) will be a big surprise to anyone who thinks of that period as one of dilution of Armstrong's talents or of inconsequential commercial throwaways. The title tune is a perfect and compact statement – an intro, a vocal chorus, an instrumental chorus with the All Stars playing a loose, jammed, New Orleans–style version of the melody with Pops in the lead, then another half-chorus of vocal, a tag, and out. Armstrong's rephrasing of the melody in the ensemble passage is a perfect example of his artistry.

Most of the twelve tracks here follow "Dolly"'s routine of vocal chorus/instrumental interlude/vocal chorus. The buoyancy of the interludes is hard to believe; Armstrong's phrasing is way behind the beat, the ultimate in both relaxation and swing (listen to his solo on "A Kiss to Build a Dream On"). The same goes for his singing. The repertoire is comprised of good pop tunes like "A Lot of Living to Do" and "It's Been a Long, Long Time," as well as remakes of some of Armstrong's best-known hits, including "Jeepers Creepers," "Blueberry Hill," and "Someday." His trumpet solo on the bright-tempoed "Be My Life's Companion" and his two vocal choruses on "Jeepers Creepers" are as thrilling as anything he ever recorded. Don't be fooled into thinking that this is a watered-down commercial greatest-hits package. There is a joy in this set that is extraordinary, even for Armstrong.

Armstrong repeated his commercial triumph a few years later with "Cabaret" and "What a Wonderful World," which achieved a second life by being featured in the film *Good Morning, Vietnam.* Both can be heard on *What a Wonderful World* (MCA MCAD-25204), a somewhat less satisfactory collection than *Hello, Dolly!* because of the addition of some ricky-tick strings and a few songs that are uncomfortably corny, several of which were written by the session's producer, Bob Thiele. Corny or not, though, Armstrong dives in as if they were masterpieces. The collection lacks the sheer elation of the *Hello, Dolly!* material, and the trumpet is spotlighted less, but it's worth having just for the title tune, especially at the budget price the set sells for.

Recorded a few weeks before Armstrong's seventieth birthday, another album also called *What a Wonderful World* (RCA/Bluebird 8310-2-RB) features Armstrong in an unlikely setting combining rock rhythms and either a string section or a big band in an eclectic program including "Everybody's Talkin'," "We Shall Overcome," and "Give Peace a Chance." By this time, Pops had set the trumpet down for health reasons, but his vocals are as good as ever, and the spirit in the studio, in which a birthday party was in progress (with guests Miles Davis, Ornette Coleman, Tony Bennett, and many others), undoubtedly contributed to his good humor. All the guests joined him in singing "We Shall Overcome," a truly moving experience. There's a lesson here, though, too. Almost none of what Armstrong recorded in his nearly fifty-year career sounds dated, but this attempt to put him into a context that seemed modern at the time (his duet with Leon Thomas on "The Creator Has a Master Plan," for example) resulted in Armstrong almost sounding corny in spots. Finally, his own transcendental hipness and genuineness carried the day, but it was a close call. The truly great is always contemporary; you don't need to update it.

No one should go through life without being acquainted with the music of Louis Armstrong. He addressed the most basic and the most exalted human questions through song, and the results can, in Wynton Marsalis's phrase, "enrich your life" beyond description. His work is as timeless as Shakespeare's or Bach's, and there is no improving on it.

## TRUMPETS NO END

An entire school of trumpet playing grew up around Armstrong and in his wake. Armstrong's language was so broad and universal that artists as different as Buck Clayton and Harry Edison, or Red Allen and Bunny Berigan, could use it to tell very different stories.

Two contemporaries of Armstrong developed styles quite distinct from Armstrong's; while neither recorded extensively, both left notable bodies of work. One, Bix Beiderbecke, was a talented player who died of alcoholism in 1931 at the age of twenty-eight. To many, Beiderbecke was a romantic incarnation of the Roaring '20s, and his reputation was inflated by certain writers and musicians after his death. Much of the confusing and adulatory writing about Beiderbecke has made it difficult to see clearly what his true worth was. Recently, it has been the fashion to disparage him somewhat. Although Beiderbecke was not the god that he was made into by some, he did have something real and valuable that was all his own.

Beiderbecke's sound was very clear, his conception precise and crisp, his solos little gems of construction, intelligence, and grace. If he had a fault as a jazz musician, it was that he was an almost complete stranger to the blues (the musical form, not the existential state). Beiderbecke was one of the few jazz musicians to figure out a way to make music that is indisputably jazz without a heavy component of the blues. But it left him a somewhat narrow musician; the blues are an antidote to sentimentality, an essential antibody.

Two easily available Beiderbecke collections showcase the cornetist in different playing situations. *Bix Lives!* (RCA/Bluebird 6845-2-RB) consists mainly of performances by the Paul Whiteman orchestra, a very large commercial dance band of the time which used several well-known hot soloists. Much of the time Beiderbecke takes his eight, or sixteen, or even thirty-two bars of solo among too-sweet violins or other jazz-inhibiting elements, but what he plays almost always sounds fresh and elegant. On "Changes," he takes his muted solo over the crooning background of the Rhythm Boys, a vocal group that included the young Bing Crosby. "Lonely Melody," a heavily arranged band piece with a full complement of strings, has Beiderbecke constructing a solo of generous length (for these records) based on a clever paraphrase of the melody. "There Ain't No Sweet Man," "From Monday On" (which features excellent writing for brass, with Bix in the lead), "Sugar," and "San" all contain especially good solos by Beiderbecke. "You Took Advantage of Me" features Beiderbecke and his soulmate, C-melody saxophonist Frank Trumbauer, in a full chase chorus, in which they toss two-bar phrases back and forth. One of the best things on the album is "Clementine" by the Jean Goldkette orchestra, a much more jazz-inflected performance than most of the Whiteman tracks, on which Beiderbecke takes a haunting solo.

*Bix Beiderbecke, Volume 1: Singin' the Blues* (Columbia CK 45450) and *Volume 2: At the Jazz Band Ball* (Columbia CK 46175) are more likely to fully satisfy those in search of flat-out jazz, although the performances here, too, have their share of overarranged sections and tricky passages that haven't aged well. The best performance on the first set, and a true jazz classic, is "Singin' the Blues," on which Beiderbecke plays a moving, storylike, perfectly constructed solo in a very small group, backed only by rhythm at a relaxed, walking tempo. This is one of the first fully realized jazz ballad performances on record; for anything from that period even close in mood, you have to turn to Armstrong's "Savoy Blues" solo, recorded later in the year. Beiderbecke also has chillingly beautiful solos on "Riverboat Shuffle," "I'm Coming Virginia," "Way Down Yonder in New Orleans," and "Ostrich Walk." *At the Jazz Band Ball* presents some real collector's items, along with some of the finest small-group things Beiderbecke recorded, including the roaring Bix and His Gang sessions that produced "Jazz Me Blues," "Since My Best Gal Turned Me Down," and "Sorry," as well as the great title track. When Beiderbecke is at his best, as he is here, his poise and eloquence can be awe-inspiring. The set includes some more fine sides with Trumbauer, as well as a few lightweight commercial sides. Beiderbecke had a large lyric gift and an ability, equaled by very few at the time, to shape a solo. There were few rough edges in Beiderbecke's playing.

One couldn't say that about Armstrong's other contemporary, Jabbo Smith; there were plenty of rough edges to be found in his playing but also plenty of excitement of a sort that was foreign to Beiderbecke's temperament. On his best-known recordings, collected as *The Ace of Rhythm* (MCA-1347, cassette only), he shows a penchant for almost reckless velocity and upper-register playing, especially on the vicious "Jazz Battle." Tunes like "Let's Get Together," "Ace of Rhythm," and "Decatur Street Tutti" display the full range of his very real talent. After these recordings (and a couple with Duke Ellington's band) were made, Smith's star faded for some reason, and he made very few records. In 1961 he made some excellent informal recordings in Chicago that showed the more mellow and lyrical side of his musical personality, revealing him to be an extremely inventive improviser. Available as *Jabbo Smith – Hidden Treasure, Volume 1* (Jazz Art TR520699) and *Volume 2* (Jazz Art TR520700), they are hard to find but are worth searching out.

### SECTION MEN

Most of the great stylists of the 1920s and 1930s made their livings as members of big bands, where they were featured for fairly short solos; often they recorded outside the context of the big band to give themselves more room for exposure. The Fletcher Henderson band always had outstanding trumpeters, beginning with Armstrong. Bobby Stark, Joe Smith, Tommy Ladnier, Henry "Red" Allen, Rex Stewart, and, later, Roy Eldridge, sparked Henderson's records. The best place to hear all of them is *A Study in Frustration: The Fletcher Henderson Story* (Columbia/Legacy C3K 57596). Each of the players mentioned is featured in solos which, together, show the Armstrong influence the way a father's facial features play through the features of his children. For more glimpses of the Henderson gang in the 1920s, especially the little-known Bobby Stark, try *Fletcher Henderson and the Dixie Stompers 1925–1928* (DRG/Swing SW8445/6).

Rex Stewart went on to have an extremely rich career and to form a distinctive style identifiable by what are referred to as half-valve, or cocked-valve, effects, on which a note is vocalized and bent by a manipulation of the trumpet's valves. His first well-known solo, on "The Stampede" (available on the Columbia/Legacy Henderson set), shows his Armstrong-based power and his edge of nervous energy, set, for interesting contrast, against Joe Smith's more legato, more melancholy sound. But Stewart's most famous recordings were made as a member of Duke Ellington's orchestra, in which his was one of the most distinctive sounds in an orchestra full of individualists. "Boy Meets Horn" on *Duke Ellington: Braggin' in Brass – The Immortal 1938 Year* (Portrait R2K 44395), is a classic example of his cocked-valve technique, and "Morning

Glory" on *Duke Ellington: The Blanton-Webster Band* (RCA/Bluebird 5659-2-RB), is a lovely, moody ballad feature for him.

The real feast for Rex Stewart fans is *The Great Ellington Units* (RCA/Bluebird 6751-2-RB), on which Stewart leads a small band of Ellingtonians from the 1940–1941 band (including Ellington himself on piano and tenor saxophonist Ben Webster) in eight of the best small-band jazz sides ever recorded. The full range of his sound is laid out here, from the blues playing on "Mobile Bay" and the plunger etude tribute to early Ellington trumpeter Bubber Miley entitled "Poor Bubber," to the exquisite lyricism of "My Sunday Gal" and "Without a Song," to the growling low notes on "Menelik (The Lion of Judah)." Stewart is also well represented by his numerous mid-1930s tracks in *The Duke's Men – Duke Ellington Small Groups, Volume 1* (Columbia C2K 46995).

Other sets with good representations of Stewart are *Djangologie/USA, Volume 2* (DRG/Swing CDSW 8424/6, yellow cover), on which Stewart and Ellington clarinetist Barney Bigard are matched up with guitarist Django Reinhardt for five mainly mellow 1939 sides, *Rex Stewart and the Ellingtonians* (Riverside/OJC-1710), on which Stewart leads a 1950s collection of Ellingtonians and non-Ellingtonians through a varied program, and *Jack Teagarden's Big Eight/Pee Wee Russell's Rhythmakers* (Riverside/OJC-1708), on which Stewart teams up with Bigard and Ben Webster under the direction of trombonist Jack Teagarden for four extended 1940 sides.

Duke Ellington's band always featured a number of contrasting stylists who set each other off. His first trumpet star, Bubber Miley, set the agenda for a whole lineage of trumpeters in the band. Miley played in a vocalized style called growl trumpet, in which the manipulation of a plunger over the bell of the horn, along with the production of a growl effect in the throat, results in a growling sound. You can hear the short-lived Miley to great effect on *Duke Ellington and His Orchestra – The Brunswick Era, Volume 1 (1926–1929)* (Decca/MCA MCAD-42325), especially on Ellington's "East St. Louis Toodle-Oo" and "Black and Tan Fantasy."

Miley's first and greatest successor in the Ellington band was Cootie Williams, who was assigned the growl parts when he replaced Miley, although he had never before used the technique. Williams is featured on Ellington's work throughout the 1930s; you can hear him growling on "Prologue to Black and Tan Fantasy" and "Jazz Potpourri" on *Duke Ellington: Braggin' in Brass – The Immortal 1938 Year* (Portrait R2K 44395), which also spots Williams batting cleanup in true Armstrong style on "Braggin' in Brass." He is also featured extensively on the essential *Duke Ellington: The Blanton-Webster Band* (RCA/Bluebird 5659-2-RB), on which his most famous moment is "Concerto for Cootie," later known as "Do Nothing Till You Hear from Me."

Williams can be heard growling on several of eight tracks recorded under the leadership of alto saxophone master Johnny Hodges on *The Great Ellington Units* (RCA/Bluebird 6751-2-RB), where he also takes a brilliant open-horn blues solo on "Things Ain't What They Used To Be." Williams and Hodges are also heard side by side on four incendiary tracks recorded under the leadership of vibist Lionel Hampton in 1937 and 1938. Available on *Hot Mallets, Volume 1* (RCA/Bluebird 6458-2-RB), "Buzzin' Around with the Bee," "Ring Dem Bells," and "Don't Be That Way" all feature Williams growling (the first two at a fast tempo), and "Stompology" has an excellent open-horn solo. Williams is at the helm for a number of tunes on *The Duke's Men – Duke Ellington Small Groups, Volume 1* (Columbia C2K 46995), which includes the haunting "Blue Reverie" and "Echoes of Harlem," as well as the fine "Alabamy Home" and "My Honey's Loving Arms" by a recording group consisting of Williams and members of the Ellington and Chick Webb big bands, called the Gotham Stompers. A number of these tracks are also to be found on the sloppily assembled *The Duke Ellington Small Bands – Back Room Romp* (Portrait RK 44094), marred by a muddy echo-chamber effect.

Williams was hired away from Ellington's band by Benny Goodman in late 1940, and he made a number of good recordings both with the big band and with the newly formed Goodman sextet, which included guitar innovator Charlie Christian. The sextet sides are especially strong and can be heard on *Charlie Christian: The Genius of the Electric Guitar* (Columbia CK 40846) and *The Benny Goodman Sextet Featuring Charlie Christian – 1939–1941* (Columbia CK 45144). Williams's horn adds an immediately identifiable coloration to the ensembles on such riff-based items as "Wholly Cats," "Benny's Bugle," and "Breakfast Feud," and he takes fine solos throughout. Several of the Goodman big-band performances on *Benny Goodman, Volume 2: Clarinet à la King* (Columbia CK 40834), especially "Superman," "Henderson Stomp," and the exciting "Pound Ridge" (which has the added benefit of Big Sid Catlett's drumming), show Williams off to advantage.

The trumpeter led his own bands in the early 1940s, one of which included the young Charlie Parker (and another of which included the young piano genius Bud Powell). The Parker band may be heard in a half-hour 1945 broadcast from the Savoy Ballroom on *Charlie Parker: Every Bit of It* (Spotlite SPJ150D, LP only). Columbia's collection *The Bebop Era* (CK 40972) contains an early (1942) performance by a Williams band of Thelonious Monk's "Epistrophy," although the open-horn trumpet solo toward the end is by Joe Guy, not Williams.

In 1962 Williams rejoined Duke Ellington's band and recorded some specialties throughout the 1960s that showed him to have become almost the equal of Bubber Miley in plunger sophistication. Some of his finest moments may be heard on *The Great Paris Concert* (Atlantic 304-2), a 1963 live performance in which Williams has long features on the slow "Concerto for Cootie" and the shuffle-rhythm "Tutti for Cootie." If RCA gets around to reissuing the mid-1960s *The Popular Duke Ellington*, which it seems they might, there's a wonderful late version of "Black and Tan Fantasy" waiting.

When Williams left Ellington's band in 1940 to join Goodman, his replacement was trumpeter-singer-violinist Ray Nance. Nance was a great talent; he stepped into the plunger role perfectly but also had an extremely personal open-horn sound and a unique way of phrasing. In his autobiography, *Music Is My Mistress*, Ellington said, "Ray Nance never played a bad note in his life." On his first solo with the band, the original 1941 version of "Take the 'A' Train" (on *Duke Ellington: The Blanton-Webster Band* [RCA/Bluebird 5659-2-RB]), Nance created a solo which became the standard solo to play, for all trumpet players, on any version of the tune. (Cootie Williams himself plays it on *The Popular Duke Ellington*.) His trumpet work can also be heard on this set on such tracks as "Main Stem," "Raincheck," "Sherman Shuffle," and, especially, the beautiful "Someone." He takes fun, jivey vocals on "Bli-Blip" and "A Slip of the Lip (Can Sink a Ship)" and a classic violin solo on the Middle Eastern–tinged "Bakiff."

Nance is featured extensively on Ellington's recordings of the 1950s and very early 1960s. On *Ellington Indigos* (Columbia CK 44444) he has a gorgeous open-horn solo on "Dancing in the Dark" and an achingly evocative violin solo on "Autumn Leaves." The 1958–1959 *Blues in Orbit* (Columbia CK 44051) shows him at length, plungering on "Villes Ville Is the Place, Man," "Pie Eye's Blues," and "In a Mellotone" to thrilling effect. He also gets in some good violin on "C Jam Blues." To hear Nance reach the heights of lyricism and poignancy on violin, listen to "Low Key Lightly," from Ellington's score to *Anatomy of a Murder* (Rykodisc RCD 10039). *Duke Ellington – The Private Collection, Volume 4: Studio Sessions, New York 1963* (SAJA 7 91044) is a full-scale Nance showcase, featuring him at length on practically every tune of an extremely varied program of previously unreleased gems. Pick this one up if you dig Nance. Ellington masterpieces such as *Such Sweet Thunder, At the Bal Masque*, and *Piano in the Background*, sporadically available in subtly different incarnations from Columbia, should be reissued in proper form; all contain great Nance. And *All Star Road Band* (Signature AGT/AGK 40012) has some uninhibited live performances by the big band featuring Nance.

Nance is also featured on a very highly recommended set by singer Jimmy Rushing, recorded in 1971, called *The You and Me That Used To Be* (RCA/

Bluebird 6460-2-RB), on which Nance (playing both cornet and violin) and tenor saxophonist Zoot Sims accompany the great ex-Basie vocalist on a program consisting mainly of popular standards. And Nance can be heard as part of an all-star trumpet section (including Clark Terry, Nat Adderley, and Harry Edison) on *Budd Johnson and the Four Brass Giants* (Riverside/OJC-209).

### SWING TRUMPETS

The 1930s flowering of trumpet styles in the wake of Armstrong was a kaleidoscope of individualists, but none was more individual than Henry "Red" Allen, who hailed from Armstrong's hometown, New Orleans. Allen had a beautiful, burnished sound and an unorthodox, rhythmically free approach to melody. He was one of the great blues players, and he could always be relied upon to do the unexpected; his playing was remarkably free of clichés.

To find Allen's early work, for the most part, you have to pick through various collections on which he is featured with big bands of the 1930s. Two good 1929 sides, "Swing Out" and "Pleasin' Paul," can be found on *Early Black Swing – The Birth of Big Band Jazz: 1927–1934* (RCA/Bluebird 9583-2-RB); their sessionmate, the fabulous blues "Feeling Drowsy," is on *Great Trumpets: Classic Jazz to Swing* (RCA/Bluebird 6753-2-RB). Allen can be heard in fine form on two early-1930s sides included on *The 1930s: Small Combos* (Columbia CK 40833) – an up-tempo "Who's Sorry Now?" with the Rhythmakers and the brooding "There's a House in Harlem for Sale" with his own small band. His melody statement and vocal on "Out Where the Blue Begins" (on *The 1930s: The Singers* [Columbia CK 40847]) are both totally characteristic – the asymmetrical phrases, the insinuating nuances and attention to detail. *The 1930s: Big Bands* (Columbia CK 40651) presents short glimpses of Allen on "Can You Take It?" with Fletcher Henderson and on "St. Louis Wiggle Rhythm" with the Blue Rhythm Band. *Hocus Pocus: Fletcher Henderson and His Orchestra 1927–1936* (RCA/Bluebird 9904-2-RB) has a great Allen solo on the title track, and there is a lot of good Allen with the bands of Fletcher and Horace Henderson on *Ridin' in Rhythm* (DRG/Swing CDSW 8453/4).

The absolute cream of mid-1930s Allen is on two hard-to-find LPs on the Collector's Classics label – *Henry Allen and His Orchestra 1934–1935, Volume 1* (CC 13) and *1935–1936, Volume 2* (CC 46), which I mention only because the material is so extraordinary. Of the two, the first is significantly the better, presenting Allen at the top of his 1930s vocal and instrumental game in all-star settings with the likes of tenor saxophonist Chu Berry and trombonists Dicky Wells and J. C. Higginbotham. The sessions have the relaxed but focused groove that so distinguished Teddy Wilson's mid-1930s recordings, a mixture of high spirits, judicious organization, and inspiration. *Volume 1* has Allen addressing such first-rate pop tunes as "Rosetta," "Body and Soul," and "I Wished on the Moon," along with more novelty-type numbers like "Truckin'" and the riotous "Roll Along, Prairie Moon," on which Allen and the band engage in some vocal call-and-response, and Allen eggs the soloists on with shouted exhortations. This is worth putting out an all-points alert for. *Volume 2* isn't quite as strong; the material is a little weaker and the accompanying cast less stellar, but it's still fine, with items like "Chloe," "On Treasure Island," and "Lost" heading up the list. These tracks have also been issued on CD on the European Classics label.

An important album, featuring what was a formidable early-1930s team for a while, is *Henry "Red" Allen and Coleman Hawkins 1933* (Smithsonian Collection R022), which includes "Jamaica Shout" and the beautiful "Heartbreak Blues" recorded under Hawk's leadership, as well as some fine tracks by the Allen-Hawkins orchestra. The music is a little more subdued than that on the Collector's Classics items but very worthwhile.

Allen kept getting better and better; by the mid-1950s his mastery of tonal shading, phrasing, and dynamics was almost unparalleled, and he had one of the most distinctive styles in jazz. *World on a String* (RCA/Bluebird 2497-2-RB), originally issued in 1957 as *Ride, Red, Ride in Hi-Fi*, is one of the best Allen sets ever issued; Allen explores the horn's full range of subtlety in performances of good pop tunes like "I Cover the Waterfront," "'Swonderful," and "Love Is Just Around the Corner," as well as his mid-1930s racehorse-tempo feature with the Mills Blue Rhythm Band, "Ride, Red, Ride." Allen is joined here by trombonist J. C. Higginbotham, clarinetist Buster Bailey, a solid rhythm section including drummer Cozy Cole, and his old friend and partner Coleman Hawkins, who very nearly steals the show, especially on the nastily swinging "Algiers Bounce."

Also fine is *Coleman Hawkins and Red Allen: Standards and Warhorses* (Jass CD-2). This late-1950s small-group recording reunion produced phenomenal music from both Hawkins and Allen on a program mixing standards like "Mean to Me," "Stormy Weather," and "All of Me" with unpromising-sounding Dixieland staples like "Bill Bailey" and "When the Saints Go Marching In." Don't be fooled by the repertoire. Allen's phrasing on things like "Frankie and Johnny" and "The Lonesome Road" reaches a very high level of abstraction and emotional expressiveness, at which stylistic pigeon-holing becomes even more meaningless than usual. Listen, too, to his use of space; he often lets several beats go by between phrases, creating a sense of surprise and suspense about where he will begin and end his ideas. A total gas.

Allen and Hawkins were together, too, for the epochal 1957 television special "The Sound of Jazz," on which Allen led a band including Hawk and trumpeter Rex Stewart through blistering versions of "Rosetta" and Armstrong's "Wild Man Blues." The readily available Columbia set *Sound of Jazz* (CK 45234), while packaged as if it were the soundtrack from the show, is not; the music here is from a recording session done four days before the live telecast with many of the same musicians and is considerably less inspired than the music actually heard in the show. While the two Allen tracks are good, the versions on the actual soundtrack of the television show, which has been issued in various incarnations, blow them out of the water. "Wild Man Blues" has truly inspired work from everyone (in addition to Allen, Hawkins, and Stewart, the group included trombonist Vic Dickenson, clarinetist Pee Wee Russell, pianist Nat Pierce, guitarist Danny Barker, bassist Milt Hinton, and drummer Jo Jones), and on "Rosetta" the rhythm section strikes a savagely swinging groove (listen to them under Allen's vocal), which doesn't let up until the end. The show itself is available on videotape, and you will want to own it.

Muggsy Spanier was a fine cornet player very much in the Armstrong/King Oliver mold. He was a master of the plunger mute and of blues playing, and he was an active figure, first in Chicago, then in New York, then all over the country, beginning in the mid-1920s. In 1939 he formed a band that recorded tunes from the New Orleans repertoire ("Dippermouth Blues," "Someday Sweetheart," "Sister Kate") along with popular songs like "Dinah" and "At Sundown" in a modified New Orleans ensemble style over a swing rhythmic background. The records, released under the sobriquet Muggsy Spanier and His Ragtime Band and available as *At the Jazz Band Ball – Chicago/New York Dixieland* (RCA/Bluebird 6752-2-RB), are some of the most enduring traditional jazz recordings ever made.

The tragically short-lived Bunny Berigan was one of the best trumpet players of the 1930s. He made his living playing with various big bands (including Benny Goodman's and Tommy Dorsey's) before forming his own, and often his solo work is found in the middle of otherwise schmaltzy arrangements. His great hit recording of the perennial "I Can't Get Started," as well as his classic solos on "Marie" and "Song of India" with Tommy Dorsey's orchestra, are available in a number of forms, usually surrounded with less satisfying performances of pop material.

But Berigan can be heard uncut with schmaltz in eight tracks on *Jazz in the Thirties* (DRG/Swing CDSW 8457/8). Four – "What Is There to Say?," "The Buzzard," "Tillie's Downtown Now," and "Keep Smiling at Trouble" – feature him at length in 1935 as a sideman in a small group led by the unique tenor saxophone stylist Bud Freeman (who also plays clarinet here). "The Buzzard" is a perfect capsule version of Berigan's style at a nice bright tempo; he gets around the horn, using the lower register comfortably, throwing in well-chosen grace notes and triplets, using the upper register very sparingly and only when it makes musical sense. The out choruses have Berigan and Freeman engaging in a spirited two-man improvisation that builds to an exciting climax. "Tillie's Downtown Now" is a sixteen-bar blues on which Berigan builds his two choruses masterfully, staying in the middle register for the first, then moving into the upper in the second. His solo on the jaunty "Keep Smiling at Trouble" is also a model of construction both logical and daring, starting out way low on the horn.

The four sides under his own leadership (also recorded in 1935) are less inspired as group performances, and Berigan's playing is not quite as fresh as on the Freeman session. Berigan was perhaps a little too generous in allotting solo space to his sidemen (Edgar Sampson on alto and clarinet, Eddie Miller on tenor, and stride pianist Cliff Jackson), but he is heard to good advantage on a tune associated with Bix Beiderbecke, "I'm Coming Virginia" (drummer Ray Bauduc sounds as if his ticket is stamped for New Orleans, not Virginia), and he serves up a mess of blues on a tune titled, simply, "Blues."

*Bunny Berigan and the Rhythm Makers, Volume 1: 1936 and 1938* (Jass J-CD-627) has lots of excellent short Berigan trumpet solos set, unfortunately, into dated-sounding arrangements of largely second-string pop tunes, like diamond chips in so many plastic rings. Berigan takes good meaty solos on a few tracks, though, among them "Dardanella" and "That's a Plenty" (a short but stunning statement). *Swing Is Here: Small Band Swing 1935–1939* (RCA/Bluebird 2180-2-RB) finds Berigan on three tunes by a studio group assembled by arranger Gene Gifford. Berigan's lead playing is wonderful to hear, but he is really featured only on "Nothin' but the Blues," on which he shows his Armstrong roots in the best possible way, along with his hallmark ability to cover the entire horn without sounding contrived.

Berigan can also be heard in perfect, extremely inventive blues choruses on "Blues in E Flat," recorded with xylophonist Red Norvo, available on *The 1930s: Small Combos* (Columbia CK 40833), and "Blues," a studio jam session with Fats Waller on piano, on *Great Trumpets: Classic Jazz to Swing* (RCA/Bluebird 6753-2-RB). He also accompanies Billie Holiday in grand style on eight 1936 tunes on *The Quintessential Billie Holiday, Volume 2* (Columbia CK 40790). He was one of the most natural players in jazz; even when he isn't in such stellar company, his work lights up any surroundings.

Hot Lips Page, a Kansas City giant who had played with Walter Page's Blue Devils and, later, Bennie Moten's orchestra, was one of the most powerful and authentic blues players on any instrument and an authoritative player on any type of material, as well as an engaging singer. Page is represented far too spottily on records, but he can be heard throughout much of *Bennie Moten's Kansas City Orchestra (1929–1932): Basie Beginnings* (RCA/Bluebird 9768-2-RB). His first-rate plunger playing sparks 1930 tunes like "That Too, Do Blues," "When I'm Alone," and "Somebody Stole My Gal," but he shines brightest on the sides from the band's famous 1932 session in Camden, New Jersey. On "Toby," he plays a leadoff solo in which he floats over the time à la Armstrong (this, by the way, is one of the most ferocious big-band recordings ever made), and his open-horn solo on "Moten Swing" is a small masterpiece, perfectly constructed, sweet-toned, and imaginative (check out his upward and downward glissandos in the last four bars). His solos on "The Blue Room," "New Orleans" (the muted one, after the vocal), "Milenburg Joys," "Lafayette" (astonishing plunger work at a high tempo), and "Prince of Wails" (on the Bluebird set, the title is misspelled "Wales," missing the pun) are just as good and by themselves would have guaranteed him a place in jazz history.

Page can also be heard at some length on the hard-to-find *All Star Swing Groups: Pete Johnson, Cozy Cole* (Savoy SJL 2218, LP only). He plays some earthshaking blues at a relentless medium stomp tempo on "Page Mr. Trumpet" with a group led by pianist Pete Johnson and figures prominently in "J.C. from K.C." and "Pete's Housewarming" from the same session. He sounds as if he was out to burn the roof off the studio. On six other tunes on the album, Page plays with another group under Johnson's direction, singing the dozens with the plunger mute on "Atomic Boogie" and "Backroom Blues." On the outstanding four-LP collection *Swing Street* (Columbia Special Products JSN 6042), Page and Johnson grill up some real Kansas City blues with singer Joe Turner on "Cherry Red" and "Baby, Look at You," two classic sides that also include Charlie Parker's teacher Buster Smith on alto saxophone. (On the same set, Page performs the blues "Walkin' in a Daze" with his own band.)

Page can be heard with tenor players Chu Berry and Lucky Thompson on *Chu Berry/Lucky Thompson – Giants of the Tenor Sax* (Commodore CCD 7004), on which Page sings a great version of the ballad "Gee, Baby, Ain't I Good to You." And for an example of Page's sly vocal blues style, listen to "Just Another Woman" on *How Blue Can You Get? – Great Blues Vocals in the Jazz Tradition* (RCA/Bluebird 6758-2-RB). That's a mellophone he's playing, by the way, not a trumpet.

Wild Bill Davison would have deserved his nickname on the basis of his cornet playing alone, even if his behavior had been sober as a church deacon's, which it wasn't. Not a major stylist in terms of melodic invention, his playing nevertheless had a razorlike edge and demonic swing that sparked the playing situations he found himself in. Often those situations were cornet-trombone-clarinet Dixieland-oriented groups playing the Oliver/Beiderbecke/Armstrong/Spanier repertoire in hot but fairly predictable fashion. Typical of the approach are the performances on *The Eddie Condon All-Stars – Dixieland Jam* (Columbia CK 45145). Even better are a number of jammed performances on *Wild Bill Davison/George Brunis – Jazz A-Plenty* (Commodore CCD 7011). But Davison's high point on record probably came on the recordings he made with Sidney Bechet for Blue Note between 1945 and 1950, available on *The Complete Blue Note Recordings of Sidney Bechet* (Mosaic MD4-110). For my taste, the best of these were recorded under the leadership of Chicago pianist Art Hodes; the interplay between the two horns on "Way Down Yonder in New Orleans," "Shine," and "Darktown Strutter's Ball," especially, stings like Chinese mustard.

Two of the most inventive and lyrical voices of the 1930s were Frankie Newton and Bill Coleman, both of whom spent time with the big band of Teddy Hill in the mid-1930s. Hill's band was a sort of seed farm for great trumpeters; at some point, Bill Dillard, Shad Collins, Roy Eldridge, and Dizzy Gillespie also passed through its ranks. Neither Newton nor Coleman became as famous as their talents warranted; Coleman settled in Europe in the mid-1930s, came back to the U.S. for most of the 1940s, then moved to France for good in 1948. Newton stayed around New York, made some topflight jazz recordings, and seems to have performed rather steadily, but he never became a headliner.

You can hear Newton's melodically inventive playing on five tracks on *Swing Is Here: Small Band Swing 1935–1939* (RCA/Bluebird 2180-2-RB). Three were recorded under clarinetist Mezz Mezzrow's leadership; of these, "The Panic Is On" is the best. Listen to the way Newton begins his first eight bars with held notes that lay across the beat and finishes the eight with punching, on-the-beat notes. On "Rosetta," recorded under the trumpeter's leadership, Newton's exuberant lead work pilots the ensemble through two wonderful out choruses in which the three front-line instruments simultaneously improvise at full tilt without getting in each other's way.

Newton makes cameo appearances on a number of collections of music from the 1930s. His opening and closing choruses on "There's No Two Ways About It" (on *The 1930s: Small Combos* [Columbia CK 40833]) are full of the best kinds of surprises and fresh ideas (check out the ascending chromatic break leading into his last solo). His four muted slow blues choruses on 1939's "The Blues My Baby Gave to Me" (on *Great Trumpets: Classic Jazz to Swing* [RCA/Bluebird 6753-2-RB]) create a fine, sustained mood; Newton plays the blues on three standout tracks on *The Complete Blue Note Recordings of Sidney*

*Bechet* (Mosaic MD4-110) and is featured throughout Mosaic's *The Complete Recordings of the Port of Harlem Jazzmen* (MR1-108). Newton takes a great up-tempo muted solo on "Dizzy Debutante" (on *John Kirby: The Biggest Little Band 1937–1941* [Smithsonian Collection R013]), but one of his best moments is the trumpet obbligato to Clarence Palmer's vocal on the 1937 "You Showed Me the Way" by Frank Newton and His Uptown Serenaders (available on the four-LP boxed set *Swing Street* [Columbia Special Products JSN 6042]), on which his trumpet forms a perfect counterpoint, weaving in and out of the vocal lines, never getting in the way, always clear and surprising.

Bill Coleman's lilting, spry playing is heard at its best on six sides recorded in Europe in 1937 under the leadership of trombonist Dicky Wells, and including guitarist Django Reinhardt, available on *Djangologie/USA, Volume 1* (DRG/Swing CDSW 8421/3, blue cover). On "Bugle Call Rag," "Between the Devil and the Deep Blue Sea," and "I Got Rhythm," Coleman is joined by two other trumpeters from the Teddy Hill band, Bill Dillard and Shad Collins. Coleman takes the second solo on "Bugle Call" and "Rhythm" and the open-horn solo on "Devil"; all three tunes are exciting. But the real knockouts here are the three Wells-Coleman performances without the other trumpets, classics of intimate, conversational improvisation – "Sweet Sue," "Japanese Sandman," and "Hangin' Around Boudon." His blues playing on "Boudon" is fine, clear-toned, and absolutely cogent; check out his closing dialogue with Wells. "Sandman" has a perfect Coleman solo, each idea flowing logically out of the previous one, and an out chorus in which Coleman and Wells improvise together beautifully. But my favorite is the chugging, relaxed, medium-tempo workout on "Sweet Sue." The format couldn't be much simpler: a chorus from Wells, followed by one from Coleman, then another chorus apiece. After Coleman's second chorus, the two horns trade four-bar ideas for twenty-four bars in which inspiration runs high – they set up each other's shots perfectly – and then riff the last eight bars together, closing out an absolutely perfect jazz record.

Coleman also gets his innings on *Djangologie/USA, Volume 2* (DRG/Swing CDSW 8424/6, yellow cover), especially on five more 1937 Paris sides with Django Reinhardt, the standout of which is his unaccompanied duet with Reinhardt, "Bill Coleman Blues," on which Coleman plays chorus after chorus of muted trumpet blues with completely characteristic chords and accents from Reinhardt. A feast for Coleman fans is *Willie Lewis and His Entertainers* (DRG/Swing SW8400/01), a collection of sides recorded between 1935 and 1937, most of which feature Coleman in fine form among mostly black American expatriate musicians in Paris. Coleman also sits in with a Lester Young small group in 1944 on *Lester "Prez" Young and Friends – Giants of the Tenor Sax*

(Commodore CCD 7002) and with both Young and Coleman Hawkins on *Coleman Hawkins/Lester Young – Classic Tenors* (Signature/CBS AK 38446).

## BASIE TRUMPETS

Buck Clayton and Harry "Sweets" Edison were the gin and bitters of the late-1930s Count Basie trumpet section. Clayton was an extremely lyrical player, an expert with cup mutes, a great blues and ballad man who could also take care of business on up-tempo numbers. Edison was a swaggering blues- and riff-based player whose sound was strong enough to be heard over the whole Basie band. His emotional range is not as broad as Clayton's, but he always swings hard, and his sound is instantly identifiable.

Clayton can be heard soloing throughout *Count Basie: The Complete Decca Recordings* (Decca/GRP GRD-3-611), Edison on the cuts made after he joined the band in 1938. Both men are featured throughout *The Essential Count Basie, Volume 1* (Columbia CK 40608), *Volume 2* (Columbia CK 40835), and *Volume 3* (Columbia CK 44150); Stanley Dance's notes guide you to the high points.

Clayton's lyricism put him in much demand for small-band recordings; some of the best of these may be found on *Lester "Prez" Young and Friends – Giants of the Tenor Sax* (Commodore CCD 7002), on which Clayton and Lester Young front the Basie rhythm section (with Eddie Durham on electric guitar in place of Basie) in 1938 for classic performances of "I Want a Little Girl" (a beautiful cup-muted melody statement from Clayton here), "Countless Blues," "Pagin' the Devil," "Way Down Yonder in New Orleans," and "Them There Eyes." This small band, called the Kansas City Six, reaches a height of ensemble coherence that has rarely been equaled and never surpassed; Clayton's solos, mostly muted, are little gems of storytelling.

The same might be said for his many perfect short solos on *The Quintessential Billie Holiday, Volume 3* (Columbia CK 44048), *Volume 4* (Columbia CK 44252), and *Volume 5* (Columbia CK 44423), in the company of the cream of the era's musicians. He gets a chance to stretch out on open horn on four 1943 titles with Lester Young, available on *The Complete Lester Young* (Mercury 830 920-2); the small band, called the Kansas City Seven, also features Dicky Wells on trombone and Count Basie's rhythm section. Clayton did the arrangements and composed three of the four tunes as well. For an interesting glimpse of Clayton shoulder-to-shoulder with Charlie Parker, listen to the four sides they recorded with Sir Charles Thompson, available on *Charlie Parker: Every Bit of It* (Spotlite SPJ150D, LP only), especially the way Clayton tears through "The Street Beat."

Clayton continued to play well and recorded some of his very best work in the 1950s. A fine example of his work from 1955 and 1956 is *Buck Clayton – Jam*

*Sessions from the Vault* (Columbia CK 44291), on which he is heard with such peers as Coleman Hawkins, Buddy Tate, Jo Jones, and trumpeter Ruby Braff in loose but controlled versions of "Out of Nowhere," "Blue Lou," and more. He was in the studio with Coleman Hawkins again in 1958 for a quintet date with the brilliant Hank Jones on piano; the results can be found under Hawkins's name on *The High and Mighty Hawk* (London 820 600-2), which is very highly recommended. A date pairing Clayton with his ex-Basie bandmate tenorist Buddy Tate produced the beautiful set *Buck and Buddy* (Swingville/ OJC-757), an example of so-called mainstream jazz at its relaxed peak. Also worthwhile is *The Classic Swing of Buck Clayton* (Riverside/OJC-1709).

Trumpeter Ruby Braff is one of the most undersung players in the music, a strong lyric stylist with a luscious sound in all registers and plenty of facility that he doesn't allow to get in the way of fiery, direct musical expression. *Braff!* (Portrait RK 44393), recorded in three small-group sessions in 1956, showcases Braff's gorgeous tone and ideas on solid standards like "Stardust," "Moonglow," and "Indian Summer." Four of the tracks feature Coleman Hawkins; all of them have nice, spare arrangements, probably by pianist Nat Pierce.

*This Is My Lucky Day* (RCA/Bluebird 6456-2-RB) is also very good and shows Braff's impeccable ear for excellent, neglected pop tunes. Here he plays "It's Been So Long," "Did I Remember?," "Marie" (these three from a 1957 album tribute to Bunny Berigan, with trombonist Bennie Morton and clarinetist Pee Wee Russell), as well as, in duets with Roy Eldridge, "This Is My Lucky Day," Armstrong's "Someday You'll Be Sorry," and "The Song Is Ended." Braff is featured as a sideman throughout *The Essential Vic Dickenson* (Vanguard), a collection of extended small-group performances from 1953 and 1954 under the leadership of one of jazz's great trombonists. The trumpeter has his say on the pop standards "Russian Lullaby" and "You Brought a New Kind of Love to Me," on Fats Waller's "Keeping Out of Mischief Now," and on an impromptu up-tempo blues, "Sir Charles at Home," named for the sessions' pianist, Sir Charles Thompson. This set is also worth having for generous helpings of Edmond Hall's astringent clarinet playing.

Buck Clayton's Basie sectionmate Harry Edison is a thoroughly distinctive stylist and has been much recorded, especially by Norman Granz in the 1970s for his Pablo label, often in very unstructured blowing situations in which not a whole lot happens. One album on which a whole lot definitely does happen is the 1962 *Ben Webster and "Sweets" Edison: Ben and "Sweets"* (Columbia CK 40853). Edison's extended muted solo on the extremely hard-swinging, medium-tempo blues "Better Go" is a virtual anthology of his favorite phrases and devices. Very few can match Sweets at this tempo on the blues; he has a certain dry way of phrasing and signifying on the horn that is his alone. Other good reasons to buy this album are the rhythm section, which includes pianist Hank Jones and bassist George Duvivier, among the finest on their respective instruments, the presence of Ben Webster's tenor saxophone (which is the main reason to buy it), and the cover photo, which tells a lot about the men involved. Another place to hear Edison in an interesting setting is *Nat "King" Cole and His Trio – The Complete After Midnight Sessions* (Capitol CDP 7 48328), on which the pianist and singer is joined, variously, by Edison, altoist Willie Smith, violinist Stuff Smith, or trombonist Juan Tizol in a program of good standards. Edison is on board for "Sweet Lorraine," "It's Only a Paper Moon," and three others. This is a very mellow set, and Cole sounds wonderful singing and playing; Sweets sets him off perfectly.

## ROY ELDRIDGE

Roy Eldridge was one of the most exciting players in the history of the music and a major stylist, representing the first true addition to Armstrong's vocabulary on trumpet. He was one of a handful of swing musicians who began to play longer lines of eighth notes and find ways to accent individual notes within those lines. In fact, he often phrased more like a saxophonist than a trumpeter.

A fiery, competitive player who sparked every situation he was in, Eldridge swung differently than any trumpeter before him; his lines of legato eighth notes, staggered with punching, on-the-beat quarter notes, used the expectations set up by the 1930s even four-four swing to create new patterns of suspense and resolution in the music. His breath control was such that he could accent individual notes out of long, even lines; he had a brilliant sound and was strong in all ranges, and he could pepper notes in the horn's stratosphere to devastating effect.

### WARMIN' UP

To hear a capsule version of what I mean, listen to the title track on the collection *Swing Is Here: Small Band Swing 1935–1939* (RCA/Bluebird 2180-2-RB). Throughout his introduction and solo (recorded in 1936), Eldridge uses punched-out notes to play off the strong four-four that Gene Krupa lays down on the drums, but he alternates them with fast lines that turn and dart unexpectedly. Listen, too, to the way he leaps into the upper register at the beginning of the second eight bars of his solo – just, it seems, on the edge of control, like a car taking corners a little too fast but still staying on the road. His playing animates the entire performance. The same remarks apply to "I Hope Gabriel Likes My Music," perhaps even more so; his lines are longer and more interesting in this only slightly slower performance. These are two tracks you don't want to miss. You can see right off the bat why Eldridge became the idol of a whole new generation of trumpet players, foremost among them Dizzy Gillespie, who initially based his entire style on Eldridge's.

Probably the best introduction to Eldridge is the Columbia set *Roy Eldridge – Little Jazz* (CK 45275), which presents an excellent sampling of the trumpeter's early years of recording, from 1935 to 1940. ("Little Jazz" was the nickname given Eldridge, by virtue of his small physical stature, by Ellington saxophonist Otto Hardwick.) Included here are the fantastic "Warmin' Up," by a recording band led by pianist Teddy Wilson and including Eldridge's companion from the Fletcher Henderson big band, tenor saxophonist Chu Berry, on which Eldridge plays a solo that was simply beyond any trumpeter playing at the time in terms of rhythmic sophistication, unpredictability of accenting, and velocity. It wasn't just a matter of running around the horn, either; listen to how logical the phrases are. Each comes out of the previous one to make a perfect, complete story in thirty-two bars (listen to the way drummer Big Sid Catlett shifts into overdrive underneath him in the last eight). Also listen to the way that Eldridge mixes up his accenting between the down beats and the up beats.

There are four fine sides by the 1936 Fletcher Henderson band with Eldridge and Chu Berry, but the seven 1937 tracks by Eldridge's own band, recorded in Chicago, are the heart of the set. "Wabash Stomp," a brooding, minor-key, medium-tempo jumper that resolves into major, is presented in two takes, both of which show Eldridge building up a fearsome head of steam. He's slower getting to it on the second take, but when he does, it raises the hair on your neck. His two choruses on the way-up-tempo "Heckler's Hop" are handled perfectly; the first, in the middle and lower range of the horn, is full of flighty ideas brimming with nervous energy, which cuts loose like a storm breaking in the second chorus, where he reaches for the sky, with the band riffing hard behind him. His ideas and equilibrium here are fabulous. The same goes for "After You've Gone," on which he deals the other trumpeters of his time some very bad cards.

Other outstanding Eldridge from this period can be heard on *Hocus Pocus: Fletcher Henderson and His Orchestra 1927–1936* (RCA/Bluebird 9904-2-RB), which contains a number of good tracks by the 1936 band, including the novelty "Knock, Knock, Who's There?" with a vocal by Eldridge. *The Quintessential Billie Holiday, Volume 1* (Columbia CK 40646) features Eldridge extensively, backing the greatest female jazz singer of all time with groups put together by Teddy Wilson and including the likes of Chu Berry, Ben Webster, and Benny Goodman. The 1935 material is sometimes insipid ("Eeny Meeny

Miney Mo" and "Yankee Doodle Never Went to Town," for example), but it doesn't matter; the sides have a freshness and exuberance that are hard to match. Eldridge shakes the rafters on "What a Night, What a Moon, What a Girl," "It's Too Hot for Words," and "Twenty-Four Hours a Day" (listen closely to him behind the vocal, too). Also fine are four sides recorded with Chu Berry for the small Commodore label in 1938, available on *Chu Berry/Lucky Thompson – Giants of the Tenor Sax* (Commodore CCD 7004), including a famous double-time Eldridge solo on "Body and Soul."

Eldridge led his own band throughout the late 1930s, then in 1941 he joined drummer Gene Krupa's big band (the earlier sides with Krupa, on *Swing Is Here*, were recorded when Krupa was the drummer with Benny Goodman's orchestra and Eldridge was a member of Fletcher Henderson's band), where he was prominently featured both as trumpeter and novelty vocalist. Krupa's band perfectly straddled the line between commerciality and serious music-making, and Eldridge recorded more than one masterpiece with the band, all of which are collected on *Roy Eldridge with the Gene Krupa Orchestra – Uptown* (Columbia CK 45448). One of the best-remembered sides from Eldridge's tenure with Krupa was his vocal duet with Anita O'Day on "Let Me Off Uptown," a real period piece but full of high spirits – the band had something special. At the end, O'Day exhorts Eldridge to "blow, Roy, blow . . ." and he does just that, with a thrilling break and solo. "After You've Gone" is an extension of Eldridge's earlier small-band arrangement (as performed on *Little Jazz*), and "Stop, the Red Light's On" is a novelty tune with a searing solo from the trumpeter.

Eldridge's version here of "Rockin' Chair" is one of the greatest ballad performances in the history of jazz; everything about his solo, which lasts for the length of the track (he plays over organlike chords from the saxophone section), is assured to the highest degree, the work of someone who has truly become himself. His tone is strong and clear at times, rasping and nasty at others; he alternates simple phrases with more complicated ones that turn on themselves, end at surprising places, and begin unexpectedly. The solo builds beautifully, too, starting with a uniquely relaxed feeling and gathering tension and complexity as it goes. Not something you want to miss. While nothing else in the collection can match "Rockin' Chair," there is a lot more good music here, including the novelty tune "Swiss Lullaby," on which Eldridge plays the part of an irate neighbor awakened by an insipid vocal duo. When he gets up and starts to blow, stand out of the way.

Some very good mid-1940s Eldridge, recorded with his own band, is collected on *Roy Eldridge – After You've Gone* (Decca/GRP GRD-605). Standouts on this album are Eldridge's readings of "Stardust," "I Surrender, Dear," "Body and Soul," and several other fine ballads, which the trumpeter makes his own. This set also includes a number of jumping trumpet showpieces with a well-rehearsed big band. Eldridge's tone and attack here are as sharp as a well-honed razor.

Eldridge also worked for a while in the mid-1940s with bandleading clarinetist Artie Shaw; seven small-group sides from that period are collected on *The Complete Gramercy Five Sessions* (RCA/Bluebird 7637-2-RB). Eldridge is featured in a carefully and imaginatively arranged group context, muted all the way, but there isn't really the room or the spirit for him to cut loose on any level.

### HAWK AND ROY

The opposite is true on a session Eldridge made with Coleman Hawkins a year earlier, in 1944, and available on *The Complete Coleman Hawkins on Keynote* (Mercury 830 960-2). Hawkins and Eldridge were a great team, both extremely fiery players; they could complement each other on ballads and goad each other to the heights on cookers. The nine tracks they share on the Mercury set, taken from sessions done for the small mid-1940s label Keynote, are all good – three takes of "I Only Have Eyes for You," two of "'Swonderful," one gemlike reading of "I'm in the Mood for Love," and three of a retooled version of "How High the Moon," entitled "Bean at the Met." Eldridge is at his most exciting on the latter number, muted and crackling with energy, especially on the third take.

Hawk and Roy also team up on a 1951 broadcast from the New York City club Birdland with one of the best rhythm sections of the early 1950s: Horace Silver on piano, Curly Russell on bass, and Art Blakey on drums. Silver and Blakey generate huge excitement behind the two horns, and they all tear their way through two Hawkins riff tunes – "Disorder at the Border" and "Stuffy" – and Rodgers and Hart's "The Blue Room." Available as *Coleman Hawkins – Disorder at the Border* (Spotlite 121, LP only), the set gives a good sense of what the pair was like on an "on" night. Also excellent, if slightly less heated, are *Coleman Hawkins and Roy Eldridge at the Bayou Club, Volume 1* (Honeysuckle Rose H.R. 5002, LP only) and *Volume 2* (Honeysuckle Rose H.R. 5006, LP only), recorded at a 1959 club appearance in Washington, D.C. Both men are at the top of their form; Eldridge's tone is clear and soaring, and he is plainly energized by Hawkins's proximity.

Eldridge and Hawkins also team up for a 1959 date under tenor saxophonist Ben Webster's leadership, available as *Ben Webster and Associates* (Verve 835 254-2). Eldridge takes wild solos on two fast blues, "De-Dar" and "Young

Bean"; his entrance on "De-Dar," especially, is startling and effective. In 1957 they were together for the historic "Sound of Jazz" telecast, which featured an unbelievable array of musicians – including an all-star band led by Count Basie (including Hawkins, Ben Webster, and Eldridge), Billie Holiday, Thelonious Monk, and Red Allen – playing in an informal setting that brought out the best in everyone. The actual soundtrack from the show, not to be confused with Columbia's *Sound of Jazz* (CK 45234), a studio recording done several days before the actual telecast, includes two peak moments from Eldridge – his stratospheric solo on "Dickie's Dream," with the big band, and his two searing blues choruses on "Fine and Mellow," with Billie Holiday.

*Roy Eldridge and the Swing Trumpets* (Mercury 830 923-2), a two-CD set, actually contains only six Eldridge tracks, on which he is teamed with the excellent but lesser-known trumpeters Emmett Berry and Joe Thomas. This collection also contains many obscure mid-1940s sides from the Keynote label by such first-rate descendants of both Armstrong and Eldridge as Berry and Thomas (both of whom have additional material here besides the Eldridge sides), Jonah Jones, Charlie Shavers, and Buck Clayton. Thomas, in particular, was a fine and underrecorded stylist; he always found something interesting to do with even the most familiar material, and his melodic invention and swing were unassailable. The four sides under his leadership here are delicious, especially "Pocatello."

Eldridge sounded better than ever in some respects in the 1950s, as you can tell from his playing on an extraordinary 1956 all-star session available as *Lester Young – The Jazz Giants* (Verve 825 672-2), on which he is truly in the company of his peers – including tenor innovator Young, trombonist Vic Dickenson, pianist Teddy Wilson, and drummer Jo Jones. Everyone sounds good on four pop tunes, including the rarely done "This Year's Kisses," which Young recorded with Billie Holiday in 1937. "Gigantic Blues" is a heated, uptempo blues with Eldridge burning it up, but everything else is taken at a variety of relaxed medium tempos which draw out everyone's most reflective, melodic sides.

A highlight of Eldridge's 1950s performances is a set recorded with the prodigious pianist Art Tatum. Tatum, who was perhaps best known and loved as a solo player, recorded a series of encounters with other instrumentalists in the mid-1950s for producer Norman Granz, which have been reissued in their entirety as *The Complete Pablo Group Masterpieces* (Pablo 6 PACD-4401-2). The sessions have also been issued individually, the Eldridge session as *Art Tatum: The Tatum Group Masterpieces, Volume 2* (Pablo PACD-2045-425-2). Included are ten tracks (including two newly discovered alternate takes of "I Won't

Dance" and Duke Ellington's "In a Sentimental Mood") by the Eldridge-Tatum pairing, backed expertly by bassist John Simmons and drummer Alvin Stoller in a program of first-rate standards by Cole Porter, Rodgers and Hart, Jerome Kern, and others. Although Tatum could be an overbusy accompanist, the sides with Eldridge (as well as an immortal session with Ben Webster) work wonderfully; Eldridge's lead playing was firm enough for Tatum's runs to bubble and swirl around in fine contrast. Highly recommended.

Also fascinating is the 1960 pairing of Eldridge, drummer Jo Jones, and pianist Tommy Flanagan with Charles Mingus, trombonist Jimmy Knepper, and alto saxophonist Eric Dolphy. Available on *The Complete Candid Recordings of Charles Mingus* (Mosaic MD3-111), this, at the time, was a totally implausible mixture of "traditional" players with seemingly far-out modernists like Mingus and Dolphy. With the perspective of thirty years, we can see just how deeply in the tradition Mingus and Dolphy were and how fresh and modern players like Eldridge will always sound. Certainly the music here is a perfect blend. Eldridge is in super form; his climactic solo on "Mysterious Blues" indicates that he was interested in making clear that any distinction between "new" and "old" in music didn't interest him at all. On two takes of "Body and Soul" he plays all over the horn, reaching down into the gravel and up into the ether. "R&R," a medium-tempo "I Got Rhythm" derivative, begins with Eldridge setting a riff with the mute in. He begins his solo with only Mingus and Jones behind him; he is joined later by Flanagan as well. His open-horn solo later in the piece contains some ferocious double-timing and leaps into the upper register. "Wrap Your Troubles in Dreams," a good, medium-up reading of the excellent standard presented in two takes, and "Me and You," a real slow blues, are both quartet performances. The two versions of "Dreams" are very different; each ends with a little out-of-tempo dialogue between Eldridge and Mingus. But "Me and You," recorded at the end of the date, is probably the best thing from the session; Eldridge's timeless and extremely authoritative blues playing is hot enough to fry eggs, and everyone digs way down.

Eldridge was active, and dangerous, as a trumpet player up until illness forced him to lay the horn down in 1980. For shocking proof, pick up *Roy Eldridge 4 – Montreux '77* (Pablo Live/OJC-373). Forty years after "Wabash Stomp" and "Heckler's Hop," Eldridge's performance at the Swiss Jazz Festival at Montreux, with pianist Oscar Peterson, bassist Niels Pedersen, and drummer Bobby Durham, scales the heights on tunes like "Between the Devil and the Deep Blue Sea," "I Surrender Dear," "Perdido," "Bye Bye Blackbird," and two up-tempo things cooked up spontaneously. Eldridge's playing on a fast blues called "Gofor" is hard to believe; at the end, he really sounds as if he wants to burn the joint down and almost does; he plainly wants to keep going even after the rhythm section stops. His sound is heard to great effect on "I Surrender Dear," which begins as a stunning duet with Peterson, then doubles in tempo. This set shows, in a nutshell, what makes jazz so exciting. Given a certain caliber of player, there is always the chance that music like this can happen; a certain spirit can settle, and everything can lift off. This was just one of those nights for Eldridge, definitely one of the most extraordinary musicians jazz has produced.

## DIZZY GILLESPIE

Like almost all trumpet players who came of age in the late 1930s, John Birks "Dizzy" Gillespie idolized Roy Eldridge. Eldridge's way of accenting notes within long, legato lines, the fire and unpredictable phrasing, and the new harmonic devices were irresistible to younger musicians with an adventuresome beat.

Gillespie used the early years of the 1940s to develop from an Eldridge imitator into one of the most distinctive stylists in the music and, along with a handful of others, a full-fledged innovator of the new idiom, usually referred to as bebop, that expanded the language of jazz. He extended the normal range of the trumpet upward by playing routinely in the highest register and greatly increased the prevailing conception of the trumpet's flexibility by executing faster, much faster, than anyone had before him on the instrument. He attributed his rhythmic sophistication to his close working relationship with Charlie Parker, and Gillespie certainly learned how to set up patterns of extremely intricate accenting within long lines of hurtling, ricocheting eighth, sixteenth, and even thirty-second notes. An avid student of the keyboard, he was known for his enthusiasm for sharing the new harmonic knowledge he worked out there. He also reintroduced Afro-Cuban rhythms as an integral part of jazz by his use of the black Cuban conga player Chano Pozo in his late-1940s band; Gillespie had a lifelong fascination with percussion and with the piano, and the merger of those two primary jazz navigational instruments made for much of Gillespie's authority.

Gillespie always had an ability to establish a rapport with audiences that many of his gifted contemporaries lacked, and he became a well-known entertainer while still upholding the highest musical standards. Although seen in the 1940s as a musical revolutionary, Gillespie was soon recognized as belonging to the jazz mainstream, a musician who contributed something irreplaceable to the music.

Gillespie was always ready to admit his debt to Eldridge, and we can hear that debt being serviced in his earliest recorded solos, of which "Hot Mallets," recorded in 1939 with Lionel Hampton, is a prime example (available on *Hot Mallets, Volume 1* [RCA/Bluebird 6458-2-RB]). Dizzy had just joined Cab Calloway's big band after a stint with Teddy Hill's orchestra (to which Eldridge had belonged earlier), and he was in the studio with perhaps the greatest saxophone section ever assembled – alto saxophonist Benny Carter and tenor saxophonists Coleman Hawkins, Ben Webster, and Chu Berry. He opens the track with a muted solo that contains a number of Eldridge mannerisms (he plays one of them twice); Gillespie plainly has no technical problem with the rapid style. But whereas in Eldridge you feel a tremendous push behind each note, Gillespie's accenting is more on top of the beat; he doesn't seem to dig into the four beats per bar as deeply as Eldridge does. One could almost posit from this solo alone that Gillespie was looking for something else.

The process by which he found it is documented brilliantly in *Dizzy Gillespie: The Development of an American Artist* (Smithsonian Collection R004). This recording presents early Gillespie solos with the big bands of Calloway, Les Hite, and Lucky Millinder; Harlem jam session material from 1941 in which you can watch his harmonic sense developing before your eyes like a photograph; "Woody'n You" and "Disorder at the Border," from what is generally considered to be the first full-fledged bebop date, recorded in 1944 under Coleman Hawkins's leadership; up through rare and fully formed 1945 recordings showing Gillespie in total command of what he was doing. The liner notes by Martin Williams, one of the deans of American jazz criticism, point you to all the right places in the music.

The Smithsonian set steers clear of the all-important recordings Gillespie made in 1945 with Charlie Parker because Parker's brilliance has tended to shadow Gillespie's. That's no reason for you to steer clear of them, however; you should drive straight for them. Most of Gillespie's recordings with Parker are discussed in the *Guide* under Parker's name, but certainly their earliest recordings together bear Gillespie's imprint at least as strongly as they do Bird's.

Available on *Dizzy Gillespie and His Sextets and Orchestra: "Shaw 'Nuff"* (Musicraft MVSCD-53), recordings like "Groovin' High," "Salt Peanuts," "Hot House," and "Dizzy Atmosphere" threw down a new kind of gauntlet for musicians in terms of the demands that would be placed on their harmonic knowledge and their ability to execute at high speeds. Gillespie bursts with ideas and energy here; his extroverted style jumps right out at you, and his rhythmic equilibrium is still startling today. Notice, too, that these recordings are all routined thoughtfully; they are not, for the most part, what many of the modern movement's records (including Parker's own) became – the head, then a series of solos, then the head and out. Each of the early records uses combinations of breaks, countermelodies, riffs, interludes, and many of the other compositional techniques that had been laid down in jazz in order to create a textured, unified whole.

The set also includes a number of sides recorded in 1946 by Gillespie's own big band, which show just how musically adaptable the boppers' devices were for a large ensemble. Performances like "Emanon," "One Bass Hit" (presented here in both small- and big-band arrangements), and, especially, "Things to Come" feature Gillespie's rocketing trumpet in an appropriately fiery setting. But the sides recorded for RCA Victor beginning in 1947, such as "Woody'n You," "Manteca," and "Cool Breeze" (mistitled "Cubano Be" on the set) show Gillespie's big band at its best, often incorporating an Afro-Cuban influence by way of conga drummer Chano Pozo (see the Ensembles section for a discussion of these recordings). They are available on *The Bebop Revolution* (RCA/Bluebird 2177-2-RB), along with four good 1946 tracks by a Gillespie small band which also features vibist Milt Jackson and the very influential tenor saxophonist Don Byas. (Another good Gillespie small-group matchup with Byas is "Good Bait" on *The Bebop Era* [Columbia CK 40972].)

As can be heard on the vocal exchanges on "Cool Breeze" as well as small-group sides like "Oop Bop Sh'Bam" and "Salt Peanuts" (on the Musicraft set), Gillespie had a buoyant sense of humor and a flair for entertaining that enabled him to become one of the most visible and publicly recognized of the bop musicians. Increasingly, he began performing bebop-flavored novelty material along with the straight-ahead jazz, especially after he broke up his big band in 1950. *Dizzy Gillespie: Dee Gee Days* (Savoy ZDS 4426) shows the most audience-conscious, good-time-oriented side of Gillespie. Comprised of tracks recorded in 1951 and 1952 for Gillespie's own short-lived independent record label (named Dee Gee), the set is heavy on such well-known Gillespie novelty items as "School Days," "Swing Low, Sweet Cadillac," "Umbrella Man," and "Ooh-Shoo-Be-Doo-Bee," most of which feature vocals by Joe Carroll and sometimes by Gillespie himself. A famous track is "Pops' Confessin'," on which Carroll does a very creditable Armstrong impression and Gillespie offers an unalloyed trumpet homage to the master. But there is good straight-ahead jazz here as well, often with a crowd-pleasing edge to it, as on "The Champ," an up-tempo blues on which the soloists are goaded by exciting riffs and Budd Johnson takes a tenor solo that sounds calculated to bring the house down, even though it was recorded in a studio. Gillespie plays some very strong stuff throughout the set, as do trombonist J. J. Johnson, vibist Milt Jackson, and the great violinist Stuff Smith. For a bonus, "We Love to Boogie" contains the first recorded solo by John Coltrane. But the accent here is definitely on entertainment.

While Gillespie always maintained the entertainment component, especially in live performances, he never let it obscure musical values, and he remained one of the premier improvisers in jazz until his death in December 1992. In the 1950s he recorded a number of albums for Norman Granz's Verve label that leave no doubt about this statement. One of the most potent is *For Musicians Only* (Verve 837 435-2), which, despite the title, can be enjoyed by musicians and nonmusicians alike. A pure jam session led by Gillespie, on which he shares the front line with Sonny Stitt on alto and Stan Getz on tenor (with a rhythm section of John Lewis on piano, Herb Ellis on guitar, Ray Brown on bass, and Stan Levey on drums), the premise here is simple – survival of the fittest. Three of the four tunes – "Wee," "Lover Come Back to Me," and the minor-key "Bebop" – are taken at killingly fast tempos, and the fourth, "Dark Eyes," at a bright medium-up-tempo that would have made it the up-tempo track on many another date.

This is pure white-hot improvisation, with nothing to draw in the listener in the way of routining, arranged interludes, vocals, or anything else; there's a theme statement for one chorus, then it's every man for himself, one at a time. Of the soloists, Getz comes in third; he swings, but he repeats a lot of phrases and doesn't show the same level of ingenuity that Stitt and Gillespie do. Both of them play at the absolute top of their games, showing total rhythmic and melodic poise at tempos that make it hard to finger the horn articulately, much less conceptualize coherently. Gillespie plays both muted and open over the entire range of the horn, in a stunning display of rhythmic, harmonic, and technical mastery. Listen, for just one example, to the degree of detail in his open-horn solo on "Wee." For those who like their jazz straight, no chaser, this is 151-proof.

The same can be said of two albums on which Gillespie is joined by Stitt and Sonny Rollins, *Duets* (Verve 835 253-2) and *Sonny Side Up* (Verve 825 674-2). Recorded in December 1957, they also show Gillespie at peak form, goaded on by the presence of two master improvisers. *Duets* has Rollins and Stitt on different songs; *Sonny Side Up* features them together. *Duets* has the great fast blues "Wheatleigh Hall" with Rollins, on which Gillespie begins his solo at low volume and low on his horn, building in excitement, volume, and intensity as he goes along, reaching way into the horn's upper reaches and executing some ridiculously intricate turns, as well as the Latin-flavored "Con Alma," on which Stitt plays some beautiful tenor and Gillespie makes the most of the undulating rhythmic background.

But for sheer excitement, it's hard to beat *Sonny Side Up*, if for nothing else than for "The Eternal Triangle," a cutting contest between the tenors of Rollins and Stitt, both of whom were at their best and in an extremely carnivorous mood. At another take-no-prisoners tempo, Rollins solos first for five brilliant choruses, then Stitt comes on for eight absolutely roasting ones. After that, Rollins returns and the two saxophones square off for six choruses of exchanges – three choruses of four-bar exchanges and three of eight-bar exchanges. It's a dead heat until about the third chorus, when I would begin to score Rollins ahead on points. This is the closest musical equivalent to the Muhammad Ali–Joe Frazier "Thrilla in Manila" that I can think of. Oh yes . . . Gillespie comes in after the tenors and blows the roof off the studio.

The album also includes a version of "I Know That You Know," on which Rollins plays a phenomenal extended stop-time solo and Gillespie plays some thrilling stuff, in places seeming to holler on the horn just for the joy of hollering. Stitt's solo here is almost the equal of Rollins's. "After Hours" is a slow blues on which Stitt takes the tenor honors and Gillespie plays a mess of blues. (By the way, on "On the Sunny Side of the Street," the first tenor soloist is Stitt, not Rollins, as the liner notes say.) This set is one of the most satisfying jazz discs you can buy.

*Portrait of Duke Ellington* (Verve 817 107-2) features a Gillespie-led big band doing fine readings of Ellington and Billy Strayhorn material, including rarely played items such as "Johnny Come Lately," and is well worth having. But Duke Ellington's *Ellington Jazz Party* (Columbia CK 40712) has Gillespie sitting in with the Ellington orchestra in 1959 on two tunes, Strayhorn's lovely "U.M.M.G." and an impromptu blues also featuring singer Jimmy Rushing, called "Hello, Little Girl." The prize of the two is "U.M.M.G.," on which Gillespie takes over the part usually played by Clark Terry and brings a whole new dimension to it in an ingeniously paced performance that builds to a real climax.

*Swing Low, Sweet Cadillac* (MCA/Impulse MCAD-33121) is a 1967 set recorded live, in which Gillespie's talent for humor is again in the forefront with a long version of the title tune, featuring some funny, impressionistic Afro-Cuban-style chanting and jive from Gillespie and saxophonist James Moody. The other four quintet performances include the samba "Mas Que Nada" and the polyrhythmic "Kush," an exercise in the pentatonic scale over a six-eight rhythmic background. This album gives a good look at Gillespie in other rhythmic bags besides the straight-ahead four-four of the Verves.

For a real uncut rhythmic workout try *Max Roach + Dizzy Gillespie – Paris 1989* (A&M CD 6404), an unaccompanied duet performance between Gillespie and the architect of modern drumming, in which Gillespie's rapid-fire trumpet lines intertwine with Roach's endlessly inventive patterns, echoing them, bouncing off them, and creating an ongoing rhythmic counterpoint. Gillespie's embouchure seems to be weak here, though, and he has trouble articulating at the rapid tempos. He sounds best on the cuts where he has the mute in, and his scat vocal on "Oo Pa Pa Da" is a gas.

## FATS NAVARRO

The greatest trumpeter to arrive in the late 1940s, after Dizzy Gillespie, was Fats Navarro. Navarro, who died at age twenty-six in 1950, had one of the most beautiful trumpet sounds of his time and was able to articulate the most complicated kinds of harmonic and rhythmic material with ease, while always swinging. He also had a true grandeur and stateliness in his phrasing that reached back to Armstrong and the New Orleans players; he had a full, clear tone which instantly made any ensemble sound distinctive, and he was a very melodic player as well, not just a slinger of formulaic patterns.

There is not a lot of Navarro available, but nearly all of it is excellent. The all-around best are surely *The Fabulous Fats Navarro, Volume 1* (Blue Note 81531) and *Volume 2* (Blue Note 81532), on which the trumpeter is heard in a number of different recording situations, nearly all of which are led by pianist-composer Tadd Dameron. Navarro's rich tone makes tracks like *Volume 1*'s "Our Delight" and "Dameronia" into some of the most luscious-sounding performances of the late 1940s. *Volume 1* also features two takes of both "The Chase," on which the trumpeter takes two crackling up-tempo choruses, and "The Squirrel," a medium-tempo blues with three terrifically relaxed and stinging trumpet choruses. Also present here is the famous "Casbah," a Dameron original on the chords of "Out of Nowhere," on which vocalist Rae Pearl sings a wordless melody and Navarro takes a fine half-chorus.

*Volume 2* includes five tracks matching Navarro with another well-known bop trumpeter, Howard McGhee, who made several records with Charlie Parker in the late 1940s. The best things from the date are undoubtedly the two takes of "Double Talk," an up-tempo composition by the two trumpeters on which they trade ideas in an escalating match of wits, technique, and imagination. "Double Talk" was recorded on a 12-inch 78-rpm record rather than the usual 10-inch type, allowing for five and a half minutes of playing time rather than the normal three or so. By the way, the liner notes have the order of trumpet soloists mixed up; Navarro takes the first chorus, then McGhee takes one, then they split a chorus before solos from piano and alto sax. After the others solo, Navarro and McGhee return and exchange sixteen-bar sections, then a chorus of eights, then a final chorus of four-bar exchanges and out. "Double Talk" is one of the most exciting records of the late 1940s. On *Volume 2*, Navarro also takes great solos on both takes of the Dameron-led "Jahbero," which features the conga drumming of Chano Pozo, the Cuban drummer whom Dizzy Gillespie introduced in his big band, and "Lady Bird," a well-known Dameron composition.

Navarro and piano innovator Bud Powell teamed up a number of times; certainly their most famous meeting was the 1949 session, including a young Sonny Rollins on tenor, which produced the bop classics "Wail," "52nd Street Theme," "Bouncing with Bud," and "Dance of the Infidels." Available (in several takes apiece) on *The Amazing Bud Powell, Volume 1* (Blue Note 81503), they are landmark sides for all concerned. Navarro is joined by both Powell and Dameron on various sides collected on *Fats Navarro: Fat Girl* (Savoy SJL 2216; the title makes reference to a nickname of Navarro's). Among the Dameron-led sides here are "Nostalgia," which is another lovely line based on "Out of Nowhere," "The Tadd Walk," an up-tempo Dameron line based on the tune "Sunday" and containing two fantastic muted trumpet choruses, and several sides recorded with the seldom-heard baritonist Leo Parker. Navarro and Powell are together here for four 1946 performances by a recording group called the Bebop Boys, which also included Sonny Stitt on alto and a young Kenny Dorham on trumpet. Originally released as two-part performances on both sides of 10-inch discs, these, too, give the soloists extended time to play. Navarro is in top form here, especially on the Powell original "Webb City." If you like Navarro, this set is highly recommended.

The Bebop Boys, with only one minor difference in personnel, had gone into the RCA studios the day before the Savoy session and recorded four tunes under the name Kenny Clarke and His 52nd Street Boys. Available on *The Bebop Revolution* (RCA/Bluebird 2177-2-RB), the tracks, while shorter, have better sound than the Savoys. On "Royal Roost" (which Sonny Rollins and John Coltrane would record together ten years later as "Tenor Madness"), Navarro follows Kenny Dorham's two trumpet choruses with two extremely brilliant ones of his own. The set also contains a 1947 track on which Navarro plays Dameron's "Half Step Down, Please" with a recording group led by Coleman Hawkins, always one to encourage the younger musicians of the 1940s.

Other intriguing Navarro guest appearances may be found on *Dexter Gordon: Long Tall Dexter* (Savoy SJL 2211), on which the trumpeter teams up with the great bop tenor player for four 1947 sides, and *The Bebop Era* (Columbia CK 40972), on which Navarro can be heard with both Bud Powell and Charlie Parker in a live performance from Birdland recorded in the summer of 1950, not long before the trumpeter died. Navarro takes a characteristic solo, and he and Parker trade electrifying fours at the end of the tune. The rest of the material from this evening goes in and out of print regularly, often on various marginal labels. Look for it; it is one of the very best of the best matchups of giants you'll ever hear.

Also worth picking up if you like this style is *Fats Navarro with the Tadd Dameron Band* (Milestone MCD-47041-2), a collection of 1948 broadcasts by the Dameron band from the Royal Roost. The sound isn't that great, since the performances were taken from broadcasts, but the set contains some stunning work from Navarro throughout, as well as good glimpses of other bebop stalwarts such as trombonist Kai Winding, tenor saxophonist Allen Eager, and the little-heard altoist Rudy Williams.

## MILES DAVIS

Miles Davis is arguably the most influential musician and bandleader who emerged after Charlie Parker. Although he gained his first major exposure playing with Parker, he was the center of a kind of countertradition, usually called cool jazz, that developed just after bebop. At a time when nearly everyone of a certain age was trying to play a highly charged, emotionally intense version of the complicated new music, Davis put together both an instrumental and an ensemble style that captured emotional territory left up for grabs by most of his contemporaries. Others at the time were thinking along the same lines, but Davis had the vision and the unique instrumental voice to focus those thoughts.

But "cool," like most such labels, is no more than a shorthand for certain stylistic and temperamental tendencies. Throughout his career, Davis would swing back and forth between the aerated sounds of *Birth of the Cool* and *Kind of Blue* and the hot sounds of the "Conception" and "Walkin'" sessions. So beware all labels.

Davis recorded copiously over a period of about forty-five years; his career went through a number of discrete phases, like Picasso's, and it was largely this constant changing and artistic urgency that make him such a fascinating figure. In the late 1960s he discovered electric music, and he recorded little of value afterward. But almost everything he recorded before then, with a few exceptions, is worth having.

Much of it has been issued in several different forms, and the choices can be confusing. I will give the titles and numbers of the records and discs in their most easily available form. One note: I give the Original Jazz Classics series titles and numbers for all of Davis's Prestige recordings of the early 1950s, but all have been collected on the eight-CD box *Miles Davis Chronicle: The Complete Prestige Recordings 1951–1956* (Prestige PCD-012-2).

### BEGINNINGS

We get a first real glimpse of what Davis was about on Charlie Parker's Savoy and Dial recordings. Davis's sensibility was, obviously, set strongly in a certain direction at a very young age (he was nineteen at the time of his first session with Bird). Davis leaves lots of space in his solos on "Billie's Bounce" and "Now's the Time" (available on *Bird/The Savoy Recordings (Master Takes) Volume 1* [Savoy ZDS 4402]); his lines are legato, full of long notes, and not heavily accented. His playing is as different from Bird's in tone and affect as lime sherbet is from pork chops.

For someone that young to play in such a different style from the leader on their first recording together says something about Davis's character, especially because the new music aesthetic of that time placed so much emphasis on dexterity (one of Bird's tunes was named for it) and quick rhythmic and harmonic thinking. His cup-muted solo on "Thriving from a Riff" shows that he had those qualities to call on, too, when he wanted to; the underplayed, cool style was a matter of choice. A footnote: Davis's "Now's the Time" solo was quoted thirteen years later by Davis's pianist Red Garland in his solo on "Straight, No Chaser" on the 1958 *Milestones* (Columbia CK 40837) album.

By 1947, after some time with singer Billy Eckstine's big band, Davis was sharing the front line of the most important jazz group of the day with Charlie Parker. On the recordings the quintet made for Dial records (available as *The Legendary Dial Masters, Volume 1* [Stash ST-CD-23] and *Volume 2* [Stash ST-CD-25] and as *Bird on Dial, Volumes 1–6* [Spotlite 101–106]), especially, the contrast between his tone and Bird's is refreshing, and Davis makes some classic statements. Listen to the way he comes in after Bird's solo on "Scrapple from the Apple" (the "alternate" – actually the take originally released on 78-rpm record – on *The Legendary Dial Masters, Volume 2*); this is a fully conceived melodic statement. Dizzy Gillespie went toe-to-toe with Bird on the Musicraft recordings, matching technique and fiery inventiveness against the same; but in Davis, Bird had found someone to complement him rather than express the same solo sensibility. The rhythm section, too, provided a cooler setting for Bird's melodic inventiveness but a very swinging one. Much of the credit goes to drummer Max Roach. Two years later, when Davis put some of his ideas together in the *Birth of the Cool* sessions, he'd use Roach again on drums.

Most great soloists seem to be playing a couple of parts at the same time, balancing their phrases with others that echo or counterbalance them, as if in an ongoing gloss on their own thoughts. Davis learned, I'm sure, about internal answering phrases from Bird. Listen to Bird's solo on "Dewey Square" – behind the beat, warm, full of parallel and answering phrases – followed by Davis's legato, almost melancholy statement. On these sides, Bird is reined in, making complete and controlled melodies. Could Davis have had anything to do with it? The Dial sides are classics of the music. The records the quintet made for Savoy are less consistently melodically inventive, and the sound quality is starker. But they made classic music for both labels.

One interesting session they made together during this period, for Savoy, was with the regular working group (with Nelson Boyd instead of Tommy Potter and John Lewis instead of Duke Jordan) but under Davis's leadership and with Bird playing tenor (available on *First Miles* [Savoy ZDS 1196]). "Milestones," "Little Willie Leaps," "Half Nelson," and "Sippin' at Bell's" are all listed as Davis compositions, although researcher Phil Schaap claims that "Milestones" was penned by John Lewis. They have a coolness about them, too, especially "Milestones," on which the whole sound, with Bird playing low and in unison with a cup-muted Miles, is shady and cool. What makes it cool? There are not a lot of notes, the tempo is moderate, and the lines are legato and evenly accented rather than heavily accented and staccato. Bird's sound on tenor wasn't as piercing as his alto sound, either. "Sippin' at Bell's" is a blues with interesting substitute changes; Miles plays open horn on this one. "Sippin'" was also recorded in a session under pianist Sonny Clark's leadership ten years later (available on *Cool Struttin'* [Blue Note 46513]), with trumpeter Art Farmer and altoist Jackie McLean.

By 1949 Miles was ready to feature himself in an orchestrated setting that would bring out his "Milestones" side – harmonically sophisticated, legato and lightly accented, unison between high and low instruments, a cushioned sound. The result was what became known as the *Birth of the Cool* sessions (available as *Birth of the Cool* [Capitol 7 92862 2]).

In the Ensembles section, I noted that the *Birth of the Cool* sides were to the rest of the modern movement what the 1927 Bix Beiderbecke–Frank Trumbauer sides were to the other small-group jazz of their day. Note also the similarities between Beiderbecke's cornet sound on "Singin' the Blues" (available on *Bix Beiderbecke, Volume 1: Singin' the Blues* [Columbia CK 45450]), for example, and Davis's on any number of sides from the 1951–1953 era, such as "Dear Old Stockholm" on Blue Note or "When Lights Are Low" on Prestige. Lester "Pres" Young felt a special affinity for Frank Trumbauer's playing; Davis was certainly a temperamental heir of Young's; both sound like men who are very sensitive inside and hide it one way or another on the outside, men with certain androgynous qualities who like to surprise people, great melodists, whose lyrical and melodic strengths were combined with a softness or delicacy of tone.

Many of the players who became associated with the so-called cool school were in fact strict Lester Young devotees. The poise involved in coming up with those graceful, perfectly balanced melodic inventions was what they were going for, rather than flat-out or percussive expressionism. In fact, the leadoff tune of *Birth of the Cool*, "Jeru," by baritone saxophonist Gerry Mulligan, who was to go on from there to make a large name for himself, is based on a phrase that Young played at the end of his 1944 Keynote recording of "Sometimes I'm Happy" (Young quoted it himself from an old song called "My Sweetie Went Away").

As for Davis himself, his sound is sharper and more piercing than it is on the Parker recordings; it has, in fact, hardened into what it would be until about 1954, when it would again shift, take on a little more of a Clifford Brownish, clarion type of sound on open horn and when he would begin using the Harmon mute in earnest. At times his dexterity is reminiscent of Fats Navarro's (for an illustration of Davis bopping at full throttle, listen to his solos on "Move," "Hot House," and "Ornithology" – with an all-star group including Bud Powell, Sonny Stitt, and Max Roach – on *Charlie Parker and the Stars of Modern Jazz at Carnegie Hall, Christmas 1949* [Jass J-CD-16]), but his sound on long held notes is unmistakable, the articulation is softer, the notes slur into each other more, and there is more space left in his solos.

Davis doesn't try to fill every moment with notes; sometimes he lets a little time pass, which focuses attention on what the rhythm section is doing, i.e., on the background. An example of that is the Davis/Sonny Rollins version of "Oleo" from June 1954 (available on *Bags Groove* [Prestige/OJC-245]), in which Rollins sometimes lets two measures go by without playing. Thelonious Monk was also an exponent of this philosophy, which all great players use in their way. Some just put more of an emphasis on it than others do.

Davis also used space in another way, which is, in a sense, percussively. Sometimes in these recordings (in "Venus de Milo" particularly) he will lead you to expect a note in a certain place, usually by playing a repeated rhythmic figure, then he leaves out the note, often an accented note and often at the end of a phrase. No wonder he was a good boxer, one of his big hobbies (he was friends with Sugar Ray Robinson). He would use this device throughout his career.

Not long after these epochal recordings, Davis's career went into a kind of eclipse. There are a number of recordings from the next five years, but he sometimes had trouble getting work, and this was compounded by personal problems – 1950s parlance for drug addiction. He wasn't at the helm of a project as ambitious as the *Birth of the Cool* sessions again until 1957.

### BLUING

The first session after *Birth of the Cool* that is worth buying is what is usually called the "Conception" session, with Sonny Rollins and nineteen-year-old Jackie McLean, from October 1951. But a few other sessions that took place before that one should at least be mentioned.

In May 1950 Davis went into the studio to record some sides with Sarah Vaughan and with a small group including Budd Johnson and trombonist Bennie Green. Available on *The Divine Sarah Vaughan: The Columbia Years, 1949–1953* (Columbia C2K 44165), the eight sides recorded that day feature Davis very sparingly, although he does take a nice sixteen-bar solo on a medium-tempo version of "Nice Work If You Can Get It." His eight-bar bridge on "Ain't Misbehavin'" is full of a huge sadness.

January of 1951 found Davis and Max Roach in the studio again with Charlie Parker; they recorded a medium-tempo blues, "Au Privave," a themeless, up-tempo ride through the chords of "Out of Nowhere," which they called "She Rote," one of Bird's favorite tunes, "Star Eyes," and a slow walking-tempo "K.C. Blues," available on *Charlie Parker, The Verve Years, 1950–51* (Verve 821 684-1). Davis makes cogent statements on all four tunes, and Bird is in top form.

On his first Prestige session as a leader (available on *Miles Davis and Horns* [Prestige/OJC-053]), from May 1951, Davis was teamed with new tenor star Sonny Rollins for the first of several studio occasions, and Bennie Green shows up again, too. There's a pleasant, medium-tempo version of "Whispering," two poignant takes of Rodgers and Hart's "The Blue Room," and a relaxed blues called "Down." "Morpheus," by pianist-composer John Lewis, later of the Modern Jazz Quartet, is interesting, as many writers have noted, for its combination of up-tempo bebop playing and its formal, almost modern classical structure. Not an entirely successful piece, but an interesting one.

Some of the same kind of experimenting with an almost contemporary classical sound can also be heard on Davis's next session (included on *Miles Davis/Stan Getz/Lee Konitz – Conception* [Prestige/OJC-1726]), where he recorded as a sideman with alto saxophonist Lee Konitz. Two of the pieces were composed by George Russell, an important modern composer. But if you're looking for Davis, there are better places to look.

One of those places is definitely on Davis's next Prestige session, from October 1951 (available as *Miles Davis Featuring Sonny Rollins: Dig* [Prestige/ OJC-005]), with a sextet including Sonny Rollins again, altoist Jackie McLean on his first recording, and a rhythm section of Walter Bishop, Jr., Tommy Potter, and Art Blakey. Blakey is largely responsible for making this session a cooker, a definite departure from the so-called cool approach. If there was anything Blakey liked to do more than swing, it was to swing some more.

There's a lot to listen for here in Davis's playing, a lot you can learn about the way he thinks. A good place to start is in his long solo on "Bluing," a medium, walking-tempo blues where he really reaches into his bag of tricks and pulls out a classic blues solo. His tone is very clear here. Listen to the fluttering device he uses to make a rhythmic point as he goes from his second chorus into his third. Perhaps because Blakey is such an aggressive presence, Davis seems to be thinking in terms of rhythmic shapes. In his fourth chorus, listen closely to how he staggers percussive, broken phrases one after the other, as if trying to elicit a response from Blakey. This technique of playing only a part of a phrase, stopping at odd places (usually on the up beat), and picking it up a beat or two later was probably something he learned from Bird, who made scintillating use of it four years earlier on the Dial "Klactoveed-sedstene," to name one example when Davis was standing next to him in the studio. In any case, it's fun and instructive to notice how Rollins, in his solo, does the same thing; it is a technique that he has used throughout his career.

Davis sounds happy, even buoyant, on this session. He sounds especially so on his beautiful reading of the medium-tempo standard "It's Only a Paper Moon." Some of the buoyancy of this session, again, must be attributed to Blakey, who accents on the second and fourth beats of every measure (instead of Roach's even four), which imparts a different, often more swinging feeling to the rhythm section and tends to elicit different accenting from the soloists.

You can hear this, too, on "Out of the Blue," based on the chords of the standard "Get Happy." On this tune, as elsewhere in this session, Davis shows off some half-valve effects, used for expressive effect, and on his second solo, listen for the way he gets all over the trumpet, from the middle to the high register. In "Dig," based on the chord changes to "Sweet Georgia Brown," you can hear how he uses space; at several points he just stops playing for several beats. All in all, this is a swinging, mature bebop date and definitely one of the essential Davis records.

### COMPULSION

In the early months of 1953 Davis recorded with two different pairs of well-known saxophonists; the sessions played back-to-back make for some instructive contrast. The second of the two, recorded in February and available on *Miles Davis and Horns* (Prestige/OJC-053), finds Davis with the two-tenor team of Al Cohn and Zoot Sims, disciples of Lester Young above all, doing some charts prepared by Cohn. Kenny Clarke plays drums here, and his evenly accented four-to-the-bar approach is an interesting contrast to Blakey's playing on the "Conception" date. The best cut is "For Adults Only," which has a lyrical, sweet Davis solo. "Willie the Wailer" and "Floppy" are probably most valuable for Cohn's and Sims's Lester Young–inspired tenor solos, but in general there isn't a whole lot going on here.

The previous month's date, available as *Collectors' Items* (Prestige/OJC-071), is another story. Davis led a group including his old boss Charlie Parker on tenor sax, playing next to the rapidly growing Sonny Rollins, in front of a murderously swinging rhythm section of Bird's pianist Walter Bishop, Jr., bassist Percy Heath, and drummer Philly Joe Jones, who would later play with Davis's great quintet of the late 1950s, here recording with Davis for the first time.

Almost every mention of this date discusses how screwed up the session was, how Bird got drunk and fell asleep, how Davis was in a bad mood and almost left because producer Ira Gitler made a salty remark to him. Somehow, though, some extremely hot music got recorded that day. The results are discussed in detail in the Ensembles section from an ensemble point of view, but it is worth owning just for Davis's fine playing. Throughout, he is in a swinging, bluesy, sassy frame of mind; Rollins and Parker are in excellent shape, too, and it is a treat to hear Bird in one of his few tenor recordings. Each plays great stuff on "Compulsion"; on both takes of "The Serpent's Tooth," Rollins quotes the tune "Anything You Can Do, I Can Do Better," a not-so-subtle message for Bird. In fact, on take two of "Serpent" he does just that, playing a swaggering, imaginative solo, while Bird seems to be having a little trouble – notice the silence toward the beginning of his solo and the slight trouble he seems to have with articulation. At that, it's a fine solo.

Thelonious Monk's "'Round Midnight" was the last tune on the date and is a performance full of sadness. But overall, this is a swinging session, with a lot happening. Davis wouldn't record with Philly Joe Jones again for a couple of years, but when he did, look out.

## TUNE UP

Davis was doing some heavy wrestling with his demons during 1953 and 1954; he made a string of recordings for Prestige and Blue Note (some of the latter were in 1952), mostly quartet sides, that contain beautiful open-horn work and constitute Davis's Blue Period. In a sense he was biding time until he could kick his heroin habit and really come into his own, but he recorded some fine music.

*Miles Davis, Volume 1* (Blue Note 81501) and *Volume 2* (Blue Note 81502) are both worthwhile for Davis lovers. The first volume consists of a 1952 sextet session with trombonist J. J. Johnson and altoist Jackie McLean and a 1954 quartet set with Horace Silver on piano. The sextet sides include beautiful, moody Davis features on "Dear Old Stockholm," "Yesterdays," and "How Deep Is the Ocean," as well as McLean's line on "Sweet Georgia Brown," recorded the year before as "Dig" and titled "Donna" here. "Chance It," by the way, was a bebop favorite also called "Max Is Making Wax" and "Something for You." The quartet sides are somewhat less satisfying, since Davis seems in places to be having some trouble with his embouchure or lip.

*Volume 2* consists entirely of tracks recorded at a 1953 session with J. J. Johnson, tenor saxophonist Jimmy Heath, pianist Gil Coggins, bassist Percy Heath, and drummer Art Blakey. There are two takes apiece of the cookers "Ray's Idea," Bud Powell's "Tempus Fugit," and Jimmy Heath's "C.T.A.," as well as two excellent Johnson originals, the lyrically orchestrated cooker "Kelo" and the lovely ballad "Enigma." There is also a lone take of the Dizzy Gillespie/ Walter Fuller ballad "I Waited for You." The whole session has an inspired feel to it, with Blakey stirring up all kinds of ideas in the rhythm section and very good solo work from all involved. Davis's sound was particularly clear and singing on this day. The arrangements are well thought-out and contribute to the excitement. Highly recommended.

In 1953 and 1954 Davis recorded two quartet sessions for Prestige, which are available as *Blue Haze* (Prestige/OJC-093). He plays open horn on both sessions. On the first, John Lewis plays piano, Percy Heath is on bass, and Max Roach plays drums. "Smooch," a Charles Mingus composition on which Mingus replaces Lewis at the piano, is one of the most haunting recordings Davis ever made, a ballad taken at a very slow tempo, with Roach's cymbals seeming almost to breathe behind the heartbreaking melodic line. Don't miss this.

The other session is fine, too. Davis's "Four" is a jazz standard; the vocal group Lambert, Hendricks, and Ross did a version in which they put words to Davis's and pianist Horace Silver's solos. Notice, on "Old Devil Moon," the use of what is called a pedal tone, which has the effect of building up tension, with the repeated rhythmic phrase the rhythm section plays, until the soloist takes a break and everything goes back into straight-ahead four-four. (Davis and Silver do the same thing on "Take Off" and "The Leap" on *Miles Davis, Volume 1* [Blue Note 81501].) Davis always liked using these kinds of implicit suspensions of time and would later make much of exploring the technique further, as his protégé John Coltrane would.

Davis recorded a lot of lasting music in 1954. One tune on *Blue Haze* is from the next session after the "Four" session, at which Davis is joined by the rarely heard altoist Dave Schildkraut, Silver, Heath, and drummer Kenny Clarke. "I'll Remember April" is an exciting track and is, along with "Smooch," enough of a reason to buy the album. The other tracks from this session, "Solar," "You Don't Know What Love Is," and "Love Me or Leave Me," are available on one of the essential Davis albums, *Walkin'* (Prestige/OJC-213).

Davis plays the whole session with a cup mute, which he had last used consistently on record with Parker. He plays beautifully throughout, very lyrically; the mute doesn't bring out a different side of his personality, exactly, but at that time it cushioned his tone, which was sometimes a little cloudy and brittle sounding when he played open horn. This session is worth hearing, also, just for Dave Schildkraut, who plays some melodically inventive, moody alto, definitely straight out of Parker but original in its way. "Solar," written on the chords of "How High the Moon" and taken at a relaxed walking tempo, became a jazz standard, and Davis's reading of "You Don't Know What Love Is" has the intimacy and smoldering mood for which he later became famous. When Davis played ballads like this, back then, on open horn, the quality of pain in his playing could be almost too much to take – see "The Blue Room," from 1951, or even "Smooch." The mute was a way of wearing musical sunglasses to hide some of the vulnerability.

In April 1954 Davis went into the studio with tenorist Lucky Thompson, J. J. Johnson, Horace Silver, Percy Heath, and Kenny Clarke to record two tunes, a medium, walking-tempo blues titled, appropriately, "Walkin'" and an up-tempo blues recorded nine years earlier by Dizzy Gillespie called "Blue 'n' Boogie." Both are available, along with the Schildkraut material, on *Walkin'* (Prestige/OJC-213). Beyond containing accomplished modern blowing, the session had a very definite "roots" feeling, much of which is due to Horace Silver's presence; his solos are relatively simple, harmonically, using lots of blue notes, and his percussive, riffing feel suffused the proceedings ("Walkin'" makes an interesting comparison to "Bluing," from two-and-a-half years earlier).

Lucky Thompson's playing provides the high points of both tunes; the riffs behind him on "Blue 'n' Boogie" make this one of the most exciting jazz records of the 1950s. On "Walkin'," which is about half the speed of "Blue 'n' Boogie," he sets a deep and creative groove; Davis comes in for a second helping after Silver's solo. This is an example of a performance heating up as it goes along.

Davis's next session, available on *Bags Groove* (Prestige/OJC-245) had the same rhythm section as the "Walkin'" session, but the front line was just Davis and Sonny Rollins. In some ways, it's really Rollins's date; three of the four tunes they recorded were his compositions, all of which became jazz standards, and he solos brilliantly throughout. By this time he was really getting something of his own together. After 1955, when he entered a correctional facility in Kentucky and kicked dope, it all fell into place. But he must have known at this time that, as well as he was playing and as distinctively, it was time to make sure he didn't kill himself.

"Airegin" starts out with a vamp by Rollins, Heath, and Clarke; the changes, like those of Lester Young's "Tickle Toe" (available on *The Essential Count Basie, Volume 2* [Columbia CK 40835]), go from major to minor, providing a kind of built-in drama. Rollins and Davis are both very into the changes here, but on two other tunes, "Oleo" and "Doxy," Davis seems to be playing more simply than Rollins, harmonically speaking, almost as if he were already hearing the different harmonic notion, built on one scale rather than on a series of chord changes, that would guide his thinking after 1957. Davis takes "Oleo," a Rollins line based on "I Got Rhythm," with the Harmon mute.

On every chorus on "Oleo," Horace Silver lays out (stops playing) except for the bridge, so that both Davis and Rollins are free to stroll, which means to play with only bass and drum accompaniment. Rollins, in particular, leaves a lot of space in his solo. Kenny Clarke's playing has a very even four-four feeling here, and it gives the proceedings an almost static feeling. Notice in "Oleo," in Rollins's second chorus, how Clarke starts at one point playing the high hat on two and four, putting a more accented, dance-oriented feeling into things. Listen also to how, when Horace Silver comes in, Clarke deftly switches to brushes; shortly thereafter, Percy Heath is playing high notes on the bass. It's as if the group is a mechanism that has shifted into another gear.

Miles took the scale notion farther on his next session, on Christmas Eve of 1954, when he brought in a piece called "Swing Spring." The whole melody of the tune consisted of a repetition of a scale fragment, which Davis said he got from Bud Powell (you can hear Powell play this fragment in the middle of his solo on "Un Poco Loco" on *The Amazing Bud Powell, Volume 1* [Blue Note 81503]). The session is split between *Bags Groove* (Prestige/OJC-245), which has two takes of the tune for which the album is named, and *Miles Davis and the Modern Jazz Giants* (Prestige/OJC-347), which contains the balance of the material, including "Swing Spring." The cast of characters included Thelonious Monk on piano and Milt Jackson on vibes, with Percy Heath and Kenny Clarke held over from the other session. As Dan Morgenstern says in his liner notes for *Miles Davis Chronicle: The Complete Prestige Recordings 1951–1956* (Prestige PCD-012-2), the sound Miles got on this session is the one he had been working to achieve.

This session has always been a favorite with critics, but it has never been one of mine. Davis has said a number of times that he doesn't like the way Monk plays behind horn players. Here, Davis has Monk lay out behind his solos, except on "Bemsha Swing," which is Monk's tune. To my ears, it gives the session an uncohesive feeling, as if Davis gets up and does his thing while Monk sits there bound and gagged.

The hottest cut is "The Man I Love"; Milt Jackson plays wonderfully, and Monk's accompaniment sounds fine. It starts out very slowly, with Miles playing the melody and Jackson sharing it with him. As soon as the melody is over, there is a break, in which Jackson suggests the slightest acceleration, like a top-spin on a tennis serve. After Jackson's solo, Monk plays a famous abstraction of the melody; at one point he stops playing for a while and Davis comes in, seemingly to cue him or to bring him back to earth. Monk finishes out the solo with a swinging riff that Davis comes in on top of. In the middle of his solo, Davis decides to put in his Harmon mute. It just doesn't add up to a whole picture to me, although there is some great music here.

### CHANGES

In 1955 a number of pieces came together for Davis, the most important of which was the formation of his quintet with John Coltrane, one of the greatest groups in jazz history. Davis would have Coltrane in his band until 1960, with a shifting personnel in the rhythm section. But before he found the exact balance he wanted, Davis had a little more wandering to do.

*The Musings of Miles* (Prestige/OJC-004), recorded in June 1955, shows Davis getting very close to the sound he ended up with in his quintet. Pianist Red Garland is here, along with drummer Philly Joe Jones; both would be with Davis full-time by year's end. The legendary Oscar Pettiford is keeping the bass chair warm for Paul Chambers, probably his greatest disciple, although still a relative unknown at this point. Pettiford takes a fantastic solo on the slow blues "Green Haze."

The repertoire on this album, too, prefigures the quintet's predilection for pop and jazz standards; beautiful but lesser-known tunes such as "Will You Still Be Mine" and "I See Your Face Before Me," played open and with his signature Harmon mute, respectively, show a joy in melody that would help Davis make some immortal records and a lot of money. They coexist with "A Night in Tunisia" and "I Didn't," which is based on the harmonies of Thelonious Monk's "Well You Needn't," both cooking performances. Garland's crisp accompanying style, Pettiford's round and swinging bass lines, and Philly Joe Jones's drumming keep things from flagging, as they did on some of the 1952–1953 sides. Davis's tone is so much better, too. If you like Miles on the rocks, uncut with other horns, this set is a good choice.

In July Davis went into the studio as a sideman with Charles Mingus to record an album that is available under Davis's name as *Blue Moods* (Debut/ OJC-043). It is a strange record, the front line consisting of Davis and trombonist Britt Woodman, vibist Teddy Charles in place of a pianist, Mingus on bass, and young Elvin Jones on drums. The program consists of four top-quality standard tunes – "Nature Boy," "Alone Together," "There's No You," and "Easy Living." Despite the intriguing instrumentation and repertoire, for some reason the session just didn't come off, and Davis says as much in his autobiography.

Maybe it's the chords from the vibes, hanging there in midair, instead of piano chords, that gives the album a kind of sticky-sweet, hothouse quality, or maybe it's the doubling of trumpet with trombone. Every year and a half or so I pull this set out, look at the tunes and the personnel, and think, "This has got to be better than I remember it being." It never is. Note: the material on this album, despite being part of the Original Jazz Classics series, is not included on the *Miles Davis Chronicle* set, since it was originally recorded for Mingus's Debut label, not Prestige.

The album *Miles Davis and Milt Jackson: Quintet/Sextet* (Prestige/OJC-012), recorded in August, reunites Davis with two of his favorite front-line mates, vibist Jackson and alto saxophonist Jackie McLean. The rhythm section consists of the fine pianist Ray Bryant, bassist Percy Heath, and drummer Art Taylor. McLean is present on two tunes, both his compositions, the medium-tempo blues "Dr. Jackle" (which Davis would record later – at a much faster tempo – on his *Milestones* [Columbia CK 40837] album, with John Coltrane and Cannonball Adderly) and "Minor March," a fast, minor-key performance with a good solo from Milt Jackson. "Changes," a blues by Ray Bryant, is a good, relaxed track with unusual chord changes, great muted Miles, and Jackson on his turf, the blues.

A very good live item from this period is a set recorded at Boston's Hi-Hat Club, released under the title *Hi-Hat All Stars; Guest Artist: Miles Davis* (Fresh Sound FSR-302). Davis appears with Jay Migliori, a Lester Young–inspired tenor saxophonist who would later play with Woody Herman's big band, and a local rhythm section. The repertoire consists mostly of straight-ahead bebop standards associated with Davis – "Ray's Idea," "Dig," "Tune Up" – and a couple of ballads. The set is valuable because it showcases Davis playing crackling-hot bebop trumpet to an extent we rarely hear; the rhythm section isn't the most subtle in the world, but it swings hard, due largely to the propulsive bass of Jimmy Woode, who would shortly be cooking up some masterpieces with the orchestra of Duke Ellington.

Before looking at the Davis quintet with Coltrane, I'm going to jump ahead to March 1956, as the *Miles Davis Chronicle* does, to one of my favorite Davis sessions, with Sonny Rollins, pianist Tommy Flanagan, bassist Paul Chambers, and drummer Art Taylor. They recorded three tunes, "No Line," "Vierd Blues," and Dave Brubeck's "In Your Own Sweet Way," available on *Collectors' Items* (Prestige/OJC-071). It's a perfect set – in order, an up-tempo blues, a slow blues, and a ballad. Davis is in top form throughout, as is Sonny Rollins, who had really come into his own by this time, the most melodically inventive tenor saxophonist since Lester Young. Flanagan, one of the best pianists in jazz, makes every note shine like a pearl, swings hard, and makes melodic sense, and the rhythm section could hardly be much better. This, along with the Davis/Rollins/Parker session that accompanies it, makes *Collectors' Items* an essential set.

### BLUES BY FIVE

Davis's classic quintet, with John Coltrane, Red Garland, Paul Chambers, and Philly Joe Jones, made its first recordings in 1955 and very quickly laid down a vocabulary of group interplay that affected all the young straight-ahead musicians who followed. Davis and Coltrane together were one of the great horn teams in jazz history, a perfectly balanced contrast of sensibilities. Davis had found the ideal sparring partner: voluble where he was laconic, hot where he was cool (at least on the surface). Yet at the heart of each man's playing lay a paradox; Davis, for all his cool, could make you cry by playing eight bars of a ballad, and Coltrane, for all his fire, at least during this period had something cold at the center of his piercing tone.

The rhythm section was a triumvirate which quickly became *the* rhythm section of its day, often in demand for independent recording sessions backing up other musicians. (When California alto saxophonist Art Pepper recorded with Garland, Chambers, and Jones in 1957, the album was titled *Art Pepper Meets the Rhythm Section* [Contemporary/OJC-338].) Garland's spare, swinging touch and distinctive block-chord style, Chambers's huge sound and melodic accompanying lines, and Jones's snare drum accents and extremely swinging way of playing the ride cymbal made for an absolutely authoritative, and even definitive, summation of the bebop rhythm section style.

The five albums the quintet recorded for Prestige – *The New Miles Davis Quintet* (Prestige/OJC-006), *Cookin'* (Prestige/OJC-128), *Relaxin'* (Prestige/OJC-190), *Workin'* (Prestige/OJC-296), and *Steamin'* (Prestige/OJC-391) – are, collectively, a kind of summa of bebop knowledge. The rhythm section provides a complete network of support for Davis and Coltrane, making each performance a perfectly integrated five-way conversation. The quintet was one of those occasions in the history of the music on which each instrument understood its role in the ensemble, contributed solo statements of its own, and made up a cohesive democracy of very individual voices. All the logic of the bebop group concept had found a kind of resting point, a balance, in this band, a sort of miniature golden age before the assumptions of the music began to be questioned again – by no one more than by Davis and Coltrane themselves.

The quintet repertoire consists almost entirely of well-chosen pop tunes and ballads such as "How Am I to Know," "It Never Entered My Mind," "It Could Happen to You," and "When I Fall in Love," as well as jazz standards of the 1940s and 1950s, such as "Salt Peanuts," "Woody'n You," "Well You Needn't," "Stablemates," and "Airegin." It would be practically impossible to choose only one of the five Prestige albums on any objective basis, as all are consistently excellent. My personal favorite, for what it's worth, is probably *Relaxin'*, with cookers like "If I Were a Bell" (listen to Paul Chambers's bass-line melodies under the soloists here), "Oleo," and "Woody'n You," and muted Davis readings of "I Could Write a Book" and "You're My Everything." But all five albums are worthwhile.

In June and September of 1956 the quintet recorded its first album for Columbia, *'Round about Midnight* (CK 40610), which includes the classic performance of the title tune along with Davis's ballad readings of "Bye Bye Blackbird" and "All of You." Davis uses the Harmon mute, which was becoming one of the most recognizable sounds in jazz, on all three. The album also contains a roaring version of Charlie Parker's contrapuntal "Ah-Leu-Cha" and Tadd Dameron's "Tadd's Delight," as well as a mid-tempo look at "Dear Old Stockholm," which includes a long solo by Paul Chambers.

Coltrane left the quintet for a while in 1957 to get his personal life together and to play with the quartet of Thelonious Monk, which he later said was a critical learning experience for him. Davis made several recordings while Coltrane was gone; one of the very best is the brooding and atmospheric soundtrack for Louis Malle's movie *Ascenseur pour l'echafaud*. Recorded in Paris at the end of 1957 with the excellent European musicians Barney Wilen on tenor, Rene Urtreger on piano, and Pierre Michelot on bass, along with American drummer Kenny Clarke, who was then living in Europe, the recording (*Ascenseur pour l'echafaud* [Fontana 836 305-2]) features the full soundtrack as originally issued on the Columbia album *Jazz Track* (no longer available) along with numerous alternate takes of the selections. The album doesn't have the same quality of completion that the Prestige and Columbia sets do, but there is unique and beautiful music on it, and it is highly recommended.

By 1958 Coltrane was back with Davis, sounding more distinctive than ever; he had evolved into one of the preeminent tenor players of the time. Early in 1958 a new member was added to the group, alto saxophone phenomenon Julian "Cannonball" Adderley, making it a sextet. Their first album, *Milestones* (Columbia CK 40837), is one of the essential jazz albums, showing all aspects of the group's abilities (except for ballads). Beginning with a ridiculously fast-paced "Dr. Jackle" (Jackie McLean's tune, spelled "Dr. Jekyll" on the disc) and moving through a slow blues ("Sid's Ahead"), Dizzy Gillespie's up-tempo "Two Bass Hit," the haunting, perennially fresh-sounding "Miles," a trio feature for Red Garland ("Billy Boy"), and a strong, medium-tempo Thelonious Monk blues ("Straight, No Chaser") that uses the sextet horn voicings to good effect, the disc is paced like a good club set. Listen to the way Red Garland and Philly Joe Jones set up little riff patterns behind the soloists on "Two Bass Hit" for an example of their approach at its best. Coltrane's and Adderley's chase choruses on "Dr. Jackle" are stunning and give some idea of the power the group must have generated in live performance. And "Miles," in which the soloists play off of a couple of scales instead of off a set of chord changes, previews the radical extension of the modal approach that was to come on *Kind of Blue* (Columbia CK 40579). Davis's playing on this track is especially beautiful and timeless.

That summer the sextet appeared at the Newport Jazz Festival with two important personnel changes: the major new piano voice Bill Evans replaced Red Garland, and Jimmy Cobb replaced Philly Joe Jones on drums. Evans's style was somewhat more introspective than Garland's; it wasn't as rooted in Bud Powell, and it was to give the group a different coloration, although it wouldn't be felt strongly for a little while. Cobb wasn't the colorful, flamboyant player that Jones was; he had a cooler, more laid-back feeling on the ride cymbal. Although he tried to sound like Jones at first, his true nature would come out and, combined with Evans's sound, make a very important contribution to Davis's music over the next year or so.

Five tunes recorded at the 1958 Newport performance appear on *Miles and Coltrane* (Columbia CK 44052), showing the horn players in very strong shape; Davis is in an extroverted mood, even quoting several of Dizzy Gillespie's pet phrases on "Ah-Leu-Cha." Coltrane has begun what critic Ira Gitler calls his "sheets of sound" phase, attacking long, whirlwind, multinote phrases with a phenomenal intensity, and Adderley's singing sound conveys his blues-soaked ideas perfectly. The set also contains the first two sides the original quintet ever recorded, from October 1955, before even the Prestige sessions. The tracks

"Little Melonae" and "Budo" are excellent, although Coltrane hasn't quite developed the strong voice he soon would.

The 1958 sextet is heard in all its true splendor on one of the essential Davis sets, *Miles Davis '58 Sessions: Featuring "Stella by Starlight"* (Columbia CK 47835). Recorded half at a May studio date and half at a live July session at New York's Plaza Hotel, this set captures the group at its most lyrical and at its hardest cooking. The first three tunes, "On Green Dolphin Street," "Fran Dance," and "Stella by Starlight," are pensive tracks with a unique mood; Davis has the Harmon mute in, and all the soloists make statements that are both subdued and extremely inventive. "Love for Sale," the fourth track from that session, is a cooker that goes through bright sunlight and shade. Adderley, especially, is bursting with ideas and energy here; the statements from Coltrane and Evans are more oblique and analytical, making for a fascinating mix of flavors in one track. Two of the three tunes from the Plaza date, "Straight, No Chaser" and "Oleo," are straight-ahead burners all the way; the ballad "My Funny Valentine" rounds out the set.

In the spring of 1958 Davis appeared as a sideman (a rare event, indeed, at this point in his career) on an album by his new sideman, Cannonball Adderley. *Somethin' Else* (Blue Note 46338) is a very mellow, moody set, on which the two horn players are accompanied by pianist Hank Jones, bassist Sam Jones, and drummer Art Blakey. It is definitely Adderley's album, but Davis has some great moments, particularly his Harmon-muted melody statements on "Autumn Leaves" and "Love for Sale" and his open-horn work and call-and-response sections with Adderley on "Somethin' Else." Added to the five tunes of the original LP is "Alison's Uncle," a brisk-tempoed, bebop-flavored line different in character from the rest of the material recorded at the session. Davis plays a happy open-horn solo here. Adderley and the rhythm section all sound great throughout.

### MILES AHEAD

After Davis's eclipse in the early 1950s and his reemergence as a full-fledged star with his quintet in the mid-1950s, he was recognized as one of jazz's most distinctive stylists and as such found himself in demand for numerous special projects that would feature him as a solo voice in different settings. The most famous of these were a series of big-band recordings arranged by Gil Evans and featuring Davis as the solo voice. The three best-known albums to come out of their late-1950s collaboration (which had begun, actually, with the *Birth of the Cool* recordings in 1949) are *Miles Ahead* (Columbia CK 40784), *Porgy and Bess* (Columbia CK 40647), and *Sketches of Spain* (Columbia CK 40578).

Of the three, the one with the most varied program is *Miles Ahead*, which covers a range of moods from the fast "Springsville" to the profoundly moving "The Maids of Cadiz" in only the first two tunes on the disc. Evans's orchestrations are the work of a master; his extremely varied palette of tonal colors always creates a mood, out of which Davis speaks with unerring appropriateness. Davis's melody statement on Kurt Weill's fine ballad "My Ship" is indelibly poignant. Evans fashions a dense counterpoint to Davis's melodic lead on "Miles Ahead" and an intriguingly shifting background to "New Rhumba." But the high points here are too many to list.

*Porgy and Bess* is, of course, Gershwin's opera translated by Evans, with Davis assuming the various solo voices. This is as beautiful and integrated a jazz album as you will ever hear; fans of the opera will certainly want it, as the familiar material is both treated with respect and given a whole new life through Evans's and Davis's magic. And Davis's fans will find no better showcase for his open-horn lyricism on trumpet and fluegelhorn. His melody statements on "Bess, You Is My Woman Now," "Summertime" (which he plays muted), and "Fishermen, Strawberry and Devil Crab," to say nothing of "It Ain't Necessarily So," throw a new but completely valid light on Gershwin's work. Don't miss this.

*Sketches of Spain* is the least successful of the three Davis/Evans collaborations, although it has been a very popular album. The very long (over sixteen minutes) version of "Concierto De Aranjuez" is static to the point of being boring; there is little or no harmonic movement for much of it. (In this, it prefigures Davis's very static 1969 "In a Silent Way.") The music is an impression of the drone-oriented aspects of Spanish music and works mostly off of one scale, with vamps in the bass and percussion. If you like that kind of thing, you'll probably like this album. It points more toward trance, however, than toward mood. In *Porgy and Bess*, for example, there always seems to be a balance of opposites in mood; here the effect seems to point in one emotional direction, like devotional music (or, in the case of "Saeta," martial music).

In 1958 the French composer, pianist, and arranger Michel Legrand made a series of large-band recordings in New York using the cream of the city's jazz and studio musicians to play a program of recast jazz standards. The album that resulted, *Legrand Jazz* (Philips 830 074-2), is disappointing; parts of it haven't aged well, and Legrand sometimes gets too cute. Other parts are good, but three of the four tunes on which Davis is featured (along with Coltrane and Bill Evans) – a promising program including "Wild Man Blues," from Louis Armstrong's repertoire, Fats Waller's "Jitterbug Waltz," and "'Round Midnight" – unfortunately suffocate under a fussy ensemble burdened with the presence of both vibes and harp. Only John Lewis's "Django" really works; the opening, in particular, sets an unforgettable mood.

In 1956 Davis was the featured soloist on an extended piece for large brass orchestra written by John Lewis (the pianist and musical director of the Modern Jazz Quartet) called "Three Little Feelings." Over the nearly eleven-minute course of this through-composed piece (available on *The Jazz Arranger, Volume 2* [Columbia CK 45445]), Davis plays brilliantly and lyrically against Lewis's meditative backgrounds.

## KIND OF BLUE

In the spring of 1959 Davis went into the studio with Coltrane, Adderley, Chambers, Cobb, and Bill Evans (Wynton Kelly was present for one tune, as well) and recorded one of his best albums, one of the most perennially popular jazz albums ever recorded and certainly one of the most influential. Others had made use of what came to be known as the modal approach before, notably Charles Mingus and composer George Russell, but the Davis sextet on *Kind of Blue* (Columbia CK 40579) produced a complete and wholly successful aesthetic statement, opening the floodgates on a new technique that was to have a profound influence on the way jazz sounded.

The modal approach is discussed in the Ensembles section at some length. What it stemmed from seems largely to have been a sense that the harmonic map dictated by the commonly used chord-progression approach was becoming denser and denser and making the music a kind of obstacle course, robbing it of some of its melodic beauty. Davis had always been a lover of melody; the modal approach simplified the harmonic map by giving the soloists a single scale to play on for long stretches, challenging them to use their melodic imagination rather than strut their harmonic knowledge and technical prowess.

The time would come when the modal approach would be done to death and become more of a prison than the chord-changes approach may have seemed at the time. But the music on *Kind of Blue* was a powerful argument for the incorporation of the new techniques into musicians' repertoires. Over thirty years after it was recorded, the album still sounds fresh and emotionally and intellectually moving. "So What," perhaps the most famous song on the album, is an extended, medium-tempo blowing vehicle on two scales; Davis, Coltrane, and Adderley take solos that startle with invention and fresh ideas. "Freddie Freeloader," a blues at the same tempo as "So What," features Wynton Kelly, one of the best pianists of the 1950s and early 1960s. "Blue in Green" is one of the most delicate and beautiful things Davis ever recorded; his muted statement of the melody is unforgettable. "All Blues" is a blues waltz with a unique sonority due to the modal approach, and "Flamenco Sketches" is, like "Blue in Green," a performance of rare delicacy and mood, nearly out of tempo and played over a series of hushed, Spanish-sounding vamps from the piano and bass. (By the way, the descriptions of "All Blues" and "Flamenco Sketches" in the album notes are reversed; the remarks about the one actually apply to the other.) *Kind of Blue* would rank in just about anyone's list of the top ten (or top five, for that matter) jazz albums ever recorded; if you don't know the album, you are missing one of the greatest musical statements ever made in the idiom.

Two sets of 1960 concert performances recorded in Sweden document Coltrane's last days with the band and a short-lived incarnation of the group featuring Sonny Stitt in Coltrane's place. *Miles Davis and John Coltrane Live in Stockholm 1960* (Dragon 90/91) and *Miles Davis and Sonny Stitt Live in Stockholm 1960* (Dragon 129/130), both featuring the rhythm section of Chambers and Cobb with Wynton Kelly in place of Bill Evans, are deeply interesting if not wholly successful. By the time the Coltrane set was recorded, the saxophonist was unhappy in the band and wanting to leave to form his own group. Here he solos at a dizzyingly fast pace no matter what tempo the rest of the group is playing; on tunes like "On Green Dolphin Street" and "So What," which once brought out his most lyrical side, he sounds as if he is trying to play every possible permutation of every scale as quickly as possible, while the rhythm section just cooks along without anything to grab onto from Trane. Davis sounds just fine. The Stitt set has plenty of good playing from all concerned, but Stitt doesn't fit in that well with the more modal approach of the group.

Davis's next studio album, 1961's *Someday My Prince Will Come* (Columbia CK 40947), while hardly the epochal event that *Kind of Blue* was, and is, is excellent nonetheless. Davis plays three extremely atmospheric slow ballads with the Harmon mute in – the standards "Old Folks" and "I Thought About You" and an original called "Drad-Dog" – as well as a medium-tempo blues ("Pfrancing"), on which Wynton Kelly sets a strong and funky groove, and two waltzes – the lovely version of the title tune and the modal "Teo," which Davis plays open. Although Coltrane had left the band by this time, he appears on the title track and "Teo" for memorable solo spots, alongside Hank Mobley, who was, by then, the band's regular tenor player. If you like Davis's muted ballad style, this is one to pick up right away.

The Davis-Mobley-Kelly-Chambers-Cobb band appeared at San Francisco's Blackhawk jazz club in April 1961; the two discs recorded at that appearance – *In Person at the Blackhawk, Volume 1* (Columbia CK 44257) and *Volume 2* (Columbia CK 44425) – show the most cooking side of this group, the other side of *Someday My Prince Will Come* so to speak. The repertoire basically consists of the classic quintet tunes ("Oleo," "Well, You Needn't," "If I Were a Bell") mixed in with *Kind of Blue*–vintage material ("So What" and

"Teo," called "Neo" here). Everyone stretches out for long solos that give a good feeling for the kind of excitement the band could generate. If the solo work isn't always as focused and deliberate as it is on the studio sets, it is certainly fiery. Davis, in particular, shows how he could generate maximum heat on tunes like "Walkin'" by just playing strings of coupled, iambic eighth notes. Still, these aren't at the top of the heap of Davis performances.

*Live Miles* (Columbia CK 40609) presents material from a May 1961 Carnegie Hall concert; the Blackhawk quintet performs "Teo," "Walkin'," and "I Thought About You," and there is a long version of "Concierto De Aranjuez," with a big band led by Gil Evans, a re-creation of the same long piece that appeared on *Sketches of Spain* (Columbia CK 40578). None of it is particularly inspired, and the sound isn't too great, either. It's weak, as Davis albums go. A compilation album of material mostly from 1962 and 1963, entitled *Ballads* (Columbia CK 44151), draws almost entirely from the albums *Seven Steps to Heaven* and *Quiet Nights* (another Gil Evans collaboration, not on the level of *Miles Ahead* or *Porgy and Bess*). The material from *Quiet Nights* makes a jarring contrast to the fine muted performances from *Seven Steps to Heaven* ("Baby Won't You Please Come Home," "I Fall in Love Too Easily," and "Basin Street Blues"), recorded with a 1963 band including new bassist Ron Carter and tenorist George Coleman.

The personnel of the Davis band finally stabilized in 1964 with what is usually thought of as his next great quintet, consisting of Wayne Shorter on tenor saxophone, Herbie Hancock on piano, Ron Carter on bass, and the very young Tony Williams on drums. But for a while before this lineup jelled, the same band, with George Coleman on tenor in place of Shorter, hit some very high water marks in group playing. Probably the highest was a concert at New York's Philharmonic Hall in 1964, the results of which are contained in *The Complete Concert: 1964 – My Funny Valentine + Four and More* (Columbia C2K 48821). Working with a repertoire that had been more or less in place for at least five years ("So What," "All Blues," "Walkin'," "Four," "All of You," "Stella by Starlight"), the quintet plays at a sustained level of fire and invention that is hard to believe. Coleman is a volcano of swing and ideas, and Davis plays with a heat and near recklessness that is still startling thirty years later.

But the most amazing thing about this set may be the way the rhythm section adapts itself to every nuance suggested by the soloists, and by each other. Hancock was a virtuoso with lightning-fast reflexes and incredible rhythmic and harmonic flexibility. Tony Williams, at age seventeen, combined the fire of Philly Joe Jones and the polyrhythmic brilliance of Elvin Jones with something all his own. And Carter was one of the preeminent young bass players, especially noted for some recordings with the radical reed player Eric Dolphy. Here, again, was a perfect rhythm section with a way of setting up patterns of the greatest subtlety and flexibility for the soloists to play off of. Davis, in particular, seems to be basing many of his phrases on Williams's ride cymbal patterns. Hancock and Williams were, in fact, a true extension of the Red Garland–Philly Joe Jones approach, a sort of abstraction of it, capable not just of generating intense straight-ahead four-four swing (listen to the mind-bending mutual understanding, wit, and imagination the two exhibit during Hancock's solo on "Walkin'," for just one example) but of suggesting all kinds of multiple rhythms and cross-rhythms from within the basic tempo they were playing. The technique created great excitement because it implied many different directions for the music to go in at any given moment. The group was able to shift tempos almost at will by playing in half time or triple meters against the basic pulse of the tune, everyone keeping track of where they were in the form and coming back to the original tempo by a process which at times seems uncanny. *The Complete Concert* marks the culmination of a phase of Davis's career and is one of the most intense jazz recordings ever made.

### E.S.P.

When Wayne Shorter joined the band later in 1964, other avenues would begin opening up. Shorter brought with him a compositional gift and a unique sensibility that did for Davis what the advent of Billy Strayhorn seems to have done for Duke Ellington. The band began exploring new kinds of sonorities and compositional techniques. The implications of the kinds of flexibility possible with the new rhythm section could now be extended into the actual forms of the pieces they played; a lyricism was liberated that contributed a new feeling to jazz.

In January 1965 the new quintet went into the studio to make its first album, the stunning *E.S.P.* (Columbia CK 46863). Extrasensory perception was what this group often seemed to have; certainly it was a supergroup in a sense, although its members were still very young: Shorter was already a significant composer and player who had made a big impact while with Art Blakey's band; the same remarks apply to Hancock (except for the Blakey credential), whose recordings for Blue Note had included the rock-flavored hit "Watermelon Man," made under Hancock's name with Dexter Gordon as special guest (available on *Takin' Off* [Blue Note 46506]). With them, Davis was able to extend the kind of work he had been doing on *Kind of Blue* (Columbia CK 40579) and take it much farther, with a lot of input from Shorter's and Hancock's compositional talents (although Carter and Williams also contributed fine things to the group's book). They extended the modal concept, explored vamps, and created unusually structured tunes and tunes with flexible structures, songs where the melody was repeated throughout by the horns and improvised around by the rhythm section – freedom, in short, but always with a rationale based in extensions of the kinds of music Davis had grown up with.

Some of the compositions here, notably the title tune and the Davis-Carter collaboration "Eighty-One," echo the work of Ornette Coleman in their free melodic quality and deceptive simplicity. Hancock's "Little One," which can also be heard in a very different version on his own album *Maiden Voyage* (Blue Note 46339), is a fine, quiet ballad, and Carter's "R.J." is a straight-ahead tune over a series of scales. "Agitation," another basically up-tempo piece with all kinds of shifting patterns in the rhythm section (listen especially to Carter here) which make for a fine tension throughout the performance, begins with a fantastic drum solo. Shorter's "Iris" is a haunting, unique ballad, as is Carter's "Mood," which features some interesting interplay between Davis and Shorter.

*E.S.P.* is challenging music; it will reward as much attention as you are willing to pay it and then some. The same may be said for the quintet's astonishing *Nefertiti* (Columbia CK 46113), recorded in 1967. The title tune, composed by Shorter, has no improvisation by the horns, who merely repeat the simple, songlike melody over and over as the rhythm section changes the context, varying the density, the dynamics, and the rhythmic implications of what is, plainly, no longer just the accompaniment. "Fall," another Shorter masterpiece, is one of the best mood performances in all of Davis's recorded work, a real milestone of jazz ballad playing in which the solo statements are compact and melodically imaginative and the work of Hancock, Carter, and Williams is subtle beyond measure. Williams's "Hand Jive," an up-tempo piece, gives a great view of the way Davis and Williams could strike sparks off of each other; the drummer's fills are always unexpected and unusual. Hancock's "Madness" has the rhythmic feel of a straight-ahead, up-tempo piece, with Williams's even ride cymbal beat and Carter's four-to-the-bar walking, but Hancock doesn't play during Davis's solo, and there is a strangely static feel about it. "Riot" is another Hancock composition, this one with multiple rhythms implied, a tension running underneath because of the vamp patterns played by the bass and drums. Shorter's "Pinocchio" is the most traditional-sounding piece on the record, a medium-tempo swinger in which Davis and Williams again engage in inspired dialogue.

Davis's playing with this group had become more rhythmic, even more pointed toward the drums, than it had been before; his old technique of playing fragments of melodic lines, interrupting them, and picking them up at unpredictable places, has been recast with less traditionally melodic content and more purely rhythmic value, as he seems to be trying to go head-to-head with Williams's aggressive accenting. Notice, too, that Davis doesn't use the mute once in all of *Nefertiti*. This aggressive side of Davis's playing comes out especially on *Miles Smiles* (Columbia CK 48849), a strong set by the quintet in which they explore vamp-based material extensively, including some very different approaches to the blues in Shorter's "Footprints," Jimmy Heath's "Gingerbread Boy," and Eddie Harris's salty "Freedom Jazz Dance."

In December 1965 the quintet was recorded live at the Chicago nightclub the Plugged Nickel. Some of this material is available as *Cookin' at the Plugged Nickel* (Columbia CK 40645); it is this band's version of *In Person at the Blackhawk* – long performances of tunes made famous by the original quintet ("If I Were a Bell," "Stella by Starlight," "Walkin'," and "Miles") with long, exploratory solos again lacking some of the focus of the studio recordings. Listen, for just one example of their amazing flexibility, to the way the rhythm section collectively shifts into what sounds like a slower tempo as Shorter enters on "If I Were a Bell," cued by Carter's playing of half-note triplets, on top of which Williams plays a slower walking rhythm designed to make them sound like quarter notes. This is a fascinating record for fans of the quintet, but it lacks the careful structuring that the studio sides have.

The landmark 1968 *Filles de Kilimanjaro* (Columbia CK 46116) picks up where much of *Miles Smiles* left off – the generation of mutating, spontaneous vamps in the rhythm section creating a very dense, heavy ensemble sound in "Frelon Brun" and yet a surprisingly delicate and flexible one in most of the other tunes, with some accenting borrowed from rock and funk music. Hancock shifts back and forth between acoustic and electric piano, and Chick Corea and Dave Holland replace Hancock and Carter on two tunes. This was the last album Davis made before he dived headlong into electric music and flat-out rock-derived rhythms. The electric piano is used as a tonal color among acoustic instruments. The album moves through an extraordinary range of moods on a very abstract level; there is no straight-ahead four-four on it at all, yet the accenting and the rhythmic feeling are clearly rooted in the jazz tradition. On "Tout De Suite," Davis plays an open-horn solo, most of which could fit over a straight-ahead background, but the rhythm section instead plays an assortment of vamps and abrupt accents, the only time-keeping function being Williams's chattering sock cymbal. Again, much of the melodic freedom here seems to owe something to Ornette Coleman's music, which Davis at the time was putting down in public statements.

*Filles de Kilimanjaro* is a fantastic listening experience, very challenging and full of surprises. It is also the last album in which Davis was dealing primarily with rhythms and melodic elements that had their roots in the jazz tradition. Later albums such as *In a Silent Way* (Columbia CK 40580) and the famous *Bitches Brew* (Columbia G2K 40577) are credited, rightly, with ushering in the hybrid form known as fusion, which took musicians in a direction that I don't feel is consistent with the kinds of implicit musical values that jazz stands for, no matter what the stylistic persuasion or individual temperament involved.

There is an elegance, a constant mixing of the bitter and the sweet, the sweet in the teeth of the bitter (and vice versa), that marks jazz and that is absent from fusion music, with a very small handful of exceptions. The music on *In a Silent Way* and Davis's subsequent records points in the direction of trance and stasis, and I find it kind of boring. The jazz world is split on the subject of Davis's later work; plenty of people think it's good, and that's fine with me. But I can't recommend Davis's post-1968 work as jazz.

## CLIFFORD BROWN

Of all the trumpeters who came to prominence in the 1950s in the immediate wake of bebop, Clifford Brown was perhaps the most respected and imitated. His crisply articulated style and broad, singing tone grew most noticeably out of the style of Fats Navarro, yet there was something more intimate and warmer about Brown's playing, and he is still a potent influence to this day.

Unlike Navarro, whose early death was brought on by dissipation, Brownie was killed in an auto accident in June 1956 while only twenty-five years old. On listening to his long, perfectly controlled, swinging, and imaginative lines, as well as to his sensitive and mature way with ballads, you can hear why he is remembered and missed by all who knew and played with him. Except for a few early recordings with a rhythm-and-blues band, Brown's recording career encompassed barely three years, from 1953 to 1956. But he recorded some extremely beautiful and exciting music in that short time.

Perhaps the best place to start is with the *Clifford Brown Memorial Album* (Blue Note 81526). The album contains the results of two 1953 sessions, one pairing Brown with alto saxophonist Lou Donaldson and drummer Philly Joe Jones, the other with Gigi Gryce and Charlie Rouse on alto and tenor, respectively, and Art Blakey on drums. The sides with Lou Donaldson also feature the seldom-heard pianist Elmo Hope. Brownie plays well on both sessions, although the one with Gryce and Rouse has the edge. Listen particularly to the two stunning trumpet choruses on the first take of "Hymn of the Orient"; the swing Brownie generates, the logic of his ideas, the way each phrase grows out of the one before, the attention to detail, and his crisp attack are all definitive of his playing.

His handling of the very fast bebop test piece "Cherokee" also shows his mighty chops, as well as his taste. Everything here is to a musical effect; his exchanges with Blakey at the end are particularly cogent. And his glorious ballad playing on "Easy Living" and Quincy Jones's "Brownie Eyes" reveals one of the fullest and most beautiful open-horn sounds in history. "Easy Living," in particular, is a moving story, in which Brown uses the entire range of the horn and the full range of dynamics, from loud to soft, even throwing in some triple-time passages that offset his clarion held notes and fit perfectly with the mood he has set up.

The hardest-swinging side of Brown's personality is shown on two discs, recorded live at Birdland in 1954, by a quintet led by Art Blakey. *A Night at Birdland, Volume 1* (Blue Note 46519) and *Volume 2* (Blue Note 46520) contain some of the most explosive small-group jazz of the 1950s. Brown shares the front line, again, with Lou Donaldson; the rhythm section includes Blakey, pianist and future bandleader Horace Silver, and bassist Curly Russell. In a program consisting mainly of medium- and up-tempo cookers (including jazz standards like Charlie Parker's "Now's the Time" and "Confirmation" and Dizzy Gillespie's "A Night in Tunisia," as well as characteristic Silver originals like "Quicksilver" and "Split Kick"), Brown gives out a staggering display of pure invention and swing. His one ballad feature, "Once in a While," is also fine, but the set belongs to the swingers.

Brown's solo on the fast blues "Wee Dot" is exhilarating; he surfs with amazing authority on top of the constantly cresting wave formed by Silver's gospel/riff-based piano and Blakey's driving ride cymbal. The same might be said for his playing on the slightly slower "Split Kick," which, if anything, swings even harder and is even more inventive, as Brown bounces accents off of Blakey's snare drum and tom-tom commentary. At one point, after a particularly inspired phrase in Brown's solo, you can hear someone in the audience yell "yeah!" in surprise. Both volumes are essential.

More excellent work by Brown can be found on *The Eminent Jay Jay Johnson, Volume 1* (Blue Note 81505), which contains the complete results of a June 1953 recording session led by the great trombone innovator and including tenor saxophone master Jimmy Heath, his brother Percy Heath on bass, and drummer Kenny Clarke. Brown takes excellent solos on every tune (except for "Lover Man" and "It Could Happen to You," two Johnson ballad features), especially on the two takes of the up-tempo "Get Happy." The very fast Johnson original "Turnpike" is a riff based on Thelonious Monk's "Thelonious." On "Sketch 1," a composition by John Lewis, who plays piano on the date, Brown takes a nice cup-muted solo.

All the material mentioned so far is included on a deluxe set from Mosaic

Records, one of the most important and imaginative independent jazz companies in existence, entitled *The Complete Blue Note and Pacific Jazz Recordings of Clifford Brown* (Mosaic MR5-104, LP only). In addition, this boxed set includes some fine and somewhat more mellow sides recorded in the summer of 1954 in Los Angeles, with Brown in the very sympathetic company of tenor saxophonist Zoot Sims and some other good West Coast men. If you are already a Brown fan, this set is a wise investment.

Brown's lyrical side is up front on Prestige's *Clifford Brown Memorial* (Prestige/OJC-017). The first four tunes here were recorded in the fall of 1953 in Sweden and pair Brown with another important trumpeter of the time, Art Farmer. Farmer is extremely lyrical and inventive, but, as good as he is, I would not have wanted to be another trumpeter in the same studio as Clifford Brown. The clarity and grandeur of Brown's conception are in a class of their own. On "'Scuse These Blues," on which the two trumpeters trade ideas back and forth, Brown sneaks in a quote from Fats Navarro's solo on "The Squirrel" (on *The Fabulous Fats Navarro, Volume 1* [Blue Note 81531]). The other five tracks are from a date led by composer Tadd Dameron, with Philly Joe Jones on drums and tenor saxophonist Benny Golson taking some roaring solos. Brownie solos brilliantly and at length on "Philly J.J." and "Choose Now," and his beautiful lead work on "Dial 'B' for Beauty" and "Theme of No Repeat" is something to hear.

Three albums recorded during the same 1953 European sojourn on which the material with Farmer was recorded (Brown and Farmer were both playing with Lionel Hampton's big band that fall) are quite uneven: *The Clifford Brown Quartet in Paris* (Prestige/OJC-357), *The Clifford Brown Sextet in Paris* (Prestige/OJC-358), and *The Clifford Brown Big Band in Paris* (Prestige/OJC-359). The quartet set is marred by the rhythmically unsure piano playing of the young Henri Renaud and unimpressive drumming by Benny Bennett, but Brownie turns in good performances on all the tunes, especially the second take of the whirlwind "The Song Is You" and all three takes of "You're a Lucky Guy." The recording quality is a little harsh here, and there is a hurried feeling to the proceedings which, according to the liner notes, echoes the conditions under which the date was recorded (Brownie was rushing to catch a plane).

The sextet album, recorded two weeks earlier, has Brownie in more relaxed shape, although there isn't quite as much of him, since he shares solo space with alto saxophonist Gigi Gryce and guitarist Jimmy Gourley. The rhythm section, again, is a little sodden (except for bassist Pierre Michelot), but the sound is better. Brownie plays beautifully on Gryce's original ballad "Strictly Romantic" and cooks on "Baby" and "Salute to the Bandbox." The big-band set has some of Brown's best playing of the three albums. Two takes of

"Brown Skins" have him wailing, at length, on the chords of "Cherokee," and "Keeping Up with Jonesy" again has him trading ideas with Art Farmer. But for the most part, the set leaves you wanting more Brownie and less of the big band and other soloists.

### BROWN-ROACH, INCORPORATED

In 1954 Clifford Brown joined forces with drummer Max Roach, who had first come to prominence with Charlie Parker, and formed a quintet that would be Brownie's musical home until the trumpeter's death in 1956. The rhythm section included Bud Powell's brother Richie on piano and bassist George Morrow, in addition to Roach, and Brownie shared the front line first with the underrated Harold Land, then with the impossible-to-overrate Sonny Rollins; this second incarnation of the band was certainly one of the classic small groups in jazz history.

You can hear the quintet with Rollins at its best on *Sonny Rollins Plus Four* (Prestige/OJC-243). This set has all concerned, especially Brown and Rollins, playing at the highest level; although they had been together only three months at the time the recording was made, the two horn players shared something special and set each other off perfectly. Their exchanges at the end of the up-tempo "Kiss and Run" are literally breathtaking. Brown's playing on the wickedly fast "I Feel a Song Coming On" is awesome, as is another set of exchanges with Rollins at the end of the tune. This set also includes Rollins's standards-to-be "Pent-Up House" and the jazz waltz "Valse Hot," both of which elicit customary brilliance from Brownie. A true landmark recording.

For a true Clifford Brown fan, the ultimate treasure trove is the ten-CD box *Brownie – The Complete EmArcy Recordings of Clifford Brown* (EmArcy/Polygram 838 306-2). In addition to a generous helping of material by Brown's last quintet (including "Gertrude's Bounce," several takes of "I'll Remember April," and the delicious "Flossie Lou"), the set includes material by the quintet with Harold Land, including "Joy Spring," "Jordu," and "Daahoud," some California studio jam session material with altoists Herb Geller and Joe Maini, albums featuring Brown with singers Sarah Vaughan, Dinah Washington, and Helen Merrill, and a gorgeous set featuring Brownie in front of a string orchestra playing standards like "Stardust," "Willow Weep for Me," "Where or When," and "Embraceable You." His maturity on ballads is hard to believe, considering he was twenty-four when the session was recorded; this is one of the most sublime trumpet ballad sets you can find.

The set with Dinah Washington is a special highlight; Brown shares the trumpet spotlight with the first-rate Clark Terry and the high-note artist Maynard Ferguson. A telling moment is the section of three-way trumpet exchanges on "I've Got You Under My Skin," which Terry leads off with sixteen bars, followed by Ferguson for sixteen noisy bars in which he reaches into the high register for no particular reason. When Brown comes on, he plays twenty-four bars that completely erase what the others have done; his phrases are totally logical and swinging, covering the horn's entire range, reaching into the upper register for an emotional high point, while maintaining by far the most beautiful sound of the three. After this, Terry and Ferguson come back in to trade fours all around, and Brownie sounds like he's out for blood. Terry plays some triple-time figures in his first four, Ferguson follows suit, as does Brownie, again winning the imagination and coherence contest; when Ferguson reaches into his high-note bag on the next round, Brownie answers with some mind-boggling ascending and descending glissandos, followed up with some more treacherous triple-timing. Make sure you hear this. And don't miss the scorching performance of "Lover Come Back to Me," at the end of which Dinah shouts out the closing chorus with all the horns blowing like mad behind her, a moment that conveys the kind of nearly apocalyptic glory jazz can rise to when the vibes are right. A fair amount of this material is available in single-disc sets such as *Study in Brown* (EmArcy 814 646-2), *At Basin Street* (EmArcy 814 648-2), and *Brown/Roach, Incorporated* (EmArcy 814 644-2), but the box is worth the investment. Wherever you start, be sure to get to know Clifford Brown's playing.

## LEE MORGAN

Clifford Brown influenced countless younger trumpeters, but none more than the supremely talented Lee Morgan. Not yet nineteen when he made his first splash with Dizzy Gillespie's mid-1950s big band, Morgan quickly became an in-demand sideman for recording sessions and the star trumpet player in Art Blakey's Jazz Messengers, which he played with off and on throughout the late 1950s and early 1960s.

Morgan had a brash, bravura style rooted solidly in Brown's playing but with an extra sassy edge, an inclination to always take the extra chance, which makes listening to him a little like watching a daring young man on a flying trapeze. But he could play lyrically, too, and he was certainly one of the most all-around talented trumpeters in jazz.

One of the best albums Morgan recorded under his own leadership is the 1964 *Search for the New Land* (Blue Note 84169), where he was teamed with tenor saxophonist Wayne Shorter, guitarist Grant Green, and a rhythm section of Herbie Hancock, Reggie Workman, and Billy Higgins in a program consisting entirely of his original compositions. The title tune is a pentatonic theme played alternately rubato and over a moderate six-eight vamp for blowing, an extended performance with good work from the entire sextet. "The Joker" is a very relaxed, swinging performance of some "I Got Rhythm" changes with a "Honeysuckle Rose" bridge. "Mr. Kenyatta" is a modal vamp that goes into swing for the bridge, "Melancholee" is a slow ballad played unison by Shorter and Morgan, again with a pentatonic basis, and "Morgan the Pirate" is a swinging waltz.

*Search for the New Land* was recorded when Morgan was at the peak of his powers – still full of youthful freshness and brilliance but in command of the story he wanted to tell. His sound is strong but expressive at the same time; listen to the way, on "Melancholee," he shows such control and logical musical use of the lower range of the trumpet. The accompanists couldn't be much better; Higgins, especially, is a joy to listen to. And Shorter, who was to join Miles Davis's quintet later in the year, had mastered his own brand of very unorthodox lyricism – always unpredictable, melodically inventive, and with a tone influenced by John Coltrane's but recognizable as his own. This is an extremely satisfying jazz album.

Just as good in its way is the 1966 *Cornbread* (Blue Note 84222), which has Hancock and Higgins in the rhythm section again, with Larry Ridley on bass; Morgan shares the front line with no less than altoist Jackie McLean and tenorist Hank Mobley. The results are exciting; everyone was really "on" that day, it seems. The title track is a wailing blues theme over a vamp/gospel rhythmic background, with all three horns playing some very strong stuff. Morgan's lovely, gentle samba "Ceora" is a real highlight, with a great piano introduction by Hancock. The album also has two bright-tempoed, straight-ahead swingers, "Our Man Higgins" and "Most Like Lee," on which all the horns turn the heat up in true hard-bop fashion; Mobley and McLean really spur each other on, and Morgan soars over it all. And check out the trumpeter's beautiful muted reading of the standard "Ill Wind." This is a highly recommended album.

Morgan scored a bona fide jazz hit with his album *The Sidewinder* (Blue Note 84157), recorded only two months before *Search for the New Land*, with a quintet including Joe Henderson on tenor, Barry Harris on piano, Bob Cranshaw on bass, and Higgins, again, on drums. The album has a good assortment of material, including various blues forms, Latin vamp backgrounds, and a fine, straight-ahead swinger ("Hocus-Pocus") that will please bebop fans. The title tune is an interestingly accented, catchy twenty-four-bar blues with great solos by Morgan, Henderson (both of whom play masterfully with the vamp background set up by the rhythm section), Harris, and Cranshaw (both of whom reach down into the funk). "Boy, What a Night" is a fast blues waltz that swings as hard as a straight-ahead four-four blues, due largely to Cranshaw's sharp, buoyant bass. Henderson plays very well on all of it, matching Morgan idea for idea. Morgan's tone, exuberance, and sheer instrumental control are a great pleasure.

*Take Twelve* (Jazzland/OJC-310) is not quite up to the level of the previously mentioned Blue Notes, but it is very good nonetheless, showcasing a somewhat less bravura side of Morgan's playing. Accompanied by tenorist Clifford Jordan, Harris, Cranshaw, and drummer Louis Hayes, Morgan plays some tasty stuff on tunes that, characteristically, include waltz sections, Latin vamps, and a good dose of straight-ahead blowing.

### FREEWHEELIN'

Much of Morgan's strongest playing was done as a sideman with some of the preeminent musicians of the time. Some of the best known of that work was recorded with Art Blakey's Jazz Messengers on *The Big Beat* (Blue Note 46400), *Indestructible* (Blue Note 46429), and, especially, *Moanin'* (Blue Note 46516). Morgan's solo on the title track of *Moanin'* is a classic of blues preaching, full of half-valve effects, daring leaps and swoops covering the whole range of the horn, and unexpected melodic touches. The CD issue of this album includes an alternate take of "Moanin'" with an intriguingly different Morgan solo. "Calling Miss Khadija" on *Indestructible* is a Morgan composition featuring some very exciting trumpeting over a churning six-eight background. But all three Blakey sets will be big favorites with Morgan fans.

Morgan has guest shots on more albums than I can list. Some of the very strongest include John Coltrane's famous 1957 *Blue Train* (Blue Note 46095), on which Morgan takes memorable solo after memorable solo, digging way down into the blues on the title track, leaping and dipping at a high tempo on "Lazy Bird," and delivering some gorgeous and assured ballad playing on "I'm Old Fashioned." *No Room for Squares* (Blue Note 84149), a 1963 album by tenor man Hank Mobley, shows the trumpeter in top form having a ball bouncing accents off of the infectious drumming of Philly Joe Jones in a program mixing Mobley and Morgan originals – modal ("No Room for Squares"), an "I Got Rhythm"–based cooker ("Three-Way Split"), a gospelish, Horace Silver–style blues ("Me 'N You"), and a beautiful Morgan ballad ("Carolyn"), among others. Tenor saxophonist Joe Henderson's 1966 album *Mode for Joe* (Blue Note 84227) has some brilliant Morgan in a slightly larger band context with Henderson, trombonist Curtis Fuller, vibist Bobby Hutcherson, and a rhythm section of Cedar Walton on piano, Ron Carter on bass, and Joe Chambers on drums. Morgan's solo on "Caribbean Fire Dance" is especially exciting; notice how at the beginning of his solo he plays some high notes that are actually two notes at once, in imitation of a tonal effect Henderson achieves on tenor elsewhere on the album.

The very young Morgan has some moments of high fire on tenor saxophonist Johnny Griffin's 1957 *A Blowing Session* (Blue Note 81559), on which he is in the fast company of tenorists Griffin, Hank Mobley, and John Coltrane, playing in front of a murderously swinging rhythm section of Wynton Kelly, Paul Chambers, and Art Blakey; it was a hot day in April, obviously. As the title implies, this is a loosely organized session – three up-tempo cookers, including a very fast "The Way You Look Tonight," and a medium-tempo ballad ("All the Things You Are"). Morgan's cocksure, even arrogant playing is arguably the best thing about a very good, if very casual, album.

Some of the same looseness can be found on two jam session–type albums by organ master Jimmy Smith, *The Sermon* (Blue Note 46097) and *House Party* (Blue Note 46546), recorded in 1957 and 1958, respectively, and including the standards "Just Friends," "What Is This Thing Called Love?," and a burning version of "Cherokee" (on *House Party*), on which Morgan clearly shows his Clifford Brown roots. My favorite Morgan work here is his pecking, preaching solo on the classic twenty-minute-long blues which is the title cut of *The Sermon*; this medium-tempo shuffle-beat workout also has a definitive organ solo by the leader, as well as fine work from guitarist Kenny Burrell, altoist Lou Donaldson, and the little-known tenor master Tina Brooks. Morgan can also be heard in absolute top form on a whole album of material on the extremely worthwhile four-record set *The Complete Blue Note Recordings of the Tina Brooks Quintets* (Mosaic MR4-106), featuring a crackling-hot Morgan next to the fluent, unique Brooks, in front of a first-rate rhythm section of pianist Sonny Clark, bassist Doug Watkins, and drummer Art Blakey, doing a blazing "The Way You Look Tonight," two other standards, and two originals.

## BLUE MITCHELL

With a melodic conception, like Morgan's, coming basically out of Clifford Brown's but more lyrical, with less of a bravura quality and, at times, an almost shy aspect that may have owed something to Miles Davis, Blue Mitchell was a wonderful if lesser-known trumpeter of the 1950s and 1960s. That lyrical quality did not, by the way, overshadow his abilities as one of the better blues players of the time. He got his first big exposure as a member of pianist Horace Silver's late-1950s quintet.

Mitchell's best record – certainly the one that features him at the greatest length – is *Blue's Moods* (Riverside/OJC-138), a 1958 date with the ideal rhythm section of Wynton Kelly, Sam Jones, and the often overlooked Detroit drummer Roy Brooks. Mitchell is at his best here, with his sweet, pointed tone and relaxed phrasing, scoring big points for melodic invention on bright-tempoed rides through neglected standards like "I'll Close My Eyes" and "I Wish I Knew," as well as Charlie Parker's "Scrapple from the Apple" and Mitchell's funky original blues titled "Sir John." Wynton Kelly seemed to be having an especially good day, and his solos (as well as his comping) are another big reason to pick up this album, which will be a favorite with fans of chord-changes-oriented, bebop-rooted playing.

Mitchell's *The Thing To Do* (Blue Note 84178) is also excellent, a somewhat harder-edged 1964 set with two of his compatriots from the Silver group, tenor saxophonist Junior Cook and bassist Gene Taylor, along with drummer Al Foster and a very young and very hot Chick Corea on piano. The album features Mitchell's happy calypso "Fungii Mama" and Jimmy Heath's "The Thing To Do," which has a gospel-tinged theme that goes into a bright swing for the solos, which include a relaxed, footloose sortie by Mitchell. Joe Henderson's walking-tempo "Step Lightly" is a good vehicle for everyone as well, and Corea's "Chick's Tune" alludes to Tadd Dameron in a Latin-flavored melodic setup. Corea is brilliant throughout, by the way; you hear Thelonious Monk, Randy Weston, Horace Silver, Wynton Kelly, and countless others in his extroverted, unusual, and highly swinging playing. When Corea plays acoustic piano, his touch and control are all his own.

*The Cup Bearers* (Riverside/OJC-797) is another outstanding disc teaming Mitchell with Junior Cook and Gene Taylor; Roy Brooks (also from Horace Silver's group) rounds out a rhythm section to which Cedar Walton contributes perfectly on piano. Except for two good standards ("Why Do I Love You?," played medium-tempo, on which Mitchell sounds a bit like Fats Navarro with the cup mute in, and "How Deep Is the Ocean"), the set consists of jazz originals, tastily arranged, by the likes of Thad Jones, Charles Davis, the underappreciated Tom McIntosh, and Walton himself. This is a very relaxed and very focused disc.

A newly assembled Mitchell collection, *Blues on My Mind* (Riverside/OJC-6009), presents material taken from three late-1950s Mitchell LPs in which the trumpeter is heard with tenorists Benny Golson, Johnny Griffin, and Jimmy Heath, with Wynton Kelly on piano throughout and either Art Blakey or Philly Joe Jones on drums. One of the highlights is Mitchell's quartet reading of Benny Golson's haunting ballad "Park Avenue Petite," but there is plenty of good cooking Mitchell here as well, and, as the title implies, a preponderance of blues. Anyone who likes Mitchell will want this one.

Like Lee Morgan, Mitchell always added to sessions on which he was a sideman. Certainly that is true of his exciting work with Horace Silver's group on

*Blowin' the Blues Away* (Blue Note 46526), *Finger Poppin'* (Blue Note 84008), and, especially, *Doin' the Thing: The Horace Silver Quintet at the Village Gate* (Blue Note 84076), on which Mitchell blazes a wide and extremely swinging, funky swath through what is perhaps Silver's most infectious performance (no small claim), "Filthy McNasty." Mitchell can also be heard on six seminal performances by Jackie McLean recorded in 1960 and available on *Jackie's Bag* (Blue Note 46142), including "Appointment in Ghana," a modal masterpiece, and "Ballad for Doll." The third member of the front line on these is, again, the brilliant tenor saxophonist Tina Brooks. Like Morgan, Mitchell is heard on the highly recommended *The Complete Blue Note Recordings of the Tina Brooks Quintets* (Mosaic MR4-106, LP only). Mitchell is Brooks's partner for the legendary "Back to the Tracks" session, a classic Blue Note quintet date that was announced in the Blue Note catalog but never released. The session has a wonderful, unique sound, a kind of keening, mournful quality that doesn't impede the crisp swing one bit.

## KENNY DORHAM

Kenny Dorham was one of the most durable and flexible trumpeters to come out of the bebop era. Unlike some musicians, Dorham never stopped listening and growing; he was as involved in some of the most adventuresome music of the mid-1960s as he was in the music of the mid-1940s, as comfortable playing with Andrew Hill and Herbie Hancock as he had been playing with Charlie Parker and Bud Powell.

Late-1940s Dorham recordings like those with the Bebop Boys (available on the Fats Navarro album *Fats, Bud, Klook, Sonny, Kinney* [Savoy SV-0181]; others by the same group under the name Kenny Clarke and His 52nd Street Boys are included on *The Bebop Revolution* [RCA/Bluebird 2177-2-RB]) and Charlie Parker (*Bird at the Roost* [Savoy ZDS 4411-4]) reveal a journeyman bebop trumpeter with neither the technical brilliance and full sound of Fats Navarro nor the ability to project mood and nuance that even the young Miles Davis had. It really took Dorham until the early mid-1950s to carve out a distinctive style, but Dorham at his best was a strong and unique voice.

As a leader, Dorham's best albums are two he recorded for Blue Note, eight years apart, the 1955 *Afro-Cuban* (Blue Note 46815) and the 1963 *Una Mas* (Blue Note 46515). Both make extensive use of Latin and Afro-Cuban rhythms, which seemed to bring out Dorham's most inventive side, and both are comprised almost entirely of Dorham's own compositions.

*Afro-Cuban* features a powerhouse group including tenorist Hank Mobley, trombonist J. J. Johnson, Horace Silver on piano, and Art Blakey on drums, augmented by conga player Carlos "Patato" Valdes; the first five tracks are full of excellent solos by the horns over a churning background set up by Blakey and Valdes and anchored by bassist Oscar Pettiford. The remaining four tracks, sans Valdes and Johnson and with Percy Heath in place of Pettiford, are in a more straight-ahead groove but are also top-notch. Throughout this set, which is a smoker from start to finish, you can hear what made Dorham special: an expressive sound that sometimes became grainy or smoky, an extroverted rhythmic sense coupled with an appealing lyricism, and a witty melodic vocabulary. He is at his most dexterous here; his up-tempo ride on "La Villa" is impressive, as is his work on all five tracks with the conga, especially the two takes of his own "Minor's Holiday."

*Una Mas* has Dorham with some of the next generation's most exciting and important players, including pianist Herbie Hancock, drummer Tony Williams, and tenor saxophonist Joe Henderson, with Butch Warren on bass. The tunes are longer here than on *Afro-Cuban*, where they range from four to six minutes; the title track on *Una Mas* is a fifteen-minute exploration of a samba-based vamp/riff tune with gospel overtones. Dorham seems to love working off the accents in Latin-based music; the seventeen-year-old prodigy Tony Williams gives him plenty to work with here, and he plays and plays. Henderson's solo work (it was his first recording) is outstanding as well. "Sao Paulo" alternates between swing and Latin rhythms, but the aptly named "Straight Ahead" is fast bebop-style swing all the way, based on a familiar riff often used, as Dorham points out in the album notes, as a background for soloists in jam sessions. It is not unlike the little figure on which "Una Mas" is based. Dorham really deals out some interesting playing on "Straight Ahead," constantly engaging Williams, feeding him little rhythmic figures to work off of. Check out the way the baton is handed to Henderson here, by the way – very slick. The set is rounded out by a lovely version of Lerner and Loewe's "If Ever I Would Leave You."

*Trompeta Toccata* (Blue Note 84181) looks like a good set, with personnel including Henderson and piano master Tommy Flanagan, but Dorham's chops are in iffy shape; at times he picks off assured high notes, and at other times his articulation is weak even in the middle register. Still, he plays some very interesting stuff throughout a set with two vamp-based tunes (the title track and Henderson's "Mamacita") and slow and fast straight-ahead tunes ("Night Watch" and "The Fox," respectively). Dorham is very strong on the punishingly fast "The Fox."

Another, very different meeting between Dorham and Tommy Flanagan is *Quiet Kenny* (New Jazz/OJC-250), on which Dorham plays beautiful versions of standards like "Alone Together," "Old Folks," and "I Had the Craziest

Dream" in a quartet setting rounded out by bassist Paul Chambers and drummer Art Taylor. This is a rewarding, intimate album. The excellent *Kenny Dorham Quintet* (Debut/OJC-113) also shows off Dorham's way with ballads on "Darn That Dream," "Be My Love," and two fabulous versions of Thelonious Monk's "Ruby, My Dear." But my favorite things on this are two tracks on which the quintet (with Jimmy Heath on tenor, Walter Bishop, Jr., on piano, Percy Heath, and Kenny Clarke) cook to the boiling point – "An Oscar for Oscar" and, especially, "Osmosis."

Two very promising-looking albums for Riverside – *Blue Spring* (Riverside/ OJC-134) and *Jazz Contrasts* (Riverside/OJC-028) – are disappointing, although each has its moments. The sound leaves a lot to be desired after the Blue Notes, but there are other problems. On *Blue Spring*, Dorham doesn't sound very inspired, and the rhythm section is muddy-sounding. Alto saxophonist Cannonball Adderley is the guest star here, and he gets some fire started, but most of the album doesn't take off. The exceptions are two tracks – "Spring Cannon" and "Passion Spring" – on which Philly Joe Jones replaces Jimmy Cobb at the drums and the focus sharpens.

*Jazz Contrasts* looks truly formidable, and about half of it almost is, featuring, as it does, tenor saxophonist Sonny Rollins, pianist Hank Jones, Oscar Pettiford on bass, and Max Roach on drums. "Falling in Love with Love," "I'll Remember April," and "La Villa" are all good performances, but one can't escape the feeling that they should have been great. Rollins plays well, but he isn't inspired, and he isn't well miked either. Dorham plays very well, though. On the three other tunes, a harp is inexplicably added; it must have seemed like a good idea at the time, but it really wasn't.

Dorham was very much in demand as a sideman during the 1950s and, as with Lee Morgan, some of his best records were made under others' leadership. Some of the best of the best are three sets recorded mostly in 1955 with a group including Hank Mobley, Horace Silver, bassist Doug Watkins, and Art Blakey: *Horace Silver and the Jazz Messengers* (Blue Note 46140) and *The Jazz Messengers at the Cafe Bohemia, Volume 1* (Blue Note 46521) and *Volume 2* (Blue Note 46522). These sides, which are discussed in some detail in the Ensembles section, are cooking, swinging, small-group hard bop at its best and most typical. Dorham is in extremely good form; his chops are in shape, and his invention runs high. All are worth picking up.

Dorham was teamed with Sonny Rollins frequently, both on Rollins's own mid-1950s records and in the Max Roach quintet, where Dorham replaced Clifford Brown after Brown's death. Dorham can be heard on the Rollins albums *Moving Out* (Prestige OJC-058) and *Rollins Plays for Bird* (Prestige/OJC-214). *Sonny Boy* (Prestige/OJC-348) lists Dorham as playing on "The House I

Live In," but he takes no solo. *Moving Out* is one of Rollins's lesser albums, a 1954 quintet performance with the rarely heard Elmo Hope on piano, recorded before Rollins had really come into his own, although he sounds very good. Dorham is featured on two up-tempo tunes, "Moving Out" and "Swingin' for Bumsy," but his best playing is on the medium-tempo blues "Solid," on which he plays an idea-packed solo that ranges over the entire horn.

*Rollins Plays for Bird* was recorded in 1956 by the Roach quintet under Rollins's leadership; Rollins had, by this time, turned into himself. The main event of the album is a twenty-seven-minute medley of standards associated with Charlie Parker, on which Dorham is featured for "My Melancholy Baby" (Bird recorded it with Dizzy Gillespie in 1950), "Just Friends," and "Star Eyes." His tone is very clear and his chops in excellent shape; his playing has more than a little hint of Clifford Brown's style in it here. Dorham also plays a good solo on the sweet waltz "Kids Know."

Two albums by the Max Roach quintet that recorded *Rollins Plays for Bird*, but with pianist Wade Legge replaced either by Ray Bryant or Bill Wallace, are *Jazz in 3/4 Time* (Mercury 826 456-2) and *Max Roach Plus Four* (Mercury 822 673-2). *Jazz in 3/4 Time* is, as the title states, an album of swinging waltzes. Included are a blues ("Blues Waltz"), the well-known Rollins original "Valse Hot," and several popular standards done as waltzes ("Lover," "I'll Take Romance," and "The Most Beautiful Girl in the World").

Unique as these performances are, *Max Roach Plus Four* works a lot better, set, as it is, in a much more straight-ahead groove; everyone in the band sounds as if they were out for blood that day. Ray Bryant was probably the strongest pianist the Roach quintet ever had, and he provides a very swinging center to the group. Dorham is at his best throughout, making sense even on the ridiculously breakneck-tempoed "Just One of Those Things" and taking cogent, imaginative solos on "Woody'n You," "Body and Soul" (an especially beautiful spot), and "Ezz-Thetic," although he is a bit overshadowed by Rollins. This is a hot album.

Another hot album is *Presenting Ernie Henry* (Riverside/OJC-102), a 1956 showcase for the little-known altoist that features Dorham in absolute top shape, with a rhythm section of pianist Kenny Drew, bassist Wilbur Ware, and drummer Art Taylor. Consisting mainly of Henry originals along with the standards "Gone with the Wind" and "I Should Care," the album is well recorded and features Dorham in truly inspired form.

Two of the most interesting albums featuring Dorham as a sideman are Joe Henderson's 1963 *Page One* (Blue Note 84140) and a 1964 masterpiece by pianist-composer Andrew Hill, *Point of Departure* (Blue Note 84167). The Hill album also features Henderson, as well as multireed man Eric Dolphy, drummer Tony Williams, and bassist Richard Davis, in a program of compositions which are never predictable and which engage the intellect as well as the emotions and body. Dorham takes all kinds of chances throughout; the material obviously inspired him. *Page One* includes what is probably Dorham's most famous composition, "Blue Bossa," along with Henderson's famous "Recorda Me." Dorham plays strongly on everything, from the two bossa novas through a fast blues called "Homestretch" and the pretty ballad "La Mesha." This album features pianist McCoy Tyner as well. Dorham also wrote the album's notes.

True Dorham freaks will want to pay attention to his work on nine 1952 tracks on *Thelonious Monk – Genius of Modern Music, Volume 2* (Blue Note 81511), four little-known 1954 tracks with alto saxophonist Lou Donaldson on Donaldson's *Quartet/Quintet/Sextet* (Blue Note 81537), including the smoker "Caracas," Tadd Dameron's fine large-band *Fontainebleau* (Prestige/OJC-055), and a good 1962 set by vibist Milt Jackson, *Invitation* (Riverside/OJC-260), on which Dorham makes the most of limited solo space.

## ART FARMER

One of the most lyrical trumpet voices of the 1950s and since, Art Farmer was part of a half generation that was a little younger than the front-line bebop players like Dizzy Gillespie, Fats Navarro, and Kenny Dorham and yet older than the firebrands like Lee Morgan and Freddie Hubbard who came along in the late 1950s. Farmer's sound, delicate and a little grainy, contains almost no elements of the explosiveness of the latter-named men. Although he can swing very hard and play at the fastest tempos, he is basically an introverted, exquisitely melodic player.

A good all-around introduction to his playing is the appropriately named *Portrait of Art Farmer* (Contemporary/OJC-166), a quartet date from 1958 featuring Farmer in front of a great rhythm section of Hank Jones on piano, Farmer's brother, Addison, on bass, and Roy Haynes on drums, performing a mixed program of blues, rarely done standards (Dietz and Schwartz's "By Myself" and Jerome Kern's "Folks Who Live on the Hill"), Benny Golson's jazz standard "Stablemates," and various originals by Farmer and composer George Russell. Fans of straight-ahead, chord-changes-based blowing will like this honest, horn-with-rhythm set. And it is always a great pleasure to hear Hank Jones in this kind of setting.

Even better in some ways is *Live at the Half-Note* (Atlantic 90666-2), a 1963 set recorded at a famous New York City club, on which Farmer plays the more mellow-toned fluegelhorn in the company of guitarist Jim Hall, bassist Steve

Swallow, and drummer Walter Perkins. It is a more sprawling, relaxed set, featuring the popular standards "What's New," "I Want To Be Happy," and "I'm Getting Sentimental over You," along with "Stompin' at the Savoy" and a version of Miles Davis's "Swing Spring," on all of which Farmer's legato approach is demonstrated to perfection. This set also demonstrates a high degree of group interaction; the breaking down of foreground and background in group playing that the avant-garde players of the time were making their business was having its effect on more traditional ensemble playing as well.

A very good 1955 date is *The Art Farmer Quintet Featuring Gigi Gryce* (Prestige/OJC-241), on which the Bird-influenced alto master joins Farmer and a rhythm section of pianist Duke Jordan, bassist Addison Farmer, and the mighty Philly Joe Jones in a program of Gryce originals (plus one by Jordan) with unusual structures and interesting metric devices. This is an extremely rewarding album, many cuts above the average "let's just get into the studio and blow" type of session. Farmer is at his most inventive here.

Farmer may also be heard in two challenging, thoughtful small-group sessions that still sound fresh today: *Art Farmer/Benny Golson – Meet the Jazztet* (MCA/Chess CHD-91550) and *The George Russell Smalltet – Jazz Workshop* (RCA/Bluebird 6467-2-RB). The former is a 1960 date by one of the best small bands of the time, an extremely varied and rich session distinguished above all by saxophonist Golson's writing, which makes the three-man front line (filled out by trombonist Curtis Fuller) sound as full as a big band on standards like "Avalon," "Easy Living," and "It Ain't Necessarily So," as well as on originals like "Blues March," the wonderfully atmospheric "Killer Joe" (on which Farmer's haunting muted statement of the main theme and ensuing solo are truly masterful), and Golson's ballad "Park Avenue Petite," which deserves to become a jazz standard. Farmer plays great stuff throughout in one of the best integrated, most satisfying programs on record.

The Russell set was a very adventurous record for its time (1956), and it still makes interesting listening, full of unorthodox harmonic and rhythmic elements, arranged backgrounds for solos, breaks, riffs, and other elements of jazz combined and used in an unusual way. Much so-called experimental work of that time sounds contrived or forced today, but this set, for the most part, sounds fresh and natural. Farmer and saxophonist Hal McKusick are the horns, and pianist Bill Evans is featured extensively in this program of originals by one of jazz's most respected and individualistic composers.

Pianist Sonny Clark's *Cool Struttin'* (Blue Note 46513) contains some fine blowing by Farmer in a straight-ahead, bop-oriented context. His front-line partner here is Jackie McLean, and the very strong rhythm section includes Paul Chambers and Philly Joe Jones. This is an extremely swinging set (in-

cluding a version of the rarely done Miles Davis blues "Sippin' at Bells").
Farmer can also be heard in two earlier sets – *Clifford Brown Memorial* (Prestige/OJC-017) and *Wardell Gray Memorial, Volume 2* (Prestige/OJC-051) – that
are less interesting for his presence than for the work of the leaders. Four
tracks on the Brown set feature Farmer and trumpeter Clifford Brown
shoulder-to-shoulder in Sweden in 1953; good as Farmer sounds, it is Brown
who gets the attention here. The set by Wardell Gray, an excellent Lester
Young–inspired tenor player, includes six 1951 tracks with Farmer not yet fully
formed, among which is one of the records that first brought the trumpeter
some notice, a blues called "Farmer's Market."

## BOOKER LITTLE

In many ways Booker Little may have turned out to be the most talented
trumpeter to arrive in the wake of Clifford Brown, but his full potential was
never realized; he died in late 1961 at the age of twenty-three. His best-known
records were made with saxophonist and flutist Eric Dolphy; he also played
with one of drummer Max Roach's late-1950s groups.

Dolphy's *Far Cry* (New Jazz/OJC-400) features Little at length at the peak of
his powers. Listen to the extraordinary range and breath control on his solo in
the first track, a bright-tempo blues by the session's pianist, Jaki Byard, called
"Mrs. Parker of K.C." (usually referred to as "Bird's Mother"); Little's melodic
conception was all his own, and his sound was already easily identifiable – a
beautiful, tart upper register that could give way in cascades of notes to pungent figures in the middle and lower registers. His playing throughout this
varied set (which stays within a swinging, straight four-four rhythmic context) is on the same high level, abetted by Byard, bassist Ron Carter, and master drummer Roy Haynes.

Three Eric Dolphy albums recorded live at New York's Five Spot eight
months later, *Eric Dolphy at the Five Spot Volume 1* (New Jazz/OJC-133), *Eric
Dolphy at the Five Spot Volume 2* (Prestige/OJC-247), and *Eric Dolphy and
Booker Little Memorial Album* (Prestige/OJC-353), maintain a similar conception of group playing, with all members of the ensemble (besides Dolphy and
Little, the group includes pianist Mal Waldron, bassist Richard Davis, and
New Orleans drummer Ed Blackwell) contributing to an overall group sound
rather than just accompanying, yet still maintaining a swinging pulse. *Memorial Album* contains only two tunes, the sixteen-and-a-half-minute "Number
Eight," which alternates between a Latin vamp and straight-ahead swing, and
the bright-tempo "Booker's Waltz."

*At the Five Spot Volume 1* has another waltz, Mal Waldron's "Fire Waltz," along with the churning, up-tempo "Bee Vamp" (on which Little swings very hard) and the side-long performance of Dolphy's shifting-tempo "The Prophet," which has written into the melody an interval of a minor second for the trumpet and alto sax to play against each other. This track has some of the best Little of all three Five Spot sets (and check out Ed Blackwell's playing behind his solo). *Volume 2* has side-long versions of "Like Someone in Love" (with an excellent, lyrical trumpet solo and fine Dolphy flute playing) and Little's own "Aggression," an exciting, turbulent, up-tempo piece. By the way, a listen to Mal Waldron's introduction and solo on "Like Someone in Love" will show why musicians so often complained (and complain) about the untuned pianos in jazz clubs.

A younger, somewhat less-formed but already brilliant Booker Little can be heard on Max Roach's *Deeds, Not Words* (Riverside/OJC-304). Although the level of musicianship on this album, which also features tenor saxophonist George Coleman, bassist Art Davis, and tuba player Ray Draper, is very high, it's still a disappointing set, both for the absence of a piano and for the presence of Draper's tuba, which, to my ears, inevitably muddies what need to be crisp-sounding ensemble lines.

## FREDDIE HUBBARD

One of the most influential trumpeters of the last thirty years, Freddie Hubbard, like Lee Morgan before him and many others after him (including Wynton Marsalis), got his first extended public exposure while with Art Blakey's Jazz Messengers, which he joined in 1961 at the age of twenty-three. He had, however, been one of the young cats to watch since his arrival in New York City in 1958.

Hubbard's sound is full, brassy, and piercing, and he plays with great authority and hardly ever a tentative note. His music is usually very busy and full of energy; in this way, his music prefigured that of the fusion players of the 1970s. Not surprisingly, Hubbard was one of the players of his generation who got most involved in incorporating rock elements into jazz in the late 1960s and 1970s. Many of these elements were extensions of the vamp- and modal-oriented work of Blakey and Horace Silver but without the rhythmic lift and sense of exhilaration that had been part of jazz. Beginning with his 1966 album *Backlash* (Atlantic 90466-2), Hubbard plugged in heavy rock elements, and in 1970 he scored a big hit with *Red Clay* (CBS ZK 40809). This section will look at his earlier work, which was more steeped in the jazz tradition.

Definitely one of the most undiluted and impressive examples of Hubbard's abilities is the mid-1960s Herbie Hancock album *Empyrean Isles* (Blue

Note 84175), on which the trumpeter plays with Miles Davis's rhythm section of Hancock, bassist Ron Carter, and Tony Williams. The set is full of subtle interplay among the members of the rhythm section and between Hubbard and drummer Williams. The essentially percussive nature of Hubbard's playing is really pointed up here, as are his extraordinary range and strength of tone and conception. This is a furiously cooking and, at times, very lyrical record. Hubbard is also heard on Hancock's *Takin' Off* (Blue Note 46506), on which he is paired with Dexter Gordon, and *Maiden Voyage* (Blue Note 46339), which again features the Hancock-Carter-Williams rhythm section, along with tenor saxophonist George Coleman, in a masterfully balanced set. Hubbard's work here, from a purely technical standpoint, will leave trumpet players and fans alike slack-jawed with admiration.

Early on, Hubbard had strong credentials both in the hard-bop school and with the more avant-garde players of the time; it is a little startling to notice that in November of 1960 he played on one of tenor saxophonist Hank Mobley's best albums, *Roll Call* (Blue Note 46823), with such stalwarts as Wynton Kelly, Paul Chambers, and Art Blakey, then appeared five weeks later on Ornette Coleman's seminal *Free Jazz* (Atlantic 1364-2), regarded at the time as one of the most radical and avant-garde recordings ever made. He did something similar in mid-1965, recording *Maiden Voyage* with Herbie Hancock in May, then appearing on John Coltrane's notorious *Ascension* in June. Hubbard, to my ears, never really fit in with the farther-out players, but it is to his credit that he explored those forms and certainly a testament to his huge talent that he was accepted and sought after by players of all persuasions.

Two of Hubbard's best mid-1960s recordings under his own name are *Hub Cap* (Blue Note 84073) and *Here to Stay* (Blue Note 84135). Both feature pianist Cedar Walton and drummer Philly Joe Jones; on *Hub Cap*, the trumpeter shares the front line with trombonist Julian Priester and the excellent and too-seldom-heard Jimmy Heath on tenor (Larry Ridley's bass rounds out the rhythm section). Hubbard's front-line mate on *Here to Stay* is his Blakey bandmate, tenor saxophonist Wayne Shorter. *Hub Cap* also spotlights Hubbard's talents as a composer. Both sets are very hard swinging; *Here to Stay* also includes the standards "Body and Soul" and "Full Moon and Empty Arms."

Hubbard's ballad ability is heard to good advantage on his version of Hoagy Carmichael's "Skylark" on the Art Blakey album *Caravan* (Riverside/OJC-038); you can hear his great trumpet control here, especially a perfectly modulated vibrato on his held notes, and his full tone in all registers. This album also features two takes of his original tune "Thermo." Two Hubbard originals can be heard on Blakey's *Mosaic* (Blue Note 46523), the back-beat-inflected "Down Under" and the complex and fascinating vamp-based

"Crisis." Notice how, in "Crisis," a number of contrasting thematic elements are combined in a short span of time and brought into balance with each other. Both of these albums also feature Hubbard at his best, along with Shorter, Walton, trombonist Curtis Fuller, Blakey, and either Jymie Merritt or Reggie Workman on bass.

Shorter's album *Speak No Evil* (Blue Note 46509) is, by any measure, a classic date, featuring Hubbard and the leader with Herbie Hancock, Ron Carter, and drummer Elvin Jones in a program consisting entirely of Shorter's unorthodox but wholly logical compositions, full of surprises, changes in dynamics, and unsentimental lyricism. They bring out the trumpeter's most supple aspect. Two albums with tenorist Hank Mobley also have Hubbard at his best, 1960's *Roll Call* (Blue Note 46823) and 1965's *The Turnaround* (Blue Note 84186). *Roll Call* has the powerhouse rhythm section of Wynton Kelly, Paul Chambers, and Art Blakey; *The Turnaround* has the excellent Barry Harris on piano and Billy Higgins on drums, with Chambers still in the bass chair.

One of Hubbard's regular associates in the early 1960s was multireed man Eric Dolphy, who had played a very important role in Charles Mingus's band as well as in a number of important avant-garde situations, notably Ornette Coleman's *Free Jazz* (Atlantic 1364-2), on which Hubbard was also a participant, and John Coltrane's small groups. Dolphy was as strong a musical personality as Hubbard; the two make a pungent aesthetic combination. Dolphy's 1960 *Outward Bound* (New Jazz/OJC-022) is a very swinging date on which the two horn players are accompanied by pianist Jaki Byard, bassist George Tucker, and drummer Roy Haynes. Two standards, "Green Dolphin Street" and "Glad To Be Unhappy," are along for the ride with four Dolphy originals, including the engaging "Miss Toni." Despite the claim in the liner notes that "this is the sound of tomorrow, the sound of the Atlas missile, the sound of the Pioneer radio blip from outer space," the music, today, reveals its true strengths, which come not from its power to shock but from the effectiveness with which the musicians found their own ways of expressing enduring truths. Hubbard sounds very fresh on this session, which has a good mix of slow and fast tempos and different moods.

Dolphy's 1964 *Out to Lunch* (Blue Note 46524) is a more challenging set for ears used to the older forms. The program is made up entirely of Dolphy originals, which make use of unusual structures and time signatures. The Dolphy-Hubbard team is augmented by the extremely inventive and flexible bassist Richard Davis and drummer Tony Williams. Bobby Hutcherson's vibes take the role usually filled by piano. This album is difficult but very rewarding; often the pulse is entirely implied, with the rhythm players offering an ongoing commentary on what the horn players are doing. It is improvised music of a very high order, although sometimes Dolphy's way of accenting and playing melody seems to have left the arena of jazz and African American conception entirely. Hubbard's work, here, is in many ways the least interesting on the album; he doesn't seem entirely comfortable with this particular kind of group improvisation. Hubbard and Dolphy are together also for one of the strongest sessions of the 1960s, Oliver Nelson's *Blues and the Abstract Truth* (MCA/Impulse MCAD-5659).

Hubbard is heard in a straight-ahead, cooking context on the 1961 Jackie McLean album *Bluesnik* (Blue Note 84067), on which the great altoist and Hubbard go toe-to-toe on a program of blues in different hues, backed by a first-rate rhythm section of Kenny Drew on piano, Doug Watkins on bass, and Pete La Roca's Kenny Clarke–influenced drumming. Hubbard plays with great power and excitement on every track. This album is a good reminder of the variety possible with the inexhaustible wellspring of jazz, the blues: there is the up-tempo bebop-style title tune, the slow "Goin' Way Blues," Kenny Drew's three very different pieces, and Hubbard's own gutbucket "Blues Function."

The presence of older horn giants often seemed to inspire Hubbard's most thoughtful, inventive statements. Four months after the McLean session, Hubbard was a sideman on a classic album by Dexter Gordon, *Doin' Allright* (Blue Note 84077). Hubbard is heard, again, in a straight-ahead context here, contributing a nice spot on the ballad "You've Changed," as well as some grits-and-gravy blues cooking on the Gordon original "Society Red" and an exciting ride on the up-tempo standard "It's You or No One." A much more unusual meeting between Hubbard and an older horn man is Sonny Rollins's strange *East Broadway Run Down* (MCA/Impulse MCAD-33120); Hubbard plays a brilliant long solo accompanied only by drummer Elvin Jones and bassist Jimmy Garrison on the twenty-minute-long, medium-tempo title track, which certainly has one of the weirdest Rollins solos ever recorded.

# THE REED SECTION

### SIDNEY BECHET

Sidney Bechet's career spanned over four decades, from the New Orleans of the early days of jazz to fame and adulation as an expatriate in France, where he died in 1959. Although he was one of the premier New Orleans clarinetists, he is perhaps better known as the greatest soprano saxophonist who ever lived. A profound influence on musicians as far apart in age as Johnny Hodges and John Coltrane, Bechet was the only musician in the early 1920s who could compare to Louis Armstrong in knowing what to do with an improvised solo. Duke Ellington referred to him as "one of the truly great originals." His sound on soprano was wide, full of vibrato, and bursting with emotion.

Another thing to know about Sidney Bechet is that he didn't make bad records. Everything he did shows the same joie de vivre, understanding of the blues, overwhelming swing, pathos, and intensity. He was most commonly found in a New Orleans or "traditional" jazz format, with a trumpet, trombone, and rhythm section, playing mostly repertoire from the 1920s and earlier. But Bechet was at home with all manner of popular songs, blues, and ragtime pieces; on the traditional New Orleans–style ensemble, his soprano could always be heard cutting through even the densest grouping of horns.

A perfect introduction to his work is *The Legendary Sidney Bechet* (RCA/Bluebird 6590-2-RB), which features Bechet's soprano and clarinet in various settings between 1932 and 1941, including sessions with pianists Jelly Roll Morton and Earl Hines, and one of the famous 1941 "one-man band" sides, on which Bechet accompanies himself, through overdubbing, playing clarinet, soprano, tenor, piano, bass, and drums. From the first notes of the earliest sides here, scorching versions of "Maple Leaf Rag" and "I Found a New Baby" made with New Orleans trumpeter Tommy Ladnier in 1932 and released as by the New Orleans Feetwarmers (a recording name Bechet would keep for the next ten years), Bechet goes for broke, playing to the hilt, his wide, reedy sound dominating the ensembles and lending his solos an exhilarating lift that still have the power to awe. He is at his most rhapsodic in a 1940 performance of the popular song "Indian Summer," his long, held notes almost trumpet-like in their power and emotional weight, and he illuminates Duke Ellington's "The Mooche" and "Mood Indigo" in a way that makes both tunes sound al-most as if Ellington had written them with Bechet in mind (not impossible – Bechet had worked with Ellington briefly in the 1920s, and the bandleader had a life-long admiration for him).

But it is Bechet's way of playing in, against, and through a New Orleans en-semble, as here on "Shake It and Break It," for just one example, that remains per-haps the most exciting aspect of his playing; he had such a strong sense of how to fit into a group counterpoint while at the same time projecting his own per-sonality. He gives the ensembles a life they would not have had without him.

If you already like Bechet, you may want to skip *The Legendary Sidney Bechet* and proceed directly to *Sidney Bechet/The Victor Sessions – Master Takes 1932–43* (RCA/Bluebird 2402-2-RB), a three-CD set that includes every-thing on *The Legendary Sidney Bechet* as well as everything else recorded at the same sessions (except for alternate takes) and the results of a couple of other sessions. This set is a real feast for anyone who has a taste for Bechet; it includes all four sides from the 1939 Jelly Roll Morton session with Bechet (two alternate takes from the session are included on *The Jelly Roll Morton Centennial* [RCA/Bluebird 2361-2-RB]), the six 1932 titles with Ladnier, the famous tracks from 1938 with Ladnier and clarinetist Mezz Mezzrow, and much more.

The continued adventures of Bechet are chronicled on a truly first-class set from Mosaic, *The Complete Blue Note Recordings of Sidney Bechet* (Mosaic MD4-110). This four-CD box has Bechet in a number of different settings recorded between 1939 and 1953; some of the most interesting are five 1945 tracks with rediscovered New Orleans trumpet legend Bunk Johnson, a hard-charging set of 1920s jazz standards ("Copenhagen," "China Boy," "Mandy, Make Up Your Mind") with cornetist Wild Bill Davison and pianist Joe Sullivan, an incendiary 1945 date with Davison and pianist Art Hodes, and a very solid 1953 date with trumpeter Jonah Jones (who always seemed to bring out Bechet's hardest-swinging side). But you wouldn't want to miss Bechet's deep, woody blues clarinet classic "Blue Horizon," his gorgeous "Dear Old Southland," accompanied only by Teddy Bunn's guitar, Pops Foster's bass, and Big Sid Catlett's drums, or any of the rest of this fine set.

## JOHNNY HODGES

Johnny Hodges was the first great alto saxophonist in jazz. Nicknamed "Rabbit" and "Jeep" (after a mythic character in the comic strip "Li'l Abner"), he came to prominence with Duke Ellington's late-1920s band. Except for a brief period in the early 1950s, he remained with Ellington for the rest of his life.

Hodges recorded frequently outside the Ellington context, but he was always set off to the best advantage in Ellington's musical universe. His twin fortes were the blues and ballads, both of which he could play with heart-piercing expressiveness. A perfect introduction to Hodges's ballad style is the essential Ellington album . . . *And His Mother Called Him Bill* (RCA/Bluebird 6287-2-RB), a 1967 set composed entirely of compositions by Billy Strayhorn, Ellington's musical alter-ego. "After All," "Day Dream," and, especially, the supernaturally beautiful "Blood Count" show Hodges to perfection. His sound alone is one of the monuments of jazz music.

Almost every album Ellington recorded after Hodges rejoined the band in 1955 has at least one excellent feature for the altoist. "Prelude to a Kiss," from the 1957 *Ellington Indigos* (Columbia CK 44444), is on a level with the previously mentioned tracks, as is all of Hodges's work on the incomparable *Anatomy of a Murder* (Rykodisc RCD 10039), Ellington's 1959 score for the Otto Preminger film of the same title, and *The Far East Suite* (RCA/Bluebird 7640-2-RB), on which he makes a classic statement on "Isfahan." Hodges also has unforgettable ballad moments in "The Degas Suite," from *Duke Ellington – The Private Collection, Volume 5 – The Suites* (SAJA 7 91045), and several features ("On the Sunny Side of the Street," "All of Me," and "The Star-Crossed Lovers") on *The Great Paris Concert* (Atlantic 304-2).

A definitive example of Hodges's way with the blues is "Jeep's Blues" from *Ellington at Newport* (Columbia CK 40587), on which his insinuating, preaching style electrifies the crowd at the 1956 Newport Jazz Festival. More Hodges blues playing (and topflight ballad work as well) can be heard throughout the ten individually available volumes of SAJA's *Duke Ellington – The Private Collection*, except for *Volume 6* (SAJA 7 91230), for which Hodges was absent. *Volume 9* (SAJA 7 91233) has an especially fine "Sophisticated Lady."

But no fan of Hodges's blues playing will want to miss *Back to Back – Duke Ellington and Johnny Hodges Play the Blues* (Verve 823 637-2), a small-group date from 1959 on which the two leaders are joined by trumpeter Harry Edison and a rhythm section including Jo Jones on drums for readings of old stand-bys such as "Beale Street Blues," "Royal Garden Blues," and "Wabash Blues." The tempos are moderate and the groove is mellow for the most part; the tracks are all between five and eight minutes long, leaving plenty of room for unhurried statements from everyone. A companion set, *Side by Side: Duke Ellington and Johnny Hodges* (Verve 821 578-2), features the same band on three tracks and six tracks with a group including trumpeter Roy Eldridge and tenor saxophonist Ben Webster. Good as this sounds, the set isn't quite the equal of *Back to Back* for relaxed blowing.

Hodges was heavily featured on Ellington's recordings of the 1930s and 1940s as well; the densest concentration of masterpieces from this earlier period can be found on *Duke Ellington: The Blanton-Webster Band* (RCA/Bluebird 5659-2-RB), which covers the years 1940–1942. Such tunes as "Never No Lament" (which later became "Don't Get Around Much Anymore"), "Warm Valley," and "I Got It Bad (And That Ain't Good)" show why Hodges is regarded as one of the very greatest ballad players in all of jazz. On "Blue Goose," a tone poem featuring Hodges on the soprano saxophone, he shows the influence of one of his inspirations, Sidney Bechet. This is an essential set for any reason you can think of. Its natural companion is *The Great Ellington Units* (RCA/Bluebird 6751-2-RB), a collection of 1940 and 1941 small-band dates under the leadership of Hodges, trumpeter Rex Stewart, and clarinetist Barney Bigard, drawing their personnel from the Ellington band. The eight Hodges titles, including the ballads "Passion Flower" and "Day Dream," the blues "Things Ain't What They Used To Be," and the jump tune "Squatty Roo," show off all sides of Hodges's work and rank as classics.

For a good glimpse of 1930s Hodges outside the Ellington context, check out his kicking solo on "Honeysuckle Rose," a jam session from Benny Goodman's 1938 Carnegie Hall concert available on *Benny Goodman Live at Carnegie Hall* (Columbia G2K 40244) that, like "Squatty Roo," shows how hard Hodges could swing. Several all-star tracks on *Hot Mallets, Volume 1* (RCA/Bluebird 6458-2-RB) – including "Buzzin' Around with the Bee" and "Stompology" – illustrate the same point. Hodges's performance of "On the Sunny Side of the Street" on the same set underlines the debt he owed to Bechet for much of his phrasing.

Hodges's 1967 set *Triple Play* (RCA/Bluebird 5903-2-RB) draws from three small-group sessions involving Ellingtonians Ray Nance, Paul Gonsalves, Cat Anderson, Buster Cooper, and Harry Carney, along with ringers like trumpeter Roy Eldridge and pianist Hank Jones. This is one of Hodges's best late-career small-group dates; he is in his prime on a mixed program that leans toward the blues and swingers and has excellent work from everyone involved. Three previously unreleased tracks add to the set's value. The up-tempo, "I Got Rhythm"–based "Monkey on a Limb" has especially good Nance and Gonsalves. Hodges's most extended moments come on the blues "Sir John" and the previously unreleased ballad "Figurine." Don't miss his preaching solo on the gospel-based "On the Way Up," either.

A 1966 collaboration with organist Wild Bill Davis, *In a Mellotone* (RCA/Bluebird 2305-2-RB) features some good playing from a live gig in Atlantic City but is marred by Davis's too-heavy hands on the Hammond. The recording balance, too, is a little casual. Oliver Nelson's tense and overarranged 1970 big-band album *Black, Brown and Beautiful* (RCA/Bluebird 6993-2-RB) was one of Hodges's last dates; the altoist plays well, but the rearrangements of Ellington classics like "Rockin' in Rhythm" seem pointlessly tricked-up. Skip this one.

One not to skip is Mosaic's *The Complete Johnny Hodges Sessions 1951–1955* (Mosaic MR6-126, LP only), a collection of everything recorded under Hodges's leadership for Norman Granz's Clef and Norgran labels during the period in which the altoist was absent from Ellington's orchestra. The repertoire, played by big small-bands (trumpet, trombone, alto, tenor, and rhythm) of shifting personnel, includes blues, ballads, and jump tunes, as well as remakes of Ellington and Strayhorn tunes associated with Hodges from his earlier days with the band, such as "Warm Valley" and "I Got It Bad." Especially good here is a 1952 session including Ben Webster in ferocious form on the blues "Jappa." Some of the material here is inspired, some is merely workmanlike, but any Hodges fan will absolutely need it.

Another set from this period that is not to be missed is *Jam Session* (Verve 833 564-2), an all-star date on which Hodges is teamed with the other great altoist of the swing era, Benny Carter, and the preeminent altoist and musician of the bop era, Charlie Parker, in a program of four extended workouts – a fast and a slow blues, an up-tempo version of "What Is This Thing Called Love?," and a medley of ballads on which Hodges plays "I'll Get By." Others on the date include tenorist (and Hodges disciple) Ben Webster, Webster's tenor disciple Flip Phillips, trumpeter Charlie Shavers, and a rhythm section of pianist Oscar Peterson, guitarist Barney Kessel, bassist Ray Brown, and drummer J. C. Heard. The set is fascinating for the contrast in styles among the altoists. Hodges doesn't compete in rapid-fire articulation with Parker (or with Benny Carter, for that matter) but uses his singing tone strategically to hold his own. On his ballad feature and the slow blues (entitled "Funky Blues"), he is on his own best turf. On "Funky Blues," Hodges, Parker, and Carter solo back-to-back, and I'm sure neither Parker nor Carter particularly wanted to follow the mess of perfect blues Hodges laid down (although both do, very well).

## BENNY CARTER

Benny Carter is surely one of the most prodigiously gifted musicians in jazz; best known as one of the preeminent alto saxophonists, arrangers, and composers in the music, he has also recorded extensively on trumpet. In addition, Carter recorded and performed on tenor, clarinet, trombone, and piano, but it is for his alto stylings that most jazz fans search out his recordings.

Carter's arrangements were important to the late-1920s Fletcher Henderson orchestra; with the coming of the swing era, Carter became one of the most active arrangers around, eventually producing arrangements for almost every major band. Born in 1907, Carter is still extremely active. In the summer of 1990 he composed an original work for vibraphonists Milt Jackson and Bobby Hutcherson, which was premiered at Lincoln Center's Classical Jazz series.

As an altoist, Carter was, and is, remarkable for his pure tone, perfect intonation, harmonic knowledge, and impeccable execution of unexpected melodic swoops and turns. A great showcase for his playing and writing is *Jazz Giant* (Contemporary/OJC-167), on which he plays both alto and trumpet with a small band including tenorist Ben Webster and trombonist Frank Rosolino in a program of older jazz standards such as "Old Fashioned Love," "I'm Coming Virginia," and "Blue Lou," as well as several Carter originals. Carter really stretches out in fine form on "Ain't She Sweet" and "Blues My Naughty Sweetie Gives to Me," on which the other horns lay out and the leader's alto is spotlighted.

Some good Carter-led big-band tracks from 1933 can be found on *Ridin' in Rhythm* (DRG/Swing CDSW 8453/4). Tenor saxophonist Chu Berry graces "Swing It" and "Six Bells Stampede"; some slightly later sides feature pianist Teddy Wilson. But Carter's fine orchestrations, especially for the reed section (check out "Blue Lou"), are the main attraction. *Coleman Hawkins – Ben Webster – Benny Carter: Three Great Swing Saxophones* (RCA/Bluebird 9683-2-RB) has a generous sampling of Carter's alto in various settings from 1929 through 1946, including a famous 1939 side ("Early Session Hop") with Lionel Hampton on which all three saxophonists are featured, with the additional presence of Chu Berry. "Cadillac Slim," a 1946 track pairing Carter and Webster (and loosely resembling Billy Strayhorn's "Rain Check"), has some exciting four-bar exchanges between the saxophonists, and three sides by the 1940–1941 Carter big band are worthwhile for his playing and writing.

His playing and writing are shown in top form on *Coleman Hawkins and Benny Carter in Paris* (DRG/Swing CDSW 8403), on which his justly famous reed orchestration of "Honeysuckle Rose" and his loose frameworks for "Crazy Rhythm," "Out of Nowhere," and "Sweet Georgia Brown" help inspire a group including Hawkins and guitarist Django Reinhardt to produce several classics. Carter's own solos are exemplary as well. *The Complete Benny Carter* (Mercury 830 965-2) presents the results of two April 1946 sessions featuring Carter on alto with only a rhythm section playing standards like "Moonglow," "Stairway to the Stars," and "Lady, Be Good." If you like Carter, this set is essential. On the first eight sides, the pianist is the litle-known Arnold Ross, whose opening solo on "Lady, Be Good," recorded with Jazz At The Philharmonic in 1946, is a classic (it precedes an equally classic Charlie Parker solo and is available on the ten-CD box set *Bird: The Complete Charlie Parker on Verve* [Verve 837 141-2]).

## WILLIE SMITH

Another highly regarded alto saxophonist of the swing era was Willie Smith, whose major recognition came as a member of the 1930s Jimmie Lunceford orchestra. For most of the 1940s and 1950s he was featured in trumpeter Harry James's big band, with some time out to play in other bands, most notably Duke Ellington's (for part of Johnny Hodges's period of absence). He was a very good blues player and was at his best on slow and medium bounce tempos; he was also one of the best lead players in the music.

A good showcase for his abilities is *Willie Smith with the Harry James Orchestra – Snooty Fruity* (Columbia CK 45447), on which Smith is featured throughout, mostly in big-band readings of jazz standards like "Moten Swing," "Tuxedo Junction," "Stompin at the Savoy," and Ellington's "Cotton Tail." Fans of solid big-band jazz will enjoy this set, which also includes plenty of James's trumpet in a straight-ahead jazz setting. *The 1930s: Big Bands* (Columbia CK 40651) includes a Smith performance of the slow and haunting "Uptown Blues," recorded in 1939 with Lunceford's band, which suggests that Smith might have been able to give Johnny Hodges a run for his money on the blues. *Nat "King" Cole and His Trio – The Complete After Midnight Sessions* (Capitol CDP 7 48328) features Smith on four intimate, relaxed tracks with the pianist-singer and his trio from 1956.

An interesting coda to this discussion of Carter and Smith can be found on the Charlie Parker album *Yardbird in Lotus Land* (Spotlite SPJ 123, LP only). The three altoists appeared together in a 1946 radio broadcast, backed by the Nat Cole trio, with Buddy Rich on drums. Smith plays "Tea for Two" and Carter "Body and Soul" – both lovely renditions in their recognizable styles. After Carter's last note there is a brief moment of rest, the tempo suddenly shoots up under a Cole piano introduction, and Parker dives into a breakneck version of Ray Noble's "Cherokee." Although Carter was a virtuoso, Parker threw down a new gauntlet for presence of mind, speed of articulation, and velocity of thought; he shifted the aesthetic in other words. Good as Carter and Smith are, there is no question about where the excitement was on that particular night.

## CHARLIE PARKER

Charlie "Yardbird" Parker, or Bird, as he is universally called, represented the culmination of one tendency in jazz and the beginning of another. In his playing you hear all the exhilaration and heat of the late-night Kansas City jam sessions, which he took part in and witnessed, the heroic swing and dance rhythms of the traveling big bands, and the romanticism and lyricism expressed in the popular songs of the 1930s. You also hear the blues, particularly the blues of the Southwest, in which a note both triumphal and ironic is usually sounded.

But there was also a quality inherent in Bird's playing that hadn't been heard before, although it had been hinted at. Bird was one of the first to find an adequate way of expressing a new mood in the post–World War II air, and his mixture of death-defying technical ability, exhilarating rhythmic drive, and poignant self-consciousness expressed the attitude of a more disillusioned audience after World War II. Eventually, it led to the attitude of the so-called cool players, foremost among whom was Miles Davis, who began as a protégé of Bird's.

The melodic forms, or building blocks, that Parker came up with constituted a new grammar for the music; a generation of musicians used that grammar to fashion their own individualized statements. Parker himself made up countless new melodies by combining and recombining these melodic building blocks over the new things he discovered about scales and chords, while keeping all the fire and the swing that had been part of his Kansas City background.

Parker was an almost endlessly inventive improviser; in the recording studio, when his groups did a number of takes of the same tune, Parker would more often than not use entirely different strategies on every take rather than following one outline and making variations on it. This kind of unrelenting creativity became part of the aesthetic of the music, for better and for worse.

The down side of it was that people were so spellbound by Parker's inventiveness that a disproportionate emphasis began to be put on the individual soloist. Ensemble concepts began to reflect this, with compositional frameworks too often amounting to nothing more than a frame for a string of solo improvisations. Every soloist was tacitly expected to be a virtuoso with an inexhaustible well of fresh ideas. But very few artists are blessed with Parker's creativity, and jazz spent thirty years trying to deal with that fact. Paradoxically, the musicians who heard Parker most deeply, perhaps – Miles Davis and Charles Mingus, for example – seemed to realize that the individual virtuoso aspect of Parker's style represented the end of something as much as it did the beginning, and they began to think more in terms of group sound and compositional frameworks.

Fans and musicians went to great lengths to record Bird in live appearances and off the radio because his well of inspiration was so deep that he created brilliant new melodies in almost all settings. One such fan, Dean Benedetti, followed Parker around the country with a tape recorder, showing up at Bird's engagements and recording only Bird's solos. (These recordings, only a legend for years, have recently been unearthed and issued by Mosaic as a seven-disc set, *The Complete Dean Benedetti Recordings of Charlie Parker* [Mosaic MD7-129], a monumental work of scholarship and love.) There were enough people who wanted to preserve Bird's inventiveness on the wing that there is a tremendous amount of Parker's music currently available.

It wasn't always so. When I first started listening to jazz in the late 1960s, there were very few Charlie Parker records in print, and those in print were all but unavailable in stores. But the last ten years have seen a literal explosion in the amount of material that has been brought out, and the release of Clint Eastwood's movie *Bird* has certainly encouraged companies to issue any and all Parker material. Today just contemplating the Bird section in your local record store is enough to make you dizzy.

### EARLY BIRD

Bird's earliest recordings were made with the Jay McShann big band, a Kansas City outfit that toured the Midwest and eventually came to New York. The band's commercial recordings, made in 1940 and 1941, are available as *Jay McShann Orchestra: Blues from Kansas City* (Decca/GRP GRD-614). On them, Parker shows the influence of tenor saxophonist Lester Young; Parker had spent a summer in the Ozark Mountains not long before, memorizing all of Young's solos from his Count Basie records (much as a later generation would memorize Bird's solos), and the lessons he learned, of melodic inventiveness and cool grace, show up in his solos with McShann. You can also hear the influence of his teacher Buster Smith, a great Kansas City alto player who can be heard on "Cherry Red" and "Baby, Look at You" with Pete Johnson's Boogie Woogie Boys on the album *Swing Street* (Columbia Special Products JSN 6042). Some of the phrases Bird invented at this time still form part of musicians' basic vocabulary.

On "Hootie Blues," Bird plays a haunting, urbane blues solo at a slow medium tempo as the brass play comments behind him. His solo on "The Jumpin' Blues" was copied by every young saxophone player, and its opening phrase became the basis for Benny Harris's tune "Ornithology." "Swingmatism" and "Sepian Bounce" also have excellent solos, full of phrases that found their way into the vocabularies of younger players such as Dexter Gordon and Sonny Stitt.

Bird left McShann, joining first Earl Hines's, then Billy Eckstine's big bands, both of which were important gathering places for the modernists. No recordings seem to have survived of Bird with either band, but a fascinating record called *The Complete "Birth of the Bebop"* (Stash ST-CD-535) documents Bird playing in extremely informal situations during the period – in a hotel room with Dizzy Gillespie, for example, and playing along with a recording of pianist Hazel Scott. On the tracks with Gillespie, Bird plays tenor, which was his instrument in the Hines big band, and we can hear his style starting to turn into itself, stripping away the unneeded aspects and strengthening and exploring the implications of the most essential parts. There is also a great short rendition of "Cherokee" from 1942 on which Bird plays several ridiculously inventive choruses backed only by rhythm guitar and drums. Also not to be missed are some searing exchanges on a live version of "Sweet Georgia Brown" with Gillespie and tenor saxophonist Don Byas in front of a wildly responsive crowd.

Bird's next studio date was with a small group led by guitarist Tiny Grimes. On this 1944 date (available on *Bird/The Savoy Recordings (Master Takes) Volume 1* [Savoy ZDS 4402]), his sound is in place – strong, diamond hard – and he swings ardently on "Tiny's Tempo" and "Red Cross," but the last touches of rhythmic flexibility are still to come.

### NOW'S THE TIME

Bird made some of his best-known recordings in 1945. The series of records he made with Dizzy Gillespie's small group (available on *Dizzy Gillespie and His Sextets and Orchestra: "Shaw 'Nuff"* [Musicraft MVSCD-53]) established much of the core repertoire of the music that was already being called bebop.

Recorded for the small labels Guild and Musicraft, performances such as "Salt Peanuts," "Shaw 'Nuff," and Tadd Dameron's "Hot House" (with Big Sid Catlett playing drums), "Groovin' High," and "Dizzy Atmosphere" set the basic format for the recorded bop performance – a group reading of an intricate melody (also called a head), often at a fast tempo, usually based on the harmonic structure of an existing popular song or the blues (the first two are based on the harmonic structure of "I Got Rhythm"; "Hot House" is based on the chords of "What Is This Thing Called Love?" and "Groovin' High" on "Whispering"), then a string of solos.

These early recordings are actually routined more interestingly than the head-solos-head approach that quickly became standard; unison introductions for the horns, small fanfares to announce instrumental breaks, and countermelodies such as the one at the end of "Dizzy Atmosphere" are a holdover from the big-band approach, in which the arrangement was critical to maintaining interest and setting off the various solo statements. Bird plays brilliantly on all these tracks; his solos are anthologies of melodic statements that would become standard material for every young saxophonist.

By November Bird had it all together for a studio date under his own leadership (available on *Bird/The Savoy Recordings (Master Takes) Volume 1* [Savoy ZDS 4402]), with Miles Davis and Max Roach, both of whom would become regular members of his classic quartet of 1947. Here is Bird laying down a new language, a new standard for articulation, a new velocity of thought. His solos on "Now's the Time" and "Billie's Bounce" were memorized by hundreds of young players on every instrument. His two choruses on "Thriving on a Riff" (later called "Anthropology") are masterpieces of controlled drive. The ballad fragment "Meandering" shows a characteristic feeling, something close to the mood and weight of tragedy, expressed through extremely lyrical melody. But the session's masterpiece is "Ko Ko," a blazing excursion through the chords of the popular song "Cherokee." A convoluted head, played in unison with Gillespie on muted trumpet, a break by each of them, then Bird takes off and never looks back. No one had ever played like this; the effect on musicians was comparable to that of Louis Armstrong's "West End Blues" or the first recordings of Lester Young. It was incontrovertible evidence that there were new possibilities of playing and of feeling.

In 1945 Parker and Gillespie were *the* important new musicians on the scene, and they were often invited to participate as guests on other musicians' recordings. You can hear the results of several of these occasions on the possibly hard-to-find *Every Bit of It* (Spotlite SPJ 150D). Standout moments are to be found on "Seventh Avenue" and "Sorta Kinda," under trombonist Trummy Young's leadership, and on some tracks with the eccentric vocalist Rubberlegs

Williams. At some point during this session, according to a widely circulated story, Gillespie surreptitiously put benzedrine in Williams's coffee; you can hear the singer get progressively wilder as the session goes on. *Every Bit of It* is also worthwhile for the tracks Parker recorded (sans Gillespie) with pianist Sir Charles Thompson and his all stars, which also feature Buck Clayton, the great trumpeter from Count Basie's band, and new tenor star Dexter Gordon. Bird takes fantastic solos on "20th Century Blues" and "The Street Beat."

An interesting study in contrast is a 1945 session for the small Comet label, on which Bird and Dizzy appeared in extended performances with older musicians such as Teddy Wilson, Red Norvo, and Flip Phillips. Several takes of "Hallelujah," "Get Happy," "Slam Slam Blues," and the exciting "Congo Blues" go in and out of print on various labels. All the musicians in the studio that day seem to have gotten along fine musically, although at the time much was made of the difference between the jazz generations.

Bird went to California with Gillespie's band late in 1945 for an engagement at Billy Berg's nitery. Three tracks from a California broadcast are included on *The Complete "Birth of the Bebop"* (Stash ST-CD-535). The band, with Milt Jackson playing vibes, performs "Shaw 'Nuff," "Groovin' High," and "Dizzy Atmosphere." Before Gillespie left California, he and Bird recorded some tunes with the novelty singer and instrumentalist Slim Gaillard; the sides – "Dizzy Boogie," "Poppity Pop," "Flat Foot Floogie," and "Slim's Jam" – are available on *Bebop's Heartbeat* (Savoy ZDS 1177). On all of these Bird blows extremely strong, cogent solos, and on "Slim's Jam" you can hear him talk a little with Gaillard, who introduces each member of the ensemble in turn.

After Gillespie left, Parker recorded his first of many sessions for the small California label Dial Records; this outing produced the classics "Yardbird Suite," "Ornithology," "Moose the Mooche," and "A Night in Tunisia," the last of which contained a famous break for Bird's alto. The break on the issued take was great, but a legendary break from an unissued take has been included on reissues as the "famous alto break," a brief miracle of rhythmic and harmonic inventiveness and equilibrium. (A break at that spot is part of the tune's compositional structure, and it is fun to compare what different musicians do with it. Pianist Bud Powell plays a tremendous one on *The Amazing Bud Powell, Volume 1* [Blue Note 81503].) On this date, Parker is in the company of Miles Davis and the fine tenor saxophonist Lucky Thompson, whose gruff, asymmetrical phrases make an interesting contrast to Parker's gliding, unflappable lines.

These sides, along with the rest of the material Bird recorded for Dial, are available on *The Legendary Dial Masters, Volume 1* (Stash ST-CD-23) and *Volume 2* (Stash ST-CD-25), as well as on a series put out by the English Spotlite label,

*Bird on Dial, Volumes 1–6* (Spotlite 101–106). The Stash CDs supposedly contain only the master takes issued on 78-rpm records at the time, although in some places the producers substituted alternate takes for the actual master takes, for no apparent reason. The alternates still offer excellent music, though. The Spotlite issues contain all alternate takes. The alternate takes are important, because Bird played completely fresh things on each take.

Bird's next session (for Dial) produced four tracks ("Max Is Making Wax," "Lover Man," "The Gypsy," and "Bebop") which were recorded while Parker was having a physical and nervous breakdown. The results are painful to listen to. After that session he was committed to Camarillo State Hospital, where he mended for a while. When he was released, he recorded a good session for Dial with pianist Erroll Garner (who went on to become a star and a major influence in his own right), which produced "Cool Blues," "Bird's Nest," and two vocals by Earl Coleman, "This Is Always" and "Dark Shadows." Bird doesn't seem quite as flexible or comfortable here; Garner's rhythms aren't really appropriate to Parker's style, but Bird blows with great energy nonetheless.

A week later Bird recorded four more tunes for Dial, "Carvin' the Bird," "Stupendous," "Cheers," and "Relaxin' at Camarillo," the last an intricate, ingenious blues line dedicated to the place where he convalesced. He is spelled in the front line by his West Coast trumpet companion Howard McGhee and the fine tenor saxophonist Wardell Gray; the mix made for a swinging, happy session.

Bird came back to New York to get his classic quintet together and make some of his most enduring statements. The quintet, composed of Miles Davis, Duke Jordan (sometimes replaced by John Lewis or, on one session, Bud Powell), Tommy Potter, and Max Roach, made most of their records for Savoy and Dial. On a few Dial sides, trombonist J. J. Johnson was added.

The majority of the material on these sides is based either on the harmonic structure of the blues or "I Got Rhythm," interspersed with ballads either named as themselves ("Embraceable You," "Out of Nowhere," "Don't Blame Me") or retitled ("Quasimodo," based on "Embraceable You," and "Bird of Paradise," based on "All the Things You Are"). You can see how fertile Bird's mind was just by comparing the different melodies he wrote on the same material. His blues were as different as the happy, Latin-flavored "Bongo Beep," the cooler, rhythmically shifting "Bongo Bop," the white-knuckle, up-tempo "The Hymn," and the straight-ahead "Drifting on a Reed" (not to mention the Savoy classics "Barbados," "Parker's Mood," "Perhaps," and "Another Hair-Do").

In his solos on successive takes, Parker constantly used different strategies and different beginnings, like different chess openings, from which each solo would unfold differently. You can hear this best on the Spotlites and on the Savoy boxed set *The Complete Charlie Parker Savoy Studio Sessions* (Savoy ZDS 5500), in both of which all alternate takes of the same tune are programmed continuously. To take an example, listen to "Bongo Beep" on *Bird on Dial, Volume 6* (Spotlite 106). Bird opens his solo on the second take with a completely different phrase than the one he uses on the first, and his solo develops in a very different direction. On the other hand, trombonist J. J. Johnson, who follows Bird, uses exactly the same opening phrase in both takes. This quality of inventing fresh melodies is not necessarily the most important gauge of a soloist's worth – many great soloists varied their solos very little, just making minor variations in emphasis and phrasing. But in the bebop era, spontaneous creation of melody was at a premium.

Other examples of Bird's phenomenal melodic inventiveness are the two takes of "Embraceable You" (on *Bird on Dial, Volume 4* [Spotlite 104]) that he recorded on October 28, 1947. From the first notes, both are completely new melodies, based on the harmonic structure of the Gershwin standard. Certain phrases and melodic fragments recur, but they are twisted and recast.

In general, I find the Dial sides more relaxed, carefully routined, varied, and satisfying than the Savoy recordings of the same year, although the Savoys can't be avoided, containing some of Bird's most famous lines as well as much fine playing. But in general they haven't the same frothy sound you find on the Dials and tend to consist only of a head (melody) and a series of solos (almost always alto, trumpet, piano, and then the head again and out).

That being said, two Savoy sessions from 1947 are indispensable. One is a session with the Dial quintet but with Bud Powell substituted for Duke Jordan. Bird and Bud didn't work together a lot; both were leaders, both geniuses, and the sparks flew, although the sparks seemed to fly between Bud and everybody during this time. On the four tracks recorded at this session – "Donna Lee," "Chasin' the Bird," "Buzzy," and "Cheryl" – they are both fired up.

The other session is by the Dial quintet, which included Miles Davis, and has John Lewis, later to be the leader of the Modern Jazz Quartet, on piano, Nelson Boyd on bass, and Bird playing tenor saxophone, one of the few occasions he recorded on the bigger horn. The results of this session are available under Davis's name, with all alternate takes, as *First Miles* (Savoy ZDS 1196). The tunes were all written by Miles, and they have a cooler, more sinuous sound than most of the hard-charging bop lines of the day. The other Savoy sides contain no less a performance than the slow blues "Parker's Mood," fascinating alternates and breakdowns on "Another Hair-Do," and whirlwind showpieces like "Klaunstance" and "Bird Gets the Worm."

This group was also caught live, unfortunately in grotesquely distorted and painfully difficult-to-hear sound. Released as *Bird on 52nd Street* (Fantasy/OJC-114), it catches the quintet in some very freewheeling playing that is much looser than either the Dial or Savoy sides. This material is included, along with much more from other sources and with better sound, on the connoisseur's feast *The Complete Dean Benedetti Recordings of Charlie Parker* (Mosaic MD7-129). An essential live performance from this time, September 1947, can be found on *Bebop's Heartbeat* (Savoy ZDS 1177). Parker was added as a guest artist at a Gillespie concert in Carnegie Hall and plays with tremendous ferocity on "A Night in Tunisia," "Dizzy Atmosphere," "Groovin' High," "Confirmation," and an unbelievable "Ko Ko." Not for the fainthearted, this is some of the most intense Bird available.

Later that same month Bird and Diz were together for two all-star radio broadcasts put together by critic Barry Ulanov as a fund-raising effort for U.S. Savings Bonds. Available as *Lullaby in Rhythm* (Spotlite 107), these are worth having, especially for a blazing "Fine and Dandy," with Bird and Diz outblowing each other over a harried announcer's final words, and a unique version of "Tiger Rag," with Bird and Diz playing Dixieland. The set-up on these broadcasts was to pair an all-star "traditional" band with an all-star "modern" band – at the time, the division couldn't have been more marked in most fans' minds. At a point in each broadcast, the modernists called a tune for the traditionalists to play, and the traditionalists returned the favor. On the second broadcast, the traditionalists called for "Tiger Rag."

In November of that same year there was another "Bands for Bonds" broadcast involving Parker (on *Anthropology* [Spotlite 108]). This time his front-line mate was trumpeter Fats Navarro. Although there isn't a lot of Bird here, what there is is excellent, and Navarro plays a definitive version of "Fats Flats," his showpiece on the chord changes of "What Is This Thing Called Love?" Sarah Vaughan is also heard singing "Everything I Have Is Yours."

By the end of 1947 Bird had more or less made his contribution; he had laid down the language for a new generation of musicians and helped add a new subtlety to small-group playing. After that, his style was in place, and it was heard in many different settings. The period in which he was changing the face of the music was over, but he continued to refine his playing, and some of his best work was recorded in the years following 1947.

### IN THE STUDIO

Beginning in 1948, Charlie Parker recorded a series of sessions for producer Norman Granz, with whose touring jazz concert series, Jazz At The Philharmonic, Bird had played in 1946 in California. Bird would record for Granz's labels, which included Clef, Norgran, and Mercury – these recordings would later be re-released on Verve – until he died, his last session being just three months before his death on March 12, 1955. All of this material is collected on a ten-CD box, *Bird: The Complete Charlie Parker on Verve* (Verve 837 141-2), which includes every scrap of studio dialogue, every false start, and every alternate take of everything Parker recorded for Granz. Verve combines and recombines this material in a number of single CDs as well, which seem to go in and out of print. Rather than breaking down every "greatest hits" and "essential Bird" package, I'll discuss the recordings session by session; Bird rarely recorded the same tune in different sessions in Granz's studios (although his live recordings contain countless versions of his best-known tunes from the 1945–1947 period), and you should be able to tell what's what on these packages by the tune titles.

One disc that does seem to stay stable is the mighty *Now's the Time* (Verve 825 671-2), which is probably the best all-around Verve album for those who want Bird with no distractions. Recorded partly in 1952 with a rhythm section of Hank Jones, Teddy Kotick, and Max Roach and partly in 1953 with Al Haig, Percy Heath, and Roach, the album is pure invention and pure swing, a kind of summing-up of Bird in an unbuttoned but focused quartet setting. The rhythm section, thanks to Roach, has the frothy, relaxed, but concentrated swing of the Dial sides, but Bird solos at greater length.

The program consists of medium-up blues ("Chi-Chi," "Now's the Time"), relaxed, down-home blues ("Cosmic Rays," "Laird Baird"), standards ("The Song Is You," "I Remember You"), a bop standard ("Confirmation"), and an up-tempo showpiece ("Kim"). It is one of the best-recorded Bird albums, with the slightest quality of echo setting off Bird's tone, which was a marvel on this occasion. He plays a lot in the middle register here; on "I Remember You" he almost sounds like a tenor during the theme. One thing to listen for is how much attention Bird pays to detail. Rarely will he play a long line of eighth notes without throwing a flourish into the middle of the line – a triplet figure or a little double-time section – for variety and greater expressiveness. He never plays the obvious.

Also excellent is a pair of sessions originally issued on LP as *Swedish Schnapps*. On five tunes from 1951 featuring Red Rodney on trumpet, Bird's sound is heavy and throaty, and he tends to play in the middle register. Rodney, too, plays mainly in the middle register, with a kind of poise that's an attractive counterpoint to Bird. This is an example of Parker just below his peak form; he plays very well, but he tends to rely on his stock phrases, creating variety by ending them with interesting melodic turns. "Si Si," a fine, rarely played blues, "Swedish Schnapps," "Blues for Alice," "Back Home Blues," and a remake of "Lover Man" are the selections.

The other session, also from 1951, finds Bird paired again with Miles Davis and Max Roach. Bird's playing on "She Rote," a workout at up-tempo on the chords of "Out of Nowhere," is fleet and beautifully lucid, full of surprising turns of phrase; this set of changes isn't usually played at this fast a tempo. "Au Privave" is still a favorite Bird blues among musicians. "K.C. Blues" is another blues masterpiece, taken at a relaxed walking tempo, full of warmth and intensity.

### SOME OTHER HAIR-DOS

Norman Granz had the imagination and the wherewithal to experiment with musicians he found interesting, putting them in different settings. One experiment was recording Bird with a string section, performing standards such as "They Can't Take That Away from Me," "Laura," "April in Paris," and "Just Friends." The resulting album, usually referred to as "Bird with Strings," brought Bird a degree of public recognition he'd never had. The strings brought out a sunny, romantic side of Bird, which must have seemed quite foreign to those for whom Bird was the flamethrower of "Ko Ko" only. But we can hear them now for what they are: some of the most beautiful music Bird ever recorded. They are currently available on the Verve box set and on various "best of" collections.

The basic routine for these sides is that Bird plays the melody straight but with embellishments and variations in phrasing, and then there is limited time for him to improvise. On some, such as "Everything Happens to Me" and "They Can't Take That Away from Me," he sticks close to the melody throughout, often ending the melodic phrase with a fillip or answering phrase of his own. On others, such as "I Didn't Know What Time It Was" and the masterpiece "Just Friends," he has more room to improvise.

His melody statements here put him up in the top rank of melody expositors of jazz, like Ben Webster and Lester Young. In fact, the sense of grandeur, release, and exhilaration in playing sheer melody on cuts like "East of the Sun" and "Easy to Love" is almost the equal of Louis Armstrong's, a facet of Bird that would have been very hard for fans to hear three years earlier. His Dial ballads, such as "Don't Blame Me" and "Embraceable You," were radical reworkings, abstractions of the song based on the harmonic structure almost exclusively.

Parker also used his string section on live gigs for a period, until finances forced him to stop, and there are several records of Bird playing live with his string section. The best of these are five tunes issued originally as *Midnight Jazz at Carnegie Hall.* They are well recorded and contain some stunning Bird improvisations on "What Is This Thing Called Love?" (with the strings riffing behind him like the reed section of a big band) and "Rocker."

One unlikely sounding experiment that worked amazingly well was a session with a chorus arranged by jazz singer Dave Lambert, later of the group Lambert, Hendricks, and Ross. The three tunes that were released, "In the Still of the Night," "Old Folks," and "If I Love Again," were unusual material for Bird, and he sounds as if he's having a ball as he swoops over, under, around, and through the chorus. "In the Still of the Night," especially, is one of Bird's most exciting performances. The Verve box contains seven takes of this song, complete with false starts and breakdowns, and nine takes of "Old Folks." It's a fascinating glimpse of Bird in the studio.

Lastly, Granz put Bird in a Latin-music setting several times, first with the Latin band of Machito, one of the most popular Latin big bands to combine a fiery, authentic jazz feeling with Afro-Cuban rhythms. Bird plays brilliantly on "Okiedoke" and "Mango Mangue." Granz also recorded Bird's regular small group in 1951 with Latin percussion added, calling the group Charlie Parker and His South of the Border Orchestra. The resulting sides are a little strange, with tunes like "La Cucaracha" and "Tico-Tico" providing unusual fodder for him, to say the least.

### LIVE

There is a huge amount of live Bird available, either taped off the radio or recorded informally on portable equipment, with his own group or in jam sessions or sitting in with other people's groups. Among this material is some of Bird's greatest playing. People who heard Bird live at the time say that you can't really appreciate Bird's genius from his studio recordings, and in these live dates he often stretches out at length and with a sense of freedom and exhilaration that you don't find in many of the studio sides.

So much of this material has been issued, in so many forms – bootlegged, legitimate, mislabeled, painstakingly annotated, utterly unidentified beyond tune titles, combined and recombined in different packages – that it would take an entire book to unravel it all. I will concentrate on just a few of the highlights, and after that you are, of necessity, on your own. Be warned: the sound on many of the live Bird records, including some essential ones, ranges from bad to really bad. Some of these, however, contain such brilliant playing that they are worth owning anyway.

One of the best Bird records available, *Bird at St. Nick's* (Jazz Workshop/ OJC-041), falls into this category. The sound is horrible; either you can hear Bird and nobody else except drummer Roy Haynes or the piano and bass are right in your face and Bird sounds like he's two blocks away. But the music . . . Bird's playing is so inventive and fresh; he was truly "on" on this night, a dance at New York's St. Nicholas Arena in 1950. It sounds as if Bird could play anything that came into his head on this evening; he plays like a dancer on a high wire doing leaps and pirouettes, quoting from odd songs that pop into his head, playing incredibly intricate and balanced double-time phrases, starting familiar phrases at unexpected places in the measure, floating entirely above the rhythm sometimes, as Louis Armstrong could, and making up wholly original melodies, all while relating to what the other musicians are playing. Listen particularly to "Hot House" and "Now's the Time" for medium-up-tempo magic and "I Didn't Know What Time It Was" for a ballad. On "Visa," Bird stops playing at one point and then inserts, verbatim, Louis Armstrong's trumpet introduction to "West End Blues." At the end of his solo on "Now's the Time," which features some truly unbelievable double-timing, he even makes the horn yodel. On a night like this, his well of ideas was inexhaustible. Here is one definition of freedom.

Also breathtaking, if a little less subtle, is *Charlie Parker Live at Rockland Palace*, originally issued as *Bird Is Free* on Charlie Parker Records and subsequently issued in as many formats as Lon Chaney had faces. The sound here is almost as bad as it is on the St. Nick's set; like the St. Nick's material, it was recorded at a dance, in 1952, where Bird had both his regular group and his string section on some tunes. Listen to the way he sears through "Cool Blues," "Moose the Mooche," "Rocker," "This Time the Dream's on Me," and, especially, the legendary performance of "Lester Leaps In," four minutes of white-hot improvisation. The fluency and authority of this performance are really unbelievable. One way of identifying this material on unidentified bootleg sets is by the presence of the calypso "Sly Mongoose"; this is the only time Bird was recorded playing it.

Savoy has issued four CDs of 1948 Parker radio broadcasts from the Royal Roost, one of the best-known of the bop venues, collectively titled *Bird at the Roost* (ZDS 4411-4). There is some excellent stuff on these sides, as well as some very expendable stuff. Most of the material consists of performances by his regular working quintet, with either Kenny Dorham or Miles Davis on trumpet. All the on-the-air patter by the radio announcers, one of whom is the legendary Symphony Sid, has been kept in; this is fun for the first couple of tunes, but it gets annoying quickly if you just want to hear the music.

Also excellent is *Charlie Parker and the Stars of Modern Jazz at Carnegie Hall, Christmas 1949* (Jass J-CD-16), which features a relaxed Bird with his regular quintet (Rodney, Haig, Potter, and Haynes) at Carnegie Hall playing "Ornithology," "Cheryl" (on which he again paraphrases Armstrong's "West End Blues" introduction), a blazing "Ko Ko," "Now's the Time," and a slower "Bird of Paradise," a beautiful, relaxed, cogent performance, reminiscent of the Dial masterpiece.

Not to be missed are two sets available only as imports on French CBS and titled *One Night at Birdland* and *Summit Meeting at Birdland*. *One Night* has Bird in one of the most electrifying sets ever recorded, in the company of trumpeter Fats Navarro and pianist Bud Powell, doing phenomenal versions of "Ornithology," "'Round Midnight," "The Street Beat," and much more. *Summit Meeting* has Powell again on piano and Dizzy Gillespie on trumpet. The juice isn't cranked up quite as high here as it is on *One Night*, but it's fabulous, nonetheless, especially for a whirlwind version of "Anthropology."

Bird was an inveterate jammer, and some of his most unbuttoned and stretched-out playing happened in this kind of context, where he wasn't fronting a band and could be very experimental, playing long solos without worrying about pacing a show. One of the best of these sets was originally issued as *The Happy Bird* on Charlie Parker Records. Recorded in Framingham, Massachusetts, at a club called Christy's, the album shows Bird at his most relaxed and inventive on "Happy Bird Blues," "Scrapple from the Apple," "I May Be Wrong," and "I'll Remember April." Also present are the great and short-lived tenor saxophonist Wardell Gray (throughout the record, during Gray's solos, you can hear someone – is it Bird? – yelling, "*Go*, Wardell . . .") and, on "I'll Remember April," bassist Charles Mingus.

A somewhat less relaxed but more fiery session is chronicled on *One Night in Chicago* (Savoy ZDS 4423). Taped on primitive equipment at a Chicago dance in 1950, Bird is accompanied by local musicians, and they must have made him feel at home. His brilliance, especially on the whirlwind "Keen and Peachy" (based on the chord changes of "Fine and Dandy"), will leave you stunned. A fun thing to listen for here is the reaction of an obviously hip crowd, who register amazement at appropriate places and laugh at Bird's musical jokes and references.

*Charlie Parker "More Unissued," Volume 1* (Royal Jazz RJD 505) contains lots of interesting odds and ends; especially good are two informal duets between Parker and pianist Lennie Tristano on "All of Me" and "I Can't Believe That You're in Love with Me" and two tunes recorded at sculptor Julie McDonald's Hollywood apartment. *Volume 2* (Royal Jazz RJD 506) has six excellent broadcast titles by the Parker quintet with Red Rodney on trumpet and Art Blakey on drums, along with three subpar tracks with trumpeter Tony Fruscella. The alto saxophonist sounds drugged here, and in places he plays phrases that are uncharacteristic of Bird; there is at least the possibility that it isn't Bird at all. I nominate Dave Schildkraut, a close associate of Fruscella's.

*Apartment Sessions* (Spotlite SPJ146) is for hard-core Bird fans, consisting as it does of almost nothing but extended Parker blowing on his standard repertoire ("Scrapple from the Apple," "Donna Lee," "Out of Nowhere," "Chero-kee"). Ernest Hemingway once spoke of Bach "emitting" counterpoint; there is the same sense here of Bird emitting chorus after chorus of unbelievably inventive, logical melody in a new language. I wish that someday someone would take three choruses at random from, say, "Little Willie Leaps" in this set, have three saxophonists play them simultaneously, and see what kind of counterpoint it would make. The sound here is good; the set was recorded in a private apartment in New York in 1950.

In the 1950s Bird would tour, land in a city for an engagement at a local club, and play the gig with a local rhythm section. Some fantastic examples of Bird in this kind of setting can be heard on *The Bird You Never Heard* (Stash ST-CD-10), particularly the first four titles, which were recorded at Boston's Hi-Hat club in 1954. Parker plays "My Funny Valentine," the only known recording of him playing that standard, with staggering inventiveness, almost on a par with the St. Nick's material, and an equally amazing "Cool Blues." Also notable is a slow, medium-tempo blues from a 1950 engagement, which the producers call "Parker's Mood," after his famous Savoy recording. For some reason, Bird rarely played blues at this tempo in live gigs.

This collection also features two live tracks from Birdland in 1953, with Bud Powell, Charles Mingus, and conga player Candido; these alone would be worth the price of the collection, which is rounded out by three 1953 concert performances at the University of Oregon with trumpeter Chet Baker, subject of his own hagiographic movie treatment, Bruce Weber's excellent *Let's Get Lost*.

Bird and Baker can be heard in a 1952 Inglewood, California, jam session context on *Bird and Chet: Inglewood Jam* (Fresh Sound TI-9801). Baker plays some very credible bebop trumpet, and Bird is inspired in places (the accompaniment of one of his favorite pianists, Al Haig, couldn't have hurt), but the really interesting thing is the presence of Sonny Criss, a highly regarded West Coast alto player who comes straight out of the Parker mode. It is rare to hear such a direct face-off between Parker and one of his disciples. Criss works in Parker's language, using his vocabulary, but without Bird's flexibility; you can really hear what set Bird apart from everyone else.

Another collection that should be mentioned, although none but the most fanatical Parker head will want it, is *Rara Avis (Rare Bird)* (Stash ST-CD-21). It consists of three broadcasts, from 1949, 1952, and 1954, the first two recorded from New York television shows. One of the tracks has Bird blowing a couple of scorching choruses on Cole Porter's "Lover" with a studio band behind a tap dancer. There are a couple of throwaway numbers, too, including an intriguing-sounding "Blues Jam Session" on which Parker is supposedly paired with Sidney Bechet; Bird is inaudible, if he's even present. Rounding out the disc is some more 1954 material from Boston's Hi-Hat club that is good but not equal to the stuff on *The Bird You Never Heard*.

### BIRD AND DIZ REVISITED

Parker and Gillespie were reunited many times over the years, almost always with thrilling results. Their last studio meeting took place on June 6, 1950; available as *Bird and Diz* (Verve 831 133-2), it is the only time Bird recorded in a studio with pianist Thelonious Monk.

The program consists of new material as well as a reading of the unlikely "My Melancholy Baby." The blues "Bloomdido" is still a popular line among musicians. "Mohawk" is also an excellent blues, at a slower tempo. The most exciting cut is "Leap Frog," a themeless, up-tempo ride through the chords of "I Got Rhythm," on which Bird and Gillespie each take one chorus, then spend the rest of the track trading four-bar phrases at lightning speed and high intensity. The Verve box contains eleven takes of "Leap Frog," six of which are breakdowns complete with conversation and expressions of consternation; they provide a fascinating insight into the way things come together (or don't) in the studio.

Even more satisfying musically, although recorded without the benefit of studio conditions, is *Jazz at Massey Hall* (Debut/OJC-044), on which Parker and Gillespie are heard in a 1953 Toronto concert in front of a rhythm section of Bud Powell, Charles Mingus, and Max Roach. In this case, the music is every bit as good as the personnel might indicate. The days when bebop was a novelty were over; it had become a classic language, and its four principal architects (and Mingus, one of its principal descendants and codifiers) play at length on the music's classic repertoire – "A Night in Tunisia," "Hot House," "Salt Peanuts," and others. The combination of relaxation and intensity makes this one of the idiom's most fulfilled statements, a definitive performance.

More for the confirmed fan because of spotty sound quality is the hard-to-find LP collection *Charlie Parker Volume 2: Bird Meets Birks* (ZuZazz ZZ1003), in which Bird and Gillespie are glimpsed together in a number of unusual and high-voltage settings. The best cuts are "A Night in Tunisia" and "52nd Street Theme," recorded at Carnegie Hall in November 1952; Parker was really "on" that night, as he had been at the same place five years earlier (see *Bebop's Heartbeat*, discussed earlier). The most interesting track is probably "The Bluest Blues," recorded at a 1953 Gillespie gig at Birdland, when Parker dropped in accompanied by Miles Davis; they both solo on this novelty number.

Bird was often thrown into all-star playing situations in which he was placed among other giants, often from earlier generations. One of the best known of these set-ups was producer Norman Granz's Jazz At The Philharmonic (JATP) concert series. The idea behind JATP was to tour an all-star lineup, having them play in a jam session–type format in a loosely organized structure. This string-of-solos approach wears thin very quickly on record, although the concerts were, on the evidence of the audible audience response, very exciting. Often the stuff that excited the audience the most is the most difficult to listen to now.

Nonetheless, when JATP presented great soloists, it gave them room to stretch out, and Bird made some fabulous recordings with JATP. All of them are available on the Verve box and, as of this writing, in otherwise shifting form on Verve. The 1946 concerts have a number of high spots, the highest of which is "Oh, Lady Be Good," on which Bird's solo is a masterpiece of development. Versions of "JATP Blues" and "I Got Rhythm" (recorded at a concert in which Bird shared the stage with Lester Young and Coleman Hawkins) are both excellent, but on "Blues for Norman," "Sweet Georgia Brown," and "After You've Gone" Bird sounds nervous and his intonation is a little off. It was a period of tremendous strain for him; later in the year he would have a breakdown that would land him in a sanitarium.

A 1949 concert presents Bird with Lester Young and Roy Eldridge on a program including "Lester Leaps In" and a gorgeous "Embraceable You." It's a great example of Bird at close to his most flexible and songlike, without the tension of the 1946 concerts. The most exciting moment is probably in "The Closer," an up-tempo blues. The performance seemingly ends after a screaming trumpet solo by Eldridge, with the crowd going crazy. Buddy Rich closes things out with a big thump on the drums, but there has been no Bird solo. After a moment's pause, Rich starts the beat up again, waiting for the crowd to settle down. After a few more moments of just Rich's drums, Bird starts a solo with a short opening phrase, then a long, cascading run that sounds like the cavalry's reinforcements coming over the hill.

Granz also put together a series of studio jam sessions along the same lines as the JATP concerts. Bird was on hand for one of these dates, available as *Jam Session* (Verve 833 564-2). The 1952 Los Angeles session also includes alto giants Benny Carter and Johnny Hodges, both idols of Bird's, and the great tenor player Ben Webster. Even though it was 1952 and Bird had to be considered part of the jazz mainstream along with the others, his freshness and inventiveness still stand out with bracing clarity. Benny Carter even shows that he had been listening to Bird, especially on "What Is This Thing Called Love?" On the up-tempo tunes – a blues and "What Is This Thing Called Love?" – Bird outswings everyone and has the most logical sense of how to organize a chorus of anyone in the room. On the slow "Funky Blues," however, he gets some serious competition from Hodges, one of the best blues players who ever lived. Still, when Bird comes in, right on Hodges's heels, well . . . you be the judge. Later in the same cut, Ben Webster follows his imitator Flip Phillips and takes solo honors for the whole track, probably even cutting Bird.

A satisfying example of Bird at the peak of his powers in an all-star setting in 1949 can be found on *The Metronome All-Star Bands* (RCA/Bluebird 7636-2-RB). Two tunes, "Overtime" and "Victory Ball," were recorded in long and short versions by a big band assembled under the auspices of *Metronome* magazine, which had been doing this kind of thing for years. In 1949 the modernists held the turf. Aside from Parker's brilliant playing, the sides are most notable for a trumpet section consisting of Dizzy Gillespie, Fats Navarro, and Miles Davis, all of whom engage in a three-way chase chorus at the end of "Overtime." It is worth buying this disc for these sides alone, although there is excellent earlier material on it as well.

One essential confrontation between Bird and a younger giant occurred in January 1953, when Bird encountered Sonny Rollins at a Miles Davis date for Prestige. Available on *Collectors' Items* (Prestige/OJC-071), the four tunes are rare examples of Bird playing tenor saxophone. The session is analyzed in some detail in the discussion of Miles Davis. Creative sparks fly throughout between Parker and Rollins, who had certainly absorbed and assimilated Parker's language as well as anybody had before or since and who had made something of his own out of it, young as he was. Bird, then only thirty-two, must already have felt the hot breath of time on his neck. He would be dead in just over two years.

### CODA

Because there is so much Bird available, in such overlapping and sometimes confusing form, it may be worthwhile to have some suggestions as to where to begin. My picks would be *Now's the Time* (Verve 825 671-2), *The Legendary Dial Masters, Volume 1* (Stash ST-CD-23), *Original Bird – The Best of Bird on Savoy* (Savoy ZDS 1208, which includes "Ko Ko," "Parker's Mood," and other classics), *Bird at St. Nick's* (Jazz Workshop/OJC-041, bad sound notwithstanding), and *Jazz at Massey Hall* (Debut/OJC-044, with Dizzy Gillespie, Bud Powell, Charles Mingus, and Max Roach). But wherever you start, you will end up sitting in front of your speakers marveling at one of jazz's greatest geniuses.

# ORNITHOLOGISTS

Charlie Parker's effect on the musicians of his era was similar to Louis Armstrong's on those of two decades earlier: suddenly musicians everywhere were struggling to master Bird's additions to the jazz language. Alto saxophonists, especially, were hit hard; most of the prominent altoists who arrived in the 1950s were devoted ornithologists, dedicated to the study of Bird lore. Almost all found something of their own to take away from Bird's work. Some were influenced by Bird's melodic inventiveness, some by his approach to scales and chords, some by his blues feeling, some by his romantic way with ballads on the "Bird with Strings" sessions.

Lou Donaldson was, and is, certainly one of the bluesiest Parker disciples. Perhaps his best single album is the quartet-plus-conga-drum date *Blues Walk* (Blue Note 46525), which includes his lilting, medium-tempo jukebox favorite, "The Masquerade Is Over," along with a galloping ride on the bop standard "Move" and the mysterioso title cut. His *Quartet/Quintet/Sextet* (Blue Note 81537) features the altoist in 1952 and 1954 dates with rhythm sections including pianists Horace Silver and Elmo Hope and drummers Art Taylor and Art Blakey, as well as with trumpeters Blue Mitchell and Kenny Dorham. The blues "Down Home" really shows Donaldson's Parker roots. The 1967 *Alligator Boogaloo* (Blue Note 84263) is set in a definite grits-and-gravy, organ-combo groove, with several vamp-based and rock-flavored tunes, as well as a shuffle-beat blues ("The Thang"), a ballad ("I Want a Little Girl"), and an up-tempo gospel-type tune called "Rev. Moses," on which Donaldson shows why he is an uptown favorite to this day. George Benson plays guitar on this set. Donaldson has stellar guest shots on *Milt Jackson* (Blue Note 81509), Jimmy Smith's twenty-minute-long blues jam "The Sermon" from *The Sermon* (Blue Note 46097), and the immortal Art Blakey albums *A Night at Birdland, Volume 1* (Blue Note 46519) and *Volume 2* (Blue Note 46520), on which he shares the front line with trumpeter Clifford Brown.

Gigi Gryce was a highly regarded altoist active in the 1950s very much in the Parker mode and a composer who always brought something interesting to a session. His *The Rat Race Blues* (Prestige/OJC-081) is a fine quintet record with trumpeter Richard Williams; the up-tempo title track finds the pianist soloing in A♭, Williams soloing in F, and Gryce soloing in B♭, an example of Gryce's constant attempt to make the small-group bebop setting more interesting than a mere procession of solos. The record as a whole has a great variety of moods and musical grooves. The same can be said of *The Art Farmer Quintet Featuring Gigi Gryce* (Prestige/OJC-241), an excellent album on which all but one of the six compositions are by Gryce. This is a very satisfying, well-programmed set of mid-1950s jazz, with an unusual rhythm section of Duke Jordan (of Charlie Parker's 1947 quintet), Addison Farmer, and Philly Joe Jones, as well as the fine trumpeting of the leader. Gryce was the leader, originally, on a quartet session available under Thelonious Monk's name (*Thelonious Monk and Herbie Nichols* [Savoy ZDS 1166]). The four tunes, recorded in 1955 (Gryce's "Nica's Tempo," and Monk's seldom-played originals "Brake's Sake," "Shuffle Boil," and "Gallop's Gallop"), are a good showcase for the altoist's singing tone and melodic imagination. Gryce can also be heard on *Monk's Music* (Riverside/OJC-084), in the saxophone section next to Coleman Hawkins and John Coltrane.

Phil Woods was a large presence in the late 1950s; his sound was penetrating and intense, and he recorded a good amount. The 1955 *Woodlore* (Prestige/OJC-052) features him in a quartet setting playing standards like "Get Happy" and "Slow Boat to China," along with bop-inflected originals. *Bird Feathers* (New Jazz/OJC-1735) is a collection of 1957 odds and ends by various ornithologists, with Woods and his alto soul brother Gene Quill featured on two 1950s jazz standards, "Solar" and "Airegin." Woods also takes an excellent solo on "Little Rootie Tootie" on *The Thelonious Monk Orchestra at Town Hall* (Riverside/OJC-135). His 1974 *Musique Du Bois* (Muse MCD 5037) is an adventuresome quartet outing full of shifting tempos, dynamics, and instrumental densities, on which Woods is abetted by the extremely flexible and responsive rhythm section of Jaki Byard, Richard Davis, and Alan Dawson. The repertoire includes Sonny Rollins's "Airegin" again, as well as Wayne Shorter's "Nefertiti" and other tunes that lend themselves to stylistically eclectic treatment. Woods's tone here is marvelous, strong and expressive in all registers; a very satisfying set.

Ernie Henry was a short-lived and little-known player who came up in the late 1940s, playing with Tadd Dameron and Dizzy Gillespie. He made several albums for Riverside in the mid-1950s that show a strongly Bird-influenced sound and imagination with a keening tone. *Presenting Ernie Henry* (Riverside/OJC-102) is a solid 1956 set which also features trumpeter Kenny Dorham in a quintet setting, playing mainly Henry originals in a bop vein, as well as two standards ("Gone with the Wind" and "I Should Care"). Henry's *Seven Standards and a Blues* (Riverside/OJC-1722), recorded the next year, is in the same groove; Henry, backed by the great rhythm section of Wynton Kelly, Wilbur Ware, and Philly Joe Jones, plays straight-ahead, Parker-style alto on tunes like "I Get a Kick Out of You," "Like Someone in Love," and "Lover Man." Both albums will make bebop fans happy. Henry can also be heard at some length on Thelonious Monk's *Brilliant Corners* (Riverside/OJC-026).

Charles McPherson, a somewhat younger player than those listed previously, has a luscious tone that seems to owe a lot to Parker's "Bird with Strings" sound. McPherson's language comes straight out of Bird's, and he has perhaps mastered and absorbed the nuances of Parker's style better than anyone, yet he is instantly identifiable. His set *Bebop Revisited!* (Prestige/OJC-710) pairs him with his mentor, Detroit bebop professor Barry Harris, on piano, and the gifted trumpeter Carmell Jones in a selection of tunes drawn from the heart of the bop repertoire – Tadd Dameron's "Hot House," Fats Navarro's "Nostalgia," Bud Powell's "Wail," Charlie Parker's seldom-played "Si Si," and the ballads "Embraceable You" and "If I Loved You." The set also includes a tune titled "Variations on a Blues by Bird," learned by McPherson from a rare Charlie Parker record which recently surfaced, for the first time since 1952, on the Verve ten-CD Charlie Parker box under the name "Passport (Tune Y)." *Bebop Revisited!* is an energetic and authentic set of classic bop; McPherson soars throughout, showing off his hardest-driving side. Everyone else contributes importantly as well to this extremely satisfying disc.

McPherson's more romantic side is in the foreground on *Siku Ya Bibi* (Mainstream MDCD 713), a set of tunes associated with Billie Holiday on which McPherson is again backed by Barry Harris and, on half the tracks, a string section. The altoist is at his singing best on fine standards like "For Heaven's Sake," "I'm a Fool to Want You," and "Good Morning Heartache." Two sets recorded for Don Schlitten's Xanadu label in the mid-1970s may be available in imported versions: *Beautiful!* is a brilliant collection of choice standards like "But Beautiful," "This Can't Be Love," and "It Had To Be You," on which McPherson, at his most inventive and lyrical, is accompanied by a rhythm section of Duke Jordan, Sam Jones, and Leroy Williams. If you can find it, buy it. As good, maybe even better, is *Live in Tokyo*, another quartet date, again with Barry Harris, on which they perform a couple of blues, a samba, good ballad versions of "These Foolish Things" and, especially, "East of the Sun," and a broiling version of Bud Powell's "Bouncing with Bud."

McPherson and Harris are together for a great 1973 album by trumpeter Red Rodney, *Bird Lives!* (Muse MCD 5371). Rodney spent a good amount of time in Parker's quintet, and the repertoire here consists entirely of tunes either composed by or associated with Bird – his blues "Big Foot," his breakneck line on the chords of "Indiana" called "Donna Lee," the popular standard "I'll Remember April," Thelonious Monk's " 'Round Midnight," and others. This is a small masterpiece of an album; the rhythm section, which includes bassist Sam Jones and neglected giant Roy Brooks on drums along with Harris, couldn't be much better, and Rodney and McPherson consistently inspire each other to heights of fire and invention. For an example of the possibilities in the bop approach to group playing, listen to the interplay between piano, drums, and soloists on "I'll Remember April," an example of improvised group counterpoint at its best; Rodney's and McPherson's two choruses of exhilarating four-bar exchanges at the end of this track are a high point of a set that can't be recommended highly enough.

McPherson spent several years, on and off, with Charles Mingus's bands, in which he was always pushed to do his best. He took part in a few of the sessions included on *The Complete Candid Recordings of Charles Mingus* (Mosaic MD3-111), including the one that produced "MDM," a jumping blues on which McPherson has an exciting dialogue with Eric Dolphy. Probably the best recording the altoist made with Mingus is *Mingus at Monterey* (Prestige P-34001), recorded at the 1964 Monterey Jazz Festival, on which McPherson plays a long solo on "Orange Was the Color of Her Dress, Then Blue Silk," during which an unforgettable mood settles. McPherson would have an honored place in jazz history even if he had never recorded another thing.

Two very little known altoists of the post-Parker era are Sonny Red and John Jenkins. Sonny Red's melodic conception was very close to Parker's, as was his tone. His 1961 album *Images* (Jazzland/OJC-148) is a recommended set for any bebop fan. Red is not just a scale-pattern player; his solos consist of real ideas. He is joined on *Images* by trumpeter Blue Mitchell and pianist Barry Harris, among others. Red is also featured on Curtis Fuller's excellent album *New Trombone* (Prestige/OJC-077), a quintet date featuring Hank Jones on piano. John Jenkins also followed Bird's conception very closely, adding a strong Jackie McLean influence. Jenkins can, in fact, be heard on a couple of albums with McLean – *Alto Madness* (Prestige/OJC-1733) and *Bird Feathers* (New Jazz/OJC-1735) – on which they are hard for even a practiced ear to tell apart.

Sonny Stitt, unquestionably one of Parker's foremost disciples, is discussed with the tenor players, since his main influence was felt on the larger instrument. But he made at least two records exclusively on alto that must be mentioned here. *Stitt Plays Bird* (Atlantic 1418-2) is a virtuoso ride through a program of eleven Parker standards – from the slow blues "Parker's Mood" to the lightning-fast "Ko Ko," by way of "Scrapple from the Apple," "Yardbird Suite," and others – accompanied by John Lewis, Richard Davis, and Connie Kay, with Jim Hall along on guitar. Stitt's playing on Dizzy Gillespie's *For Musicians Only* (Verve 837 435-2), on which Stan Getz rounds out the front line, is even better, a staggering display of technique and presence of mind on "Bebop," "Dark Eyes," "Wee," and "Lover Come Back to Me," all of which except "Dark Eyes" are taken at breakneck tempos.

Stitt also plays mostly alto on *Sonny Stitt Sits In with the Oscar Peterson Trio* (Verve 849 396-2), a set of material from two sessions in 1957 and 1959 in which swing is the key word on standards like "I Can't Give You Anything But Love" and "I'll Remember April," Charlie Parker's blues "Au Privave," and more. Ray Brown's bass puts a deep keel in the water here. Stitt's early alto solos with Gillespie's 1946 band ("That's Earl, Brother" and "Oop Bop Sh'Bam") can be heard on *Dizzy Gillespie and His Sextets and Orchestra: "Shaw'Nuff"* (Musicraft MVSCD-53).

### COUSINS

Art Pepper was highly regarded by many jazz fans for his sweet tone and jaunty, bouncing rhythmic feeling. The natural comparison was with Bird, but when he switched to tenor from time to time one could hear a large helping of Lester Young in his style, too. His autobiography, *Straight Life*, is a lurid look at the West Coast jazz scene of the 1940s and 1950s. Later in life his sound became more penetrating, even harsh sometimes, yet he could play ballads beautifully.

One Pepper set that everyone should own is *Art Pepper Meets the Rhythm Section* (Contemporary/OJC-338), where pianist Red Garland, bassist Paul Chambers, and drummer Philly Joe Jones take a brief holiday from Miles Davis's 1957 quintet to accompany the altoist on a very satisfying, laid-back program consisting mainly of popular and jazz standards like "Imagination," "Tin Tin Deo," and "You'd Be So Nice to Come Home To." The set has a fresh, spontaneous feeling to it and is highly recommended. Three years later he had a rendezvous with another Miles Davis rhythm section of Wynton Kelly, Paul Chambers, and Jimmy Cobb (*Gettin' Together* [Contemporary/OJC-169]), with trumpeter Conte Candoli added. This is a less interesting date, by and large, although two ballads, "Diane" and "Why Are We Afraid?," are fine. Wynton Kelly was having an especially good day, and *Gettin' Together* is recommended for Kelly fans. One set to stay away from, although it looks very promising, is *Art Pepper + Eleven: Modern Jazz Classics* (Contemporary/OJC-341), on which the altoist plays jazz standards by Parker, Gillespie, Monk, and others, accompanied by a big band consisting of crack West Coast men. The arrangements, by Marty Paich, are unfailingly corny, and nobody sounds particularly interested, with the exception of drummer Mel Lewis, who broils away behind the lackluster proceedings.

Lee Konitz is a master of improvisation, with an instantly identifiable sound that has broadened since his late-1940s days with Stan Kenton's big band (of which Pepper, too, was an alumnus). He was one of the archetypal cool players, involved in Miles Davis's *Birth of the Cool* sessions as well as recording as a guest with Gerry Mulligan's pianoless quartet in the early 1950s. He was involved, also, with pianist and theorist Lennie Tristano, with whom he made some interesting 1949 sides, available on *Lee Konitz* (Prestige/OJC-186). Also included on this set are several highly intuitive and contrapuntal sides with tenor player Warne Marsh. Konitz teams up with Tristano again for five exceptional live tracks from 1955 on *Lennie Tristano/The New Tristano* (Rhino/Atlantic R2 71595), on which the altoist and pianist engage in some truly inspired improvised counterpoint.

Konitz loves collective improvisation and spontaneous counterpoint; his *The Lee Konitz Duets* (Milestone/OJC-466), which includes unaccompanied duets with tenor saxophonists Richie Kamuca and Joe Henderson, violinist Ray Nance, drummer Elvin Jones, and others, is a very rewarding album that runs the stylistic gamut from Armstrong's "Struttin' with Some Barbecue" to totally spontaneous "free" playing. My favorite Konitz album is the 1976 *Figure and Spirit*, originally issued on Progressive Records and available again on CD as a Japanese import. It may be a little tough to find, but it is worth any effort. Konitz and tenorist Ted Brown match wits backed by a great rhythm section of pianist Albert Dailey, bassist Rufus Reid, and drummer Joe Chambers on a swinging and extremely supple set of essays on disguised standards like "I'll Remember April" and "You Stepped Out of a Dream." Konitz and Brown sometimes engage in simultaneous improvisation that sounds like a bebop version of New Orleans polyphony. The seven-minute-long title cut (a meditative, profound, themeless improvisation on the harmonic structure of "Body and Soul") is a bona fide masterpiece.

Paul Desmond, usually identified with pianist Dave Brubeck's small group, is in some ways an alto saxophone version of tenorist Stan Getz. His tone is very pure and cushioned, sweet and sometimes ironic, and never strident. He was a stranger to the blues, but he was a fine ballad player. His most famous recording is unquestionably "Take Five" from the Dave Brubeck album *Time Out* (Columbia CK 40585), a collection of pieces in unusual meters. But the ballads and coolly swinging standards that make up Desmond's own *Easy Living* (RCA/Bluebird 2306-2-RB) will be appreciated by any fan of sweet, romantic playing on high-quality tunes like "Easy Living," "Polka Dots and Moonbeams," and "Here's That Rainy Day." Desmond is accompanied here by guitar master Jim Hall, among others. This is not the most challenging music, but it is a warm and mellow, cognac-on-a-fall-afternoon set.

## JACKIE McLEAN

Jackie McLean arrived in the early 1950s very much under the influence of Bird, but he was destined to grow far beyond the status of mere disciple. McLean is one of the best players in jazz to this day, a serious artist who has constantly challenged himself. His sound is full, broad, and urgent; sometimes he almost sounds more like a tenor than an alto. His swing can be irresistible, especially on straight-ahead, bebop-influenced material, on which his long lines of eighth notes ride the harmonic contours like a surfer timing a wave perfectly. He has recorded prolifically, covering a spectrum of styles from the straight-ahead bebop that he grew up with through the modal approach of the early 1960s and even the "free" experiments of that time. McLean's playing is nearly always of a very high quality; the differences in his recordings have to do mainly with the accompanists and the material.

McLean's many recordings for Prestige/New Jazz are uneven in quality. He plays extremely good bebop on *Jackie's Pal* (Prestige/OJC-1714), on which McLean and trumpeter Bill Hardman are backed by Mal Waldron, Paul Chambers, and Philly Joe Jones in a program including four originals and an exciting version of Charlie Parker's seldom-played "Steeplechase." The originals are all interesting, especially the minor-key "Dee's Dilemma," which puts the set in a different class from some of McLean's other Prestige recordings, in which familiar standards are given an unrehearsed, workaday treatment. McLean plays very fresh melodic lines in his solos; this is an excellent example of what he can do in this kind of setting when he is at his best.

*McLean's Scene* (New Jazz/OJC-098) is an example of a session in which familiar standards are given an unrehearsed, workaday treatment. The altoist relies, for the most part, on stock phrases, although he plays a startlingly hot solo on "Gone with the Wind." *Makin' the Changes* (New Jazz/OJC-197) is better overall because of three tracks recorded with an expanded group, including trumpeter Webster Young and trombonist Curtis Fuller, to which a little more care and planning were obviously devoted. "Jackie's Ghost" is a fine, up-tempo, minor-key original arranged well for the three horns, with interludes between the solos, and "Chasin' the Bird" is one of Parker's two contrapuntal compositions, with an extra line added here for trombone. *4, 5 and 6* (Prestige/OJC-056) is a solid album of straight-ahead blowing, in which McLean leads a quartet, a quintet, and a sextet (hence the title). This one includes a nice medium-tempo, cooking quartet performance of the rarely played standard "Why Was I Born?" and a version of Bird's "Confirmation" on which McLean is joined by tenor saxophonist Hank Mobley.

*Lights Out* (Prestige/OJC-426) has McLean with trumpeter Donald Byrd and pianist Elmo Hope. This is one of the best of the Prestiges, largely due to Hope's supportive playing behind McLean. The title cut is a blues recorded in a darkened studio. Despite the absence of anything above a medium walking tempo, *A Long Drink of the Blues* (New Jazz/OJC-253) is also one of the best in this series. The second side consists of three slow ballad performances

("Embraceable You," "I Cover the Waterfront," and "These Foolish Things") by a quartet with Mal Waldron at the piano which have McLean in a soulful and inventive groove; side one is taken up by a long blues by the same band that performed "Jackie's Ghost" on *Makin' the Changes,* prefaced with a snatch of a studio argument among the musicians. This is a thoroughly rewarding set. Lastly, McLean teams up with fellow ornithologist John Jenkins for *Alto Madness* (Prestige/OJC-1733), a straight-ahead blowing session during the course of which you will hear enough bebop alto to last you for a while, played expertly, to be sure. If this style is your bag, this set is worth buying. Another track from the same session, not included on *Alto Madness,* shows up on *Bird Feathers* (New Jazz/OJC-1735), a collection of bebop alto also featuring cuts by Hal McKusick and the team of Phil Woods and Gene Quill.

## ONE STEP BEYOND

McLean's work for Blue Note is, in general, fresher, better recorded, and more interesting than his Prestige recordings. The Prestige sets mostly have the air of a bunch of guys coming into the studio, blowing on some standards, collecting their money, and leaving; even the loosest Blue Notes are more thought-out and pulled together. McLean had been doing some real growing musically; his playing could be mistaken for no one else's at this point, and his originals tend to be real originals, not just new lines on familiar changes.

*Jackie's Bag* (Blue Note 46142) may be the all-around best and most varied of the Blue Notes. It consists of material from a 1959 quintet date with Donald Byrd on trumpet and a rhythm section of Sonny Clark, Paul Chambers, and Philly Joe Jones, as well six titles from a 1960 date with trumpeter Blue Mitchell, neglected tenorman Tina Brooks, and a rhythm section of Kenny Drew, Chambers, and Art Taylor. The three 1959 tracks really sparkle; they include McLean's "Quadrangle," a very unusual composition which the altoist says he originally conceived of as a modal tune, to which he put the "I Got Rhythm" chord changes at the last moment, "Fidel," a happy, AABA swinger with a surprising melody, and "Blues Inn," a durable blues. McLean is still more or less in his bebop bag, harmonically.

The 1960 date shows that McLean had been thinking about the modal work that was influencing many in jazz at the time, in which soloists would play on only one or two scales during their solos, rather than negotiating a harmonic obstacle course. This session produced McLean's famous modal piece "Appointment in Ghana," as well as the extremely beautiful "Ballad for Doll," a feature for Kenny Drew's piano. McLean plays very strongly, evoking tenor player Dexter Gordon at times. His abilities as a composer and leader had developed to a high degree by this time, and the set is a good example of the possibilities in the small-band format when some time is taken to plan an interesting context. Highly recommended.

*New Soil* (Blue Note 84013) is an exceptional 1959 quintet date with Donald Byrd on trumpet, Walter Davis, Jr., on piano, Paul Chambers on bass, and drummer Pete La Roca. The set includes four good Davis originals and two by McLean, including the up-tempo "Minor Apprehension," on which La Roca takes a staggering five-chorus Cubist drum solo that has to be heard. Everyone swings hard, no one harder than the leader.

*Bluesnik* (Blue Note 84067) was recorded in 1961 with Freddie Hubbard on trumpet and a fine rhythm section consisting of Kenny Drew, Doug Watkins, and, again, the brilliant Pete La Roca. This is a set of blues and blues-derived tunes in different rhythmic settings, including the way-up title track, the six-eight-accented, after-hours-groove "Goin' Way Blues," and the gospel-inflected "Torchin'." It, too, is first-rate both in its solo work and the extraordinary variety presented in what could have been a repetitive program. McLean preaches and exhorts in top form throughout.

*Let Freedom Ring* (Blue Note 46527), from 1962, consists of three McLean compositions and one by Bud Powell ("I'll Keep Loving You," a favorite of McLean's to this day). The brooding, somewhat eerie "Melody for Melonae" is a McLean classic, with an out-of-tempo, conducted theme (faintly reminiscent of Monk's "Brilliant Corners"), which shifts into a straight-ahead, minor scale for blowing. McLean is working with an extended repertoire of techniques here, overblowing to achieve some extraordinarily high pitches, as well as occasionally using alternate fingerings in which the same pitch can be fingered in two ways with a subtly different sound. His playing here, as throughout, is amazingly intense. You can tell he had been hearing Ornette Coleman in his playing and writing (check out his witty blues line "Rene"). Pianist Walter Davis, Jr., bassist Herbie Lewis, and drummer Billy Higgins are exemplary.

*One Step Beyond* (Blue Note 46821) was recorded in 1963 with an unusual instrumentation of trombone (Grachan Moncur III), vibes (Bobby Hutcherson), Eddie Khan's bass, and the extraordinary drumming of Tony Williams, who would soon go on to make a large name for himself with Miles Davis's quintet. This set continues the compositional adventurousness of *Let Freedom Ring* and never stops swinging. McLean's "Saturday and Sunday" is an interesting piece with contrasting slow and fast themes, which shifts into up-tempo for blowing, and his "Blue Rondo" is a contrapuntal blues. The altoist was obviously continuing to experiment with his sound and had obtained fantastic control in all registers. This album and *Let Freedom Ring* are great examples of the way some of the devices and techniques of the avant-garde of the time could be used by thoroughly schooled musicians to broaden the music's canvas.

Two of McLean's best Blue Note albums are currently available only as Japanese imports, but you should at least know that they are out there. For McLean at his bebop best, track down *Swing, Swang, Swingin'*, a 1959 quartet date on which pianist Walter Bishop, Jr., Jimmy Garrison (who later played bass in John Coltrane's great quartet), and drummer Art Taylor grill up a take-no-prisoners groove under McLean's versions of tasty standards like "I Remember You," "I Love You," and "What's New." This album consists of the highest level of straight-ahead swinging and melodic invention on chord changes, in the tradition of Charlie Parker's quartet album *Now's the Time* (Verve 825 671-2), and is worth having at any price. The same rhythm section, with Paul Chambers on bass in place of Garrison, powers 1960's ferocious *Capuchin Swing*, on which McLean is joined by trumpeter Blue Mitchell in a hard-cooking set. The highlight is probably the very hot "Francisco," which cuts back and forth between a Latin groove and some straight-ahead swinging.

McLean was in demand as a sideman throughout the 1950s, recording at various times with the groups of Charles Mingus, Miles Davis, and Art Blakey. With Mingus, McLean can be heard to advantage on *Pithecanthropus Erectus* (Atlantic 8809-2) and, especially, on *Blues and Roots* (Atlantic 1305-2). With Davis, McLean made his first recording session at the age of nineteen, available as *Miles Davis Featuring Sonny Rollins: Dig* (Prestige/OJC-005). He also guests with the trumpeter on *Miles Davis, Volume 1* (Blue Note 81501) and *Miles Davis and Milt Jackson: Quintet/Sextet* (Prestige/OJC-012). With Blakey, McLean can be heard on *Theory of Art* (RCA/Bluebird 6286-2-RB). He is also a sideman on any number of Blue Note records of the late 1950s and 1960s; one famous date to which he contributes heavily is pianist Sonny Clark's *Cool Struttin'* (Blue Note 46513), a cooking, bebop-based 1958 session with Art Farmer on trumpet and a rhythm section rounded out by Paul Chambers and Philly Joe Jones.

But McLean's finest hour as a sideman must be the 1960 quartet recording of the music from the Off-Broadway show *The Connection*, in which McLean also acted. The session, under the leadership of pianist Freddie Redd, who composed the music, is available on *The Complete Blue Note Recordings of Freddie Redd* (Mosaic MD2-124). In addition to the music from the show, which consists mainly of furious, up-tempo cooking in a bebop vein, this set contains the music from another 1960 Redd session, long out of print as *Shades of Redd*, which pairs McLean with tenorist Tina Brooks, as well as a previously unissued 1961 session featuring McLean, Brooks, and trumpeter Benny Bailey. Redd is a limited piano soloist, but as an accompanist he is just fine, and his compositions, especially the ballads (check out "Just a Ballad for My Baby" from the *Shades of Redd* session), are invariably interesting and sensitive, full of attention to dynamics, tempo shifts, and harmonic alertness. They certainly inspire McLean to heights of expression. This set is absolutely essential for McLean fans.

## CANNONBALL ADDERLEY

Julian "Cannonball" Adderley exploded onto the New York music scene in 1955, having just arrived from Florida, where he was a music teacher. He was a fiery player, a florid and romantic improviser who was unquestionably influenced by Bird, but he also had strong roots in swing and blues approaches. He loved to swoop up into the high reaches of his horn for emotional effect, and his work sometimes had an almost giddy exultation in it. He gigged around New York with his own groups for a couple of years before joining Miles Davis's band (which included John Coltrane) in 1958, expanding the quintet to a sextet. When he left Davis it was to lead his own band, most of the time with his brother, Nat, on trumpet.

*Spontaneous Combustion* (Savoy ZD70816) contains the first session Adderley recorded, days after he arrived in the Apple, under drummer Kenny Clarke's leadership, as well as a session from several weeks later under his own leadership. The set contains a wide spectrum of material, including the up-tempo "Chasm," Oscar Pettiford's mysterioso minor-key line "Bohemia After Dark," the ballad "Willow Weep for Me," and two tunes that show Adderley's penchant for riff-based, roots-and-blues home cooking – "Hear Me Talkin' to Ya" and "Spontaneous Combustion." Adderley's preaching, shouting style is heard to good advantage here, in a true blowing-session setting.

Adderley's tenure with Miles Davis's band is well documented and includes two indisputable jazz classics, *Milestones* (Columbia CK 40837) and *Kind of Blue* (Columbia CK 40579). Adderley's playing on both sessions set standards that he would approach but never surpass for inventiveness and lyricism. His blistering exchanges with Coltrane on *Milestones'* "Dr. Jackle" (a Jackie McLean tune called "Dr. Jekyll" on the disc), his soaring leadoff solo on the same album's "Miles," and every note he plays on *Kind of Blue* are high points of his career and of jazz history. Both sets are essential for anyone interested in jazz.

Adderley plays wonderfully on every track of *Miles Davis '58 Sessions: Featuring "Stella by Starlight"* (Columbia CK 47835), especially on "Love for Sale," where he fairly bursts with imagination and swing. Three tunes recorded by the sextet at the Plaza Hotel that summer are also very hot. *Miles and Coltrane* (Columbia CK 44052) consists mainly of five tracks recorded at the

1958 Newport Jazz Festival by the sextet, on which Adderley takes hard-hitting solos throughout – not an essential item, but a valuable supplementary document of the band's activities.

Adderley recorded two very good albums under his own leadership using his cohorts from the Davis band. *Somethin' Else* (Blue Note 46338) features Miles Davis in the unaccustomed role of sideman, side-by-side with the altoist in front of a dream rhythm section of Hank Jones, Sam Jones, and Art Blakey, for a truly all-star date. The results are as good as you might expect, generally on the mellow side, with tunes like "Autumn Leaves," "Dancing in the Dark," and the blues "One for Daddy-O" setting a moody, late-afternoon groove that is unique to this session. The set also includes a fine version of "Love for Sale" and an extra tune recorded that day, "Alison's Uncle," which was not released on the original LP, perhaps because its up-tempo, bop-flavored melody and chord changes make it so different in mood from the rest of the music here. This is one of those sets that everyone should own.

Recorded a year later, *Cannonball and Coltrane* (EmArcy 834 588) features the Davis band of the time minus its leader. There is a lot of good music here, including some high-velocity Adderley-Coltrane exchanges on "Limehouse Blues" that rival those on *Milestones'* "Dr. Jackle" and a gorgeous Adderley ballad performance of "Stars Fell on Alabama." Something about this set is a little tiring, though, despite the uniformly high quality of the playing. I think it is that the horn players are both intense, multinote players; they don't provide enough of a contrast to each other. With Davis rounding out the front line, there was the perfect tart counterweight to all that heat. Pianist Wynton Kelly fills that role to some extent here, but still the set feels a little lopsided.

Adderley made many records as a leader, a good number of them fairly casual situations in which a loose, blowing atmosphere reigned. *Cannonball's Sharpshooters* (Mercury 826 986-2) is one of the best (and best organized) of these, a highly charged set in which the altoist is paired with his brother, trumpeter Nat, and a rhythm section including a surging, well-recorded Sam Jones on bass. This is one of the lesser-known Adderley albums, but it is a true smoker. The repertoire is drawn mainly from jazz standards associated with the boppers – Tadd Dameron's "Our Delight" and "Stay On It" and Monk's "Straight, No Chaser," for example. Adderley flies high (especially on his aptly named original, "Jubilation"), and the group put some effort into working out arrangements that would enhance the album's cooking ambience. A highly recommended set.

*Portrait of Cannonball* (Riverside/OJC-361) has Adderley with trumpeter Blue Mitchell in front of an interesting-looking rhythm section of Bill Evans, Sam Jones, and Philly Joe Jones, but this is one of 'Ball's lesser efforts. It has a thrown-together feeling about it. *Things Are Getting Better* (Riverside/OJC-032), a collaboration with vibist Milt Jackson and an ace rhythm section of Wynton Kelly, Percy Heath, and Art Blakey, is somewhat better, although still a bit casually assembled. The sheer firepower of talent in the studio seems to have put Adderley on his mettle, though, and Jackson plays well, as always, in a basically blues-oriented program.

Recorded late in 1959 with Adderley's working band, *The Cannonball Adderley Quintet in San Francisco* (Riverside/OJC-035) is a minor jazz classic for the presence of the gospel-influenced waltz "This Here," written by the band's pianist, Bobby Timmons. "This Here" became a big hit for the band and pointed Adderley toward the soul/roots bag he was to follow increasingly for the rest of his life. Also included are new versions of "Bohemia After Dark" and the blues "Spontaneous Combustion." This is punchy, energetic music all the way, if not especially subtle. *The Cannonball Adderley Sextet in New York* (Riverside/OJC-142), recorded in 1962 with a band including brother Nat, Yusef Lateef on reeds, and Joe Zawinul on piano, fits the same description, as does *The Cannonball Adderley Quintet Plus* (Riverside/OJC-306), which has two takes of the sprightly favorite "Lisa."

## ERIC DOLPHY

Multireed man Eric Dolphy was known primarily for his alto saxophone playing, although he was more than proficient on flute and bass clarinet. Dolphy came along toward the end of the hard-bop period, and he was one of those who, like John Coltrane, became part of the 1960s avant-garde after serving a thorough apprenticeship in earlier forms. An extremely fiery player given to unusual interval leaps rather than straight-ahead scale passages or standard arpeggios, Dolphy sometimes used these unusual note intervals to undercut the conventional tonality of a piece; in some respects, his almost perverse way of outlining a song's harmonies resembles that of alto player Benny Carter. But where Carter's attack was always smooth, Dolphy's was piercing and aggressive.

A good place to get introduced to Dolphy's playing is *The Complete Candid Recordings of Charles Mingus* (Mosaic MD3-111). The reed man is to be found here in several very different settings, the most famous of which is certainly the quartet date, available on its own as *Mingus Presents Mingus* (Candid CD 9005), which produced "Folk Forms No. 1," "Fables of Faubus," "All the Things You Could Be by Now If Sigmund Freud's Wife Was Your Mother," and the amazing "What Love," which contains an extraordinary dialogue between Dolphy's bass clarinet and Mingus's bass. This material, as well as most of the rest of the box, is discussed in some detail in the Ensembles section. Besides the quartet tracks, Dolphy is heard with a larger ensemble on the surging, riff-based blues "MDM" and on a small-band date on which trumpeter Roy Eldridge sits in. In every session, Dolphy's playing is immediately identifiable, very vocal-sounding on both alto and bass clarinet, adventuresome, and challenging to listen to.

Dolphy was seen, or at least promoted, as a somewhat far-out player in the early 1960s, as the titles of some of his albums – *Outward Bound, Far Cry*, and *Out There*, for example – attest. The liner notes for *Outward Bound* claim that "this is the sound of tomorrow, the sound of the Atlas missile, the sound of the Pioneer radar blip from outer space." At times some of Dolphy's compositions, such as "The Prophet" on *Eric Dolphy at the Five Spot Volume 1* (New Jazz/OJC-133) or "Straight Up and Down" on *Out to Lunch* (Blue Note 46524), sound as if he were trying to live up to this description. As a result, such tunes sometimes sound downright corny, as often happens when a deliberate attempt is made to come up with unusual sounds. But much of this music sounds surprisingly mainstream today.

Probably most enjoyable are *Far Cry* (New Jazz/OJC-400) and *Outward Bound* (New Jazz/OJC-022). Both sets find Dolphy in the company of the extremely flexible, inventive, and spontaneous pianist Jaki Byard and the undersung drummer Roy Haynes. *Far Cry* has the brilliant Booker Little playing trumpet; *Outward Bound* has Freddie Hubbard. Both present a good mixture of original cookers and ballads (and one or two standards) in straight-ahead time signatures, with lots of interesting commentary from the rhythm section. *Far Cry* has two Byard compositions dedicated to Charlie Parker, a tricky medium-up-tempo blues known as "Bird's Mother" and a lovely ballad, "Ode to Charlie Parker," on which Dolphy plays flute. The standard ballad "Tenderly" is a great showpiece for Dolphy's unaccompanied alto and shows his expressive tone in all its glory. The quartet performance of "It's Magic" does the same for his bass clarinet playing. *Outward Bound* has a similar mix of good material, including Dolphy's reading of the standard "Green Dolphin Street."

On records like *Eric Dolphy at the Five Spot Volume 1* (New Jazz/OJC-133), *Volume 2* (Prestige/OJC-247), and *Eric Dolphy and Booker Little Memorial Album* (Prestige/OJC-353), all recorded in 1961 at the famous downtown New York jazz club, Dolphy has more room to indulge his vice, which is to play multinote patterns full of his own stock scale passages and devices. I think that many times, in the rush of expressing all that fire he had inside, Dolphy loses sight of the actual content of what he is saying. This is not to say that what he plays is random, only that it can be repetitive and studded, at its worst, with corny-sounding devices. But there is much exceptional music on the Five Spot sets, despite this tendency, and these have been some of the most popular items among true Dolphy fans.

One of the most extreme records Dolphy made, and one that is still challenging to listen to, is *Out to Lunch* (Blue Note 46524), recorded in 1964 with Hubbard again on trumpet, Bobby Hutcherson's vibes in place of a piano, Richard Davis's bass, and the drums of the young genius Tony Williams. The set is full of unusual song forms, shifting rhythmic patterns, and an unusual group sound. Particularly interesting here is the way in which Williams works off of the various rhythmic motifs that are set up throughout, especially on the title track. The interest here is primarily cerebral.

## ORNETTE COLEMAN

In the 1960s Ornette Coleman's name was almost synonymous with what was called, variously, the New Thing, the avant-garde, or free jazz. He provoked widely varying and even violent reactions for years after his arrival on the scene in 1959; in the late 1960s *Down Beat* magazine was still full of argument over his merits. Many, including Miles Davis, said he was a charlatan with no knowledge of music; others, including John Lewis of the Modern Jazz Quartet, felt that Coleman was a true innovator who had unlocked a way of playing melody that was not based primarily on the chord-changes approach of bebop.

I agree wholeheartedly with the second group. Almost everything about Coleman's music is songlike, natural, and emotionally direct. Moreover, it uses all of the compositional devices integral to jazz – riffs, breaks, backgrounds to solos – as well as the other elements – swing, blues techniques, a call-and-response sensibility, the sensitivity to Latin rhythms that Jelly Roll Morton called the Spanish tinge – that define the music. In his playing, Coleman had, and has, a lyricism that aims for the heart as well as the head, with one of the most expressive sounds of any instrumentalist in jazz.

Coleman's first two records – *Something Else!!!* (Contemporary/OJC-163) and *Tomorrow Is the Question!* (Contemporary/OJC-342) – have been somewhat passed over by critics in favor of the slightly later recordings with his classic quartet that included trumpeter Don Cherry (who appears on the first two, as well), bassist Charlie Haden, and either Billy Higgins or Ed Blackwell on drums. But as showcases for his alto playing – and as complete musical statements – both sets are highly recommended. Coleman's alto always swings, and he takes a number of different tacks in his solos, depending on the material (which consists exclusively of his compositions). Sometimes he plays pure melody; at other times his solos sound like abstracts of bebop solos, phrases darting here and there, posing questions and answering each other. Notice how much Coleman uses dynamics in his playing; within one solo he will move from a shout to a muttered aside to a singing, lyrical line. One has to think hard before one can think of another "modern" saxophonist who paid so much attention to dynamics.

There is a lot to listen for in both records. After *Something Else!!!*, his first album, Coleman did not record with a pianist for quite a while. Although Coleman jettisoned the keyboard from his band in order not to be directed by the chordal framework the piano almost inevitably set up at the time, pianist Walter Norris doesn't get in the way here, and the set is a kick. Coleman's lines, played with trumpeter Don Cherry, who would be his musical companion for the next few years, are still deeply bebop-influenced, except for "The Sphinx," a two-part song with contrasting thematic material, which suggests the direction Coleman's writing would take. Throughout, Coleman's sound is drenched in the cry of the blues and is also intensely rhythmic at the same time as it is most melodic – another key to his music's jazz character. Many of the tunes incorporate breaks for the drummer (Billy Higgins) into the melody. To hear Coleman swinging hard on the most traditional material there is, listen to his solo on "When Will the Blues Leave?"

*Tomorrow Is the Question!*, recorded a year later, in 1959, moves a little farther out; the piano is no longer present, and the compositions move away a few steps from the bebop-oriented material of the previous set (although material like "Tears Inside," "Giggin'," and "Endless" refer unmistakably to bebop). The title tune shows just how deeply Coleman was steeped in the jazz tradition; it incorporates a rhythmic figure that goes back to James P. Johnson's stride piano showpiece "Carolina Shout," as well as bebop figures, breaks, a Charleston beat, and even the suggestion of a Spanish tinge in the way the horns are voiced in thirds. But increasingly the relation between lead and background is being implicitly questioned, as in the shifting accompaniments to the solos on "Tears Inside." Compositions like "Compassion" and "Lorraine" extend the freedom of line of "The Sphinx." Yet on "Giggin'," Coleman takes a solo that shows clearly just how acquainted he was with Parker's language.

A little later in the year, Coleman began his great series of recordings for Atlantic, in which his group conception really crystallized. Everything he did for Atlantic is collected on *Beauty Is a Rare Thing – The Complete Atlantic Recordings* (Rhino/Atlantic R2 71410), a six-CD set that includes a number of previously unreleased performances and things issued only in Japan. This is one of the best collections of its type, not just for the music but for the beautiful design of the box itself and the excellent booklet contained therein.

If you miss the intelligent programming to be found on the original albums, several of them are available individually. One of these, which everyone should hear, is *The Shape of Jazz to Come* (Atlantic 1317-2), probably the greatest album Coleman recorded. It is discussed in the Ensembles section. Coleman is even more adventuresome in his playing here, as on "Eventually" and "Focus on Sanity," where he sometimes plays groups of notes that form shapes, or gestures, rather than discrete lines, or on "Peace," where his songlike melody leads wherever it likes, not hewing to a set of chord changes yet never discordant sounding. He never, even at his most abstract, seems to be playing anything just for effect, as Dolphy, for example, often seems to. This is, finally, extremely joyous music. *Change of the Century* (Atlantic 7 81341-2) is another of Coleman's best quartet records; it includes the classic blues "Ramblin'," the Latin-flavored "Una Muy Bonita," and a homage to Charlie Parker called "Bird Food."

Coleman and Dolphy may be heard side-by-side on 1960's *Free Jazz* (Atlantic 1364-2), which is discussed at some length in the Ensembles section. *Free Jazz* presents two trumpeters (Freddie Hubbard and Don Cherry), two altoists (Coleman and Dolphy), two bassists (Charlie Haden and Scott La Faro), and two drummers (Billy Higgins and Ed Blackwell) in a "collective improvisation" punctuated by Coleman's ensemble interludes. This set may sound initially like chaos, but when you begin to hear what's going on, its roots in the entire jazz tradition become clear.

*The Art of the Improvisers* (Atlantic 7 90978-2) is an extremely worthwhile set made up of quartet items from 1959 through 1961 that didn't make it onto the originally released albums, but there is nothing inferior about the material. The set tends toward the more convoluted of Coleman's compositions, such as "The Alchemy of Scott La Faro," "Moon Inhabitants," and "The Circle with the Hole in the Middle." But it also includes one of the most beautiful things Coleman ever recorded, the ballad "Just for You," on which Coleman and Don Cherry phrase around each other at a slow tempo in a way that recalls the exquisite beauty of Charlie Parker and Miles Davis in the final chorus of "Bird of Paradise" (available on *The Legendary Dial Masters, Volume 1* [Stash ST-CD-23]; another take can be found on *Volume 2* [Stash ST-CD-25]). For those who may already own the LP, the CD is worth having for two additional tracks, "Music Always" and "Brings Goodness."

If you like Coleman, you can hear a few different sides of him on a number of albums. *At the Golden Circle, Volume 1* (Blue Note 84224) and *Volume 2*

(Blue Note 84225) present Coleman in a trio setting with bassist David Izenzon and drummer Charles Moffett. Coleman's alto is given the freest rein possible here, and the results are a feast for anyone who likes the way he plays. The somewhat later *New York Is Now!* (Blue Note 84287) has Ornette paired with tenor saxophonist Dewey Redman, a good foil for him, and Jimmy Garrison and Elvin Jones, a team in John Coltrane's famous quartet, on bass and drums, respectively. This is a freewheeling and enjoyable set that includes the humorous riff "Broad Way Blues" and the very humorous "We Now Interrupt for a Commercial." Finally, the 1987 *In All Languages* (Caravan of Dreams CDP 85008) features an interesting contrast between his original quartet (with Cherry, Haden, and Higgins reunited) and his electric band, Prime Time (with two drummers, two bassists, and two guitarists). The quartet has ten tracks to itself, and Prime Time gets thirteen; certain tunes are performed once by each band, for a very revealing contrast. The quartet is as coherent and musical as ever, although none of its selections runs over four minutes. Prime Time, on the other hand, sounds kind of lumpy and confused, as if the various instruments are working at harmonic and rhythmic cross-purposes; it is hard to focus on Coleman in the middle of it all. But the quartet tracks are compact, elegant statements, albeit no match for the earlier masterpieces.

# TENORS

### COLEMAN HAWKINS

Coleman Hawkins was the first musician to play jazz successfully on the tenor saxophone, which had been used mainly as a novelty instrument in popular music up until his arrival. His career ranged from the early 1920s to his death in 1969, and he was active in the serious work being done in all eras, playing with everyone from blues singer Mamie Smith to Thelonious Monk.

Hawk, or Bean, as he was called, defined the style of the tenor saxophone for the 1920s and most of the 1930s, until Lester Young began to make his presence felt. His sound was heavy, very throaty and bearlike, with a big vibrato. It was authoritative and instantly identifiable. At faster tempos, especially as his career went on, his swing was irresistible, his accents usually falling on the beat; at ballad tempos, his ideas were sensuous, and his sound opened into a wide, rhapsodic vibrato. Hawkins never stopped developing and experimenting; he was a dynamic force in the music and encouraged many younger musicians throughout his career.

#### THE STAMPEDE

The earliest Hawkins solos on record are to be found on recordings he made with the Fletcher Henderson orchestra, the preeminent big jazz orchestra of the 1920s. His early solos, on tunes such as "Dicty Blues" (available on *A Study in Frustration: The Fletcher Henderson Story* [Columbia/Legacy C3K 57596]), tend to sound stiff; Hawkins didn't really find his style until after Louis Armstrong had joined the Henderson band in 1924 and showed everyone how to construct a solo that swung and made sense.

Hawkins learned quickly and well. In 1926 the Henderson band recorded a Don Redman arrangement of "The Stampede" (also available on the Columbia/Legacy set), which features Hawkins at length. His phrasing has smoothed out, and he bursts with ideas; the solo established Hawkins as *the* influence on the instrument. Hawkins recorded innumerable excellent solos with Henderson right up until his departure in 1934; some of the best can be found on *Fletcher Henderson and the Dixie Stompers 1925–1928* (DRG SW 8445/6), especially the rip-roaring "I'm Feelin' Devilish" and "Goose Pimples." More good Hawkins with Henderson may be found on a collection of 1931 titles called *Fletcher Henderson: The Crown King of Swing* (Savoy SJL 1152) and on *Hocus Pocus: Fletcher Henderson and His Orchestra 1927–1936* (RCA/Bluebird 9904-2-RB). On this latter set, listen especially to Hawk's solo on the title tune, recorded in 1934, a masterpiece of blues-inflected playing. An alternate take of this can be found on *Coleman Hawkins – Ben Webster – Benny Carter: Three Great Swing Saxophones* (RCA/Bluebird 9683-2-RB); it is just as good as the one on *Hocus Pocus* and a fascinating contrast. The two Bluebird sets also contain alternate takes of a 1931 recording of "Sugar Foot Stomp" (Henderson's reworking of King Oliver's "Dippermouth Blues"), with roaring solos from Hawkins. Both solos begin with the same phrase; overall, the solo on the take on *Hocus Pocus* is superior – listen to the energy with which he tears into the second chorus of this up-tempo blues.

Toward the end of the 1920s, Hawkins was developing his own florid ballad style, full of a romantic, heavy vibrato. One of the earliest examples of his ballad playing is his solo on "One Hour," recorded with a small recording group called the Mound City Blue Blowers, assembled by singer Red McKenzie. Available on *Three Great Swing Saxophones*, the tune shows Hawkins creating an entirely new set of melodies based on the harmonies of the song rather than on its melody. At its best this approach resulted in lyric masterpieces such as "It's the Talk of the Town," recorded with Henderson in 1933 and available on *Ridin' in Rhythm* (DRG/Swing CDSW 8453/4). At its worst it sounded turgid and choked; his tendency to ornament the melodic line with arpeggios, glissandos, and grace notes could clutter up any feeling of continuity. "The Day You Came Along" (also on *Ridin' in Rhythm*) is an example of this approach applied unsuccessfully. Throughout the 1930s he smoothed out his ballad playing until, although he always played many notes, none of them was wasted, resulting in the 1939 masterpiece most identified with him, "Body and Soul."

Hawkins was in demand as a guest star in the recording studios, as well as with Henderson. "One Hour" is an example of this kind of activity, as is "Hello Lola," recorded at the same session and included on *Three Great Swing Saxophones.* "Hello Lola" contains a ferocious Hawkins solo, in which he plays his notes staccato, swinging heavily and accenting almost invariably on the down beat. Other examples of this approach are "Wherever There's a Will, Baby," with McKinney's Cotton Pickers (available on the same set), and "Jamaica Shout," recorded under Hawkins's own leadership in 1933 (available on *Ridin' in Rhythm*).

The combination of staccato phrasing and down-beat accenting made for a very heavy, insistent swing beat, characteristic of jazz before musicians (with the exception of Louis Armstrong) had really learned how to use the four beats per measure in a smoother way. You can hear Hawkins working this out himself if you compare his solo on "Jamaica Shout" with his performance of "Lady, Be Good" from a year later, also included on *Ridin' in Rhythm*. Over a chugging mid-tempo swing approximately the same as that of the earlier number, Hawkins's lines on "Lady, Be Good" are more legato and more evenly swinging, and he is learning to use the one-two-three-four beat not just as something to hammer home but as a set of expectations to alternately fulfill and subvert. By the time he recorded "Crazy Rhythm" with Benny Carter and Django Reinhardt in Paris in 1937, he would be one of the great masters of this.

"Jamaica Shout," "The Day You Came Along," and the beautiful "Heartbreak Blues" are also available on a fine set entitled *Henry "Red" Allen and Coleman Hawkins 1933* (Smithsonian Collection R022), along with a number of sides recorded by a cooperative band under the joint leadership of Hawkins and Allen, a New Orleans trumpeter who was one of the greatest disciples of Louis Armstrong.

*Ridin' in Rhythm* is a treasure trove of mid-1930s Hawkins, containing, in addition to the titles mentioned earlier, a series of recordings with a big band under the direction of Fletcher Henderson's brother Horace, two duets with pianist Buck Washington, and a number of records made during Hawkins's long mid-1930s residence in Europe, including some fine duets with pianist Stanley Black and two sides with the English dance orchestra of Jack Hylton. The latter two are interesting because, despite a very contemporary, slick, big-band ensemble sound, the rhythm section hasn't learned to swing yet. Hawk sounds unfazed and swings in fine fettle.

The best recordings Hawkins made in Europe, however, are the previously mentioned sides with Benny Carter and Django Reinhardt, available as *Coleman Hawkins and Benny Carter in Paris* (DRG/Swing CDSW 8403; also on *Djangologie/USA, Volume 1* [DRG/Swing CDSW 8421/3]). Set off by gorgeous writing for saxophones by Benny Carter (the two are joined by French altoist

Andre Ekyan and tenorist Alix Combelle, to form a fine sax section), Hawk plays a fantastic solo on "Honeysuckle Rose," totally in command of his now-ripe legato swing style, using the accents of the background to create patterns of expectation, suspense, and release. "Crazy Rhythm" is even better, an up-tempo romp in which he enters his solo with a short phrase announcing himself, then hammers on a riff, which he shortens, then extends, then tears away from. The head of steam he builds up makes for one of the most exciting recorded solos in jazz.

As if that weren't enough, Hawkins plays a classic ballad solo on "Out of Nowhere," without any of the arhythmic, cluttered arpeggios of a few years before. He learned how to dovetail phrases, answering himself, in effect, as he plays – playing a phrase, then echoing it with the next in such a way as to lead him into a new line of thought, each sentence, as it were, coming out of the one before it, a technique learned from Armstrong. Almost as an after-thought, there is a loose, jammed version of "Sweet Georgia Brown" to round out the set.

### BODY AND SOUL

By the time Hawkins returned to the United States he had spawned a school of followers, including such strong individualists as Chu Berry and Ben Webster. A very different approach to the tenor sax and to swinging had been opened by Lester Young. But Hawkins was at the height of his powers, and Young's influence was not to be pervasive for another couple of years.

Hawkins appeared on one of Lionel Hampton's most famous all-star dates in 1939, recording "Early Session Hop," "When Lights Are Low," and "Hot Mallets" in the company of his two greatest disciples, Berry and Webster. The tunes are available on *Hot Mallets, Volume 1* (RCA/Bluebird 6458-2-RB) and are interesting also for the presence of the young Dizzy Gillespie.

His popularity was such that he was able to lead a big band for a while, and in 1939 he recorded his most famous side, "Body and Soul." At a slow tempo, after a four-bar piano intro, Hawkins slides into the harmonies of the song, using only the briefest reference to its melody, and, turning up the flame slowly, he spins out a three-minute improvisation that has proved to be one of the most enduring of all jazz masterpieces. It is available on *Body and Soul* (RCA/Bluebird 5717-2-RB), accompanied by an armada of other notable early-1940s tracks, as well as some 1950s material with an orchestra. Particularly en-joyable here are four small-group sides recorded in 1940 with the trombonist J. C. Higginbotham which have a loose, jammed feeling to them and on which Hawkins really stretches out. His solo on "The Sheik of Araby" could almost define the classic swing tenor feel.

Throughout the 1940s Hawkins was a dominant figure in the music. Two highly recommended sets document his activities during the years of World War II: *Coleman Hawkins/Lester Young – Classic Tenors* (Signature/CBS AK 38446) and a monumental four-disc set called *The Complete Coleman Hawkins on Keynote* (Mercury 830 960-2). *Classic Tenors* contains at least two sides that are Hawkins landmarks, versions of "The Man I Love" and "Sweet Lorraine," recorded in 1943 with Oscar Pettiford on bass. Both tunes were released originally on 12-inch 78-rpm records rather than the standard 10-inch; the larger format allowed for more playing time, and these records are extended explorations of the harmonies of two great pop tunes. On both, Hawkins paces himself carefully, unleashing more and more imagination and passion as the performances go on. Listen, on "The Man I Love," to Oscar Pettiford breathing between the phrases of his bass solo as if he were a horn player. "Get Happy" and "Crazy Rhythm," from the same session, are also excellent, and there are several other good Hawk tracks included here, along with four beautiful Lester Young sides.

*The Complete Coleman Hawkins on Keynote* contains the results of eight 1944 sessions for the small Keynote label, including multiple takes of many items. The sessions find Hawkins in various settings, with trumpeters Buck Clayton, Charlie Shavers, Joe Thomas, and Roy Eldridge, one of Hawk's favorite musical companions. The tracks with Eldridge here, especially the "How High the Moon"–derived "Bean at the Met," are very exciting and bring out the most aggressive and hard-driving side of both men. Pianist Teddy Wilson is featured extensively on five of the eight sessions; Earl Hines is at the keyboard for another session, which produced "Father Co-operates" and "Through for the Night." Anyone who likes Hawkins or small-group swing in general is advised to pick this up.

At the same time as the above sides were being recorded, the developments pioneered by Charlie Parker and Dizzy Gillespie were slowly becoming part of the jazz language. Hawkins was always very receptive to the best of the newcomers, and he made records with trumpeters Gillespie, Miles Davis, Fats Navarro, and Howard McGhee, as well as pianist Thelonious Monk and others associated with the bebop movement. Two sides with Gillespie, from what is often called the first full-fledged bebop session, are included on *Dizzy Gillespie: The Development of an American Artist* (Smithsonian Collection R004). "Woody'n You" and "Disorder at the Border" also feature Max Roach's drums along with Gillespie's rocketing trumpet and Hawkins sounding as roaring and full-bodied as ever. *Hollywood Stampede* (Capitol CDP 7 92596 2) consists of tracks from 1945 and 1947 with Howard McGhee and Miles Davis, including a number of fine, abstract ballad interpretations and the riffs

"Stuffy" and "Rifftide," the latter of which showed up later in Thelonious Monk's repertoire as "Hackensack." *Body and Soul* (RCA/Bluebird 5717-2-RB) contains two 1947 tracks with electric Fats Navarro solos, "Half Step Down, Please" and "Jumping for Jane."

A fascinating but probably hard-to-find album of material recorded slightly later is *Coleman Hawkins – Disorder at the Border* (Spotlite 121, LP only), which features two 1952 broadcasts from the New York nightclub Birdland. On one, Hawk's front-line partner in the quintet is Howard McGhee; on the other, more explosive one it's Roy Eldridge. Despite what the notes say, Art Blakey, not Connie Kay, is the drummer on the evening with Eldridge; Kay is the drummer on the McGhee tracks. This set contains some of the most ferocious Hawkins to be found anywhere, due in large part to the exhilarating drive of the rhythm section, which includes pianist Horace Silver and bassist Curly Russell on both nights. The rhythm section of Blakey, Silver, and Russell is the same one that powered Blakey's fantastic *A Night at Birdland, Volume 1* (Blue Note 46519) and *Volume 2* (Blue Note 46520), with trumpeter Clifford Brown and altoist Lou Donaldson.

### LATE HAWK

Hawkins made some of his best records in the 1950s and 1960s. His tone had aged like fine cognac; his ballad performances grew more reflective, but he could still turn up the heat as high as ever. One of his best sets of the 1950s is *The High and Mighty Hawk* (London 820 600-2), an extremely well recorded 1958 session with trumpeter Buck Clayton, pianist Hank Jones, bassist Ray Brown, and drummer Mickey Sheen. Brown, especially, gives lustre to this varied set by his imaginative and melodic accompaniment; listen closely to him throughout. "Bird of Prey Blues" is a swinging, medium-tempo blues riff by Hawkins on which the leader tears off no fewer than seventeen mean, swaggering choruses, and Hawk's ballad interpretations of "My One and Only Love" and "You've Changed" are both lyric masterpieces. Two bouncy Hank Jones originals elicit good playing from everyone as well. This is an example of mature musicians playing in a style with which they are completely comfortable, having a ball, telling stories, swinging.

*Hawk Eyes!* (Prestige/OJC-294), from 1959, contains some more roaring Hawk in a sextet with trumpeter Charlie Shavers, guitarist Tiny Grimes, and pianist Ray Bryant. Standouts are the churchy title track, the midnight blues "C'mon In," which Hawk begins accompanied only by George Duvivier's bass (Hawk really plays a mess of blues here), and the hollering "Stealin' the Bean." Also excellent is 1958's *Soul* (Prestige/OJC-096), with guitarist Kenny Burrell and with Bryant again on piano, a mixture of blues, ballads (a great version of "Until the Real Thing Comes Along"), and an up-tempo riff. This set includes a haunting version of the ballad "Greensleeves." But fans of Hawkins's ballad playing will love *At Ease with Coleman Hawkins* (Prestige/OJC-181) above all. Hawkins plays with a rhythm section including pianist Tommy Flanagan, doing gorgeous and uncommon standards like "Trouble Is a Man," "For You, for Me, for Evermore," "Then I'll Be Tired of You," and Alec Wilder's "While We're Young." This is one of the finest things Hawkins recorded.

*The Genius of Coleman Hawkins* (Verve 825 673-2) is an outstanding date with Hawkins playing standards like "I'll Never Be the Same," "Ill Wind," "There's No You," and "You're Blase" in front of the Verve house rhythm section of Oscar Peterson, Herb Ellis, Ray Brown, and Alvin Stoller. Hawk is at ease and very inventive in this relaxed and happy set. A mellow mood also prevails on *Coleman Hawkins Encounters Ben Webster* (Verve 823 120-2), which features the two in front of the same Verve rhythm section. This is a loose, laid-back conversation between the two big-toned horns, mostly on familiar material. No fireworks here. The two tenor men lock horns again on *Ben Webster and Associates* (Verve 835 254-2), on which they are joined by trumpeter Roy Eldridge and a third tenorist, the undersung Budd Johnson, who outplays both Hawkins and Webster! This one is a real feast for tenor fans.

A live nightclub recording from 1959, *Roy Eldridge and Coleman Hawkins at the Bayou Club* (Stash ST-CD-531) has exciting work by both horn players despite a pretty dull rhythm section. This set contains seventy-five minutes of full-bodied blowing on Hawkins/Eldridge favorites such as "Rifftide," "How High the Moon," and "Just You, Just Me." Just as good are two late-1950s studio dates with his 1930s trumpet partner Henry "Red" Allen, combined on one CD called *Coleman Hawkins and Red Allen: Standards and Warhorses* (Jass CD-2). Don't be put off by the corny-looking repertoire (it includes things like "Bill Bailey" and "Battle Hymn of the Republic"); this has Hawk (and Allen) blowing at full throttle. Best of all, though, is *World on a String* (RCA/Bluebird 2497-2-RB), a 1957 set originally issued as *Ride, Red, Ride in Hi-Fi*, featuring both horns playing fantastic stuff throughout a program of standards and blues. Hawkins is in dangerous shape on this one; his solo on "Algiers Bounce" alone is worth the price of the disc.

Hawk is truly in top form as well on four tunes recorded at a German jazz festival in 1960 with pianist Bud Powell, who was living in Europe at that time, bassist Oscar Pettiford, and drummer Kenny Clarke. Available under Powell's name as *The Complete Essen Jazz Festival Concert* (Black Lion BLCD 760 105), this set has Hawk swinging through medium-tempo versions of "All the

Things You Are" and his riff "Stuffy" as if his life depended on it, accompanied by one of the best bop-oriented rhythm sections imaginable. Essential stuff.

## BEN WEBSTER

Ben Webster, only four years Hawkins's junior, was perhaps Hawkins's greatest disciple, with a sound so identifiable and a sensibility so inimitable that the notion of discipleship is misleading. He was without peer as a ballad player, having learned as much, or more, about phrasing from alto saxophonist Johnny Hodges (his sectionmate in the Duke Ellington orchestra, where Webster was a star member from 1940 to 1943) as from Hawkins, and his blues playing was also hard to match. This big, hard-drinking, pool-playing man, one of whose nicknames was "The Brute," was in fact one of the greatest lyric voices in the history of the music. His playing on ballads could have a tenderness and a romantic quality that were all the more moving for the sense of strength that lay behind them. Flip the coin and his sound could swell with passion and force.

For an example of Webster at his all-time best, proceed directly to *Soulville* (Verve 833 551-2). The 1957 set consists of a slow, after-hours blues (the title track), a charging, medium-tempo blues, three stunningly lyrical ballads ("Time on My Hands," "Where Are You," and "Ill Wind" – on this kind of material Webster was unbeatable), and relaxed readings of the standards "Lover Come Back to Me" and "Makin' Whoopee." He is accompanied by Oscar Peterson's piano, Herb Ellis's guitar, Ray Brown's bass, and Stan Levey's drums. This is one of the most cohesive "mood" albums ever recorded. For good measure, Verve included three informally recorded piano solos by Webster – two stride pieces and a boogie-woogie – that break the deep mood of the rest of the album but which are fun to have anyway.

For more Webster on this level, pick up *Art Tatum: The Tatum Group Masterpieces, Volume 8* (Pablo PACD-2405-431-2), from a series of group recordings that Tatum led in the mid-1950s with such guests as Benny Carter, Lionel Hampton, and trumpeter Roy Eldridge (the Eldridge set runs the Webster a fairly close second). *Volume 8* features Webster with Tatum, bass, and drums in one of the very best encounters of this sort in the history of the music. Where some of Tatum's other guests in the series tried to match him technique-for-technique, run-for-run, Webster underplayed it, singing the gorgeous melodies with his fullest sound, a perfect complement to the pianist's florid, multinote approach. Together they play the most beautiful of popular standards, like "Gone with the Wind," "Have You Met Miss Jones," "My

Ideal," and "Where or When," and produce one of the music's masterpieces. Don't miss this.

Webster came to New York City in December 1932 with the great Kansas City orchestra of Bennie Moten (which included young Count Basie and trumpeter Hot Lips Page), stopping off in Camden, New Jersey, to make some famous recordings available now as *Bennie Moten's Kansas City Orchestra (1929– 1932): Basie Beginnings* (RCA/Bluebird 9768-2-RB). This was one of the great bands of its time, and you can hear its spirit blasting through the seven tracks included on this set (the other tracks here are by earlier incarnations of the band). Webster takes several solos, sounding very much like Hawkins. Through the rest of the decade Webster was much in demand as a sideman for the best big bands of the 1930s, including Fletcher Henderson's and Cab Calloway's. He also played saxophone on many of the small-band dates led by pianist Teddy Wilson and featuring the vocals of Billie Holiday; some of the best of these may be heard on *The Quintessential Billie Holiday, Volume 1* (Columbia CK 40646) and *Volume 3* (Columbia CK 44048).

But Webster really hit his stride as a voice on recordings during his years with Duke Ellington's orchestra, beginning in 1940. The classic recordings by this band are all on *Duke Ellington: The Blanton-Webster Band* (RCA/Bluebird 5659-2-RB), a three-CD set that is one of the basics of any jazz library. The up-tempo showpiece "Cottontail" features Webster in one of his most famous performances, tearing up the track on "I Got Rhythm" chord changes. "All Too Soon" and the brooding "Blue Serge" contain unforgettable ballad interpretations by the tenor player, and "Conga Brava," "Bojangles," "Raincheck," "Main Stem," and "Just A-Settin' and A-Rockin'" all have favorite Webster statements. He was one of the most distinctive, strongest voices in a band that placed a premium on individuality.

You can hear this band recorded live in 1940, in full roar, on the two-CD set *Duke Ellington and His Famous Orchestra: Fargo, North Dakota, November 7, 1940* (Vintage Jazz Classics VJC-1019/20-2). One of the miracles of jazz history, this set was recorded on acetate discs at the Crystal Ballroom by a young fan and shows the band on an unmistakably "on" night just after cornetist-violinist Ray Nance joined. (This set includes every scrap of music recorded that evening, not just the tracks that have been available in helter-skelter form until now. The sound is the best so far, too.) Webster plays hard throughout, but nowhere harder than on the finale, "St. Louis Blues," on which he follows singer Ivie Anderson's vocal with five choruses that will clear your sinuses. Webster also took part in some small-group studio dates in 1940 and 1941 led by fellow Ellingtonians Rex Stewart and clarinetist Barney Bigard. Collected on *The Great Ellington Units* (RCA/Bluebird 6751-2-RB), they are small-group jazz at its best. Webster scores with a charging, cogent solo on "Linger Awhile," a smoldering blues solo on "Poor Bubber," and an intriguing passage on the minor-key "Lament for Javanette."

Webster was a sideman on countless recording dates in the 1940s and a leader on quite a few more. *Ben Webster/Don Byas: Giants of the Tenor Sax* (Commodore 7005) contains some excellent 1944 sides by Webster with drummer Big Sid Catlett and is well worth owning. But Webster did his best playing in the 1950s and 1960s. He had arrived at a point at which his control of nuance and sound was absolute; sometimes he would trail out his notes on ballads until all you hear is the air going through his mouthpiece – it was one of the most human sounds ever produced.

Webster got better and better as he got older. Three sets from the 1950s–1960s period are absolutely essential for anyone who likes his playing. *Ben Webster with Strings: "The Warm Moods"* (Discovery DSCD-818) is one of the best things he ever recorded, Webster in front of a fine string section arranged by ace orchestrator Johnny Richards, playing rarely done and beautiful romantic standards like "The Sweetheart of Sigma Chi," "Time After Time," and "With Every Breath I Take." It is hard to beat this set for a mixture of strength and tenderness. *King of the Tenors* (Verve 314 519 806-2) shows both the fierce and the lyrical sides of Webster's temper in sessions with an Oscar Peterson rhythm section and, on several tunes, added commentary from trumpeter Harry Edison and altoist Benny Carter. Big Ben surges through his solo on "Jive at Six," one of his hardest-swinging solos ever, and makes definitive ballad statements on "That's All" and "Danny Boy." *See You at the Fair* (Impulse/GRP GRD-121) is a 1964 collector's item, dedicated to the 1964–1965 World's Fair, that is as good as *King of the Tenors*, with Webster in his fullest roar on the medium-tempo-blues title track and at his gentlest on Duke Ellington's rarely done "Single Petal of a Rose." The rhythm section features pianist Hank Jones.

*Ben Webster and "Sweets" Edison: Ben and "Sweets"* (Columbia CK 40853) is an excellent 1962 set pitting Webster against the pungent playing of the ex-Basie trumpeter, in front of a fine rhythm section including Hank Jones. The swinging, buoyant blues "Better Go" is a standout (Ben really surges along here, a definitive solo), as are the ballad readings, especially "How Long Has This Been Going On?" The set is almost worth having for the cover photo alone, which shows Webster, listening to Edison, in a dark blue suit with a starched white shirt open at the neck, French cuffs, a cigarette angled down from his mouth, and a gray hat perched on his head.

Another first-rate set is *Ben Webster/Joe Zawinul: Soulmates* (Riverside/OJC-109, LP only). Webster and the young Viennese pianist Joe Zawinul (who was playing with Cannonball Adderley at the time and who would go on to form the band Weather Report with saxophonist Wayne Shorter) are accompanied by good rhythm players, including drummer Philly Joe Jones. Webster's ballad playing, again, takes the honors on the beautiful and rarely done tunes "Trav'lin' Light" and "Too Late Now."

*Ben Webster Meets Oscar Peterson* (Verve 829 167-2), a quartet date recorded in 1959 with Peterson, bassist Ray Brown, and drummer Ed Thigpen, is a nice set, consisting of standards like "The Touch of Your Lips," "Bye Bye Blackbird," and "In the Wee Small Hours of the Morning." Webster takes "Blackbird," "Sunday," and "This Can't Be Love" at swinging mid-tempos. *Coleman Hawkins Encounters Ben Webster* (Verve 823 120-2) is a little disappointing, although there is nothing wrong with it; it just doesn't seem to take off. A more charged meeting between the two took place on *The Big Reunion*, recently available on the imported Fresh Sound label, a late-1950s re-creation of the Fletcher Henderson big band, conducted by Rex Stewart, on which they trade choruses on "Sugar Foot Stomp" for some truly gladiatorial thrills. And *Ben Webster and Associates* (Verve 835 254-2) is a real surprise, an all-star session with Hawkins, trumpeter Roy Eldridge, and the mighty Budd Johnson, who steals the show from the two better-known players.

*Ben Webster at the Renaissance* (Contemporary/OJC-390), a live recording at a Los Angeles nightclub, is somewhat marred by a recording balance unfavorable in many places to the leader, who, with characteristic generosity, gives too much solo space to his accompanists. This isn't in any way to demean the extraordinary talents of pianist Jimmy Rowles, bassist Red Mitchell (these two work togther so well), guitarist Jim Hall, or drummer Frank Butler, only to wish that there were more Webster here. This is a problem, by the way, on some of the live recordings he made after moving to Europe in 1964. In any case, this isn't one of the best Webster sets available.

*Big Ben Time* (Philips 814 410-2), recorded in London in 1967, is a good set, very well recorded, the only problem being the presence on three tracks of what is apparently a fugitive church organist; the effect of hearing him with Webster is like discovering that someone has put whipped cream in your beef soup. The other tracks have pianist Dick Katz in place of the organist. Again, there are great ballads, like "How Deep Is the Ocean" and "Solitude," as well as a languorous version of "Honeysuckle Rose."

Anyone with what Duke Ellington called "a yen for Ben" will want to pick up *Ben Webster Plays Ballads* (Storyville STCD 4118), on which Webster does what you might expect, mostly with European musicians, in both small-group and big-band settings, recorded between 1967 and 1971 (Webster died in Amsterdam in 1973). His 1971 version of "For Heaven's Sake" is breathtaking. On a 1968 meeting with tenor player Don Byas (a fellow expatriate), available as *Ben Webster Meets Don Byas* (MPS 827 920-2), Webster sounds as if he had had one too many reunion drinks. But a version of the original ballad "When Ash Meets Henry," on which he is accompanied only by bassist Peter Trunk, is exceptional.

As a sideman Webster never failed to raise the temperature at least a few degrees. *Jam Session* (Verve 833 564-2) is a 1952 date that brought Webster into the studio for a memorable encounter with altoists Johnny Hodges, Benny Carter, and Charlie Parker; Webster quiets everyone down with his solo on "Funky Blues." The tenorist provides some great moments on one of Billie Holiday's best albums of the 1950s, *Songs for Distingué Lovers* (Verve 815 055-2), including a fine, abstract solo on "Just One of Those Things." Webster also contributes generously to four 1957 tracks with vibist Red Norvo included on Norvo's *Just a Mood* (RCA/Bluebird 6278-2-RB), as well as to a good small-group date under the leadership of trombonist Bill Harris, *Bill Harris and Friends* (Fantasy/OJC-083). The former date is extremely mellow and has great blues and ballad playing from Webster; the Harris session is looser and includes a stomping tenor solo on "Crazy Rhythm." Jimmy Rowles is the fine and original pianist on both dates.

## CHU BERRY

Like Ben Webster, Leon "Chu" Berry was a heavy-toned disciple of Hawkins's and one of the dominant tenor players of the 1930s. Berry made a large name for himself playing with the big bands of Benny Carter, Teddy Hill, and, especially, Fletcher Henderson and Cab Calloway; Berry played with Calloway from 1937 until his death, at age thirty-one, in 1941. He was one of the most swinging of swing tenor players, with a fluent technique the match of any clarinetist's and a rolling, propulsive rhythmic feel that made him a perfect match for trumpeter Roy Eldridge, his bandmate from the Henderson orchestra, with whom he made some of the best small-group jazz records of the time. His authoritative swing at even the fastest tempos, his superior harmonic knowledge, and his alert, fresh sense of where to begin and end phrases made him a favorite musician of Charlie Parker's.

You can hear Berry at greatest length on the small-group sides he recorded with leaders like Teddy Wilson, Lionel Hampton, Gene Krupa, and Red Norvo; many of these are available on compilations that include excellent music by others as well. A perfect place to begin is *Roy Eldridge – Little Jazz*

(Columbia CK 45275), which includes two classics by a Teddy Wilson small band ("Warmin' Up" and "Blues in C Sharp Minor"), as well as four tracks by the Henderson band with good Berry solos. The interplay between Berry and Eldridge really makes the opening ensemble jump on "Warmin' Up"; when Berry begins his solo, with a repeated riff, listen for the way the entire rhythm section, powered by drummer Big Sid Catlett, seems to lift to meet the increased swing level. Berry and Eldridge also collaborated on four sides for the small Commodore label in 1938, which show off Berry's ballad abilities. Available on *Chu Berry/Lucky Thompson: Giants of the Tenor Sax* (Commodore CCD 7004), the session includes a famous version of "Body and Soul," on which the tempo doubles for Eldridge's solo, as well as two swingers that feature Berry at length, one of which, the ferocious "Tiger Rag"–based "Sittin' In," begins with some spoken patter between Eldridge and Berry. The set also includes four tracks on which Berry is joined by trumpeter Hot Lips Page.

For sheer excitement, it is hard to beat two 1936 tracks by a studio group assembled by drummer Gene Krupa including Eldridge, Berry, and Benny Goodman, available on *Swing Is Here: Small Band Swing 1935–1939* (RCA/Bluebird 2180-2-RB). Again, listen for the way Eldridge and Berry use riffs in the improvised opening ensembles to create an urgent counterpoint; this was the height of swing as a musical style. Berry could generate huge momentum by, at one moment, hammering home the underlying four-four pulse and at the next moment playing a long, fluid line that contained all kinds of cross-accenting. This was Eldridge's way, too, and the reason they made such perfect partners. The set also includes three 1939 tracks by New Orleans trumpeter Wingy Manone that feature Berry. For further adventures of Berry and Eldridge in their Henderson days, pick up *Hocus Pocus: Fletcher Henderson and His Orchestra 1927–1936* (RCA/Bluebird 9904-2-RB). Berry takes solos on several of the 1936 tracks here; listen especially to his twenty-four bars on "Sing, Sing, Sing" – Berry usually entered with a very clear, original phrase designed to capture attention from the outset, like a good first sentence of a story – and to "Knock, Knock, Who's There?," which contains the only Chu Berry baritone sax solo on record.

*Lionel Hampton, Volume 2: The Jumpin' Jive* (RCA/Bluebird 2433-2-RB) contains one of the most famous recordings Berry ever made, the 1939 "Sweethearts on Parade," on which Berry blows for the entire length of the performance, under the melody statement by Hampton's vibes as well as under the leader's vocal. "Shufflin' at the Hollywood," recorded at the same session, also has lots of Berry throughout. Several other tracks on this collection of all-star performances led by Hampton include Berry as well. An alternate take of "Shufflin' at the Hollywood" may be found on the Hampton collection *Hot*

*Mallets, Volume 1* (RCA/Bluebird 6458-2-RB), along with four 1939 tracks from one of the most all-star sessions in jazz history, which united Berry with Hawkins and Webster as well as alto master Benny Carter, trumpeter Dizzy Gillespie, and guitarist Charlie Christian.

*The 1930s: Small Combos* (Columbia CK 40833) has the fine "Chuberry Jam," by Chu Berry and His Stompy Stevedores, a group of musicians from the Cab Calloway band, where Berry was the star soloist. *Red Norvo – Featuring Mildred Bailey* (Portrait Masters RK 44118), a collection of mid-1930s sides from sessions led by one of jazz's few xylophonists, includes several cuts with Berry, including "Bughouse" and "Blues in E-Flat." Berry also has some good moments with a Teddy Wilson-led small group, including Roy Eldridge, assembled to back up Billie Holiday, on *The Quintessential Billie Holiday, Volume 1* (Columbia CK 40646); check out his solo on "Twenty-Four Hours a Day."

## BUDD JOHNSON

Tenor saxophonist, multireed man, and arranger Albert "Budd" Johnson had one of the longest, most varied, most interesting, and least publicly recognized (in proportion to accomplishment) careers of any major jazz musician. Born in 1910, Johnson taught Ben Webster the rudiments of the horn in the late 1920s, was a primary architect of the great Earl Hines band's sound in the 1930s and again in the early 1940s, played with Dizzy Gillespie on 52nd Street in the mid-1940s (Johnson was as open-minded and adaptable as Coleman Hawkins in embracing bebop when it came along), was constantly in demand as a sideman and arranger for many big bands through the late 1940s and 1950s, returned to small-group activity with Earl Hines in the 1960s while also taking time to play with bands organized by Gil Evans and Randy Weston, and continued an extremely active schedule until his death. Although almost never mentioned in the same breath as Hawkins, Webster, Young, or the other innovators of the tenor, Johnson was one of the instrument's great players, very melodically inventive from his early solos with Louis Armstrong through recordings he made in his late sixties.

Probably the best demonstration of Johnson's instrumental power currently available is the 1965 quartet set *Earl Hines Live at the Village Vanguard* (Columbia CK 44197). On "Sometimes I'm Happy," taken at a medium-up tempo, Johnson starts out low and soft for his first chorus, then builds in volume, pitch, and intensity while maintaining a lilting, dancing, rhythmic feel, playing over the bar lines and behind the beat, at times sounding much like

Lester Young, gradually and judiciously throwing in trills, honks, and shouting blues phrases, turning up the excitement and the heat while never losing his composure. This six-minute performance, Johnson all the way, is a perfect introduction to his style. "Moten Swing," on the same set, is every bit as inspired, with Johnson driving home chorus after chorus of inventive, preaching, insinuating, relentlessly swinging tenor. "Red River Remembered" is a slow blues that Johnson wails on soprano saxophone. Listen to the way he will hold a long, curving note, letting it finally wobble a little with vibrato before cutting it off; Johnson was a master of the expressive effects of vibrato, and his tone was one of the most penetrating and human sounds in jazz.

Another great showcase for Johnson is his own 1960 quintet set *Let's Swing* (Prestige/OJC-1720), on which he is joined by his brother, trombonist Keg Johnson, pianist Tommy Flanagan, bassist George Duvivier, and drummer Charlie Persip. Johnson's theme statements on tunes like "Serenade in Blue" and "Falling in Love with Love" are models of relaxation and songlike phrasing. Again, the similarity to Lester Young's conception may be noted, although the sound and choice of notes are immediately identifiable as Johnson's. *Budd Johnson and the Four Brass Giants* (Riverside/OJC-209) is good, too, with Johnson set off by the trumpets of Clark Terry, Harry Edison, Ray Nance, and Nat Adderley, playing his arrangements in a program half made up of Johnson's own compositions. The only problem with this one is that there isn't enough Johnson because of the shared solo responsibilities.

One occasion on which Johnson made the most of his shared solo responsibilities was his appearance alongside Coleman Hawkins and Ben Webster on the 1959 *Ben Webster and Associates* (Verve 835 254-2). Listen to the way he uses dynamics during his first chorus on "In a Mellotone," starting softly, varying his lower-volume phrases with louder ones, becoming more forceful in his second chorus, coming up with some really extraordinary melodic turns. He takes the saxophone solo honors by a mile on this one, as he does on the other three tunes he plays on (two medium-up-tempo blues and a slow blues); his phrases are more coherent and definite, more swinging and imaginative than anything anybody else (with the possible exception of Roy Eldridge) was playing that day.

Johnson was a sideman on countless recording dates during his more than five decades of activity, and he always contributed solos that stood out, no matter whether the context was Louis Armstrong's 1933 big band, Dizzy Gillespie's 1951 small group, or Gil Evans's 1961 big band. *Laughin' Louie* (RCA/Bluebird 9759-2-RB), a set of early-1930s Armstrong items, features Johnson soloing on several tunes, especially the buoyant "Mahogany Hall Stomp" and "Some Sweet Day," on which his solo elicits a shout of joy from the leader. Not many saxophonists thought in such songlike, coherent melodic phrases in 1933; it would be 1936 before Lester Young would cut his first records and delineate an entire conception of soloing based on the same approach, although refined to an even higher and more stylized degree and stripped of the heavy, Hawkins-like tone.

*Piano Man: Earl Hines, His Piano and Orchestra* (RCA/Bluebird 6750-2-RB), a collection of tracks by the pianist's big bands of 1939–1942, contains a number of classic arrangements by Johnson, including the exciting and ingenious "Grand Terrace Shuffle," and some good, if short, solo spots for his tenor and alto. His full chorus on "Call Me Happy" is a gem, and his clarinet playing over the ensemble after Billy Eckstine's vocal on "Jelly, Jelly" is extremely hip. *Lionel Hampton, Volume 2: The Jumpin' Jive* (RCA/Bluebird 2433-2-RB) contains a 1938 track, "Rock Hill Special," on which several members of Hines's band join Hampton in the studio; Johnson takes two good choruses on this medium-tempo blues.

On Dizzy Gillespie's exciting 1951 version of "The Champ," included on *Dizzy Gillespie: Dee Gee Days* (Savoy ZDS 4426), Johnson bats cleanup (after vibist Milt Jackson, Gillespie, and trombonist J. J. Johnson), with seven wild choruses that get progressively louder and higher pitched, kicked along by Gillespie's background riffs. Johnson was also a favorite section man and featured soloist of arranger Gil Evans. On the 1959 Evans album *Great Jazz Standards* (Pacific Jazz CDP 7 46856 2), Johnson plays some beautiful clarinet on a reorchestrated version of Don Redman's "Chant of the Weed" and takes an extended tenor outing on the modal "La Nevada" that is the solo highlight of the entire album. When Evans recorded the tune again in 1961 for his album *Out of the Cool* (MCA/Impulse MCAD-5653), Johnson again took the tenor solo.

Two later sets featuring Johnson as a sideman are the 1964 Earl Hines small-band session *Up to Date* (RCA/Bluebird 6462-2-RB), on which Johnson is featured on tenor, soprano, and baritone saxophones, and an outstanding 1971 album by singer Jimmy Rushing, *The You and Me That Used to Be* (RCA/Bluebird 6460-2-RB), on which Johnson plays soprano exclusively. The Rushing album is one of the nicest things you could possibly do with twelve dollars or whatever you have to pay; he is accompanied by two bands – one with tenorist Al Cohn and Johnson, the other with trumpeter-violinist Ray Nance and tenor man Zoot Sims – in a program of little-done standards like "Home," "Thanks a Million," and "Linger Awhile." Johnson takes fine solos on the title track and on "All God's Children Got Rhythm," but everybody sounds great on this one.

# LESTER YOUNG

From his first recordings in 1936, Lester Young, known as "Pres" (a nickname given to him by Billie Holiday, short for "the President"), brought a new way of swinging to jazz, a gliding, dancing, melodically inventive style that had a new relation to the passage of time within the bar line. He brought what saxophonist Dexter Gordon called a new "philosophy" to playing, and it changed the way many people sounded, not the least of whom was a young Charlie Parker, who spent one summer learning all of Young's recorded solos. He also sired an entire school of tenor players that included Stan Getz, Zoot Sims, Brew Moore, Paul Quinichette, and quite a few others.

Listening to Pres is one of the best experiences jazz has to offer. On early recordings with Count Basie and as a guest star on many of Billie Holiday's greatest records, Young's solos stand out like gems, each shaped differently, each a coherent, complete poem in sound. He invented entirely new melodies as he played, which still surprise with their unexpected logic and lyricism. Phrases from his solos found their way into almost every young musician's melodic vocabulary; it is next to impossible to listen to a record of Dexter Gordon's, or Sonny Stitt's, or Illinois Jacquet's, without hearing quotes from Lester Young.

His sound, too, was different and wholly appropriate to his melodic and rhythmic innovations. The opposite of Hawkins's heavy, broad sound, Pres's was cooler, lighter, with almost no vibrato. Whereas Hawkins's lines, and those of his followers, tended to accentuate a heavy four-four beat, Young's called for a lighter four-four, over which he could dance and construct melodies that started and stopped in surprising places. Pres got the lighter, more implicit four-four he needed from the matchless rhythm section of the Count Basie orchestra with which he came to New York: Basie on piano, Walter Page on bass, Jo Jones on drums, and, slightly later, Freddie Green on rhythm guitar. For a discussion of their work and the Kansas City rhythmic feeling, see the Ensembles section.

## LESTER LEAPS IN

Most of Pres's greatest recordings were made in the late 1930s during the time he was with Count Basie's orchestra. He recorded classic after classic with Basie, as well as with Billie Holiday and various small groups. He made plenty of great recordings in the 1940s and 1950s, but his style shifted just a bit. In some people's opinion he was just as good, or better, later. It may be enough to say that his style was different, with different (yet some of the same) virtues.

But during his Basie period he seemed to generate fresh melodies endlessly. A good place to start is with *The Essential Count Basie, Volume 1* (Columbia CK 40608). It includes one of the best, if not the best, single records Young ever made, his first one, the 1936 "Oh, Lady Be Good," with a small Basie-led band. For two choruses at a swinging, medium-bounce tempo, Young weaves pure magic, a whole new song on the harmonies of the old. Another song recorded at the same session is "Shoe Shine Swing," available on *The 1930s: Small Combos* (Columbia CK 40833). At a way-up-tempo, Young sails through two electrifying choruses, utterly relaxed and creating a momentum of swing that few others had ever achieved. The Basie set includes three rare tracks by another small group, from 1939, in which Pres plays wonderfully on both tenor and clarinet, an instrument at which he was a master, along with a number of full-band tracks from the same year, on which Pres takes classic solos on tunes like "Taxi War Dance" (on which he begins his famous solo with a quote from "Old Man River"), "Twelfth Street Rag," "Miss Thing," and the blues "Pound Cake." All of these solos (especially "Pound Cake") contained phrases that young musicians memorized for years afterward.

The same could be said for many of his solos on the three-CD set *Count Basie: The Complete Decca Recordings* (Decca/GRP GRD-3-611). On tracks like "One O'Clock Jump," "Time Out," "Jumpin' at the Woodside," "Jive at Five," "Shorty George," "You Can Depend on Me," "Doggin' Around," "Texas Shuffle" (on which he plays clarinet), and, especially, "Roseland Shuffle," on which Young's tenor and Basie's piano engage in a dialogue of doctoral-level swing and melodic invention, Young made his place in musical history.

*The Essential Count Basie, Volume 2* (Columbia CK 40835) contains further adventures of Pres with Basie, from 1939 and 1940, including the small-group classics "Lester Leaps In" and "Dickie's Dream" (named for trombonist Dicky Wells), Pres's original composition "Tickle Toe" for the full band, and other good Young solos on "I Never Knew," "Louisiana," and "Blow Top." *Volume 3* (Columbia CK 44150) has some more good Young, but half this volume is devoted to the band after Young's departure late in 1940.

The musical affinity between Young and Billie Holiday made for one of the great pairings in the music's history. Their first recording session together, under the leadership of pianist Teddy Wilson (who assembled bands made up of the best musicians of the time for many of Holiday's 1930s recording dates), was held in January 1937, just after the Basie band landed in New York City; it was love at first sight. The four tunes recorded that day – "He Ain't Got Rhythm," "This Year's Kisses," "Why Was I Born?," and "I Must Have That Man" – are available on *The Quintessential Billie Holiday, Volume 3* (Columbia CK 44048). Listen especially to Pres's melody statement on "This Year's Kisses" and his solo on "I Must Have That Man," certainly one of the greatest jazz solos of all time for balance and melodic grace (and everything else).

That magic was to last for nearly two years, with the results audible in *Volume 4* (Columbia CK 44252), *Volume 5* (Columbia CK 44423), and *Volume 6* (Columbia CK 45449). If you are trying to decide which to buy first, I would recommend *Volume 4*, which contains the ballads "Easy Living" (a reasonable nomination for Holiday's greatest single recording), "Foolin' Myself," and "I'll Never Be the Same," as well as "Me, Myself and I," which has Pres accompanying Holiday's second vocal chorus in ecstatic counterpoint. *Volume 5* contains fantastic Young on "Trav'lin' All Alone," "Back in Your Own Backyard," and, especially, "When You're Smiling," to name just three. *Volume 6* is a bit less heavy on the classics but still worthwhile.

### COUNTLESS BLUES REVISITED

Young was present at Benny Goodman's famous 1938 Carnegie Hall concert along with Basie colleagues Buck Clayton, Walter Page, Freddie Green, and the Count himself. They joined with Ellington saxophonists Johnny Hodges and Harry Carney for a jam session on Fats Waller's "Honeysuckle Rose" (available on *Benny Goodman Live at Carnegie Hall* [Columbia G2K 40244]). Pres takes the leadoff solo on the fourteen-minute jam, and it is a perfect illustration of a major aspect of his musical technique. Young's timing often worked the way a boxer's or a juggler's does; by repeating certain musical phrases, or rhythmic patterns, he leads the listener into expecting a pattern. When he then breaks the pattern with a variation, the effect is one of surprise and satisfaction. He makes exhilarating use of this technique in his two choruses here.

Another of Pres's very best sessions was a 1938 date with fellow Basie-ites Buck Clayton, Freddie Green, Walter Page, Jo Jones, and trombonist Eddie Durham playing electric guitar in place of Basie's piano. The Kansas City Six, as this group was called, recorded five masterpieces which are included on *Lester "Prez" Young and Friends: Giants of the Tenor Sax* (Commodore CCD 7002). Pres plays clarinet as well as tenor here and takes exquisite solos on both instruments; he was really on his mettle for this particular date. The atmosphere is mellow but spirited, conversational, and buoyant. There's nothing loud here, but the swing this small group generated, not to mention the melodic inventiveness, is awesome. With the delicate ensemble interplay on "Way Down Yonder in New Orleans," the propulsive riffs of "Countless Blues," the thick mood of "Pagin' the Devil," the lyricism of "I Want a Little Girl," and Pres's uncanny solos on "Them There Eyes" (which was recorded at the same date as the others, despite what the notes say), this date ranks with the best in jazz history. It was, by the way, the first recording of a jazz electric guitar. The set also includes some very good 1944 sides, on which Young leads a sextet including trombonist Dicky Wells, trumpeter Bill Coleman, and drummer Jo Jones.

Several sets document the early-1940s period of Young's musical life. The best of these, by far, is *The Complete Lester Young* (Mercury 830 920-2), which contains the results of two important sessions for the small Keynote label, from 1943 and 1944. The first is a quartet date with Johnny Guarnieri on piano, Slam Stewart on bass, and Big Sid Catlett on drums, which produced two takes apiece of the standards "Just You, Just Me," "I Never Knew," and the ultra-relaxed "Sometimes I'm Happy," along with an up-tempo original called "Afternoon of a Basie-ite." This session is a favorite with all fans of Pres because everyone seems so at ease on it, and Young's phrasing is a marvel of grace throughout. His melody statements alone are worth the price of admission.

The other session, recorded three months later with members of the Basie band (including the Count himself), which Young had briefly rejoined, is excellent, too. Trumpeter Buck Clayton provided the sketches for a band including himself, Young, trombonist Dicky Wells, and the Basie rhythm section, with Rodney Richardson on bass in place of the temporarily absent Walter Page. Pres is in high spirits, and the eight tracks from this session have a happy feel about them.

*Lester Young – Master Takes/Savoy Recordings* (Savoy ZDS 4419) has some nice moments on it, but as a set it falls well below the Keynote material. Three titles from Young's brief 1944 return to the Basie band are unremarkable; another session (from the same day) with Johnny Guarnieri, trumpeter Billy Butterfield, and clarinetist Hank D'Amico has some nice Pres, as does a session from the next month with the Basie rhythm section. Four titles from 1949, featuring Young in the company of some younger musicians, including drummer Roy Haynes, have some very good moments, too. But all in all, this is second-string Pres. All these tracks are available, with numerous alternate takes, on a two-LP set, *Lester Young, Pres/The Complete Savoy Recordings* (Savoy 2202).

*Coleman Hawkins/Lester Young – Classic Tenors* (Signature/CBS AK 38446) has four great December 1943 tracks by a small group with a front line of Young, Dicky Wells, and trumpeter Bill Coleman, with Pres in top form on the bouncy "Hello Babe" and "Linger Awhile," a ferocious "I Got Rhythm," and the blues "I'm Fer It, Too." The swing Pres musters on "Linger Awhile" is truly something to hear. This set, with its classic Hawkins tracks, is an excellent introduction to the contrasting styles of these two giants.

Young's work from the 1950s is very spottily available, and in some cases this is just as well; as the decade went on (he died in 1959), illness and alcoholism took their toll on his embouchure and, on the evidence of the recordings, on his agility of mind. Still, some of his 1950s work counts as first-rate jazz. One example is the extraordinary *The President Plays with the Oscar Peterson Trio* (Verve 831 670-2), recorded in 1952. From the first notes of "Ad-Lib Blues," Pres is in control of his game, playing with a bouncing swing and a happy and cagey imagination in a set that rivals anything he did after leaving Basie. In addition to the opener and several other medium- and up-tempo tracks, including a masterful "Indiana," the set features a number of definitive performances of standard ballads like "These Foolish Things," "On the Sunny Side of the Street," and "I'm Confessin'." As a bonus, an informal version of "(It Takes) Two to Tango" shows up, with a funny vocal by Pres and some studio conversation.

*Lester Young – The Jazz Giants* (Verve 825 672-2) is a 1956 session featuring Pres in the company of his true peers, trumpeter Roy Eldridge, trombonist Vic Dickenson, pianist Teddy Wilson, guitarist Freddie Green, bassist Gene Ramey, and drummer Jo Jones. Although his embouchure shows signs of weakness here and there, what he plays is very definite and beautiful; the program includes four fine standards (including "This Year's Kisses," a rarely done tune recorded almost twenty years earlier by Pres on his first session with Billie Holiday, under Wilson's leadership) and an up-tempo blues. Everyone is in good form, especially Teddy Wilson, and the set is an excellent example of the continuing vitality of the small-group style these men had pioneered in the 1930s.

*Pres and Teddy* (Verve 831 270-2) was recorded the very next day, with only Young, Wilson, Ramey, and Jones, and is also a strong program, consisting of standards like "Taking a Chance on Love," "Louise," and "Prisoner of Love." Wilson really sparkles here, and Young's phrasing of the melodies is as relaxed and swinging as can be. My favorite track is a CD-only bonus recorded at the same session, a medium-tempo blues called "Pres Returns," on which the President weaves a fantastic blues sermon through which an unmistakable note of triumph is sounded. That is as it should be; despite all the pain and bad news in his life, Lester Young left the world an irreplaceable beauty.

## DON BYAS

In his way, Don Byas was as big an influence on younger tenor players as Lester Young was. Three years younger than Pres (whom he replaced in the Basie band, after tenorist Paul Bascomb's brief stay), Byas was more in the Hawkins mode, heavy-toned but never rough, with a harmonic sophistication that led him into the company of the still-younger bop players of the time, foremost among them Dizzy Gillespie, with whom he made some important early recordings. Byas's predilection for running changes, his exploration of the new and so-called substitute chord progressions favored by younger musicians in the 1940s, his fleet execution at even the fastest tempos, and his often unusual interval leaps and note choices had a big effect on younger players such as Lucky Thompson, Paul Gonsalves, Benny Golson, and Johnny Griffin, and he has not received his due in jazz history as a major stylistic influence.

There isn't a lot of Byas currently available. Perhaps the most revealing examples of his playing are three tracks, included on *Ben Webster/Don Byas: Giants of the Tenor Sax* (Commodore 7005), from a 1945 Town Hall concert, which pair Byas with bassist Slam Stewart (pianist Teddy Wilson joins them for one). Byas's and Stewart's whirlwind five-minute treatment of "I Got Rhythm" shows Byas's facility, his warm tone, his mastery of scalar sequences, and also, despite his harmonic affinity for what the boppers were doing, his steadfast roots in swing's rhythmic approach. "Candy" is a great example of his sensuous ballad style with further evidence, in his occasional choice of wide intervals, of his exceptional ear.

Byas participates in a thrilling, privately recorded 1946 jam session on "Sweet Georgia Brown" with Dizzy Gillespie and Charlie Parker, included on *The Complete "Birth of the Bebop"* (Stash ST-CD-535); he holds his own in the electric exchanges that are all we have of this performance, swinging hard in his instantly identifiable style. He also participated in a February 1946 recording session with Gillespie; four tracks from this session are included on *The Bebop Revolution* (RCA/Bluebird 2177-2-RB), including two takes of the "I Got Rhythm"–based "52nd Street Theme," on which Byas plays many of the same scalar patterns he plays on the Town Hall "I Got Rhythm."

The hard-to-find two-LP set *Don Byas – Savoy Jam Party* (Savoy SJL 2213) brings together several sessions from the 1944–1946 period, with solid, deeply felt blowing from the leader on cookers and ballads alike. A listen to this set will leave you wondering why Byas isn't better known. He was a master storyteller on the horn. It includes a stunning "Cherokee," on which Byas shows why he was held in such high esteem by the younger players. A quartet date from 1946, with Max Roach on drums, includes some fascinating interplay between Byas and the little-known pianist Sanford Gold, who went on to become a widely respected piano teacher.

*Don Byas on Blue Star* (EmArcy 833 405-2) is a mixed bag of performances recorded in Paris between 1947 and 1952. With the exception of one year, Byas was an expatriate from the late 1940s until the end of his life in 1972. These tracks showcase his ballad playing especially; check out his specialties "Laura" and "Old Folks" (not "Old Folks at Home," as the notes say). This set includes an excellent booklet with rare photos of Byas with Dizzy Gillespie, Ben Webster, Paul Gonsalves, and others. *Ben Webster Meets Don Byas* (MPS 827 920-2), a late-1960s meeting between the two expatriates, is a little disappointing because Webster is in somewhat rocky shape, but Byas plays very well.

Some of the best Don Byas on record languishes in Columbia's vaults, a 1961 Paris session with Bud Powell on piano, available briefly in the early 1980s as *A Tribute to Cannonball.* Let's hope some hip soul sees fit to reissue it.

## TEXAS TENORS

When Lester Young came to New York with Count Basie in 1937, he wasn't the only tenor player in the band. Herschel Evans also played tenor with Basie but in a very different style – heavy-toned, Hawkins-influenced, and even more steeped in the blues – and the contrast between his style and Young's was a great element of the Basie band's sound. You can hear them together throughout *Count Basie: The Complete Decca Recordings* (Decca/GRP GRD-3-611), which includes Evans's classic ballad performance of "Blue and Sentimental."

While nothing like the innovator that Pres was, Evans, who was from Denton, Texas, became the prototype of a sort of loose subschool of tenor saxophonists, usually called Texas tenors. Like most such terms, it is a convenience and best when used only half-seriously. But it does point to the dominance of the blues in the Texas/Oklahoma area in the 1920s and 1930s (and beyond), and players such as Buddy Tate (Evans's replacement with Basie), Arnett Cobb, and Illinois Jacquet, as well as younger men such as David "Fathead" Newman, bear a definite family resemblance.

Buddy Tate, from Sherman, Texas, can be heard very much in the Evans mold in brief solos on the three volumes of Columbia's *The Essential Count Basie.* But a much fuller picture of Tate's big talent and sound may be had from *Tate-a-Tate* (Prestige/OJC-184), on which he is joined by trumpeter Clark Terry, who is truly inspired here, pianist Tommy Flanagan, and a good rhythm section, in a solid, varied program of blues, swingers, and a poignant Tate version of Duke Ellington's ballad "All Too Soon." Tate and Terry engage in some exciting exchanges on "Take the 'A' Train." Equally good is *Buck and Buddy* (Swingville/OJC-757), a session in which Tate shares the front line with his old Basie cohort, trumpeter Buck Clayton.

Tate is present also for an all-tenor album under Coleman Hawkins's name, *Very Saxy* (Prestige/OJC-458), on which Tate and Hawkins share the solo space with Eddie "Lockjaw" Davis and Arnett Cobb (they are accompanied by organist Shirley Scott, bass, and drums). Cobb was a star with Lionel Hampton's big band in the 1940s and had a good-sized hit with an instrumental called "Smooth Sailing." Here he nearly steals the show from his better-known colleagues on a program of jumping tunes including "Lester Leaps In." This set, however, is almost too much of a good thing – four heavy-toned, aggressively swinging tenor saxophonists, cooking away relentlessly. It's a bit like eating four steaks at one sitting. Keep some Bach piano music close at hand to restore your perspective afterward.

Cobb's own *Party Time* (Prestige/OJC-219) is a very good showcase for his extroverted, witty style. It consists mainly of blues and standards in medium grooves, most of which Cobb grills up to a strong climax. His up-tempo "Lonesome Road" is exhilarating, but he really turns up the heat on the riff tune "Flying Home," which had been a big feature for him with Hampton (he inherited it from Illinois Jacquet); this is the kind of roaring, infectious playing that could make people jump out of theater balconies in ecstasy. *Party Time* is as good a definition as anything could be of the essence of Texas tenor. Both Hampton versions of "Flying Home" (Jacquet's 1942 original and Cobb's 1944 remake, called "Flying Home No. 2") are available on *Lionel Hampton: Flying Home* (Decca/MCA MCAD-42349). An interesting Texas footnote is that on the original 1942 "Flying Home," Jacquet pays tribute to none other than Herschel Evans by leading into the bridge of his solo with a phrase Evans used in his 1938 "Texas Shuffle" solo with Basie.

Illinois Jacquet, born in New Orleans but raised in Texas, managed (and manages) to combine the Texas feeling and certain strategies of phrasing with influences from Lester Young and the bop players of the late 1940s. A good introduction to his playing is *Illinois Jacquet: The Black Velvet Band* (RCA/Bluebird 6571-2-RB), which includes a number of honking, shouting sides by his late-1940s small big-band. This set also includes a version of "Flying Home" recorded at the 1967 Newport Jazz Festival, on which Jacquet is reunited with the Hampton big band for a very raucous and exciting performance which sounds as if it nearly precipitated a riot.

*Banned in Boston* (Portrait RK 44391) is a good 1962 set of well-recorded sides by a small Jacquet band including trumpeter Roy Eldridge. "Frantic Fanny" shows the real Texas side of Jacquet, while on the title tune he sounds much more like Pres. There are a couple of nice ballads here, too, and a fast "Indiana" on which Jacquet plays some startlingly Parkerian alto. On 1968's *Bottoms Up: Illinois Jacquet on Prestige!* (Prestige/OJC-417), the tenorist single-handedly (with the help of a super rhythm section of Barry Harris, Ben Tucker, and Alan Dawson) generates as much momentum as the entire Hampton band on such Jacquet favorites as "Port of Rico," "Jivin' with Jack the

Bellboy," and the title track. Harris is a consummate bop pianist and a perfect foil for Jacquet's swinging, riff-based work. The party-time groove of the title track is the essence of Jacquet, on the rocks, no chaser.

## DEXTER GORDON

When Dexter Gordon really began leaving his mark in the mid-1940s, after a five-year apprenticeship in the big bands of Lionel Hampton, Louis Armstrong, and Billy Eckstine, it was as the first tenor player who was neither primarily Hawkins- nor Young-derived, playing within the framework of the new music called bebop. Still, Gordon's biggest inspiration, he once told me, was Young's playing – not his sound or even his specific phrasing but rather his "philosophy" of playing. By this, I think, Gordon was referring to Young's attitude toward the beat, legato attack, and emphasis on melodic creativity wed to harmonic sophistication. Once Gordon found his own voice, though, it didn't resemble Young's; his sound was harder, his swing more driving.

Gordon was one of jazz's aristocrats, a suave man well over six feet tall (hence one of his nicknames, Long Tall Dexter), whose career was a varied course of ups and downs that included a late-1940s tenor reign (during which he was a profound influence on younger players like Jackie McLean and, especially, John Coltrane), an early-1950s California prison stay for a narcotics conviction, a classic string of 1960s albums, a long period as an expatriate living in Copenhagen, a triumphant late-1970s homecoming to the United States during which he became a hero to a whole new generation of jazz fans, and even a 1987 Academy Award nomination – not for a musical score but as Best Actor, for his portrayal of saxophonist Dale Turner in the 1986 Bertrand Tavernier film *Round Midnight*.

Gordon's best recordings were made during the 1960s for Blue Note and Prestige. He still owned all his early fire and had added to it a maturity that made him one of the great ballad players in jazz. The best of the best are *Go!* (Blue Note 46094) and *A Swingin' Affair* (Blue Note 84133), recorded two days apart with the same excellent rhythm section of Sonny Clark, Butch Warren, and Billy Higgins. You can't go wrong with either album; both have Gordon showing earthshaking swing and ultra-warm ballad wisdom. Of the two, *A Swingin' Affair* may have a slight edge, if only for the unique and pungent "Soy Califa," on which Gordon is endlessly inventive, dancing over the fascinating beat, a kind of Moorish samba, with a hint of Brazil and Haiti in there, too. The set also includes fantastic versions of the ballads "Don't Explain" and "Until the Real Thing Comes Along," on which Gordon actually seems to be singing the lyrics as he plays, and cooking versions of the standard "You Stepped Out of a Dream" and Gordon's blues "McSplivens." It's hard to recommend this set highly enough.

But *Go!* has the irresistible minor-key swinger "Cheese Cake," on which Gordon is shockingly inspired – dodging, bobbing, and weaving. The two ballads here are as good as the ones on *A Swingin' Affair* (although "Don't Explain" is hard to top), and there are exciting versions of "Love for Sale" and "Second Balcony Jump" (which was originally done by Earl Hines's big band – the version here is as inventive as "Cheese Cake") and a witty, tasty one of "Three O'Clock in the Morning." Both albums show Gordon's strong sound to full advantage; don't miss them.

Very nearly as good is the 1969 *The Tower of Power* (Prestige/OJC-299), a quartet set (with Barry Harris, Buster Williams, and Albert Heath) on which tenorist James Moody sits in for an extended workout on a minor-key original called "Montmartre," which is worth the price of the album. It also includes a good straight-ahead blues, "Stanley the Steamer," and a beautiful and warmly lyrical original called "The Rainbow People." The rhythm section is top-notch, and Barry Harris's piano solos are another strong reason to pick this up. There was another album's worth of material recorded with this band, issued as *More Power*; one hopes Original Jazz Classics will get around to putting it out, too.

Gordon's 1970 Prestige outing, *The Panther* (Prestige/OJC-770), with pianist Tommy Flanagan, is also one of his strongest records. The title track is a swaggering blues based on a riff from the Jay McShann orchestra's recording of "Swingmatism," with an almost New Orleans rhythm-and-blues rhythm underlying it, on which Gordon spins inventive chorus after chorus. He was really on fire for this session. His ballad versions of "Body and Soul" and, especially, "The Christmas Song" also help make this one of the essential Gordon sets.

Gordon is a sideman for tenorist Booker Ervin's *Settin' the Pace* (Prestige 24123), possibly the wildest date Gordon ever participated in. The rhythm section here consists of Jaki Byard, Reggie Workman, and Alan Dawson, and the mood is adventuresome to say the least. The twenty-three-minute-long version of Gordon's classic "Dexter's Deck" contains a nine-and-a-half-minute solo by Gordon that is one of the most exciting things he recorded. The original liner notes, by David Himmelstein, are almost as wild as the music.

*Dexter Calling . . .* (Blue Note 46544) is a good 1961 quartet set with Kenny Drew, Paul Chambers, and Philly Joe Jones, but it is neither as relaxed nor as spirited as the next year's *Go!* and *A Swingin' Affair*. This and *Doin' Allright* (Blue Note 84077), recorded three days earlier, were comeback albums of sorts for Gordon, who had been off the scene for most of the 1950s. His tone would harden some over the next year and become more penetrating and assured. This is a perfectly good set, just not one of the very best. The 1963 *Our Man in Paris* (Blue Note 46394) is a fairly disappointing quartet set. With a rhythm section of pianist Bud Powell, bassist Pierre Michelot, and expatriate drum innovator Kenny Clarke, this looks like a dream session. But Powell wasn't in the best shape, and he is undermiked to boot, and this one never quite takes off, despite a good "Stairway to the Stars."

*Doin' Allright* is a more satisfying, varied set than *Dexter Calling . . .*, with two good Gordon originals, "For Regulars Only" and "Society Red," as well as a fetching, walking-tempo reading of the rarely done Gershwin tune "I Was Doing All Right" and a cooking "It's You or No One," on which Gordon really digs in. This set pairs the tenorist with new star trumpeter Freddie Hubbard, who sounds very good. *One Flight Up* (Blue Note 84176) was recorded in Paris in 1964 in a studio that lends a cavernous echo to the sound. Gordon plays very creatively here, next to trumpeter Donald Byrd and in front of a rhythm section featuring pianist Kenny Drew. Drew's tune "Coppin' the Haven" brings out the best in everybody, and Gordon plays a version of "Darn That Dream" on which he sounds as relaxed as Lester Young, which is very relaxed, indeed. This set has a unique mood about it. *Gettin' Around* (Blue Note 46681) is probably the least of the Blue Notes, despite such good companions as vibist Bobby Hutcherson and a rhythm section of Barry Harris, Bob Cranshaw, and Billy Higgins. The material isn't as strong, and it never quite lifts off, for me at least.

*Homecoming* (Columbia C2K 46824), recorded in 1976 during the season of Gordon's triumphant return to the U.S., has its moments but lacks the relaxation of the earlier Blue Note and Prestige sets. This may be partly because it was recorded live, partly because of the accompanying group's chemistry, but whatever the reason, there is a livid feeling about the set that is at odds with Gordon's best instincts.

Gordon's excellent mid-1940s small-group sides are collected on *Dexter Gordon: Long Tall Dexter* (Savoy SJL 2211); they include sessions with many of the best younger musicians of the time, including some very hot tracks with Bud Powell and equally hot ones with Fats Navarro. Gordon's solos here are, for the most part, gems within these three-minute performances. The sound, of course, is not as good as the things from the 1960s, but anyone with a taste for Gordon will enjoy these examples of young Dexter, the firebrand. For other glimpses of the Long Tall One at a young age, *Dizzy Gillespie and His Sextets and Orchestra: "Shaw 'Nuff"* (Musicraft MVSCD-53) has a brief but brilliant Gordon solo on "Blue and Boogie," and the Billy Eckstine set *Mr. B. and the Band* (Savoy ZDS 4401) has an electrifying 1945 big-band performance of "Lonesome Lover Blues," with chase choruses by Gordon and tenorist Gene Ammons.

## GENE AMMONS

Gene "Jug" Ammons, Gordon's sectionmate with Eckstine, was a heavy-toned, blues-oriented player – Herschel Evans, in a way, to Gordon's Lester Young, although Ammons, like any player of his generation, knew his Pres. In his recordings from the 1950s through the 1970s, he moved effortlessly between smoky, late-night ballads, grits-and-gravy organ-trio workouts, peerless blues playing, and straight up-and-down bebop jamming.

His all-around best album is probably *Boss Tenor* (Prestige/OJC-297), one of the great tenor sax albums of all time. On this 1960 date, Ammons has the benefit of an incomparable rhythm section of Tommy Flanagan, Doug Watkins, and Art Taylor, with conga player Ray Barretto added for a perfect accent. From Ammons's first lazy, growling notes on the album's slow blues opener, "Hittin' the Jug," he draws a definitive portrait of himself and, in fact, of a kind of subschool of tenor playing. It's safe to say that the Ammons approach, as presented in this set, can still be heard in the playing of countless tenors in uptown establishments across the country. The set offers a delicious, medium-tempo workout on "Close Your Eyes," a ballad ("My Romance"), a reading of the semiexotic "Canadian Sunset," a blues in a medium groove, and two cookers, Charlie Parker's "Confirmation" and the swing-era standard "Stomping at the Savoy," in which Ammons mines the Lester Young by-way-of Illinois Jacquet territory. *Boss Tenor* is one of those perfect albums. Don't miss it.

*Blue Gene* (Prestige/OJC-192) has the same rhythm section as *Boss Tenor* (including Barretto), with Mal Waldron in place of Flanagan (not a fair trade) and trumpeter Idrees Sulieman and baritone saxophonist Pepper Adams added. Ammons generates some real excitement on the fast blues "Scamperin' "; notice that he quotes from Lester Young's solo on Count Basie's "Riff Interlude" (available on *The 1930s: Big Bands* [Columbia CK 40651]). Listen to the way he will take a short motif, extend it by a note or two, then change that extension slightly, adding to the intensity all along; he digs in, and keeps digging in, with the band riffing behind him. This track is worth the price of the set, which otherwise is pretty ordinary. *Jug* (Prestige/OJC-701) is a solid set, if a little monotonous in its choice of medium walking tempos. A refreshing change is the rarely done pop tune "Tangerine," which really moves along here at a bright clip.

To hear Ammons firing away in an organ-combo setting, pick up *Richard Holmes and Gene Ammons – Groovin' with Jug* (Pacific Jazz CDP 7 92930 2). Recorded live in 1961 in front of a responsive Los Angeles crowd (except for three studio cuts), Holmes's throbbing chording and the exhortations from the audience ("Work!" "Let's go!") bring out Jug's most down-home side and make for an exciting set, despite an occasionally shaky rhythm section. Another organ meeting, with Brother Jack McDuff (*Brother Jack Meets the Boss* [Prestige/OJC-326]), looks promising but is disappointing. There is some absolutely great Ammons with organ, though, on *The Boss Is Back!* (Prestige 24129), including a smoldering, chitlins-and-greens version of "He's a Real Gone Guy," on which Ammons really cranks up the soul over a shuffle groove.

Ammons recorded a number of all-star jam sessions for Prestige in the 1950s, all of which have good moments, with the likes of altoist Jackie McLean and trumpeters Art Farmer and Donald Byrd. *Gene Ammons All Star Sessions* (Prestige/OJC-014) has Farmer and altoist Lou Donaldson sharing the front line with Jug in 1955, but the real reasons to pick this one up are the seven 1950–1951 tracks on which Ammons goes toe-to-toe with fellow titan Sonny Stitt. "Blues Up and Down" and "You Can Depend on Me," especially, are prototypical tenor battles, the jam session equivalent of heavyweight bouts, tests of imagination, stamina, and presence of mind. Ammons is the first soloist on all takes of both tunes; Stitt's tone is slightly drier, a little more like Dexter Gordon's.

### BLUE AND SENTIMENTAL

If you like Ammons's approach to the tenor, especially on the *Boss Tenor* album, you should also hear Ike Quebec's wonderful album *Blue and Sentimental* (Blue Note 84098), an ace program of ballads, blues, and standards, played by a neglected tenor giant. Quebec was very much in the Ammons bag, and in this 1961 set, accompanied by guitarist Grant Green, bassist Paul Chambers, and drummer Philly Joe Jones, he came out with a minor classic. The title track is a ballad associated with the short-lived Basie tenorist Herschel Evans, and Quebec and company summon an unforgettable mood. Quebec cooks very well on "That Old Black Magic," "It's All Right with Me," and his original "Like," but he shines brightest on the title tune and the fine ballad "Don't Take Your Love from Me."

Another son of Jug is the tough and prolific Stanley Turrentine. His *Look*

*Out!* (Blue Note 46543) is an excellent 1960 quartet album that fans of *Boss Tenor* and *Blue and Sentimental* will enjoy. His big sound and fluid ideas are illuminated from a number of different angles; the ballads "Yesterdays" and "Journey into Melody" are standouts, as is the Turrentine original "Minor Chant," a swinging, medium-tempo piece that gathers steam as it goes along. His albums *Blue Hour* (Blue Note 84057) and *Z.T.'s Blues* (Blue Note 84424), which has Tommy Flanagan on piano, are favored by his fans as well, but for Turrentine at his bluesy best, pick up organ master Jimmy Smith's *Midnight Special* (Blue Note 84078); Turrentine preaches a blues sermon on the title cut and builds up a big Jug of steam on "One O'Clock Jump," goaded on by Smith's organ riffs.

## SONNY STITT

Equally proficient, and prolific, on alto and tenor, Sonny Stitt had the misfortune to be one of the very earliest and very best musicians to grasp Charlie Parker's language in the 1940s; as a result, he was seen for much of his career as a sort of second-string Bird. An extremely agile and swinging improviser, he certainly was not a genius of Bird's order of inventiveness and rhythmic flexibility (who ever was?); he was more a master of swing and suspense, with a repertoire of thousands of phrases, scale patterns, chord inversions, and sundry tricks of the trade, all of which he could call to mind with lightning speed. Consequently, he was a very hard man to beat in a jam session, and there is recorded evidence of his giving even Sonny Rollins a bad time.

Stitt could generate great heat through his swing, but one didn't really feel one was getting to know Sonny by listening to his playing, as one might feel about most of jazz's great players; he was among the most impersonal of the music's giants, which may partly explain his undeservedly low standing among some critics. As Stitt got older, when the vibes were right, more of his lyrical side came out. He recorded many, many albums, many of which are just ho-hum; here is the cream of the crop.

*Sonny Stitt/Bud Powell/J. J. Johnson* (Prestige/OJC-009) is a collection of blistering sides from 1949 and 1950 with two bands, one of which is a quartet with Powell, Curly Russell, and Max Roach, the other of which is a quintet with Johnson, John Lewis, Nelson Boyd, and Roach. Stitt plays tenor all the way, swinging, swinging, swinging, on tune after tune, mostly standards favored by the boppers, like "All God's Chillun Got Rhythm," "Fine and Dandy," and "Strike Up the Band," as well as blues- and "I Got Rhythm"–based originals. You can hear Stitt's mastery of the Parker/Lester Young tradition very clearly (he had lots more Parker in his style than did his colleague Dexter

Gordon). Bud Powell was in death-defying form when these were recorded; this set will make your amplifier break out in a sweat.

The same can be said for Dizzy Gillespie's 1957 album *Sonny Side Up* (Verve 825 674-2), which features one of the great tenor battles of all time (maybe the greatest) – "The Eternal Triangle," a fourteen-minute up-tempo workout on which Stitt and Sonny Rollins are paired off against each other in true gladiatorial style. In Stitt's eight choruses (and the subsequent exchanges with Rollins), you can hear that he had a seemingly unlimited number of ways to negotiate the chord changes, breathing fire all the way. Stitt also has some good moments with Gillespie on *Duets* (Verve 835 253-2), as well as on the stunning *For Musicians Only* (Verve 837 435-2), where Stitt, on alto, cuts a game but badly overmatched Stan Getz to ribbons.

Stitt's overall most satisfying album is probably *Constellation* (Muse MCD 5323), recorded in 1972 (not 1971, as the CD liner notes say) with an ideal rhythm section of Barry Harris, Sam Jones, and Roy Brooks. Alternating between tenor and alto on a program of standard ballads ("Ghost of a Chance," "It's Magic") and jazz standards, mostly from the bop era (Parker's "Constellation," Bud Powell's "Webb City," Tadd Dameron's gorgeous "Casbah"), Stitt shows the full range of emotion and technique throughout, in a relaxed but very exciting session. His tenor balladry on "Ghost of a Chance" is wondrous, as is his delicious playing on "Casbah," which critic Ira Gitler called a "jasmine-scented, night-wind line" in the album's original notes. So is his two-fisted playing on the swinging blues "By Accident" and the minor-key Basie favorite "Topsy," as is his quicksilver alto on the ultrafast title tune. Harris's piano solos are characteristically bright throughout. This album was produced by Don Schlitten, who had a knack for getting the best out of musicians of a bebop persuasion. He also produced the slightly earlier, and slightly less satisfying, *Tune Up* (Muse MCD 5334), recorded with the same group, but with Alan Dawson on drums in place of Roy Brooks, and with a similar repertoire. But "slightly less satisfying" than *Constellation* means very good and worth having.

Stitt's fine all-alto tribute to Parker, *Stitt Plays Bird* (Atlantic 1418-2), is discussed earlier. His three tenor tracks on the mostly alto *Sonny Stitt Sits In with the Oscar Peterson Trio* (Verve 849 396-2) include a good "Moten Swing." To hear him in a varied program recorded in the early 1950s playing tenor, alto, and baritone saxophones, check out *Kaleidoscope* (Prestige/OJC-060). And, in the wish department, keep an eye out for a Stitt album called *Personal Appearance* on Verve; recorded in the late 1950s and long out of print, this has Stitt in steaming-hot form on alto and tenor. If you like Sonny, and Verve decides to reissue this, run, don't walk, to the store and grab it.

# LUCKY THOMPSON

Critics have questioned for years whether Eli "Lucky" Thompson's nickname was appropriate. An extremely gifted and uncompromising musician who has never received recognition commensurate with his talent, Thompson has several times disappeared from the music scene in order to meditate and escape various pressures for which, by all reports, he has no taste. He has been off the scene for a decade and a half, and those who would know say he hasn't even picked up the horn for years. When you listen to him play, you will feel as badly about this as every other Thompson fan does.

Thompson came to prominence in the 1940s, an unclassifiable player who obviously loved Coleman Hawkins and Don Byas, and throughout his career he continued to grow and deepen. He had a very expressive, warm sound, and his ideas ran in unorthodox directions; he was a thinker in addition to being a swinger, the kind of musician who brought out the best in those around him. Thompson's presence on a record, whether as sideman or leader, almost invariably coincided with above-average work from everyone concerned.

His 1964 album *Lucky Strikes* (Prestige/OJC-194) is a thing of beauty, a quartet session with a golden rhythm section of Hank Jones, Richard Davis, and Connie Kay. Thompson plays tenor and soprano saxophones, and he composed six of the eight tunes. This is not your basic blowing date, although the music swings hard in a number of grooves; Thompson came up with interesting arranging touches for all the tracks, which add variety and challenges while also allowing great latitude for improvisation. Some of the music is Latin-tinged, some is straight-ahead swinging, there is a waltz, and there are a couple of exquisite ballads, including a version of Duke Ellington's "In a Sentimental Mood," which Thompson plays on soprano at a slow tempo with Jones and Davis embroidering pretty patterns around his unimaginably pure held notes. Soul, fire, swing, deep emotion, imagination, lyricism – Thompson had it all, and it's all here. This set is impossible to recommend highly enough.

The same goes for Thompson's *Tricotism* (Impulse/GRP GRD-135), which brings together the results of four legendary 1956 dates with bassist Oscar Pettiford. On eight of the sixteen tracks, Thompson plays in a trio with Pettiford and guitarist Skeeter Best for a sound that is unique to these performances – relaxed yet alert, warm yet astringent. The opportunity to hear Pettiford, one of jazz's greatest bassists, at such length and so much in the foreground is reason enough to pick this up. The other tracks are performed by a sextet in which Thompson is joined by trombonist Jimmy Cleveland and, on four, pianist Hank Jones. Thompson composed all but two of the pieces here (and one of the two is a collaboration between Thompson and Pettiford); each is a gem, especially the ballad "A Lady's Vanity" and two unusual blues, "Mister Man" and "Old Reliable." This is one of the essential Thompson items.

Another excellent Thompson set is *Lucky Thompson Paris 1956, Volume 1* (Swing SW 8404), which features the tenorist in several settings, mostly with European musicians. French pianists Henri Renaud and Martial Solal, tenorist Guy Lafitte, and ex-Fletcher Henderson trumpeter Emmett Berry are featured; the best tracks have Thompson playing with just a rhythm section (on one track he plays accompanied by only bass and drums). Again, most of the material was composed by Thompson himself, and, as on *Lucky Strikes*, Thompson makes an exception for a Duke Ellington ballad – "Sophisticated Lady," this time. His sound is so original, his ideas so fresh. His playing on the original ballad "One Last Goodbye" is fabulous – emotionally moving, aesthetically convincing, and intellectually satisfying. Thompson's further European adventures are chronicled on *Kenny Clarke in Paris, Volume 1* (Swing SW 8411); here he plays four jazz standards ("Now's the Time," Tadd Dameron's "The Squirrel," "Stompin' at the Savoy," and "Four") with a small group under the leadership of drummer Clarke and four tunes with a small big-band. The tracks are all three and a half minutes and under, though, and this set isn't as satisfying as any of the previously mentioned Thompson albums.

Four 1947 tracks under Thompson's leadership appear on *Esquire's All-American Hot Jazz Sessions* (RCA/Bluebird 6757-2-RB); among them is one masterpiece, Thompson's famous version of the ballad "Just One More Chance," a ballad interpretation on a level with Coleman Hawkins's "Body and Soul." Thompson takes a number of hot choruses on the up-tempo "Boppin' the Blues." This track is an example of how brilliant playing can transcend even the most ordinary material.

Thompson, as noted, was a heroic sideman on many a record date, but none more so than the great 1954 Miles Davis session that produced "Walkin'" and "Blue 'N' Boogie." Available on Davis's *Walkin'* (Prestige/OJC-213), these two tracks feature the tenorist at the top of his game. His blues solo on the title track has been much celebrated, but I enjoy his stampeding romp on "Blue 'N' Boogie" even more; Davis and trombonist J. J. Johnson back him up with exciting riffs (borrowed from Coleman Hawkins's original recording of "Disorder at the Border"), and Thompson wails on top of them. Again, not to be missed. Thompson and Davis were together also for the 1946 Charlie Parker date that produced "Ornithology" and "A Night in Tunisia" (available on *The Legendary Dial Masters, Volume 1* [Stash ST-CD-23]). Thompson's rambunctious playing here is a startling contrast with Bird's lines, which sound almost cool by comparison. Thompson also makes a significant contribution to some 1952 Thelonious Monk recordings (including the wonderful "Skippy"), available on *Thelonious Monk – Genius of Modern Music, Volume 2* (Blue Note 81511).

Thompson and vibraphone master Milt Jackson were old friends and musical partners, and they hooked up for several good sessions. Jackson's *Plenty, Plenty Soul* (Atlantic 1269-2) features Thompson on four 1957 tracks, along with trumpeter Joe Newman, bassist Oscar Pettiford, and drummer Connie Kay (the pianist, unaccountably left off the personnel listing, is Horace Silver), the best of which is the infectious "The Spirit-Feel." Thompson really gets a groove going on this up-tempo blues and builds to a great climax. Thompson is also on board for the Jackson set *Second Nature* (Savoy SJL 2204), a collection of blowing-session-style items from 1956, mostly popular and jazz standards like "Now's the Time," "Sometimes I'm Happy," and "Flamingo," mixed in with a number of originals. Thompson and Jackson are accompanied by Hank Jones, Wendell Marshall, and Kenny Clarke (Wade Legge replaces Jones on several tunes), and everything moves along in a very casual and swinging manner. Several tracks from this set turn up also on the Jackson set *From Opus de Jazz to Jazz Skyline* (Savoy ZD 70815), including a good version of "Lover," on which the melody statement switches back and forth between a waltz and a brisk four-four.

## BENNY GOLSON

Another of jazz's undersung heroes is Philadelphia-born composer and tenor player Benny Golson. Although well known as the composer of jazz standards such as "Stablemates," "I Remember Clifford," "Killer Joe," and "Blues March," Golson, like Thompson, has never really received his due as a saxophonist. One reason for this is that both men represent something of a countertradition to the Lester Young–through–Charlie Parker approach that came to be seen as the mainstream of modern jazz playing on all instruments. Their conception of melody ran differently, coming more out of Don Byas and Coleman Hawkins; their approach was fuller toned, less legato, heavier sounding, in a time in which most musicians wanted to sound airborne.

Still, fellow musicians were very aware of Golson both as composer and saxophonist, and even the jazz public at large woke up to him after he joined Art Blakey's Jazz Messengers in 1958. Blakey's *Moanin'* (Blue Note 46516), perhaps the strongest single album Blakey ever recorded, is a Golson showcase; four of the set's six tunes are Golson originals, and he takes fiery, surprising solos throughout. A listen to his solo on the title track, pianist Bobby Timmons's bluesy "Moanin'," shows what a brilliant player Golson is; he starts with simple phrases in the lower range of the horn, then combines them into ever more complex sentences, using the musical equivalent of subordinate clauses to comment on what he has just played as he goes along, the phrases never ending up quite where you expect them to, getting more and more heated, higher pitched, faster, covering the entire range of the horn, finally, like a preacher building a sermon to a climax. Trumpeter Lee Morgan's solo on this is justly famous, but Golson's is a masterpiece, too.

The album also includes Golson's fine swinger "Are You Real?," his cool-as-a-breeze walking tempo "Along Came Betty," and his appropriately titled "Blues March." On all of them, the tenorist's contributions are extremely inventive, and he really doesn't sound like anyone else. This album is one of the essential jazz recordings and is a perfect place to check out Golson's unique style.

Another album that nicely balances Golson's writing and playing skills is *Art Farmer/Benny Golson – Meet the Jazztet* (MCA/Chess CHD-91550), recorded in 1960. Trombonist Curtis Fuller is also present in the front line, giving Golson a third voice to work with (in addition to trumpeter Farmer) on his ingenious arrangements of originals like "I Remember Clifford," "Killer Joe," and the haunting ballad "Park Avenue Petite," as well as on standards like "It Ain't Necessarily So" and the rarely done "Serenata." Golson is a volcano of ideas and fire in his playing; listening to him is sometimes like riding a roller coaster, as his lines twist abruptly, never settling into predictable patterns. His solo on "Serenata" is especially exhilarating. But Golson is one of the master ballad players, too; his version of "Easy Living" here is lovely. This album is one of the neglected landmarks of the music.

*Benny Golson's New York Scene* (Contemporary/OJC-164) is a nice 1957 set including quartet and quintet items (with Wynton Kelly on piano and Art Farmer on trumpet), as well as several cuts with an expanded band including Julius Watkins's French horn and Gigi Gryce's alto sax. Although this wasn't a working band, the same care is taken with arrangements (some of which were written by Gryce or Ernie Wilkins), the music never turns into a string of boring solos, and Golson sounds wonderful as always. Again, he scores with a gorgeous ballad performance of "You're Mine, You."

*The Other Side of Benny Golson* (Riverside/OJC-1750), an especially cooking 1958 set on which Golson gets a chance to solo at somewhat greater length, has Curtis Fuller on trombone, Barry Harris on piano, Golson's Blakey colleague Jymie Merritt on bass, and Philly Joe Jones on drums. If you like Golson's playing, this one is a real feast. Check out, too, what a big and varied sound he gets in his ensemble sketches here, writing for only tenor and trombone. The same remarks apply to *Groovin' with Golson* (New Jazz/OJC-226), one of the loosest Golson sets available, on which Golson and Fuller are accompanied by Ray Bryant, Paul Chambers, and Art Blakey. The repertoire here consists of three blues at different tempos and two medium-tempo ballads ("I Didn't Know What Time It Was" and "Yesterdays"). *Benny Golson* (Swing 8418) contains material from two 1958 dates, one recorded in New York and one in Paris. The New York sides have Lee Morgan on trumpet, with Philly Joe Jones again on drums; the Paris sides find Golson and pianist Bobby Timmons (his bandmate from the Blakey group) with three French musicians, including bassist Pierre Michelot. Golson plays very well here, as does Morgan. The three Paris tracks are a bit less interesting, but the album is certainly worth having.

## LESTORIAN MODE

Lester Young was a large and direct influence on many young musicians and not just tenor players, especially beginning in the early 1940s. Although his was far from the only influence – Don Byas and Coleman Hawkins, for example, had just as many adherents – a whole school of young tenor players undeniably fashioned themselves in Young's image with acolytic fervor. One of the best of them was even quoted as saying that any tenor player who didn't play like Pres was playing wrong.

The statement is obviously somewhat unsound, but it gives an idea of the kind of nearly fanatical devotion Young could inspire. One semilegendary character around the New York jazz scene, a nonmusician now in his sixties, is famous for his instant recall of almost any Lester Young solo; on the least provocation, and under almost any circumstances, he will collar his listener and begin singing Young solos from memory.

Other musicians have inspired this kind of adulation, but only a handful; they tend to be jazz's prophetic voices: Armstrong, Parker, Coltrane. Young certainly belongs in their company; the elements of his style were fundamental to the music's development, implying what writer Stanley Crouch has termed "a fresh logic." In any case, the 1940s saw a whole armada of young Pres devotees arrive on the scene, many of whom went on to forge very identifiable voices for themselves, but few, if any, of whom ever lost that identifying stamp of the President in their sounds, their ideas, and their approach to swinging.

The most famous seed farm for these Youngsters was the Woody Herman big band of the late 1940s, the so-called Four Brothers band, referring to the three tenors of Herbie Steward, Zoot Sims, and Stan Getz and the baritone of Serge Chaloff, Pres devotees all. Later Al Cohn would become one of the

Herman Brothers as well. The 1947 recording of the tune named for them, "Four Brothers," can be heard on *Woody Herman – The Thundering Herds, 1945–1947* (Columbia CK 44108); the arrangement and melody, by reed man Jimmy Giuffre, are bop-influenced, but the tenor solos come straight out of Pres (baritonist Chaloff is the most Parker-influenced of the soloists). This is one of only two tunes by this edition of the Herman band on this set, by the way; the others are by a slightly earlier gang, and, for me, they hold up a bit less well.

In any case, the records the Brothers made under their own names afford them more room to stretch out. Getz, Sims, and Cohn all got much more interesting as they got older, but many of their recordings of the 1940s and early 1950s are enjoyable, if not earthshaking. A good sampling of their sound from this early period is *Stan Getz/Zoot Sims – The Brothers* (Prestige/OJC-008), which contains the results of two sessions, a 1952 Al Cohn–Zoot Sims date and a 1949 summit meeting involving Getz, Cohn, Sims, and fellow Pres followers Allen Eager and Brew Moore. In the Five Brothers tracks, the differences among the players' styles are so slight as to be negligible to all but specialists, and no one gets much chance to stretch out; the Cohn-Sims tracks are more satisfying. This is swinging, easy-to-listen-to jazz, happy and melodically pleasing at its best, somewhat boring at its worst. In any case, a little of it goes a long way. All involved are featured to better advantage elsewhere. The same remarks apply to *Brothers and Other Mothers* (Savoy SJL 2210), which is valuable for its 1947 tracks by Serge Chaloff, the very talented baritone Brother, and its generous sampling of tracks by Pres cult figure Brew Moore (the titles are "Blue Brew," "Brew Blue," "More Brew," and "No More Brew"). Still, this is hardly essential stuff.

Brew Moore, perhaps the most elusive of the Lestorians (with the exception of Allen Eager, who is fondly remembered by those around at the time for his appearances with Tadd Dameron's band), was a natural, warmly swinging player who led a more or less tragic life and never achieved any public recognition to speak of. His album *Brew Moore* (Fantasy/OJC-049), for some reason available only on LP, is an extremely relaxed, happy session presenting Moore in tandem with an obscure West Coast tenorist and Pres devotee named Harold Wylie. Together they play chorus after chorus of swinging, inventive tenor with a special lyrical edge. Moore's version of the ballad "Nancy with the Laughing Face" is reason enough to pick this one up. No history being made, just very good jazz. Another Moore set, *The Brew Moore Quintet* (Fantasy/OJC-100, LP only), is good, too, but neither as relaxed nor as inspired as *Brew Moore*. Let's hope that Fantasy decides to bring out *Brew Moore*, at least, on CD.

Wardell Gray was not a part of the Woody Herman gang, but he took a backseat to no one as a disciple of Lester Young's. *Wardell Gray Memorial, Volume 1* (Prestige/OJC-050) and *Volume 2* (Prestige/OJC-051) contain Gray in various small-group settings recorded between 1949 and 1953. *Volume 1* is probably the better of the two; it includes Gray's medium-tempo blues solo "Twisted," which became a hit for singer Annie Ross (with lyrics added) and, later, Joni Mitchell. Throughout, Gray's evenly swinging, bop-flavored but essentially Lestorian playing is very tasty.

### THE BROTHERS

Zoot Sims was one of the most consistent players in jazz until his death in 1985. Like Moore, he had a natural spark, a buoyant swing, and an inner warmth that tended to suffuse any session he was involved in, especially as he got older and his tone broadened. Sims really loved to play; a good example of his go-for-broke spirit is the famous 1951 "Zoot Swings the Blues" (included on *Zoot Sims Quartets* [Prestige/OJC-242]), one of the first jazz records to be made using the extended time available on what was then the new medium of the long-playing record. While this number was being recorded, Sims was supposed to be watching for a signal from the control booth to let him know when to stop his solo; he forgot to look up, according to writer Ira Gitler, who was there, and by the time he remembered to look, the producer just waved him to keep going. The result was an exhilarating long tenor blowout on an up-tempo blues; Art Blakey's drums were a key factor in goading Sims onward.

A very good Sims set, recorded in 1956, is *Zoot Sims in Paris with Henri Renaud and Jon Eardley* (Swing SW 8417). His beautiful sound really comes through here, and he is in inspired form on these quintet sides with the obscure trumpeter Eardley and a French rhythm section. The repertoire is a nice mix of swinging originals and standards, a walking-tempo blues on which Sims excels, and a fine ballad, "My Old Flame." This set is a perfect capsule lesson in what made Zoot Sims so special – he swings effortlessly, his ideas always take interesting turns, and his sound is warm and expressive. Pres is present in the always-melodic quality of the tenor improvisations and in the light-footedness of the swing, but this could be no one but Sims. *Zoot!* (Riverside/OJC-228) is another nice 1956 quintet date with several originals by pianist-composer George Handy; this, too, is well recorded, and Sims plays very well, if not quite as inspired as on the Swing set.

In his later years Sims recorded many albums for producer Norman Granz's Pablo label; Sims always played well, but many of Granz's productions in the 1970s have a thrown-together air about them, and often either the recording balance or the mix of musical personalities isn't all it could have been. But on the 1975 *Zoot Sims and the Gershwin Brothers* (Pablo/OJC-444), there are no problems, and Zoot is in super form on an all-Gershwin program ranging from swingers ("The Man I Love," "Lady, Be Good") that feature Sims at his most exciting, to ballads like "How Long Has This Been Going On?" His rhythm section includes Oscar Peterson, and this is a jazz album for all seasons. Even better is *Zoot Sims Meets Jimmy Rowles: If I'm Lucky* (Pablo/OJC-683), on which Sims is paired with the pianist for a beautifully programmed set of ballads and swinging pop tunes in which Sims's tone is a thing to marvel at. "You're My Everything" and "Gypsy Sweetheart" are my personal favorites, but the entire set is superb. Sims communicates an almost ecstatic joy here, a sheer exhilaration.

Sims was often at his best with another saxophonist with whom he could exchange ideas, and the saxophonist with whom he exchanged the most ideas over the course of his life was his Brother from the Herman band, Al Cohn. Two excellent albums by this duo, recorded sixteen years apart almost to the day, are 1957's *Al and Zoot* (Decca/MCA MCAD-31372) and 1973's *Body and Soul* (Muse MCD 5356). Cohn was a musician's musician, a talented composer and arranger as well as a tenor player of rare imagination and lyricism. The earlier of these two sets is a happy, swinging jaunt for the two Brothers, with good two-horn arrangements provided by Cohn. The emphasis here is on straight-ahead blowing; the album even includes an ingenious tune that features them both on clarinet.

*Body and Soul* is a more varied program, with several extraordinary ballad performances. The rhythm section is an unusual one of Jaki Byard, George Duvivier, and Mel Lewis, players who rarely played together, but they really provide an extra spark here. The opening swinger, "Doodle-Oodle," has muscular solos from both horns and exciting exchanges with drummer Lewis; there's also a fast waltz, a bossa-nova medley, a beautiful duet on Johnny Mandel's "Emily," and a gorgeous Sims soprano sax reading of the ballad "Jean." Highly recommended. Sims and Cohn both play, in separate groups, on an album by singer Jimmy Rushing, *The You and Me That Used To Be* (RCA/Bluebird 6460-2-RB), a showcase for one of jazz's best voices, singing standards in all-star instrumental settings.

Cohn made several excellent albums on his own; of them, the most impressive must be the hard-to-find *Heavy Love* (Xanadu 145, LP only), an album of unaccompanied duets with pianist Jimmy Rowles. This is a stunning display of musicianship and soul; on the opening "Them There Eyes," for example, the two generate as much momentum as it is possible to generate, and without anyone spelling out the rhythm. Both men have such sure command of the musical pulse that the underlying beat doesn't need to be stated. The rest of the program consists mainly of standards like "Taking a Chance on Love" and "These Foolish Things." *Al Cohn's America* (Xanadu 138, LP only), also consisting mostly of standards, is a fine quartet outing with Barry Harris, Sam Jones, and Leroy Williams. Perhaps the most unusual and delightful track here is a muted bossa-nova version of "America the Beautiful"; it may sound strange, but they bring it off.

## STAN GETZ

Of all the Brothers, Stan Getz was by far the most commercially successful. Few jazz musicians since the days of the big bands have enjoyed such popularity with the general public; in 1963 Getz had a gigantic hit with the Brazilian tune "The Girl from Ipanema," and his albums have been consistently popular. Although his penchant for accessible material and lyrical, melodic improvising led some critics and fans, especially during the 1960s, to dismiss Getz as a merely pleasant and unchallenging player, Getz was in fact a great stylist, with an instantly identifiable, light, Pres-influenced sound that grew more and more full-bodied as his career progressed.

Although his playing gained in heat and passionate expressiveness in the 1960s, Getz always strove for beauty first. He seldom played his best at ultra-fast tempos, at which he tended to rely on repeated scalar patterns rather than fresh combinations of melodic ideas, and he was never a blow-all-night tenor battler. Rather, he shone in settings that displayed his beautiful sound and his inventive, melodic ideas at more relaxed tempos. One of the earliest devotees of the bossa nova, a samba-based Brazilian music that came to the United States early in the 1960s, Getz was a romantic first and last.

His 1967 *Sweet Rain* (Verve 815 054-2) is probably the best album he ever recorded, a quartet set with Chick Corea on piano, Ron Carter on bass, and Grady Tate on drums. The rhythm section is extremely flexible here, able to move from meditative sections, in which the pulse is only implied, to charging, cooking passages, and Getz responds with playing that ranges from gorgeous, round-sounding lyrical phrases to aggressive shouts, even yodeling some here and there. None of it is forced; all of it works as a whole. Two adventuresome Corea originals, the Latin-tinged Dizzy Gillespie tune "Con Alma," the bossa nova "O Grande Amor," and the title track, a haunting ballad, make up a set that can't be recommended highly enough. Corea's "Litha" is notable for its contrasting meditative and cooking sections, not just in the melody statement but underneath the solos; listen here, and throughout, to

Ron Carter's masterful way of playing melodic figures underneath Corea and Getz. This is a great mood album that will also repay the closest listening.

*Jazz Samba* (Verve 810 061-2), which pairs Getz with guitarist Charlie Byrd, was the first and best of Getz's bossa-nova records, certainly the one with the best jazz-to-samba ratio. From the first notes of the lovely "Desafinado," this is a different kind of jazz, as refreshing as an ocean breeze. The album contains a number of moods – reflective, bluesy, joyous, urgent, just plain happy. Getz's sensuous sound is the perfect vehicle for the very romantic and sweet melodies heard here. *Getz/Gilberto* (Verve 810 048-2), recorded a year later with Brazil's major bossa-nova figures Joao Gilberto and Antonio Carlos Jobim, contains the original version of "The Girl from Ipanema," with Astrud Gilberto's memorable vocal. This set is a little lighter on the jazz than *Jazz Samba*, but it is very listenable.

Somewhat more challenging is the 1964 meeting between Getz and pianist Bill Evans, available as *Stan Getz and Bill Evans* (Verve 833 802-2). This set is interesting especially for the presence of drummer Elvin Jones, at that time a member of John Coltrane's classic quartet; on tunes like "Night and Day" and "My Heart Stood Still," his polyrhythmic style contrasts, not altogether successfully, with the more lyrical tendencies of the two principals. Still, there is some very good music here, including a fine performance of the ballad "But Beautiful."

Many Getz fans feel that 1961's *Focus* (Verve 821 982-2) is one of the saxophonist's great statements. Getz improvises his way around, over, under, and through music written for a large string ensemble by veteran Eddie Sauter, which was supposedly designed to be able to stand on its own as well as provide half of a stimulating dialogue for the star. This set isn't a favorite of mine; the string arrangements sound stilted, sometimes like an attempt at contemporary European classical music, sometimes like an uneasy mixture of watered-down Impressionism and movie music. Getz's playing here, to me, is ironically unfocused, since the compositions offer him no melodic meat to transform, little harmonic motion, and no rhythmic momentum.

For a taste of the young Getz at his most Lester Young–like in 1949 and 1950, playing standards like "There's a Small Hotel," "My Old Flame," and "Too Marvelous for Words," with several good bebop rhythm sections including one with pianist Al Haig and drummer Roy Haynes, check out *Stan Getz Quartets* (Prestige/OJC-121). And for evidence of his vitality in the 1970s, *The Lyrical Stan Getz* (Columbia CK 44047) offers a grab bag of the tenorist in various settings, including two tracks from 1972's *Captain Marvel* album, with Chick Corea playing electric piano, a 1977 "Willow Weep for Me," recorded at the Montreux Jazz Festival, and a beautiful version of "Lover Man," with the little-known but brilliant Albert Dailey on piano.

## TENOR MADNESS

With all these influences – Coleman Hawkins, Lester Young, Don Byas, Charlie Parker, Sonny Stitt, and the rest – the 1950s saw a real explosion of tenor talent. The common language had incorporated Bird's additions, and it was a period of consolidation, in which many excellent players spoke the same language in a variety of voices. The 1950s culminated in the emergence of the twin colossi Sonny Rollins and John Coltrane as the dominant players on the instrument, although both had been on the scene since the beginning of the decade. Before we get to them, here's a look at some of the players who made the 1950s and early 1960s a golden age for the tenor saxophone.

In some ways, Hank Mobley was the archetypal 1950s tenorist. A strong swinger who sometimes sounded like a one-man encyclopedia of hard-bop strategies for dealing with chord changes, Mobley played with most of the best-known bands of the time, including those of Art Blakey, Horace Silver, Miles Davis, and Max Roach. Beginning in 1960, he also made a series of classic albums for Blue Note under his own name. These records have been somewhat overlooked by most critics; by the time they were made, Sonny Rollins, John Coltrane, and the New Thing players were dominating critical vision, and Mobley's records weren't seen as being on the cutting edge anymore. With today's perspective, though, it's obvious that they include some of the best straight-ahead, bop-rooted tenor playing ever recorded. Mobley's smoky tone, mastery of chord changes, and even-footed rhythmic attack light up his versions of popular standards (of which he chose some of the best and most neglected) as well as his own originals.

One of the best of this series of albums is the 1960 quartet session *Soul Station* (Blue Note 46528), on which Mobley has a killer rhythm section of Wynton Kelly, Paul Chambers, and Art Blakey. The program here is split between Mobley originals designed for cooking and two rarely done standards ("If I Should Lose You" and Irving Berlin's "Remember") that have Mobley in a certain rhythmic pocket that brings out his tastiest work. He was a master at setting exactly the right tempo for a tune, like a cook setting exactly the right amount of flame under a pan; these two are taken at slightly different medium tempos (notice that "If I Should Lose You" is just a hair faster) that make for perfect momentum. A tune taken even a bit too slowly may drag; the same tune taken just a bit too quickly may sound rushed. This sense of the right tempo is an important part of a jazz musician's equipment and is developed only with experience. The originals here include the fast romp "This I Dig of You" and the bluesy title tune. Highly recommended.

Just as good, maybe better, is *Another Workout* (Blue Note 84431), a 1961 quartet set with Kelly and Chambers again but with Philly Joe Jones on drums this time; Jones lends a certain kind of rhythmic freshness to things here that is his alone. Again, two unusual popular standards ("Hello, Young Lovers" and "Three Coins in the Fountain") are given cooking, medium-tempo treatments, and the former, especially, finds Mobley at his best in chorus after chorus of exciting but controlled swinging. The set also includes an up-tempo original, "Out of Joe's Bag," which incorporates breaks for Jones's drums into the melody and has some very strong blowing from Mobley, a fine version of the ballad "I Should Care," a mostly modal Mobley original called "Gettin' and Jettin'," and Mobley's minor-key "Hank's Other Soul."

Throughout, the Kelly-Chambers-Jones rhythm section inspires the tenorist, as they do on another fine set also recorded in 1961, *Workout* (Blue Note 84080). Here, with the addition of guitarist Grant Green, the group plows through a set consisting mostly of Mobley originals. "Workout," like "Out of Joe's Bag," uses Jones's drum breaks in the head; "Uh Huh" is a funky, backbeat-flavored piece using a call-and-response figure at a surging medium tempo. "Smokin'" is an appropriately titled up-tempo blues, and "Greasin' Easy" is a walking-tempo blues. The set also includes another of those well-chosen pop tunes in medium tempo, "The Best Things in Life Are Free." Again, a very satisfying quartet outing.

*Roll Call* (Blue Note 46823), recorded in 1960, is one of the most exciting jazz albums ever recorded. Mobley is joined by trumpeter Freddie Hubbard and the mighty Kelly-Chambers-Blakey rhythm section in a strongly swinging set in which Mobley's toughest edge is brought out. From the first notes of the title tune, this one takes off and keeps going, the rhythm section laying down an absolutely irresistible rolling groove. Blakey, especially, was in an explosive mood that day, and his drum interjections, rolls, and cymbal splashes goad the soloists to heights of invention. All the tunes here are Mobley originals with a strongly blues- or gospel-inflected base, with the exception of another fine medium-tempo standard, "The More I See You." Strongly recommended as an example of hard bop at its hardest.

*No Room for Squares* (Blue Note 84149) is a 1963 date with Lee Morgan on trumpet and a rhythm section of Andrew Hill, John Ore, and Philly Joe Jones, featuring a variety of material, including the modal title track, a vamp blues called "Me 'N You," and a beautiful Lee Morgan ballad called "Carolyn." Listen to the fascinating accenting interplay between Mobley and Jones's snare drum on the previously unreleased "Syrup and Biscuits" (only on the CD issue).

*The Turnaround* (Blue Note 84186), recorded a year and a half later, features Freddie Hubbard again, and a Barry Harris–Paul Chambers–Billy Higgins rhythm section. This one consists entirely of Mobley originals, including the beautiful ballad "My Sin," and is thoroughly enjoyable.

Some of Mobley's best earlier playing may be heard on three 1954–1955 sets by the first edition of the Jazz Messengers, when it included pianist Horace Silver and drummer Art Blakey; bassist Doug Watkins rounded out the rhythm section, and trumpeter Kenny Dorham was Mobley's companion in the front line. *Horace Silver and the Jazz Messengers* (Blue Note 46140) and *The Jazz Messengers at the Cafe Bohemia, Volume 1* (Blue Note 46521) and *Volume 2* (Blue Note 46522) are all classics of hard bop and are discussed under Jazz Messengers in the Ensembles section. Some other albums on which Mobley really shines as a sideman are Lee Morgan's *Cornbread* (Blue Note 84222), Kenny Dorham's *Afro-Cuban* (Blue Note 46815), and *The Eminent Jay Jay Johnson, Volume 2* (Blue Note 81506). He can also be heard as a member of Miles Davis's quintet on *Someday My Prince Will Come* (Columbia CK 40947) and *In Person at the Blackhawk, Volume 1* (Columbia CK 44257) and *Volume 2* (Columbia CK 44425).

An excellent player of the time, with a somewhat similar conception to Mobley's but with his own characteristic approach to intervals and an identifiable, keening sound, was the short-lived and lesser-known Tina Brooks. Best known for his work on *The Sermon* (Blue Note 46097) by organist Jimmy Smith, Brooks also made a number of quintet dates for Blue Note under his own name, all of which are collected on a fantastic four-LP set from Mosaic, *The Complete Blue Note Recordings of the Tina Brooks Quintets* (Mosaic MR4-106). Much of the material included was heretofore unissued, for obscure reasons; certainly the music is consistently rewarding.

Brooks is featured with four different groups, recorded from 1958 through 1961, including trumpeters Lee Morgan, Freddie Hubbard, Blue Mitchell, and Johnny Coles, pianists Sonny Clark, Kenny Drew, and Duke Jordan, bassists Doug Watkins, Paul Chambers, Wilbur Ware, and Sam Jones, and drummers Art Blakey, Philly Joe Jones, and Art Taylor. In other words, these are truly all-star sessions. Brooks sets a fast pace with some very attractive writing for the ensembles, as well as with his deft, moving, and always swinging horn playing. Most of the tunes are Brooks originals; his playing and writing alike had a certain characteristic cry. Everything here is excellent, although I would call special attention to the legendary material from Brooks's *Back to the Tracks* album, announced by Blue Note thirty years ago but never issued. This is small-group jazz of the highest order, with a unique flavor. Brooks also has large roles in Freddie Hubbard's *Open Sesame* (Blue Note 84040), Jackie

McLean's *Jackie's Bag* (Blue Note 46142), Kenny Burrell's jam session *Blue Lights, Volume 1* (Blue Note 81596) and *Volume 2* (Blue Note 81597), and the Blue Note album *Shades of Redd* included on *The Complete Blue Note Recordings of Freddie Redd* (Mosaic MD2-124).

Philadelphian Jimmy Heath is part of a musical family that includes his brothers, bassist Percy and drummer Albert; his tenor always added a welcome and distinctive voice to recording sessions. For much of the 1950s he was inactive, and he didn't record as much as some other players during that decade. But in the late 1970s and 1980s the Heath Brothers became a working band, making several very nice albums, and Heath could be heard fairly regularly in New York. One of his best albums as a leader is the hard-to-find 1975 *Picture of Heath* (Xanadu 118, LP only), a straight-ahead quartet date with Barry Harris, Sam Jones, and Billy Higgins. This is a very satisfying, swinging set, which includes a great version of "Body and Soul," on which Heath plays both tenor and soprano saxes. *Really Big!* (Riverside/OJC-1799) and *The Thumper* (Riverside/OJC-1828) have Heath, variously, among trumpeters Clark Terry and Nat Adderley, trombonist Curtis Fuller, and pianists Tommy Flanagan, Cedar Walton, and Wynton Kelly, in programs that combine standards with Heath originals.

Some of Heath's most exciting work was recorded as a sideman. One classic set is on the CD issue of *Miles Davis, Volume 2* (Blue Note 81502), in which Heath is part of a 1953 sextet with Davis, trombonist J. J. Johnson, brother Percy on bass, and Art Blakey on drums. They play his composition "C.T.A.," but my favorite solos here are Heath's two choruses on each of two takes of the fast "Ray's Idea." Heath, Johnson, and Percy Heath are together also on *The Eminent Jay Jay Johnson, Volume 1* (Blue Note 81505), another excellent 1953 sextet set, this one featuring Clifford Brown on trumpet. Heath is also featured on two very good albums under the leadership of trumpeter Kenny Dorham, *Kenny Dorham Quintet* (Debut/OJC-113) and *Showboat* (Time/Bainbridge BCD-1043), a nice quintet workout on the melodies from Jerome Kern's musical. Freddie Hubbard's hot 1961 set *Hub Cap* (Blue Note 84073) features Heath extensively, and Heath is heard to good effect on several cuts included on Milt Jackson's 1964 *Statements* (Impulse/GRP GRD-130), especially a burning version of his own fast blues "Gingerbread Boy."

A St. Louis native with strong roots in the swing approach, Jimmy Forrest was a big-band veteran who also incorporated many of the melodic and rhythmic elements of bebop into his big-toned style, which somewhat resembled that of Illinois Jacquet. His best album is probably *Out of the Forrest* (Prestige/OJC-097), a quartet date which includes the famous "Bolo Blues," as well as cooking versions of "I Cried for You" and "This Can't Be Love" on which Forrest uses all his late-night club experience to build excitement in his solos. The set also has a good version of the ballad "That's All." *Most Much!* (Prestige/OJC-350) is also excellent, again a quartet date, but with Ray Barretto's conga drum added. This one includes a roiling version of the calypso "Matilda," as well as such sentimental standards as "My Buddy" and "Sonny Boy," which Forrest transforms into the stuff of jazz. He also tips his hat to Jacquet with an unhurried but very swinging "Robbins' Nest."

The legendary and little-known James Clay qualifies as a Texas tenor by birth. He never had the recognition he should have had in the 1950s, since he stayed in Dallas except for a 1956 visit to Los Angeles. On that visit (he was barely twenty-one years old), he recorded an album that shows why he became an underground legend. Now available as *The Lawrence Marable Quartet Featuring James Clay: Tenorman* (Blue Note 84440), this quartet date featuring Sonny Clark on piano is a real collector's item. Clay swings like mad but is also very inventive, with an unusual sense of phrasing that owes something to Sonny Stitt (as does his tone) and is very definite and melodic. Here he cooks on "The Devil and the Deep Blue Sea," as well as on some tasty Sonny Clark originals (Clark plays extremely well here, too), and shows uncanny maturity on his ballad versions of "Easy Living" and "Lover Man." This one is not just another blowing session.

Clay also participated, with fellow Texan David "Fathead" Newman, in an extremely tough 1960 two-tenor album, *The Sound of the Wide Open Spaces: James Clay and David "Fathead" Newman* (Riverside/OJC-257, LP only). The two tenors cook for chorus after chorus on the opening blues and continue to do so for the rest of the album, aided and abetted by the swing-or-die rhythm section of Wynton Kelly, Sam Jones, and Art Taylor. Their medium-tempo "They Can't Take That Away from Me" is a standout, and they go toe-to-toe on the "Indiana"-based "Figger-ration." Clay is also featured on guitar player Wes Montgomery's *Movin' Along* (Riverside/OJC-089), playing flute for the most part, although his tenor is heard on the surging "So Do It!," which many will fondly remember as the opening theme music for New York disc jockey Ed Beach's show in the 1960s and 1970s.

James Moody made his name with Dizzy Gillespie's late-1940s big band (he also spent a good deal of time with later Gillespie small groups). Equally proficient on alto and flute, he is best known as a cooking, inventive bop tenor player (and sometime vocalist). *Wail, Moody, Wail* (Prestige/OJC-1791), *Hi Fi Party* (Prestige/OJC-1780), and *Moody's Mood for Blues* (Prestige/OJC-1837) are all solid examples of his talent; often he is joined here by his alter ego, the vocalist Eddie Jefferson. Moody's solo on "I'm in the Mood for Love" was fitted out with lyrics (and retitled "Moody's Mood for Love") and may be heard in vocalist King Pleasure's version on *King Pleasure Sings/Annie Ross Sings* (Prestige/OJC-217).

Charlie Rouse is best remembered as the tenorist in Thelonious Monk's classic quartet of the 1960s (which he joined in 1959), but he had played with Duke Ellington, Dizzy Gillespie, and Tadd Dameron as far back as the 1940s. Somewhat undervalued critically, Rouse had an instantly identifiable sound from the big-voiced school; he was a swinger and a fantastic ballad player. He can be heard at length on most of Monk's Columbia recordings, such as *Monk's Dream* (CK 40786) and *Underground* (CK 40785).

If you like his playing, check out either or both of two sets under his own name – *Takin' Care of Business* (Jazzland/OJC-491) and *Unsung Hero* (Epic/Columbia EK 46181). The Jazzland set is more varied in repertoire and sound; it also features trumpeter Blue Mitchell and includes cooking originals, a very interesting ballad by pianist Randy Weston called "Pretty Strange," and a solid, medium-tempo version of the standard "They Didn't Believe Me." *Unsung Hero* consists of quartet tracks from two different 1960–1961 sessions; the standouts here are the ballads, especially the opener, "When Sunny Gets Blue." Rouse is also featured prominently on an excellent album by pianist Sonny Clark, *Leapin' and Lopin'* (Blue Note 84091).

By any measure, Paul Gonsalves must be counted as one of the major tenor voices of the 1950s and 1960s. Equally formidable on the blues, up-tempo wailers, and romantic ballads, Gonsalves had a sound that was unforgettable and a harmonic approach that seemed to have been influenced substantially by the unusual and fluid playing of Don Byas. His reputation is inevitably linked to his recordings (and live performances) with Duke Ellington's orchestra, which he joined in 1950 and remained with until his death in 1974.

By far the most famous one is the epic performance of "Diminuendo and Crescendo in Blue" recorded at the Newport Jazz Festival in 1956 and available on *Ellington at Newport* (Columbia CK 40587). Ellington opened up the middle section of his 1937 extended piece and had Gonsalves play the blues at a rocking swing tempo for as long as he wanted. Gonsalves closed his eyes, reared back, played twenty-seven choruses, and nearly started a riot. This is one of the most infectious jazz performances ever recorded and an essential set.

Most of Gonsalves's other recordings with Ellington are discussed in the Ensembles section, but special attention must be called to his sinuous, passionate solo on the "Mount Harissa" segment of *The Far East Suite* (RCA/Bluebird 7640-2-RB), his beautiful reading of "Where or When" on *Ellington Indigos* (Columbia CK 44444), and his wild ride on the "Ready Go!" section of Ellington's "Toot Suite," included on *Jazz Party* (Columbia CK 40712), on which he is goaded on by the band's riffs. No Gonsalves fan will want to miss

*Duke Ellington and His Orchestra Featuring Paul Gonsalves* (Fantasy/OJC-623), on which Gonsalves is given his head for an entire program with the band; he gets to solo at length on tunes, like "Take the 'A' Train," on which he usually didn't solo. Gonsalves can be heard playing the blues at a rocking tempo with just the Ellington rhythm section on a track carelessly labeled "Diminuendo and Crescendo in Blue" on *The Best of Duke Ellington* (Signature/CBS AK 45257). Gonsalves's own album *Gettin' Together!* (Jazzland/OJC-203), which features him with a rhythm section of Wynton Kelly, Sam Jones, and Jimmy Cobb, is a nice set; his ballad versions of "I Surrender Dear" and "I Cover the Waterfront" take the honors here. Another album, *Paul Gonsalves and Roy Eldridge: Mexican Bandit Meets Pittsburgh Pirate* (Fantasy/OJC-751), recorded in 1973 with the trumpet giant, is quite disappointing; Gonsalves was in ill health at the time, and he sounds it.

Chicagoan Clifford Jordan's smoky lyricism has been heard in any number of settings, from Charles Mingus's adventuresome mid-1960s group with Eric Dolphy and Jaki Byard to a 1980s quartet with Barry Harris, which explored the classic bop repertoire of the 1940s. His 1961 album *Starting Time* (Jazzland/OJC-147) is a nice introduction to his playing and his composing (three of the eight tunes are his). His guests are trumpeter Kenny Dorham and a rhythm section of Cedar Walton, Wilbur Ware, and Albert Heath; the set is varied and interestingly programmed. Jordan's perhaps hard-to-find 1984 *Repetition* (Soul Note SN 1084), recorded with the Barry Harris–Walter Booker–Vernel Fournier rhythm section with which Jordan was working at the time, is a fine mix of Jordan originals and jazz standards like Thelonious Monk's "Evidence." Jordan can also be heard to advantage on Charles Mingus's 1964 *Town Hall Concert* (Jazz Workshop/OJC-042) and trumpeter Lee Morgan's *Take Twelve* (Jazzland/OJC-310).

Jordan's fellow Chicagoan Johnny Griffin was one of the strong presences on the scene during the late 1950s and early 1960s; he spent a long time in Europe but has been appearing (and recording) regularly in the United States since the late 1970s. Griffin is a voluble player who had something of a "fastest gun in the West" reputation because of his awesome technique and torrential ideas. A good place to hear Griffin is on the Thelonious Monk album *Thelonious in Action* (Riverside/OJC-103), recorded live at New York City's Five Spot in the summer of 1958 when Griffin was a member of Monk's quartet. This set features the tenorist at length on Monk favorites "Blue Monk" and "Rhythm-A-Ning," as well as on the lesser-known compositions "Light Blue" and "Coming on the Hudson." "Rhythm-A-Ning," an up-tempo ride on the chords of "I Got Rhythm," underlines Griffin's weaknesses as well as his strengths: his technique is prodigious, and he is never at a loss for something to play, but sometimes he lacks taste – a way of saying he didn't leave enough space in his solos. The companion album *Misterioso* (Riverside/OJC-206) is also good; these are not among the essential Monk items, but they are worthwhile, as was everything Monk recorded.

Griffin's own *The Little Giant* (Riverside/OJC-136) is a nice, varied set with Blue Mitchell on trumpet and Wynton Kelly on piano, marred somewhat by a bad recording balance. *A Blowing Session* (Blue Note 81559) is just what the title implies: an all-star date with the emphasis on extended solos. In this case the lineup is truly daunting: Lee Morgan on trumpet, Griffin, Hank Mobley, and John Coltrane on tenors, and a rhythm section of Wynton Kelly, Paul Chambers, and Art Blakey. Many, many notes are played, not all of them meaningful. Morgan plays some of the most interesting stuff here, but of course there is much excitement along the way from all involved. Tenor fans will also enjoy an album made by the quintet Griffin led with tenorist Eddie "Lockjaw" Davis in 1960, *Griff and Lock* (Jazzland/OJC-264), a straight-out blowing session (with arranged touches), a little short on subtlety but full of swing and good times. And Griffin has an effective guest role on Wes Montgomery's 1962 live album *Full House* (Riverside/OJC-106), backed by Miles Davis's rhythm section of that time (Wynton Kelly, Paul Chambers, and Jimmy Cobb).

## SONNY ROLLINS

From the time of his most important early recordings in August 1949 with Bud Powell and Fats Navarro (available on *The Amazing Bud Powell, Volume 1* [Blue Note 81503]), Sonny Rollins had something different. Most tenor players at that time who were influenced by Charlie Parker were equally influenced by Lester Young in their way of accenting eighth notes; they also tended to play with a dry, hard sound, like Dexter Gordon or Sonny Stitt. Rollins had the same freedom of accenting that Bird had, but his heavy tone was modeled on Coleman Hawkins's sound.

Rollins didn't really come into his own until the mid-1950s, after a year-long absence from the scene during which he lay low in Chicago to get himself together personally and musically; when he did, it was as the tenor player who had most perfectly digested Bird's way of accenting, as well as his conception of melody. By 1956 Rollins was arguably the greatest melodic improviser in jazz. He also had a gigantic sound that could seemingly do anything Rollins wanted it to; it could sing romantic ballads, tell stories, ski effortlessly through difficult harmonic terrain at impossible speeds, shout, honk, squeal, laugh derisively, imitate cellos and bassoons, all the while maintaining an awareness of form in his solos that sometimes made it hard to believe they could have been improvised.

During the 1950s Rollins played and recorded with Miles Davis, Thelonious Monk, Dizzy Gillespie, and Max Roach, among others. In 1957 he left Roach's group and became a leader himself. At the end of the decade, Rollins retreated from the jazz scene, going into seclusion for two years to practice, study, meditate, and keep his own counsel (he even practiced some on New York City's Williamsburg Bridge). When he returned, in 1962, he had plainly been influenced by some of the tonal and timbral implications of the avant-garde players of the time, such as Ornette Coleman. The 1960s were a strange time for Rollins; he produced some brilliant work and some that seems to be striving for an effect that never really comes off. At the end of the decade he disappeared again.

He returned in 1972, and no one who heard him at the time will ever forget the power and brilliance with which he played, strolling around bandstands spinning extended unaccompanied cadenzas while everyone held their breath as if they were watching someone do ballet on a high wire with no net. On Rollins's *Next Album* (Milestone/OJC-312), recorded soon after his reemergence, the version of Hoagy Carmichael's "Skylark" contains an extended cadenza that gives some idea of what he can do when he is really inspired.

Rollins has been on the scene ever since, and when he is "on" he is still the greatest improviser alive. When he isn't "on," he is capable of astonishingly dull playing. The latter side of Rollins has almost invariably been the dominant one on his recordings after *Next Album*. While most of these have at least one worthwhile track on them, there is a whole lot of Rollins to listen to before bothering with his recordings of the 1970s and 1980s. But if he comes through your town, always make it a point to gamble on a ticket. If you hit him on the right night, you are liable to hear something you'll never forget.

### SAXOPHONE COLOSSUS

Rollins's all-around greatest album is probably *Saxophone Colossus* (Prestige/OJC-291), recorded in 1956. A quartet session with Tommy Flanagan, Doug Watkins, and Max Roach, *Saxophone Colossus* spotlights Rollins while he was still featured with the Clifford Brown/Max Roach quintet and had put together all the elements of his style into a coherent and irresistible extension of the entire tenor saxophone tradition. You can hear everything here that makes Rollins a giant: his colossal, expressive sound (which he uses to forge a masterpiece version of the slow ballad "You Don't Know What Love Is"), his utterly compelling swing (obvious throughout, and especially on the fast

"Strode Rode" and his famous calypso "St. Thomas"), his endless melodic invention, which invariably made use not only of the harmonic structure of a piece but of its melody as well (especially evident on "You Don't Know What Love Is" and the mysterioso blues "Blue Seven"), and his humor.

Rollins has returned to the calypso throughout his career (listen also to "The Everywhere Calypso" on *Next Album* [Milestone/OJC-312] and "Hold 'Em Joe" on *On Impulse!* [MCA/Impulse MCAD-5655 JVC-458]), but *Saxophone Colossus*'s "St. Thomas" is probably his best-known composition and performance in this genre. The first section of the track is in calypso rhythm. Midway through the drum solo, Roach shifts into straight-ahead four-four; when Rollins comes back in, soloing over the swing rhythm, the effect is like a tidal wave sweeping everything before it. And listen to how naturally Rollins phrases the melody of "You Don't Know What Love Is," as if he were a singer, to the way he leaves space in his playing, and to the way he builds intensity through the track. The matter of leaving space is important; some players feel as if they have to be playing something all the time, but Rollins builds his solos with conversational logic, staggering short, choppy phrases with exquisite held notes and long, labyrinthine lines that rarely go where you would expect them to but which always make sense.

"Strode Rode," taken at a bracing tempo, shows how Rollins can take a motif and instantly extend it, alter it, add to it, invert it, in a thrilling extended improvisation. Rollins takes his first thirty-two bars accompanied only by bass; listen to the way he brings Roach into the performance afterward by playing a repeated figure that mimics Roach's ride cymbal pattern. "Moritat" is better known as the pop song "Mack the Knife"; the quartet takes it at a relaxed medium tempo. "Blue Seven," a blues at a walking tempo, has received much attention because of Rollins's "thematic improvisation." He takes the simple, harmonically ambiguous opening saxophone motif, built on the major third, flat seventh, and flat fifth of the B♭ scale, and uses it as the organizing principle of his solos, in extremely ingenious fashion. This track, like all the others, will repay as much close listening as you want to give it.

Finally, what makes this album so good is the grandeur in Rollins's conception, a sort of nobility and exultation in the act of organizing melody spontaneously that is almost Armstrong-like. And, significantly, it finds Rollins addressing each of the fundamentals of jazz: swing at slow ("You Don't Know What Love Is"), medium ("Moritat"), and fast ("Strode Rode") tempos, the blues ("Blue Seven"), the ballad ("You Don't Know . . ."), and Afro-Hispanic rhythms ("St. Thomas"). The album was made at a moment at which Rollins knew exactly what he was doing and why. Not to be overlooked are the contributions of the sidemen, especially pianist Tommy Flanagan, who provides such perfect accompaniment throughout, as well as some lovely solos. *Saxophone Colossus* is unquestionably one of the landmarks of the music.

### WORKTIME

Recorded six and a half months before *Saxophone Colossus*, Rollins's *Worktime* (Prestige/OJC-007) is also a quartet outing, with Roach again on drums, pianist Ray Bryant, and bassist George Morrow. It hasn't quite the Olympian grandeur of the later set, but it comes very close; one difference is that it contains only one Rollins original (the Latin-tinged "Paradox") as opposed to *Saxophone Colossus*'s three. But the choice of tunes is characteristically unusual: "There's No Business Like Show Business" (Rollins loves to pick out songs no other jazz performer would think of doing; he takes this one at a punishingly fast tempo), Billy Strayhorn's "Raincheck," the ballad "There Are Such Things," and a galloping version of Cole Porter's "It's All Right with Me."

Rollins's coordination, presence of mind, and soul are stunning throughout. He does all kinds of things with time and rhythmic expectations; on the lightning "Show Business," he sometimes plays at half tempo while the rhythm section races away, then suddenly doubles up with a run of rapid-fire eighth notes. Sometimes he just floats way above the tempo in the manner of Lester Young or the Louis Armstrong of "I've Got a Right to Sing the Blues" (on *Laughin' Louie* [RCA/Bluebird 9759-2-RB]). Listen to the way Rollins uses certain motifs throughout "There Are Such Things" to give the performance unity. In his unaccompanied closing cadenza, after the initial ascending line, he plays a sliding descending rhythmic figure, answered immediately by its mirror image, ascending; at the end of the cadenza he plays truncated versions of both lines, only reversed (i.e., ascending, then descending), turning the cadenza into a unified summation, perfectly framed, of the entire track. Genius at work.

Between *Worktime* and Rollins's retreat from the scene in 1959, he recorded an enormous amount of good music. Some of the best was recorded with only bass and drum accompaniment. Before turning to these trio sets, here is a look at some of Rollins's other late-1950s dates.

*Sonny Rollins Plus Four* (Prestige/OJC-243) is a March 1956 date under Rollins's leadership by the Clifford Brown/Max Roach quintet, of which Rollins was then a member. Clifford Brown was a genius of the trumpet; until his death in June 1956, he and Rollins were a fantastic team in this band. This set captures their brilliance, as well as that of Roach; it contains Rollins's jazz standard "Valse Hot," one of the first jazz tunes written in waltz time, as well as his "Pent-Up House." Rollins's and Brown's crackling exchanges at the end

· · · · · · **300** *Tenors*

of both "Kiss and Run" and "I Feel a Song Comin' On" are startlingly sharp and empathetic, and "Count Your Blessings" is a fine, walking-tempo feature for Rollins.

*Tenor Madness* (Prestige/OJC-124), recorded in May 1956, has a happy, relaxed Rollins playing with Miles Davis's rhythm section of the time (Red Garland, Paul Chambers, and Philly Joe Jones) in a program of three standards ("When Your Lover Has Gone," "The Most Beautiful Girl in the World," and the beautiful and rarely done "My Reverie"), a Rollins original ("Paul's Pal"), and the title track, on which Rollins is joined by none other than John Coltrane for their only meeting on record. Both men take good, long solos on this medium-tempo blues (once known as "Royal Roost"), then engage in some delicious exchanges. Nobody seems to be out for blood here; they set up each other's shots, echoing and amplifying what the other has said. This is a perfect place to study the differences and similarities in the styles of the two dominant tenor players of the time. On the other tracks, Rollins gives lots of solo space to the members of the rhythm section, and there isn't as much of him here as there is on some other records. What there is, though, is fine; listen to the way he floats above the tempo as he phrases the melody of "The Most Beautiful Girl in the World."

*Rollins Plays for Bird* (Prestige/OJC-214) was recorded in October 1956 less than three months after Clifford Brown's death in an automobile accident along with the Brown/Roach band's pianist, Richie Powell (Bud Powell's brother). Its main feature is a twenty-seven-minute medley of tunes associated with Charlie Parker, who had died a year and a half earlier. Rollins begins the medley by quoting Bird's opening phrase from "Parker's Mood" (available on *Bird: The Savoy Original Master Takes* [Savoy ZDS 8801]) and goes immediately into a lovely reading of "I Remember You." Rollins's sections here are separated by statements by trumpeter Kenny Dorham (Brown's replacement in the quintet) and pianist Wade Legge, so you need patience if it's Sonny you want to hear, although everyone else plays very well. The album also includes a nice waltz by Rollins called "Kids Know" and his great performance of "I've Grown Accustomed to Your Face."

*Sonny Boy* (Prestige/OJC-348), recorded only two months later, is in its way another kind of tribute to Bird. Two tracks here – "B.Quick" and "B.Swift," themeless workouts on the chords of "Cherokee" and "Lover," respectively – are staggering examples of Rollins's coordination and presence of mind at the fastest tempos, as fast as anything Parker ever played, somewhat reminiscent, in fact, of Parker's themeless "Bird Gets the Worm" and "Klaunstance" (also available on *Bird: The Savoy Original Master Takes*). Rollins seems to have been in an aggressive mood on this particular day; the opening blues, "Ee-ah," is based almost entirely on a short, jagged, one-note rhythmic motif, and Rollins sounds agitated, tearing off intricate runs in quadruple time, hoarse shouts, and squeals. An interesting set.

*The Sound of Sonny* (Riverside/OJC-029), from June of the next year, has Rollins with a very good rhythm section of Sonny Clark, Percy Heath, and Roy Haynes, in a program consisting mostly of relatively short versions of standards like "The Last Time I Saw Paris," "Every Time We Say Goodbye," and "Toot, Toot, Tootsie." He plays very well throughout, but he doesn't get as much room to stretch out as he does in many other sets. This one includes an unaccompanied version of "It Could Happen to You." Nice, but not quite as satisfying as some others.

*Sonny Rollins and the Contemporary Leaders* (Contemporary/OJC-340), from October 1958, has Rollins in a swinging mood accompanied by the cream of Los Angeles's rhythm section men (Hampton Hawes, Leroy Vinnegar, and Shelley Manne, with Barney Kessel on guitar). This session has a buoyant, happy feel about it; Rollins picked unusual standards again, like "I've Told Every Little Star," "You," and "Rock-A-Bye Your Baby with a Dixie Melody" (a companion piece to *The Sound of Sonny*'s "Toot, Toot, Tootsie"). This isn't one of Rollins's most challenging albums, but it swings hard and is fun to listen to.

Rollins made a series of sessions for Blue Note during this period. *Volume 1* (Blue Note 81542), recorded a week after *Sonny Boy* in December 1956, is a quintet date with Donald Byrd on trumpet and a rhythm section of Wynton Kelly, Gene Ramey, and Max Roach. The repertoire, except for a beautiful "How Are Things in Glocca Morra?," consists of Rollins originals. The pick of the litter is the tenorist's extended improvisation on his up-tempo "Sonnysphere," based on "I Got Rhythm" with a "Honeysuckle Rose" bridge; he is all over the place here, reeling off extended bebop lines, short, percussive yelps, and swaggering rhythm-and-blues phrases. At the end, he and Roach trade four- and two-bar exchanges for some real excitement. A good, well-recorded set.

*Volume 2* (Blue Note 81558), recorded the next spring, is an unusual date on which Rollins is paired in the front line with trombonist J. J. Johnson. The rhythm section has Paul Chambers on bass, an explosive Art Blakey on drums, and either Horace Silver or Thelonious Monk on piano; on Monk's blues "Misterioso," *both* pianists play. There isn't as much Rollins here as there is on many other records, since he is dividing the solo duties with Johnson, but what there is is excellent, if somewhat tense-sounding. His solo on the up-tempo "You Stepped Out of a Dream" is top-notch, but the real prizes are the two tracks with Monk – the previously mentioned blues and Monk's ballad "Reflections," on which the two men have a classic musical conversation.

*Newk's Time* (Blue Note 84001) is a 1958 quartet date with Wynton Kelly, Doug Watkins, and Philly Joe Jones. This is especially worthwhile for the interaction between Rollins and Jones, although Rollins doesn't sound as inspired here, overall, as he can be. An unusual track is "Surrey with the Fringe on Top," which Rollins and Jones play as a duet for tenor and drums. "Namely You" and "Wonderful! Wonderful!" are both good and seldom-done standards. Not essential, but nice.

### TRIOS

Three of Rollins's records during this period were made with only bass and drum accompaniment: *Way Out West* (Contemporary/OJC-337), *Freedom Suite* (Riverside/OJC-067), and *A Night at the Village Vanguard, Volume 1* (Blue Note 46517) and *Volume 2* (Blue Note 46518). Rollins wanted the harmonic (and rhythmic) freedom that a pianoless group could afford, and he made the most of it, probably more than anyone ever has. The moods, approaches, repertoires, and meanings of the three albums are as different as can be; each is a masterpiece of a different sort.

*Way Out West*, recorded in Los Angeles in March 1957, features bassist Ray Brown and drummer Shelley Manne and is a happy-feeling blowing session with such unusual tunes as "Wagon Wheels" and "I'm an Old Cowhand." The date began at three in the morning; something – perhaps the late hour – encouraged an extremely uninhibited and imaginative side of all three men, a kind of relaxed, late-night jam session feel, an anything-goes vibe. Rollins takes "Cowhand" at a loping medium tempo and "Wagon Wheels" at a walking pace. The set also includes a gorgeous reading of Duke Ellington's "Solitude," the standard "There Is No Greater Love," and Rollins's originals "Come, Gone" (a fast cooker) and the medium-tempo "Way Out West." His inspiration runs high; this is a very undiluted presentation of his inventiveness, humor, and meditative fire.

*Freedom Suite*, a New York City studio date from February 1958 with the virtuosos Oscar Pettiford on bass and Max Roach on drums, is most notable for the nineteen-and-a-half-minute title piece, a shifting masterpiece of structured improvisation. The first section consists of a repeated eight-bar "chorus," in which a four-bar melodic fragment, consisting of two phrases in a call-and-response relationship, alternates with four bars of improvisation; during the solos, a four-bar pedal-tone section alternates with a simple four-bar chord progression. The second section is a passage in six-eight meter, faintly suggestive of a work song, again using call-and-response-type phrases. This leads directly into a walking-tempo ballad, which contains a fantastic Pettiford solo and ends with a brief reference to the first theme, then a reprise of the six-eight theme. The final section is very fast, again alternating four-bar theme sections with four-bar improvised sections before launching into a solo section that alternates four bars of pedal-tone, four bars of chord-changes blowing, and four bars of drums, all finally ending with the answering phrase from the first theme. This is an ingeniously structured piece that hangs together perfectly and is a model of what an organized framework for improvisation could be. The rest of the set finds the same trio playing good tunes like "Will You Still Be Mine?," "Till There Was You," and two waltzes, "Shadow Waltz" and Noel Coward's "Someday I'll Find You."

*A Night at the Village Vanguard, Volume 1* and *Volume 2*, recorded live at the New York City nightclub in November 1957 with bassist Wilbur Ware and drummer Elvin Jones, is a series of extremely adventurous extended patrols into the innards of such standards as "Get Happy," "What Is This Thing Called Love?," "Old Devil Moon," "I Can't Get Started," and "A Night in Tunisia." These two discs contain some of the wildest, wooliest, and freest Rollins improvising available; Rollins's surprising explorations into the familiar material are not for the faint of heart, but if you're willing to follow, this is an exciting trip. Wilbur Ware's sound is so big and his intonation so sure that you are never in doubt about the harmony, and Elvin Jones's drums form a brilliant, dense rhythmic counterpoint to Rollins's horn; the interaction among the three instruments here is some of the most exciting and challenging ever recorded.

*Sonny Rollins Brass/Sonny Rollins Trio* (Verve 815 056-2) has three 1958 tracks by a Rollins trio with Henry Grimes on bass and Charles Wright on drums; although these tunes highlight Rollins's tenor sound very well, they fall well below the level of inspiration of the previously mentioned sets. This set also has four tracks with a brass section arranged by Ernie Wilkins, which are nice but not earthshaking, and an unaccompanied Rollins solo on "Body and Soul," which never seems to lift off.

Two imported sets, recorded in early 1959 during a European tour, should be mentioned, although they may be difficult to find. *St. Thomas: Sonny Rollins Trio in Stockholm 1959* (Secret CD 479003) has Henry Grimes on bass and the excellent and little-known Pete La Roca on drums. The standout of this set is a version of "St. Thomas," recorded at a Swedish nightclub, on which Rollins really stretches out. The other tracks (including "Oleo," "There Is No Greater Love," and "I've Told Every Little Star"), recorded in a studio for broadcast on Swedish radio, feature Rollins in a relaxed, swinging mood for the most part. *Sonny Rollins, Aix en Provence 1959* (Royal Jazz RJ 502), recorded a week later at a French nightclub with Kenny Clarke on drums in place of La Roca, contains some truly abstract extended playing from Rollins; the three tracks here (Dizzy Gillespie's "Woody'n You," George Gershwin's "But Not for Me," and Tadd Dameron's "Lady Bird") are each over fifteen and a half minutes long and feature Rollins almost without a break. Rollins plays things that make you gasp in surprise at their daring. This set is for serious jazz fans only, but one no Rollins fan will want to miss. The sound is good, too.

### THE BRIDGE

*The Bridge* was Rollins's first recording after returning from the self-imposed period of absence that began in 1959. Available on *Sonny Rollins – The Quartets Featuring Jim Hall* (RCA/Bluebird 5643-2-RB), along with two other 1962 cuts, the album presents a different Rollins, just as brilliant in a different way. His sound is different, more speechlike, and he is more prone to go into the horn's extreme registers, both high and low. He also uses overblowing and other effects to distort his sound. In a year or two, many of his attempts in this direction would begin to sound forced (to my ears, at least), but in 1962 they were still well integrated into an expressive style.

This set consists of four standards, including "Without a Song" and "God Bless the Child," along with Rollins's adventurous, up-tempo originals "The Bridge" and "John S." The two extra tracks are a samba version of "If Ever I Would Leave You," and a lighter, bossa-nova-tinged "The Night Has a Thousand Eyes," both of which are lovely. The LP version of this set has several more tracks on it, including the famous calypso "Brownskin Girl." Throughout, Jim Hall's guitar is a sensitive counterpoint to the tenor, and Bob Cranshaw and Ben Riley contribute good background on bass and drums, respectively.

Another set, *All the Things You Are* (RCA/Bluebird 2179-2-RB), consists of material recorded in 1963 and 1964, including the famous, or infamous, date pairing Rollins with his hero Coleman Hawkins, one of the weirdest recordings in jazz history. Rollins sounds like he's straining for effect; only Hawkins and bassists Bob Cranshaw and Henry Grimes really deliver the goods consistently in this program of standards like "Yesterdays," "Just Friends," and "All the Things You Are." Six 1964 small-group sides with pianist Herbie Hancock are somewhat better; Rollins plays convincingly on " 'Round Midnight," "It Could Happen to You," and Charlie Parker's blues "Now's the Time," but still there is the sense that he is being intentionally, pointlessly, oblique, even perverse in spots. One of the weakest pre-1974 Rollins sets available.

Rollins's three mid-1960s albums for Impulse – *On Impulse!* (MCAD-5655

JVC-458), *Alfie* (MCAD-39107), and *East Broadway Run Down* (MCAD-33120) – are a real mixed bag, containing both great Rollins and monumental weirdness, often within the same eight bars. *On Impulse!* contains the wailing calypso "Hold 'Em Joe," along with a haunting, slow performance of "Everything Happens to Me" (at times Rollins changes and distorts his sound so much that he seems, literally, to be speaking through the horn) and adventuresome, up-tempo versions of "On Green Dolphin Street" and "Three Little Words," on which Rollins seems to be using asymmetrical melodic shapes more for their rhythmic and timbral effects than for the kind of cumulative storytelling purposes toward which he had spun melodies a few years earlier. It is definitely interesting, sometimes exhilarating, but overall I get the feeling that Rollins was, to paraphrase Picasso, seeking rather than finding.

The same can be said, in italics, for *East Broadway Run Down*, a 1966 set on which Rollins plays with bassist Jimmy Garrison and drummer Elvin Jones (both of whom had spent most of the decade with John Coltrane's groundbreaking group) and, on the title track, trumpeter Freddie Hubbard. On the twenty-minute title track, based on a simple repeated riff, Rollins plays a solo in which he takes the kind of timbral manipulation he was exploring on *On Impulse!* to an extreme, often sounding choked and distorted. The medium-tempo "Blessing in Disguise" is also based on a simple repeated riff, which Rollins takes off from, playing over the tonic and subdominant chords for the improvised segments, except for several out-of-tempo interludes. "We Kiss in a Shadow" is a very individual version of a lesser-known Rodgers and Hammerstein tune, alternating between a Latin feel and a walking tempo. A strange album, the height of Rollins's abstract expressionist phase (in the studios at least).

*Alfie* is a favorite of many Rollins fans; it is in some ways the most conventional of the Impulse sets. It contains Rollins's music for the film of the same name, orchestrated for large ensemble by Oliver Nelson, mostly in a straightahead groove. Rollins plays some inspired stuff here; "Alfie's Theme" is a bluesy Rollins line that he still plays today, and Rollins takes an extended, exploratory solo. But the lesser-known items here are worth checking out, too.

### LATER AND EARLIER ROLLINS

Rollins's 1972 *Next Album* (Milestone/OJC-312) is, in my opinion, the last really strong album Rollins recorded, and even it has more weak tracks than strong ones. But the two strong ones are more than worth the price of the set. "The Everywhere Calypso" is one of his best calypso performances; he builds up steam by using the underlying two-beat as accenting in his eighth-note lines, varying the pattern little by little and keeping the tension taut, like a master game fisherman playing a sailfish. And "Skylark" is one of Rollins's great ballads; he uses Hoagy Carmichael's gorgeous melody as a jumping-off point for two fullbodied meditations and ends with an extended unaccompanied cadenza which gives a picture of what Rollins might do in a club on a hot night, suspending the rhythm and using the tune's melodic motifs as a basis for a totally improvised theme-and-variations. Throughout, Rollins's phenomenally quick, allusive mind pulls rabbits out of hats as melodic fragments remind him of other melodies, which he quotes or paraphrases on a moment's notice; knowledgeable listeners will be tickled and awed by Rollins's references to other tunes and other solos remembered from records. This is one of Rollins's classic recordings.

Two Rollins sets recorded nearly twenty years earlier, before his watershed return in 1955 from seclusion in Chicago, contain solid bebop tenor. *Sonny Rollins with the Modern Jazz Quartet* (Prestige/OJC-011) features Rollins in 1953 with the first incarnation of the MJQ (Milt Jackson, John Lewis, Percy Heath, and Kenny Clarke) for three fine swingers and an excellent slow "In a Sentimental Mood." All of Rollins's ingredients are here – the wit, the allusiveness, the big tone, the imagination – but he hasn't quite coalesced into the grand and distinctive stylist he would become. Some 1951 quartet tracks with Kenny Drew, Percy Heath, and Art Blakey (recorded when Rollins was barely twenty-two) are somewhat less developed, but they're good nonetheless. For a hint of his later mastery of time, listen to the floating way he phrases the melody of "With a Song in My Heart."

*Moving Out* (Prestige/OJC-058) contains four August 1954 cuts – the fast title cut and "Swingin' for Bumsy," the ballad "Silk N' Satin," and the blues "Solid" – with trumpeter Kenny Dorham and a rhythm section of Elmo Hope, Percy Heath, and Art Blakey. These are fine, but not on the highest level for Rollins. A fifth track, "More Than You Know," was recorded two months later with bassist Tommy Potter, drummer Art Taylor, and Thelonious Monk on piano; Monk's presence must have inspired Rollins, for he turns in an especially reflective performance, an early masterpiece.

Two other tunes from this session (exultant, up-tempo rides on "The Way You Look Tonight" and "I Want To Be Happy") can be found on an album under Monk's name, *Thelonious Monk and Sonny Rollins* (Prestige/OJC-059); both contain exciting, inventive bebop tenor. Another track, "Friday the Thirteenth," is from the November 1953 session that also produced "Let's Call This" and "Think of One," available on *Monk* (Prestige/OJC-016). This session paired Rollins with French horn player Julius Watkins. But for Rollins's best work with Monk you need *Brilliant Corners* (Riverside/OJC-026), a classic Monk session from October 1956 that contains great Rollins on the medium-tempo blues "Ba-Lue Bolivar Ba-Lues-Are," the tricky, whipsawing title track, and especially the Monk ballad "Pannonica," on which Rollins's passion and intellect both run high.

Rollins was a favorite recording companion of Miles Davis's throughout the 1950s. Their first date together, recorded in 1951 and available on *Miles Davis and Horns* (Prestige/OJC-053), is notable especially for a haunting, Lester Young–like Rollins solo on the ultra-slow "Blue Room (Take 1)" and the swinging "I Know," based on Charlie Parker's "Confirmation"; this track, the first one ever released under Rollins's name, has Davis playing piano. Later that same year they were together for a session that also included the nineteen-year-old Jackie McLean; five of the tunes are on *Miles Davis Featuring Sonny Rollins: Dig* (Prestige/OJC-005). Rollins takes one of his best early solos on "Out of the Blue" (check out his bold entering phrase; attention-grabbing opening statements were a Rollins trademark) and also plays well on "Bluing," a blues tune, the "Sweet Georgia Brown"–based "Dig," and the bouncing "It's Only a Paper Moon." *Collectors' Items* (Prestige/OJC-071) is an essential set, containing the results of two Davis/Rollins dates, one from 1953 and one from 1956. The 1953 date was the only time Rollins ever recorded with Charlie Parker, who joins him on tenor sax instead of his customary alto; this date is discussed in some detail in both the Miles Davis and the Ensembles sections. The 1956 session is a fine quintet date with Tommy Flanagan on piano, which produced three truly great tracks: the fast blues "No Line," the slow "Vierd Blues," and the ballad "In Your Own Sweet Way." Rollins takes fantastic solos on all of them (listen to his entering phrase on "In Your Own Sweet Way"); 1956 was a vintage year for him. Lastly, the June 1954 quintet sides with Horace Silver on piano, collected on Davis's *Bags Groove* (Prestige/OJC-245), including the classic Rollins compositions "Airegin," "Oleo," and "Doxy," as well as two takes of an up-tempo "But Not for Me," contain searching, extremely cogent Rollins solos.

Finally, some of the best Rollins of the 1950s can be found on two Dizzy Gillespie albums recorded in December 1957: *Duets* (Verve 835 253-2) and, especially, *Sonny Side Up* (Verve 825 674-2). Both albums also feature tenorist Sonny Stitt; the former has the two tenors on separate tracks, and the latter throws them together for one of the most exciting sessions in jazz history. *Duets*'s main selling point is the up-tempo blues "Wheatleigh Hall," on which Rollins and Gillespie both blow the walls down. But *Sonny Side Up* is the genuine item; Rollins and Stitt face off on a breakneck "I Know That You Know" (on which Rollins plays a hair-raising stop-time passage, a masterpiece of breath control, imagination, and soul), the slow blues "After Hours," a jolly, medium-tempo "On the Sunny Side of the Street" (on which Rollins takes the second solo and Stitt the first; the liner notes have the order backward), and, above all, the ferocious, up-tempo "The Eternal Triangle," on which Rollins and Stitt each take extended solos, then come back for chorus after chorus of exchanges that are the stuff of myth. Rollins pulls out all the stops; his big-toned style and percussive lines are perfectly complemented by Stitt's even, sinuous straight bop lines, each one's brilliance drawing out even greater brilliance from the other. This is one of the greatest cutting contests ever captured by recording equipment. Rollins probably ends up on top, but not by a whole lot. Please don't miss this.

## JOHN COLTRANE

John Coltrane was certainly one of the most influential tenor saxophonists in jazz, an intense, searching player with an instantly identifiable sound. But beyond that, he was a dedicated artist who practiced incessantly and never stopped growing; he became influential not just as an instrumentalist but as a bandleader in the early 1960s, leading a quartet with McCoy Tyner, Jimmy Garrison, and Elvin Jones.

Coltrane began his musical life in the late 1940s steeped in the bebop idiom, as well as in all the other music that had come before (Sidney Bechet was his inspiration in picking up the soprano saxophone); by the early 1960s he was one of the elder statesmen of the avant-garde, or free jazz, movement of the time. Coltrane was, from all reports and from the aural evidence, a hard-working craftsman whose dedication to the craft was a channel for enormous vital energy. Everything Coltrane played, until the final phase of his career, was extremely ordered and even mathematical in its formal preoccupation.

He was fascinated with the technical sound-producing qualities of the tenor itself and expanded the conception of what could be done on the horn, even playing more than one note at a time (as he does on "Harmonique," on the album *Coltrane Jazz* [Atlantic 1354-2]). More important, he was obsessed with the mathematical aspects of linear harmony and seemed to have set himself the task, for a while at least, of playing every permutation of every possible scale on every chord change in the popular songs and jazz standards he performed. This produced a sort of musical blur comprised of carefully articulated melodic elements played at high speed, a technique critic Ira Gitler dubbed "sheets of sound." It was as if Coltrane were trying to get to a place beyond harmony by running harmony out to its limit, pointing toward a drone effect by using chord changes to their logical extreme, just as many different colors projected on a blank wall will combine to produce white.

The particular musical dilemma he found himself in as the 1950s drew to a close had wide implications for jazz as a whole. Coltrane's musical development is discussed in some detail in the Ensembles section; this section will focus on mapping out the best recordings he made as a leader and sideman.

<h3 style="text-align:center">EARLY TRANE</h3>

Coltrane began more or less as a Dexter Gordon imitator, and throughout his career (at least until its final phase) Gordon's influence was audible both in Coltrane's sound and in his legato, chord-changes-oriented approach to improvising. His first recorded solo, on "We Love to Boogie," a 1951 Dizzy Gillespie record, may be heard on *Dizzy Gillespie: Dee Gee Days* (Savoy ZDS 4426). The Gordon influence is obvious, although Trane's characteristic wail is there already, along with one or two typical harmonic turns of mind in his second chorus.

Our real interest in Coltrane begins when he joined the Miles Davis quintet in late 1955. Although he had played with Gillespie and with Johnny Hodges's band, he was hardly well known. The records he made with the quintet put him on the map; his volubility and fire were the perfect contrast to Davis's lyricism and spare playing, and the sound of the band, with Red Garland's popping piano, Paul Chambers's full, brilliant bass, and the galvanic drumming of Philly Joe Jones, is irresistible and not dated in the least.

The albums they made for Prestige – *The New Miles Davis Quintet* (Prestige/OJC-006), *Cookin'* (Prestige/OJC-128), *Relaxin'* (Prestige/OJC-190), *Workin'* (Prestige/OJC-296), and *Steamin'* (Prestige/OJC-391) – are discussed in the Miles Davis section, as is their first Columbia set, *'Round about Midnight* (CK 40610). They are excellent, full of great solos by all. In them we can hear Coltrane working out his sound and his approach to playing on changes. He stayed with Davis until early 1957 when he left to free-lance, working during the summer and fall with the Thelonious Monk quartet.

Until recently, the only surviving recordings of that Monk quartet, which played a legendary engagement at New York's Five Spot, were some studio titles included on *Thelonious Monk with John Coltrane* (Jazzland/OJC-039). Coltrane plays fabulous things on Monk's "Nutty," the intricate "Trinkle, Tinkle," and the lyrical, gorgeous masterpiece "Ruby, My Dear." Essential Monk, essential Coltrane. This set also includes alternate takes of two tunes from the session that produced *Monk's Music* (Riverside/OJC-084), a large-band date that paired Coltrane with tenor patriarch Coleman Hawkins. In 1993, though, Blue Note released some recordings that Coltrane's wife made of the Monk quartet at the Five Spot in the summer of 1957, with Ahmed-Abdul Malik on bass and Roy Haynes on drums in place of Wilbur Ware and Shadow Wilson, respectively. *The Thelonious Monk Quartet Featuring John Coltrane –*

*Live at the Five Spot: Discovery!* (Blue Note CDP 0777 7 99786 2 5) has fairly bad sound, but the music contained therein is tremendous, with Coltrane really roaring through five Monk standards (including another version of "Trinkle, Tinkle"). Coltrane rejoined Davis in 1958.

In 1957 Coltrane commenced a career as an amazingly prolific recording artist, along with his duties in the Davis and Monk bands. In 1957 and 1958 alone he made countless recordings both as a leader and a sideman for seemingly every label in existence. His playing from this period, during which he was evolving the sheets of sound technique, is brilliant, but Coltrane is depending more on the harmonic outline of the tunes than on their melodic nature for the shape of his improvisations – as opposed, say, to Sonny Rollins's playing, which took the tunes' melodic, rhythmic, and lyrical aspects into account during the improvisation.

Rollins's records of the time have radically different qualities; many of Coltrane's have a sort of sameness, which is partly due to the continuity in sidemen, often consisting of the Miles Davis rhythm team of Red Garland and Paul Chambers, with Art Taylor on drums. These records, most of which were made for Prestige, contain extraordinary music, but I will concentrate on what I consider to be the strongest and most representative and will only briefly outline what's on most of the rest.

One of the best recordings of this period, perhaps the very best, is *Blue Train* (Blue Note 46095), recorded in September 1957 with a fine band including Lee Morgan on trumpet, Curtis Fuller on trombone, and a rhythm section of Kenny Drew, Paul Chambers, and Philly Joe Jones. The session was obviously carefully worked out and consists of four Coltrane originals nicely arranged for the sextet and one standard ballad ("I'm Old Fashioned"). All the ingredients combined to form a session that loses none of its freshness with repeated playing.

The justly famous title track is a medium-tempo blues that evokes the classic blues subject of the train. The hauntingly voiced call-and-response theme gives way to one of Coltrane's greatest solos, in which he is abetted by an alert rhythm section that keeps the terrain interesting and, at one point, by a lonesome midnight train whistle background from Morgan and Fuller. Trane mixes up straight eighth notes with faster passages of sixteenth notes, which then give way to eighth notes again. The structures of phrases that he plays are the same, but in the passages where he plays faster, more information needs to be absorbed more quickly, sometimes so quickly that it nearly becomes a blur. The effect is similar to being on a train, watching buildings in the distance, then going through a small town at the same speed but where the buildings are much closer. Listen to the way, when the other horns first come in for their background riff, Trane (and Philly Joe, who has been playing a little double-time figure) downshifts, in effect, back into a brief passage of shorter phrases with more held notes, as if he has come out into open country again.

The rest of the album is great also. "Moment's Notice" was, at the time, the same kind of gauntlet to musicians that "Giant Steps" was to be a couple of years later – a rapidly shifting harmonic obstacle course in which the chords changed twice per measure for most of the tune, posing a real challenge to the musicians' presence of mind and harmonic knowledge, as if they were forced to play the bridge of "Cherokee" for an entire chorus. Still, the nature of the chord movement in "Moment's Notice" was relatively conventional, whereas that in "Giant Steps" was very unusual for the time. "Moment's Notice" also incorporates breaks for each soloist at the beginning of choruses. Everyone plays beautifully on this, especially Coltrane, who takes the hurdles effortlessly, and Morgan, who leaps and runs, setting off firecrackers and sparklers along the way. "Lazy Bird" and "Locomotion" are both up-tempo Coltrane originals of unusual structure. Although the album notes call the latter a blues, it isn't, exactly; it is, rather, a forty-four-bar chorus made up of two twelve-bar blues "choruses," an eight-bar bridge, and another twelve bars in the blues form. And "I'm Old Fashioned" is a warm, reflective Coltrane ballad. All in all, a landmark album, essential to any jazz collection.

Probably the best balanced of all the quartet albums Coltrane recorded with the rhythm section of Red Garland, Paul Chambers, and Art Taylor is *Soultrane* (Prestige/OJC-021), from February 1958. Here Trane is at the beginning of his sheets of sound period; on the opener, a walking-tempo version of Tadd Dameron's "Good Bait," Trane is a whirlwind of mighty, searching, double- and triple-timed passages, involving a fabulous command of scales and breath control. "I Want to Talk about You" was a ballad associated with Billy Eckstine; Coltrane's version here shows off his beautiful tone and his soul. He returned to this tune over and over throughout his career. The other ballad, "Theme for Ernie," is dedicated to altoist Ernie Henry. "You Say You Care" is a dazzling, surging, medium-up-tempo performance on which Coltrane struts his stuff in grand style, moving back and forth between straight bebop tenor and the sheets of sound approach. "Russian Lullaby" is a punishingly fast ride on Irving Berlin's melody; Coltrane here defies gravity and the laws of physics. This album is programmed very intelligently, like a good set in a nightclub, the faster tunes spelled by the more relaxed items. If you like Coltrane, you will love this one.

*Coltrane* (Prestige/OJC-020; not to be confused with the Impulse album of the same name) is an excellent, varied set including several tracks on which Coltrane is joined by trumpeter Johnny Splawn and baritonist Sahib Shihab, the standout of which is probably a churning version of trumpeter Cal Massey's "Bakai." "Time Was" is a medium-up swinger, on which Trane peels off chorus after chorus of solid bebop tenor. He was especially good at this kind of thing, as he also showed on "I Hear a Rhapsody," recorded at the same session and included on *Lush Life* (Prestige/OJC-131), and "My Shining Hour" on *Coltrane Jazz* (Atlantic 1354-2). Another standout here is "While My Lady Sleeps," with its mysterioso, late-night groove.

The rest of the Prestige titles are, for the most part, more workaday affairs, often with a somewhat thrown-together feeling about them. Still, they all contain good playing. The following titles feature Trane backed by the Garland-Chambers-Taylor rhythm section. *Black Pearls* (Prestige/OJC-352), from May 1958, which also features trumpeter Donald Byrd, is probably most notable for "Sweet Sapphire Blues," an example of the sheets of sound technique taken to its extreme, a blur of scalar passages played with utmost facility. Listen to the rhythm section play away in time-honored rock-the-joint fashion, while Coltrane speeds past our ears like a train speeding past a building too near to focus on. *Settin' the Pace* (Prestige/OJC-078), from March 1958, contains a good ballad, "I See Your Face Before Me," and a racehorse run on "Rise and Shine," but Coltrane plays his best on Jackie McLean's "Little Melonae," on which the soloists play mainly on one scale rather than a set of chord changes. Trane builds a powerful solo here out of motifs which he turns, turns again, double times, plays in different registers and different places in the scale, before transmuting them or countering them with different motifs. *Traneing In* (Prestige/OJC-189), recorded in August 1957, has very strong Trane on the title track, a rocking, medium-tempo blues on which the tenorist plays a solo that grows in complexity as it proceeds. "You Leave Me Breathless" is a fine ballad on which Coltrane shows great control of the horn's upper reaches, and "Soft Lights and Sweet Music" is another ultra-fast set of standard changes, through which Coltrane makes his way seemingly effortlessly. *Bahia* (Prestige/OJC-415), from December 1958, has two great tracks: the title tune, on which Coltrane plays some very strong stuff over a mambo vamp that occasionally, teasingly, slides into swing, and "Goldsboro Express," a tenor-bass-drums outing that consists almost entirely of rapid-fire exchanges between Coltrane and Art Taylor, prefiguring Trane's later high-energy duets with Elvin Jones.

Three albums recorded late in 1957 and early in 1958 under Red Garland's name feature Coltrane and Donald Byrd, with George Joyner (later known as Jamil Nasser) replacing Paul Chambers on bass. *All Mornin' Long* (Prestige/OJC-293) is probably the best, with its long, walking-tempo blues title track (once recorded by Sir Charles Thompson, with Charlie Parker guesting, as "20th Century Blues"), a relaxed "They Can't Take That Away from Me," and a very hot version of Tadd Dameron's "Our Delight" (listen to how Joyner, at the end of the first eight bars of Coltrane's solo, juggles the time slightly by sliding a few notes downward on the bass). Everyone gets a chance to stretch out throughout. *High Pressure* (Prestige/OJC-349) features a rolling, up-tempo, fourteen-minute version of the blues "Soft Winds," on which Garland, especially, shines, and a swinging "Two Bass Hit," on which Trane scores. *Dig It!* (Prestige/OJC-392) is the most ordinary of the three; a long (sixteen-minute), slow blues called "Lazy Mae" dominates the set, which also features Trane wrapped in his sheets of sound for Charlie Parker's "Billie's Bounce," a short trio version of "Crazy Rhythm" sans Coltrane, and a fast run-through of Jimmy Heath's "C.T.A."

Lastly, *Lush Life* (Prestige/OJC-131) and *The Last Trane* (Prestige/OJC-394) are sets that combine material from several sessions. *Lush Life* is the more satisfying of the two, with its three trio tracks with bassist Earl May and drummer Art Taylor (including the excellent, self-descriptive "Trane's Slo Blues"), a gorgeous version of Billy Strayhorn's ballad "Lush Life," and the medium-up cooker "I Hear a Rhapsody." *The Last Trane* has not one but two long, slow blues, back-to-back, as well as a ballad ("Come Rain or Come Shine") and a blistering, up-tempo reading of "Lover." It's all fine, individually, but taken together it makes for an unbalanced set. Two 1958 Savoy sets issued under the joint leadership of Coltrane and trumpeter Wilbur Harden, *Countdown* (ZD 70529) and *Africa* (ZD 70818), contain plenty of good Coltrane (along with pianist Tommy Flanagan), but he has to split the solo duties with Harden, under whose leadership the sessions were originally recorded. They are nice but hardly the first Trane to jump on.

Two albums featuring Coltrane as a sideman are also worth mentioning. Pianist Sonny Clark's October 1957 *Sonny's Crib* (Blue Note 46819) has some fine Trane in the company of Donald Byrd, trombonist Curtis Fuller, and the rhythm team of Paul Chambers and Art Taylor playing three standards and a couple of good Clark originals. And *Chambers' Music* (Blue Note 84437) contains some interesting earlier glimpses of Coltrane, from 1955 and 1956, in quartet and sextet sessions led by bassist Paul Chambers.

### KIND OF BLUE

By January 1958 Coltrane was again a member of Miles Davis's band, now expanded to a sextet including altoist Julian "Cannonball" Adderley. Coltrane would remain with the band until mid-1960, when he would go on his own with epochal results. But the things he learned and worked out while with Davis during this second stint were to be of the utmost importance to him.

The first recording the new sextet made was the landmark *Milestones*

(Columbia CK 40837); it was also the last recording Davis would make with the Garland-Chambers-Jones rhythm section that had been in place since 1955. They definitely ended on a high note. It is discussed in the Miles Davis section of this book, along with the other Davis albums with Coltrane. Trane takes great solos throughout, but two things should be underlined here – his staggering, high-velocity exchanges with Adderley on Jackie McLean's "Dr. Jackle" (called "Dr. Jekyll" here) and his beautiful solo on the unforgettable "Miles," a first taste of the modal approach that would be explored fully a year later on *Kind of Blue* (Columbia CK 40579). In the summer of 1958 the sextet, with Bill Evans replacing Red Garland and Jimmy Cobb replacing Philly Joe Jones, appeared at the Newport Jazz Festival. Five tracks recorded at that appearance are available on *Miles and Coltrane* (Columbia CK 44052), along with two 1955 quintet tracks. The Newport items show the band in a hard-charging mood, a satisfying glimpse of them in actual performance.

But 1959 was the watershed year for Coltrane, a year in which he both explored the running-the-changes approach about as far as it could be explored and began to investigate a way out of that approach that would have a huge impact on the way young jazz players would sound for years to come. Before discussing these twin aspects of Coltrane's development, I should mention two albums he recorded as coleader at the beginning of that year, *Cannonball and Coltrane* (with Cannonball Adderley; EmArcy 834 588) and *Bags & Trane* (with Milt Jackson; Atlantic 1368-2). The album with altoist Adderley, by the Miles Davis band without Davis, is discussed in the Adderley section of the *Guide*; it is full of good Coltrane in his *Milestones* bag. *Bags & Trane* is highly recommended; it includes some very swinging Coltrane (in the company of vibes player Jackson, one of the most swinging musicians in jazz, as well as a rhythm section of Hank Jones, Paul Chambers, and Connie Kay) on tasty versions of "Three Little Words," the medium-tempo "The Late, Late Blues," a very fast version of Dizzy Gillespie's "Bebop," and several other fine tracks.

But Miles Davis's *Kind of Blue* (Columbia CK 40579) and Coltrane's own *Giant Steps* (Atlantic 1311-2), recorded within a month of each other in the spring of 1959, are the seminal albums of this period, pointing to the exhaustion of one approach and the opening of another. The Ensembles section looks at this phase of Coltrane's career in some detail and discusses the significance of both sides of Trane's searching at this time.

*Giant Steps*'s title tune is an extension of the approach Coltrane took on *Blue Train*'s "Moment's Notice": a rapid-fire steeplechase of changing harmonic terrain, only with much more unusual chord movement than in the earlier performance. Coltrane here is a volcano of ideas and swing; it is a startling, up-tempo workout that gives full exercise to Coltrane's peerless harmonic knowledge. His sound had never been as open and forceful as it is on this album, which consists entirely of his own compositions. Aside from the title tune (and "Countdown," which involves a similar, complex harmonic plan), the set includes several tunes with harmonic and rhythmic devices that point up Coltrane's harmonic development. The ballad "Naima" uses suspended chords and pedal tones; both devices make the harmonic destination ambiguous, allowing the soloist to take a number of different routes rather than the single tortuous one prescribed in such obstacle courses as "Giant Steps." "Spiral" also uses a pedal-tone device over a vamp, which alternates with swing rhythm. Another highlight of this landmark set is the minor blues "Mr. P.C.," on which Coltrane tears off sixteen thrilling choruses of furiously swinging tenor over a surging background laid down by Tommy Flanagan, Paul Chambers, and Art Taylor. He returns at the end for some really exciting exchanges with Taylor.

In the two months before most of *Giant Steps* was recorded, Coltrane was in the Columbia studios with the Davis band recording the historic *Kind of Blue*, which popularized the modal approach to improvising that certain musicians were beginning to explore, in which one would play only over one or two scales for long stretches of a tune rather than negotiating a harmonic obstacle course. The sound the Davis band got here, on "So What," "Freddie Freeloader," "Blue in Green," "All Blues," and "Flamenco Sketches," is like a blast of crisp air, and the techniques involved pointed a way for Coltrane out of his, by this time, obsessive mining of the ore in every possible twist and turn of the classic bebop approach. His solos on all the tunes on this album find him playing with an unprecedented lyricism and sensitivity.

Throughout his career, however (until, perhaps, the very end), Coltrane was never locked into one approach; his modal experiments went hand-in-hand with new ways of exploring chord changes, and his most searching playing almost always left room for lighter-hearted work in a more lyrical or swinging vein. *Coltrane Jazz* (Atlantic 1354-2), recorded at the end of 1959, is a very listenable combination of approaches and an excellent introduction to Coltrane's playing. It includes the straight-ahead swingers "My Shining Hour" and "Little Old Lady," as well as "Fifth House," which, like *Giant Steps*'s "Spiral," moves between a pedal-point vamp and swing, and the unique "Harmonique," a blues waltz, the melody of which finds Coltrane using the saxophone's natural harmonics to produce more than one note at a time (he uses the same technique at the end of "Fifth House"). The accompanying group is, for the most part, a quartet consisting of Wynton Kelly, Paul Chambers, and Jimmy Cobb, the rhythm section from the Miles Davis band, of which Coltrane was still a member.

*Coltrane Plays the Blues* (Atlantic 1382-2), recorded late in 1960, is an important album in many respects, not the least of which is that Coltrane by this time had his classic quartet of the early 1960s almost entirely in place. He had left Miles Davis's band and now used McCoy Tyner on piano and Elvin Jones on drums, both of whom would remain with him for the next few years; bassist Steve Davis would be replaced before too long by Jimmy Garrison. This set, consisting of a number of different approaches to blues-based material, finds Coltrane further exploring his use of what sound like Moorish, West African, and Indian scalar patterns, as well as other ways of overlaying different scales on the basic tonality of the piece, as in the fast, pianoless "Blues to You," on which he switches keys like an express train switching tracks at a moment's notice, going farther and farther from the tonal center but building on what has come before and never becoming indecipherable. He is exploring the horn's technical side, too, inserting false or alternate fingerings into his long lines, playing the same note twice with slightly different sounds.

His rhythmic sense is becoming more defined as well; he breaks up his lines into different groupings of notes. Whereas most bop-rooted players tended to play phrases that were fairly closely tied to the multiple-of-four pattern suggested by the four-four beat characteristic of the music, Coltrane had started breaking up his lines into three- and five-note groupings as often as the more standard patterns. This gave his melodies polyrhythmic implications that fit in perfectly with Elvin Jones's way of accenting. Often, a kind of six-eight beat was implied against the four-four, a technique that Coltrane would develop more and more. Coltrane also plays soprano saxophone on several titles.

Listen to the subtle distinctions, too, that are made in tempo here. The first two slow blues, "Blues to Elvin" and "Blues to Bechet," are very close in tempo, but the second is ever-so-slightly faster, contributing to its different mood (as does Coltrane's choice of different saxophones, of course). This kind of attention to detail was to set Coltrane apart over the next few years. Harmonically, the band explores the suspensions, pedal tones, and incantatory vamp forms that Coltrane had been increasingly attracted to (especially on the hypnotic "Mr. Knight," another tune, like "Fifth House" and "Spiral," in which vamps and swing trade off with each other). This tendency was encouraged by the presence of McCoy Tyner, whose ideas ran along the same lines and whose chord voicings were often suspended, open chords that were harmonically ambiguous. His touch reminds me of Wynton Kelly's, the notes popping out, but his work was leading to a different place. All in all, this is an important set that showed clearly where Coltrane was heading. Incredibly, the same week in October 1960 in which Coltrane recorded *Coltrane Plays the*

*Blues*, he recorded two other classic sets, *My Favorite Things* (Atlantic 1361-2), one of his most popular albums, and *Coltrane's Sound* (Atlantic 1419-2).

*My Favorite Things* consists of extended treatments of four popular tunes: Rodgers and Hammerstein's "My Favorite Things," Cole Porter's "Everytime We Say Goodbye," and George Gershwin's "Summertime" and "But Not for Me." All of them are radically transformed by Coltrane's emerging harmonic, rhythmic, and group-organization concept, in a fresh version of the kind of appropriation that jazz always has worked at its best. In this set we can see, with even more focus than in *Coltrane Plays the Blues*, how Coltrane's sensibility was developing in the direction of an incantatory approach. The title tune gives perhaps the best evidence; Coltrane's higher-pitched soprano plays the melody over a swirling six-eight background, with a two-chord harmonic base from Tyner and Davis. The two-chord base has the effect of a breath in and a breath out; consequently, the tune has a much more static feeling than the standard bebop chord-progression, four-four rhythm performance. Instead of a series of lines leading forward in time, the effect of this track is of waves rippling outward from a central source. Coltrane's increasing interest in Eastern religion and African culture seems to have echoed and reinforced a view of things that was based not on progress and forward, or linear, horizontal movement but on stasis and upward, or vertical, movement. Coltrane's emerging spiritual orientation is implicit in the musical choices he was making at the time.

"Everytime We Say Goodbye" and "Summertime" reflect the same techniques and preoccupations in their own way; in the former, the harmony is such that bassist Steve Davis can use the same pedal note for much of the tune, as Tyner, especially, lays various shifting suspended chords on top of it. The effect builds a tension that is then released as the group moves away from that tonal center. "Summertime" is taken on tenor at a swinging, medium-up tempo, which alternates with another pedal-tone vamp; Trane's solo here is in his wailing, sheets of sound bag. Finally, Gershwin's "But Not for Me" is treated to a complete reharmonization and played in swing tempo. One of the essential jazz sets.

*Coltrane's Sound* is a somewhat less cohesive album, a more conventional set than the other two, yet it may be my personal favorite of the three. It has perhaps the strongest, most aggressively rhythmic Coltrane blowing of the three, as well as a couple of classic ballads. The opener, a powerhouse version of "The Night Has a Thousand Eyes," follows the by now familiar pedal-tone-vamp-and-suspended-chords-alternating-with-swing format, but Coltrane really roars here, as he does on "Liberia," with its out-of-tempo intro that evolves into a churning, rhythmic foray with Coltrane sweeping away everything in his path. On this one, check out the break he takes leading into his solo, a startling dive off the high board using several of the alternative-fingering tricks mentioned earlier. This set also includes the beautiful, unique Coltrane ballad composition "Central Park West" and his reworking of the standard "Body and Soul," which uses a piano vamp and substitute harmonies that have gone on to become standard equipment on the tune.

### A LOVE SUPREME

Beginning in the spring of 1961, Coltrane recorded for the new Impulse label, which was to become home for many of the farthest-out players of the 1960s avant-garde, including Archie Shepp, Marion Brown, and Albert Ayler. He was encouraged to take as many chances as he wanted, which he did, producing some of the most passionately driven and adventuresome music of the time. Much of Coltrane's music from this period provoked genuinely perplexed, even angry, responses from listeners. We can see why: his music was moving away from the straight-ahead, bebop-rooted music most listeners were accustomed to, with its harmonic and rhythmic structures that spoke of movement through time and eventual resolution, into forms that spoke of incantation, stasis, even trance, a true change in worldview, expressed through harmony and rhythm. His music was moving away from a style that said it was important to move ahead, to get somewhere, toward a style that said one should sit where one was and breathe. Yet he also produced several albums that include the most lyrical statements he ever made on standard popular tunes.

Before looking at the Impulse sets, two other albums must be mentioned. One is Coltrane's final session with Miles Davis's group, *Someday My Prince Will Come* (Columbia CK 40947), which contains two brilliant Coltrane solos – a stunningly melodic one on the title tune and a probing, intense one on the Spanish-flavored "Teo." *Olé* (Atlantic 1373-2) is Coltrane's last date for Atlantic; here he uses Eric Dolphy on flute and alto and Freddie Hubbard on trumpet, as well as Tyner, Elvin Jones, and both Art Davis and Reggie Workman on bass. This is a sort of bridge album, sounding more like his later Impulse sets; the title tune is eighteen minutes long (it took up a full side on the original LP) and is another two-chord, vamp-oriented piece, like "My Favorite Things." This one has an ominous, flamenco-like feeling about it. There's not quite as much Trane here as in many other sets because of the other horns; all in all, it's one of his lesser efforts.

Coltrane's first session for Impulse, available as *Africa/Brass, Volume 1 & 2* (MCA/Impulse MCAD-42001), is best known for the three tunes on the original *Africa/Brass*, "Africa," "Greensleeves," and "Blues Minor." "Africa" features

Coltrane wailing on tenor over an African-flavored vamp, occasionally accompanied by a large ensemble including Booker Little's trumpet and four French horns. This sixteen-and-a-half-minute performance took up an entire album side originally and maintains what Coltrane termed a "drone" effect in the background, over which the tenorist sends out a strong message. "Greensleeves" is another drone- and vamp-based performance; Coltrane takes the beautiful folk melody for a long ride on soprano. And "Blues Minor" is a full-blown, up-tempo, minor-key blues, on which the rhythm section generates a fantastic drive.

*Coltrane "Live" at the Village Vanguard* (MCA/Impulse MCAD-39136) was recorded in performance at the New York City nightclub in November 1961, and it offers three revealing looks at the live Coltrane of the time. "Spiritual" opens the album with a prayerful, out-of-tempo introduction, which leads into a sort of polyrhythmic waltz over a vamp/drone background from Tyner, Jones, and bassist Reggie Workman. Eric Dolphy joins the band for this track on bass clarinet. McCoy Tyner's solo here, and elsewhere in this set, shows just how much he had been absorbing Coltrane's manner of phrasing. After Tyner's solo, Trane comes back on soprano. This nearly fourteen-minute track shows how different this music must have sounded to an audience weaned on bebop.

"Softly as in a Morning Sunrise" is more conventional, couched in a traditional medium-up-tempo four-four groove, with Jones playing brushes behind Tyner's opening solo; he switches to sticks when Coltrane comes steaming in on soprano. But "Chasin' the Trane" is the prize of the set, an up-tempo blues, completely improvised, which Coltrane plays on tenor, a long patrol into a dense musical jungle, with Coltrane playing with five- and four-note motifs and other note groupings, twisting them back and forth in short bursts in a rhythmic counterpoint with Jones's fabulous drumming. (According to Stanley Crouch, Reggie Workman says that it is Jimmy Garrison keeping the strong bass pulse here, not Workman as the notes say. Tyner sits this one out.) You can hear some of Ornette Coleman's melodic influence in places, but nobody had ever played like this before; as Coltrane gets into the solo, he produces all kinds of unusual timbres from the horn, yodeling, squawking, constantly swinging. As the track progresses, he moves farther and farther out harmonically, rhythmically, and timbrally, with Jones on him all the way. This thrilling track has Coltrane blowing constantly for just over sixteen minutes and gives a sense of how compelling he must have been to see live.

*Impressions* (MCA/Impulse MCAD-5887) has two tunes recorded a few days later at the same November 1961 Vanguard gig: "India," another vamp/drone-based piece, again featuring Dolphy, and the up-tempo, modal "Impressions" (structured like Miles Davis's "So What" on *Kind of Blue* [Columbia CK 40579], which qualifies as the first tune recorded by the classic quartet, with Tyner, Jones, and bassist Jimmy Garrison. This is another of those extended tenor forays, like "Chasin' the Trane," on which Coltrane and Elvin Jones really go at it. The album is rounded out by a 1962 blues, which Tyner sits out, and a 1963 quartet ballad.

But it is with 1962's *Coltrane* (MCA/Impulse MCAD-5883) that we enter the era of the classic recordings by the John Coltrane Quartet. From the first notes of the vamp waltz "Out of This World," the sound is in place – Trane blowing full held notes, spelled by leaps into the upper register and rhythmic note clusters, Tyner backing him up with patented voicings that would influence pianists as definitively as Bud Powell's work did in the 1940s, Garrison playing a repeated vamp figure, varying it slightly according to what was going on around him, and, through it all, Jones's polyrhythmic fusillade. This is a classic small-group approach, rooted in the jazz tradition, but bringing something truly new to it.

The set's other tunes are no less remarkable; "Soul Eyes" is a fine, haunting ballad by pianist Mal Waldron, with Coltrane playing the melody at the top end of the tenor's range and returning after Tyner's solo for some searching improvisation; "The Inch Worm" is another vamp-based waltz, a bit slower than "Out of This World," a playful melody that Coltrane renders on soprano; "Tunji" is a meditative, drone-based piece (actually a blues) based on one Eastern-sounding scale; and "Miles' Mode" is a medium-up-tempo modal swinger. The album is a major statement; Coltrane had figured out a new way to play jazz. He had made all his experimenting come together, and the next three years would be a kind of golden age for him.

My favorite album by the quartet is probably *Crescent* (MCA/Impulse MCAD-5889), from April 1964. By this time the group really thought with one mind and had digested many of the lessons of their new concept. The set has an extremely relaxed yet focused air about it. "Crescent," "Wise One," and "Lonnie's Lament" (mainly a feature for Tyner and Garrison) all open with meditative cadenzas, in which Coltrane's tenor is couched in out-of-tempo playing by the other three, before sliding into slightly different walking tempos. Coltrane here combines his rhythmic, note-cluster approach with a thoughtful, lyrical aspect that bespeaks a great strength. On "Crescent," Coltrane plays a solo that lays triplet accents over the relaxed, walking-tempo four-four pulse in an ingenious way, creating a built-in polyrhythmic melodic aspect for Elvin Jones to play against. Listen to the way, after Tyner drops out, that Jones keeps the tempo going on the ride cymbal while answering all of Coltrane's rhythmic figures with his other stick on the snare drum. "Wise

One"'s undulating, almost bossa-nova-like rhythmic feel brings out a very warm side of Coltrane. "Bessie's Blues" is a happy, up-tempo blues on which Coltrane gradually moves farther and farther out as Tyner stops playing, going head-to-head with Jones before cueing the rest of the band to come back in. A relatively short tune, this is a gem. In all, this is one of the most satisfying sets Coltrane ever recorded.

*The John Coltrane Quartet Plays* (MCA/Impulse MCAD-33110) is another outing in which the probing, polyrhythmic side of the group comes out. The selections include a version of the popular song "Chim Chim Cheree," which Coltrane plays on soprano. By this time, early 1965, a change had begun to take place in Coltrane's sound; an emotionally high-pitched, somewhat choked element had entered, and the foundations of his playing were shifting away from a concern with swing and blues tonality. This is, to me, one of the quartet's least satisfying Impulse recordings.

A perennial favorite set by the quartet is the exquisite *Ballads* (MCA/Impulse MCAD-5885), from 1962, certainly one of the greatest mood albums ever recorded. Coltrane and the others play with ultimate lyricism and sensitivity on eight of the best standard ballads, such as "It's Easy to Remember," "Nancy (With the Laughing Face)," and "You Don't Know What Love Is." These performances are short, as Coltrane's work from this period goes; only one track is over five minutes. His assignment here was to play melody, to sing on his horn, which he does with consummate grace, producing an album as serene and reflective as *"Live" at the Village Vanguard* is searching and relentless. This is one of those sets that everyone ought to own.

Much the same might be said for Coltrane's March 1963 collaboration with singer Johnny Hartman, called, simply, *John Coltrane and Johnny Hartman* (MCA/Impulse MCAD-5661 JVC-466). This is, if anything, an even greater mood album than *Ballads*, although there is somewhat less from the saxophonist here, proportionately, since he shares the spotlight with Hartman's smooth-as-brandy baritone. The tunes, "They Say It's Wonderful," "Dedicated to You," "My One and Only Love," Billy Strayhorn's "Lush Life" (probably the best version ever recorded of this unique ballad), "You Are Too Beautiful," and "Autumn Serenade," are a well-chosen lot of popular standards, played here at slow, romantic tempos. But the album never drags, never bogs down; it's a marvel of strength and delicacy. Highest recommendation.

*Coltrane Live at Birdland* (MCA/Impulse MCAD-33109) is another of the quartet's best, recorded live (except for two added studio cuts) in extremely good sound at the famous nightclub in 1963. Everyone is in great shape here; Tyner gets a long workout on "Afro-Blue," a real chance to hear the trio on an extended outing before Coltrane comes back in on soprano. The version of the old ballad associated with Billy Eckstine, "I Want to Talk about You," one of Trane's favorites, is extremely revealing, with Coltrane's closing unaccompanied tenor cadenza one of his most dazzling statements. "Alabama," one of the two studio performances, is a dirge full of deep sadness, written after a racially motivated bombing at a Birmingham, Alabama, church left four young girls dead.

*Dear Old Stockholm* (GRP/Impulse GRD-120) is interesting for its glimpse of what the quartet might have sounded like had Elvin Jones not been available. Roy Haynes takes over the drums for these five tracks, two of which are from 1963, the remainder from 1965. Haynes is one of jazz's most unjustly neglected drummers, among the public, at least. Here he lights his own kind of fire under the band, especially in the swinging title track and the go-for-broke "One Down, One Up." This is a very enjoyable set, a refreshing change of pace for those who already know the classic Impulse albums backward and forward.

*Duke Ellington and John Coltrane* (MCA/Impulse MCAD-39103) is a historic 1962 meeting between jazz's greatest composer and the music's foremost avant-gardist. Many at the time were surprised that the meeting came off so well. They needn't have been; Coltrane had served a full apprenticeship in the music and had built his innovations solidly on what he knew of the music's full sweep. Likewise, it should be no surprise to anyone that Ellington's piano sounds as fresh and "modern" as Tyner's, or anyone's, could. His essentially percussive, rhythmic accompanying style fits in perfectly in these quartet performances that use different combinations of Garrison and Jones and Ellington's bassist, Aaron Bell, and drummer, Sam Woodyard. The program consists of Ellington and Coltrane originals (as well as one by Billy Strayhorn), including a brilliantly arranged "In a Sentimental Mood," the charging "Take the Coltrane," and the happy, Latin-tinged "Angelica." But every tune here could be singled out; this was a one-time experiment of the sort that often doesn't satisfy expectations. This time, though, it really worked out. Highly recommended.

One of Coltrane's most famous recordings is certainly the overtly spiritual *A Love Supreme* (MCA/Impulse MCAD-5660 JVC-467), a suite in four parts titled "Acknowledgement," "Resolution," "Pursuance," and "Psalm." Recorded in December 1964, this, too, presents the quartet as a single organism that breathes and thinks together; Jimmy Garrison sets things rolling on "Acknowledgement" by intoning the album's signature four-note melody like a heartbeat. On top of it, Jones, Tyner, and Coltrane play with an extraordinary degree of ordered freedom. This is, obviously, something other than good-time music; it is music that draws on jazz's fundamentals to make a serious devotional statement. And yet, no one can deny the overwhelming swing of

"Resolution." And no one will escape a case of the chills as Coltrane enters with the melody on that track. "Pursuance" opens with an extended drum solo and turns into an up-tempo modal exploration; the power and concentration that Coltrane and Jones generate are nothing short of staggering. And "Psalm" is an incantatory offering around one tonal center. This is powerful stuff, certainly one of the classic statements of the music.

Not quite a year later, Coltrane recorded *Meditations* (MCA/Impulse MCAD-39139), another album centered on spiritual concerns. Its five sections – "The Father and the Son and the Holy Ghost," "Compassion," "Love," "Consequences," and "Serenity" – make use of an expanded ensemble with a second drummer, Rashied Ali, and another tenor player, Pharoah Sanders, in a program that takes things much farther out than anything Coltrane had released before, with the exception of *Ascension*, which was Coltrane's answer to Ornette Coleman's *Free Jazz* (Atlantic 1364-2). Here Coltrane has moved away from the roots of jazz almost entirely into forms that sound more like Tibetan devotional music or Indian ragas or Middle Eastern music. From this point on, what he recorded is more or less in this other territory. This was his choice, and no one can reasonably question his sincerity in moving that way. It seems to me that Coltrane's final work was an attempt to make a sort of spiritual separate peace in a language that was, finally, not usable by the largest part of the community he was addressing. Whether one agrees with this estimate or not, Coltrane's contributions, over the ten or so years of the heart of his career, were immense; he was one of the most serious artists jazz has ever known. He died in July 1967 at the age of forty.

## MORE TENORS

Great as they were, Rollins and Coltrane were not the last word in the 1960s, although no one has really extended the saxophone's range or ground rules beyond what those two did. A number of excellent stylists came along in their wake, combining elements from both their styles as well as from those of older players.

One of the best of these, and an important jazz composer as well, is Wayne Shorter. He was first heard at length with Art Blakey's Jazz Messengers, then as a member of Miles Davis's great mid-1960s quintet with Herbie Hancock, Ron Carter, and Tony Williams; he composed lasting tunes for both bands, as well as forging a very personal style with roots in Coltrane's playing. Among his own albums, the 1966 *Adam's Apple* (Blue Note 46403), a quartet set with Herbie Hancock, Reggie Workman, and Joe Chambers, showcases his playing at its best, in a varied program including the funky title tune, the bossa-nova-flavored "El Gaucho," an eerie ballad by pianist Jimmy Rowles called "502 Blues," Shorter's famous six-eight blues "Footprints" (which he recorded with Miles Davis later in the year), his gorgeous ballad "Teru," in which his tone is pebble-smooth in the upper register, and more. This is a perfect introduction to his playing.

Perhaps an even more interesting set, from a compositional point of view, is the 1964 *Speak No Evil* (Blue Note 46509), which is made up entirely of Shorter tunes played by a group including trumpeter Freddie Hubbard and a rhythm section of Herbie Hancock, Ron Carter, and Elvin Jones. One thing to listen for here is the attention to dynamics, both in the compositions and in the solos; Shorter obviously likes to surprise, and he will spike a cool-sounding tune like "Fee-Fi-Fo-Fum" with unexpected accents or build to a hysterical crescendo from a cocky, I-don't-care theme in "Witch Hunt." This set also includes Shorter's ballad "Infant Eyes." Shorter's playing here isn't as smooth as on *Adam's Apple*; his lines are full of speechlike turns of phrase and timbral manipulation, changes from loud to soft. He thinks as a composer while he plays, too, which means he knows how to play and listen at the same time. Very little of what he sets up in a solo gets lost; he tends to remember the motifs he uses, bringing them up again just when you've forgotten them. If he plays some melodic fragment that strikes you, listen for it to pop up again, subtly transformed.

*Juju* (Blue Note 46514), recorded about five months before *Speak No Evil*, is a quartet session with McCoy Tyner and Elvin Jones, borrowed from John Coltrane's quartet, and bassist Reggie Workman, again consisting entirely of Shorter originals. The title tune is a waltz based on a whole-tone scale, very much in the Coltrane mode compositionally. "Yes or No" is an up-tempo cooker that echoes the Coltrane of the Atlantic period – especially "The Night Has a Thousand Eyes" from *Coltrane's Sound* (Atlantic 1419-2), alternating, as it does, a pedal-point vamp with chord-changes-based swinging. Shorter plays very strong stuff here and throughout.

Shorter has an extremely high batting average as a sideman, having made classic statements as composer and soloist with both Blakey and Davis, as well as on recording dates with others. Blakey's *The Big Beat* (Blue Note 46400) has several Shorter tunes, including the haunting "Lester Left Town," and his *Caravan* (Riverside/OJC-038) has Shorter's exquisitely voiced tribute to Bud Powell, "This Is for Albert." The compact disc of Blakey's *Ugetsu* (Riverside/OJC-90) has no fewer than four Shorter tunes, including the lovely ballad "Eva," never before released. All of these also feature Shorter's tenor, of course.

Miles Davis's 1967 album *Nefertiti* (Columbia CK 46113) features the Shorter-

Hancock-Carter-Williams quintet and includes three Shorter tunes on which the saxophonist really shows how far he has come both as player and writer. Especially beautiful is "Fall," a thing of unparalleled delicacy of mood; Shorter's solo here, brief and quiet as it is, is worthy of Lester Young at his greatest. "Nefertiti" 's structure is worth noting; the idea here was to turn the usual conception of melody and solos on its head. Davis and Shorter play Shorter's walking-tempo, sing-song line over and over, varying the dynamics and (ever so slightly) the timing, while the rhythm section gets louder, softer, denser, and sparser around it. This is a fascinating eight minutes. *E.S.P.* (Columbia CK 46863), recorded in 1965 by the same band, is also top-notch; Shorter's ballad "Iris" is a standout.

Shorter went on to form the fusion band Weather Report with pianist Joe Zawinul, but their work falls outside the range of this book. One album Shorter recorded on his own during this period, entitled *Native Dancer* (Columbia CK 46159), is a collaboration with Brazilian singer Milton Nascimento and contains some lovely things, especially the ethereal "Ponta de Areia" and the rock-based "Beauty and the Beast," on which Shorter plays some roaring soprano saxophone.

### JOE HENDERSON

Tenor saxophonist Joe Henderson arrived in New York City in 1962 at the age of twenty-five and made a big splash. He was, and is, a strong stylist with a big debt to Sonny Rollins but has a way of phrasing and constructing melodies that is as personal and unpredictable as Shorter's. He also has the same interest in timbral effects as Coltrane and the avant-gardists, but these are always used as a way of expanding his options within a more or less straight-ahead context.

His two best and most characteristic albums are probably *Inner Urge* (Blue Note 84189) and *Mode for Joe* (Blue Note 84227). *Inner Urge* is a quartet set that, like Wayne Shorter's *Juju* (Blue Note 46514), uses McCoy Tyner and Elvin Jones from John Coltrane's quartet, along with bassist Bob Cranshaw, one of Sonny Rollins's favorite accompanists. It includes three Henderson originals, including the turbulent title track, the swinging blues "Isotope," and the two-chord, Spanish-feeling "El Barrio." A standout on the album is a cooking version of "Night and Day." Like Shorter, Henderson doesn't waste material, and his solos are both adventuresome and coherent; his control in all registers is impressive, to say the least.

Good as the quartet album is, the 1966 *Mode for Joe* is even more interesting. Henderson had grown substantially as a player, and the accompanying group is formidable, consisting of trumpeter Lee Morgan, trombonist Curtis Fuller, vibist Bobby Hutcherson, and a rhythm section of Cedar Walton, Ron Carter, and the excellent Joe Chambers. The ensemble passages are lent a fascinating texture because of the way the vibes are used, and the rhythm section provides maximum flotation under the solos. The tunes (three by Henderson, two by Walton, and one by Morgan) are unfailingly interesting; they tend to be in the modal bag rather than based on chord changes, and they tend to end up in straight four-four, usually at medium or fast tempos. Lots of care was given to the overall shapes of the performances; not everyone solos on every tune, and there are nice arranging touches behind the solos in places. Henderson is intense and fiery throughout; he sometimes leaps into the upper register unexpectedly, to great effect, and he always swings like mad. (Listen to the head of steam he builds on Walton's "Black," especially when he comes back in after Walton's piano solo. On the alternate take of this tune included on the compact disc, Henderson makes use, less successfully, of some of the same motivic material, and it is interesting to see how his conception coalesces on the originally issued take.) His phrasing is as personal and unpredictable as Shorter's, and his control of the horn's sound is phenomenal. This is a great jazz album.

Henderson's first album under his own name, *Page One* (Blue Note 84140), is fine, too; it includes his own bossa nova, "Recorda Me," a smoking, up-tempo blues called "Homestretch," and two good tunes by trumpeter Kenny Dorham – the fine ballad "La Mesha" (which Henderson plays beautifully) and "Blue Bossa," which has become a jazz standard. The accompanying band consists of McCoy Tyner on piano, Butch Warren on bass, and Pete La Roca on drums, as well as Dorham himself on trumpet. Dorham was a close associate and supporter of Henderson's, and they ended up on quite a few recording dates together. One of the best is Dorham's *Una Mas* (Blue Note 46515), the first record Henderson ever made, on which the trumpeter and tenorist are backed by Herbie Hancock, Butch Warren, and Tony Williams on the title tune (a highly spiced bossa nova), "Straight Ahead" (an up-tempo riff based on "I Got Rhythm"), Dorham's moody, medium-tempo "Sao Paulo," and a CD bonus track of Lerner and Loewe's "If Ever I Would Leave You," taken at a deliciously relaxed walking pace spurred by Williams's brushes. Henderson explodes with ideas and soul throughout. He is also featured to advantage on Dorham's *Trompeta Toccata* (Blue Note 84181) and pianist Andrew Hill's *Point of Departure* (Blue Note 84167), on which Dorham also takes part. He is on hand for Lee Morgan's very popular *The Sidewinder* (Blue Note 84157); the title tune on this one bears a close resemblance to Dorham's "Una Mas," by the way. Henderson also played for a while in pianist Horace Silver's small group, and he appears on Silver's *The Cape Verdean Blues* (Blue Note 84220) and *Song for My Father* (Blue Note 84185). As you might expect, he burns it up on all of these.

### BOOKER ERVIN AND RAHSAAN ROLAND KIRK

Booker Ervin's playing is not as well known today as it should be. At his best he was a strong, intense tenor voice who could be mistaken for no one else. Some of his best work can be found on the mid-1960s recordings called "Books" that he made for Prestige – *The Space Book*, *The Freedom Book*, *The Song Book*, etc. *The Song Book* (Prestige/OJC-779) and *The Blues Book* (Prestige/OJC-780) are both available, and both are worthwhile. *The Song Book* has Ervin playing tasty standards like "Just Friends" and "The Lamp Is Low" with a rhythm section of Tommy Flanagan, Richard Davis, and Alan Dawson; *The Blues Book* substitutes Gildo Mahones for Flanagan and adds trumpeter Carmell Jones. Ervin's playing is full-bodied, sometimes strident, always emotional, usually on top of the beat; he rarely sets a finger-popping groove.

Another Prestige set, *Setting the Pace* (Prestige 24123), features Ervin at his wildest in epic tenor battles with Dexter Gordon on the title track and on the old Gordon bebop signature tune "Dexter's Deck," on which Gordon takes a nine-and-a-half-minute solo. Ervin's keening, fervent tenor obviously had been keeping up with the avant-garde players of the time. The ultraflexible, amphibious rhythm section of Jaki Byard, Reggie Workman, and Alan Dawson could adapt themselves to any circumstances, setting themselves for Naturalism, Cubism, or Abstract Expressionism; here they play a constantly evolving, shifting, contrapuntal background that could have been matched by few rhythm sections for imagination and sheer go-for-broke spontaneity. This set is worth having for them alone.

Ervin also recorded a good quartet set for Candid, entitled *That's It!* (CCD 79014); the repertoire consists of several Ervin originals, including the eerie ballad "Uranus," and two standards, "Poinciana" and Kurt Weill's "Speak Low." Charles Mingus valued Ervin enough to use him regularly; he appears on Mingus's *Blues and Roots* (Atlantic 1305-2), as well as on several of the sessions included in *The Complete Candid Recordings of Charles Mingus* (Mosaic MD3-111). Listening to Ervin for too long can wring you out a little; the emotional pressure is relentless. But he is more than worth a listen.

Another musician beloved by Mingus was the reed prodigy Roland Kirk, later known as Rahsaan Roland Kirk. Kirk initially gained attention with his ability to play as many as three reed instruments at the same time, sometimes harmonizing like the reed section of a big band, sometimes even playing counterpoint with himself. As has been said many times, what at first was regarded as something of a gimmick came to be seen for what it was – the honest musical expression of a phenomenally gifted player.

Kirk was a strong, big-toned tenor player, with definite roots in rhythm and blues as well as jazz; he spelled the big horn with passages played on his two other reed instruments, the manzello and the stritch, as well as flute, on which he was an innovator. He wasn't necessarily the most melodically inventive of saxophonists, but his music was always highly charged, spiritually and emotionally. It had humor and a wide range of moods, and he knew more about the music's history than many musicians and writers. The quality of his recordings varies widely, but the best of them are kaleidoscopes of deeply human emotions and images.

Of Kirk's available recordings, the ones that give the broadest and most jazz-based sense of his playing are *Rip, Rig and Panic* (EmArcy 832-164-2) and *We Free Kings* (Mercury 826 455-2). Both sets have a wide variety of repertoire and approach. *Rip, Rig and Panic*, recorded in 1965, is perhaps the more interesting; Kirk is accompanied by pianist Jaki Byard, who is as much of an eclectic as Kirk was, capable of taking the music through its various historical periods as well as out into spaceville. Both men have a strong streak of gallows humor. The group is rounded out by bassist Richard Davis and drummer Elvin Jones. "No Tonic Pres" is an exciting, up-tempo blues with an ambiguous key center, on which Kirk takes off like a bull set loose in the streets, careening off of Jones's accents; in the middle of Byard's solo, the band stops and Byard launches into some unaccompanied stride piano. It's that kind of session. Kirk states the melody of "From Bechet, Byas, and Fats" on the high-pitched stritch (reminiscent of Sidney Bechet's soprano saxophone), then goes on another tenor rampage, using circular breathing techniques that allow him to play continuously where most others would have to stop for a breath, achieving a sort of extension of Coltrane's sheets of sound effect. In the middle of one of those sorties he ingeniously incorporates the accents Elvin Jones is playing into his line. The album is full of interesting material, including some nonmusical sounds patched in for a kind of dreamlike narrative effect.

*We Free Kings*, from 1961, is somewhat more conventional. It is also a quartet session, using either Hank Jones or Richard Wyands on piano. The opener, "Three for the Festival," is an up-tempo, minor-key blues that Kirk plays on three horns at once; during his solo he switches to flute. Here and on "You Did It, You Did It" he shows the technique he added to flute playing, a way of combining sung vocal lines with the actual flute notes. He exhumes Charlie

Parker's rarely done "Blue for Alice" and the pop tune "Moon Song," one of pianist Art Tatum's favorites. This set, *Rip, Rig and Panic*, and everything else Kirk recorded for Mercury are available in a deluxe set from Polygram.

*Kirk's Work* (Prestige/OJC-459) is a nice quartet set with organist Jack McDuff, bassist Joe Benjamin, and drummer Art Taylor, generally in a more straight-ahead, blues-dominated groove than the two previously mentioned sets. In the middle of certain solos, Kirk inserts sax-section riffs with all three horns playing simultaneously, often using these brief interludes as excuses to change horns, in a kind of spontaneous one-man big-band head arrangement. *Introducing Roland Kirk* (MCA/Chess CHD-91551) is a good 1960 date on which the reed man is paired with multi-instrumentalist Ira Sullivan, who plays mainly trumpet here. Again, this is a fairly straight-ahead set, with a variety of material: a shuffle blues, an unusually slow version of "Our Love Is Here to Stay," which doubles in tempo, and several cookers.

In the late 1960s and 1970s Kirk began to incorporate a wider range of musics into what could be called his act, including some rock and funk elements and some good old vaudeville aspects. His recordings and performances were in actuality an early form of performance art, combining Kirk's spontaneous raps, quick changes of idiom, and broad humor – sometimes successfully, sometimes not. One of his most popular albums is *The Inflated Tear* (Atlantic 7 90045-2), a grab bag of blues, sing-song flute tunes, even a self-duet on Duke Ellington's "Creole Love Call." But his unique personality and sensibility are given their freest rein on *The Case of the 3 Sided Dream in Audio Color* (Atlantic 1674-2), a wild melange of tape overdubs, commentary from Kirk, rock, funk, and even Kirk himself playing trumpet in a pastiche of Miles Davis's style on "Bye Bye Blackbird." It's interesting, but this kind of project depended on the personal projection of Kirk; to me, it hasn't stood up that well as the years have passed.

# THE PIANO

## PIANISTS

Jazz piano exists in something of its own orbit; it is equally an accompanying instrument that functions as part of the group's rhythm section, a solo voice within the group that can make its own melodic solo variations during a group's performance, and a self-sufficient solo instrument, capable of providing both lead and accompaniment, harmony and rhythm.

The piano is, in a way, the cerebral cortex of the jazz group, coordinating the activities of the different elements of the band. It functions this way because of its unique nature as both a percussion instrument (the piano's sound is produced by striking, however softly, keys which then cause hammers to strike strings located inside the piano) and a harmonic instrument capable of playing chords (and thereby outlining the harmony of a song) or a melody – or many melodies at the same time. In practice, these aspects – the percussive, the harmonic, and the melodic – never function separately. In jazz, melody almost always has a strongly percussive quality; the accenting within the melody or melodies sets up a rhythmic pattern that gives the drummer something to play off of, much as a poet's deliberate use of a pattern of accented syllables sets up a rhythmic pattern in a poem. Moreover, these accented notes also have an important harmonic function, often serving as signposts in a melodic line to tell us where we are harmonically.

The piano is at the center of this complex network of harmonic and rhythmic significance in a jazz group. During another instrument's solo, the pianist keeps up an ongoing commentary on what the soloist plays, in keeping with the call-and-response quality of a jazz group's interaction; the pianist comments harmonically, as well as rhythmically, on what the soloist plays by echoing or answering the soloist's accents.

But this dialogue with the soloist is only part of what the pianist is thinking about; as part of the rhythm section, the piano carries on separate but related relationships with both the bass and the drums. You will often hear a pianist and a drummer set up a little pattern of accents behind a soloist (for an example of this, listen closely to the way pianist Red Garland and drummer Philly Joe Jones play behind the soloists on "Two Bass Hit" on the Miles Davis album *Milestones* [Columbia CK 40837]). And the pianist also has to be thinking about what the bassist is playing, so that they agree harmonically on the route to be taken through a song's chordal steeplechase.

Unaccompanied piano presents its own challenges. The solo pianist needs to be able to maintain a pulse whether or not he or she is actually spelling it out; he or she needs tremendous harmonic knowledge in order to keep the performance from becoming boring, an orchestrator's sense of balance and density, a juggler's coordination, a basketball coach's ability to think in simultaneous lines, phenomenal stamina, and the concentration of a stunt pilot. The solo jazz piano is like a jazz group in microcosm; often, especially in dance-oriented styles like stride and boogie-woogie, a pianist can develop the same kind of call-and-response effect, the making of complex shapes out of simple repeated phrases, of a big band in full roar.

Perhaps for this reason, many of jazz's preeminent composers and orchestrators – Jelly Roll Morton, Duke Ellington, and Thelonious Monk are the most obvious examples – have been pianists. Many of jazz's most important pianists are discussed in the Ensembles section because their greatest significance was the effect they had on the ensemble concept in the music.

Anyone looking for an overview of the jazz piano will be well served by the Smithsonian's four-CD set *Jazz Piano*; almost all the major figures are represented, from Jelly Roll Morton through Fats Waller, Earl Hines, Art Tatum, Bud Powell, Thelonious Monk, Bill Evans, McCoy Tyner, and Herbie Hancock. The seventy-eight-page accompanying booklet is full of expert commentary by the late Martin Williams, one of the deans of jazz criticism, and pianist Dick Katz. Like *The Smithsonian Collection of Classic Jazz*, *Jazz Piano* covers a lot of ground in a dauntingly small space, managing to give a meaningful view of a complex subject. A useful, if much less comprehensive, set is *Classic Jazz Piano* (RCA/Bluebird 6754-2-RB), which is weighted toward styles that developed before bebop.

From its beginnings, jazz piano has been contrapuntal in nature and has used the instrument's percussive qualities to bring out the call-and-response and polyrhythmic aspects of the music. The earliest players tended to set up rhythmic expectations with the left hand, then use the right hand to play shifting patterns off against the underlying pattern. This created a drama of tension and release that was often specifically designed to encourage dancing.

Jelly Roll Morton, whose work is discussed in some depth in the Ensembles section, was one of the most important early pianists to record. His 1923 piano solos, available on *Jelly Roll Morton 1923/24* (Milestone MCD-47018-2), are a very high level example of early jazz piano, with strong roots in the structures of ragtime but incorporating many of the compositional elements of jazz, such as breaks, riffs, and shout choruses. You can hear how his left hand mostly alternates between bass notes and chords, creating a momentum and a set of expectations against which his right hand plays endless intriguing variations. The same could be said, in the abstract, for stride piano and boogie-woogie, except that the nature of what each hand plays is quite different.

For an example of the Spanish tinge that Morton said was indispensable to jazz, listen to his "New Orleans Joys" and "Tia Juana," on which the left hand plays a rhumba beat instead of the alternating bass/chord, bass/chord pattern; Morton plays some extremely ingenious variations with his right hand here. In other places in this set, his left hand incorporates what amounts to a countermelody in the bass, sometimes imitating the trombone part in a typical New Orleans ensemble (a good example of this is "Kansas City Stomp"). In all cases, Morton sets up a tension between the rhythmic pull of the left hand and the right. Morton's solos and band performances on the slightly later *The Pearls* (RCA/Bluebird 6588-2-RB) and on the monumental, for-collectors-only *The Jelly Roll Morton Centennial* (RCA/Bluebird 2361-2-RB) are also classic examples of his style.

A treasure trove of Morton's piano playing, including his examples of how jazz developed out of earlier forms of music, is Rounder's four-disc series of Morton's 1938 recordings for the Library of Congress. *The Library of Congress Recordings, Volume 1 (Kansas City Stomp)* (Rounder 1091) has his famous illustration of how "Tiger Rag" evolved from a French quadrille, as well as versions of "Maple Leaf Rag" played in different styles. *Volume 2 (Anamule Dance)* (Rounder 1092) has the charming title track but is generally the lightest of the four on essential pianistics. *Volume 3 (The Pearls)* (Rounder 1093) contains a version of the title tune, one of Morton's greatest compositions, as well as other Morton standards like "King Porter Stomp" and "Wolverine Blues." *Volume 4 (Winin' Boy Blues)* (Rounder 1094) has his definitive illustrations of the Spanish tinge, especially "The Crave," and his study in "advanced" chords called "Freakish." One thing to be aware of here is that many of the performances are incomplete; when Morton recorded these, the piano and vocal sections often grew naturally out of Morton's reminiscences, and it is too bad that these aren't present. It is not uncommon for tunes to cut off in mid-chorus. For the serious-minded student, it's not that much of a problem, but if you are listening for enjoyment primarily, it can be annoying. *Volumes 3* and *4* are probably the easiest to listen to in this respect.

**STRIDE**

Stride piano, as practiced largely in New York City by pianists like James P. Johnson, Willie "The Lion" Smith, and Fats Waller, somewhat resembles Jelly Roll Morton's playing, incorporating as it does the bass/chord, bass/chord way of keeping time in the left hand, but it has a different rhythmic emphasis, a more headlong forward propulsion. This comes from a slightly different way of accenting. In the bass/chord, bass/chord pattern, Morton tended to accent the bass note; the stride players tended to accent the beat that the chord falls on. Musicians would say that Morton tended to accent one and three, the stride players two and four, out of every group of four beats.

For an example of stride piano at its best, check out the 1929 "Handful of Keys" on the Fats Waller set *The Joint Is Jumpin'* (RCA/Bluebird 6288-2-RB). You can hear how Waller's left hand keeps up a bouncing tempo by alternating bass notes with chords, while his right hand plays swinging, repeated riffs in both single notes and chords. Sometimes, instead of a simple bass note in the left hand, Waller (like most stride pianists) plays the interval of a tenth with his pinky and thumb, giving a fuller sound than just the bass note. Listen, too, for the way Waller sometimes constructs a countermelody in the bass. The combined shapes of the left-hand rhythm and the right-hand riffs create an exciting series of patterns, the way a juggler's simple actions combine to produce a complicated total effect. Much of the pleasure in this style lies in listening for the way the pianist varies the patterns he sets up. Waller's other recordings are discussed in the Ensembles section, where he is also discussed as the fine band pianist that he was. If you really like the stride style and want to study his playing in depth, the two-CD set *Fats Waller Piano Solos – Turn On the Heat* (RCA/Bluebird 2482-2-RB) is essential.

Waller was the best-known stride pianist by virtue of his great showmanship, songwriting, and singing ability, but anyone with a taste for this style must listen to some of the older men he learned from, especially James P.

Johnson. Johnson was thought of as the father of the stride piano; he was a prolific composer of classical pieces and popular songs as well (he wrote "Charleston" and "If I Could Be with You One Hour Tonight"). Unfortunately, much of Johnson's best recorded work is only spottily available. *Snowy Morning Blues* (Decca/GRP GRD-604) is the best collection currently in print; it contains one of his most exciting stride performances, the irresistible 1930 "Jingles," as well as several other 1930 solos and a slew of 1944 performances on which he is accompanied by a drummer. He is not in peak form on the 1944 tracks, eight of which are Fats Waller tunes recorded as a tribute after his protégé's death the previous year, but some of them are excellent anyway, especially the Johnson classics "Keep Off the Grass" and "Carolina Shout," and the thrilling "Over the Bars." In general, though, Johnson's mighty left hand isn't as prominently displayed on the 1944 cuts as one might wish.

You can also hear Johnson sounding good on a number of solo sides included on *The Complete Edmond Hall/James P. Johnson/Sidney De Paris/Vic Dickenson Blue Note Sessions* (Mosaic MR6-109); the two best, from a stride point of view, are probably the arrogantly swinging "Mule Walk" and the impossibly up-tempo fingerbuster "Caprice Rag." Johnson was a master at varying his left-hand patterns, suggesting all kinds of polyrhythms and countermelodies. His technique was awesome, and his swing overpowering. He also plays a couple of boogie-woogie numbers here; this is surprising because some schooled musicians (which Johnson certainly was) tended to look down on the relatively simple, blues-based boogie-woogie form (more on this in a while).

Willie "The Lion" Smith, like Johnson, a hero of Duke Ellington's (both Johnson and Smith had befriended the young Ellington when he arrived in New York City in the mid-1920s), was a flamboyant, colorful personality and a strong, florid stride pianist. His unique style can be heard at length in his album *Piano Solos* (Commodore CCD-7012), a collection spotlighting his lyric side as well as his stomping side. He is also in fine form on six 1958 tracks on *Luckey and The Lion – Harlem Piano Solos by Luckey Roberts and Willie "The Lion" Smith* (Good Time Jazz 10035), a lovely set that he splits with one of his few peers, Charles Luckeyeth Roberts. Duke Ellington's 1965 solo piano tribute to Smith, called "The Second Portrait of The Lion," full of canny appropriations of The Lion's style, may be heard on *Duke Ellington: Solos, Duets, and Trios* (RCA/Bluebird 2178-2-RB). Both Smith and James P. Johnson may be heard in late-1930s small bands in the set *Swing Is Here: Small Band Swing 1935–1939* (RCA/Bluebird 2180-2-RB).

The stride style became part of a complete pianist's bag of tricks for many years, even if he or she spent most of the time playing in a very different style.

Pianists as different as Earl Hines, Art Tatum, and Thelonious Monk have used stride as an integral part of their styles (Monk's version of "Nice Work If You Can Get It," included on *Standards* [Columbia CK 45148], is a good, humorous example of his way of handling it). Even Count Basie, who was known for making a few notes say a lot, can be heard in 1932 playing some ferocious stride on "Toby," "Lafayette," and "Milenburg Joys" on *Bennie Moten's Kansas City Orchestra (1929–1932): Basie Beginnings* (RCA/Bluebird 9768-2-RB). For a stunning example of Duke Ellington's ability to play two-handed stride, listen to the 1932 "Lots O' Fingers" on the album *Duke Ellington: Solos, Duets, and Trios* (RCA/Bluebird 2178-2-RB).

## BOOGIE

Like stride, boogie-woogie piano gets its effects by combining a regular pattern in the left hand with a series of riff-based variations in the right. Boogie-woogie, which is almost always based on blues progressions and forms, is much easier to play than stride, and it was a staple of unschooled pianists who played for dances and parties in the South and Southwest of the 1920s and 1930s. At its best, it is a wildly exciting style, too, and some thoroughly trained pianists have found it fascinating. In the late 1930s and early 1940s it became a popular musical fad through the success of boogie-woogie tunes like Mary Lou Williams's "Roll 'Em" and, later, novelties such as "Beat Me, Daddy, Eight to the Bar" and "The Boogie Woogie Bugle Boy of Company B."

Boogie-woogie was sometimes called eight-to-the-bar because of its characteristic accenting, a rocking rhythm that accented what musicians call the back beat, or the "and" half of every beat (in a four-beat measure, if you count the beats "one and two and three and four," the "ands" would get the emphasis). This pattern is hammered home, in boogie-woogie, by the pianist's left hand, which plays a repeated bass line or pulsating chords over simple blues progressions while the right hand plays riffs against the pattern. It is a fairly simple principle, but a skilled player can make almost endless variations using this technique.

A classic boogie-woogie performance, and a perfect capsule summary of the style, is Meade Lux Lewis's "Honky Tonk Train Blues," included on the essential boogie-woogie anthology *Barrelhouse Boogie* (RCA/Bluebird 8334-2-RB). Against a steady, rocking chordal boogie pattern in his left hand, Lewis sets a procession of ingenious, shifting right-hand riffs that are exhilarating in the way they set up expectations and then shift them. This collection also includes ten cuts by the Chicago master Jimmy Yancey and nine by the two-piano team of Pete Johnson and Albert Ammons. Yancey's approach was in many ways the most basic of all boogie-woogie players'; he usually used only single-note, broken bass lines in the left hand and single-note melodies in the right hand, as opposed to the rolling basses and chordal work of some other pianists. He tended to be at his best on slower blues pieces, of which there are several here.

Johnson and Ammons were, individually, probably the greatest boogie-woogie pianists who ever lived; when they played together, as they do here, the swing they generated could be overwhelming. Anyone who has tried to play piano duets knows how hard it is to keep things from getting muddy; unless the two players know each other very well, musically, bass parts can cancel each other out, chords can lead in different directions, and melody lines can send out mixed messages. But Johnson and Ammons speak the same language and know how to complement each other, handing the lead back and forth like basketball players moving a ball down the court. A performance like "Boogie Woogie Man" shows each of them digging way down into their bags of tricks.

Lewis, Johnson, and Ammons recorded quite a bit on their own. Some of the most important recordings Lewis made are included in *The Complete Edmond Hall/James P. Johnson/Sidney De Paris/Vic Dickenson Blue Note Sessions* (Mosaic MR6-109); he is featured not on piano but on the high-pitched celeste with the Edmond Hall Celeste Quartet, a small group led by one of jazz's best clarinetists and including Charlie Christian on acoustic guitar as well as bassist Israel Crosby. Of the four tunes they recorded (five, if you count the extra take of "Profoundly Blue"), all of which are blues, "Celestial Express" has the highest boogie quotient. You can hear Lewis backing Hall's clarinet with celeste riffs that sound like the trumpet section of a big band. *The Blues Piano Artistry of Meade Lux Lewis* (Riverside/OJC-1759) is a disappointment, containing only one full-fledged boogie out of ten selections. Unfortunately, the fantastic *The Complete Blue Note Recordings of Albert Ammons and Meade Lux Lewis* (Mosaic MR3-103), a limited edition, like almost all of Mosaic's sets, has sold out and will not be reprinted.

Pete Johnson is pretty well represented on records. He has six tracks to himself on *The Pete Johnson/Earl Hines/Teddy Bunn Blue Note Sessions* (Mosaic MR1-119), among which are two powerhouse boogies, "Holler Stomp" and "Barrelhouse Breakdown." The probably hard-to-find collection *All Star Swing Groups: Pete Johnson, Cozy Cole* (Savoy SJL 2218) has two full sides of Johnson, mostly at the helm of a 1946 session spotlighting a different musician on each title; the musicians include trumpeter Hot Lips Page and tenor saxophonist Ben Webster. "1280 Stomp," made at a different 1946 session, with Hot Lips Page and Budd Johnson, builds up a good head of boogie-woogie steam.

Johnson is best known for his collaborations with blues shouter Big Joe Turner. Against Turner's loud, tough, jubilant vocals, Johnson's left hand kept a steady rocking rhythm and from his right pealed ringing treble riffs. Some of the best of these pairings, including their classic duet "Roll 'Em Pete," are either unavailable or hard to find. Two exceptional 1939 tracks, "Cherry Red" and "Baby, Look at You," may be found on the fine four-LP boxed set *Swing Street* (Columbia Special Products JSN 6042); these are quintessential Kansas City boogie-woogie, with Turner cutting loose over a Johnson-led band including Hot Lips Page and alto legend Buster Smith, Charlie Parker's early inspiration. One 1940 track featuring Turner, Johnson, and Page, the spellbinding "Piney Brown Blues," shows up on *Joe Turner Volume 1: I've Been to Kansas City* (Decca/MCD MCAD-42351); Johnson's piano fills here are 151-proof Kansas City blues.

The Kansas City pianist and bandleader Jay McShann was, and is, capable of serving up a great mess of blues and boogie-woogie. The collection *Jay McShann Orchestra: Blues from Kansas City* (Decca/GRP GRD-614) has him at the helm of his early-1940s band, which included alto saxophonist Charlie Parker. McShann's playing on cuts like "Vine Street Boogie," "Confessin' the Blues" (with its Walter Brown vocal), and "One Woman's Man" are definitive of the Kansas City approach to blues and boogie-woogie piano.

Mary Lou Williams, who made her name playing with the Kansas City big band of Andy Kirk, is sadly underrepresented on compact disc. One can hear her fine piano with the late-1930s Kirk band on *Andy Kirk and Mary Lou Williams: Mary's Idea* (Decca/GRP GRD-622), which includes a number of her imaginative and advanced arrangements for the band, including the classic "Walkin' and Swingin'." Williams only got better as she grew older, and she was active well into the 1980s. Fantasy/OJC should really reissue her fantastic Pablo album, *My Mama Pinned a Rose on Me*, from the late 1970s, on which she performs an all-blues program, showing her ability to play in all idioms of jazz while keeping the taproot of the blues intact.

## STEPPING OUT

Stride piano and boogie-woogie both require the pianist to keep time with his or her left hand and to play riff-based variations in the right. Both styles show how jazz piano is percussive in its nature, the contrast between the right- and the left-hand rhythms producing complicated effects. By the late 1920s, though, some pianists were learning that the rhythm didn't always have to be spelled out by the left hand, that it could be implied, and that the right hand could play melodies that were freer, more like improvised trumpet solos, say, than the intricate riffs used by earlier players.

The pioneer of this thinking was Earl "Fatha" Hines, a Chicago pianist who came to prominence with Louis Armstrong in the late 1920s. Hines had deep roots in stride and often used it in his performances, but it was more characteristic of him to break up the left-hand's rhythm, to insert a series of stabbing, off-the-beat left-hand chords or a jabbed, held bass note or a slurred left-hand run against a right hand that was playing not riffs but loud, trumpetlike melodies, often voiced in octaves. His style was, in fact, called trumpet-style piano. The independence of Hines's two hands made it seem as if each were controlled by a separate brain that could read the other's mind.

*Louis Armstrong, Volume 4: Louis Armstrong and Earl Hines* (Columbia CK 45142) is a document of the year 1928, when Hines turned the piano world upside down. Matched here with the greatest instrumental genius jazz has ever known, Hines redefines the possibilities of his own instrument in terms that still have the power to shock. Only Hines would have jumped into the medium-tempo waters of "Savoyagers' Stomp" with those off-the-beat triplets, followed them with such a willingness to leave space, ended his first eight bars with a splashing succession of descending chordal arpeggios, or even been able to conceive of what he does at the beginning of his second eight, the line that rises out of the bass, like a fish surfacing, to meet the spitting, jabbing series of right-hand notes for that harmonized phrase. Hines was a genius, no question about it. The fact is argued further on every track of this collection but nowhere more strongly than on "Weather Bird," one of the greatest jazz recordings ever made, an unaccompanied duet between Hines and Armstrong on a tune Armstrong used to play with King Oliver. The two trade the lead back and forth, Hines constantly changing the background for the trumpeter, providing a pulsating rhythmic base, although the rhythm is seldom directly spelled out.

Hines was an important bandleader in the 1930s and early 1940s as well as a major pianist. Five solo performances from 1939 through 1941, a trio track with Sidney Bechet, and a number of big-band performances are collected on *Piano Man: Earl Hines, His Piano and His Orchestra* (RCA/Bluebird 6750-2-RB), an introduction to Hines at the peak of his popularity; this set is discussed in more detail in the Ensembles section for its great band tracks. Of special pianistic interest among the band cuts are "Piano Man," an up-tempo tour de force for Hines, and "Boogie Woogie On 'St. Louis Blues,'" one of Hines's most popular recordings and one of his few in the boogie mode. The solo cuts show Hines's stride roots, his absolute rhythmic mastery, and his daring. Two fantastic 1939 solo tracks on *The Pete Johnson/Earl Hines/Teddy Bunn Blue Note Sessions* (Mosaic MR1-119), "The Father's Getaway" and "Reminiscing at Blue Note," are worth the price of the set.

Hines rarely recorded as a sideman until he broke up his big band and rejoined Louis Armstrong as a member of the All-Stars in 1948; however, the few times he did guest on others' dates were memorable. He plays some extraordinary stuff on five tunes recorded with clarinetist and soprano saxophonist Sidney Bechet in 1940, available on *Sidney Bechet/The Victor Sessions – Master Takes 1932–43* (RCA/Bluebird 2402-2-RB); check out his wild exchanges with Rex Stewart on "Ain't Misbehavin'." Hines is also in peak form on some 1944 recordings with Coleman Hawkins, included on the four-CD set *The Complete Coleman Hawkins on Keynote* (Mercury 830 960-2), such as "Blue Moon," "Just One More Chance," "Thru' for the Night," and four takes of the up-tempo "Father Co-operates," on which Hines gets very abstract as well as digging into his stride bag.

Hines endured a period of relative obscurity for most of the 1950s, but in the 1960s he made a strong comeback, appearing to greatest effect as a solo pianist. Hines's style was most suited to solo work; the unaccompanied setting gave the best spotlight to his unique rhythmic sense (which often resulted in much of his playing sounding like a series of intricate breaks), his awareness of dynamics, and his timbral shading.

Still, over the right background, he could make many of the same points with a rhythm section, which he does on the essential 1965 *Earl Hines Live at the Village Vanguard* (Columbia CK 44197), recorded at the New York landmark with Eddie Locke on drums, Gene Ramey on bass, and, on some tracks, the mighty Budd Johnson on tenor and soprano saxophones. Any of Hines's solo recordings that you can find from the 1960s or 1970s are worth owning; two of the best, *Quintessential Recording Session* and *Quintessential Continued*, made for the small Chiaroscuro label, may be re-released before long.

## ART TATUM

Ask ten pianists to name the greatest jazz pianist ever and eight will tell you Art Tatum. The other two are wrong. Tatum, who moved to New York from Ohio in 1932, was the most technically awesome pianist who ever played jazz; his understanding of harmony and voice-leading and his rhythmic equilibrium have never been equaled.

Through his style, which combined strong elements of stride as well as techniques evolved by Earl Hines, Tatum gave piano a greatly expanded language with which to treat the popular romantic songs that were the most common repertoire of the time. Like Hines, he was at his greatest as a solo player; a group situation rarely gave him the elbow room to shape the flow and pace of a performance with his sense of dramatic contrast, of timing and dynamics. Tatum often played the first chorus of a tune out of tempo, speeding up the phrasing then slowing it down, as naturally as breathing, before easing it into a walking pace or jumping into an impossibly fast ride studded with breaks full of his trademark arpeggios and scale passages, played with equal facility in both hands. Tatum took familiar material and invariably transformed it into something new, finding surprising ways of reharmonizing standard tunes – seemingly on the wing, although many of his most famous performances were worked out in advance.

Tatum, as pianist Ellis Marsalis implies in his fine notes to the essential *Art Tatum – Solos 1940* (Decca/MCA MCAD-42327), was not the most blues-oriented of players; to use Albert Murray's terms, his music has less of the percussion and incantation that Murray has located at the center of the blues sensibility. Still, the blues are there, as are the qualities of swing and pulsation that always accompany a jazz performance. Anyone who has any sense at all of what is going on at a keyboard listens to Tatum in awe.

*Solos 1940* is one of the best individual Tatum sets available, and it showcases him at his most swinging, with plenty of stride still present in his style (it tended to recede in importance in later years). The stride at the end of "Elegie" may be the most startling in its impact, but it's no more powerful than the stride on tunes like "Get Happy," the rocking "Emaline" (listen to the way he makes a countermelody with the thumb of his left hand for much of the tune), or the apocalyptic "Tiger Rag." There's even a boogie-woogie performance of "St. Louis Blues" that opens with the same device with which Meade Lux Lewis opens "Honky Tonk Train Blues," then proceeds very much in Lewis's bag. His ballad playing is heard here in such titles as "Moonglow" and "Love Me"; notice that his time is so strong that from the first notes of, say, "Moonglow," a tempo is set that one feels as a pulse whether or not it is being spelled out. These are complete arrangements, with contrast between parts, transitions, changes in mood, and constant variety in texture.

Just as good as *Solos 1940* is *Art Tatum: Classic Early Solos (1934–1937)* (Decca/GRP GRD-607). This set is particularly valuable for several alternate takes of tunes like "Liza" and "After You've Gone" on which you can hear Tatum adjust his approach to his satisfaction, thinking like a composer who hears the entire shape of the performance in his or her head. This set also includes the mind-boggling stride showpiece "The Shout," one of the most exciting and compelling things he ever recorded. Don't miss this.

As Tatum went along he began to perfect his ballad style into a florid, highly ornamented approach, in which his technique itself sometimes seemed to determine the shape of the performance. The 1949 solos collected on *Art Tatum – The Complete Capitol Recordings, Volume 1* (Capitol Jazz CDP 7 92866) and *Volume 2* (Capitol Jazz CDP 7 92867) show this aspect of his style at its peak in a program of standards such as "You Took Advantage of Me," "Nice Work If You Can Get It," "I Cover the Waterfront," and "Dancing in the Dark." Tatum's hands, by this point, were even more independent than Earl Hines's; you can hear throughout this set how Tatum will begin a careening, skittering run in his right hand, continuing it down the keyboard with his left, as his right proceeds to block out against-the-beat chords or contrary-motion arpeggios. These two discs also include some performances by his trio, with guitarist Everett Barksdale and bassist Slam Stewart, which are generally less interesting than the solo tracks.

One of the best Tatum sets ever recorded is available, but perhaps hard to find, as *20th Century Piano Genius* (EmArcy 826 129-1; no CD). The two-record set, also available on cassette, originally issued on 20th Century Fox Records, was recorded at a private party in Beverly Hills in 1955 and features Tatum at his most relaxed and inventive. It also has a strong feeling of presence, stemming perhaps from the reaction of the guests and the snatches of conversation but also from Tatum's willingness to vary the routine and take breathtaking, high-wire chances even on his most familiar material. Tatum plays all kinds of games with the harmonies of tunes like "Sweet Lorraine," "Someone to Watch Over Me," and "I'll Never Be the Same"; the set will reward whatever level of musical knowledge you bring to it. Dan Morgenstern once wrote that listening to Tatum in depth temporarily spoils one for other pianists; this is the kind of playing that will do it. Listen closely and be amazed. The liner notes by Felicity Howlett are outstanding.

Five tunes from the EmArcy set found their way onto a grab-bag Tatum album issued by the Smithsonian, entitled *Pieces of Eight* (Smithsonian Collection R029). Despite the duplication, the Smithsonian set is worth having for some fine 1939 performances and some nice mid-1940s tracks, including two fascinating back-to-back takes of "Hallelujah." The album's one trio track, "Exactly Like You," contains, as Howlett's excellent liner notes point out, a rare passage of boplike eighth-notes from the pianist's right hand. For a glimpse of Tatum in an unaccustomed role (at least on recordings), check out *Joe Turner Volume 1: I've Been to Kansas City* (Decca/MCA MCAD 42351), on which Tatum backs up the blues singer on six cuts, including the rocking "Corrine, Corrina" and the eerie "Lonesome Graveyard."

The greatest source of Tatum piano is the epic series of solo recordings he made for Verve in the 1950s (later reissued on Pablo). They are available as *The*

*Complete Pablo Solo Masterpieces* (Pablo 7 PACD-4404-2), a seven-CD boxed set, also available volume by volume in eight individual CD packages. This is the Tatum Grand Tour – hours and hours of standards played without the time restrictions of 78-rpm records (from which the Decca and Capitol material is taken), giving the most comprehensive view available of Tatum's genius. He has more time to develop his themes and ideas, and he revisits a number of tunes he recorded earlier in more compact versions. If you can afford the set and you love piano, buy it. Otherwise, any of the individual discs will only whet your appetite for the others.

*The Complete Pablo Group Masterpieces* (Pablo 6 PACD-4401-2), a six-CD companion set, also available as eight individual CDs, contains the results of all the group recordings Tatum made with various guest stars in the 1950s for Verve (again, as reissued by Pablo). Tatum, as noted, was not always as satisfying in a group context as he was solo, and only the confirmed Tatum freak will want this entire box. But all Tatum fans, and jazz fans in general, would be well advised to pick up *Art Tatum: The Tatum Group Masterpieces, Volume 2* (Pablo PACD-2405-425-2), on which Tatum is paired with trumpeter Roy Eldridge, and, especially, *Volume 8* (Pablo PACD-2405-431-2), the classic matchup with tenor saxophonist Ben Webster.

## TEDDY WILSON

Of the dominant piano stylists of the 1930s, Teddy Wilson is in some ways the easiest to overlook. He didn't have Hines's percussive extroversion or Tatum's supernatural technique or Fats Waller's overwhelming, riff-based swing. What he did have was exquisite, perfect taste, a brilliant melodic imagination, a subtle harmonic sense, and a peerless ability to accompany (especially vocalists) and to function as part of a group.

Perhaps because of this, there isn't a lot of Wilson available under his own name; to find most of his best work today, one buys recordings by Billie Holiday, Coleman Hawkins, Lester Young, Benny Goodman, and others. Herewith is a survey of where to find Wilson at his best.

Probably the most Wilson per minute can be found on the late-1930s recordings of the Benny Goodman trio and quartet, with Wilson, vibist Lionel Hampton, and drummer Gene Krupa. Wilson can be heard throughout, even when not soloing; because the trio consisted only of clarinet, piano, and drums, Wilson had a big responsibility for maintaining the harmonic base of the music while also providing variety in the ensemble texture, answering and extending Goodman's melodies (later, Hampton's vibes would distribute the work load a bit). Wilson evolved a way of using his left hand to make the fullest possible sound in this group, which lacked a bass player: he often played in a manner that suggested stride (a succession of tenths one right after the other) but that had more than a trace of Hines's and Tatum's broken runs and arpeggios. When he did solo, Wilson displayed a great talent for inventing melodies in single-note right-hand lines; these lines were the equal in melodic invention of what almost any saxophonist or trumpeter was playing at the time.

The Goodman sets *Trio and Quartet Sessions, Volume 1: After You've Gone* (RCA/Bluebird 5631-2-RB) and *Avalon – The Small Bands, Volume 2, 1937–1939* (RCA/Bluebird 2273-2-RB) present the trio and quartet in their studio recordings, doing the standards and swing specialties that made them a regular feature of Goodman's act – "China Boy," "Moonglow," "Stompin' at the Savoy," and others. *Volume 2* has only eight tracks by the original quartet and trio; on the rest of the album, various drummers come and go (including the wonderful Dave Tough), and John Kirby's bass is added for several tracks. *Volume 1* is the original two groups all the way. An interesting track for stride fans is the quartet's translation of Fats Waller's stride showpiece "Handful of Keys" on *Volume 2*; here you can hear Wilson's "walking tenths" approach especially clearly, as well as the degree of respect he had for Waller. Although it is all but useless to single out tracks because of their uniform high quality, the trio sides present Wilson in a less diluted context. But throughout, Wilson's work is, to me, the highlight of the small groups' performances. Given the demands of the bassless ensemble (as well as Goodman's reputation as a harsh taskmaster), he is the operative definiton of grace under pressure.

The trio and quartet both have fantastic moments on *Benny Goodman Live at Carnegie Hall* (Columbia G2K 40244), the famous 1938 concert performance; "China Boy" (trio) and "Dizzy Spells" (quartet), both taken at a breakneck tempo, show what the groups were capable of when they got a chance to stretch out. A 1963 reunion of the quartet, available as *Together Again!* (RCA/Bluebird 6283-2-RB), is fairly disappointing, although Goodman sounds like he's having fun; Wilson, for the most part, seems to be only going through the motions.

During the 1930s Wilson was hired to lead a series of small-band recording dates, using the best musicians available from the top big bands (black and white), for the Brunswick company; quite a few of these are available today, usually under the names of the more famous performers who were guests. One of these guests was Billie Holiday; the series of recordings she made as vocalist with Wilson-led small bands in the mid-1930s stand as perhaps her greatest work and certainly rank with the best jazz ever recorded. All nine volumes of Columbia's *The Quintessential Billie Holiday* contain excellent Wilson; some contain more than others, since Holiday sometimes recorded under her own name with other pianists.

*The Quintessential Billie Holiday, Volume 3* (Columbia CK 44048) features Wilson on all sixteen cuts, including four of Holiday's best recordings, "He Ain't Got Rhythm," "This Year's Kisses," "Why Was I Born?," and "I Must Have That Man," from a famous 1937 date with Lester Young and Benny Goodman. *Volume 4* (Columbia CK 44252) features Wilson on all but one track and contains the masterpieces "Mean to Me," "Foolin' Myself," "Easy Living," and "I'll Never Be the Same" (on which Wilson plays a full chorus, one of his finest). *Volume 1* (Columbia CK 40646) has Wilson on all but two tracks; he really romps on these 1935 cuts, over, under, around, and through Holiday's optimistic vocals (check out "What a Little Moonlight Can Do") and the solos of an all-star cast, including Ben Webster, Roy Eldridge, Chu Berry, and many others. His solos are outstanding here; for just one example of his storytelling powers and his swing, listen to what he does with his chorus on "Twenty-Four Hours a Day." The other volumes in the series are also excellent, but these are probably the standouts.

Wilson is the bandleader for four 1936 titles on a collection under trumpeter Roy Eldridge's name, entitled *Roy Eldridge – Little Jazz* (Columbia CK 45275). The classics here are "Warmin' Up" and "Blues in C Sharp Minor," but the throwaway pop tune "Mary Had a Little Lamb" has a great Wilson solo as well. And any student of the piano, or any Wilson fan, will want to pick up the monumental four-CD set *The Complete Coleman Hawkins on Keynote* (Mercury 830 960-2). Wilson is present here for five sterling 1944 sessions with the tenor patriarch; his rippling lines of pearl-like notes are a constant pleasure, and he is, as always, the perfect accompanist, adding pretty fills between Hawk's lines and shouting right-hand riffs in the out choruses of the swingers. Another compilation set on which Wilson contributes is *The Complete Edmond Hall/James P. Johnson/Sidney De Paris/Vic Dickenson Blue Note Sessions* (Mosaic MR6-109). Wilson is the pianist for six 1944 small-group tracks (two of the four titles are presented with alternate takes) under the leadership of clarinetist Edmond Hall, including the electrifying "Seein' Red," named for vibist Red Norvo, who plays on the session. This hopping, up-tempo blues has Wilson walking tenths in his left hand for all he's worth during his solo; at the end, he and Norvo goad Hall through a succession of riff-based shout choruses that will leave you hollering for more.

Two recordings from the 1950s that find Wilson in the company of his peers, both under Lester Young's name, are *Lester Young – The Jazz Giants* (Verve 825 672-2) and *Pres and Teddy* (Verve 831 270-2), recorded on consecutive days in 1956. *Pres and Teddy* has a little more Wilson on it, proportionately, than *The Jazz Giants*, on which he has to share solo space not only with Young but with trumpeter Roy Eldridge and trombone master Vic Dickenson. The bassist and drummer on both are Gene Ramey and Jo Jones, respectively. In both cases, the repertoire consists of fine standards; Wilson is consummately graceful, supportive, and lucid throughout.

## COUNT AND DUKE

The two greatest bandleaders of the swing era, Count Basie and Duke Ellington, were also two of its greatest pianists. Neither has been given his proper due; neither made a point of showing off his technique, leading some to assume that they didn't have technique. Both, however, were not just distinctive but great jazz pianists, and both had profound influence on musicians and styles that followed them.

Count Basie's recordings with his own big band are discussed in the Ensembles section; *Count Basie: The Complete Decca Recordings* (Decca/GRP GRD-3-611) and the three volumes of Columbia's *The Essential Count Basie* (CK 40608, CK 40835, CK 44150) contain masterpiece after masterpiece. Basie was both one of the best accompanists and one of the best big-band pianists. He had a way of inserting jabbed, trenchant punctuations between horn phrases at just the right moments; his choices were based on a call-and-response conception rooted in African American church music and the blues.

You can hear his approach in fine relief in various small-group recordings as well as in the previously mentioned big-band sides. *The Complete Decca Recordings* contains the great series of blues that Basie recorded with his rhythm section of bassist Walter Page, guitarist Freddie Green, and drummer Jo Jones, including "How Long Blues," "The Fives," and "Oh! Red." *Charlie Christian: The Genius of the Electric Guitar* (Columbia CK 40846) contains a number of first-rate tracks by Benny Goodman's sextet, featuring Basie as guest pianist along with Christian, the innovator of the modern guitar. Basie is also on board for a famous 1938 jam session version of "Honeysuckle Rose," available on *Benny Goodman Live at Carnegie Hall* (Columbia G2K 40244), on which his powerfully swinging accompaniment is a major reason for the high swing level behind soloists like Lester Young, Buck Clayton, and Johnny Hodges. His own solo, built mostly on right-hand riffs borrowed from Fats Waller, interspersed with Basie's own patented pointillistic motifs, draws applause midway on the basis of the sheer overwhelming swing he is able to generate, sometimes only using perfectly placed single notes.

One of the best small-group dates Basie was ever involved in was a 1944 Lester Young session for the small Keynote label, on which Basie appeared under the pseudonym Prince Charming for contractual reasons. Available on *The Complete Lester Young* (Mercury 830 920-2), the eight tracks by the Kansas City Seven (Young, Basie, trumpeter Buck Clayton, trombonist Dicky Wells, guitarist Freddie Green, bassist Rodney Richardson, and drummer Jo Jones) are fantastic small-band swing with inspired solos from all the horn players, and Basie as well. Collectors will be thrilled with the newly issued alternate takes of "After Theater Jump" and "Six Cats and a Prince." Basie plays tremendous solos throughout, as well as providing full and exciting accompaniment. His solo on "Lester Leaps Again," a compendium of riffs, is especially characteristic. In his second chorus, he trickily begins the riff that occupies his second four bars a beat early, fooling the ear into thinking he is in a different place than he actually is; Basie was a master of time. He and Young engage in some fine exchanges at the end of this track, too.

Another Kansas City Seven session, with completely different personnel except for guitarist Freddie Green, was recorded in 1962 with some latter-day Basie-ites like trumpeter Thad Jones and reed men Frank Wess and Frank Foster. *Count Basie and the Kansas City Seven* (MCA/Impulse MCAD-5656 JVC-457) is a thoroughly pleasant date, quietly swinging, revisiting a few classic Basie small-band tunes ("Oh, Lady Be Good," "Shoe Shine Boy") as well as new material. Basie illustrates the wisdom of the notion that an artist is only as good as what he or she can leave out. He leaves almost everything out of his solos here and achieves a high degree of abstraction, indeed. The band plays very well, without fireworks but swinging very solidly. Not essential, by any means, but nice.

You can't really compare Basie and Duke Ellington any more than you can compare Matisse and Picasso. What Basie did, he did better than anyone; he distilled swing down to its barest, most concentrated essence, and he showed as well as anyone ever has that blues techniques could be applied to just about any material. There could never be a better Count Basie on piano, because he himself defined a certain style of playing and took it to its limit.

That being said, it would be wrong not to acknowledge that Duke Ellington's achievement was broader in scope, ran across a broader spectrum of mood and sensibility than Basie's – or anyone's, for that matter. There is no question in my mind that, of the two, Basie swung harder at the keyboard, and Ellington tacitly admits as much in his autobiography, *Music Is My Mistress*; nor can there be a lot of argument over who was more soaked in the blues

(Basie had, after all, spent his formative musical years in Kansas City, blues territory). And yet Ellington could swing much harder than most people realize (listen to his accompaniment to Paul Gonsalves's solo on "Diminuendo and Crescendo in Blue" on *Ellington at Newport* [Columbia CK 40587] for just one example), and, although Basie could get to the very gravitational center of the blues with two notes, no one has ever done as much with the blues as a musical form as Duke Ellington. While Basie's blues tended to mine the same territory – better than anyone – Ellington wrote blues in every color, every shape, every emotional and timbral pitch, and did so for fifty years. And he was a great blues pianist as well.

In fact, Ellington was one of the most complete pianists in jazz history. He could play strong stride, he was a perfect big-band pianist, he had an immediately identifiable style, and he was a great ballad player (one of the best who ever lived) with an unerring and very sophisticated harmonic mind and an extremely expressive touch. It would be impossible to attempt a comprehensive tour of Ellington's piano work here; what follows is a highly selective look at examples of various aspects of his piano playing.

One of the best single discs you can buy for Ellington's piano is *Duke Ellington: Piano Reflections* (Capitol Jazz CDP 7 92863 2), recorded in 1953 with Wendell Marshall on bass and Butch Ballad on drums for all but three of the fifteen tracks. This is one of those magical sets, not widely known but legendary among those who do know. It contains strong blues playing at various tempos ("B Sharp Blues," on which he seems to be sending Basie a message, "Things Ain't What They Used To Be," and a smoking "Kinda Dukish" not on the original issue of this material), but it is mainly a mood album. Ellington standard ballads like "All Too Soon," "Prelude to a Kiss," and "In a Sentimental Mood" (an exceptional version of this) are revisited; more important, however, are the unique and haunting originals that appeared for the first time here – "Retrospection," "Reflections in D," "Melancholia," and "Janet."

The first three of these tunes, each exquisite in its own way, are studies in suspension of time, as if Ellington were trying, musically, to stretch one or two fleeting instants over three or four minutes. Although they bear a family resemblance, with their suspended chords and bowed pedal tones from Wendell Marshall, each conveys a subtly, but markedly, different mood. "Melancholia," especially, is a thing of amazing delicacy and strength, a precursor, in its way, to some of the things Wayne Shorter was to write in the 1960s, such as "Fall," which Miles Davis recorded and included on *Nefertiti* (Columbia CK 46113). "Melancholia" can be listened to over and over; its pattern of voice leading is as dense and poignant as the pattern of memories of friends and relationships recalled on a long afternoon. Wynton Marsalis has recorded two versions of this tune on his albums *Think of One* (Columbia CK 38641) and *Hot House Flowers* (Columbia CK 39530). "Janet" is something special and is different from the other three; it begins right on an up-tempo riff for thirty-two bars, then suddenly stops and turns into a pensive, walking-tempo ballad, with a completely contrasting theme for sixteen bars. At the end of this section, the trio goes right back into the up-tempo section, which ends in a fadeout. It works very logically; this selection, recorded three and a half years before Thelonious Monk's two-tempoed "Brilliant Corners" (on *Brilliant Corners* [Riverside/OJC-026]) – and six years after Ellington's own abstract masterpiece "The Clothed Woman" (currently unavailable), which also contains several tempos – underlines how few people have bothered to think in terms of changing tempos within a selection as well as underlining, once again, Monk's debt to Ellington. Charles Mingus, one of the few who have seriously addressed this kind of compositional complexity, was, of course, a confirmed Ellingtonian.

Another essential Ellington piano set is *Duke Ellington: Solos, Duets, and Trios* (RCA/Bluebird 2178-2-RB). It's a grab bag, containing material from as early as 1932 and as late as 1967, but it gives an excellent indication of the scope of Ellington's abilities at the keyboard. It contains the early stride showpiece "Lots O' Fingers" as well as the 1965 tribute to Willie "The Lion" Smith, "The Second Portrait of The Lion." It offers comparison between two 1941 versions of Ellington's classic mood piece "Solitude" and the very beautiful, heartfelt 1967 solo version of Billy Strayhorn's ballad "Lotus Blossom" (taken from . . . *And His Mother Called Him Bill* [RCA/Bluebird 6287-2-RB]). The main attraction here is the presence of all the results of Ellington's October 1940 duet session with bass innovator Jimmy Blanton, which is discussed in the Ensembles section.

An especially interesting track is the 1945 "Frankie and Johnny," a trio selection with bassist Junior Raglin and drummer Sonny Greer. This is a miniature suite based on folk material; it opens with a fast section in two parts – a theme statement over a sort of pastiche of boogie-woogie, then a second chorus over a cool, modern-sounding rhythm section, which segues immediately into the slow middle section. Ellington makes variations on the material here, teasing the ear with sporadic references to the earlier, fast tempo, and there is room for some Raglin-Ellington dialogue (including some jokey references to the "Salt Peanuts" riff that was in the air that spring) before they return to the faster tempo (a couple nods to Basie here). Ellington inserts various stride figures before winding up with some exciting three-way riffing involving Raglin and Greer. Ellington manages to introduce several themes at two tempos, make sly variations on them while maintaining the blues-based compositional integrity of the piece, engage in memorable improvisation, and use the resources of the piano trio fully, in well under three minutes.

*Money Jungle* (Blue Note CDP 7 46398 2), a 1962 session teaming Ellington with his disciple Charles Mingus (on bass) and drum master Max Roach, is one of the pianist's best-known albums if only because of the sheer weight of talent assembled in the studio that day. For me, this is one of those all-star dates that doesn't quite come off; the three parts of the trio don't really blend, for the most part, and Ellington sounds as if he's having trouble settling in, at least on the medium- and up-tempo blues tunes that comprise much of the set. The exceptions are the fine ballad performances of "Fleurette Africaine," "Solitude," and the rarely done "Warm Valley." My guess is that Mingus and Roach were able or willing to follow the leader a little better in these classics, which bear the mark of Ellington's compositional genius. The other Ellington originals here – such as "REM Blues," "Very Special," "Switch Blade," "Backward Country Boy Blues," and "Wig Wise" (which begins as a bop-flavored thing reminiscent of Dizzy Gillespie's "Woody'n You" but turns into a blues during the blowing section) – have a very thrown-together feel about them, as if Ellington just sketched out the barest of ideas and then they rolled the tape; none of them really goes anywhere. One note – "Backward Country Boy Blues" is a funny title because this twelve-bar blues is, literally, backward; the harmony goes to the dominant, or "five," chord in the middle four bars of each chorus and to the subdominant, or "four," chord in the last four bars, reversing the usual progression. But all in all, I have the feeling that, for whatever reason, Ellington wasn't able to exert the kind of control in this session that he needed to in order to pull together something cohesive.

Throughout Ellington's work with his own big band, late and early, there is more great piano playing than I could possibly mention. All the recordings discussed in the Ensembles section contain examples of his keyboard genius. But a couple should be pointed out again for special interest. One of these is his eleven-and-a-half-minute romp on "Ad Lib on Nippon," from 1966's *The Far East Suite* (RCA/Bluebird 7640-2-RB). This ingenious piece, despite its unusual tonality, is a blues all the way, and Ellington puts the piano through its paces, using the pedals and varying his touch to produce an astonishing range of percussive attacks. Ellington's influence on Thelonious Monk has been noted often, and this performance underscores the link in sensibility, although by this time, of course, Ellington had had the opportunity to think about what Monk was doing, too. For an example of just how directly Ellington influenced Monk, listen to the piano introduction to 1940's "Blue Goose" on *Duke Ellington: The Blanton-Webster Band* (RCA/Bluebird 5659-

2-RB). According to trumpeter Ray Nance, Ellington said, on first hearing Monk, "Sounds like he's stealing some of my stuff." Here's some pungent evidence. Another example may be heard on a recording Ellington made as a guest with the Tommy Dorsey big band in 1945, "The Minor Goes Muggin'," available on the Dorsey set *Tommy Dorsey/Yes, Indeed!* (RCA/Bluebird 9987-2-RB).

Two early-1960s sessions have Ellington at the keyboard in summit meetings with, respectively, Louis Armstrong and John Coltrane. *Louis Armstrong and Duke Ellington: The Complete Sessions* (Roulette CDP 7938442) has Ellington guesting with Armstrong's All-Stars (which included Ellington clarinet alumnus Barney Bigard) in an all-Ellington program. It is a relaxed, friendly session, including some lesser-done Ellington gems like "I'm Just a Lucky So and So" (a great vocal from Armstrong on this, with Ellington's delicious piano in the background), the beautiful "Azalea," and "Drop Me Off in Harlem." *Duke Ellington and John Coltrane* (MCA/Impulse MCAD-39103), too, is a real standout session for both principals, even better, on the whole, than *Louis Armstrong and Duke Ellington*, mainly because the accompanists are exceptional. Instead of Armstrong's good but not outstanding bassist and drummer, we get various permutations of Ellington's and Coltrane's rhythm teams, which included bassists Aaron Bell and Jimmy Garrison and drummers Sam Woodyard and Elvin Jones. It makes a difference.

The program, again, consists entirely of Ellington tunes, except for Coltrane's fetching soprano specialty "Big Nick" and Billy Strayhorn's "My Little Brown Book." Ellington, Bell, and Jones weave a haunting background around Coltrane's tenor on "In a Sentimental Mood," a classic performance of this ballad. "Take the Coltrane" is an up-tempo tenor blues riff, "Stevie" is a medium, minor blues, "Angelica" is a happy, Latin-flavored tune which Ellington also recorded as "Purple Gazelle" on his *Afro-Bossa* (Discovery 71002) album, "My Little Brown Book" rivals "In a Sentimental Mood" as a mood piece, and "The Feeling of Jazz" is a mellow, walking-tempo tune. Coltrane contributes adventuresome solos as well as lovely ballad work, and Ellington shows rhythm section sophistication of the highest degree, shifting his approach subtly but noticeably depending on which bassist and which drummer he finds himself with. Coltrane's language presents no problem for Ellington the accompanist and vice-versa. An essential set.

One last recommendation, although there is no particular point to it other than to steer you toward one of my favorite Ellington performances – be sure to listen to "The Single Petal of a Rose" from "The Queen's Suite," available on *The Ellington Suites* (Pablo/OJC-446), which you are going to want to own anyway. Duke is accompanied only by Jimmy Woode's bowed bass in one of the most moving things he ever recorded.

# BUD POWELL

Certainly one of the most influential musicians in the history of jazz, pianist Bud Powell was never as well known to the public as were his contemporaries Charlie Parker, Dizzy Gillespie, and Thelonious Monk. Throughout his career, he suffered from mental illness, and periods of amazing fluidity and brilliance alternated with times when he couldn't think clearly or, if he could, couldn't articulate what he was thinking.

But Bud Powell's best work is a unique listening experience in jazz, one of almost unparalleled intensity and beauty. His most distinct contribution to the music was a way of translating the melodic language developed by Charlie Parker into sharply etched single-note lines for the piano's right hand. His right-hand technique was so strong that he could articulate the complex accents of the new style of the time with a percussive force that made them stand out in great relief. In his most characteristic medium- and up-tempo work, Powell used his left hand to punctuate his right-hand figures with chords, much as an accompanist would add accents behind a soloist. At slow tempos, he had a rhapsodic, florid approach to chording, with dense inner voices closely harmonized. He was also, like his good friend Thelonious Monk, an important composer who added a number of standards to the jazz repertoire.

Almost without exception, every pianist who came after Powell shows his influence, especially those who are right-hand melody players. For all his technique and rapid-fire execution, Powell was basically a melodic player, as Bird was. Many players who developed strong right hands à la Powell were more arpeggio, or "sequence," players, using repeated melodic fragments for percussive effect – see, for example, Horace Silver's solo on "Filthy McNasty" from *Doin' the Thing: The Horace Silver Quintet at the Village Gate* (Blue Note 84076). But the mainstream of postwar pianists, such as Tommy Flanagan, Hank Jones, Barry Harris, Wynton Kelly, Sonny Clark, Bobby Timmons, Red Garland, Chick Corea, and Herbie Hancock, all owe a huge debt to Bud Powell.

Powell arrived on the scene almost fully formed around 1945. After 1953, because of his personal problems, his recordings became very erratic. After he moved to Europe in 1959, his situation improved somewhat, and there is some great Powell available from the 1960s.

## WAIL

Probably the best all-around introduction to Powell's sound and ideas is the Verve set *The Genius of Bud Powell* (Verve 827 901-2). Featuring Powell in both a solo and a trio setting, these 1950 and 1951 tracks show very clearly, in good sound, what made Powell unique. The opening trio tracks – "Hallelujah" and "Tea for Two" – show Powell at his most fiery, breathtakingly sure-footed at breakneck tempos, accompanied by bassist Ray Brown and drummer Buddy Rich. The three takes of "Tea" allow you to see just how inventive he was; he plays completely different ideas on each version.

"Parisian Thoroughfare," recorded here as a solo, is something of a jazz standard. Listen to the way Powell's finger control makes accents pop out of lines of notes that, in other hands, might just sound like unaccented scales. Compare it, for example, to Lennie Tristano's piano solos on the two takes of "Victory Ball," on *The Metronome All-Star Bands* (RCA/Bluebird 7636-2-RB). It is the difference between someone talking expressively and someone accenting all their syllables the same. This is the most characteristic aspect of Powell's single-note lines, and it is why they are so interesting to listen to. Notice how Powell inserts triplets into a line of eighth notes in order to vary the rhythm and shape his ideas in more detail.

The same can be said for all the solo performances here, including "Hallucinations" (which Miles Davis recorded as "Budo" on both *Birth of the Cool* [Capitol CDP 7 92862 2] and *Miles and Coltrane* [Columbia CK 44052]), "Oblivion," and the others. On the popular song "The Last Time I Saw Paris," Powell even plays some stride piano in his left hand while playing bop single-note lines in his right, showing the continuity underneath the changing assumptions of jazz.

At opposite ends of the spectrum, but characteristic of the extremes of Powell's temperament, are "Dusk in Sandi" and "Just One of Those Things." "Dusk" is a ballad written by Powell and voiced in lush, florid chords with patented voicings. "Just One of Those Things" is a reading of Cole Porter's great standard at a tempo no other pianist but Tatum would dare; Powell's right-hand lines have the force of something under tremendous pressure coming out through a very small opening. The tension is exhausting; it's hard to imagine someone thinking coherently, not to mention brilliantly, at this speed.

*Jazz Giant* (Verve 829 937-2) is a fine companion piece to *The Genius of Bud Powell*, consisting entirely of trio sides recorded in 1949 and 1950, with Max Roach on drums and either Ray Brown or Curly Russell on bass. Powell is in a somewhat mellower mood here than he was with Brown and Rich, although there are several up-tempo showpieces, like the fine "Sweet Georgia Brown" and Powell's own "Tempus Fugit," also recorded by Miles Davis for Blue Note. But basically this set is most valuable for the medium-tempo readings of Powell originals such as "Celia" and "So Sorry Please" and the beautiful readings of several standard ballads, including a solo version of "Yesterdays" and a great trio version of "Body and Soul," which shows Powell's melodic inventiveness perhaps more clearly than some of the up-tempo numbers. Also not to be missed is his solo version of his own ballad "I'll Keep Loving You."

Almost as good as *The Genius of Bud Powell* (some would say better) is *The Amazing Bud Powell, Volume 1* (Blue Note 81503) and *Volume 2* (Blue Note 81504), culled from several recording sessions, with Powell at the helm of both trios and a quintet including trumpeter Fats Navarro and a nineteen-year-old Sonny Rollins on tenor sax. Some of his greatest statements are here, including the amazing, Latin-inflected "Un Poco Loco," presented in three electrifying takes in which you can hear the trio's conception develop right before your ears. His trio version of "A Night in Tunisia," recorded at the same session, is classic Powell, driving and endlessly inventive, as are two takes of Charlie Parker's "Ornithology" and a trio version of "Parisian Thoroughfare," which Powell plays on *The Genius of Bud Powell* set as a solo.

The quintet sides present several Powell compositions – "Bouncing with Bud," "Wail," and "Dance of the Infidels" – that became jazz standards and a Monk composition, "52nd Street Theme." Along with excellent solos from Powell and the others, these well-recorded sides give you a chance to listen closely to the choices Powell made when accompanying a soloist, the answering chords always contributing to the rhythmic momentum and forward movement of the solo and commenting on the soloist's harmonic choices; listen to how when Navarro or Rollins finishes a phrase, Powell will insert a short answering rhythmic phrase in chords. This technique is discussed more fully in the Ensembles section. Finally, some tracks by his 1953 trio with George Duvivier and Art Taylor, including "Reets and I," Oscar Pettiford's "Collard Greens and Black Eyed Peas" (also called "Blues in the Closet"), and the fine "I Want To Be Happy," are only slightly less excellent.

Powell was used widely as a sideman on some of the best, most famous small-group bop dates of the late 1940s. Albums such as *Fats Navarro: Fat Girl* (Savoy SJL 2216), *Dexter Gordon: Long Tall Dexter* (Savoy SJL 2211), *J. J. Johnson: Mad Bebop* (Savoy SJL 2232), *The Complete Charlie Parker Savoy Studio Sessions* (Savoy ZDS 5500), *The Be Bop Boys* (Savoy SJL 2225), and *Sonny Stitt/Bud Powell/J. J. Johnson* (Prestige/OJC-009) all present Powell in the company of other giants; he never failed to raise the stakes at a session. When Powell was there, a certain intensity and pressure were on that simply weren't there with any other pianist of the time.

One of Powell's best trio dates, recorded for the small Roost label, is available as *The Bud Powell Trio Plays* (Roulette CDP 7939022). Eight sides from a 1947 session with Curly Russell and Max Roach present Powell at his electrifying best on popular and jazz standards like "I'll Remember April," "Nice Work if You Can Get It," "Bud's Bubble," Monk's "Off Minor," and "Somebody Loves Me." These share a berth with eight mostly funereal 1953 sides that can't match the earlier ones for intensity, invention, or precision of execution. But piano and bebop fans will find the set essential for the earlier eight. Also worth checking out is *Charlie Parker and the Stars of Modern Jazz at Carnegie Hall, Christmas 1949* (Jass J-CD-16), which features Powell in one trio track and as the pianist for a jam session including Miles Davis, Sonny Stitt, baritone saxophonist Serge Chaloff, and others.

Although Powell and Parker don't play together on *Christmas 1949*, there are several recordings of the two together, live. They brought out the most fiery sides of each other. The sparks fly especially hard on a 1950 session at Birdland that has been issued in as many different forms as John Dillinger had aliases, often on budget and bootleg labels. Columbia issued the complete session in the late 1970s as *One Night at Birdland*. Look for the combination of Bird, Powell, and trumpeter Fats Navarro; the three only recorded together once, so you'll know you have the right session (Curly Russell and drummer Art Blakey rounded out the band). It produced some of the most intense bebop you'll ever hear. Powell's solos on "Ornithology" (available on *The Bebop Era* [Columbia CK 40972]; the collection is worth buying for this track alone), "The Street Beat," "I'll Remember April," "Move," "Dizzy Atmosphere," and the other fast numbers generate a drive that overshadows even that of Bird and Navarro. His solo on the very slow " 'Round Midnight," on the other hand, is an almost frightening look deep into Powell's soul. Often when Powell's demons were out and about they blunted his ability to articulate what he was seeing. Not so, here; Powell was never in better form, and this solo is worthy of the nightmares in Goya's *Caprichos*.

Easily available, and at the top of the heap, is one of the unquestioned classics of the music, *Jazz at Massey Hall* (Debut/OJC-044, usually filed under Parker's name in stores), a 1953 Toronto concert which finds Powell in the company of Parker, Dizzy Gillespie, Charles Mingus, and Max Roach, easily one of the greatest all-star bands ever assembled. Powell's solos on "Wee," "Hot House," and "A Night in Tunisia" are right up with his best work, and his accompaniments are perfect. Some trio tracks from the same concert are available on *Bud Powell Trio: Jazz at Massey Hall, Volume 2* (Debut/OJC-111), which is also well worth owning, although some inferior material from a different session is along for the ride. Slightly earlier the same year, Powell and Mingus appeared at a club in Washington, D.C., with Roy Haynes on drums; the album assembled from the tapes of that afternoon, *Inner Fires* (Elektra/

Musician E1-60030), contains some excellent, lucid Powell at near-peak form, but the sound is really hard to take. Good as Powell's playing is, I find myself taking this one off after a cut or two.

## DRY SOUL

For the next seven years, Powell's career went into something of an eclipse. His mental problems were plaguing him, and often his playing suffered. None of the material he recorded before he moved to Europe in 1959 can stand up to his early recordings, although some of it is quite beautiful in its own way, if you're not expecting 1950-vintage Powell. But even at his best, his playing lacked an assurance that it would regain – and lose again – when he moved to Europe.

Powell recorded several more times for Verve, but the results are unavailable currently; there is some good material, especially an album released originally as *Piano Interpretations*, but it all falls short of what he could do. On this, some recordings for Victor, and two of Powell's late-1950s Blue Note sessions, he sounded, pianistically, like someone slurring his words.

Two albums that are worth passing up are *The Amazing Bud Powell, Volume 3: Bud!* (Blue Note 81571) and *Volume 4: Time Waits* (Blue Note 46820). On the first, from 1957, he is heard with a trio including Paul Chambers and Art Taylor; they are joined for three tunes by trombonist Curtis Fuller, but Powell was just not in good shape. "Blue Pearl" is a nice original by Powell, and he plays some good things, but you can tell that he is hearing so much more than he is able to play: phrases get garbled before they end, fingerings disintegrate. It's painful to listen to. The same is true of the 1958 *Time Waits*, another trio album, although there are some good originals, including the haunting title cut and the up-tempo "John's Abbey," which became a staple of his repertoire in the following years.

Somewhat better is *Time Was* (RCA/Bluebird 6367-2-RB). This material, recorded in 1956 and 1957 with George Duvivier and Art Taylor, is often either overlooked or put down, but I find it superior to the previously mentioned Blue Notes from the same period, as well as to the mid-1950s Verve material. Powell plays with a lot more authority on the 1956 titles, although sometimes his phrases end up not quite working out. But his swing on standards like "There Will Never Be Another You" and "I Cover the Waterfront" is beautiful and unforced, and he plays fresh ideas, sometimes in a block-chord style (in which a melodic line is voiced all in chords). "Blues for Bessie" affords a rare chance to hear Powell dig into some slow blues, with interesting results.

He has a harder time on the 1957 titles, where you can hear him struggling to stay on the horse during a runaway version of "Salt Peanuts" that he counted off at too fast a tempo. On the swingers here, such as "Swedish Pastry" and "Midway," you can hear the main difference between early Bud and Bud from this period: in the earlier days he accented individual notes in the middle of his long lines of eighth notes; here he tends to play them more evenly, and it is why the music sounds less intense. Still, if you don't expect the Powell of "Bud's Bubble," this is worth buying for its excellent sound and a relaxed side of Powell that isn't heard too often.

The 1958 session released as *The Amazing Bud Powell, Volume 5: The Scene Changes* (Blue Note 46529) is very good Powell; he seems in complete control here, where he is accompanied by Paul Chambers and Art Taylor. The all-original program elicits probably the best music he had recorded since 1953. It wouldn't be in my top five Powell picks, but it is worth owning.

An important note: this album, along with the classic 1949 quintet date with Fats Navarro and Sonny Rollins, the 1951 trio date that produced "Un Poco Loco" and "A Night in Tunisia," and all the other Blue Note Powell, as well as the Roost trio sides, is available in a deluxe four-CD set from Blue Note entitled *The Complete Blue Note and Roost Recordings* (Blue Note CDP 7243 8 30083 2 2). For a Powell fan, this collection is essential. It includes a fine booklet with recording-session photos and an interview with Blue Note producer Alfred Lion about Powell, and the sound is excellent.

### THE SCENE CHANGES

When Powell moved to Europe in 1959, he took a turn for the better; he was surrounded by people to whom his genius was apparent and respected, and he was given all the playing opportunities he wanted. His recordings from the 1960–1962 period reflect this relative well-being.

Probably the all-around most satisfying Powell album from this period was recorded in April of 1960 at a jazz festival in Germany. Available as *The Complete Essen Jazz Festival Concert* (Black Lion BLCD 760 105), it features Powell in a trio with bassist Oscar Pettiford and drummer Kenny Clarke; on four tunes – "All the Things You Are," "Yesterdays," a stomping riff called "Stuffy," and "Just You, Just Me" – they are joined by a roaring Coleman Hawkins. The sound is good, and Powell sounds happy. His accompaniments and solos on the cuts with Hawkins are especially thrilling, and Pettiford's bass gives the rhythm a buoyancy that really goads Bud.

Neck and neck with *Essen*, and in some ways even better, is *Bouncing with Bud* (Delmark DD-406). Recorded two years later in Copenhagen, the album is a program of medium- and up-tempo bop standards such as "Bouncing with Bud," "Move," and "Hot House," along with one ballad, Benny Golson's "I Remember Clifford." When Powell was at his best in the late years, he played with a crispness of articulation and swing that had been missing for most of the 1950s, but he often relied on familiar scalar patterns in his solos. But here Powell is extremely inventive, full of fresh melodic ideas, especially on "Bouncing" and "Straight, No Chaser."

Also from Powell's stay in Copenhagen, recorded in April 1962, are five volumes on the Steeplechase label, entitled *Bud Powell Trio at the Golden Circle*. Passages of great inventiveness come cheek-by-jowl with periods where Powell phases out completely; listening at these moments is a disturbing experience. One example is a long version of Pettiford's "Blues in the Closet" on volume 2. You can hear Powell getting interested in what he is playing, then losing interest. On one version of Charlie Parker's "Moose the Mooche," also on volume 2, Powell will stop playing for a couple of bars at a time, then pick up a melodic line right in the middle, as if it had been going through his head but he had just forgotten to play it. At such moments, we are afforded a glimpse straight down into the void of time over which good music usually rocks us in steady arms. (All jazz musicians experience moments when they are playing more or less automatically, without meaning what they are saying, the way you might walk down the street and pick up your laundry, buy a paper, and let yourself back into your apartment without really being present in those actions.) Powell is accompanied by a local bassist and drummer who aren't too swinging, and the performances bog down sometimes. But then there are other tracks where he is extremely aware of what he is doing, full of allusions and new melodies.

A very good album of live Powell, recorded in a French nightclub in 1961, is *A Portrait of Thelonious*. Out of print, it is still sporadically available and should be re-released by Columbia sooner or later. Powell, accompanied by the French bassist Pierre Michelot and drummer Kenny Clarke, who was making his home in Europe at that point, performs Monk's "Off Minor," "Ruby, My Dear," "Thelonious," and "Monk's Mood" with an understanding that is rare for any pianist other than Monk to achieve. But that's what twenty years of friendship and mutual respect will do for you. The other tracks are good, too. *Shaw 'Nuff* (Xanadu CD FDC 5167) contains much swinging but not always super-inventive Powell from his first year in Europe, including two unaccompanied duets with tenor saxophonist Johnny Griffin. The sound isn't very good, and Powell's characteristic grunting and growling are often as audible as his piano.

Powell recorded several times as a sideman in Europe. The most interesting is probably a long version of "I'll Remember April" recorded at a jazz festival in Antibes in the summer of 1960, when Powell sat in with Charles Mingus's band. Available on *Mingus at Antibes* (Atlantic 90532-2), the tune features a fine extended solo by Powell, as well as the chance to hear him accompanying Eric Dolphy and Booker Ervin. Powell isn't quite as sparkling on Dexter Gordon's *Our Man in Paris* (Blue Note 46394), which is too bad; they had struck hot sparks off each other on their 1946 sides for Savoy (on *Dexter Gordon: Long Tall Dexter* [Savoy SJL 2211]). But the "Stairway to the Stars" here is almost worth the price of admission.

## ALL BUD'S CHILDREN

As noted earlier, Bud Powell influenced just about every pianist who came along after him (as did Art Tatum). Most pianists who came of age in the 1950s accompanied soloists using Powell's principles, if not his actual sound, and their solos (in group performances) were also based on his solo approach: single-note right-hand lines rooted in bebop, accompanied by percussive and broken chords in the left hand.

The number of exceptional pianists who came along in Powell's wake is startling. Often they made their most remembered statements as sidemen with horn-playing leaders (as Red Garland did with Miles Davis, for example); often, too, they made trio sessions that are worth tracking down. Because so many good jazz records were made in the 1950s, and almost all of them used someone from the stable of fine pianists, a comprehensive list of where to find whom is impossible here. This is a highly selective guide to some of these pianists' best dates as leaders, as well as to really outstanding sessions on which they appear as sidemen.

One of the most influential of the 1950s pianists was Wynton Kelly, who was one of everybody's favorite accompanists. Kelly lent a special crispness and heat to rhythm sections; as a soloist, he had a popping, sharply articulated, very bluesy style, which can be heard on two small-group sessions under his leadership: *Wynton Kelly Piano* (Riverside/OJC-401), with Paul Chambers, Philly Joe Jones, and guitarist Kenny Burrell, and *Kelly Blue* (Riverside/OJC-033), which features both a trio with Chambers and Jimmy Cobb and a sextet that adds Nat Adderley's trumpet and the saxes of Benny Golson and the too little known Bobby Jaspar. The sets were cut in 1958 and 1959, respectively, when Kelly was a member of Miles Davis's band. Both show off Kelly's incisive, staccato, on-top-of-the-beat approach to good advantage.

Good as these sets are, Kelly was probably at his best as a member of a rhythm section supporting one or more strong solo voices; he was certainly one of the best accompanists ever to play jazz, as a rundown of some of the recordings to which he contributed proves. With Davis (who loved Kelly's playing), Kelly recorded one track on *Kind of Blue* (Columbia CK 40579), "Freddie Freeloader," and the wonderful *Someday My Prince Will Come* (Columbia CK 40947); his playing is like fresh spring air throughout the latter set. John Coltrane was playing tenor in Davis's band at the time, and he used Kelly on his own 1959 session that was released as *Coltrane Jazz* (Atlantic 1354-2), a very strong set in which it is easy to see how much Coltrane's subsequent pianist, McCoy Tyner, learned from Kelly. Kelly takes an especially swinging solo on "My Shining Hour." The Miles Davis rhythm section of Kelly, Chambers, and Jimmy Cobb does an excellent job of showing alto saxophonist Art Pepper in the best light on the 1960 *Gettin' Together* (Contemporary/OJC-169), worth buying for Kelly alone.

Kelly is the pianist on Sonny Rollins's *Volume 1* (Blue Note 81542) and *Newk's Time* (Blue Note 84001); the latter is a quartet set that has Kelly at his best, and at some length. Another tenorist who loved Kelly's playing was Hank Mobley; they are together for Mobley's classic albums *Soul Station* (Blue Note 46528), *Workout* (Blue Note 84080), the highly recommended quartet cooker *Another Workout* (Blue Note 84431), and the incendiary *Roll Call* (Blue Note 46823), on which Mobley is joined by trumpeter Freddie Hubbard. See the Mobley section for further details. Some of Kelly's best playing may be found (if you can find the record, that is; it isn't yet on CD) on an outstanding album by trumpeter Blue Mitchell, *Blue's Moods* (Riverside/OJC-138). Kelly's solos on the medium-up swingers "I'll Close My Eyes" and "I Wish I Knew" are definitive and would be worth buying the record for themselves. He is also a major factor in the savage swing level on a 1954 date under trombonist J. J. Johnson's leadership, available on *The Eminent Jay Jay Johnson, Volume 2* (Blue Note 81506); the six cuts with Kelly, including "Old Devil Moon," "Too Marvelous for Words," and the up-tempo blues "Jay," are outstanding. Kelly shares the rhythm duties with bassist Charles Mingus and drummer Kenny Clarke; conga drummer Sabu gives the rhythm an extra kick that really makes these go. On "Jay," by the way, notice how in the final riff choruses Johnson thought to build excitement by raising the key a half step each chorus; the effect is thrilling.

Finally, no picture of Wynton Kelly would be complete without *Smokin' at the Half Note* (Verve 829 578-2), recorded with guitar giant Wes Montgomery at the New York City club in 1965. Accompanied by Paul Chambers and Jimmy Cobb, Kelly and Montgomery turn up the heat in a mixed program of ballads and cookers; Kelly's solo on the medium-up "No Blues" is an especially good example of his ability to sustain a soulful, swinging groove. They are together, too, for an exciting 1961 date pairing Montgomery with vibes giant Milt Jackson; *Bags Meets Wes* (Riverside/OJC-234) is a great showcase for the guitarist's unique sound, achieved by often playing his melodic lines in octaves rather than single notes. The excellent rhythm section is Kelly, Sam Jones, and Philly Joe Jones. Also fine is the 1962 Montgomery album *Full House* (Riverside/OJC-106), recorded live, with Kelly, Paul Chambers, and Jimmy Cobb, and tenorist Johnny Griffin as special guest.

If anyone could rival Wynton Kelly in the sideman derby, it would be the Detroit master Tommy Flanagan. Flanagan is, to this day, one of the most respected musicians in jazz; pianists always speak of him with reverence. His chordal sense is just about unrivaled, and his touch is capable of almost infinite gradation; at his best he is fantastically inventive, and he is comfortable playing with anyone.

Flanagan has been the pianist on a dauntingly high number of classic jazz albums; he has a way of bringing out the best in other musicians, and a number of giants have made either their greatest, or one of their greatest, statements with Flanagan at the keyboard. He was the pianist on Sonny Rollins's *Saxophone Colossus* (Prestige/OJC-291), John Coltrane's *Giant Steps* (Atlantic 1311-2), Gene Ammons's *Boss Tenor* (Prestige/OJC-297), *At Ease with Coleman Hawkins* (Prestige/OJC-181), the three 1956 Miles Davis quintet sides with Sonny Rollins included on *Collectors' Items* (Prestige/OJC-071), Dexter Gordon's *The Panther* (Prestige/OJC-770), Kenny Dorham's *Trompeta Toccata* (Blue Note 84181), and Wes Montgomery's *Incredible Jazz Guitar* (Riverside/OJC-036), to name just a handful. Flanagan always brings a sympathetic set of ears to a session, and his accompaniments are perfectly adapted to whomever he is playing with. His solos are often as memorable as those of the headliners on these records; for just three examples, listen to his unique, moody solo on "D Natural Blues" on the Montgomery album, his exquisite statement on "In Your Own Sweet Way" on *Collectors' Items*, and his solo on the up-tempo blues "No Line," also on the Davis set. These are the work of a truly creative artist.

Flanagan had recorded only sparingly as a leader before the end of the 1970s, when he began to record, and perform, prolifically at the helm of a trio. I have yet to hear anything by him that isn't first-rate. Special mention might be made of his all-Ellington (and Strayhorn) *The Tommy Flanagan Tokyo Recital* (Pablo 2310-724), the 1978 *Something Borrowed, Something Blue* (Galaxy/OJC-473), and a live 1986 recording, *Nights at the Vanguard* (Uptown UP27.29). Another Flanagan talent is revealed by his choice of material; the Vanguard set, for example, includes lesser-known tunes by Thelonious Monk, Benny Golson, Lucky Thompson, Phil Woods, and Thad Jones, as well as the standard bebop test piece "All God's Children Got Rhythm." Also very rewarding are two volumes of unaccompanied duets with pianist Hank Jones, *Our Delights* (Galaxy/OJC-752) and *More Delights* (Galaxy GXY-5152, cassette only).

Hank Jones is on the highest level as a pianist. A Detroiter, like Flanagan, who came to New York in the mid-1940s, he is the brother of drummer Elvin Jones and trumpeter Thad Jones. He can play authoritatively in any idiom of the music; he has been the pianist in the popular musical *Ain't Misbehavin'*, with its Fats Waller–based repertoire, has recorded albums of ragtime and spirituals, has worked with possibly every great jazz horn player, including Lester Young, Coleman Hawkins, Miles Davis, and Charlie Parker, and has recorded with musicians of every stylistic persuasion. His harmonic sophistication, melodic inventiveness in solos, and sensitivity in accompaniment are the equal of Flanagan's; the range of styles at which he is convincing is, if anything, even greater.

Jones, too, has been a sideman on an extraordinary number of first-rate recordings. His crisp, inventive soloing and accompaniment can be heard on *Ben Webster and "Sweets" Edison: Ben and Sweets* (Columbia CK 40853), Wes Montgomery's *So Much Guitar!* (Riverside/OJC-233), Cannonball Adderley's *Somethin' Else* (Blue Note 46338) with Miles Davis, *Bags & Trane* (Atlantic 1368-2), Lucky Thompson's phenomenal *Lucky Strikes* (Prestige/OJC-194), and an album by bassist Paul Chambers, *Bass on Top* (Blue Note 46533), on which the bass is the lead instrument, accompanied by Jones, guitarist Kenny Burrell, and drummer Art Taylor. Jones and Burrell get a fair amount of solo room as well. Jones is a hero of all these sessions. For three examples, listen to his ballad work on "In a Sentimental Mood" from *Lucky Strikes*, his delicate yet absolutely smoking solo on "Better Go" from the Webster-Edison set, and his quiet magic on "Autumn Leaves" from *Somethin' Else*. Pure beauty, pure soul.

Jones, like Flanagan, has had a renaissance of activity as a leader since the late 1970s. Of special interest is a set of unaccompanied solos, recorded in 1977 and 1978, entitled *Tiptoe Tapdance* (Galaxy/OJC-719). The album mixes fine standards like "I'll Be Around" and "I Didn't Know What Time It Was" with moving versions of three spirituals, "It's Me Oh Lord," "Love Divine, All Loves Surpassing," and "Lord, I Want To Be a Christian." And make sure to hear his two volumes of unaccompanied duets with Tommy Flanagan, mentioned earlier.

Another Detroit pianist who has contributed to many an excellent session is Barry Harris. Of all the pianists discussed here, Harris is the most steeped in the vocabulary of Bud Powell and Charlie Parker, a bebop player first, last, and always. While he is perhaps not as adaptable to as wide a range of styles as either Jones or Flanagan, Harris has no equal when it comes to a bop sound. Two prime examples of this are the classic 1972 Sonny Stitt quartet album *Constellation* (Muse MCD 5323) and trumpeter Red Rodney's 1973 quintet date *Bird Lives!* (Muse MCD 5371). Both have Sam Jones on bass and the underrated Roy Brooks on drums; the Rodney album also features alto saxophonist Charles McPherson. Throughout, Harris's choices in accompaniment, his timing, and his sense of where to place chords under soloists are straight from Powell. In his solos, his way of fitting scales to chords is straight Parker and Powell, but Harris's touch is all his own. A real high point is his solo on "I'll Remember April" on the Rodney set, an extended outing at a cruising, medium-up tempo on which his ideas and inspiration run hot. The Stitt set, recorded a year earlier, finds Harris playing with a slightly more percussive touch; the change was likely due to his decision, around that time, to begin studies with a classical teacher. The somewhat earlier *Bebop Revisited!* (Prestige/ OJC-710), a fiery 1964 album by Charles McPherson, has Harris on piano for a program consisting of classic bop repertoire like Bud Powell's "Wail," Tadd Dameron's "Hot House," Fats Navarro's "Nostalgia," and several others. Harris plays 100 percent pure bebop throughout an excellent small-group jazz set.

Two trio albums for Riverside show an even younger Harris bopping resolutely through sets that mix good pop tunes, bop standards, and a few originals. *Preminado* (Riverside/OJC-486) is probably the better of the two, if you can overlook the slightly out-of-tune piano; Joe Benjamin and Elvin Jones give Harris strong support on a varied program including a fast "What Is This Thing Called Love?" and a groovy, medium-tempo "My Heart Stood Still." *At the Jazz Workshop* (Riverside/OJC-208) has Harris's rhythm sectionmates from the Cannonball Adderley group of the time, Sam Jones and Louis Hayes, joining the pianist on bop standards like "Woody'n You," "Moose the Mooche," and "Star Eyes."

Harris also lends strong support on albums as different as Lee Morgan's 1963 *The Sidewinder* (Blue Note 84157), *Bottoms Up: Illinois Jacquet on Prestige* (Prestige/OJC-417), and Dexter Gordon's *The Tower of Power* (Prestige/OJC-299). In the mid-1970s Harris was the house pianist at the small Xanadu label, run by veteran producer Don Schlitten, who also produced the Jacquet, Gordon, Stitt, and Rodney recordings just mentioned. Schlitten's devotion to bebop equals Harris's; for Xanadu, Harris made a number of albums as a leader, the best of which are *Live in Tokyo* (Xanadu 130) and *Barry Harris Plays Barry Harris* (Xanadu 154), a trio date (with George Duvivier on bass) comprised entirely of Harris's own beautiful compositions. Harris is the perfect accompanist for his one-time student Charles McPherson on *Charles McPherson Live in Tokyo* (Xanadu 131) and for tenorist Al Cohn on *Al Cohn's America*

(Xanadu 138). These Xanadu items may be hard to track down, but they are all worth it.

Certainly one of the best pianists of the 1950s, and a gifted composer as well, was Sonny Clark. Clark's playing was rooted in Powell's vocabulary; he was an inventive spinner of right-hand melodies, especially effective at medium tempos. Two trio sets, both called *Sonny Clark Trio*, are highly recommended for all pianists and piano fans. The one on Blue Note (Blue Note 46547) has Paul Chambers on bass and Philly Joe Jones on drums and consists of pop and jazz standards like "I Didn't Know What Time It Was," "I'll Remember April," and "Two Bass Hit." It is an archetypal bebop piano trio outing. The other *Sonny Clark Trio* (Time/Bainbridge BCD 1044) has Clark with the equally formidable support of George Duvivier and Max Roach in a program consisting entirely of Clark originals. If I had to choose one, it would be the second one; the Time set has a presence and inventiveness that put it just ahead of the other for me. Clark's tunes always sound fresh, and they inspire him and his sidemen to equally fresh blowing. Listen to the way Clark cooks his way through chorus after chorus of "Blues Mambo" or to his slower "Blues Blue." And his unaccompanied "My Conception" is something else. Fantastic stuff.

Clark assembled several small-group recording dates for Blue Note featuring all-star casts playing a mixture of Clark's own tunes and standards. The best known of these is *Cool Struttin'* (Blue Note 46513), a 1958 date with trumpeter Art Farmer, altoist Jackie McLean, and Paul Chambers and Philly Joe Jones in the rhythm section. The CD issue of this adds two tracks to the familiar "Cool Struttin'," "Blue Minor," "Sippin' at Bells," and "Deep Night" (a trio performance) from the original LP. This set has the feeling of a blowing session, but everyone makes very pointed, cohesive statements; it is a quintessential hard-bop date, cooking all the way.

Somewhat less well known (perhaps because it lacks the all-star element of *Cool Struttin'*) is the great *Leapin' and Lopin'* (Blue Note 84091), a 1961 date with trumpeter Tommy Turrentine and tenorist Charlie Rouse, with Butch Warren and Billy Higgins providing their customary fine accompaniment. Clark's tunes here are all excellent, from the opening minor blues "Somethin' Special," through the happy, cool-sounding, modal "Melody for C" and the mysterioso but humorous "Voodoo" (which tips its hat to Thelonious Monk), to the previously unreleased swinger "Zellmar's Delight," which echoes Tadd Dameron beautifully. Clark's accompaniment here is always extremely alert and smart; you can hear him thinking compositionally, setting up patterns under the soloists (as always, Rouse presents his credentials as a major tenor voice) and working off of Higgins's accents. His solos are all gems, as well.

*Sonny's Crib* (Blue Note 46819), from 1957, is the least interesting of the three group sessions, despite the presence of John Coltrane's tenor saxophone in the front line with Donald Byrd's trumpet and Curtis Fuller's trombone (Paul Chambers and Art Taylor fill out the rhythm section); it contains two long takes apiece of "With a Song in My Heart" and "Speak Low," and a long version of "Come Rain or Come Shine." The set gains its main distinction from the presence of one of Clark's best tunes, the tantalizingly arranged "News for Lulu."

Clark was very active as a sideman throughout the 1950s and the early 1960s. If you like his playing and would like to hear him as a sideman on a session that gives satisfaction on every level, pick up tenorist Dexter Gordon's quartet masterpieces *Go!* (Blue Note 46094) and *A Swingin' Affair* (Blue Note 84133), recorded two days apart in 1962. Gordon is in top form, Clark is in top form, bassist Butch Warren and drummer Billy Higgins are in top form, and together they laid down some immortal jazz. Clark's work on *The Complete Verve Recordings of the Buddy De Franco Quartet/Quintet with Sonny Clark* (Mosaic MD4-117), from 1954 and 1955, is in a slightly less developed vein than the material mentioned previously, although these sides with one of the few bop clarinetists are enjoyable.

A unique and unclassifiable pianist and composer of the 1950s who recorded very little was Herbie Nichols. Nichols made most of his living playing with traditional jazz bands or in any other honorable situation that would sustain him financially. But he made a series of trio recordings for Blue Note in 1955 and 1956, with either Art Blakey or Max Roach on drums, that show him to have been an interesting composer and pianist, obviously influenced by Monk and Ellington but with a wryness and formal originality that were all his own. These recordings are collected on *The Complete Blue Note Recordings of Herbie Nichols* (Mosaic MD3-118), a worthwhile set for anyone interested in jazz piano or the possibilities of jazz composition. By all accounts, Nichols was a soft-spoken, very intelligent man; his playing and compositions reflect both qualities. His work is an acquired taste, but very rewarding. Young musicians, in particular, will find in Nichols many interesting ideas, as well as some healthy challenges to tried-and-true formulas.

Red Garland, the pianist with the original Miles Davis quintet, with John Coltrane, Paul Chambers, and Philly Joe Jones, is one of the most underrated pianists in jazz. He was a distinctive stylist, a fine accompanist, an arsonist in a rhythm section, and one of the hardest-swinging soloists around in the late 1950s. For evidence of this last claim, acquire a copy of his album *High Pressure* (Prestige/OJC-349) and proceed directly to the first track, the popping, up-tempo blues "Soft Winds." For over seven minutes (until John Coltrane enters with a roaring solo), Garland serves up a graduate-level lesson in blues-ology, swing, and riffsmanship. Like tenorist Sonny Stitt, Garland sometimes seems to be an encyclopedia of well-known phrases and devices; what sets both of them apart from average players is not only the phenomenal reper-toire of phrases they command but the flexibility and wit with which they de-ploy them and the pure swing and exhilaration in that deployment.

Garland was, in Davis's group, a member of one of the most famous rhythm sections that ever existed; you can hear them at work in the Prestige quintet sets (see the Davis section), on 'Round About Midnight (Columbia CK 40610) and, especially, on Milestones (Columbia CK 40837), with Garland's up-tempo version of "Billy Boy." (A technical note: Garland's signature sound, al-though usually referred to as a block-chord technique, comes not from block chords, in which all the notes move as the melody moves, in harmony and counterpoint. What Garland does is to play the melody either in octaves or in a line of single notes, along with chords that remain constant until the back-ground harmony shifts.) A funny moment in this album occurs in "Straight, No Chaser," when Garland inserts a two-chorus-long quote from Davis's solo on Charlie Parker's 1945 "Now's the Time," available on Bird/The Savoy Re-cordings (Master Takes) Volume 1 (Savoy ZDS 4402). The Garland-Chambers-Jones trio occasionally found itself backing other horn players, as it did on an excellent album by the California altoist Art Pepper, Art Pepper Meets the Rhythm Section (Contemporary/OJC-338).

When Garland recorded on his own – as he did, copiously, for Prestige in the late 1950s – he usually used Art Taylor on drums and either Chambers or George Joyner (later known as Jamil Nasser) on bass. It is possible to be happy in life with only a few of the many albums that Garland cut; a certain sameness begins to be apparent after a while. Still, one needs at least one or two Garland sets around, just as one needs an umbrella, or a jar of peanut butter, or a spring-weight jacket. You won't die without them, but they improve the qual-ity of life. Certainly the version of the blues ballad "Please Send Me Someone to Love" on Red Garland's Piano (Prestige/OJC-073), with its perfect dance-floor, belly-rub, walking tempo, is not the kind of thing you want to go too long without hearing. The rest of this set is fine, too, a mixture of ballads like "The Very Thought of You" and medium-tempo groovers like "Stompin' at the Savoy" and "But Not for Me." This is a classic example of the piano trio genre.

The same can be said for the ace set Red in Bluesville (Prestige/OJC-295), on which Sam Jones replaces Paul Chambers on bass. This one has Garland ex-ploring six different blues, material as traditional as the slow "See See Rider" and "Trouble in Mind." Garland's quintet albums with John Coltrane, High

*Pressure* (Prestige/OJC-349), the fine *All Mornin' Long* (Prestige/OJC-293), *Dig It!* (Prestige/OJC-392), and *Soul Junction* (Prestige/OJC-481), are all worth having. If one has a yen for Garland, John Coltrane's *Black Pearls* (Prestige/OJC-352) should be procured for the pianist's long solo on the swinging "Sweet Sapphire Blues."

## OTHER STYLISTS

Garland's replacement in the Davis group was Bill Evans, who was to become one of the more influential players of the 1960s. Evans had a subtle touch, a brilliant harmonic mind, and a real lyric talent. He was not the most blues-oriented pianist who ever lived, but perhaps he compensated for this by articulating a certain autumnal melancholy that he proved could have a place in the music.

Bill Evans is more or less idolized by many pianists, although he is less in vogue today than he once was. He was a serious artist, with a near-genius for voice leading and a personal ear for harmonies involving major-seventh chords. He also introduced some new techniques into the vocabulary of the piano trio. But I must admit that I have trouble sitting still for his work for very long. He doesn't swing enough, he can't play the blues, and I don't feel close to his soul. But everyone, especially pianists, should at least hear him; I'll recommend a few places to start, and from there you're on your own. His recordings are very consistent, so you'll have few disappointments if you like his playing.

A good place to start is with *Waltz for Debby* (Riverside/OJC-210), recorded in June 1961 at the Village Vanguard by Evans's most famous trio, with Scott La Faro on bass and Paul Motian on drums. This group was remarkable for the way in which the virtuoso La Faro intertwined his lines around Evans's playing; the three men truly evolved a way of turning the piano trio into a sort of improvisational chamber music group. One could argue that La Faro's influence, which was profound and widespread, did more harm than good in making the bass solo an inevitable feature of every tune in a jazz group's performance and in steering younger players' attention toward the upper ends of their basses and away from the roundness and depth of sound that is indispensable to a jazz group's swing. We have had to wait until very recently to see a revival of youngsters who could walk strong and varied bass lines with a broad, rich sound as well as playing interesting solos. But taken on his own terms, La Faro was a real stylist, and his interplay with Evans is justly renowned.

On this set, as in almost all of Evans's sets, choice popular and jazz standards comprise the repertoire; here we are offered "My Foolish Heart," "My

Romance," and the fine and seldom-done "Detour Ahead," as well as Evans's own composition "Waltz for Debby," and Miles Davis's "Miles" (called "Milestones" here). It is a mood set, finally, like most of what Evans did; those who listen closely to piano players' chordal work and who know harmony will find a lot to listen for. If these performances were short stories, though, one might say they were long on setting and mood and short on plot. It's a question of what you're looking for. The trio's studio recordings are a bit better balanced in terms of sound; *Portrait in Jazz* (Riverside/OJC-088) and *Explorations* (Riverside/OJC-037) are good examples of their studio work.

Evans's swinging side, such as it is, comes out on *Everybody Digs Bill Evans* (Riverside/OJC-068), on which he is joined in a 1958 trio by bassist Sam Jones and drummer Philly Joe Jones. Even more swing-minded is *New Jazz Conceptions* (Riverside/OJC-025), a 1956 set with bassist Teddy Kotick and drummer Paul Motian on which Evans sounds at times like Red Garland; this resemblance also comes out on a 1958 Newport Jazz Festival appearance by the Miles Davis sextet with Evans, available on *Miles and Coltrane* (Columbia CK 44052). Evans's work on Davis's epochal *Kind of Blue* (Columbia CK 40579) is justly celebrated for its sensitivity and beauty. Finally, the 1963 *Conversations with Myself* (Verve 821 984-2) is a fascinating set; on it, through overdubbing, three Evanses converse at the keyboard in dense, ingenious performances of three Thelonious Monk tunes ("'Round Midnight," "Blue Monk," and "Bemsha Swing") and on a number of good standards like "Just You, Just Me," "How About You," and the too-seldom-done "A Sleeping Bee."

Erroll Garner was a unique talent, one of the most distinctive stylists in the history of jazz piano. He projected a certain joy and buoyancy that made him a great favorite with audiences that ordinarily didn't pay much attention to jazz. But musicians, too, held Garner (who supposedly was unable to read music) in awe for his inventiveness and spirit. The pianist Mary Lou Williams, whose Harlem apartment was a kind of salon for musicians in the 1940s and 1950s, told me that Bud Powell went to hide in her kitchen after hearing Garner play during one session there.

Garner also contributed certain devices to the vocabulary of jazz piano, the most well known being his way of using his left hand as a rhythm guitar, playing four chords to the bar, while his right played characteristically voiced chords a hair behind the beat. You can hear this technique clearly on his witty version of "When Johnny Comes Marching Home" on *Long Ago and Far Away* (Columbia CK 40863). His sensibility was primarily romantic, but he could swing hard on up-tempo numbers; he was truly unclassifiable stylistically. Although he came up in the time of bebop (he made some 1946 recordings with Charlie Parker, including the famous "Cool Blues," available on *The Legendary Dial Masters, Volume 1* [Stash ST-CD-23]) and he incorporated some bop devices in his playing, the spirit and attitude of his music went back to earlier forms of jazz.

*Long Ago and Far Away* is a wonderful set and a perfect introduction to Garner's playing. The repertoire on these beautifully remastered 1951 sides (trio performances with bassist John Simmons and drummer Shadow Wilson) consists almost entirely of standards such as "It Could Happen to You," "Lover," "Poor Butterfly," and "When You're Smiling" (a quintessential performance). This is extremely listener-friendly music; it obviously made Garner feel good to play it, and it is designed to make you feel good when you listen. The message communicates itself directly, and anyone can understand it. All but one of these performances is under four minutes, but Garner, like all truly great artists, could say a lot in a small space. Highly recommended.

Garner's 1955 *Concert by the Sea* (Columbia CK 40589), recorded at a live performance in Carmel, California, is his most enduringly popular album and one of the best-selling jazz albums of all time. It's no mystery why; Garner was in an expansive mood, and he really stretches out to heights of invention and swing on this program of standards such as "Autumn Leaves," "I'll Remember April," and "April in Paris." The sound is not as good here as it is on *Long Ago and Far Away*, but you get a chance to hear Garner's characteristic grunt in action. And, anyway, the immediacy of the occasion and the pure fun of the proceedings more than make up for any deficiency in sound. While *Long Ago and Far Away* is one of the most romantic, candlelight-and-wine jazz albums you can buy, this has a little more of a party feeling.

Another pianist who has achieved a strong reputation and following outside of the ranks of jazz connoisseurs is the mighty Oscar Peterson. He is also one of the most prolific jazz recording artists of all time, a sort of house pianist for probably the most prolific jazz record producer of all time, Norman Granz, whose Verve and Pablo labels would have been at quite a loss without Peterson. The pianist has been a sideman on recordings by, it seems, everyone who recorded for Granz – Ben Webster, Coleman Hawkins, Lester Young, Roy Eldridge, and others too numerous to mention. He has also recorded countless albums under his own name, for Granz and others as well.

A phenomenal technician whose first and biggest model was Art Tatum, Peterson can execute intricate, rapid-fire single-note lines at brutally fast tempos, sometimes with both hands playing in unison. He is the archetypal piano-trio pianist and has led several classic groups, the most famous of which had Ray Brown on bass and Ed Thigpen on drums. At his best, he can generate a huge, tidal-wave swing. He has many, many fans.

So I am not necessarily in the majority in saying that I find his playing almost unrelentingly devoid of real ideas. His single-note right-hand lines resemble bebop the way wood-grained formica resembles wood. His solos don't build, or tell a story, yet he can emit line after line of notes, ad infinitum, the way a computer could generate sentence after sentence if you programmed it with a dictionary and the rules of grammar. Listening to a performance like, say, "If I Were a Bell" on *Blues Etude* (Limelight 818 844-2) is like witnessing an extraordinary musical perpetual-motion machine.

And yet there is a kind of greatness about him. I have seen him live twice, once playing solo at Carnegie Hall and once in a reunion with bassist Ray Brown, guitarist Herb Ellis, and drummer Bobby Durham at the Blue Note in New York, and both times his energy and the swing he generated carried the day and made for big-time excitement. But it is hard to recommend his playing as long as there is a Hank Jones or a Tommy Flanagan around. If you're curious about him, he is at his best on *Night Train* (Verve 821 724-2), with the Ray Brown/Ed Thigpen edition of the trio. Peterson's swing here is compelling on tunes like the fast "C Jam Blues" and the walking-tempo title track. *Very Tall* (Verve 827 821-2) features the same trio with vibes player Milt Jackson as a guest for some good home cooking. And if Polygram ever gets around to reissuing a set originally recorded for MPS called *Hello Herbie*, with Herb Ellis on guitar, Sam Jones on bass, and Bobby Durham on drums, there will be at least one truly great Peterson album available; here he takes his propensity for swing to its limit on cookers like "Seven Come Eleven" and "Naptown Blues," and there's no arguing with it.

A pianist who has gotten nothing like the acclaim he deserves is Ray Bryant. A master of the blues, with a distinctive touch and way of swinging, Bryant was a very active sideman in the late 1950s, recording with Coleman Hawkins and Miles Davis on Prestige, for two; he is the pianist on Sonny Rollins's classics *Worktime* (Prestige/OJC-007) and *On Impulse!* (MCA/Impulse MCAD-5655 JVC-458), and he keeps all the pots cooking on one of the greatest recording dates of the 1950s, Dizzy Gillespie's *Sonny Side Up* (Verve 825 674-2), with Sonny Rollins and Sonny Stitt. "After Hours" here affords a good look at his blues playing.

But for a good look right down into Bryant's big soul, track down his *Alone with the Blues* (New Jazz/OJC-249, no CD), a solo recording from 1958 on which the repertoire consists of the blues in several tempos as well as two slow ballads, "Lover Man" and "Rockin' Chair." This is a first-rate solo piano album; Bryant's blues playing is absolutely authentic, the sound of someone who grew up steeped in the idiom. There's nothing affected, no mannerisms or posturing – just the real goods, delivered hot. His style is not richly ornamented but rather a percussive, call-and-response-based sound rooted in old-time blues piano and gospel music. Yet he can pour on the heat with right-hand single-note lines à la Bud Powell. Check this one out.

Bryant's trio set *Con Alma* (Columbia CK 44058) is a more uneven set, but some of it is fine. His version of John Lewis's lovely ballad "Django" is memorable, as are his solo reading of "Ill Wind" and his trio version of "Autumn Leaves." My favorite track on this set is the tantalizing arrangement of Bryant's own "Cubano Chant," which consists of a minor-key, chantlike melody in the right hand set against a left-hand riff played unison with the bass. Any piano fan will enjoy this set.

Cedar Walton also has not received his due, either as a pianist or a composer. His 1967 disc *Cedar!* (Prestige/OJC-462) presents his credentials in a program made up of four originals, two Ellington/Strayhorn tunes, and Kurt Weill's "My Ship," played by a group that includes Kenny Dorham on trumpet, Junior Cook on tenor, and Leroy Vinnegar and Billy Higgins rounding out the fine rhythm section. The record is very good, but Walton was also one of the most in-demand sidemen of the 1960s, and his playing on records like Freddie Hubbard's *Hub Cap* (Blue Note 84073), Joe Henderson's *Mode for Joe* (Blue Note 84227), and Blue Mitchell's *The Cup Bearers* (Riverside/OJC-797) is so good that it threatens to steal the spotlight away from the front-line players. Listen, for just one example, to his solo on "Dingbat Blues"on the Mitchell set. Walton was also the pianist for Art Blakey's Jazz Messengers for a good stretch in the 1960s; listen to him on the great *Mosaic* (Blue Note 46523), *Indestructible* (Blue Note 46429), and *Caravan* (Riverside/OJC-038).

The brilliant and eclectic Jaki Byard is another unfathomably neglected figure. When Byard is in a rhythm section, anything can happen, from straight-ahead swing to avant-garde fireworks to stride piano, sometimes within the same chorus. As a solo pianist, Byard is one of the most interesting compositional thinkers out there. His 1965 album *Jaki Byard Quartet Live!* (Prestige 24121), recorded at a Massachusetts nightclub with saxophonist Joe Farrell, bassist George Tucker, and drummer Alan Dawson, is an explosive, kaleidoscopic view of what happens when Byard is on the stand. The set is of its time in the way all the members of the group contribute to an overall compositional effect and in the group's willingness to shift tempo and texture, but Byard is, finally, a tonal thinker, and one thoroughly grounded in the history of the music.

Byard was one of the most active recording sidemen of the 1960s and contributed to a number of the best sessions of the time, including Rahsaan Roland Kirk's *Rip, Rig and Panic* (EmArcy 832-164-2), Booker Ervin's *Setting the Pace* (Prestige 24123), Eric Dolphy's *Outward Bound* (New Jazz/OJC-022) and, especially, *Far Cry* (New Jazz/OJC-400), Al Cohn and Zoot Sims's *Body and Soul* (Muse MCD 5356), and Phil Woods's *Musique Du Bois* (Muse MCD 5037). He was a favorite pianist of Charles Mingus's and is prominent on many of the great bassist-composer's 1960s recordings, especially the famous *Town Hall Concert* (Jazz Workshop/OJC-042).

## THELONIOUS MONK

Thelonious Monk and Horace Silver were two of the most important pianists, bandleaders, and composers of the 1950s and 1960s. Both provided alternatives to the mainstream of piano thinking of the time, playing in a less florid and ornamental style than many of the Powell/Tatum disciples, reaffirming some of the basic elements of the jazz piano tradition – especially the essentially percussive nature of the piano. Silver was noted for his incorporation of church-oriented phrasings and voicings, as well as call-and-response patterns, in his playing. Monk's affinity for the players of the stride school has been widely remarked. But for both men, less was often more; they tended to use fewer notes in their chords and to play those chords with a different philosophy than did most players of the time. Silver's accompaniments usually consisted of a constantly shifting barrage of riffs, Monk's of almost Basie-like surgical-strike chords. And in solo, both men tended to strip melody down to its essentials.

Silver's work is discussed in the Ensembles section. Monk's band recordings, as well as his piano style in accompaniment, are also discussed in the Ensembles section; what follows is a brief look at some of Monk's best recordings in a solo or trio setting.

Monk's 1959 solo set *Thelonious Alone in San Francisco* (Riverside/OJC-231) is one of his most relaxed and satisfying all-piano recordings; it is a good illustration of what Albert Murray, in his book *Stomping the Blues*, calls the "empty ballroom etude" quality of Monk's playing. "Thelonious Monk," Murray writes, ". . . is in a sense also a very special descendent of the old downhome honky-tonk piano player who likes to sit alone in the empty ballroom and play around with unconventional chord combinations and rhythms for his own private enjoyment." That describes the mood of this album perfectly; it was, in fact, recorded in an empty meeting hall on a fall day in California, and it finds Monk taking his time, and having a good time, poking around and reharmonizing a number of standards (including "Everything Happens to Me"), as well as doing some unbuttoned versions of originals like "Blue Monk," "Ruby, My Dear," and "Pannonica." On "Blue Monk" he even slips into some stride playing. Very highly recommended.

*Thelonious Himself* (Riverside/OJC-254) is in some respects a less satisfying set than *Thelonious Alone in San Francisco*. Monk seems less engaged for much of this 1957 session; the performances are not as relaxed and expansive. It includes, again, a mixture of standards and Monk originals. One of the more interesting aspects of this set is a twenty-two-minute take of Monk working out an arrangement for his own " 'Round Midnight," on which you can hear him trying things, making choices and rejecting them. It is a more interesting than pleasurable listening experience. The album also includes a version of "Monk's Mood," on which he is joined by John Coltrane and bassist Wilbur Ware, and a good blues called "Functional." But much of this set is almost funereal in pace.

Much better is *Solo Monk* (Columbia CK 47854), with its spirited stride version of "Dinah" and its great ballad interpretations of standards like "I Surrender, Dear," "I Should Care," and Monk's own "Ask Me Now." A bonus on this CD is the seldom-heard Monk original "Introspection," which was not on the original LP. If you are looking for the essence of Monk's solo style, this is almost as good a place to look as *Thelonious Alone in San Francisco* – lighter on mood, perhaps, but better recorded.

*Standards* (Columbia CK 45148) contains a number of solo performances from the mid-1960s taken from Monk's numerous Columbia albums, many of which are hard to find. The 1964 "Nice Work if You Can Get It" shows off Monk's stride to its fullest, and the wonderful 1967 "Between the Devil and the Deep Blue Sea" also has more than a glimpse of it, as do others here (check out "Sweetheart of All My Dreams," one of Monk's most joyous performances). But everything on this album is engaging; Monk enjoyed finding his own way around in these standards, and his enthusiasm jumps out at you.

*The Complete Black Lion and Vogue Recordings of Thelonious Monk* (Mosaic MR4-112) contains early (1954) and late (1971) solo tracks that are not up to the level of the Riverside or Columbia material. The 1954 cuts have pretty rough sound, and the 1971 cuts have Monk sounding a little spacy. He plays well on these later tracks – Monk always sounded like himself, which is reason enough to listen – but some part of him sounds as if it were out to lunch. Still, "Something in Blue" is a thoroughly enjoyable blues, and "Little Rootie

Tootie" has more Monk stride. "Chordially," a unique, extended chordal study at a very slow tempo, is just about unlistenable for pleasure but is intriguing musically. The trio tracks recorded at the same session, with bassist Al McKibbon and drummer Art Blakey, are unremarkable.

For good Monk trio playing, the 1955 *Thelonious Monk Plays Duke Ellington* (Riverside/OJC-024) is hard to beat. Monk is accompanied by bassist Oscar Pettiford and drummer Kenny Clarke in an all-Ellington program in which the mood is mostly mellow; this was one of the first Monk recordings to introduce him to a wider audience, after years of being regarded as "difficult" to listen to. This set is very easy to hear. *Thelonious Monk* (Prestige/OJC-010), a trio set recorded in 1952 and 1954 with either Max Roach or Art Blakey on drums, contains some very uninhibited and percussive Monk piano; the Latin-flavored "Bye-Ya," especially, is a celebration of the piano's tuned-percussion qualities, with Monk setting up one rhythmic pattern after another against Blakey's churning drum rhythms. This is about as far away from the traditional European conception of piano playing as you can get and still be playing piano. The version of "Little Rootie Tootie" included here is one of Monk's most famous recordings; his solo was transcribed by arranger Hall Overton and played by a large ensemble under Monk's direction in a 1959 Town Hall concert, available as *The Thelonious Monk Orchestra at Town Hall* (Riverside/OJC-135).

## SCATTERED SEEDS

The 1960s began, in jazz as in America in general, with an unprecedented array of possibilities and hope. The decade ended with most of those hopes in pieces and with many of the best minds and hearts in retreat from the kinds of responsibilities implied by the opportunities the decade offered. In jazz, some who seemed most promising ended the decade with retreats from the peculiarly American sophistication of jazz into ersatz tribal music, or rock and roll, or imitation European chamber music. There were many reasons, subtle and not so subtle, for these various tangents, among them the desire to make money and to be popular with a new, affluent audience, the rise of interest in African culture among many black Americans, and the increasing power of critics who thought of the music either in purely political terms or in terms more appropriate for European concert music.

At any rate, the decade's four most influential pianists – McCoy Tyner, Herbie Hancock, Chick Corea, and Cecil Taylor – each, in his own way, ended the decade involved in music that bore slim resemblance to anything I would call jazz. Tyner was playing what often sounded like a combination of African and South American music, Hancock and Corea wanted to be liked by many rather than loved by a few and found rock a good way to achieve that, and Taylor, who had begun as an Ellington acolyte, was playing a serious but finally not very blues-inflected form of semi-improvised chamber music. Taylor's work is discussed briefly in the Ensembles section; he is a serious artist but, as I say elsewhere, the musical choices he has made place him outside the frame of reference of this book.

Of the four, Tyner probably had the most influence on other acoustic jazz pianists. In his early-1960s work with John Coltrane's quartet, as well as in numerous albums as a sideman, Tyner outlined a style of accompanying and soloing that constituted the first meaningfully new (in jazz terms) approach to the piano since Bud Powell and Thelonious Monk. With a touch that originally resembled Wynton Kelly's staccato, crisp, on-top-of-the-beat style, Tyner began to incorporate the pentatonic scale, with its overtones of African scales, into his playing, as well as phrasing in different note groupings from the beboppers; in this way, he fit in with Coltrane's melodic concept. The pentatonic approach, as well as his way of chording with open fourths, contributed to the evolution of the static time feeling, discussed in the Ensembles section, that many players were working toward at the time.

In any case, Tyner's playing with Coltrane, on albums such as *Coltrane's Sound* (Atlantic 1419-2), *Crescent* (MCA/Impulse MCAD-5889), *Coltrane* (MCA/Impulse MCAD-5883), *My Favorite Things* (Atlantic 1361-2), *Ballads* (MCA/Impulse MCAD-5885), and *A Love Supreme* (MCA/Impulse MCAD-5660 JVC-467), is truly innovative jazz piano playing. So is his work on countless Blue Note albums of the 1960s, such as Wayne Shorter's *Juju* (Blue Note 46514) and Joe Henderson's *Inner Urge* (Blue Note 84189) and *Page One* (Blue Note 84140), as well as his own *The Real McCoy* (Blue Note 46512) and *McCoy Tyner Plays Duke Ellington* (MCA/Impulse MCAD-33124). In much the same way as young tenor players almost invariably chose Coltrane as their model during the last years of the decade and for the entire 1970s, so young pianists almost invariably voiced their chords as Tyner did, accompanied as he did, and soloed as he did.

Herbie Hancock and Chick Corea were the electric twins of the 1970s, the avatars of so-called fusion, sired by Miles Davis out of Jimi Hendrix (or vice versa). Both were extremely talented acoustic jazz pianists with varied experience in the early and mid-1960s. Of the two, Hancock probably had the more impressive pedigree, having been part of Davis's last great quintet, with Wayne Shorter, Ron Carter, and Tony Williams, as well as the leader on several classic 1960s dates such as *Maiden Voyage* (Blue Note 46339) and *Empyrean Isles* (Blue Note 84175) and sideman on countless more; their names read like a list of Blue Note's greatest hits – Hank Mobley's *No Room for Squares* (Blue Note

84149), Lee Morgan's *Search for the New Land* (Blue Note 84169) and *Cornbread* (Blue Note 84222), Wayne Shorter's *Speak No Evil* (Blue Note 46509) and *Adam's Apple* (Blue Note 46403), and Kenny Dorham's *Una Mas* (Blue Note 46515), to name just a few.

Hancock had prodigious technique and harmonic understanding, and he found a way of playing in a rhythm section, most famously along with Carter and Williams, that was a true and supple extension of the Red Garland–Paul Chambers–Philly Joe Jones conception, tailored for the Davis band's new sense of dynamics and form. He used tone clusters, ambiguous and complex harmonies, and a fine sense of the gradations of touch in fashioning a very complete approach to the keyboard. Almost from the beginning he showed an interest in rock-flavored elements (he recorded his famous composition "Watermelon Man" on his 1962 album *Takin' Off* [Blue Note 46506]); by the time he participated in Miles Davis's last great album, *Filles de Kilimanjaro* (Columbia CK 46116), he was firmly committed to electronic music and would stay that way for several years, recording albums, like the famous *Headhunter* (Columbia CK 32731), that had little to do with jazz. In more recent years, he has applied his talents to harmonically interesting music again; a good sampling of the results can be heard in *Herbie Hancock – A Jazz Collection* (Columbia CK 46865), which includes some revealing 1978 acoustic duets with Chick Corea (what I think they reveal is how much better both of them sounded on acoustic piano). Probably the most revealing of those duets is their outing on George Gershwin's "Liza," a nine-minute fantasy that begins as stride, moves through bebop, gets increasingly harmonically sophisticated, and ends up in outer space before making a successful landing. This is a real tour de force, a treat for the ear, the mind, the heart, and the nervous system.

Corea had a technique almost as prodigious as Hancock's, plus more melodic inventiveness as a soloist, a certain extroverted quality, and a Latin-flavored tang that were hard to resist. You can hear what he sounds like in a very straight-ahead jazz context on trumpeter Blue Mitchell's excellent 1964 album *The Thing To Do* (Blue Note 84178), with the exciting calypso "Fungii Mama" and Corea's own swinger "Chick's Tune," as well as Jimmy Heath's title tune. Throughout, Corea's solos always surprise, melodically; they swing like mad, and they show a knowledge of the tradition.

Two years later, in material later released on *Inner Space* (Atlantic 2-305-2), Corea was showing Tyner's influence in the use of the pentatonic scale and in certain left-hand chord voicings; this set has some very good, swinging music on it, including a version of Corea's "Litha," a modal tune that alternates sections of walking tempo with sections of up-tempo improvising by Corea, tenorist Joe Farrell, and trumpeter Woody Shaw. In 1967, as a member of Stan

Getz's quartet, Corea would record "Litha" again, on what is arguably Getz's best album, *Sweet Rain* (Verve 815 054-2). Corea's acoustic piano work on this set is consistently excellent. The next year Corea, like Hancock, would take part, on electric as well as acoustic piano, in Miles Davis's *Filles de Kilimanjaro* (Corea also recorded a stunning acoustic trio album, *Now He Sings, Now He Sobs* [Blue Note 90055] with bassist Miroslav Vitous and drummer Roy Haynes). The year after that brought Davis's all-electric *Bitches Brew* (Columbia G2K 40577), and the rest is history, or histrionics, depending on how you look at it. In the early 1970s Corea formed his own electric band, Return To Forever. Lately he has made some return trips from forever to lead, once again, a trio consisting of Miroslav Vitous and Roy Haynes, which he calls Trio Music, with whom he has proven that he can still play brilliantly within the jazz idiom.

# EPILOGUE

**AT THE END** of his book on bullfighting and Spain, *Death in the Afternoon*, Ernest Hemingway wrote a lyrical, elegiac chapter about all the things he wasn't able to include, and I have to admit to some of the same feelings. I wish there were a way to give some sense of what it was like to see Duke Ellington rehearse his band, or to accompany the great Basie trombonist Dicky Wells on his rounds as a Wall Street messenger (we visited Fats Waller's clarinetist Rudy Powell, who was pushing a mail cart in the Merrill Lynch building; a number of older musicians worked down there, it was a sort of fraternity), or to be sixteen and see Sonny Stitt and Dexter Gordon square off at Radio City Music Hall while two middle-aged Harlemites hollered constant encouragement and poured me shots of Tanqueray gin from a bottle they carried in a doctor's bag. I wish there were room to convey the sense of anticipation that hovers in the odd twilight of the recording studio, the strange foreshortening of sounds, the muffled quality of nearby voices, and the unexpected crispness and presence of voices from the studio as they come over the speakers. I'd love to show what certain jazz clubs are like long after closing, or the reactions of a school bus full of swing-era musicians en route to a concert at the old New York World's Fair grounds when they found out the bus driver was lost (earlier, Gene Krupa had opened his wallet and pulled out a well-creased photograph of Louis Armstrong and Big Sid Catlett, which he always carried around with him; he showed it to Jo Jones, who was sitting next to him on the bus seat, and the two of them looked at it silently, the way old college friends at a reunion might look at a photo of classmates long gone). These kinds of experiences are, in their way, almost as much a part of being involved with the music as the music itself is, and everyone who hangs around enough has his or her own stories to tell.

But, finally, what lingers most for me are the occasions when I first heard something that I knew would be part of my life forever – Roy Eldridge's ecstatic solo at the end of "Let Me Off Uptown" (with Gene Krupa's band) on my grandparents' old record player, for instance, or Charlie Parker suddenly swooping out of the speakers in a used-record booth at a Long Island farmers' market when I was about twelve (it was his solo on "I'll Remember April," from *The Happy Bird*; I bought the album immediately), or the shock of hearing the urgency in John Coltrane's tenor as he peeled off chorus after chorus of "Mr. P.C." on the *Giant Steps* album. All of these recordings have become a part of my life; I revisit them regularly, and I never tire of hearing them. But the surprise, the exhilaration of hearing them for the first time, has been one of the nicest things in life, for me, and that is something I can share with you, through this book.

In that respect, I'm luckier than Hemingway was with Spain; the sounds and the spirit that this book addresses are out there to be had, as close as your nearest record store, and they are as fresh now as they were when they were first set down. The spirit that jazz embodies will never die; as long as we can touch a button and begin again, at the beginning, of Duke Ellington's "Ko-Ko," or John Coltrane's "Crescent," or Louis Armstrong's "West End Blues," we will have proof that the individual and the group can be reconciled, that African and European cultural streams are compatible, and that the blues can be held at bay. And when the balance sheets are toted up for this country, and this century, let no one miss the sweet justice that the greatest artistic expression of the American ideal has come from the descendants of slaves, who found the true meaning of democracy and the essence of freedom.

# INDEX

*A page number in **boldface** indicates a major entry, which may continue on the pages following.*